Canadian Entrepreneurship

& Small Business Management

FIFTH EDITION

D. Wesley Balderson
University of Lethbridge

 **McGraw-Hill
Ryerson**

Toronto Montréal Boston Burr Ridge, IL Dubuque, IA Madison, WI New York
San Francisco St. Louis Bangkok Bogotá Caracas Kuala Lumpur Lisbon London
Madrid Mexico City Milan New Delhi Santiago Seoul Singapore Sydney Taipei

McGraw-Hill Ryerson Limited

A Subsidiary of The McGraw·Hill Companies

Statistics Canada information is used with the permission of the Minister of Industry, as Minister responsible for Statistics Canada. Information on the availability of the wide range of data from Statistics Canada can be obtained from Statistics Canada's Regional Offices, its World Wide Web site at http://www.stat.can.ca, and its toll-free access number 1-800-263-1136.

ISBN: 0-07-089427-2

2 3 4 5 6 7 8 9 10 TCP 0 9 8 7 6 5 4 3

Printed and bound in Canada.

Care has been taken to trace ownership of copyright material contained in this text; however, the publisher will welcome any information that enables them to rectify any reference or credit for subsequent editions.

Vice President and Editorial Director: Pat Ferrier
Sponsoring Editor: Lenore Gray Spence
Managing Editor, Development: Kim Brewster
Director of Marketing: Jeff MacLean
Supervising Editor: Anne Macdonald
Copy Editor: Nancy Carroll
Production Coordinator: Jen Wilkie
Photos and Permissions: Alison Derry, Permissions Plus
Composition: Michelle Losier, Finelines
Cover Design: Dianna Little
Cover Image Credits: Courtesy of Spin Master Toys, Nuytco Research Ltd., Death by Chocolate, Tilley Endurables, Royal Group Technologies Ltd., and Clearly Canadian Beverage Corporation.
Printer: Transcontinental Printing

Cover: Note that all cover images are representative of products manufactured by Canadian companies profiled in this text. (Clockwise from top: Spin Master Toys, Clearly Canadian, Royal Group Technologies Ltd., Tilley Endurables, Death by Chocolate, and Nuytco Research Ltd.)

National Library of Canada Cataloguing in Publication Data

Balderson, D. Wesley (David Wesley), 1948-
        Canadian entrepreneurship and small business management

5th ed.
First ed. published under title: Canadian small business management.
Includes bibliographical references and index.
ISBN 0-07-089427-2

    1. Small Business—Canada—Management. 2. Small business—Canada.
3. New business enterprises—Canada—Management. I. Title.

HD62.7.B34 2002   658.02'2'0971   C2001-904211-6

Contents

Part I
The Small Business Decision   1

Part II
Preparing for Small Business Ownership   93

Part III
Managing the Small Business   231

Part IV
Looking to the Future   407

Preface

Canadian Entrepreneurship and Small Business Management, Fifth Edition, is a result of many years of teaching entrepreneurship business classes at the college and university level, of working closely with numerous owners of small businesses in a consulting role, of direct, personal small business management experience, and, of course, a result of experience with all the previous successful editions. This edition has been improved by making it more current, interesting, and instructional, practical and theoretically sound, and rigorous yet easy for the student to follow and absorb.

To accomplish these sometimes diverse aims, the text incorporates standard small business start-up and management fundamentals and introduces the reader to many Canadian entrepreneurs and their businesses through over 50 real-life small business incidents and 15 profiles of Canadian entrepreneurs. Each individual profiled started his or her business small. All have succeeded, and some have expanded into large businesses.

Numerous cases illustrate the small business management concepts discussed in the text. These concepts are stated at the beginning of each case in the Instructor's Manual to aid in teaching. Each case proceeds in a logical order from start-up of the business to management of the existing business and finally to planning for the future.

WHAT'S NEW IN THIS EDITION

The fifth edition introduces several improvements to the previous editions based on professor and student feedback. Specifically, the fifth edition includes:

- A new chapter: Chapter 9, Small Business and Electronic Commerce

- More information on such contemporary topics as Internet marketing, home-based businesses, youth and female entrepreneurs, new business opportunities and trends for entrepreneurs, and franchising

- Updates of statistics, examples, charts, information sources, government programs, and taxes

- The addition of several new video cases, new incidents, and examples

- Updating and/or replacement of previous small business profiles at the beginning of each chapter. Several new entrepreneurs are profiled in this edition.

This text is appropriate for any entrepreneurship or small business management class at the college or university undergraduate or graduate level. It can also be adapted easily to continuing education classes for those who are thinking about or are currently involved in running their own businesses. In many cases, the text would also be a useful resource book for practitioners outside the classroom setting.

CHAPTER STRUCTURE OF CANADIAN ENTREPRENEURSHIP AND SMALL BUSINESS MANAGEMENT

Canadian Entrepreneurship and Small Business Management is divided into four parts. Each part covers an essential aspect of starting and/or managing a small business.

Part I provides background information essential to the decision to undertake small business ownership. Chapter 1 reviews the characteristics of small business and its contribution to Canadian society. Chapter 2 covers areas required for a personal evaluation of one's suitability for small business ownership. Chapter 3 presents a systematic procedure for determining whether a small business opportunity is feasible. It includes numerous sources of information essential in carrying out a feasibility analysis.

The four chapters in Part II discuss important aspects of starting or obtaining a business. Chapters 4, 5, and 6 review the three methods of establishing a small business. Chapter 4 discusses organizing the small business from scratch, including a special emphasis on the preparation of the business plan. Chapter 5 covers buying a business. Chapter 6 deals with franchising as a type of small business ownership. Chapter 7 discusses financing concerns in starting the business and includes a complete listing of sources of financing for entrepreneurs.

Part III includes six chapters that discuss the fundamental management practices in operating the already established business. Chapter 8, 9, 10, 11, and 12 cover in detail the small business applications in marketing, e-commerce, finance, internal operations, and personnel management, respectively. Chapter 13 focuses on tax considerations for the small business owner-manager.

Part IV appropriately discusses future and long-term aspects of the small business. Chapter 14 deals with the principles underlying effective growth management. Chapter 15 discusses methods of terminating or transferring the ownership of the enterprise, with a special emphasis on family businesses.

SUPPLEMENTAL MATERIAL FOR STUDENTS AND INSTRUCTORS

CBC Videos—New to this edition, CBC video segments are available on VHS tape for instructors, and in video streaming for students and instructors from the Online Learning Centre. All segments are tied in by concept to the chapters in the text.

Online Learning Centre—A student and instructor website at *www.mcgrawhill.ca/college/ balderson* contains useful study tools and instructor assistance. **Students** can do self-testing of key concepts and exam preparation using online quizzes and Internet exercises. We also offer a full set of web links, CBC video streaming, and a searchable key terms glossary. **Instructors** are invited to download supplements such as the Instructor's Manual and PowerPoint® Presentations, and view the CBC video streaming.

Instructor's CD-ROM—New to this edition, this CD-ROM combines all the supplements into one instructor's management system. It includes: Brownstone Diploma's Computerized Test Bank, PowerPoint® Presentations, and the Instructor's Manual.

Instructor's Manual—The Instructor's Manual has been carefully prepared to provide the instructor with helpful information while allowing considerable flexibility. Notes relating to each chapter include the following components:

- Chapter objectives—reproduced from the text chapters

- Summary points—key concepts summarized from text chapters

- Key terms and concepts from chapter material

- Power Point slides and software

- Transparency list—a list of transparencies appropriate for each chapter

- Answers to end-of-chapter questions
- Case solutions—for end-of-part and comprehensive cases
- Test bank for use as class discussion or examinations
- Video case teaching notes

The solutions to the supplementary case questions are included toward the end of the Instructor's Manual, and transparency masters, enlarged reproductions of the text materials, are included at the end.

Acknowledgements

Many people contributed to *Canadian Entrepreneurship and Small Business Management*, Fifth Edition. I am grateful to the many students and colleagues who have offered input and critical analyses of our small business course over the years. I also appreciate those owner-managers with whom I have had an opportunity to work in a consulting role. They have provided considerable insight regarding the pertinent problems small business owners face. Reviewers of the fifth edition and reviewers and users of the previous four editions also provided valuable suggestions. Reviewers include:

Perley Brewer, New Brunswick Community College
Victoria Calvert, Mount Royal Community College
Dorothy Derksen, Red River Community College
Denny Dombrower, Centennial College
Jim Doucette, Northern Alberta Institute of Technology
Lydia Dragunas, Champlain College
Glenn Fraser, Durham College
Kim Galvin, Nova Scotia Community College
Maureen Gerber, British Columbia Institute of Technology
Brad Hill, St. Lawrence College
Brian Hobson, Georgian College of Applied Arts and Technology
Walter Isenor, Acadia University
Peter Johnson, McGill University
Peter Kaglik, Red River Community College
Reid MacWilliam, Mohawk College
Catherine McCougan, Conestoga College
Gordon McFarlane, Langara College
Lissa McRae, Bishop's University
John Morrison, Seneca College
Tom O'Connell, Concordia University
Garfield Pynn, Memorial University of Newfoundland
David Ross, Kwantlen University College
Dennis Sullivan, Fanshawe College
Barrie Tober, Niagara College
Randy Vandermark, British Columbia Institute of Technology
Rick Wagman, Saskatchewan Institute of Applied Science and Technology
Keith Wallace, Kwantlen University College
Leslie Wilder, Red River College

Several people made direct contributions to this edition of the text. Research assistant, Miranda Selinger, collected data, checked references and permissions, and entered text material into the word processor. Professor Jim Clark, Faculty of Management, University of Lethbridge, wrote the initial draft of Chapter 9: Small Business and Electronic Commerce. Professor Gordon Dixon, Associate Professor in the Faculty of Management, University of Lethbridge, once again reviewed the taxation chapter and provided valuable input. Norman Robinson allowed me to use his business as the basis for writing the comprehensive case. To all of these people I express my gratitude for their valuable contributions.

I thank those who authored some of the cases: Cam Roberts, and Rick Heyland, research assistants at the University of Lethbridge; Malika Das, Mount Saint Vincent University; Gordon McDougall, Wilfrid Laurier University; William Rudelius, University of Minnesota; Fred Crane, QMA Consulting Group Ltd.; Morris Borts, Marketec Business consultants Ltd.; James Nelson, University of Colorado; and Robert Wykham, Simon Fraser University. I also thank S. Shapiro, J. McCarthy, and Richard D. Irwin, Inc., for allowing some of their cases to be adapted for this text.

I thank the many authors and entrepreneurs who granted us permission to use diagrams, tables, profiles, and article excerpts to illustrate the text concepts.

I am extremely grateful for the support and assistance the Faculty of Management at the University of Lethbridge provided in allowing computer research and office administrative time for this project.

I thank the staff of McGraw-Hill Ryerson for their encouragement and support.

Wes Balderson

McGraw-Hill Ryerson
Online Learning Centre

McGraw-Hill Ryerson offers you an online resource that combines the best content with the flexibility and power of the Internet. Organized by chapter, the BALDERSON Online Learning Centre (OLC) offers the following features to enhance your learning and understanding of Business:

- Online Quizzes
- Web Links
- CBC Video Streaming
- Internet Exercises
- Searchable Key Terms Glossary

By connecting to the "real world" through the OLC, you will enjoy a dynamic and rich source of current information that will help you get more from your course and improve your chances for success, both in the course and in the future.

For the Instructor

Downloadable Supplements

All key supplements are available, password-protected for instant access!

PageOut   **PageOut**

Create your own course Web page for free, quickly and easily. Your professionally designed Web site links directly to OLC material, allows you to post a class syllabus, offers an online gradebook, and much more! Visit www.pageout.net

Online CBC Cases and Video Streaming   CBC

New to this edition, view the CBC segments online as chosen by the author to illustrate key concepts and demonstrate how these concepts work in the world of business. The video notes and discussion questions are also available for downloading.

Online Resources

McGraw-Hill Ryerson offers various online resource tools such as CBC video streaming and web links to help you get the latest information for immediate use in class.

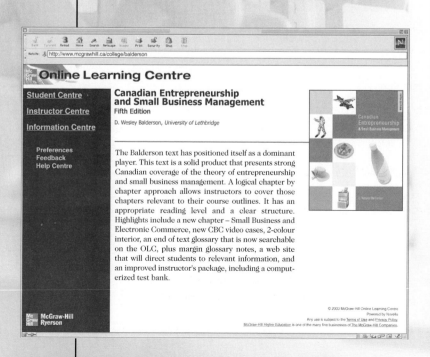

Part I

The Small Business Decision

The decision to start one's own business is a difficult one. It often involves leaving secure employment to face an uncertain financial future. Such a decision can have far-reaching effects on the physical, emotional, and financial aspects of one's life. To provide a better understanding of the implications and preparation for this decision, Part I discusses three topics.

Chapter 1 reviews the role of small business in Canadian society. It examines current trends and the probable future environment for small business.

Chapter 2 describes the characteristics of successful and unsuccessful small businesses, and the personal capabilities of the majority of successful entrepreneurs. The chapter also reviews the potential advantages and dangers of operating one's own business. Understanding this information can help one make an informed small business career decision.

Once an individual understands the relative merits of starting a small business and feels suited for such a career, he or she can do several things in the pursuit of the best business opportunity. Generally, a person needs to gather a considerable amount of information in order to evaluate business opportunities. Chapter 3 presents ideas that can improve information collection and analysis skills for this purpose.

Chapter 1

The Role of Small Business in Canada

Chapter Objectives

- To discuss the evidence of increased interest and activity in the small business sector.

- To review common methods of defining small business and explain why a definition is important.

- To understand the current extent of small business in Canada.

- To discuss the benefits a healthy small business sector can offer society.

- To explain the probable future environment for the small business community.

Small Business Profile

Alex Tilley
Tilley Endurables Inc.

Tilley Endurables Inc.
www.tilley.com

Just over 20 years ago, Alex Tilley sold his first wide-brimmed hat at a boat and tradeshow. His indestructible cotton creations became an instant success, and earned the entrepreneur the supplemental income he desired.

While continuing his day job of selling and renting Canadian art to businesses, Tilley expanded his home-based venture. The success of the Tilley hat prompted Tilley to develop and sell a line of hardy sailing shorts. Response to the pocket-laden and pricey shorts was poor, and Tilley feared he would have to give up his creation. However, Tilley's shorts eventually gained the recognition they deserved. In 1983, the America's Cup yachting team was featured wearing the khaki shorts. This provided Tilley's innovation with the credibility it deserved.

Soon people were demanding more than just hats and shorts. In 1984, Alex Tilley quit his day job and committed himself to his Toronto-based company, Tilley Endurables Inc.

Tilley immediately expanded his line of easy-care travel clothing. Now Tilley manufactures and retails an entire line of clothing; items guaranteed for life. From hats to trousers to underwear, customers' clothing needs can be satisfied by Tilley's innovations.

Tilley refers to his customers as clients and friends. The 63-year-old appreciates the loyalty of his clientele and enjoys catering to the needs of this particular market. In fact, Tilley Endurables caters mainly to older travellers who seek high quality, but easy-to-care-for clothing. Tilley, an extensive traveller himself, understands the needs of his clients, which is why he always strives to produce only clothing of the highest quality and maximum comfort.

The success of Tilley Endurables is international. Tilley products have penetrated the market of 17 countries. In Canada, durable Tilley products can be found in four family stores and are available through a catalogue and web site. Customers who frequent the Toronto-based store also have the opportunity to tour Tilley's manufacturing facilities. Close to 4,000 hats a week are produced in a facility adjacent to the Toronto location. Manufacturing of all other Tilley products including shorts, skirts, jackets, vests, and underwear occurs in Canada.

Consumers familiar with advertisements containing Mr. Tilley's smiling bearded face are now seeing the face of a younger, attractive woman. Alex Tilley has spent the last 20 years cultivating his clothing empire and is now preparing for the day he will turn the business over to his daughter. Thirty-two-year-old Alison Tilley is currently vice president of marketing and merchandising for Tilley Endurables, and one day she will be in charge of overseeing all aspects of the family business, a challenge that her father believes Ms. Tilley is more than capable of accomplishing.

THE ENTREPRENEURIAL REVOLUTION

Since the mid-1970s a reawakening of interest in entrepreneurship and small business ownership has occurred in both North America and abroad. Since the Second World War, the philosophy in many circles has been that bigger was better in both business and government. As a result, for several years government increased in size and the climate for big business improved.

The critics of "bigness" since the 1970s, however, have gathered more support as big government and big business failed to provide the expected panacea for society's economic problems. The result has been that more people and more governments are looking to small business to provide a catalyst for their stagnant economies and to enable faster economic growth. As John Naisbitt has stated in *Global Paradox*, "The entrepreneur is the most important player in the building of the global economy, so much so that big companies are decentralizing and reconstituting themselves as networks of entrepreneurs. Huge companies such as IBM and GM must break up to become confederations of small, autonomous, entrepreneurial companies if they are to survive."[1]

The resulting rapid growth in small business formations and activity has continued through the 1980s and 1990s and shows no sign of slowing down well into the millenium. In a recent survey conducted by Ernst and Young, 8 out of 10 influential North Americans indicated that they believe entrepreneurialism will define twenty-first century business.[2] Many other countries have shared in this growth and increased awareness.[3]

This trend is solidly entrenched in Canada as well. The Global Entrepreneurial Monitor rates Canada as second in the world in entrepreneurial activity behind only the United States.[4] Statistics Canada indicates that nearly half a million new small businesses are started in Canada each year.[5] The importance of the small business sector of Canadian society is now more widely acknowledged than at any time since the turn of the century.

What has fueled this growth? Throughout this text, descriptions of many entrepreneurs will illustrate examples of the reasons why an increasing number of people are establishing their own businesses. The dream of starting small and developing a successful business, such as Alex Tilley (see Small Business Profile), is shared by many. On the other hand, many individuals have become successful entrepreneurs due to downsizing of larger organizations. An example of such a situation appears in Incident 1-1. During the past recessions, and recent downsizing, many individuals who lost their jobs and many college and university graduates unable to secure employment started their own businesses. A recent labour force survey found that 12 percent of self-employed individuals were "pushed" into business ownership because there was no work available.[6] Others chose to leave secure employment and strike out on their own because of a natural interest or a desire for a challenge. Incidents 1-2 and 1-3 illustrate examples of this.

Although the above examples provide anecdotal evidence of the growth of small business, a more detailed discussion regarding the evidence of small business growth follows.

Increases in the Number of Business Establishments

Considerable research has been done to determine the number of new businesses established each year. This has proved a difficult, if not impossible, task because of the many different types of businesses as well as the varied methods of estimating business start-ups. Some indicators of business start-ups that researchers have used are tax returns, new employer registrations, phone hookups, new incorporations, and business registrations.[7]

Incident 1-1

A Business with Soul

Sometimes corporate downsizing and restructuring have a happy ending, and even an element of philanthropy as well.

Take Save-On Foods and its now-defunct shoe repair service, for example. Kevin Waites, Save-On manager in Lethbridge, says the service wasn't making money corporation-wide so Save-On decided to close all its shoe repair outlets.

This was fine with most stores, where shoe repair was a bit of an albatross, but not in Lethbridge where the service was successful.

When Save-On decided to close all its shoe repair outlets, the decision in Lethbridge was tough as a result of such success.

"Our customers value that service and we didn't want to take that away from them," Waites says.

So how to stitch corporate reality together with customer need?

Simple.

Save-On sold Lorri Kubick and her husband Dave hundreds of thousands of dollars in shoe repair equipment for next to nothing.

Meanwhile, although the location has changed, the service that made the Kubicks so successful and helped them dodge the swipe of the corporate axe is the same as it always was. This has led to a successful business and allows the Kubicks the chance to be entrepreneurs.

SOURCE: Clayton Grose, "A Business with a Soul," *Southern Alberta Business*, Fall 1998, p. 14.

Incident 1-2

A Fresh Idea

After working together at Starbucks, Jason Cunningham, 24, and Derek Brock, 28, launched Calgary-based Jugo Juice in 1998 as a healthy alternative to fast-food and coffee bars. The two entrepreneurs wanted to tap into the growing market for healthy, natural food and beverages. Jugo Juice offers sandwich-style wraps and 17 flavours of fruit smoothies. Juice smoothies include mouth-watering names like *Berry Binge* and *Watermelon Wiggle* that can be fortified with ginseng and echinacea extracts upon request.

Offering a trendy alternative to traditional food-court options has proven to be a successful endeavour for Cunningham and Brock. Since Jugo Juice's opening in 1998, three stores have been launched in Calgary and one in Vancouver. Three additional locations are soon to be opened in both cities. Jugo Juice occupies locations in office tower food courts, thus, catering to a mainly professional market.

Jugo Juice sports a unique "un-food court" look. Sleek silver, black counters and upbeat Latin music from a station in Los Angeles create a trendy atmosphere that attracts the attention of potential customers. Cunningham and Brock encourage staff to bond with customers. Offering customized fruit smoothies and individualized wraps helps to foster bonding. To accomplish this goal, Jugo Juice places great emphasis on training and development.

Cunningham and Brock's exceptional service and unique food and beverage concept has not gone unnoticed. In fact, the dynamic duo has received the Cadillac Fairview's 1999 retail ARC Award for outstanding achievement in new retail concepts. Establishment of a fresh, new idea in the existing restaurant and fast food industry has brought success to young entrepreneurs willing to act on their fantasies.

SOURCE: Adapted from Rhea Seymour, "Winners," *Profit*, June 2000, p. 10.

Incident 1-3

The BlackBerry

The BlackBerry is a wireless handheld device designed by Research in Motion (RIM) to meet the organization and communication needs of today's high-tech world. Waterloo, Ontario-based RIM employs over 1,400 people, is worth $7 billion, and has won both an Emmy and an Oscar for outstanding technical product development. However, RIM cannot boast that it became successful overnight. Founder, president, and co-CEO, Mike Lazaridis, and his partner, Doug Fregin, vice-president of operations, experienced eight or nine failures before developing and launching their greatest wireless triumph, the BlackBerry.

Beginnings were modest for Research in Motion. When the company first began, it consisted of two employees, Lazaridis and Fregin, friends since grade six. Both share fond memories of their childhood electronics shop teacher, Mr. Micsinszki. Micsinszki ran the local ham radio and amateur television club in the boys' home city of Windsor, Ontario. It was this teacher who encouraged Lazaridis and Fregin's interest in electronics and wireless technology. In fact, Lazaridis remembers Mr. Micsinszki saying, "Don't get too captivated by computers. In the future, the people who put computers and wireless technology together are really going to come up with something."

Both Lazaridis and Fregin attended university to study engineering. During their university careers, the two entrepreneurs took a year off to develop automated television, a technology that allowed information to be transferred over the air. This development was inspired by a transmission method used by ham operators to place call letters on television screens. Both men returned to their studies, but Lazaridis never did complete his engineering education. In fact, he fell short of graduating by only one month in 1984. The young entrepreneur had difficulty balancing his education and a $600,000 contract he had landed with General Motors. General Motors contracted Lazaridis' expertise to produce a display system to communicate messages throughout GM manufacturing facilities. At this point Lazaridis committed to RIM full time.

Fresh out of university, Lazaridis and Fregin sought the business expertise necessary to operate their new company. The next 15 years were a whirlwind of failures and triumphs for the techno-oriented company. However, it is RIM's latest technological release, the BlackBerry, that has earned RIM the fame and recognition it deserves. And who knows? Maybe RIM's future holds yet another Emmy or Oscar.

SOURCE: Adapted from Laura Pratt, "Persistence in Motion," *Profit*, May 2001, pp. 18-26.

Statistics Canada
www.statcan.ca

Figure 1-1 illustrates the number of small businesses in Canada in 1999. In addition, the number of businesses with less than 50 employees has increased substantially over the last decade. Similar trends for the United States show even more marked increases in small business formations than in Canada.[8] During the 18 months ending in June, 1999, the small business segment with fewer than five employees experienced an increase of 38,000 firms. During this time the number of all other firms in other size categories actually declined.[9] Statistics Canada has also estimated that 97 percent of all existing businesses have fewer than 50 employees.[10] By 2000 there were 2.5 million self-employed persons, representing 16 percent of the total work force, an increase of 43 percent since 1990.[11] Also, the number of people who own a small business has been increasing significantly compared to the number of people employed by the government.[12] Figure 1-2 illustrates this trend.

Figure 1-1   Number of Establishments by Employment Size, December 1999

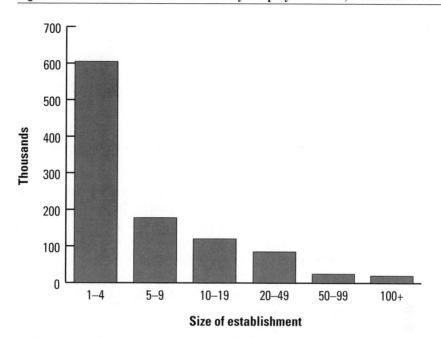

SOURCE: *Market Research Handbook* (Ottawa: Statistics Canada 2000) p. 147.

Figure 1-2   Comparison of Self-Employed to Government-Employed

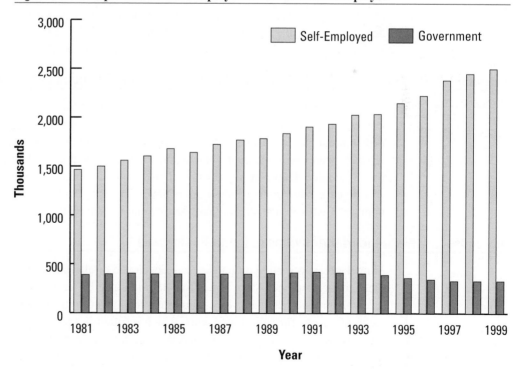

SOURCE: *Canada Labour Force Characteristics, Total Federal Government Employment* (Ottawa: CANSIM, Statistics Canada, January 4 and 16, 2001).

Increases in the Number of Employees of Small Businesses

As has already been shown, the number of Canadians employed by small businesses has grown substantially in recent years.[13] From 1989 to 1999 growth in self-employment was four times that of paid workers.[14] In addition, there is a marked shift in new job creation from a reliance on big firms and projects to small firms and entrepreneurs. Statistics Canada indicates that over 50 percent of total job growth between 1989 and 1999 was due to small businesses.[15]

Increases in Government Interest and Programs

The federal government recognizes the vital role that small business plays in the Canadian economy. Small businesses create jobs, they generate wealth, and they provide satisfying careers for a growing number of entrepreneurs. To realize their full potential as an engine for growth, however, they need a favourable environment that allows them to prosper and expand. They also need forms of support that are tailored to helping them meet the challenges of a changing and competitive economy. While extensive assistance is already provided to Canada's small businesses, the government has heard their concerns and it is moving energetically to respond.[16]

As the above quote illustrates, many politicians now recognize the importance of small business to a healthy economy and are beginning to offer various financial and nonfinancial programs to assist the small business owner.[17] Presently the Entrepreneurship and Small Business Office in the Department of Industry Canada coordinates and administers programs designed to aid small business at the federal level. Likewise, all of the provinces have departments that perform the same function for small businesses within their jurisdictions. Appendix 3B (see Chapter 3) gives a complete listing of these agencies.

Increases in the Number of Small-Business-Related Courses at Colleges and Universities

The level of interest in small-business-related courses at Canadian colleges and universities has risen dramatically in the past few years. The trend of increasing numbers of entrepreneurship courses in business schools appears to be continuing.[18] Historically such courses typically were housed in management and commerce faculties and attracted only students of those faculties. However, as a result of the growing general interest in small business in recent years, many nonbusiness majors now take such courses. In addition, there are now a number of entrepreneurship courses being taught at the high school level in Canada.[19]

Increases in Entrepreneurial Activities in Large Businesses

Many large, successful companies have developed or altered their organizations to promote creativity, entrepreneurship, and individual initiative.[20] These businesses have realized considerable productivity gains by encouraging this type of intrapreneurship. In their extensive study of successful large companies, which resulted in the best-selling book *In Search of Excellence,* Thomas Peters and Robert Waterman found that one characteristic of these organizations was their formal encouragement of entrepreneurship within and among departments. These companies were quick to recognize increases in productivity and innovativeness by rewarding employees who engaged in such entrepreneurial behaviour.[21] Canadian companies such as Bombardier and Nortel are examples of companies having incorporated these practices into their organizations.

Increases in Political Power of Small Business

Canadian Federation of Independent Business
www.cfib.ca

Collectively, the small business community is a significant economic force in Canadian society. Several organizations are currently attempting to advance the small business cause through lobbying efforts and educational programs. The largest and most visible organization is the Canadian Federation of Independent Business, which boasts a membership of over 100,000. Such lobbying has resulted in many government programs and some legislation beneficial to small business. Many industry associations made up primarily of small businesses also are very active in lobbying activities and have influenced the directions of government initiatives.

Improvement in the Image of Small Business

Small business owners and entrepreneurs are viewed more positively today than they were several years ago. As more and more people recognize the benefits which small businesses provide to society, the occupation of entrepreneur carries more prestige than it previously did. A recent survey carried out by *Business Week* found that small business leaders were more trusted by the general public than leaders of religious institutions, big business, the news media, labour unions, and the government.[22]

WHAT IS SMALL BUSINESS?

What size of business qualifies as a small business? This question is not easy to answer, because most organizations and agencies concerned with small businesses use different definitions. It is essential, however, to understand some of the common characteristics of these definitions to better appreciate what constitutes a small business. These characteristics are outlined in the following paragraphs.

Comparison and Evaluation

Statistics Canada
www.statcan.ca

Dun and Bradstreet
www.dnb.com

To compare the performance of a small business to other small businesses, it is necessary to understand the sizes and characteristics used by data collection and dissemination agencies such as Statistics Canada and Dun and Bradstreet. Ensuring that firms are relatively the same size allows a more meaningful monitoring of sales levels, performance, and productivity in relation to other similar firms in the industry. Currently Statistics Canada publishes operating data for incorporated and unincorporated businesses that have average net sales of $1 million or less.

Government Programs

Knowing how various government departments define a small business enables an entrepreneur to take advantage of the tax incentives and other government assistance programs designed for small business. Examples of differences in definitions among government agencies are given later.

Lending Programs

Business Development Bank of Canada (BDC)
www.bdc.ca

A small business owner needs to know the size of business that lenders require in their lending programs in order to take advantage of favourable small business provisions. Programs are available to small businesses from the Business Development Bank of Canada (BDC), provincial government lending agencies, and the chartered banks. Therefore, it is important to understand the criteria commonly used to distinguish a small business from a large one. At least four criteria exist.

**Business Development
Bank of Canada (BDC)
www.bdc.ca**

**Statistics Canada
www.statcan.ca**

1. Number of Employees. The Department of Industry, Science and Technology specifies a small business as one that employs under 100 people in a manufacturing industry and under 50 employees in a nonmanufacturing industry. The Ministry of State for Small Business also uses the guideline of 50 employees, while the Business Development Bank of Canada (formerly the Federal Business Development Bank) considers a business that employs fewer than 75 to be eligible in its Counseling Assistance for Small Businesses Program. Other agencies, such as the Small Business Administration in the United States and Statistics Canada, specify much larger numbers of employees, ranging from 250 to 1,500 depending on the industry.[23]

2. Total Revenue. Although the limits vary by industry, total revenue is a common basis for defining small business. The Ministry of State for Small Business uses $2 million in revenue as a benchmark. The Small Business Loans Act in Canada applies to firms with revenues of less than $2 million. The Small Business Administration in the United States uses the following revenue guidelines:

Retailing: $3.5 million to $13.5 million
Services: $3.5 million to $14.5 million
Construction: $7 million to $17 million

**Canada Customs and
Revenue Agency
www.rc.gc.ca**

3. Profits. Revenue Canada uses operating profits as a guideline to define which businesses qualify for the "Small Business Deduction." This special deduction allows a reduced tax rate (the small business deduction is discussed in detail in Chapter 13). This limit is presently set at a net operating profit of $200,000.

4. Type of Management-Ownership Structure. Another criterion used to define small business is the degree to which the owner is also the day-to-day manager of the business. With some exceptions, the majority of small business owners are also the managers.[24] Because the guidelines differ among industries and agencies, the Committee for Economic Development in the United States uses a slightly different and less specific approach in defining a small business. Its definition states that if any two of the following characteristics exist, the business may be classified as a small business:

1. Independent management (i.e., the owner is the manager)

2. Owner-supplied capital

3. Local area of operations

4. Relatively small size within its industry

It is no easy task to define the size limits of a small business. The definition used will depend on the purpose and the agency or program concerned.

CURRENT STATE OF SMALL BUSINESS IN CANADA

Although the size and extent of small business in Canada depends on the definition used, a review of the data compiled by Statistics Canada and Industry Canada illustrates that small business comprises a significant part of the Canadian economy. This is shown in Figure 1-3. The pertinent facts derived from this figure show the strong position held by the small business community (percentages are approximate):

• 97 percent of all businesses operating in Canada employ fewer than 50 employees while 78 percent of all businesses have fewer than five employees.[25]

Figure 1-3   Significance of Small Business to the Canadian Economy

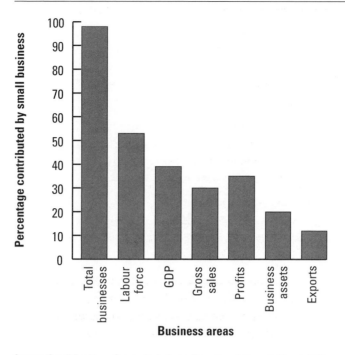

SOURCE: *Small Business Quarterly, Industry Canada,* vol. 2, no. 3, March 2001.
Small Business Primer, Canadian Federation of Independent Business, June 2001.

- 58 percent of the labour force is employed in small business.[26] This includes businesses with fewer than 100 employees.
- 38 percent of gross domestic product is provided by small business.[27]
- 32 percent of all business profits are made in small businesses.[28]
- 29 percent of gross sales in Canada are made by small businesses.[29]
- 10 percent of exports are made by small businesses.[30]
- 20 percent of all business assets are owned by small businesses.[31]

Young Entrepreneurs

Business Development Bank of Canada (BDC)
www.bdc.ca
Young Entrepreneurs Association
www.yea.ca

In addition to the large general increases in the number of small businesses in recent years, more small businesses are started by young people today. In 2000, 53 percent of the self-employed were under the age of 35 as shown in Figure 1-4 (on the next page). This represents a steady increase over the last decade.[32] This indicates that business ownership is an attractive career option for many younger Canadians. Further, a recent survey of Canada's fastest growing small businesses indicated that the average age of the owners was about 40.[33] In recent years, organizations such as the Young Entrepreneurs Association and ACE (Association of Collegiate Entrepreneurs) have been formed in Canada to provide networking and information for these young entrepreneurs. In addition, the recognition by government and private organizations of the importance of young entrepreneurs is evidenced by lending programs offered by the Business Development Bank of Canada as well as the Canadian Youth Business Foundation (see Chapter 7). Annual awards are also made to top Canadian youth entrepreneurs by the BDC.

Figure 1-4   Share of Self-Employment by Age

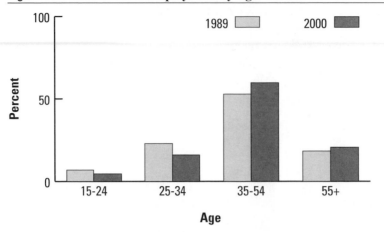

SOURCE: *Self-Employment in Canada Trends and Prospects* (CIBC Economics Division, December 2000) p. 7.

Female Entrepreneurs

Statistics Canada
www.statcan.ca

Self-employment is more prevalent among men than among women. In 2000, one in five employed men owned and operated their own business, compared with one in eight employed women. However, for both sexes, the likelihood of being self-employed has grown considerably over the last 20 years, and the rate of growth has been stronger for women. See Figure 1-5. Women now account for close to 40 percent of one person businesses and 27 percent of self-employed business owners with employees.[34]

Figure 1-5   Number of Self-Employed People by Gender, Annual Averages from 1990 to 2000

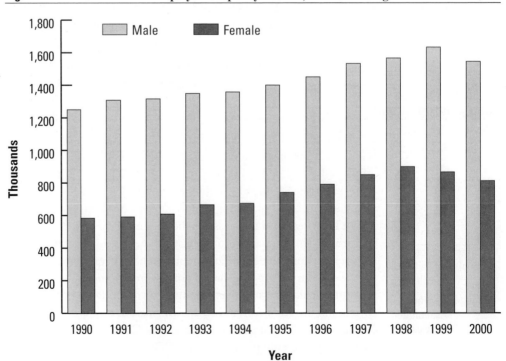

SOURCE: *Canada Labour Force Characteristics* (Ottawa: CANSIM, Statistics Canada, January 16, 2001).

A Global Economic Entrepreneurship study recently found that in 2000, 43 percent of entrepreneurs starting new businesses were female.[35]

Although the majority of self-employed men and women in 1996 worked in the service sector, 4 in 10 businesses operated by men were in the goods sector, while this was the case for only 2 in 10 self-employed women. This mostly reflects the greater concentration of men in the construction industry, since similar proportions of self-employed men (14 percent) and women (12 percent) worked in agriculture.[36]

Canadian Women's Business Network www.cdnbizwomen. com

Many females in corporate life intend to start their own business. A recent study of Canadian female managers found that 27 percent intend to leave to start their own businesses. Reasons cited are dissatisfaction and frustrations with their current employment.[37] Many of the incidents and profiles in this text illustrate the significant contributions of Canadian female entrepreneurs. Incident 1-4 illustrates some challenges female entrepreneurs face.

Immigrant Entrepreneurs

A large number of Canadian entrepreneurs are immigrants to Canada or have parents who were immigrants. More than one in five of the self-employed in Canada are immigrants, almost double the rate observed in the 1980s.[38]

Incident 1-4

It Takes Commitment and Courage

In 1986, LuAn Mitchell married her husband Fred, part owner of a family-run business, Mitchell's Gourmet Foods Inc (MGF). Shortly after their marriage, Fred was diagnosed with Cystic Fibrosis, and a 10-year family feud over the ownership of MGF ensued. Undiscouraged by Fred's condition, LuAn sought ownership with her husband's support. In 1996, Fred and LuAn reclaimed control over MGF's troubled pork-processing operations.

Within two years, the Mitchell's had averted bankruptcy and drastically improved company operations. However, LuAn's newly found success was dampened by Fred's unexpected death in 1998. Grief did not deter LuAn from participating in MGF. Rather then relinquish her shares, she went on to become company chairperson. LuAn now oversees the company's vision, budgets, and the sales office in Banff, Alberta. MGF's operations have been so successful that a $50 million processing plant was built last April. This new plant is expected to double the company's production capacity, thus, increasing sales from their current $287 million level.

In February of 2001, IBM and Los Angeles-based Star Group recognized LuAn Mitchell as one of the Leading Women Entrepreneurs of the World. This prestigious title has motivated LuAn to pursue a second career. The entrepreneur has recently joined the National Speakers Bureau and is giving motivational speeches that share her life experiences. LuAn Mitchell attributes her hard-earned success to unwavering commitment and good communication skills.

SOURCE: Adapted from "Top 100 Women Business Owners," *Profit*, October 2001, p. 26.

Entrepreneurial Activity by Industry

As in other countries, Canadian small business activity is more dominant in sectors that are not capital intensive such as the service industry. Small firms also play a significant role in the retail and construction industries. The manufacturing industry is still dominated by large firms, although this trend is beginning to change as the momentum toward smaller organizations grows.

Figure 1-6 shows the growth of self-employment for some industries in Canada in 1996 and 1999.

Entrepreneurial Activity by Region

Although small businesses exist in all areas of Canada, some regions seem to be more fertile areas for growth. Figure 1-7 shows the growth of employment contributed by small businesses. The regional distribution of growth in self-employment over the past decade shows the West and Ontario seeing the most rapid growth.

Figure 1-6 Growth of Self-Employment by Major Industry

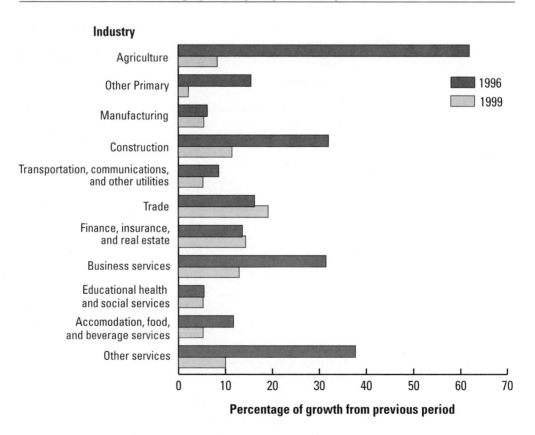

SOURCE: *Small Business Quarterly Report* (Ottawa: Strategis, Industry Canada/Statistics Canada, Spring 2000); and *Perspectives on Labour and Income, Labour Force Survey* (Ottawa: Statistics Canada, Spring 1997), p. 59.

Figure 1-7   **Percentage Increase in Self-Employed by Province, 1989 to 1999**

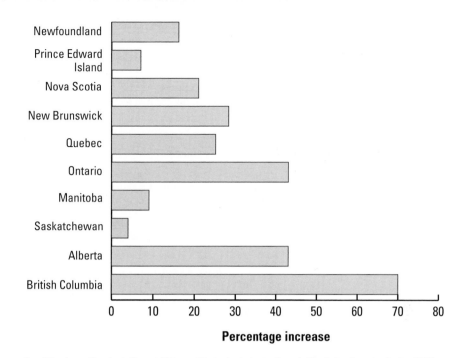

SOURCE: *Small Business Quarterly Report* (Ottawa: Strategis, Industry Canada/Statistics Canada, Spring 2000).

CONTRIBUTIONS OF SMALL BUSINESS

The size of the small business sector is not the only reason this sector is important to Canada. The following sections discuss other significant benefits of small business to Canadian society.

Labour Intensity

Small businesses are generally more labour intensive than large companies. This means they typically employ more people to produce a certain level of output than a larger business does. In addition, small firms accounted for a significant portion of the new jobs created in Canada over the last decade.[39] Statistics Canada reports that in 1997 small businesses created 353,000 more jobs than it lost.[40] In the last quarter of 2000 small businesses in Canada created 60,355 new jobs.[41] Most of these new jobs have been created in the trade and services sectors. In this era of concern about employment levels, it is not surprising that current government policy includes incentives to promote the establishment of small businesses.

Innovations and Inventions

Individuals in small businesses have been responsible for a majority of the inventions and innovations that society benefits from today. Many of these inventions were made by Canadian entrepreneurs. Even innovations made within larger companies are often done by individuals who are rewarded for their entrepreneurial creativity. Incident 1-5 (on the next page) illustrates the innovation of one Canadian entrepreneur who developed his product while working at another job.

Incident 1-5

Davnor Water Treatment Technologies Ltd.

Davnor Water Treatment Technologies Ltd., based in Calgary, Canada, is marketing a low-tech intermittently-operated slow sand filter which removes foul taste, impurities, pathogenic organisms, and toxins from drinking water. The filter does not require power or a steady supply of water to work.

Dr. David Manz, Associate Professor of Civil Engineering at the University of Calgary, and president of Davnor, invented the filter 10 years ago; and, through a licensing arrangement with University Technologies International Inc., formed the company to manufacture, market, and distribute the filter.

Sand filters have been used for centuries to clean impure drinking water; but Dr. Manz developed a system which does not require a steady flow of water to operate. Furthermore, the filter can be built on site from local materials. The filter has attracted the attention of a number of humanitarian organizations and service clubs who have supported the installation of the systems worldwide. The filter is currently in use in Canada, the U.S., Mexico, Nicaragua, El Salvador, Costa Rica, Brazil, Equador, Haiti, Indonesia, Bangladesh, Laos, Vietnam, China, the Philippines, Ethiopia, Kenya, Nigeria, Gabon, and the list continues to grow.

In 1996, Dr. Manz was awarded a Summit Project Achievement Award by the Association of Professional Engineers Geologists and Geophysicists of Alberta.

SOURCE: Don Morberg, "Bringing Clean Water to the World," *UTI Ink* VI, no. 2 (June 1998), p 6.

Productivity and Profitability

Since the turn of the century, the conventional wisdom of economics concerning productivity in organizations has been that the larger the organization, the greater the opportunity to be more productive and profitable. As a result both business and government have tended to increase in size. However, the validity of this thinking has been seriously questioned in recent years and shown to be empirically weak.

Large businesses are also recognizing the gains in productivity associated with smallness. Of the eight attributes of success listed by Peters and Waterman in their study of successful corporations,[42] no fewer than six are commonly found in small businesses.[43] These six attributes are listed below.

1. Bias for Action. These organizations have found that a preference for doing something—anything rather than sending an idea through endless cycles of analyses and committee reports—encourages new ideas and creativity. This principle seems typical of most successful businesses.

2. Staying Close to the Customer. Small businesses learn customer preferences and cater to them. They are generally closer to and have more contact with the consumer. Larger organizations spend considerable amounts of money to maintain this closeness.

3. Autonomy and Entrepreneurship. Breaking the corporation into small companies and encouraging each unit to think independently and competitively has become a strategy of many large businesses.

4. Productivity through People. Creating in all employees the awareness that their best efforts are essential and that they will share in the rewards of the company's success is a major goal of successful companies. In small businesses, owner and employees typically share in the rewards of success and the disappointments of failure in their efforts.

5. Hands On–Value Driven. Many organizations insist that executives keep in touch with the firm's essential business and promote a strong corporate culture. A popular method of management known as management by walking around (MBWA) testifies to the realization that management needs to be familiar with the firm's employees and the operation of the business. The successful owner-manager follows this principle faithfully.

6. Simple Form–Lean Staff. Few administrative layers, with few people at the upper levels, is characteristic of many successful businesses. In many small businesses, employees have a direct line of access to the owner-manager. This arrangement increases the flexibility of the organization as well as employee morale.

Flexibility

Small businesses are generally able to respond more quickly than large businesses to changes in the economy, government policies, and competition. In addition, many markets can be served only by small businesses because they are too small or too localized for large companies to serve profitably. This situation alone presents countless opportunities for entrepreneurs.

Canadian Ownership

The content of Canadian ownership, a major concern of economic nationalists in Canada, tends to be much higher in small business than in large business.[44] Of businesses operating in Canada with less than $2 million in sales, fewer than 1 percent are foreign owned while over 99 percent are Canadian owned.

Small Business Health as a Link to Economic Growth

Considerable evidence exists that those economies that provide the most encouragement for entrepreneurship and small business have experienced the highest growth rates since the 1950s.[45] Recognition of this fact by many centrally planned economies has resulted in more encouragement of entrepreneurship with the associated potential of rewards for those engaged in this type of productive activity.[46] It may also have contributed to the dramatic changes that have occurred in these countries in recent years. One of the key findings of the Second Annual Global Entrepreneurship Monitor, which examines new and growing business in 21 countries, found that a country has a better chance of achieving economic well being if entrepreneurial activities are supported by that society.[47]

Social Contributions

Small business owners often have a long-term interest in the communities in which their businesses operate. As a result, they appear to contribute to those communities in nonbusiness ways to a greater extent than an employee of a large corporation might do.

SMALL BUSINESS AND THE FUTURE

An important question for present and future entrepreneurs, as well as for policymakers is, What effects will future changes in our society have on the small business community? As mentioned at the beginning of this chapter, the 1970s and 1980s were a period of entrepreneurial revolution. Moreover, the late 1990s have determined that change to have been a permanent adjustment to the Canadian business environment.[48] Several developing trends have potentially positive implications for entrepreneurs. At the same time, many of these trends will be advantageous only if entrepreneurs' actions are the result of insight, research, and careful planning.

Some of the more significant factors that will affect the future of small business are discussed briefly in the following sections.

Change

The world is now undergoing a period of rapid change, and this trend is expected to continue. Businesses today will carry out their various activities very differently than they will 10 years from now. This means that small business flexibility likely will continue to be a competitive strength for the entrepreneur.

As the following sections discuss, changes are occurring in technology, consumer demographics and buying patterns, and the competitive aspects of markets.

Technology

Technology has revolutionized the activities of both small and large businesses. Computers allow the entrepreneur to manage large amounts of information as effectively as a larger business. Such advances have signalled significant small business opportunities. Financial management and accounting, marketing research and planning, promotion, and consulting are areas where small businesses, many of them home based, have succeeded. As computer technology becomes more affordable, more small businesses will take advantage of computer applications in these areas.

New technology has also allowed small businesses to obtain subcontracts of many services from larger businesses and government organizations that are unable or choose not to carry out these activities themselves. Despite these potential opportunities, however, small businesses must be prepared to embrace new technology or face the possibility of obsolescence and lack of competitiveness.

Increased performance in the areas of customer service, marketing, manufacturing, and improved communications are all benefits an entrepreneur can achieve through the use of technology. Incident 1-6 illustrates how new technology has revolutionized eye surgery. New opportunities are also opening for entrepreneurs as the Internet and on-line services become more widely used. This information highway is capable of delivering words, pictures, sounds, and music through the use of satellite communication and compression switches accessed by computers. It also allows users to access libraries and to transmit all forms of business communication to data banks throughout the world. The opportunities for entrepreneurs in both obtaining information and marketing products and services to both domestic and global markets are limitless. Appendix 3A (see Chapter 3) provides a complete listing of on-line assistance and Internet addresses which may be helpful to entrepreneurs. More about how small businesses can utilize the Internet is discussed in Chapter 9.

Consumer Demographics and Buying Patterns

Canadian consumers are ageing and their disposable incomes are growing. Of particular interest to most businesses is the baby-boom consumer, born between 1946 and 1964. These people are the largest and most significant demographic group, comprising close to one-third of the Canadian population. This group is currently entering its highest income-earning period, resulting in large expenditures for certain types of goods and services. Although small in number, Canadian seniors hold close to 80 percent of personal wealth and are big spenders on travel, health and fitness products, and various services. This group, however, will represent a large market for entrepreneurs when the baby-boom market moves into this age category. In addition, the ageing of the population presents implications for self-employment as the propensity for self-employment rises with age as shown in Figure 1-4 (on page 12). The

Incident 1-6

TLC Makes Perfect Better

TLC is North America's largest provider of laser eye surgery. When ophthalmologist, Jeffrey Machat, realized that lasers had the potential to revolutionize surgery, he quickly located business partner, Elias Vamvakas, and started up the venture. Correcting three common eye problems, myopia (near-sightedness), hyperopia (far-sightedness) and astigmatism has been TLC's specialty since its establishment in 1993.

Combining unfaultering entrepreneurial spirit and technology has resulted in a new use for old technology. Machat developed the Custom Lasik procedure to fix complications from previous eye surgeries and is now using the procedure to maximize the potential of the human eye. Clients willing to pay a third more than standard patient fees receive the chance to acquire vision that is better than 20/20. In fact, 20/15 and 20/10 is the expected eye enhancement for those undergoing the surgery.

TLC is targeting mainly active, athletic clients who are willing to pay about $3,000 per eye to achieve outstanding vision. Machat began offering the procedure in Toronto in the summer of 2000, but the rest of North America will have to wait until more eye surgeons obtain the required training.

Since its modest beginning in 1993, TLC has experienced an astronomical five-year growth of 28,938%. The company has expanded from one Ontario-based laser clinic to over 60 clinics in 1999. President and CEO, Elias Vamvakas, expects to see up to 15 clinics a year open their doors. Most of the new clinics will open in the U.S., and Vamvakas expects 50 percent of their sales to come from the new Custom Lasik Procedures.

Source: Adapted from Charise Clark, "Better Than Perfect," *Profit*, June 2000, p.75.

larger number of working women has created greater economic clout for females as well as heavier demand for time-saving products and convenience. All demographic groups in Canada are concerned about the environment and demand quality products at reasonable prices.

Each of these demographic and demand trends represents opportunities for entrepreneurs. Many examples of how entrepreneurs are responding to these trends are presented in the profiles and incidents in this text. Markets will become further fragmented as businesses attempt to satisfy consumer wants and needs. This increase in segmentation should favour small businesses that cater to these smaller, more specialized markets.

Competitive Aspects of Markets

Three major occurrences in the past few years have affected the already intensely competitive environment that most small businesses face. The first is the North American Free Trade Agreement, which has liberalized trade between Canada, the United States, and Mexico. The second is the worldwide movement to global markets, augmented by recent developments in Europe. The third is the response to the growth of the small business sector by large business.

The North American Free Trade Agreement (NAFTA). The Free Trade Agreement gradually removes trade barriers among Canada, the United States, and Mexico, but it also eliminates protection for certain industries. In general, Canadian small business has been in favour of the agreement because it opened up the large consumer market to the south. Beginning with the U.S. and Canadian agreement in 1989 and adding Mexico in 1993, market opportunities to over 380 million consumers to Canadian businesses were opened.[49] The agreement also eliminates tariffs, offers Canadian companies much greater and surer access to government markets in Mexico and the United States,[50] and disallows prohibitions of most services.[51] In addition, Latin American countries such as Chile and Argentina are showing interest in becoming part of NAFTA as they too are working toward the elimination of barriers to trade and investment.[52] Some Canadian entrepreneurs have already successfully penetrated these markets. Many have found, however, that they must overcome other difficulties before they can effectively compete. These problems include higher Canadian taxes and distribution costs.

Free trade with the United States and Mexico has also increased competition, particularly from U.S. firms expanding into Canada. This trend has been most noticeable in the retailing industry. Although there will likely be adjustments in particular industries in the short term, the overall competitiveness of the affected industries is expected to improve.

A recent survey of the Alliance of Manufacturers and Exporters Canada members indicated that a high majority of Canadian businesses have benefited from NAFTA.[53]

Global Markets. The world is currently experiencing a major shift to the globalization of markets. The erosion in the domestic and international market boundaries means that smaller businesses should have increased opportunities to source, produce, and deliver to international markets. This means that the many small businesses will eventually include an international aspect in their operations. Although the trend toward trade liberalization has been evolving gradually over a number of years, the defeat of communism in the Eastern bloc signalled a number of new opportunities for entrepreneurs. Consumers in these countries have an insatiable demand for Western products and services. As remaining barriers and purchasing power problems are overcome, these areas will offer huge untapped markets.

Another development that will affect Canadian entrepreneurs is the European Union (EU). The EU is an outgrowth of the six country EEC which is adding other European countries in its own free trade arrangements and has established a single currency. Some of the Eastern bloc countries seem likely to join this union which, although liberalizing trade barriers within the group, may continue with many restrictions to outside countries.

Perhaps the market with the most potential for Canadian entrepreneurs in the future is in Southeast Asia in countries such as Singapore, Thailand, Taiwan, South Korea and, most notably, China. China's population alone of over one billion represents a massive market. These areas are also increasingly receptive to Western goods and services.

Large Business Response. Small businesses have always had difficulty competing with large businesses, particularly for such things as capital, raw materials, and labour. This situation is not expected to change appreciably in some industries. Financing problems continue to plague small businesses. Despite new programs, influence over suppliers by large businesses is strong, and wage rates paid by larger organizations and government are often too high for the smaller business to meet.

In addition to the difficulty of matching wage rates, labour shortages continue. This will increase the competition for competent employees even more. Small businesses will need to find ways to retain top employees through nonfinancial methods. (Chapter 12 discusses this further.) One survey of small business owners indicated that close to half see labour shortages as a major concern for small business.[54]

One positive aspect is that many large businesses and government agencies are increasingly downsizing and subcontracting the purchase of products and services to small business. There is also evidence that many small businesses are joining together through such means as industry associations in an attempt to be more competitive. Such a collaborative relationship, however, often runs against the grain of the entrepreneur's independent nature.

Recently large businesses in some industries have adopted strategies employed by smaller businesses to recoup lost market share. The adoption of entrepreneurial programs in product development, the increased attention to customer service, and the addition of some small business operating policies have enhanced the growth and success of smaller enterprises.

The Economy

The performances of many small businesses are directly related to the Canadian economy. During the recession of 1981–1982, net increases in the number of small businesses decreased. This reflects the fact that it is harder for businesses to get established during such times and the number of failures increases because of lower revenues. The recession of the early 1990s had a similar effect on the performance of the small business sector. There is evidence, however, that those businesses that start during a recession have a greater chance of survival than those started during expansionary periods.[55] The current recession and dramatic events of 2001 have further impacted all business performance and underscores the need for careful planning. Incident 1-7 illustrates how entrepreneurs can benefit from difficult times in the economy. On the other hand, today's economy favours innovation and imagination creating fertile ground for small and medium-sized businesses with new product and service ideas.

The Political Climate

During the 1990s, the political climate for small business ownership seemed to be improving. This was evidenced by attempts to reduce the burdens of paperwork and provide tax incentives to small businesses. (These efforts are discussed in detail in Chapter 13.)

Federal government attempts to encourage entrepreneurship are also evidenced by incentives for immigrant entrepreneurs to enter the country. Special visas are provided for immigrants who invest in small business. Considerable capital has been injected into the Canadian economy through this program.

Although there is considerable interest in government circles in reducing government involvement in business and encouraging entrepreneurial activity,[56] most small business pro-

---

Incident 1-7

Does Small Business Have What It Takes?

A mini-revolution has hit the Canadian economy in the last six years and the main force driving the change has been small and medium-sized enterprises (SMEs).

We know from Statistics Canada about the huge increase in employment the SME sector has generated. And we can read daily in the financial pages about the growing number of new companies, from computer software makers to oil and gas drillers, listing on the stock markets.

In the past, many Canadians earned a living from jobs related to resource industries. And this traditional economy, which has employed our people and paid our bills for several hundreds of years, isn't dead.

But what happened is that many of the giant companies built on the traditional economy, from the railroads to the forest product firms, drastically downsized starting in the late 1980s, sending thousands of well-qualified people into the marketplace.

As the downsizing was taking place, these large companies began outsourcing. A reservoir of creative energy was unleashed of experienced, bright individuals from corporate Canada to build new companies.

Investment strategist Sebastian Van Berkon knows all about this trend because he champions the smaller companies. "There have been more new and innovative companies formed in the last five years in Canada than during the whole period since the 1930s," he said in a recent interview.

SOURCE: James Ferrabee, "Does Small Business Have What It Takes?" *Profits Magazine* 17, no. 1 (Business Development Bank of Canada, Winter 1997), p. 5.

ponents are still waiting for significant action to take place.[57] In fact, the enactment of the goods and services tax (GST) had a much more severe effect on small businesses than on larger firms. (Chapter 13 discusses the GST further.) Small businesses state repeatedly that some of the major concerns about the businesses' environment are high taxes, regulations and paper burdens imposed by the government, and ineffective government programs.[58] Continued collective lobbying efforts through organizations such as the Federation of Independent Business are required to achieve a political environment more conducive to the establishment and successful operation of the small business.

The Social Climate

Society tends to look more favourably on small business and entrepreneurial activities as a legitimate way to make a living. A recent Angus Reid survey indicated that entrepreneurs have the highest level of respect from Canadians, edging out doctors, police officers, and teachers.[59] More and more college graduates are beginning their careers by starting their own businesses, joining the ranks of the many people who left the once secure confines of large business to strike out on their own. Although this trend is expected to continue, adequate preparation and planning will be increasingly required to achieve success following this route.

The onus is now on entrepreneurs as prospective owner-managers to sharpen their skills in this competitive and rapidly changing society. An owner-manager in today's world cannot survive on guesswork. Numerous programs, courses, and types of assistance are available to allow the owner-manager to acquire this training. The remaining chapters in this book cover the critical areas a prospective owner-manager should be familiar with in starting and operating a successful small business.

Summary

1. The entrepreneurial revolution is evidenced by the growing number of business establishments, employees in small businesses, government small business programs, college and university small business classes, and entrepreneurial activities of large companies.

2. Although defining a small business is difficult, having a definition is important in comparing and evaluating small business as well as in taking advantage of various lending and assistance programs. Some common criteria in defining small business are gross sales, number of employees, profitability, and type of management structure.

3. Small business accounts for 97 percent of all businesses, 29 percent of gross sales, 38 percent of gross domestic product, and 56 percent of the labour force in Canada.

4. Small business can provide jobs, innovations, high productivity, flexibility, a higher proportion of Canadian ownership, and more contributions to a society.

5. The climate for starting a small business should continue to be strong, despite some competitve disadvantages.

Chapter Problems and Applications

1. Why do you think entrepreneurial activity has increased? Do you think these trends will continue? Why or why not?

2. Under what conditions would the various definitions of small business be more appropriate? (e.g., the level of profit may be used by the Canada Customs and Revenue Agency to determine the small business tax rate).

3. What is meant by the statement, "Small business is the backbone of the Canadian economic system?" Give evidence to support this statement.

4. The computer-consulting business is becoming more and more fragmented. In data processing; for example, there are hardware versus software consultants, batch versus time-sharing service bureaus, and mainframe versus microcomputer specialists. What effect does this type of industry fragmentation have on the small business community?

5. Ask three small business owners about their projections for the future of small business. What problems and opportunities do they foresee?

Suggested Readings

Canadian Business Magazine. Canadian Business Media Ltd., November 1995 issue.

Clemens, Jason, Fazil Mihlar, Johanna Francis. "The Government Should Get Out of Small Business." Fraser Forum, December 1998, pp. 25–29.

Drucker, Peter F. *Innovation and Entrepreneurship: Practice and Principles*. New York: Harper and Row, 1985.

Gay, Katherine. *Women Talk About What It Takes to Start and Manage a Successful Business*. Harper Collins Publishers Ltd., 1997.

Growing Small Businesses. Ottawa: Industry Canada/Statistics Canada, February 1994.

Perspectives on Labour and Income. Statistics Canada, Spring 1997, pp. 58–62.

Reid, Tim. "Giving Small Business a Fighting Chance." *Canadian Business Review*, Spring 1994.

Self-Employment in Canada, Trends and Prospects. CIBC Economics Division, December 2000.

Small Business in Canada. Ottawa: Industry, Science and Technology Canada, 1991.

Small Business Quarterly. Ottawa: Industry Canada/Statistics Canada, quarterly.

Women Entrepreneurs—Shutting the Glass Box. Statistics Canada, 1997.

Yaccato, Joanne and Paula Jubenville. *Raising Your Business: A Canadian Women's Guide to Entrepreneurship*. Scarborough, Ont.: Prentice Hall Canada, 1998.

Video Case Questions
Reaching for the Heights*

CBC

Steve Smith, a carpenter from Omeemee, Ontario, has invented a line of products he hopes will make him rich. They are add-on accessories intended to make extension ladders safer. Steve wants to get his Strong Arms products on hardware store shelves across Canada. But making the transition from tradesman/inventor to full-fledged entrepreneur is harder than he ever imagined.

1. What characteristics of a typical entrepreneur does Steve Smith possess?

2. Which of these characteristics will help him be successful? Which might contribute to the failure of his idea?

3. What would you recommend that he do to overcome his weaknesses as an entrepreneur?

*Source: CBC *Venture* #728, running time 8:24.

Chapter 2

The Small Business Decision

Chapter 2

Chapter Objectives

- To discuss the advantages and disadvantages of small business ownership as a starting point in making the small business decision.

- To review the personal and organizational attributes of a successful small business owner.

- To discuss environments which are conducive to small business success.

- To explain the reasons some businesses succeed and others fail.

- To identify the differences between an entrepreneur and a manager.

Small Business Profile

Greg Aasen
PMC-Sierra Inc.

PMC-Sierra Inc.
www.pmcsierra.com

Greg Aasen graduated from the University of British Columbia with a degree in Electrical Engineering in 1979 and began his career with Mitel Corporation in Ottawa. In 1986 he left Mitel, moved back to his native B.C. and joined MPR Teletech Ltd. "I came out here with the idea of spinning off a company," says Aasen. His idea evolved from building a business in the telecommunications market to developing chips for data communications. Two years later he convinced MPR to start their first business division PMC which was incorporated in 1992. Greg Aasen has developed PMC-Sierra into a leading supplier of semiconductor chipsets for Broadband Networking applications with sales reaching almost $694 million in 2000.

Greg predicts that within a few years people shopping for clothes will be able to view 3-D images of themselves wearing new suits and outfits even before they're sewn. Business-people will routinely converse with clients through their computers, which will by then have full video, contracts, plans, and resource materials at the click of a mouse.

Although he is PMC-Sierra's chief operating officer, he is not its chief executive officer or president—that title and job he leaves to Robert Bailey who was brought in to manage PMC-Sierra when it became clear the company would become a major player in the industry. "It's just a matter of wanting to be successful so much that you do whatever you have to to make the company a success," he says.

PMC-Sierra is accelerating the broadband revolution. Its extensive family of broadband communication semi-conductors enables the equipment that makes up the backbone of the Internet. In 1995 Greg Aasen was named the Entrepreneur of the Year for Innovation, Design, and Manufacturing in Canada and "Person of the Year" in 2000 by the B.C. Technology Industries Association. He and his company are poised to become major players in the semiconductor industry as the information superhighway becomes a reality. "I love it," says Aasen. "The idea of creating jobs and creating something that will last— that won't just come and go—it's really exciting."

THE SMALL BUSINESS DECISION: PERSONAL EVALUATION

In contemplating whether to start their own businesses, individuals are well advised to consider the potential consequences of such a move, both on themselves and on those closely associated with them. Failure to do this can lead to disillusionment, frustration, and an unsuccessful attempt to capitalize on a viable business opportunity. Frequently, the entrepreneur finds that the reasons for continuing in a small business are different from the reasons for start-up. Compare and contrast Figures 2-1 and 2-2 to note these differences. A good way, therefore, to begin this evaluation is to learn the potential advantages and disadvantages of starting and operating one's own business. In addition, an understanding of the personality characteristics and abilities required of an entrepreneur, as well as an honest self-appraisal of one's own suitability, is essential in making an intelligent small business decision.

ADVANTAGES OF SMALL BUSINESS OWNERSHIP

Running one's own business offers some unique advantages over being an employee. Numerous small business owners cite the following potential advantages.

Statistics Canada
www.statcan.ca

More Personal Contacts with People. Running a small business usually means making contact with a larger number of people, including customers, suppliers, and employees. Those who enjoy and are skilled at working with people find such interactions the most rewarding aspect of their business.

Independence. Often independence is the primary reason for going into business for oneself. This includes the freedom to make one's own decisions without having to account to a

Figure 2-1 **Main Reason for Self-Employment**

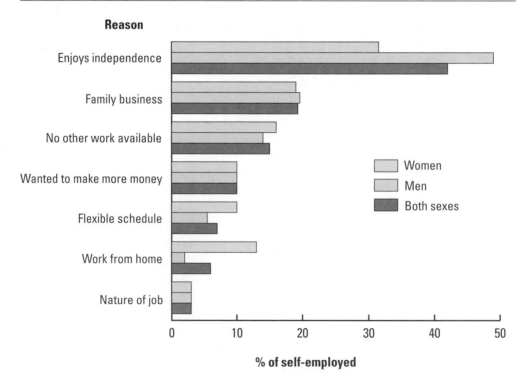

SOURCE: "Survey of Work Arrangements," *Perspectives* (Ottawa: Statistics Canada , 1995), p. 62.

Figure 2-2   Best Aspects about Your Own Business

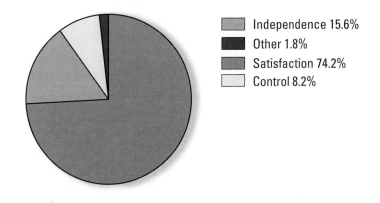

Independence 15.6%
Other 1.8%
Satisfaction 74.2%
Control 8.2%

SOURCE: Padgett Business Services of Canada Ltd., 1995 as reported in *The Globe and Mail*, July 17, 1995.

superior. One study of successful entrepreneurs indicated that the majority started their businesses to "control their own lives" or to "be their own boss."[1] Entrepreneurs should realize, however, that even though they own their businesses, they still must answer to customers, suppliers, key employees, and creditors. A more recent study found "independence" to be one of the things small business owners like the most about owning their own business.[2] (See Figure 2-2.) A recent Statistics Canada study found independence to be the number one reason for self-employment with 41.8 percent of self-employed persons stating this.[3] Incident 2-1 illustrates this trait.

Incident 2-1

Giving It All Up

For some people job security and receiving a regular paycheque is not sufficient incentive to continue working for someone other than yourself. In fact, the independence, challenge, and potential financial rewards that may be received when working as an entrepreneur is motivation enough for one to leave the corporate environment. Such was the case with Ontario resident, Hans Tammemagi. Although working as an environmental consultant provided Tammemagi with a secure lifestyle, the daily routine of consulting on behalf of a large company became tedious and suffocating. Despite being well paid and fairly high up in management, Tammemagi decided to take the risk of launching his own businesses.

In 1994, Tammemagi began conducting environmental audits of buildings for the federal government. Three years later he decided to satisfy his passion for writing by setting up Oakhill Publishing. Both his environmental consulting and publishing businesses are thriving, but such success does not come without a cost. Tammemagi works approximately 60 hours a week.

"Well, they are long hours, but…it's because you enjoy what you're doing and the reward comes straight home," explains the entrepreneur.

The financial rewards, independence, and challenge of running one's own business bring Tammemagi more enjoyment than a corporate career could have. Although the entrepreneurial lifestyle brings many rewards to the business owner, such rewards often come at the cost of lost family and leisure time.

SOURCE: Adapted from Dawn Walton, "Entrepreneurs Embrace Solo Lifestyle: Survey," *The Globe and Mail*, March 25, 1999, p. B-2.

Skill Development. Abilities in many functional areas of management are necessary in running a small business and can be developed during the process. Often the possession of such skills makes an individual more sought after in larger organizations. Today many progressive and innovative organizations look for employees who have had small business experience.

Potential Financial Rewards. The higher risk associated with operating a small business offers the possibility of obtaining a higher financial return. Many small businesses are profitable enough to make their owners financially independent. Note, however, that the promise of financial reward is seldom the sole motivating force behind a small business start-up.[4]

Challenge. Many people start small businesses for the challenge and feeling of personal accomplishment. A study of Canadian entrepreneurs' perceptions of the "ideal" work showed that work that offers a challenge is the most important factor.[5] Often these people left larger companies because their positions lacked the opportunities and challenges a small business can offer. A recent Angus Reid poll of entrepreneurs indicated that the most common reason for starting a business was "the appeal of doing something interesting and challenging."[6]

Enjoyment. Most successful entrepreneurs enjoy what they do. In fact, entrepreneurs tend to get their best ideas from their hobbies.[7] This factor explains in part why financial rewards are not necessarily the prime motivation for establishing a business. It also partly explains the large amount of time entrepreneurs devote to their businesses, as illustrated by the small business profile of Greg Aasen at the beginning of this chapter. Indeed, over 90 percent of Canadian entrepreneurs said they would start their own business again.[8] Incident 2-2 illustrates this characteristic of many small businesses.

Incident 2-2

Three Blondes and a Brownie

At 35, Candace Brinsmead was the youngest bank manager in Canada before she recently resigned to become, "a full-time blonde." Nadja Piatka wrote a newspaper food column and books on fitness and food, and has managed fitness spas. Terry Lynne Meyer has anchored her own local morning television show and has an extensive background in sales and marketing. In other words, they are not amateurs.

McDonald's
www.mcdonalds.com

They also own a low-calorie muffin recipe, developed by Piatka, that has knocked the socks off several key McDonald's executives, not to mention the buying public since March 1994 when it was introduced to McDonald's outlets across Edmonton.

Although McDonald's is their biggest client, they also work with a number of distributors, including a Vancouver distributor who serves all of Western Canada. And their fresh-baked client list is extensive, including the University of Alberta Hospital cafeteria.

They are best friends who also happen to make great business partners. Although from different backgrounds, they are both high achievers who enjoy managing their own lives. Piatka administers product development and quality-control, Meyer handles marketing, and Brinsmead counts the beans. "We want to enjoy a certain quality of life, but we don't want to run on the hamster wheel," says Meyer. "We've been there."

"We do have incredibly intense work periods," adds Piatka. "We're not afraid of work. But we enjoy the work, so it feels like play to us."

That's not to say that anyone else out there with a deadly home recipe couldn't also succeed. For them, the blondes have this advice. Don't believe what everybody tells you about how difficult it is. Don't accept your first 10 rejections. Don't take it personally when nobody in the food industry wants to talk with you. Do provide service. Do go the extra step to make sure your product is a good quality product. And do take your product directly to the marketplace and public if possible.

Source: Adapted from Donna Korchinski, "Three Blondes Cook Up Sweet Success," *The Globe and Mail,* Aug. 4, 1999, p. B10.

DISADVANTAGES OF SMALL BUSINESS OWNERSHIP

While there are many advantages in owning and operating a small business, there are several often overlooked disadvantages. A discussion of some of these and other disadvantages is found below.

Risk. The failure rate of small businesses is very high. Bankruptcy statistics for Canada have shown that smaller firms face a greater danger of bankruptcy than larger ones.[9] It has been estimated that four out of every five small businesses fail within the first few years. There are many potential reasons for these failures, but the major causes appear to be inexperience and unbalanced management.[10]

Stress. Studies show that small business owners have high stress levels, a high incidence of heart disease, and a high rate of divorce owing to the increased pressures of managing their businesses.[11] In owning a business, it is difficult, if not impossible, to confine concerns about the business to the workplace. Typically these pressures will affect one's personal life and family situation as well.

Need for Many Abilities. The acquisition of the required skills, such as accounting, finance, marketing, and personnel management, is a difficult task that many owner-managers never master. This is particularly true for the countless businesses that start out very small. In these situations, entrepreneurs generally cannot afford to hire people with specialized expertise. Failure to acquire these skills, either personally or through recruitment, can seriously hinder the growth of the business.[12] Figure 2-3 illustrates the many skills needed by the owner for a business to succeed.

Limited Financial Rewards. Although the possibility of high earnings exists, relatively few small business owners become millionaires. The financial rewards are often very meagre, especially during the first few years. Even businesses that grow rapidly are not necessarily as

Figure 2-3   Importance of Skills Required for Starting and Managing a Business

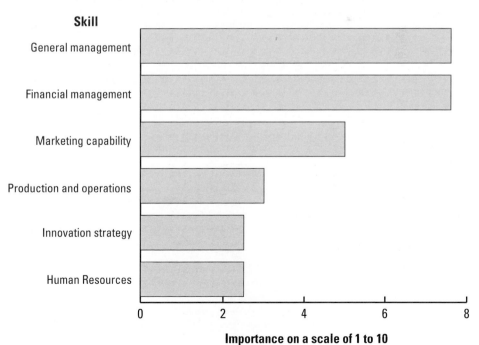

SOURCE: *Failing Concerns* (Ottawa: Statistics Canada, December 1997).

The Canadian Federation of Independent Business
www.cfib.ca

Statistics Canada
www.statcan.ca

profitable as one might think. The Canadian Federation of Independent Business reports that, while a small number of small business owners do very well financially, the majority earn less than the average paid employee.[13] Statistics Canada found this to be 91.4 percent of employed person's wages in 1996.[14]

People Conflicts. Because owning a small business tends to require more contact with people, the potential for more conflicts with employees, suppliers, and customers arises. This factor could turn what is often thought of as an advantage into both a disadvantage and a frustration.

Time Demands. At least initially, almost all small businesses require long hours of work. The work schedule in Incident 2-1 illustrates that the owner-managers of a small business often have a much longer workday than if working for someone else. A recent study of Canada's small businesses found that 50 percent of owners worked over 60 hours per week and 18 percent worked over 70 hours per week, whereas only 14 percent of paid employees work over 50 hours per week.[15] Figure 2-4 illustrates that long hours are part of owning a

Figure 2-4   Percentage of Small Business Owners Who Work More than 50 Hours/Week

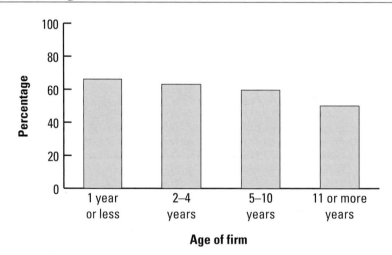

SOURCE: *Canadian Federation of International Business Survey,* April 1999; and BR Newsletter, May 2000, vol. 3, no. 6, p. 8-GD Sourcing.

Figure 2-5   Small Business Owner Advice to Start-Ups

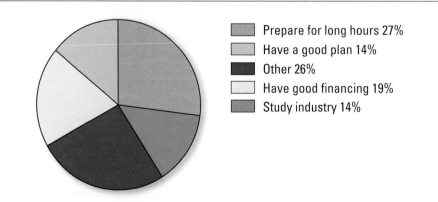

SOURCE: Padgett Business Services of Canada Ltd., 1995 as reported in *The Globe and Mail,* July 17, 1995.

small business, particularly in the early years of its existence. Another study of 650 small businesses in the service/retail sector found that the most frequently mentioned advice to potential entrepreneurs was to "be prepared to work hard and put in long hours."[16] Figure 2-5 illustrates this and other suggestions from these entrepreneurs.

DEMOGRAPHIC CHARACTERISTICS OF ENTREPRENEURS

While entrepreneurs come from all demographic backgrounds, there are some conditions which seem to be correlated with entrepreneurial activity. Entrepreneurs are more likely to come from families in which parents set high standards for their children's performance, encouraged habits of self-reliance, and avoided being strict disciplinarians.[17] A recent trend which is significant is that the greatest growth of small business start-ups come from those who have post secondary education.[18] In addition, entrepreneurs tend to be children of parents who owned their own businesses. Some of the relevant demographic characteristics of entrepreneurs are shown in Figure 2-6.

PERSONALITY CHARACTERISTICS REQUIRED BY SUCCESSFUL ENTREPRENEURS

What are the personality traits of the successful owner-manager? In his book, *Peak Performers*, Charles A. Garfield estimates that 70 percent of the 1,500 peak performers he studied were entrepreneurs. These individuals exhibited some common characteristics that confirmed the results of previous studies.

In discussing the following characteristics, note that Canadian entrepreneurs have many different traits and come from diverse backgrounds. Very few entrepreneurs, if any, possess

Figure 2-6   Characteristics of Entrepreneurs

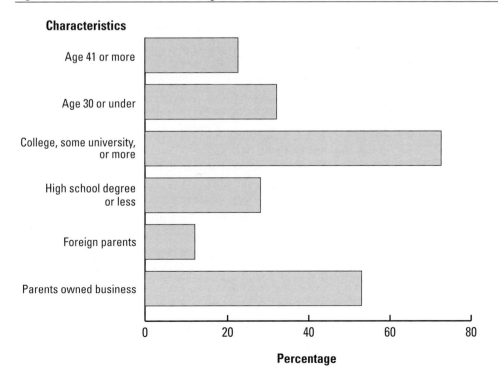

SOURCE: Arnold C. Cooper, *Entrepreneurship: Starting a New Business* (Washington, D.C.: NFIB Foundation, 1993); and Business Development Bank of Canada Survey, 1997.

all of the traits discussed, but many possess at least a few of them. On the other hand, possession of such characteristics does not guarantee success in small business.

Individuals contemplating small business ownership would do well to evaluate their own suitability to operate a small business by noting the following personality characteristics and keeping in mind, however, that being an entrepreneur is less about being a type of individual and more about possessing an attitude of "pursuit of opportunity."

Achievement Orientation.   Those who place a high value on achievement, competition, aggressiveness, and hard work may be ideal owner-managers. Such people tend to be disciplined goal setters and to have a bias for action. Entrepreneurs also tend to possess above-average focus and drive, as well as the initiative to make things happen. Because they are hard workers, they generally strive to maintain good health to sustain this high level of energy.

Risk Taking.   As previously mentioned, the very nature of small business suggests that entrepreneurs are risk takers, although they often do not think of themselves as such. Evidence shows, however, that successful entrepreneurs usually do take calculated risks. They do not fear failure but use it as a source of motivation.

Independence, Self-Confidence, and Self-Assurance.   Entrepreneurs tend to resent authority and to want to take credit or discredit for their own actions. Karl Vesper, the well-known spokesperson for entrepreneurship, states in his book *New Venture Strategies* that "The entrepreneur . . . has a basic human appetite to crave for freedom and power over his/her circumstances."[19]

Other characteristics of successful small business ownership strongly correlated with independence are self-confidence and self-assurance. Often these traits are acquired through parents who were also small business owners. A recent study found that 50 percent of Canadian entrepreneur's parents owned businesses. This is illustrated in Figure 2-6.

Innovativeness.   Successful entrepreneurs tend to be creative and willing to try new ideas. They are not afraid to evaluate an idea in a nontraditional way and to ask questions such as "why not?" Such entrepreneurs are sensitive to new trends in society and potential opportunities that result from such trends. Interestingly, the major reason given by Canadian entrepreneurs for starting their own businesses was that they had found an attractive market niche and wanted to pursue it.[20] Entrepreneurs such as Mark Skapinker, highlighted in Incident 2-3, tend to be oriented toward opportunity.

Strong Verbal and Numerical Skills.   Successful small business owners are able to communicate their thoughts well. One study of 264 Canadian entrepreneurial companies found that communication skills were judged to be the most important contributor to the success of the entrepreneur.[21] Their numerical skills aid them in solving many of the problems that arise in operating a small business.

Whether or not they have achieved a high degree of formal education, successful entrepreneurs usually have acquired the necessary skills and knowledge from various sources. Increasingly, however, the educational background of Canadian entrepreneurs is rising. The CIBC Economic Analysis division recently found that the majority of small business start-ups had at least some post secondary education.[22] Statistics Canada has also found that the growth in self-employed persons with graduate degrees was higher than other educational levels.[23]

Statistics Canada
www.statcan.ca

Selling Skills.   Most successful entrepreneurs have above-average marketing and selling skills. This skill is not only helpful in promoting the business to customers but is also essential for obtaining debt or equity capital, securing suppliers, and maintaining employee loyalty. It is also very valuable in establishing networking contacts or sources of assistance for their operations.

Incident 2-3

Balisoft Technologies

In 1995, Canada lost software pioneer Delrina Corporation to California-based Symantec. Many were disappointed by the merger including Delrina management. Within a short period of time, ex-Delrina innovators realized that Symantec was not interested in them but rather in the company's fax-software technology. Unpleasant tension caused by the merger soon resulted in a cadre of wealthy, experienced software entrepreneurs starting up their own small businesses.

Ex-Delrina President, Mark Skapinker, remained with Symantec until merger tension became unbearable. It was a family trip to Israel that ignited Skapinker's entrepreneurial instinct in 1996. During this trip the entrepreneur was struck with the realization that e-commerce businesses did not possess the capabilities to offer on-line assistance to their customers. At the time of his insight, Skapinker was consulting for an Israeli software company. This allowed him easy access to Israeli venture capitalists waiting to sink their monies into the latest technological innovation.

Skapinker quickly secured the backing necessary to start up Toronto-based Balisoft Technologies, a company that allowed dot-coms to offer on-line customer services. Soon after pioneering this technology, Balisoft merged with ServiceSoft Corps. The Boston-based company possessed the capabilities necessary to bring the new technology into full commercialization. In 1999, sales of Balisoft's technology reached $10 million, and it was at this point that Skapinker realized that it was time to move on yet again.

Skapinker continues to serve as ServiceSoft's chairman, but has now developed a business that supplies him with the entrepreneurial atmosphere he desires. Brightspark Inc. is Mark's latest business venture. The new company provides "incubation" services for technological start-ups. Brightspark guides six to eight new high-tech companies a year to the point where they can begin operating independently. During the incubation period, Skapinker and his 16 employees direct young entrepreneurs on everything from marketing to finance. When start-ups have acquired the business basics, they are ready to operate on their own. In return, Brightsparks receives a piece of each company. This arrangement allows promising new firms to start up in an e-marketplace that is otherwise difficult to penetrate.

Lesson learned: "First and foremost, I'm an entrepreneur," says Skapinker, "I'm better at starting and growing companies than at long-term management."

SOURCE: Adapted from Kara Kuryllowicz, "Founding Father," *Profit*, April 2000, p. 40.

Problem-Solving Abilities. Entrepreneurs identify problems quickly and respond with effective solutions. Typically they rank above average at sorting through irrelevant details and getting to the heart of a problem. Incident 2-4 illustrates how one Canadian entrepreneur started a business to solve the problem of communication between corporate data bases.

Strategic Planning. Successful small business owners tend to excel at setting business objectives and developing different ways of achieving them. They adapt to change easily and know their industries and products thoroughly.

Perseverance. Because of the difficulties in starting and operating a small business, successful entrepreneurs tend to have perseverance. They do not quit amid adversity. One study found that successful entrepreneurs "average 3.8 failures before the final success."[24] Incident 2-5 illustrates the perserverance displayed by Mellanie Stevens.

To assess the suitability of their personalities for starting a small business, entrepreneurs should evaluate their own capabilities in the areas just described. Making a checklist allows a quantitative evaluation of these characteristics. An example of one such checklist appears in Figure 2-7 on page 35.

Incident 2-4

DataMirror

DataMirror develops software that allows instantaneous communication between corporate databases where none would otherwise occur. DataMirror President, Nigel Stokes, identified a need for this technology while managing a software development firm called Nidak Associates Inc. Demand for immediate access to information was growing, and Stokes quickly spotted an opportunity to profit from this unmet need.

The company's first technological development was not easily accomplished. In fact, Stokes and his team of engineers spent 18 months in research and development before launching their first software product. Although DataMirror's first-year revenues in 1994 were only $117,000, by 1999 revenues had sky-rocketed to $42.2 million.

DataMirror's revolutionary database integration software has been sold to more than 1,000 companies throughout North America including U.S. bookseller Barnes & Noble and motorcycle giant Harley-Davidson. Although U.S. market share generates nearly half of DataMirror's sales, the company remains rooted in its home territory, Canada. Competitive labour costs, low employee turnover rates, world-class software engineers, and a growing pool of multi-cultural talent provide DataMirror with advantages it cannot refuse.

As the global market for database integration software continues to increase, DataMirror must remain focused on research and development. Winning global market share means meeting the needs of new corporate customers, and this can only be accomplished with the development of new software products.

Source: Adapted from Peter MacDonald, "Reflected Glory," *Profit*, June 2000, p. 72.

Incident 2-5

Failure Leads to Success

One often encounters failure before achieving success in the world of small business. At least this was the case for Mellanie Stephens. Stephens' latest business manufactures personal-care products including soap, massage oil, and medicinal creams under the name, "From the Meadow." From the Meadow has been meeting the dermatological needs of women since 1999. Operating from a renovated barn in Avon, Ontario, the entrepreneur indicates that her latest endeavour should be substantially more successful than the last two.

In the mid-1980s, Stephens was part owner of a chain of 59 stores called Kettle Creek Canvas. The successful Ontario-based franchise retailed rugged, outdoor clothing. Stephens proudly managed the chain until a bitter dispute erupted in 1988. The disagreement between Stephens and her silent partners resulted in her permanent dismissal from the company. Shock and hurt remained with Mellanie three years after her departure from Kettle Creek.

Kettle Creek Canvas declared bankruptcy the same year that Stephens began operating her second small business, Rural Route Dry Goods Inc. Semi-inspired by Kettle Creek, Stephen's second company retailed outdoor apparel. Rural Route also went out of business. Stephens claims that high costs and low sales were responsible for the demise of her second venture. Spending too much money on store fixtures in a location that did not receive enough shoppers is a mistake that the entrepreneur will never make again.

Two failures would have driven most people from seeking a career in small business. However, it was not enough to deter Mellanie Stephens. This persevering entrepreneur proclaims, "I'm a fighter. And I love business. I love that wheel going around." Working for someone else is simply not an alternative. Although sales for her latest company are nominal, the entrepreneur is positive that From the Meadow will be a success. This time Stephens' company is fulfilling a need. "There are a lot of problems out there in the air, and a lot of it we don't have any control over. But we do have control over what we put on our skin," says Stephens.

Source: Adapted from Laura Pratt, "Where Are They Now," *Profit*, April 2000, p. 44.

Figure 2-7 Personality Characteristic Checklist

1. If the statement is only rarely or slightly descriptive of your behaviour, score 1.

2. If the statement is applicable under some circumstances, but only partially true, score 2.

3. If the statement describes you perfectly, score 3.

	Score
1. I relish competing with others.	3
2. I compete intensely to win regardless of the rewards.	3
3. I compete with some caution, but will often bluff.	2
4. I do not hesitate to take a calculated risk for future gain.	3
5. I do a job so effectively that I get a feeling of accomplishment.	3
6. I want to be tops in whatever I elect to do.	3
7. I am not bound by tradition.	2
8. I am inclined to forge ahead and discuss later.	2
9. Reward or praise means less to me than a job well done.	3
10. I usually go my own way regardless of others' opinions.	2
11. I find it difficult to admit error or defeat.	2
12. I am a self-starter—I need little urging from others.	3
13. I am not easily discouraged.	3
14. I work out my own answers to problems.	3
15. I am inquisitive.	2
16. I am not patient with interference from others.	2
17. I have an aversion to taking orders from others.	2
18. I can take criticism without hurting feelings.	3
19. I insist on seeing a job through to the finish.	3
20. I expect associates to work as hard as I do.	3
21. I read to improve my knowledge in all business activities.	3

A score of 63 is perfect; 52 to 62 is good; 42 to 51 is fair; and under 17, poor. Obviously scoring high here is not a guarantee of becoming a successful small business owner, since many other personal qualities must also be rated. But it should encourage you to pursue the matter further.

THE SMALL BUSINESS DECISION: ORGANIZATIONAL EVALUATION

It is important not only to evaluate one's personal capabilities to operate a small business successfully but to investigate what makes some businesses succeed and others fail. The following discussion reviews what some businesses do right and what others do wrong. The potential small business owner should incorporate those things successful businesses do right and avoid the mistakes other businesses have made.

SMALL BUSINESS SUCCESSES

Despite the high risk associated with starting a small business, many small businesses operate successfully today. Numerous examples of these successes appear throughout this book in the incidents and profiles. These examples illustrate many of the characteristics of successful businesses and their owners. The characteristics discussed next are compiled from reviews of successful small businesses.

Alertness to Change. Small businesses that are flexible and plan ahead are able to adapt to changing environmental conditions more quickly and, in many cases, more effectively than larger businesses. The success of many small computer software companies is a good example. The computer industry is changing very rapidly, and the new needs that are emerging offer many opportunities for small business.

United Furniture Warehouse www.UFW.com

Ability to Attract and Hold Competent Employees. Small businesses tend to be labour intensive, and thus the value of employees cannot be overstated. Small businesses face increasing competition from large firms and even the government in attracting and holding good employees. Those that have mastered this skill are generally more successful. Many of the owner-managers profiled in the text have retained their good employees by using creative personnel management techniques. John Volken of United Furniture Warehouse (see the Small Business Profile in Chapter 3) has implemented personnel policies that allow the firm to retain its best employees—and have also helped United grow into a successful business.

Molly Maid www.mollymaid.com

Staying Close to the Consumer. Business owners who have a good knowledge of consumers' wants and needs and are able to incorporate them within the operations of their companies tend to be more successful. This skill involves constant monitoring of and responding to the market. Molly Maid's success (see the Small Business Profile in Chapter 6) can be attributed to the owners' knowledge of consumers' wants and needs. Molly Maid spends $80,000 a year on consumer research and is looking to expand into other areas.

College Pro Painters www.collegepro.com

Thoroughness with Operating Details. Successful businesses have a very detailed and highly controlled operating plan, whether it be in the plant or out in the market. Goals, reports, and evaluations and adjustments are made constantly. College Pro Painters' success can be attributed to the very thorough operating plan the founder, Greig Clark, set up while testing the business concept. Many successful entrepreneurs subscribe to the "management by walking around" (MBWA) technique through which they remain on top of operations details. Also most successful small business owners have a strong technical background relating to their business.

Ability to Obtain Needed Capital. A potential constraint on the operation and growth of any business is a lack of funds. Businesses destined to succeed, however, often have little difficulty obtaining start-up and operating capital. Their owners are aware of the sources of available financing and are able to make an acceptable presentation of their requirements to both equity and debt sources as the situation requires.

Effective Handling of Government Laws, Rules, and Regulations. Owners of successful small businesses keep abreast of legislation and programs that may affect their operations. They realize that ignorance of certain regulations can cost their organizations not only in a direct financial sense, but perhaps more important, in terms of a tarnished reputation or a missed opportunity.

Environments Conducive to Small Business Success

In addition to the preceding internal characteristics of successful small businesses are some important external situations that may give small businesses a competitive edge. Some of these environments are:

1. Businesses or industries in which the owners' personal attention to daily operations is essential to success. In a service business, for example, the expertise of the owner-manager is a major factor in generating revenue.

2. Businesses in which owner contact with employees is important to the motivation of staff and the quality of work done. Specialized or custom-made manufacturing processes or service businesses and other businesses in which employees have direct contact with customers fit into this category.

3. Markets in which demand is small or local, making large businesses generally reluctant to pursue them. Incident 2-6 illustrates how such a market may offer opportunities for small businesses.

4. Industries that require flexibility. These include industries with high growth rates, erratic demand, or perishable products.

5. Businesses that are more labour and less capital intensive. Because of the above points, a business that relies heavily on people rather than machines to provide its product or service may be easier to manage if it is small in size. The retail industry is a case in point.

6. Industries that receive considerable encouragement from the government in the form of financial, tax, and counselling assistance. Much of this

---

Incident 2-6

A Winning Survival Strategy

Avoiding competition with "the big guys" is the strategy choice of Diagnostic Chemicals Ltd. Thirty years ago, 67-year-old Regis Duffy launched what is now Canada's largest producer of clinical chemical reagents. DCL manufactures and sells blood sugar and cholesterol products not only to Canadian hospitals and laboratories but to those abroad as well. In fact, Duffy's global success landed him the 1999 Canada Export Award.

Seven years ago, Duffy recognized that current product demand was going to dry up with the onset of new hospital machines and analyzers. The new technologies no longer required the array of chemicals produced by DCL. Accordingly, Duffy changed his company's production focus to meet and serve the needs of pharmaceutical manufacturers. Today, DCL produces chemicals that are essential compounds required in the production of insulin, while also supplying big names such as Johnson & Johnson.

Finding the right market niche and avoiding competition with large corporate competitors has really been the key to DCL's success. "We try not to compete with the big guys," says Duffy. Development of specialized products with added value ensures the loyalty of DCL customers. Duffy finds that today companies provide customers with limitless attention. Consequently, the key to success in the pharmaceutical industry is to develop niche markets by forging relationships with companies that have specific needs. Manufacturing products that meet pharmaceutical companies' specific needs prevents competitors from easily stealing ideas and clients.

In 1992, Duffy was recognized by *Profit* magazine as one of Canada's top entrepreneurs; at the time, sales were $7 million. Since the prestigious award, DCL's sales have grown to over $20 million a year. Duffy attributes his company's success to his avoiding the "big guys" strategy, as Diagnostic Chemicals Ltd. continues to forge ahead in the pharmaceutical industry.

SOURCE: Adapted from Rhea Seymour, "Staying Power," *Profit*, April 2000, p. 32.

assistance is directed at smaller businesses in the manufacturing, processing, and exporting industries. Such industries represent potential opportunities for small businesses.

In deciding whether to start a small business, the potential owner should investigate whether any of the above environments exist or might exist. Such conditions could be a critical factor in the success of the business.

SMALL BUSINESS FAILURES

Despite the considerable appeal of operating one's own business, it can also be disappointing if adequate preparations are not made. This section discusses some of the causes of small business failure. Hopefully prospective entrepreneurs will avoid making the same mistakes as they start their own businesses.

Although higher in 2000, the number of business bankruptcies in Canada has been dropping slightly over the last five years[25] (see Figure 2-8); situations such as the one described in Incident 2-7 have been all too common in recent years. Bankruptcy figures alone, however, do not give a complete picture of business failures. Many businesses are placed in receivership, and other business owners simply close their doors and walk away from their businesses when they fail.[26] Estimates indicate that in 2000 there were 10,040 bankruptcies,[27] but close to 100,000 businesses in Canada actually ceased operations.[28]

Businesses follow much the same life cycle that products do in that both go through start-up, growth, maturity, and decline phases. The majority of businesses that fail pass completely through this life cycle within five years of start-up. Therefore, a small business owner has little time to remedy serious mistakes. Information from Statistics Canada reveals that only about 55 to 60 percent of businesses are still operating three years after their establishment[29] and that only one in five survive to the tenth year of operation.[30]

Statistics Canada
www.statcan.ca

Figure 2-8   Incidence of Business Bankruptcies

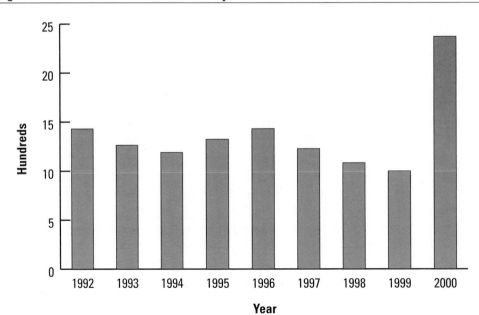

Source: *Market Research Handbook* (Ottawa: Statistics Canada 1998 and 2000), p. 94 and p. 121; and *Office of the Superintendent of Bankruptcy and Small Business Quarterly*, vol. 2, no. 3, March 2001, p. 5.

Incident 2-7

Richard Thomas

Daimler Chrysler Corporation www.daimler chrysler.com

Richard Thomas was optimistic about the new car dealership and gas station he had established in his home town of Kenora, Ontario. He had the only Chrysler dealership in the area and had just received approval from the bank to go ahead with the construction of a new building in an excellent location. He was confident that by offering gasoline at cut-rate prices he could increase customer traffic, which would eventually lead to sales of other accessories and, of course, automobiles.

Within a few months, however, problems started to surface. The cost of the new building exceeded projections, and Thomas had to use operating funds to complete construction so that he could begin operations. This led to a serious cash shortage. He could not meet operating expenses and service the current debt, which carried a high interest rate. In addition, Chrysler Corporation was experiencing its own difficulties, which were affecting its sales throughout Canada. Finally, although many people stopped to purchase gasoline, few bought anything else at Thomas's business. As a result, a year later Thomas was bankrupt and forced to give up the business that had once looked so promising.

SOURCE: D. W. Balderson, University of Lethbridge, Alberta. Although this incident is based on a factual situation, the name and location have been changed.

Entrepreneurs need to understand the reasons businesses fail so that they can avoid similar mistakes. As Figures 2-9 and 2-10 illustrate, there are both external and internal factors which contribute to business failures. More specifically, some of the internal reasons for failing small businesses include: budgeting, receivables and payables management, inventory management, fixed-asset administration, high debt load, and marketing. Chapters 8–12 are devoted to these principles of management, because failure to follow them contributes to the difficulties unsuccessful firms encounter.

Figure 2-9   External Factors Contributing to Bankruptcy

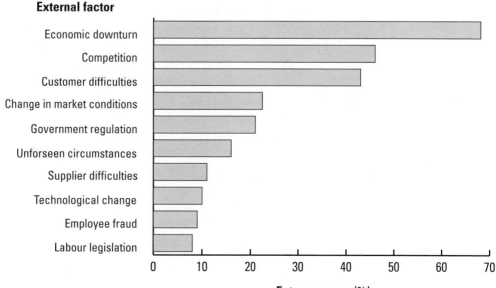

SOURCE: *Failing Concerns: Business Bankruptcy in Canada* (Ottawa: Statistics Canada), November 1997, p. 23.

Figure 2-10 Internal Factors Causing Bankruptcy

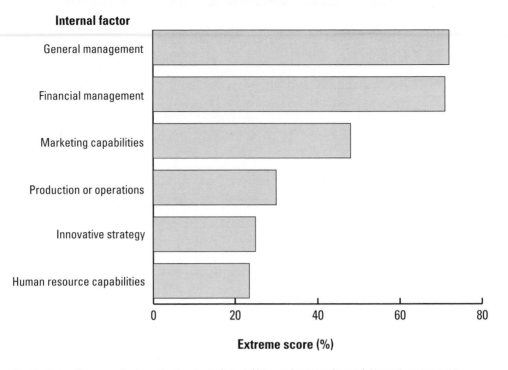

SOURCE: *Failing Concerns: Business Bankruptcy in Canada* (Ottawa: Statistics Canada), November 1997, p. 23.

ENTREPRENEURSHIP AND SMALL BUSINESS MANAGEMENT

Up to this point in the text, the terms *entrepreneurship* and *small business management* have been used interchangeably. However, considerable confusion exists between these two terms, the types of skills they describe, and the type of training required to develop such skills. This section distinguishes between these terms. Understanding this distinction can be valuable in establishing and maintaining a business. Although they differ, both entrepreneurial and managerial skills may be necessary at different stages of the business's life cycle. This is the primary reason that both types of skills and traits are discussed together earlier in this chapter.

Entrepreneurial Skills

Entrepreneurial skills are required to start or expand a business. The specific traits that describe entrepreneurship are creativity, flexibility, innovativeness, risk taking, and independence. Entrepreneurs who have a high tolerance for ambiguity and change tend to think and plan with a long-term perspective. Entrepreneurs are generally idea-oriented.

Those who start their own businesses are known as *founders* of the business and may be found in two types. The first, sometimes called the *artisan* entrepreneur has expertise in the technical or operations side of the business. They may have invented the product and tend to be passionate about the product and confident of its success. The second is the *promoter* who identifies a product or service which they feel has potential, and they team up with the founder to assist with initial financing or marketing expertise. Many small businesses are established following this pattern.

Managerial Skills

The skills of a manager are useful in maintaining and solidifying the existing product/service or business. The effective manager knows how to develop strategy, set organizational goals, and develop methods for achieving those goals. Managers require skill and knowledge in several functional areas of a business, including finance, marketing, personnel, network development, research, teamwork development, and operations. Such skills are most valuable after the business has been established.

As can be seen, although the skills the entrepreneur and the manager possess differ, they are nevertheless essential for the long-run success of the business. Entrepreneurial skills help get the business started, while managerial skills help ensure that the business continues to operate successfully. Entrepreneurial skills may be essential once again to promote growth of the business.

A major problem associated with small business is that individuals who have strengths in both areas are rare. Because most small businesses are started and operated by the same person, skills or characteristics which that person might lack must be found in others who are hired or otherwise acquired. Failure to do so may doom the venture. A study by the Harvard Business School found that only one-tenth of 1 percent of the ideas patented and listed in the Patent Gazette had actually made money or could be considered successful.[31] This suggests that many of the businesses established to develop these ideas may have lacked the necessary managerial skills. Figure 2-11 summarizes the distinction between entrepreneurial and managerial skills and the situations to which they apply. Part II of this text discusses essential considerations in starting a business (the entrepreneurial side), and these chapters refer to the individual as the entrepreneur. Part III covers the managerial skills required for the established enterprise (the management side) and refers to the individual as the owner-manager or the small business manager.

Figure 2-11 Small Business Skills

Type	Characteristics	Appropriate Situations
Entrepreneurial	Creativity and innovativeness Independence	Generating ideas or solutions to problems
	Risk taking	Starting new business
	Idea-oriented	Expanding or adding new products
Managerial	Develops strategy and goal setting	Reaching performance objectives
	Prefers to know outcomes of actions or activities	Maintaining control of operations
	Team player	
	Works through others	
	Skills in finance, marketing, personnel, operations	

Summary

1. There are many advantages and disadvantages to owning a small business. Some of the most common advantages are frequent contacts with people, independence, skill development in many areas, potential financial rewards, challenge, and enjoyment. The possible disadvantages include high risk, higher stress levels, the need for many abilities, conflicts with people, limited financial rewards, and time demands.

2. Certain personality characteristics are associated with a successful owner-manager. These include an achievement orientation, risk taking, independence, self-confidence and self-assurance, innovativeness, strong verbal and numerical skills, problem-solving abilities, strategic planning ability, and perseverance.

3. Environments conducive to small business success have the following characteristics: a good owner-manager rapport with employees, high labour intensity, personal attention to daily operations by the owner, markets requiring flexibility, markets in which demand is small or local, and industries that receive governmental assistance.

4. The major causes of business failure are generally related to incompetent or inexperienced management. Some specific areas where difficulties are found are budgeting, receivables and payables management, inventory management, fixed-asset administration, high debt load, handling personnel, and marketing problems.

5. Entrepreneurs are creative, independent, and idea-oriented whereas managers possess strengths in problem solving, working with others, and developing strategies.

Chapter Problems and Applications

1. What does your analysis suggest are the most common reasons for small business failure? Investigate the causes of failure for a small business that you are familiar with or for one of the examples in the text.

2. Which of the characteristics of successful small business owners do you think is the most important? Why?

3. How do managerial skills differ from entrepreneurial skills? When would an entrepreneur's skills be more useful than a manager's? Why?

4. Complete the checklist in Figure 2-7. Do you possess the personality characteristics necessary for successful small business ownership?

5. What characteristics does Greg Aasen in the Small Business Profile have? Are these managerial or entrepreneurial characteristics? Explain.

6. Interview a local small business owner about what he or she feels are the advantages and disadvantages of small business ownership.

7. Interview a local entrepreneur, and attempt to identify his or her entrepreneurial characteristics and leadership style.

Suggested Readings

Balwin, John, Tara Gray, Joanne Johnson, Jody Proctor, Mohammed Rafiquazzaman, and David Sabourin. Statistics Canada, Catalogue no. 61-525-XPE, November, 1997.

"Chatelaine Top 100 Women Business Owners." *Chatelaine*, November 2000.

Drucker, Peter F. *Innovation and Entrepreneurship: Practice and Principles*. New York: Harper and Row, 1985.

Garfield, Charles A. *Peak Performers*. New York: Morrow and Company, 1985.

Gerber, Michael. *The E-Myth Revisited*. New York: Harper Business Publishers, 1995.

Gould, Allan. *The New Entrepreneurs—80 Canadian Success Stories*. Toronto: McClelland and Stewart–Bantam, Ltd., 1986.

Longsworth, Elizabeth. *Anatomy of a Startup*. Goldhirsh Group Inc., 1991.

McMullan, W. Ed, and Wayne A. Long. *Developing New Adventures*. Toronto: HBJ Publishers, 1990.

Rumball, Donald. *The Entrepreneurial Edge*. Toronto: Key Porter Books, 1989.

Statistics Canada. "Profile of the Self-employed." *Canadian Economic Observer*. January–December, 1997/98.

"The Entrepreneurial Mind." *Success Magazine*, November 1993, pp. 25–27.

Vesper, Karl H. *New Venture Strategies*. Toronto: Prentice-Hall, 1990.

Comprehensive Case
The Framemakers: Part 1

Robert and Teresa Norman faced a big decision. They were contemplating Robert leaving his job as manager of his father's painting business to set up their own retail picture-framing store. As they thought about this dilemma, their minds wandered back to the events that had led up to the impending decision. Robert had been raised in a small town about 32 kilometres south of Brandon, Manitoba. His father was a painter, and Robert had worked in the painting business part time for several years. Upon graduating from high school, he completed a two-year business administration in interior design course at a college in the United States. It was there that he met and married his wife, Teresa.

Teresa had studied interior design at college. She came from a small farming community near Robert's hometown. One of her favourite pastimes while she was growing up was taking pictures of beautiful scenery and making frames for them. Teresa, an only child, had always been very independent. Her parents, farmers, spent a lot of time tending to the farm. Teresa started helping them when she was very young by doing the bookkeeping and other administrative jobs.

Although Robert had always thought he might come back to take over his father's painting business, he wanted to obtain some outside business experience first. As a result, he found a job in a Zellers store in Winnipeg after his graduation. Robert enjoyed working with people in the retail setting, but felt frustrated working for a larger company. He wanted to be on his own and dreamed of someday running his own business. While Robert worked at Zellers, Teresa had been developing her photography skills, working for local retailers preparing catalogues. Though she was fairly busy with this, she did not feel as if she was challenged.

Finally, after two years with Zellers, the Normans decided to leave Winnipeg and return to Brandon where they could begin to take over the painting business. Robert's father was pleased with their decision and, since he was approaching retirement age, allowed his son to assume a major role in the business. Norman managed the business for six years with Teresa doing the bookkeeping. But although it provided a steady income, he could see that the growth possibilities in terms of income and challenge were limited. In addition, he soon realized he didn't like painting as much as he thought he would. As a result, he and Teresa started looking around for sideline opportunities to earn a little extra money. One they particularly enjoyed was assembling and selling picture frames.

One day, while in Winnipeg to obtain some water-seal paint, Robert ran across a small retail store called U-Frame It. He went in to look around and talk to the manager about the business. He was impressed by the manager's enthusiasm and also noticed that the store was extremely busy. Robert immediately began wondering about the possibility of starting his own picture-framing store.

Excited by what he had seen, Robert returned to Brandon without even buying his paint and told Teresa what had happened. She was extremely enthused with the idea. Robert's father was skeptical and, as Robert had expected, disappointed that they wanted to leave the family business.

Robert and Teresa needed to make their decision quickly. The manager of the U-Frame It store had indicated that the franchise chain was looking at Brandon as a possible site for another outlet sometime in the future.

Questions

1. What aspects of Robert and Teresa Norman's backgrounds will contribute to their success if they decide to go ahead with the picture-framing store?
2. What further areas should Robert and Teresa explore before making this decision?

This case, based on an actual small business situation (names and location changed), was written by D. Wesley Balderson, University of Lethbridge.

Video Case Questions
Bright Lights, Deep Waters*

CBC ⬤

Scientist turned entrepreneur, David Green, has a multi-million dollar idea for solar-powered marine lighting. Now all he's got to do is get the product to market before his competitors.

1. Discuss the difference between an entrepreneur and a manager using David Green and Carmanah Lights as examples.
2. What dangers of obtaining equity financing are illustrated in this example?

*Source: CBC *Venture* #780, running time 9:58.

Chapter 3

Evaluation of a Business Opportunity

Chapter Objectives

- To review the nonquantitative aspects of evaluating business opportunities.

- To introduce the methods by which an entrepreneur can enter a market with a product or service.

- To discuss the types of information available to assist in the quantitative analysis to select a small business and illustrate how that information can be used.

- To provide a systematic way to quantitatively assess an industry and evaluate the financial feasibility of a specific small business opportunity.

Small Business Profile

John Volken
United Furniture Warehouse

**United Furniture
Warehouse
www.UFW.com**

John Volken spent his early childhood in the former Soviet-occupied East Germany. His father was a professional, so John was not allowed a high school education. This left a lasting impression on him. At 14 he moved to West Germany where he worked during the day and obtained an education at night. In September of 1960, at the age of 18, he moved to Canada with just $20. Upon his arrival he worked as a farm labourer, then as a dishwasher, and then in construction. As soon as he became comfortable with the English language he moved into sales. During the next few years he lived and worked in Ontario, Quebec, and Nevada. In 1969 he moved to B.C. and for the next 12 years operated a door-to-door frozen-food business and mail-order business.

In 1981 he started United Buy and Sell Service. The original intent was to bring sellers and buyers of used commodities together. However, some of the first merchandise he bought and sold was furniture and he saw the potential in this industry. John's research showed that there was a market for reasonably priced quality furniture in a nonpressured environment. Furniture soon became the only commodity and after four years "used" furniture was discontinued.

John Volken's philosophy is customer appreciation and commitment to employees. "We value our customers not as statistics, but with a warm sense of appreciation," he says. Though financing is available, he refuses to offer "no payments till the year 2000" loans because he feels they are not in his customer's best interests. He is proud of the fact that his customers always know where they stand. "With the ever-increasing competition for people's disposable income, you have to go the extra mile for customers," says Volken. "We try to bend over backward for the customer." In its 20 years, United Furniture Warehouse has never offered a sale nor does it employ commission salespeople. When a piece of furniture is assigned a price, it remains at a price that undercuts all competitors. As well, all of Volken's stores are closed on Sunday. "Sunday is a family day and our employees are happier and more motivated." That his formula is successful is evidenced by the fact that United Furniture Warehouse has grown to 150 locations. In 1995 Volken was selected as Entrepreneur of the Year for the Pacific Canadian Region.

Having achieved his professional goals, Volken is now employing his talents as a social entrepreneur by building Welcome Home, a $23 million long-term care facility where disenfranchised young men and women learn to become productive members of society.

Used with the permission of John Volken.

NONQUANTITATIVE ASSESSMENT OF BUSINESS OPPORTUNITIES

Chapter 2 discussed methods of evaluating one's suitability for small business ownership. Much of this chapter deals with methods of quantitative evaluation. This section examines some nonquantitative factors to consider in the selection of a small business opportunity. These factors may influence one's selection and significantly alter the quantitative analysis.

Goals. The individual should examine his or her personal goals regarding income earned from the business. The question to address is: How well will the type of business chosen allow me to achieve not only my financial goals but also my occupational status goals?

Content of Work. The individual should assess his or her suitability for the business's working conditions. What type of work will the business involve? Will the business require hard physical work or considerable contact with people?

Lifestyle. What type of lifestyle will the business allow? Will the hours be long or concentrated in the evenings or on weekends? Will the business allow family members to be involved? Remember that most small businesses take much more time to operate than the owner anticipates prior to start-up.

Capabilities. In addition to the personal characteristics needed to run a small business that were discussed in Chapter 2, at least three other capabilities are required.

The first requirement is good health. As mentioned earlier, managing a small business usually involves long hours and is often physically and mentally stressful. One will need good physical health and stamina as well as the ability to withstand high levels of stress.

The second requirement is expertise in the fundamentals of management, including administration, marketing, and finance. While numerous courses can provide valuable train-

---

Incident 3-1

The Importance of Experience

Setting goals and acquiring industry experience was the key to success for Toronto-based SunBlush Technologies. SunBlush was created in 1986 to license MAP, a shelf-life extension technology, developed by the University of British Columbia. MAP is Modified Atmosphere Packaging, a technology that reduces spoilage-inducing oxygen in sealed packages.

Selling a technology that is capable of doubling the shelf-life of fresh produce seemed like it would be an easy task. However, food processors were painfully change-resistant and convincing them to adapt a cost-and risk-reducing alternative proved to be no easy feat for SunBlush. "The food industry is extremely traditional," says president and CEO, Nigel Lees.

So how did SunBlush finally tap into the market? Through persistence, goal setting, and experience. When food processors refused to adopt MAP, SunBlush bought its own processing businesses, including a pineapple processor in Costa Rica and a cut-lettuce supplier in Boston. This approach was extremely successful, as it allowed SunBlush to demonstrate the effectiveness of its technology. "We feel the technology is fully commercializable now," says manager of SunBlush investor relations, Kathy Fischer. SunBlush has sold off several of its fruit processing plants and is once again pursuing its original licensing goals.

Since its establishment 15 years ago, Nigel Lees has learned plenty from his experiences in the food processing industry. Most importantly, the president recognizes the importance of having first-hand experience in the industry one is trying to enter. Experience provides one with invaluable knowledge, contacts, and a clear idea of how to achieve company goals. Now that the company has successfully reached food processors, it is tackling cyberspace. SunBlush has recently acquired Access Flowers, an on-line flower wholesaler. Lees says, "We want to see SunBlush Technology applied to all kinds of perishables traded on the Net."

Source: Adapted from Richard Wright, "Back to Its Roots," *Profit*, June 2000, p. 79.

Figure 3-1   Sources of Ideas for New Businesses

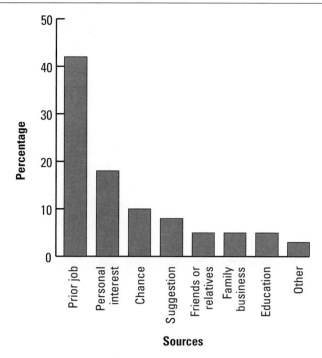

SOURCE: National Federation of Independent Business.

ing, many successful small business managers have acquired expertise in these areas through self-education.

The third requirement is a sound financial base. Except for some types of service businesses, one can seldom start a business with less than $10,000 to $50,000. This amount may, in fact, be only the equity portion, which qualifies the business to acquire the necessary capital.

Experience. Lack of experience and unbalanced experience are two major causes of business failure. One of the best preparations prospective small operators can make is to acquire knowledge in the type of business or industry they plan to enter. "An example of such an approach appears in Incident 3-1. In this example, an entrepreneur had some well-defined career goals and capabilities and experience in the field prior to establishing his business. Another benefit of experience is the personal contacts one acquires while working in a particular industry. In addition, some entrepreneurs have received assistance from mentors provided by such organizations as the Canadian Youth Business Foundation and Women's Enterprise. For many entrepreneurs, assistance from such sources can be invaluable in successfully establishing the business.

Canadian Youth Business Foundation www.cybf.ca

National Federation of Independent Business www.nfibonline.com

Many entrepreneurs establish their businesses and work in them part time while holding another job. This is an excellent way to gain experience and minimize risk. Although such an approach is not possible in some situations, many successful businesses originated from a part-time job. Entrepreneurial ideas come from many other sources. Figure 3-1 illustrates the percentages for such sources in a survey of entrepreneurs carried out by the National Federation of Independent Business.[1]

BREAKING INTO THE MARKET

Entrepreneurs have essentially three ways to enter a market by establishing a new business. The first is to offer a totally new product to the market. This involves "inventing" a product that meets a need not currently being fulfilled. Thousands of successful products have resulted from an individual's dissatisfaction with existing or a lack of existing products. An example of this type of product appears in Incident 3-2.

Many of the fad or novelty types of products also fit into this category. The needs these types of products satisfy are often emotional or subjective rather than rational. Products such as pet rocks and mood jewellery fit this description. Several periodicals provide product ideas (see Appendix 3A at the end of this chapter). Some companies sell ideas that have received preliminary market testing.

K-tel International
www.ktel.com

A second approach is to offer an existing product to a different market or industry. Phillip Kives, founder of K-tel International, was the master of this type of approach. His company achieved success initially by acquiring products currently sold abroad and marketing them in North America. Another form of this approach is to offer an existing product or service in the same geographical market, but to a different age or income group, or to use the product for a different purpose. This approach is illustrated in Incident 3-3.

Incident 3-2

Turncoat Teddies

It's always a bear market for Wendy Donchi of Millarville, Alberta., but that's fine with her. Her home business — recycling old fur coats into teddy bears — has been growing since she made her first ones in 1993 for her sister and friends. Now, she has customers from across Canada and the U.S. wanting their mothers' and grandmothers' old furs turned into one-of-a-kind bears.

"My clients tell me stories about the women who owned the coats," says Donchi, who tries to capture something of the owner's personality in her designs. That, and a distinctive scent of perfume that often still clings to the fur, provides a special connection with the owner.

A typical bear is 46 centimetres tall and costs about $300; a full-length coat can yield up to three bears. Donchi uses any type of fur, but mink works best because the hide ages better.

Business, which comes mainly from word of mouth, gets more bullish as Christmas gets closer.

Source: Leslie Goodson, "Turncoat Teddies," *Report on Business Magazine,* December 1997, p. 25.

Incident 3-3

Car Sharing—A Missing Link in the Transportation System

How can one reduce driving expenditures, pollution, and traffic congestion without taking public transportation? The answer is by becoming a member of AutoShare Ltd., an up-and-coming Toronto-based car-sharing company. Former ministry of housing worker, Liz Reynolds, and partner, Kevin McLaughlin, began AutoShare Ltd. after receiving inspiration from a similar Quebec-based operation.

Car sharing is a new way to offer an existing product to a different market. Interested persons obtain an AutoShare membership and then receive access to vehicles that sit in Toronto subway and streetcar stations across the city. A one-time fee of $500 and a monthly fee of up to $40 can reduce yearly driving expenditures by more than half, compared to owning a vehicle.

Reynolds and McLaughlin continue their quest to wean Toronto drivers from car ownership. Their current endeavours have resulted in the purchase of over 260 memberships with approximately 20 new members joining every month. The two entrepreneurs are currently solidifying a deal that will substantially sweeten AutoShare membership privileges. The creation of smart cards will allow AutoShare members access to car-sharing as well as Toronto trains, transit, and taxis. Liz Reynolds and Kevin McLaughlin have certainly developed a dynamic new way to integrate cars into an environmentally friendly transportation market.

Source: Adapted from Rhea Seymour, "Share and Save Alike," *Profit 100,* June 2000, p. 10.

The third way to enter the market is to offer a product or service similar to those already existing in the same market. In this case, the prospective small business owner attempts to obtain some competitive advantage over the existing products or businesses in the industry to maintain viability. Perhaps the market is large enough to accommodate an additional business, or the level of satisfaction with existing businesses or products in the industry is low. Examples of this type of entry into the market include establishing a retail store that stocks brand-name, conventional merchandise and manufacturing a product so that it can be sold at a lower price.

More will be discussed about carrying out an evaluation for this type of venture later in this chapter. Regardless of the approach used, it is important to look at the growth trends within the industry, the number of competitors and their relative market share, as well as their strengths and weaknesses prior to entering the market.

Following are the 10 top Canadian business ventures for the near future according to a leading industry analyst as reported in *Profit*.[2]

1. Self-diagnostic tools
2. Affordable organic foods
3. Education books, videos, and CD-ROMS
4. Technology training centres
5. Customized information services
6. Anti-ageing cosmetics
7. Pet-related products and services
8. Financial services tailored for women
9. Activewear for ageing adults
10. Home-safety devices

COLLECTION OF INFORMATION

The key to making a wise decision regarding which industry to enter and the type of business to start is the gathering and analysis of information. The more relevant the information, the greater the reduction of uncertainty about the results of this decision. One study showed that the overwhelming majority of small business owners do no formal marketing research, although many do informal, unsystematic information gathering.[3] Failure to do adequate or appropriate market research is frequently cited as the most common reason for small business failure.[4] Incident 3-4 (on the next page) illustrates how an organization was successful because of doing research prior to starting their business.

Some reasons entrepreneurs commonly cite for lack of research and investigation are that it is too time consuming, too expensive, too complicated, and irrelevant. While each of these claims has some substance, there are some simple, inexpensive, but effective methods of collecting and analyzing data available to the entrepreneur.

Sources of Information

The first thing entrepreneurs should be aware of is the many sources of information available to assist them in their investigations. Two general types of information can aid prospective small business owners in selecting the right small business. The first, secondary data, consists of data previously published by another organization. The second, primary data, is data collected by the entrepreneur. The following sections discuss both types of information in detail.

Incident 3-4

Med-Eng Systems Inc.

Med-Eng Systems Inc. has learned the value of doing market research before completing the final development of the product. This modern marketing philosophy to product development has made Ottawa-based Med-Eng Systems Inc. a world leader in bomb-disposal equipment.

Producing a helmet designed specifically for use with another manufacturer's bomb suit, in 1991 Med-Eng achieved $1 million in sales to police and military forces. However, when Med-Eng refused a takeover bid by a U.S. firm, the U.S. firm bought the suit maker, then cut off supply to Med-Eng. "They bought the company thinking they could put us out of business," says Med-Eng's co-founder, Vince Crupi. Instead of folding, Med-Eng decided to compete directly with this company by developing their own suit.

Crupi and president Richard L'Abbé took the resulting prototype—a less cumbersome, more protective suit and helmet combination with two-way radio technology—on a three-month tour to clients in 45 countries. "We asked them what they thought of it, what needed to be done and asked them for input," explains Crupi. Involving potential clients in the design process helped Med-Eng develop a superior suit and created immediate buy-in among their "consultants," most of whom placed orders. It made them much more competitive with the U.S. company and helped them survive.

With annual sales of $7 million, Med-Eng now holds 95 percent of the world market for bomb-disposal suits. The future looks even rosier. A $2 million injection of venture capital in 1997 will be used to develop equipment for the global crusade to remove land mines.

Source: Adapted from Bruce Livesey, "Great Moments in Marketing," *Profit*, February–March 1998, pp. 34–40.

Secondary Data

Statistics Canada
www.statcan.ca

Business Development Bank of Canada
www.bdc.ca

Secondary data takes the form of reports, studies, and statistics that another organization has already compiled. There is no shortage of secondary data to aid the entrepreneur, and it is usually inexpensive. A major problem, however, is finding information relevant to one's own situation. The secondary data available may be too general or may not apply to the type of business being established. Also, some reports are out of date and thus will need to be adjusted to make them useful. Such data can be updated by projecting past trends.

Secondary information is inexpensive, which makes it very attractive to the prospective small business owner. Much of the secondary information available in Canada is provided by the federal and provincial governments. However, much valuable secondary information is available from private and semiprivate sources. Appendix 3A at the end of this chapter presents a complete listing of those sources most relevant for small businesses. Figure 3-2 gives an example of using secondary data to begin the feasibility analysis for a business. This example uses Statistics Canada reports to estimate market potential for a florist shop in Toronto.

In addition to obtaining published secondary information, entrepreneurs can consult several agencies for counselling in both starting up a business and ongoing operations. The most inexpensive and often most valuable source is the counselling provided to entrepreneurs by federal and provincial governments. The Business Development Bank of Canada can provide start-up counselling as well as analysis of the already operating business. The latter service is offered through the BDC Consulting Group. The BDC Consulting Group is available to businesses and uses retired business people as consultants.

**Figure 3-2   Assessing Market Feasibility of Opening a Bookstore in Toronto Using
Secondary Data**

Problem	To estimate the size of the market for a bookstore in Toronto.	
Step 1:	Determine the population in Toronto Population of Metropolitan Area of Toronto (Source: Metro Toronto Information 2000)	= 4,700,000
Step 2:	Determine the number of families in Toronto. 4,700,000 divided by 3.1 (average size of families in Ontario) (Source: Statistics Canada Census information)	= 1,516,129
Step 3:	Estimate total bookstore sales for Toronto 1,516,129 × $50 (family expenditures on books and magazines) (Source: *Market Research Handbook* 2000, Statistics Canada)	= 75,806,450

This shows that a total of $75,806,450 could be expected to be spent in
the Toronto area in bookstores.

SOURCE: *Market Research Handbook,* 2000, Statistics Canada; Metro Toronto Information, 2000.

Most provincial governments also employ small business consultants to assist the small business (see Appendix 3B at the end of this chapter for the addresses of these agencies in each province). Many provincial agencies provide start-up and business plan preparation assistance similar to that offered by the federal government.

Another potentially valuable source of assistance comes from universities and colleges. Many universities have student consulting programs designed to aid the small business owner. Using the expertise of graduating or graduate students, these programs can assist in preparing feasibility analyses or evaluating a business problem for a minimal fee, usually the cost of materials used. (Appendix 3C at the end of this chapter lists universities in Canada that have such programs; several colleges offer similar services.)

Other helpful counselling sources are lawyers, accountants, or bankers. Some of these sources may be more expensive than government services, however. Numerous consulting firms also specialize in small business operations.

In addition to the types of assistance just described, another concept appears to promise considerable help in establishing new enterprises: the incubation centre. The incubation centre consists of an organization—usually a municipal or provincial agency—that provides essential services for new small businesses, either free or at minimal cost. Office space, secretarial services, computer capabilities, and financial and business counselling are examples of these services. One study found that eight out of 10 businesses nurtured by incubators were still operating after five years.[5] Incident 3-5 (on the next page) illustrates how business incubators are assisting new businesses and providing employment for Canadian youth.

There are currently over 500 incubators operating in North America.[6] These include more than 1,000 incubator tenants, and estimates indicate that new incubators are opening at a rate of one per week.[7] In Canada, more than 40 business incubation centres operate across the country[8] although this recent growth may be difficult to maintain due to cutbacks in funding

Incident 3-5

A Hatchery for Winners

**Communication
Research Centre (CRC)
www.crc.ca**

"Getting customers is usually the biggest problem for small companies," says David Jackson, general manager of the Toronto New Business Development Centre, a five-year-old incubator housed in the 96-year-old former Massey-Ferguson plant west of Toronto's downtown. "That's where we can give them a lot of help."

Marketing clout is what attracted Linmor Information Systems Management Inc. to Ottawa's Innovation Centre, a business incubator opened last year by the federal Communications Research Centre (CRC), a large public sector laboratory.

Linmor recently licenced some communications software from Bell-Northern Research Ltd., customized it for the general market, and plans to sell it to large corporations around the world. Already, the managers of the CRC incubator have enabled Linmor to meet with executives from Telsat, Rogers, EDS, and Stentor.

"Normally, we wouldn't have access to these people," says Shawn Ling, vice-president of marketing for Linmor. "They gave us a chance to make our pitch."

Linmor also has access to the 200 scientists and engineers employed by CRC. They're available to help with any technical problems encountered by the small company.

Next year, Linmor will probably move out of the CRC incubator and into its own quarters. "We got a kick-start at the CRC, but we'll be able to go off on our own shortly," Mr. Ling says. Indeed, most companies remain in business incubators for a maximum of two years, and some of them stay only a few months.

SOURCE: Gerry Zeidenberg, "A Hatchery for Winners," *The Globe and Mail,* June 5, 1995, p. B5.

from government sources. Business incubators allow the small business community to work, individually or collectively, through the chamber of commerce and with municipal (city or town) governments, provincial governments, universities, and colleges. Statistics show that businesses receiving assistance from incubator centres have a 30 percent greater chance of success.[9]

Primary Data

Primary data is information collected through one's own research. Although usually more costly to obtain than secondary data, it can be more relevant to one's business and more current. Primary research is essential if secondary sources do not provide information required for the feasibility analysis. It may also be beneficial to supplement information obtained from secondary sources. Despite these advantages, small business owners have traditionally hesitated to do much primary research because of their lack of knowledge about how to do it and its relatively high cost.

Some research methods, however, are not complicated and can be of great value to the entrepreneur in evaluating the feasibility of a potential business opportunity. Three general methods that can be used to collect information through primary research are: observation, surveys, and experiments.

1. Observation. Observation involves monitoring the who, what, where, when, and how relating to market conditions. For the small business, this method might involve observing auto and pedestrian traffic levels or customer reactions to a product, service, or promotion. It may also entail simply observing sales or expenditure levels. The observation method may be fairly expensive, as it requires that time be spent in monitoring events as they occur. Another limitation of observation research is that it allows one to only make inferences about the reasons people respond in certain ways. There is no two-way interaction with the subject of the research that might shed light on such motivations.

2. Surveys. To obtain more detailed information from potential consumers and to better understand their motivations in purchasing a product or service, a small business owner can carry out a survey. The entrepreneur should clearly define the objectives of the research prior to questionnaire construction and ensure that each question addresses one of the objectives. Usually it is not possible to survey each potential customer or the total market; therefore, only a part of the market is surveyed. It is essential, however, that the responses obtained be representative of the total market. Figure 3-3 illustrates a simple but accurate method for determining a representative sample for a research project for a small business. Such a survey might give the entrepreneur a general indication of the extent of demand for a new business. Of course more detailed research should be carried out before a decision to start the business would be made. Many businesses have failed because the owners acted on their own feelings or the opinions of a few acquaintances. In some cases, these responses do not represent the opinions of the total market. Incident 3-6 (on the next page) illustrates how a lack of representative information from the market created a difficult problem for a small agricultural machinery manufacturer.

Occasionally, through design or necessity (e.g., limited funds), a nonrepresentative group of people are surveyed as part of the primary research project. This could involve surveying only experts or knowledgeable people in an industry rather than an equal cross-section of consumers. This method is also often used in surveying shopping mall customers. The most obvious drawback is that the findings may not be representative of the total market.

Figure 3-3   **Calculating a Representative Survey Sample for a Small Business**

Step 1:   The following chart can be used to determine the number of surveys that should be completed to achieve a 95 percent confidence level at .05 degree of precision.

Population Size	Sample Size
50	44
100	80
500	222
1,000	286
5,000	375
10,000	385
100,000 and over	400

Step 2:   Choosing the respondents. If a phone survey is being conducted, there are two ways to choose the respondents. The first is to use the phone book and choose every nth individual. The second is to use a random number generator to come up with the phone numbers. Both of these methods have advantages and disadvantages, but both allow the surveyor to obtain a representative sample.

Incident 3-6

Kirchner Machine Ltd.

Kirchner Machine Ltd. is a well-known farm machinery manufacturer in Lethbridge, Alberta. It manufactures many successful tillage and haying implements and has built a solid reputation as a well-run small manufacturer in the farm machinery industry. In 1991 several farmers expressed concern to Kirchner about their inability to handle and transport large, round hay bales. These bales, commonly weighing about 500 kg, had become very popular with farmers and ranchers throughout North America. However, they had to be moved to the stack or a larger truck one at a time, which was quite time consuming.

In response to this concern, Kirchner designed and manufactured a bale hauler that could be pulled with a tractor that could carry six bales. Named the Big Bale Fork, it was expected to add another successful product to Kirchner's line. Unfortunately, sales were disappointing. Although those who purchased the Big Bale Fork were satisfied, sales were too few and far between. One reason was that the firm had not carried out market research to assess total market potential for the product. Those who had purchased the hauler were too small a part of the market to make it economically feasible. Those who had suggested that Kirchner manufacture the Big Bale Fork were unrepresentative of the total market.

SOURCE: D. W. Balderson, University of Lethbridge.

Three types of surveys are used to collect market information: mail surveys, telephone surveys, and personal interviews.

Mail Surveys. Mail surveys are most appropriate when

- Only a small amount of information is required.
- Questions can be answered with "yes–no," "check the box" answers, or brief responses.
- A picture of the product may be required.
- An immediate response is not required.

One problem with mail surveys is their poor response rate—typically well under 50 percent—and the lack of control over who fills out the questionnaire. Also, the preparer needs to make sure that the mail survey is not too long or too complicated. Figure 3-4 shows a simple mail survey carried out for a small business to assess initial demand for a Japanese restaurant.

Telephone Surveys. Telephone surveying has become the most popular survey method in recent years, most likely because of its low cost and quick response time. However, it is even more restricted than a mail survey in the amount and detail of information one can obtain. The telephone interviewer should follow a survey guide to ensure consistency. Figure 3-5 (on page 58) offers an example of a typical phone survey guide. As with the example of the mail survey, this phone survey might give the entrepreneur an indication of the acceptance of the concept. Further research and analysis would be required before a decision should be made.

Personal Interviews. The most expensive type of survey is the personal interview. While this method generally costs more and requires greater expertise, it is the best approach for obtaining more detailed information and opinion-oriented responses. Since the number of people surveyed typically is smaller than in mail or phone surveys, this method is more suitable for

Figure 3-4   Mail Questionnaire: Japanese Family Restaurant

1. Approximately how often does your family eat at a restaurant or dining lounge in the city of Oakville?*

    a. _____ Less than once per month

    b. _____ Once per month

    c. _____ Once every two weeks

    d. _____ Once per week

    e. _____ Two–three times per week

    f. _____ More than three times per week

2. Approximately how much do you normally spend per family when you eat out at a restaurant or dining lounge?

    a. _____ Less than $25

    b. _____ $25 – $50

    c. _____ $50 – $75

    d. _____ $75 – $100

    e. _____ Over $100

3. Are you familiar with the difference between Japanese and Chinese cooking?

    _____ Yes

    _____ No

4. If a family restaurant specializing in Japanese food was opened in Oakville, would you

    a. _____ probably never go?

    b. _____ definitely try it?

    c. _____ patronize it regularly if food, service, etc., were adequate?

5. Where would you prefer such a facility to be located?

    a. _____ Downtown

    b. _____ West Oakville

    c. _____ South Oakville

    d. _____ North Oakville

    e. _____ Does not matter

Thank you very much for your time and cooperation.

* Name of the city has been changed.

SOURCE: Academy Management Services, Lethbridge Alberta.

interviewing knowledgeable people in an industry as opposed to surveying a cross-section of potential consumers. It may involve surveying one individual at a time or, as many large companies do, surveying several people together in what is called a focus group. The personal interview may be used for purposes such as testing a new product concept or advertisement or evaluating a company's image.

Figure 3-5 Telephone Questionnaire Guide: Sporting Goods Rental Store

A sporting goods store, located in a city of approximately 65,000 people, wanted to start renting summer sports equipment. The following survey was designed to determine consumer demand for such a rental business.

Survey number: Phone number:

Hi, my name is _____; I am presently conducting a survey to determine people's summertime leisure activities in the city. A few moments of your time to answer the questions would be greatly appreciated.

1. Can you tell me if you participate in any of the following activities during the summer? List the equipment…and the responses.

2. A lot of people ski in the winter because ski equipment can be rented at a fraction of its retail price. Are there any summer activities you would participate in if the equipment was available on a similar basis?

    a.

    b.

3. Are you older than 18 years of age?

    Yes (   )   No (   )   If no, please record your age and stop doing this survey.

4. Would you consider renting the following equipment if available at reasonable prices?

    Please indicate if you have the item.

    List equipment

5. Male (   )   Female (   ) Fill in for all respondents

6. Age: 18–25   (   )

                    26–35   (   )

                    36–50   (   )

                    > 50   (   )

7. Income: Less than $20,000   (   )

                    $20,000–$40,000   (   )

                    $40,000–$60,000   (   )

                    $60,000+   (   )

    Thank you very much for participating in this survey.

Source: Student Consulting Project, University of Lethbridge.

Entrepreneurs are often unsure about what types of questions to use in a survey. Some areas in which information should be obtained are the following:

- Respondents' reactions to the product or service
- The price respondents are willing to pay for the product or service

- Respondents' willingness to purchase the product or service. Answers to such questions are often overly positive and should be adjusted downward by as much as 20 percent.

- Frequency of purchase

- Level of satisfaction with current product or service

- Demographic characteristics of respondents

3. Test Marketing. Test Marketing involves an attempt to simulate an actual market situation. For an inventor, it may mean letting a number of people try out a new product and then finding out their reactions. For a business, it may mean marketing a product on a limited basis and observing sales levels, or surveying to find out the level of satisfaction with the product or service. This method is fairly costly in that the product must be developed and marketed, albeit on a limited basis. The main advantage of experimental research, or test marketing, is that it measures what people actually do, not just what they say they will do, concerning the product. Small businesses have successfully used this method in taking prototype products to trade shows, exhibitions, or potential customers to assess potential acceptance. Test marketing is especially appropriate where little capital investment is required, such as with a small service business or on-line marketing to other businesses and consumers.

The proper collection of secondary and primary data can be invaluable to entrepreneurs as they assess business opportunities. It can provide a base of data that, if analyzed correctly, may allow the capitalization of a successful opportunity or the avoidance of a disaster. The types of market research just described require an investment in time and money, but many successful entrepreneurs are convinced they are a worthwhile investment.

Although owner-managers often use these information collection methods prior to starting their businesses, they can and should use them on an ongoing basis after the businesses have been established to stay abreast of changes in market conditions. Many successfully established businesses have become complacent, and as a result, eventually have failed because they lost touch with consumers and/or the market conditions. To avoid this, the small business should set aside the effort and money required to regularly collect and use relevant market information. Chapter 8 discusses this subject further.

QUANTITATIVE ASSESSMENT OF BUSINESS OPPORTUNITIES

Preparing the Feasibility Analysis

Once the entrepreneur has collected the relevant information about the market, the next step is to use this information as quantitatively as possible to assess the financial feasibility of the proposed venture. The purpose of this assessment is to determine whether the business will earn the amount of income the entrepreneur desires. The financial feasibility analysis as described in this section is most appropriate for starting a new business from scratch, but much of it could be applied to the purchase of an existing business or the operation of a franchise.

There are essentially three steps in estimating the financial feasibility of a proposed business venture. The first step is to determine potential revenue (demand) for the total market. The second is to estimate the share of total market revenue that the new business might obtain. The third is to subtract the associated expenses from the revenue estimate to arrive at a projected estimated net income for the prospective business. A more detailed explanation of the steps in calculating a feasibility analysis is presented next. A detailed example of such an analysis is given in Figure 3-6 (see pages 64–68). In carrying out the feasibility analysis, one should remember to be conservative with all estimates. See Incident 3-7 for an illustration of a small business that failed to do this.

Incident 3-7

Overly Optimistic Market Share Projections

"I don't dream little, I tend to dream big," says Harold MacKay, company president of Maritime Beer Co. MacKay, a former Moosehead Breweries Ltd. manager, joined Moosehead brewmaster, Kirk Annand, to launch a 42,000 square-foot craft brewery and restaurant in Dartmouth, Nova Scotia. In 1993, Moosehead's Dartmouth plant closed and both men were offered positions elsewhere in the company. MacKay remained with Moosehead, while Annand resigned the offered position. Before leaving the company MacKay offhandedly approached Annand with the idea of starting a brewery. Annand's response was, "Harold, if you get the money, we'll start a brewery."

Mackay stayed with Moosehead until 1995, while Annand taught at Chicago's Siebel Institute of Technology. By 1997, MacKay had raised the funds necessary to begin the company, and Mr. Annand joined the endeavour. With products available in New Brunswick, Prince Edward Island, the French islands of Saint-Pierre and Miquelon, as well as Nova Scotia, the two brewers hoped to obtain a healthy 3.5 percent of the market. But in an industry dominated by Molson Cos. Ltd. of Montreal and Labatt Brewing Co. Ltd., it didn't happen. In fact, the brewers fell short by a substantial amount and managed to grab only 2 percent of their projected market share. Advice from Don MacDougall, former president of Labatt Breweries, should have been heeded. MacDougall, who sits on the Maritime Beer board, proposed that projections of company market share were overly optimistic. "I tended not to listen. I thought I had all the answers," laments MacKay after realizing his company was $3 million below expected revenue projections.

Winning affection over established beer brands also proved to be difficult for Maritime Beer Co. Introducing five 100-percent malt beers at once gave the impression that the company had only one type of beer. Mistakes made early on had grave consequences on revenue generation for Maritime Beer, but the co-founders have not lost faith in their company. New, more realistic projections indicate that the brewery should capture its original 3.5 percent market share within the next 12 to 15 months. Both Mr. Annand and Mr. MacKay have learned that being "painfully naïve" in making financial predictions can result in surprisingly low revenue.

SOURCE: Adapted from Dawn Walton, "Beer Upstart Works to Uncap Potential," *The Globe and Mail*, May 25, 1999, p. B-12.

Step 1: Calculate Market Potential

The purpose of this step is to arrive at a dollar or unit sales figure for the total market. It may involve three substeps:

1. *Determine the market area and its population.* Delineate the geographic area or target market the business will serve. This can be done by obtaining a map and marking off the size of the market. Then estimate the population (numbers) within that market that might conceivably purchase the type of product or service to be offered. This process yields an estimate of the size of the target market.

Statistics Canada
www.statcan.ca

2. *Obtain revenue (sales) statistics for this market area for the product type or service.* Usually federal, provincial, or municipal governments have this information for many standard types of products or businesses. For example, Statistics Canada publishes retail expenditure and manufacturing data for many products and services. If total revenue or sales figures are not available for the proposed type of business or product, but per capita or per family expenditures are obtainable, simply multiply this figure by the population estimate obtained in substep 1 (population of market × per capita expenditures).

If the product or service is new and no secondary data is available, use secondary data about a similar product. If there is no similar product, primary research—in the form of a survey, for example—may be used to assess consumer acceptance of the concept. If the results of such a survey indicate that a certain percentage of the market shows a purchase interest, multiply that percentage by the size of the market to obtain the market potential estimate.

3. *Adjust the market potential total as necessary.* If one is able to obtain actual revenue statistics for the market, usually the only adjustment needed is to update the data. As mentioned previously, secondary data is typically a year or two out of date. A simple way to update sales and expenditure data is to increase the amount of sales by the annual rate of inflation for the years involved. This might also include a forecast of trends that will affect demand in the future. Such trends could be included in the estimate.

   If national averages of per capita expenditures are used, adjustments for local shopping patterns must be made. A common adjustment in this regard is to adjust for those living in the market area who purchase outside the market, and vice versa. For example, if it is estimated that 20 percent of the market buys the product or service outside of the market area, reduce the market potential by 20 percent.

   Projections should include one-year and five-year estimates to reflect trends that may exist in the industry. Projections should also include trends with respect to growth of the competition that might affect future market share.

Step 2: Calculate Market Share

The purpose of this step is to estimate the percentage of the total market potential the proposed business will obtain. Because the method of calculating market share differs significantly depending on the type of business, market share calculations for retail, manufacturing, and service firms are illustrated separately.

Retail Firm

1. *Estimate the total amount of selling space in the market devoted to the merchandise the new business will sell (usually in square feet or metres).* This involves taking an inventory of space of competing stores (specialty and department stores) devoted to this product. This estimate may be obtained informally by observation or by asking the owners. In some areas, secondary information about retail selling space may be available through the municipal or city government or department.

2. *Estimate the size of the proposed store (in square feet or metres).* It is likely that the entrepreneur will have a good idea of the size of the proposed store. The actual size, of course, may depend on the availability of outlets.

3. *Calculate the market share based on selling space as follows.* The information collected in steps 1 and 2 is now integrated in the following formula:

$$\frac{\text{Proposed store selling space}}{\substack{\text{Total market selling space} \\ \text{(including proposed store)}}} = \text{Percentage market share}$$

4. *Make adjustments to reflect any competitor strengths and weaknesses regarding the proposed store.* Typical adjustments might include the following:

a. Decrease percentage share if the competition has a better location, is larger in size, or has considerable customer loyalty. A decrease in the percentage should also be made, because the proposed store is new and will take time to build customer loyalty.

b. Increase percentage share if the proposed store will offer unique products, services, location, advertising, or other advantages over the competition.

The amount of the adjustments may be arbitrary and somewhat subjective, but typically they are fractions of a percentage of the market share.

5. *Multiply the revised market share percentage by the market potential estimate obtained in step 1.* The result is a dollar revenue estimate for the proposed business for the first year of operations. By applying market trends to this figure, a one- to five-year estimate can be obtained if required.

Manufacturing Firm

1. *Estimate the total productive capacity in the market for the product to be manufactured.* Typically this will be calculated in units, but it may be in dollars. This will involve estimating the production size of competitors (both domestic and foreign).

   If the product is a new innovation and no competition exists, market share obviously is the same as the market potential calculated previously.

2. *Estimate the productive capacity of the proposed manufacturing plant.*

3. *Calculate the market share based on productive capacity.* The information obtained in steps 1 and 2 is integrated into the following formula:

$$\frac{\text{Production capacity of proposed business}}{\substack{\text{Total production capacity} \\ \text{(including proposed business)}}} = \text{Percentage of market share}$$

4. *Make adjustments to reflect competitive strengths and weaknesses the proposed plant may possess.* The market share percentage estimated in step 3 will likely need to be adjusted. The strengths and weaknesses of competitors should be determined and compared with the proposed business. Often primary research may be required to obtain this type of information.

   Generally a higher market share can be obtained in industries in which competitors are smaller in size, the product can be differentiated from competitors' products, and primary research shows a particular level of dissatisfaction with existing products.

   Market share will tend to be smaller if the industry is made up of a few large and powerful competitors who hold key contracts or where consumer satisfaction with the existing product is determined to be high.

   Even though the existing market may look formidable, some sectors of the economy look favourably on purchases from small businesses. The federal government, for example, is a very large potential purchaser that should not be overlooked. These types of markets are discussed in Chapter 8. For a manufacturing firm, success at obtaining key contracts may provide the certainty required to calculate the market share and bypass some of these calculations.

5. *Multiply the estimated market share percentage by the market potential estimate obtained in step 1.* This figure projects estimated dollar sales for the first year of operations. As in the retail example, industry trends can assist in estimating this figure for more than one year.

Service Firm

1. *Estimate the total capacity of the service available in the market area.* The base used to calculate capacity will vary depending on the type of service being offered. For example, restaurant capacity may be measured by number of seats, tables, or square footage; motel capacity by number of rooms; and beauty salon capacity by number of employees or number of workstations. It is important to determine which base most accurately reflects the service capacity. This estimate can be obtained by observing existing businesses or talking to owners.

2. *Estimate the service capacity of the proposed business.* This involves projecting the size of the proposed business in terms of service capacity.

3. *Calculate market share based on the capacity base.* The information obtained in steps 1 and 2 is integrated into the following formula:

$$\frac{\text{Proposed business service capacity}}{\substack{\text{Total production capacity} \\ \text{(including proposed business} \\ \text{service capacity)}}} = \text{Percentage of market share}$$

4. *Make adjustments similar to those made for a retail store.* The adjustments in the service industry tend to be more significant than in retailing. The opportunity to differentiate from competitors in the service industry is much greater than in retailing, which tends to deal with more standardized products. Therefore, the percentage adjustments may be larger for service industry market share calculations.

5. *Multiply the estimated market share percentage by the market potential estimate obtained in step 1.* This figure projects estimated dollar sales for the first year of operations. As in the retail example, industry trends can assist in estimating this figure for more than one year.

Step 3: Calculate Net Income and Cash Flow

1. *Using the market share revenue figure obtained in step 2 as the starting point, calculate the expenses expected to be incurred for the business.* Most of these figures should be obtained by checking with suppliers and other similar businesses. However, some secondary sources, such as those provided by Statistics Canada, provide typical operating statements for many types of small businesses. Often these statements express expenses as a percentage of revenue and thus can be easily adapted to the proposed business. Some of the more important required expenses are:

   - Cost of goods sold and gross profit percentages—these can be obtained from secondary data but should be confirmed with suppliers.

   - Cash operating expenses, such as rent, wages, utilities, repairs, advertising, and insurance—these expenses can also be obtained from secondary sources but should be verified by checking with vendors of these services, as they may differ for the market area of the proposed business.

   - Interest and depreciation—a list of the costs of capital items (i.e., building and equipment) and total start-up costs will need to be made so that yearly depreciation and interest expenses can be calculated. Chapter 7 presents information on determining start-up costs and subsequent interest calculation.

One should remember that only the portion of these assets estimated to be used during that period should be included as the depreciation expenses. Using these start-up costs as a basis, an estimate of the amount of debt and annual interest costs using current rates should be determined.

2. *Subtract expenses from revenue to determine the projected net income from the proposed business in the first year and subsequent years, if required.* Once a projected income figure is calculated, the prospective entrepreneur is in a position to evaluate and compare this result with other types of available investments. Return (income) as a percentage of investment (funds put into venture) can be compared to other types of businesses or safe uses of money, such as the return obtained by placing the funds with a bank. The rate of return of the business should be higher than bank interest, however, to compensate for the risk factor that accompanies a new business.

It is conceivable—and not uncommon—that the projected income for the new business will be negative, at least in the first few years of operation. Usually the entrepreneur is taking a long-term view of the business, and thus long-term projections may be required to evaluate financial feasibility. In addition to a net income projection, many feasibility analyses include a projected cash flow statement. This document is of particular interest to potential lenders and investors. The cash flow simply describes the cash in minus the cash out on a chronological basis. Usually cash flow statements are shown monthly (see Chapter 7). The sample cash flow in schedule 4 of Figure 3-6 is shown on a yearly basis for simplicity.

A quantitative financial feasibility analysis for a retail pharmacy is presented in Figure 3-6, which follows. This example illustrates the steps described in the preceding sections.

Figure 3-6   Feasibility Analysis for a Pharmacy in Lethbridge (approximately 300 square metres)

Step 1: Calculate Market Potential

1. *Market area.* The market area is the population of Lethbridge plus outlying regions. This region includes towns within a 100 km radius of Lethbridge. The population of this total market area is about 160,000. (Source: *Lethbridge Community Profile,* 1999–2000 edition, published by the city of Lethbridge.)

2. *Sales for market area.* The per capita sales for pharmacies in the market area can be determined through two sources. First, the actual sales figures may be published and available from the municipality concerned. Second, if that information is not available, find the per capita sales by taking Canadian or provincial sales of pharmacies divided by the respective population. This information is available from Statistics Canada.

$$\frac{\text{Pharmacy sales for Canada (2000)}}{\text{Population Canada (2000)}} = \text{Per capita pharmacy sales}$$

$$\frac{\$13,000,000,000}{30,300,000} = \$430$$

Once per capita sales have been determined, this number can be applied to the market area population.

Figure 3-6   (continued)

$$
\begin{aligned}
\text{Lethbridge} \quad &= \quad \text{Population} \times \text{Per capita sales} \\
&= \quad 61{,}500 \times \$430 \\
&= \quad \$26{,}445{,}000
\end{aligned}
$$

$$
\begin{aligned}
\text{Outlying area} \quad &= \quad \text{Population} \times \text{Per capita sales} \\
&= \quad (160{,}000 - 61{,}500) \times \$430 \\
&\qquad\quad \text{(Total market)(Lethbridge)} \\
&= \quad 98{,}500 \;\times\; \$430 \\
&= \quad \$42{,}355{,}000
\end{aligned}
$$

Since only 30 percent of people in the outlying area made their purchases in Lethbridge (primary research), multiply this figure by .3:

$$
\begin{aligned}
\$42{,}355{,}000 \times .3 \quad &= \quad \$12{,}706{,}500 \\
\text{Total market potential} \quad &= \quad \$26{,}445{,}000 + \$12{,}706{,}500 \\
&= \quad \$39{,}151{,}500
\end{aligned}
$$

3. *Adjustments.* Typical adjustments might include updating secondary information regarding population and purchases by applying past trends.

Step 2: Calculate Market Share

1. *Estimate selling space in market.* There are a total of 30 pharmacies and pharmacy departments in Lethbridge, with a total estimated size of 10,000 square metres. (Primary research collected by observation.)

2. *Size of proposed store.* The size of the proposed pharmacy is 300 square metres.

3. Calculation of market share. Percentage share of the market:

$$
\frac{\text{Proposed store selling space}}{\substack{\text{Total market selling space} \\ \text{(including proposed store)}}} = 300 \text{ m}^2/10{,}000 \text{ m}^2 \text{ plus } 300 \text{ m}^2 = 3.1\%
$$

4. *Adjustments.* The percentage of market share would probably have to be decreased slightly, because the proposed pharmacy is new and would not have built up clientele and the reputation of an existing store.

Based on the above factors, market share has been adjusted to 2.3 percent.

5. *Multiply market share percentage by the market potential.*

$$
\begin{aligned}
\text{Market share} \times \text{Market potential} \quad &= \quad \text{Estimated market share} \\
2.3\% \times \$39{,}151{,}500 \quad &= \quad \$900{,}484.50
\end{aligned}
$$

Therefore, market share is approximately $900,000.

Figure 3-6 **(continued)**

Step 3: Calculation of Net Income and Cash Flow

NEW PHARMACY
Projected Income Statement
For the Period Ended December 2001

		Percent of Sales	Source of Information
Sales	$ 900,000	100. 0	From calculation in step 2
Less: Cost of goods sold	648,000	72.0	Dun and Bradstreet Key Business Ratios (2000)
Gross margin	252,000	28.0	
Expenses:			
Manager's salary	34,000	3.7	Primary information (talked to owners)
Employee wages (Schedule 1)	130,000	14.0	Schedule 1, primary information
Fringe benefits	4,450	.5	Stats Canada operating results for pharmacies (2000)
Rent	26,700	3.0	Primary and secondary operating results (talked to owners and Stats Canada 2000)
Utilities and telephone	8,000	.9	Primary (talked to owners)
Accounting, legal, taxes and licence	4,450	.5	Primary (checked with agencies)
Insurance	4,450	.5	Primary and secondary (operating results, etc.)
Repairs and maintenance	4,450	.5	Stats Canada (operating results, etc.)
Advertising	4,450	.5	Stats Canada (operating results, etc.)
Bad debts	1,780	.2	Primary and secondary (talked to owners and Stats Canada)
Depreciation (Schedule 2)	16,000	1.8	Stats Canada (operating results, etc.), Schedule 2 and Schedule 3
Interest, exchange, and bank charges	5,120	.8	Stats Canada (operating results, etc.)

Figure 3-6   (continued)

Office and store supplies	4,950	.5	Stats Canada (operating results, etc.)
Contingency	3,560	.4	Stats Canada (operating results, etc.)
Total expenses	252,360	28.0	
Net income (loss) before tax	$360		

Schedule 1 (obtained through primary research)

Employee wages

1 Full-time pharmacist	40,000
1 Part-time pharmacist	18,000
1 Full-time cashier @ $18,000	18,000
2 Part-time cashiers @ $7,500	15,000
1 Bookkeeper	18,000
1 Marker/receiver	13,000
1 Part-time stock/delivery boy (delivery expense included)	8,000
Total	$130,000

Schedule 2 Depreciation Schedule

Equipment cost = $80,000 Capital cost allowance (CCA) = 20% (obtained from Master Tax Guide)

Year	Undepreciated Amount	$\times$	CCA	=	Depreciation
2001	$80,000	$\times$	.20	=	$16,000.00
2002	64,000	$\times$	.20	=	12,800.00
2003	51,200	$\times$	.20	=	10,240.00
2004	40,960	$\times$	.20	=	8,192.00
2005	32,768	$\times$	.20	=	6,553.00

The above process is continued until the entire item is depreciated.

Schedule 3

Interest schedule

Amount borrowed = $50,000

Interest rate = 9%

Interest 2001 = 50,000 $\times$ 8%	=	$ 4,000
Estimated bank and service charges	=	$ 1,120
Total		$ 5,620

Figure 3-6   (continued)

Schedule 4

Calculation of Cash Flow
NEW PHARMACY
Projected Cash Flow Statement
For Period Ended December 31, 2001

Cash inflow	
Beginning cash	$ 20,000
Bank loan	50,000
Cash sales	510,000
Payments on credit sales	210,000
Total cash inflow	790,000
Cash outflow	
Start-up costs	50,000
Merchandise purchases	550,000
Manager's salary	34,000
Employee wages	130,000
Fringe benefits	4,450
Rent (including deposit)	27,000
Utilities and phone	
(including deposit)	8,200
Accounting, legal, etc.	4,450
Insurance	4,450
Repairs and maintenance	4,450
Advertising	4,450
Interest and bank charges	5,120
Office supplies	4,450
Other expenses	4,950
Total cash outflow	$ 835,970
Net cash flow	$ (45,970)

Another potentially important part of the feasibility analysis, particularly for the manufacturing firm, is to estimate the level of production and sales required to break even
financially. A detailed discussion of break-even analysis is included in Chapter 10. Once the
feasibility analysis is completed, the prospective entrepreneur should have enough information to decide whether to pursue a particular business opportunity. The areas covered up to
this point can be used to make this decision. Figure 3-7 presents a checklist for personal and
opportunity evaluation.

Figure 3-7   Self-Assessment for a Small Business Opportunity

Personality:	Do I possess most of the personality characteristics of successful entrepreneurs introduced in Chapter 2?
Nature:	Does this business opportunity meet my occupational and lifestyle goals and interests?
Abilities:	Do I have the expertise in the fundamentals (financial, marketing, personnel, production) needed to manage this business opportunity? If I do not, am I able and willing to acquire or hire such expertise?
Experience:	Do I have experience with the business or industry? If not, am I able and willing to obtain it or find someone who can help me get started?
Financial base:	Do I currently have or can I obtain, the necessary funds to finance the venture?
Feasibility:	Does the financial feasibility of the business opportunity meet my expectations and financial goals?

Summary

1. Before deciding which small business opportunity to pursue, the entrepreneur must consider some nonquantitative factors such as his or her goals, the content of the work, the lifestyle the business offers, and the individual's capabilities and experience.

2. There are three ways to enter a market with a new product or service. The first method is to offer a totally new product. The second is to offer an existing product to a different market or industry. The third is to offer a product or service similar to those that already exist in the same market.

3. Two general types of information are available to aid a potential small business owner in selecting a business opportunity. The first and most inexpensive method is to collect secondary data about a potential market. Many government documents and other sources can provide valuable secondary data. When little current secondary data is available, prospective small business owners can collect primary data to help determine the feasibility of their businesses. Primary data is information collected through one's own research. Although usually more costly than secondary data, it can be more relevant and current to the analysis. Three general methods of doing primary research include observation, surveys, and experiments. Surveying usually is the most effective method for a small business.

4. There are three steps in estimating the financial feasibility of a proposed business venture. The first step is to determine potential revenues for the total market. The second step is to estimate the proposed business share of that total market. The third step is to subtract the associated expenses from the revenue estimate to determine an estimated net income for the prospective business.

Chapter Problems and Applications

1. Briefly explain the ways of entering a market. List examples that fit these methods other than those mentioned in the text.

2. J&J Inc. is thinking of developing a new coin laundry. The firm first needs to do some market research to determine the demand for the product. What kind of information should it collect?

3. What could Kirchner Machine Ltd. (Incident 3-6) have done to properly develop a financial feasibility analysis for the Big Bale Fork?

4. Why is it important to make adjustments in market potential and market share figures?

5. For a small business opportunity of your choice, show how you would evaluate the nonquantitative factors such as goals, experience, lifestyle, and content of work.

6. Design a simple mail questionnaire to assess demand for a carpet-cleaning business in your city.

7. From Statistics Canada Small Business Profiles (see Appendix 3A), find the "Return on Sales, Gross Profit, and Current Ratios" for a jewellery store, a clothing manufacturer, and a grocery store.

8. Using information obtained from the Internet, develop a market potential analysis for a bakery in your area.

9. The new bakery in Problem 8 has a proposed selling space of 50 square metres. The total amount of selling space devoted to bakery products in the city is 850 square metres. From the market potential estimated in Problem 8, find the market share in dollars for the new bakery.

Appendix 3A

Small Business Reference Books and Sources of Information

ABC Assistance to Business in Canada, Business Development Bank of Canada, 204 Richmond Street West, Toronto, Ontario, M5V 1V6.

Canadian Industrial Innovation Centre, Waterloo, Ontario. Provides assessment of new product, service or process ideas by marketing experts and engineers.

Canadian Small Business Guide, CCH Canadian Ltd., 6 Garamond Court, Don Mills, Ontario, M3C 1Z5.

Canadian Federation of Independent Business, Willowdale, Ontario. Has several publications and statistics on small business.

CIBC Guide to Business Planning, Canadian Imperial Bank of Commerce. Provides a business planning workbook to assist in development of the business plan.

Compusearch Micromarketing Data and Systems provides information on population segments by lifestyle, 1,000 product categories and locations of 650,000 businesses. For a free database catalogue, call 1 (800) 268-DATA.

Handbook of Canadian Consumer Markets, The Conference Board of Canada, Suite 100, 25 McArthur Road, Ottawa, Ontario, K1L 6R3. This book includes data on provincial, rural, marital populations, and so on; employment; income; expenditures; production and distribution; and pricing.

Handbook of Grants and Subsidies of Federal and Provincial Governments, CCH Canadian Ltd., 6 Garamond Court, Don Mills, Ontario, M3C 1Z5.

How to Succeed in Your Home Business, Toronto Dominion Bank.

Index to Federal Programs and Services, Supply and Services Canada, Ottawa, Canada.

Industry, Science and Technology Canada. Provides several services for small businesses across the country. ISTC business service centres contain publications, videos, and computer databases, networking sources as well as counselling personnel.

Key Business Ratios, Dun and Bradstreet Canada Ltd., P.O. Box 423, Station A, Toronto, Ontario. Contains key business ratios for over 800 different types of businesses. Also, the U.S. affiliate of Dun and Bradstreet publishes "typical" balance sheets, income statements, and "common-size" financial figures.

Kryszak, Wayne D. *The Small Business Index,* Grolier, Inc., Sherman Turnpike, Danbury, Connecticut, U.S.A. 06816. This book is an index to American and Canadian books, pamphlets, and periodicals that contain information on starting and running a small business.

Management Tips—A Guide for Independent Business, Royal Bank of Canada. This series of books offer guidance in starting and running a business. Topics covered include "How to Finance Your Business," "Pointers to Profits," and "Good Management—Your Key to Survival."

Managing for Success Series, The Institute for Small Business Inc., 1051 Clinton Street, Buffalo, New York, U.S.A. This series contains 16 self-tutorials in business procedure written expressly for the independent business owner. It discusses important business topics such as financing, a do-it-yourself marketing plan, planning and budgeting, and advertising and sales promotion. It provides illustrative case studies and detailed examples and workbook and checklist pages that let you work out your business details along the lines given in the text.

Market Research Handbook, Statistics Canada, Ottawa, Ontario.

Minding Your Own Business, Business Development Bank of Canada, Management Services, P.O. Box 6021, Montreal, Quebec, H3C 3C3. This is a series of guides to starting and running a small business. They provide information on areas such as forecasting for an existing business, managing your current assets, retail pricing, attracting and keeping your retail customers, and buying a franchise. The Business Development Bank also publishes workbook case study pamphlets, which are used in training seminars for entrepreneurs. Some of these topics are "Total Quality Control," "Developing a Financial Forecast," and "How to Prepare a Market Study."

Periodicals and Trade Magazines Particular to the Type of Business Involved. For example, one would consult *Restaurateur* if opening a new restaurant. These magazines often provide typical start-up and operating costs for a business. In addition, there are several general small business periodicals, such as *Entrepreneur, Venture,* and *INC.*, that provide valuable ideas on starting a business.

Planning for Success, Business Development of Canada (BDC). Designed to teach entrepreneurship to youth and adults. Brochures and CD format.

Provincial Small Business Departments. These offices can be very useful to someone who operates or plans to open a small business. They can provide information on sources of financing for small business, and so on. In Alberta, for example, the government publishes pamphlets on many aspects of running a small business, as well as "Kind of Business Files" (KOB), which contain data on 100 types of small businesses such as financial ratios, market trends, and so on.

Research and Retrieval, Business Research Newsletter, G. D. Sourcing, Toronto, Ontario.

Small Business Problem Solver, Bank of Montreal. Fourteen pamphlets covering various management topics.

Small Business Quarterly, Entrepreneurship and Small Business Office. Provides a quick and easy-to-read snapshot of recent performance of Canada's small business sector. 235 Queen Street, Room 505A, Industry Canada, Ottawa, K1A 0H5.

Small Business Source Book, John Ganly, Diane Seialtana, and Andrea Pedolsky, editors. Gale Research Company, Book Tower, Detroit, Michigan, U.S.A. 48226. This book was designed as a first step toward finding information for anyone who is considering starting a small business. The book lists 100 companies as well as associations, sources of supply, statistical sources, trade periodicals, franchises, educational programs, trade shows, and conventions.

Statistics Canada, Head Office, R. H. Coats Building, Tunney's Pasture, Ottawa, Ontario, K1A OT6.

1. *Operating Results.* This report presents typical expenses, cost of goods sold, inventory, and net profit as a percentage of sales for many types of businesses. It presents results for both incorporated and unincorporated businesses and gives both mean and median results. Data is provided by both level of sales and province.

2. *Market Research Handbook.* This book presents data on selected economic indicators, government revenue, expenditures and employment, merchandising and services, population characteristics, personal income, and expenditures.

3. *Family Expenditure in Canada.* This report provides information on family expenditures in Canada for a very detailed list of items.

4. *Census Data.* This can be obtained from local city halls. Census data provides information on population growth rates, income level of schooling, and other facts. Census tracts for large centres can also be obtained from Statistics Canada.

5. *Small Business Profiles.* These provide complete financial operating reports for many small businesses.

TD Business Planner, Toronto Dominion Bank. Includes step-by-step financial and business plan preparation.

The Financial Post Canadian Markets, Maclean Hunter Ltd., 777 Bay Street, Toronto, Ontario, M5W 1A7. This book provides complete demographics for Canadian urban markets. It looks at 500 municipalities across Canada with populations greater than 5,000. It includes data on demographics; income; manufacturing activity; television, radio, and newspaper statistics; other economic statistics; average and annual growth rates of the population; and future population projections.

Suggested Periodicals for Small Business

Entrepreneur
Chase Revel
2311 Pontius Avenue
Los Angeles, CA 90064

Home Business Report
www.homebusinessreport.com
about_HBR.htm

In Business
Jerome Goldstein, Publisher
Box 351
Emmaus, PA 18049

INC.
Bernard Goldhirsh, Publisher
38 Commercial Wharf
Boston, MA 02110

Journal of Small Business and Entrepreneurship
Faculty of Management
University of Toronto
246 Bloor Street West
Toronto, ON M5B 2K3

Journal of Small Business Management
Bureau of Business Research
West Virginia University
Morgantown, WV 26506

N.E.D.I. Notes
National Entrepreneurship Development
Institute
3601 St. Jacques West
Montreal, PQ

Profit—the Magazine for Canadian
Entrepreneurs
CB Media Ltd.
70 The Esplanade, 2nd Floor
Toronto, ON

Profits
Business Development Bank of Canada
BDC Building
5 Place Ville Marie
Suite 400
Montreal, Quebec
H3B 5E7

Small Business Canada
P.O. Box 1684 Station Main
Holland Landing, Ontario
L9N 1P2

Success
Lang Communications
230 Park Avenue
New York, NY

Venture
Arthur Lipper III, Chairman
521 Fifth Avenue
New York, NY 10175

Your Money
Maclean Hunter Ltd
777 Bay Street
Toronto, ON

On-Line Sources of Assistance for Small Businesses

Alberta Business Advantage—http://Albertafirst.com—on-line source for small business profiles.

American On-line—largest commerical on-line service for business.

Bank of Montreal Entrepreneur Site—http://www.bmo.com—provides information on management aspects of running a small business as well as interaction with other entrepreneurs.

BR Newsletter—http://www.gdsourcing.com—reference for government and industry information about small business sector.

Business Development Bank Information Site— http://strategis.ic.gc.ca

Canada Business Service Centres—http://www.cbsc.org—information for government services, programs and regulations for business.

Canadian Business Map—http://commercecan.ic.gc.ca — allows access to Canadian industry statistics, market research, municipal information, Canadian and foreign newpapers, and international trade information.

Canada One—http://www.canadaone.com—provides useful business tools to start, run, and grow a successful small business.

Canadian Federation of Independent Business—http://www.cfib.ca

CANSIM Main Base Series Directory—index to latest census—http://www.statcan.ca/english/cansim

Entrepreneur on-line—www.Entrepreneur.com—general information about small business.

Export Development Corporation—http://www.edc.ca—provides information about exporting.

Export Source On-line Services—http://exportsource.gc.ca/—step-by-step guide to exporting for small business.

A Guide for Canadian Small Business—www.rc.gc.ca—federal government web site to help small businesses.

Free Management Library—www.mapnp.org/library

On-line Small Business Workshop—http://www.sb.gov.bc.ca/smallbus/workshop/workshop.html—provides guides for planning a business through to functional management of the ongoing business.

Profit on-line—www.PROFITguide.com—articles and newsletters for entrepreneurs.

Small Biz Canada—http://microsoft.com/canada/smallbiz—provides news and research articles on the benefits of technology and on issues related to marketing, financing, and general business.

Small Biz Manager—http://smallbizmanager.com—reviews, screens, and recommends business services, products, advice, etc.

Small Business Advancement National Center—http://www.sbaer.uca.edu/—research, training, consulting, and information library.

Small Business Information—http://sbinformation.about.com—a comprehensive small business web site on e-commerce start-ups.

Small Business Information Seminars—www.ccra_adrc.gc.ca/business—provides information on your responsibilities regarding customs, income tax, GST/HST, etc.

Small Business Resource Center—http://www.webcom.com/~seaquest—contains "how to" files on starting and operating small businesses.

Small Business Resource Centre—assistance on all facets of starting and operating a business sponsored by the Business Development Bank of Canada. http://www.bdc.ca

Small Business Profiles—http://strategis.ic.gc.ca/SSG/mi06756e.html—free profiles and statistics for various types of small businesses.

Small-Office and Home-Office Business Links—www.soho.ca

Statistics Canada—www.statcan.ca/Daily/English/today/daily.html—up-to-date information on releases by Statistics Canada.

Trade Commissioner Service web site—www.infoexport.gc.ca—assistance for small business in identifying markets, contacts, etc.

USENET Groups—http://www.execpc.com—bulletin board service for small businesses.

Young Entrepreneurs Association—www.yea.ca/yeaframen.html

Organizations and Trade Associations That Assist Entrepreneurs

Alliance of Independent Business Associations Canada

Association of Canadian Venture Capital Companies

Association of Collegiate Entrepreneurs (ACE) Ryerson Polytechnical University

Business Counselling Group
Communications Branch
Department of Industry, Science, and Technology

Directory of Associations in Canada

Encyclopedia of Associations

Entrepreneurship and Small Business Office
235 Queen Street
Ottawa, ON K1A 0A5

Business Development Bank of Canada (BDC)
BDC Consulting Group
901 Victoria Square
Montreal, PQ H2Z 1R1

Business Information Centre
Business Development Bank of Canada
204 Richmond Street West
Toronto, ON M5V 1V6

Canadian Association of Business Incubators

Canadian Association of Family Enterprise

Canadian Association of Home-Based Business

Canadian Association of Women Executives and Entrepreneurs

Canadian Chamber of Commerce
120 Adelaide Street West, Suite 2109
Toronto, ON M5H 1T1

Canadian Council of Better Business Bureaus
2180 Steeles Avenue West, Suite 219
Concord, ON M6P 4C7

Canadian Federation of Independent Business
4141 Yonge Street, Suite 401
Willowdale, ON M2P 2A6

Canadian Franchise Association
—www.cfa.ca

Canadian Organization of Small Business

Canadian Organization of Small Business
Toronto Office
150 Consumers Road, Suite 501
Willowdale, ON M2J 4V8

Centre for Entrepreneurial Management
29 Greene Street
New York, NY 10013

International Council for Small Business—Canada
204 Richmond Street West, 5th Floor
Toronto, ON M5V 1V6

National Association of Home-Based Businesses
(NAHBB)—http://www.usahomebusiness.com/homesite.html

National Entrepreneurship Development Institute
3601 St. Jacques West
Montreal, PQ H4C 3N4

National Small Business Institute
1070 West Broadway, Suite 310
Vancouver, BC V6H 1E7

Small Business Network
52 Sheppard Avenue West
Willowdale, ON M2N 1M2

Women Entrepreneurs of Canada

Young Entrepreneurs Association of Ontario
www.yea.ca/yeaframen.html

Appendix 3B

Provincial Departments for Small Business

Alberta
Economic Development: Small Business Assistance
17th Floor, 10025 Jasper Avenue
Edmonton, T5J 3Z3

British Columbia
Ministry of Small Business, Tourism and Culture
Business Information Centre
601 West Cordova St.
Vancouver, V6B 1G1

Manitoba
Department of Business Development
and Tourism and Small Business
and Regional Development
155 Carlton Street
Winnipeg, R3C 3H8

New Brunswick
Department of Commerce and Technology
Small Industry and Regional Development
Centennial Building
P.O. Box 6000
Fredericton, E3B 5H1

Newfoundland
Department of Development and Tourism
Local Industry Support Services
Atlantic Place, Water Street
St. John's, A1C 5T7

Prince Edward Island
Department of Industry
Business Development
Shaw Building, P.O. Box 2000
Charlottetown, C1A 7N8

Northwest Territories
Department of Economic Development
and Tourism
Business Development
P.O. Box 1320
Yellowknife, X1A 2L9

Quebec
Ministere du Commerce
Exterieur et du Development, Technologique
Place Mercantile, 6e-7e et 10e étages
770, Rue Sherbrooke Ouest
Montreal, H3A 1G1

Nova Scotia
Department of Development
200 Barrington St.
P.O. Box 1656
Halifax, B3J 2Z7

Saskatchewan
Department of Economic and
Cooperative Development
Bank of Montreal Building
2103 11th Avenue
Regina, S4P 3V7

Ontario
Ministry of Industry, Trade, and Technology
Hearst Building
900 Bay Street
Toronto, M7A 2E1

Yukon
Department of Economic Development:
Mines and Small Business
Business Development Office
2131 Second Avenue
Whitehorse, Y1A 2C6

Appendix 3C

Universities and Groups That Offer Student Consulting Programs

These programs offer consulting projects for all aspects of business conducted by senior commerce/business students under the supervision of the university faculty. These programs have two purposes: (1) to provide a low-cost consulting service to small businesses and (2) to provide a useful and practical learning experience for senior commerce/business students.

Alberta
Mount Royal College
4825 Richard Rd. SW.
Calgary, T6G 2R6

University of Alberta
Faculty of Business
202 Faculty of Business Building
Edmonton, T6G 2R6

University of Calgary
Venture Development Group
Faculty of Management
2500 University Drive N.W.
Calgary, T2N 1N4

University of Lethbridge
Centre for Management Solutions
Faculty of Management
4401 University Drive
Lethbridge, T1K 3M4

British Columbia
David Boag
University of Victoria
P.O. Box 1700
Victoria, V8W 2Y2

Geoffery Dalton/Coordinator
Faculty of Business Administration
University of British Columbia
Burnaby, V5A 1S6

Simon Fraser University
Burnaby, BC
Small Business Consulting Group

The Province of British Columbia has
several Business Development Centres.
For more information, contact Gary L. Bunney,
Director of Academic/Technical Programs of
the Ministry of Post-Secondary Education,
(604) 387-6181.

Manitoba
The Asper Centre for Entrepreneurship
Faculty of Management
University of Manitoba, R3T 5V4

Canada/Manitoba Business Service Centre
250–240 Graham Avenue
Winnipeg, R3C 4B3

Centre for International Business Studies
M.B.A. Student Consulting Program
(May–August)
Department of Business Development and Tourism
Winnipeg Enterprise Development Centre
1329 Niakwa Road, 2nd Floor
Winnipeg, R2J 3T4

Small Business Law Clinic (MB) INC.
106–167 Lombard Avenue
Winnipeg, MB R3B 0T6

Newfoundland
P. J. Gardiner Institute
for Small Business Studies
Memorial University
St. John's

Nova Scotia
Atlantic Business Consultants
Coburg Consultants
6152 Coburg Road
Halifax, B3H 1Z5

Ontario
Professor Murray Bryant
SBC Faculty Coordinator
University of Toronto
Faculty of Management Studies
246 Bloor Street West
Toronto, M5S 1V4

Dr. W. B. Crowston/SBC Faculty Coordinator
York University
Faculty of Administrative Studies
4700 Keele Street
Downsview, M3J 2R7

Faculty Coordinator
Wilfrid Laurier University
School of Business and Economics
Waterloo, N2L 3C5

Professor Jim Forrestor/Faculty Coordinator
Ryerson Polytechnical University
School of Business
50 Gould Street
Toronto, M5B 1E8

Professor Dave Gillingham/Faculty Coordinator
Laurentian University
School of Commerce and Administration
Sudbury, P3E 2C6

J. F. Graham/Faculty Coordinator
University of Western Ontario
School of Business Administration
London, N6A 3K7

Professor Clem Hobbs/Faculty Coordinator
Carleton University/School of Business
Ottawa, K1S 5B6

David Litvak/Faculty Coordinator
University of Ottawa
Faculty of Administration
Ottawa, K1B 6N5

Professor John McKirdy/Faculty Coordinator
Small Business Consulting Service
Queen's University
School of Business
Kingston, K7L 3N6

Reid McWilliam, Program Manager
Small Business Management Program
Mohawk College
P.O. Box 2034
Hamilton, L8N 3T2

Dr. M. Ragab/SBC Faculty Coordinator
University of Windsor
Faculty of Business Administration
401 Sunset Avenue
Windsor, N9B 3P4

Dr. A. W. Richardson/Faculty Coordinator
McMaster University
Faculty of Business
Hamilton, L8S 4M4

Ontario has several colleges and universities that run innovation centres. The innovation centre developed specifically for small business is listed below. For further information on other innovation centres, contact the Ontario Ministry of Industry, Trade, and Technology.

Ryerson Innovation Centre
Ryerson Polytechnic University
350 Victoria Street
Toronto, M5B 2K3

Professor P. Shonoski/Faculty Coordinator
Lakehead University
School of Business Administration
Thunder Bay, P7B 5E1

Professor Wally Smieliauskas
SBC Faculty Coordinator
University of Toronto
Faculty of Management Studies
246 Bloor Street West
Toronto, M5S 1V4

Quebec
McGill University
McGill Business Consulting Group
Montreal, PQ

Saskatchewan
Business Consulting Services
College of Commerce
University of Saskatchewan
Saskatoon, S7N 0W0

University of Regina
Faculty of Administration
Regina, S4S 0A2

The University of Regina operates a student consulting service on an informal basis. Students involved in this service have completed a number of different projects for a small number of organizations. They are now considering formally establishing the student consulting service.

Suggested Readings

Berman, Paul. *Small Business and Entrepreneurship.* Scarborough, ON: Prentice Hall, 1998.

Davidson, Jeffery P. *The Marketing Source Book for Small Business.* New York: John Wiley and Sons, 1989.

D'souza, Patricia, Rick Kang and Diana Luciani. "The Hottest Trends in Business — 99." *Profit Magazine,* December–January, 1999, pp. 38–48.

Developing a Financial Forecast. Montreal: Federal Business Development Bank, 1991.

Gray, Douglas A., and Diane L. Gray. *The Complete Canadian Small Business Guide.* Toronto: McGraw-Hill Ryerson, 1994.

Hoitz, Lou. "Winning Every Day." *Harper Business,* 1998.

How to Prepare a Market Study. Montreal: Business Development Bank, 1989.

McMath, Robert, and Thomas Forbes. *What Were They Thinking?* New York: Times-Books, 1998.

Portsmouth, Ian. "Surf's Up." *Profit Magazine,* October–November, 1995, pp. 25–30.

Researching a Small Business 2001—A Practical Guide to Small Business Research in Canada, Toronto: G.D. Sourcing. (access through web site—www.gdsourcing.com)

Comprehensive Case
The Framemakers: Part 2

After a few days of evaluating their small business decision, Robert and Teresa Norman decided to open the picture-framing retail outlet in Brandon. Robert had learned a great deal about the business from his visit with the U-Frame It franchise in Winnipeg. He convinced his father that the opportunity had promise. Both were aware that many people were now becoming do-it-yourselfers in home decorating.

His college training had taught Robert the importance of thorough investigation before starting a business. He realized he should do this even before deciding whether to start the business on his own or to become a franchisee. He contacted the Professional Picture Framers Association (PPFA) and learned that the average customer spends $32 per visit at a framing store. In checking framing costs with the U-Frame It manager in Winnipeg, he confirmed this information. A typical per-customer profit statement for a framing shop was as follows:

Revenue	$32	(100%)
Materials	15	(47%)
Overhead (rent, utilities, wages, etc.)	9	(28%)
Profit per customer	8	(25%)

Robert knew there was one other framing store in Brandon, a city of 35,000. Using Winnipeg as an example, Robert calculated that a framing store could service a population of approximately 25,000 people and earn an acceptable profit.

While Robert was collecting his information, Teresa was conducting some of her own market research. She visited the only picture framing store in Brandon and noted that the store was the busiest between the hours of 11 a.m. and 3 p.m. She also observed that many customers had some time to wait for available workstations and for the glue to dry. During this time they browsed around the store looking at the merchandise.

Robert also attended an industry supplier seminar in Minneapolis. He was encouraged to learn that the do-it-yourself framing business was experiencing rapid growth throughout North America. While there, Robert learned about several picture-framing trade magazines and bought subscriptions for them. He also made valuable contacts with suppliers and other dealers.

Things looked more positive each day, so Robert closed down the painting business, and he and Teresa began making preparations to open their new store, which they would call The Framemakers.

Questions

1. What positive things have Robert and Teresa done in investigating the feasibility of the new store?
2. What additional information might they have collected? From what sources could this information be obtained?

Video Case Questions
Beer Mitts*

CBC

Some people spend a lifetime trying to come up with the "perfect product," the idea that should sell itself. Others just stumble right into it, but as Colin King discovered from a couple of guys who found their "big idea" sipping beer, the idea's the easy part.

1. What can be learned from this example about the importance of preparing a feasibility analysis?

2. Discuss the start-up problems that occurred with this business.

3. What type of approach to starting a business was utilized in this example?

*SOURCE: CBC *Venture #720*, running time 8:24.

Cases for Part I

A Chance to Be Self-Employed   Petite Shop (B)
Bookworms Inc.   Tom's Cleaning Company
Petite Shop (A)   Westwinds Realty Ltd.

A CHANCE TO BE SELF-EMPLOYED

Morris Borts
McGill University

Situation

Martine, Chantal, and Philippe, three physiotherapists, were seated at a cafeteria table at Hôpital de Bonne Santé during their lunch break.

"Chantal and Philippe, I've been doing some thinking about my professional future and I'd like to discuss an idea with you," said Martine.

"As I see it, as physiotherapists working in a hospital we're respected, useful members of the medical community, but we're limited in terms of our earnings and chances for advancement. As public sector employees our salaries are negotiated as a group with the government and our earning power is limited. Unless our supervisor leaves or dies, there's no chance for advancement.

"Last night I read an article in an American magazine about the shortage of physios in the States.

"No! No! I'm not thinking of moving to the U.S. What interests me is that in the States, physios who are self-employed earn an average of 2.3 times as much as those who work in hospitals. I recognize that the American market is different from Quebec and what works in the U.S. may not be successful here, but perhaps there's an opportunity for us here. If you recall the annual report of the Presidente Corporation Professionelle des Physiotherapeutes du Quebec, it reported that the number of physios in private practice has increased by 500 percent in the past 10 years. [The percentages are misleading because 10 years ago there were very few members of our Corporation in private practice.]

"Although private practice seems to offer significant advantages in terms of career development and earning potential, it has some drawbacks as well. Some clinics have gone bankrupt and the owners have lost their investments. In other cases, the physio-owners earn less than they would if they remained in the public sector.

"The three of us have been friends since our CEGEP [community college] days and I hope that we can agree on staying together as partners in our own clinic. Should we decide to go into private practice, we must do it properly: develop and implement a plan that will help to ensure our success.

"First, we should evaluate the competition that we'll face if we open an office. As I see it, we have three types of competitors: hospitals such as the one where we work, other independent clinics, and for some problems chiropractors [who aren't covered by Medicare]. If a patient elects to seek treatment at a hospital, the treatment is free to the patient [i.e., paid by the Régie D'Assurance Maladie], but there's a long waiting list and the start of treatment could be delayed three to six months.

"At private clinics patients are seen in a matter of days, but a fee is charged for each visit. For some people the cost isn't a factor because their treatments are, at least in part, covered by their private health insurance policies. For other people the cost is secondary because of the pain, discomfort, and/or incapacities they're suffering. For some patients the ability to be seen early or late in the day or perhaps even on a Saturday is worth paying for. However, there's still a large part of the market who would like to be treated at a hospital because it's free.

"Although most of a physio's work comes from physician referrals, it is legal, as you know, for us to treat patients who come directly to us without first seeing a physician. If we attempt to cultivate both types of patients, we will need to develop a separate plan for direct patient business.

"Because of the necessity of physicians for their patients, some private clinics are owned, at least in part, by physicians [usually orthopedic surgeons]. Other clinics have developed good working relationships with independent physicians. To be successful we must find out what skills and/or features a physician looks for in a clinic before making referrals. Although GPs do from time to time make referrals, the majority of cases originate from a small group of specialists. Based on our experience at this hospital we know some of them, but what about the others who are affiliated with other hospitals in the city?

"In fact, like many other health professionals, we have two types of customers to deal with: the referring physician and the actual user of the service who doesn't have the expertise to accurately evaluate the treatment. They often base their evaluation on factors such as: am I getting better, is the person nice to me [friendly, polite, explains what's happening, etc.], can I get appointments at a convenient time, is the clinic easy for me to get to [location and parking]? Because of our designation, physiotherapists' patients don't usually ask what are our qualifications. Occasionally someone may ask how long we've been working.

"If we decide that we're interested in the work, there are other markets that we could pursue. We could attempt to obtain contracts from two government agencies: the CSST [Worker's Compensation] and the Régis D'Assurance Automobile du Quebec. Both of these agencies pay the clinics directly according to a predetermined fee schedule which tends to be lower than what we'd charge a private patient. However, these agencies can generate a lot of volume. In fact, according to CSST regulations, the patient must go to the clinic and contact the CSST.

"Most clinics have the expertise and equipment to treat almost all types of physio ailments. However, it seems that some clinics claim to have a special interest in treating certain types of problems. I don't know if we should be general practitioners or if we should become specialists. I don't know in which area we should specialize. If we pick a specialty that's too small, we may find that we won't have enough patients to keep us busy.

"Since I know nothing about business or marketing, I called my good friend Maurice for some advice on how to evaluate the different possible market segments. He gave me some guidelines to use. Since statistical data are limited, he suggested that we use our expertise and make assumptions. Apparently many business decisions are made using this type of data analysis. Last night when I started thinking about going into private practice, I spent a few minutes looking for some statistical data and I found this. [See Appendices A and B.] I wonder if we spent a little time on research, if we could find other useful data or even articles on the marketing of physiotherapy services.

"For each market segment that we identify, we should determine what special skills or equipment are needed. Are we capable of satisfying these needs? How big is the market? How good a job are our competitors doing in satisfying the need? Will the need grow or diminish over time?

"Since patients are referred by physicians, it won't be necessary for us to have offices that are visible from the street. However, we'll have to find out what factors may be important to our clients and pick a location for our office that satisfies these constraints.

"We also must think of how we'll promote our clinic. We must be careful in our promotion. First, the regulations of the Order of Physiotherapists must be respected. Second, we want to maintain our professional image and not undertake promotional activities that could cause negative reactions. Most other medical professionals limit themselves to calling card ads. Oh, you know the type: name, address, phone number, and business hours. Since physician referrals are the key to our profession, what should we do to get doctors to send us their patients on a regular basis?

"You think I should stop now? We have enough decisions to make. Unfortunately, opening our own practice is complex, especially for those of us who don't have any formal business training. However, there are still at least two more marketing issues that we'll have to deal with.

"One is how to develop our fee schedule for each of our procedures. The other is how do we develop a client-oriented attitude toward our patients? In the future when, hopefully, the clinic becomes too large for the three of us, we'll also have to recruit and train employees who'll accept the client orientation.

"Last night I was so excited about the possibility of being my own boss that I could not sleep. I used the time to put together some numbers which may help us to decide if we should proceed or not. I made copies for each of you [see Appendix C] to analyze and I look forward to your comments on these data.

"I just looked at my watch. Our lunch break is just about over and I have a patient scheduled in 10 minutes.

"Why don't the three of us meet Friday evening at my place and try to work on some of the decisions that have to be made. If you can be there about 6:30 we can order a pizza and hope that it's not delivered in 30 minutes and it will be free. On the other hand, if we do have to pay, it may be the first legitimate expense of our new venture.

"I have to run. See you Friday at 6:30."

Appendix A   Breakdown of Physiotherapy Services Provided (%)

Muscular skeletal	47.6
Medicine	26.0
Neurology	15.0
Arthritis	7.5
Others including fractures and multiple injuries	4.4

Appendix B   1998 Physiotherapy Statistics, Montreal Region

1,183,200 patients visits were made to physiotherapists working in Montreal Hospitals (Government of Quebec, Ministêre do Santé, vol. 3. Region de Grand Montréal).

200,000 Private practice patient visits (estimated by E. Lessard).

According to government regulations, a physio working in a hospital should see 15 patients per day.

In 1998, in the Montreal region hospitals there were:

175 full-time physiotherapists.

111 part-time physiotherapists.

36 rehabilitation technicians working under the supervision of a physiotherapist.

Appendix C   Private Physiotherapy Facility Operating Cost Projections (in constant dollars)

Estimated number of working days per person: 227 (after statutory holidays, vacation, personal development and sick leave/personal days)
Estimated percent of professional capacity utilized:

Year 1	62 percent
Years 2 and 3	90 percent

Although after year 1, demand will be 100 percent of capacity, in actual fact some people cancel on short notice and other people miss their appointments and actual utilization is estimated at 90 percent of capacity.

Estimated average fee from all types of clients for two-hour physio consultation = $40 (no GST or PST is charged on physio fees and GST paid by physios on purchases is not recovered.)

Based on Quebec medicine hospital norms a physio should see 15 patients per day.

The premises will have four treatment rooms plus an adequate waiting/reception area.

In the first year only the three physio partners will treat patients. In the third year, it is likely that demand will be large enough to employ a fourth physio at a cost of $38,000 per year plus the usual 20 percent fringe costs. Supplies for this additional person are estimated at $40 per week. After making a few enquiries, I estimate that our operating costs would be:

Rent (2,000 square metres of space)	$30 per metre per year
Business taxes + Licences	$1,500 per year

Insurance (professional and property)	$2,500 per year
Telephone—2 lines	$50 each per month plus GST and PST
Advertising (calling card ads in local paper and mailings to physicians)	$600 per month
Promotion meetings	$100 per month
Legal and accounting fees	$200 per month
Supplies (years 1 and 2)	$200 per month
Long-term equipment rentals	$600 per month plus GST and PST
Receptionist/bookkeeper salary	$2,100 per month
Three physio (partners salaries same as current hospital levels)	$38,000 per year each
Fringe salary costs — UIC, medicine pension plans, vacation, etc.	20 percent of all salaries
Depreciation on leasehold improvements	$4,000 per year
Bank charges, including interest on bank loan	$400 per month

Question

Should the three physiotherapists leave their jobs at the hospital to set up a private practice? If so, how might they best approach marketing their new venture?

BOOKWORMS, INC.

James Nelson
University of Colorado

Late one August morning, Nancy Klein, co-owner of Bookworms, Inc., sat at her desk near the back wall of a cluttered office. With some irritation, she had just concluded that her nearby calculator could help no more. "What we still need," she thought to herself, "are estimates of demand and market share ... but at least we have two weeks to get them."

Klein's office was located in the rear of Bookworms, Inc., an 1,800-square-foot bookstore specializing in quality paperbacks. The store carries more than 10,000 titles and sold more than $520,000 worth of books last year. Titles were stocked in 18 categories, ranging from art, biography, and cooking to religion, sports and travel.

Bookworms, Inc. was located in a small business district across the street from the boundary of Verdoon University (VU). VU currently enrolled about 12,000 undergraduate and graduate students majoring in the liberal arts, the sciences, and the professions. Despite national trends in enrollment, the VU admissions office had predicted that the number of entering students would grow at about 1 percent per year through the 2000s. The surrounding community, a city of about 350,000, was projected to grow at about twice that rate.

Bookworms, Inc., carried no texts, even though many of its customers were VU students. Both Klein and her partner, Susan Berman, felt that the VU bookstore had simply too firm a grip on the textbook market in terms of price, location, and reputation. Bookworms also carried no classical CDs, as of two months ago. Klein recalled with discomfort the $15,000 or so they had lost on the venture. "Another mistake like that and the bank will be running Bookworms," she thought. "And, despite what Susan thinks, the copy service could just be that final mistake."

The idea for a copy service had come from Susan Berman. She had seen the candy store next door to Bookworms (under the same roof) go out of business in July. She had immediately asked the building's owner, Ed Anderson, about the future of the 800-square-foot space. Upon learning it was available, she had met with Klein to discuss her idea for the copy service. She had spoken excitedly about the opportunity: "It can't help but make money. I could work there part-time and the rest of the time we could hire students. We could call it 'Copycats' and even use a sign with the same kind of letters we do in 'Bookworms.' I'm sure we could get Ed to knock the wall out between the two stores, if you think it would be a good idea. Probably we could rent most of the copying equipment, so there's not much risk."

Klein was not so sure. A conversation yesterday with Anderson had disclosed his desire for a five-year lease (with an option to renew) at $1,000 per month. He had promised to hold the offer open for two weeks before attempting to lease the space to anyone else. Representatives from copying-equipment firms had estimated that charges would run between $200 and $2,000 per month, depending on equipment, service, and whether the equipment was bought or leased. The copy service would also have other fixed costs in terms of utility expenses, interest, insurance, and the inventory (and perhaps equipment). Klein concluded that the service would begin to make a profit at about 20,000 copies per month under the best-case assumptions, and at about 60,000 copies per month under the worst-case assumptions.

Further informal investigation had identified two major competitors. One was the copy centre located in the Krismann Library on the west side of the campus, a mile away. The other was a private firm, Kinko's, located on the south side of the campus, also one mile away. Both offered service while you wait, on several machines. The library's price was about ½ cent per copy higher than Kinko's. Both offered collating, binding, colour copying, and other services, all on a seven-days-a-week schedule.

Actually, investigation had discovered that a third major "competitor" consisted of the VU departmental machines scattered throughout the campus. Most faculty and administrative copying was done on these machines, but students were allowed the use of some, at cost. In addition, at least 20 self-service machines could be found in the library and in nearby drugstores, grocery stores, and banks.

Moving aside the stack of books on her desk, Nancy Klein picked up the telephone and dialed her partner. When Berman answered, Klein asked, "Susan, have you any idea how many copies a student might make in a semester? I mean according to my figures, we would break even somewhere between 20,000 and 60,000 copies per month. I don't know if this is half the market or what."

"You know, I have no idea," Berman answered. "I suppose when I was going to school I probably made 10 copies a month — for articles, class notes, old tests, and so on."

"Same here," Klein said. "But some graduate students must have done that many each week. You know, I think we ought to do some marketing research before we go much further on this. What do you think?"

"Sure. Only it can't take much more time or money. What do you have in mind, Nancy?"

"Well, we could easily interview our customers as they leave the store and ask them how many copies they've made in the past week or so. Of course, we'd have to make sure they were students."

"What about a telephone survey?" Berman asked. "That way we can have a random sample. We should still ask about the number of copies, but now we would know for sure they would be students."

"Or what about interviewing students in the union cafeteria? There's always a good-sized line there around noon, as I remember, and this might even be quicker."

"Boy, I just don't know. Why don't I come in this afternoon and we can talk some more?"

"Good idea," Klein responded. "Between the two of us, we should be able to come up with something."

Questions

1. What source of information should Klein and Berman use?
2. How should Klein and Berman gather data?
3. What questions should they ask?
4. How should they sample?

PETITE SHOP (A)

D. Wesley Balderson
University of Lethbridge

Alice Wood was concerned. She had worked in a women's clothing store for several years and was now considering opening a store of her own. Her investigations had yielded considerable secondary information, but she was not sure how to go about estimating the potential for another women's clothing store in Prince George, British Columbia. Prince George was a city of 86,100 surrounded by a large trading area. Presently it had 17 clothing stores and five department stores that retail women's clothing. During the past few years, she had been saving her money and learning all she could so that her Petite Shop ladies' wear store would be a success.

In anticipation of starting her own store, Alice had enrolled in a small business management course at a local college. The instructor had stressed the importance of market research and mentioned several sources of secondary information that could assist in determining market potential for a new business. Alice had obtained the reports she felt were relevant to her prospective business from the Provincial Department of Small Business, Statistics Canada, and the city hall in Prince George. This information is presented in Figures 1 and 2.

Now that Alice had this information, however, she was not sure how to proceed. She did not want to retail all kinds of ladies' clothing but planned to cater to the "petite" woman who wore dress sizes 3 to 9. Alice herself was petite (1.55 metres), and she felt she understood the difficulties women of her size had in shopping for clothing. From her retailing experience, she estimated that about 60 percent of all clothing sales were in womens' clothing and 20 percent of all women fit in the size 3 to 9 category. She arrived at her decision to select a store directed at the petite woman after she visited all of the 17 clothing stores in Prince George and the clothing departments of the city's five department stores. She estimated that only about 10 percent of clothing stores' stock was sized 3 to 9, and the five department stores devoted only about 6,500 square feet of selling space to this size range. She believed a small shop of about 1,000 square feet could provide a much better selection to this market than those outlets presently provided.

Figure 1	Selected Data for the City of Prince George
Population	86,100
Number of families	29,200
Per capita income	$15,000
Retail sales	$737,700,000
Per family expenditure on women's clothing	$1,000

Source: *Financial Post Canadian Markets and Urban Family Expenditure Report;* and *Market Research Handbook, 2000,* Statistics Canada.

Figure 2	Estimated Retail Space for Selected Retail Establishments (in square feet) City of Prince George
Food stores	1,200,000
Apparel stores:	
Men's clothing stores	145,000
Women's clothing stores	180,000
Hardware stores	600,000
Department stores	1,650,000

Source: City of Prince George; and *Market Research Handbook*, 2000, Statistics Canada.

Questions

1. Using the information provided, prepare an estimate of the market potential for the target market at which Alice Wood is aiming.
2. What portion of this market potential could Alice expect for Petite Shop's market share?
3. What nonquantitative considerations should be brought into this analysis?

PETITE SHOP (B)

D. Wesley Balderson
University of Lethbridge

Now that Alice Wood had a better idea of market potential and market share for her proposed retail store, she wanted to be satisfied that the Petite Shop would provide an adequate return on her savings of $25,000. She began investigating the typical costs she would incur in operating the store. Alice thought she could operate her new store with one other full-time person and some part-time help at the estimated monthly cost of $2,000. In looking at potential rental costs, she came across a retail outlet for lease on a busy street in the central business district of Prince George that seemed ideal for the Petite Shop. She learned that the site leased for $20 per square foot, with no royalty payments except $550 per year to cover municipal taxes. The estimated utility expenses the owner provided were $300 per month, and the insurance for the retail shoe store that had previously been located there was $1,500 per year.

Although Alice was excited about the potential of this site, she estimated she would need to spend approximately $12,000 for leasehold improvements, of which $8,000 would be depreciable items (20 percent). When obtaining the secondary information from the Prince George city hall, she learned that the business licences would be $100. Alice estimated all miscellaneous expenses such as stationery, bad debt expense, credit expense, and telephone to be about $5,000 per year. These figures were based on her experience in the store she currently worked in.

Alice knew she would have to borrow some money to purchase inventories. She visited her local bank and found out that the interest rate for a business loan was 10 percent. She also learned that until she had a more concrete proposal, her banker was not interested in considering her for a loan. He mentioned that in addition to leasehold improvements, she would need one-fourth of the year's cash expenses as operating funds. Although a bit surprised at the bank's reaction, Alice was determined to prepare such a proposal. She knew the new store would need to be promoted, but didn't know how much she should spend on advertising. The banker had suggested the average for ladies' clothing stores was about 2 percent of sales and had given her a copy of a recent Dun and Bradstreet financial ratio sheet to assist her (see Figure 1).

Alice now found herself in the same dilemma she had been in when determining market potential and market share. She had a lot of information, but was not sure how to proceed.

Figure 1   Key Business Ratios, Canada—Corporations

Line of Business Clothing, Women's

(Number of concerns reporting)	(2,323)
Cost of goods sold	58.40%
Gross margin	41.60
Current assets to current debt	1.4
Profits on sales	2.7
Profits on tangible net worth	15.6
Sales to tangible net worth	5.9
Sales to inventory	5.7
Fixed assets to tangible net worth	63.6
Current debt to tangible net worth	127.6
Total debt to tangible net worth	177.3

Questions

1. Using the information presented in "Petite Shop (A)" and this case, prepare an estimated income statement and return on investment calculation for the Petite Shop's first year of operation.
2. What areas has Alice overlooked in her investigation?
3. Given your analysis, what would you recommend to Alice?

TOM'S CLEANING COMPANY

E. Jerome McCarthy and Stanley J. Shapiro
Michigan State University and Simon Fraser University

Tom Willis is a 26-year-old ex-army man and a lifelong resident of Brockville, Ontario. Brockville is a beautiful summer resort area situated on the St. Lawrence in the Thousand Island region. The permanent population is about 20,000, and this more than triples in the summer months.

Tom spent seven years in the Canadian Forces after high school graduation. Returning home in June 2000, Tom decided to go into business for himself because he couldn't find a good job in the Brockville area. He set up Tom's Cleaning Company. Tom felt that his savings would allow him to start the business without borrowing any money. His estimates of required expenditures were $3,900 for a used panel truck, $475 for a steam-cleaning machine adaptable to carpets and furniture, $330 for a heavy-duty commercial vacuum cleaner, $50 for special brushes and attachments, $75 for the initial supply of cleaning fluids and compounds, and $200 for insurance and other incidental expenses. This total of $5,030 still left Tom about $2,800 in savings to cover living expenses while getting started.

One of the reasons Tom chose this line of work is his previous work experience. From the time he was 16, Tom had worked part-time for Joel Bidwell. Mr. Bidwell operated the only other successful carpet-cleaning company in Brockville. (One other company was in Brockville, but it was near bankruptcy.)

Mr. Bidwell prided himself on quality work and had a loyal clientele. Specializing in residential carpet cleaning, Bidwell has been able to build a strong customer franchise. For 35 years, Bidwell's major source of new business has been retailer recommendations and satisfied customers who tell friends about the quality service received from Mr. Bidwell. He is so highly thought of that the leading carpet and furniture stores in Brockville always recommend Bidwell's for preventive maintenance in quality carpet and furniture care. Often Bidwell is trusted with the keys to Brockville's finest homes for months at a time when owners are out of town and want his services. Bidwell's customers are so loyal, in fact, that a national household carpet-cleaning franchise found it next to impossible to compete with him. Even price-cutting was not an effective weapon against Mr. Bidwell.

Tom Willis felt that he knew the business as well as Mr. Bidwell, having worked for him for many years. Tom was anxious to reach his $40,000 per year sales goal because he thought this would provide him with a comfortable living in Brockville. While aware of opportunities for carpet cleaning in businesses, office buildings, motels, and so on, Tom felt that the sales volume available there was only about $20,000 because most businesses had their own cleaning staffs. As he saw it, his only opportunity was direct competition with Bidwell.

To get started, he allocated $600 to advertise his business in the local newspaper. With this money he was able to purchase two half-page ads and have enough left over to buy daily three-line ads in the classified section, listed under Miscellaneous Residential Services, for 52 weeks. All that was left was to paint a sign on his truck and wait for business to catch on.

Tom had a few customers and was able to gross about $200 a week during the first few months. These customers were usually Bidwell regulars who, for one reason or another (usually stains, spills, or house guests), weren't able to wait the two weeks required until Bidwell could work them in. While these people did admit that Tom's work was of the same quality as Mr. Bidwell's, they preferred Bidwell's quality-care image. During April and May Tom did get more work than he could handle when resort owners were preparing for summer openings and owners of summer homes were ready to open the cottage. The same rush occurred in September and October as resorts and homes were being closed for the winter. During these months, Tom was able to gross about $200–$250 a day working 10 hours per day.

Toward the end of his first year in business, Tom began to think about quitting. While he hated to think of having to leave Brockville, he couldn't see any way of making a living in the carpet- and furniture-cleaning business in Brockville. Mr. Bidwell had the whole residential market sewed up except in the rush seasons and for people who needed fast cleaning.

Questions

1. Evaluate Tom's approach to starting his carpet-cleaning business.
2. Why was he not able to reach his goal of $40,000 in sales?
3. Is there anything Tom could do to stay in business?

WESTWINDS REALTY LTD.

D. Wesley Balderson
University of Lethbridge

Westwinds Realty Ltd. is a small, independent real estate firm located in Lethbridge, Alberta. Because of its success, the company recently decided to expand operations from residential real estate to office development. Management believed the decision to move into this area was sound because Alberta was experiencing a buoyant economy and all projections for business, population, and construction were very positive for the next decade. Although most of this activity was centred in Calgary, Edmonton, and points north, considerable spillover was affecting Lethbridge, which is located in the southwest corner of the province and has a population of 70,000. Westwinds' accountant had noticed some figures in *The Financial Post Survey* of *Markets* indicating that Lethbridge's growth rate per decade was 35 percent—significantly higher than the Canadian average of 10 percent and even 1 percent higher than the Alberta average. In the same publication, he found that Lethbridge had a market rating of 86 percent above the national average, also higher than Edmonton and Calgary. This, he surmised, was a result of high retail expenditures per capita and a large retail drawing from the smaller communities surrounding Lethbridge.

Although Westwinds' management was a bit hesitant to move so quickly, they were aware that the demand for office space rose in proportion to population, income, and retail expenditures, and all these variables were rapidly increasing. The accountant pointed out that construction in Lethbridge was proceeding briskly and this would be an ideal time for Westwinds to enter this area of office development.

As a result, Westwinds purchased a site one block from the central business district, with plans to construct an office building. Although the site contained an old building, it would be replaced with a four-story office building of about 40,000 square feet.

Before going ahead with construction, Westwinds decided to do some research on the types of facilities prospective tenants would prefer (underground parking, recreation facilities, restaurant). They believed that acting on the results of this research would increase their chances to obtain the high early occupancy rate of at least 90 percent they would require to make the project financially feasible. Their investigation revealed the following, in addition to tenant preferences regarding amenities:

1. The population of Lethbridge was growing at a rate of 35 percent per decade (*FP Survey of Markets*) compared to the Canadian average of 10 percent.

2. The market rating index of Lethbridge was 86 percent above the national average in 2000 (*FP Canadian Markets*).
3. Per capita retail sales in Lethbridge in 2000 was $5,924, considerably above the Canadian average of $3,190.
4. Population projections for Lethbridge were as follows:

2002	72,000
2004	74,000
2006	76,000
2008	78,000

5. The present supply of office space in Lethbridge (2000) was estimated at 500,000 square feet, with a vacancy rate of 20 percent.
6. Averages for other cities in Canada showed an average of about 6.5 to 7 square feet per capita in office space at 90 percent occupancy.
7. There did not appear to be a great demand for restaurant or recreation facilities; the major preference was to be close to downtown.

   In view of this information, Westwinds is still planning to proceed with construction of the building, but management is now a bit worried.

Questions

1. Should Westwinds be concerned about the results of its most recent research?
2. How should Westwinds have gone about assessing the market potential for the new office building?
3. What additional information, if any, is required at this point?
4. What would you advise Westwinds to do at this point?

Part II

Preparing for Small Business Ownership

Once the entrepreneur has assessed an opportunity, the next important consideration is selecting from among three methods of assuming ownership of the business: organizing the business from scratch, buying an existing business, or signing a franchise contract. Chapters 4, 5, and 6 provide information to help evaluate each of these methods. The last, but equally important, start-up consideration is obtaining financing. Chapter 7 discusses the critical factors the entrepreneur should consider in obtaining financing needed to establish and operate the venture.

Chapter 4

Organizing a Business— The Business Plan

Chapter Objectives

- To describe the advantages and disadvantages of organizing a business from scratch compared with purchasing a business or becoming a franchisee.

- To discuss the importance of formulating and following a business organizational plan.

- To review the essential components of a small business plan.

Small Business Profile

Clive Beddoe
West Jet Airlines Inc.

West Jet Airlines Inc.
www.westjet.com

In 1995, Clive Beddoe was a successful businessman who spotted what he thought was an opportunity for a low-cost airline in Western Canada. Despite considerable advice to the contrary by industry experts who thought there was no room for another airline, Beddoe's team member, Mark Hill, developed a solid business plan that would show an opportunity in the market for a discount airline patterned after the tremendously successful Southwest Airlines in the U.S. Plans were drawn up in early 1995 for an equity-based operation with no debt and limited overhead and Beddoe consulted extensively with David Neeleman, president of Morris Air, which was purchased by Southwest Airlines, one of the most successful low-cost airlines in the U.S.

WestJet was up and running with its first commercial flight on February 29, 1996. It shuttled 388,000 passengers in the first six months exceeding its own projections. Since then WestJet has revolutionized travel in Western Canada, radically changing the rules of competition in every market in which it has flown. This is no small accomplishment for 50-year-old Beddoe and his staff of 750. Many small discount airlines have buckled under the competition power of the larger airlines over the years. But WestJet has overcome the odds through a mixture of careful planning,

innovative employee programs, careful research, economic circumstance, and the desire of Westerners to see it succeed.

One of the keys, according to Beddoe, was to offer a low-cost operation and use bargain-basement fares to expand the market, luring the masses of people who don't travel and those who drive when they do, rather than compete head to head with the large airlines. It saves money by providing a ticketless reservation system and offering no meal services. The company flies only one type of aircraft, which cuts expenditures on maintenance crews, pilot training, and inventory, and operates with roughly 59 employees per aircraft. It also owns its own planes rather than leasing, and because of its high equity content, incurs little in interest expenses.

Today WestJet operates 21 aircraft flying to many destinations across Canada with revenues of approximately $330 million. Beddoe, along with co-founders Don Bell, Mark Hill, and Tim Morgan, were recently honoured with a national Entrepreneurs of the Year award due to their accomplishments with West Jet.

Used with the permission of Clive Beddoe.

GETTING STARTED: ESTABLISHING THE BUSINESS

Once the entrepreneur has assessed the feasibility of a business opportunity and found it to be favourable, the next step is to select the method of establishing the business. There are essentially three methods from which to choose. The first is to organize a business from scratch, the second is to purchase an existing business, and the third is to become a franchisee. This chapter discusses the essential steps in organizing a business from scratch and details the steps in creating a business plan. Chapter 5 deals with purchasing an existing business, and Chapter 6 covers franchising. Although the topics covered in Chapters 5 and 6 are treated separately, many of the aspects of business plan preparation covered in this chapter are applicable to the following two chapters.

In making the decision to organize a business from scratch, one generally opts for greater independence in the establishment and operation of the business. Figure 4-1 illustrates this concept.

Statistics Canada
www.statcan.ca

The option to organize from scratch is often chosen by an entrepreneur who wants the satisfaction of creating a business and adding his or her personal touch to all its aspects. It may also be the preferred route when few suitable businesses are for sale or there is little chance of obtaining a franchise for the market area. A recent survey of small business owners by Statistics Canada indicates that about two-thirds of them started their business from scratch.[1] In making this decision, the entrepreneur should be aware of the advantages of organizing the business from scratch as well as the potential drawbacks.

Advantages of Organizing a Small Business from Scratch

Organizing a business from scratch offers several advantages. First, this option allows the small business owner to define the nature of the business, the competitive environment in which the business will operate, the appropriate market, and the size and extent of operations. In the small business profile that opens this chapter, Clive Beddoe was free to handle each of these aspects for his new business.

Second, the owner can obtain the exact types of physical facilities—building, equipment, and location—preferred. Buildings and equipment can be tailored to meet requirements precisely. The owner can also choose the most appropriate location for the market, a very important competitive tool in retailing.

Third, the owner can obtain fresh inventory tailored to the target market. Thus, the risk of products becoming obsolete or difficult to turn over is minimized.

Fourth, the owner can personally select and train employees for the business rather than having to rely on the existing personnel of an established business.

Finally, the owner can develop his or her own information systems such as the methods used for bookkeeping and for evaluating the operation. The owner also can take advantage of the latest technology in equipment and materials.

Figure 4-1

	Organizing	**Buying**	**Franchising**
Level of independence	Higher	Medium	Lower
Level of risk	Higher	Medium	Lower
Chance of Survival	20%	70%	90%

Disadvantages of Organizing a Small Business from Scratch

Starting one's own business also carries substantial risks. First, the owner lacks historical information on which to base future plans. This can be a drawback if the owner has uncertainties regarding market demand, supplies, and operations. It is also generally more difficult to obtain financing if projections are based on estimates rather than on the extension of trends from existing operations.

Second, the advantage of personally assembling physical facilities can become a liability because of the time required. In some industrial situations where prompt establishment is critical, purchasing a business or signing a franchise contract may be more advisable.

Third, a new business always has start-up problems or bugs that have to be worked out. Incident 4-1 illustrates some of the problems one Canadian entrepreneur experienced because she didn't start out with a business plan..

Fourth, establishing outside relationships with financial institutions, suppliers, and other key professionals is often time-consuming. For example, new small businesses typically are

---

Incident 4-1

Planning for the Future

Heidi Lang declares, "Planning is the name of the game in a world that is rolling with the forces of economic upheaval." Eight years ago Heidi found out just how important a solid business plan is, especially when trying to obtain financing from the bank. "No one would talk to me because I didn't have a clearly laid out vision of where I was going and what I wanted to do with the new money I was seeking."

Lang's willingness to embrace long-term planning was incited by the loss of her husband's job in 1993. At the time, Heidi was successfully managing an independent sales agency. While good, the earnings were not enough to solely support the Lang family, and it was not long before Heidi began dipping into her savings account. During her continued employment at the sales agency, Heidi noticed a small niche market for interesting lines of photo frames. Outsourcing the frames proved to be unsuccessful, and soon Heidi took a personal interest in her new discovery.

Heidi and her husband decided to use the last $10,000 of their life savings to make a business out of the trendy photo frames, and so the Transatlantic Marketing Group (TMG) was born. A person who could make the frames was contracted, while Heidi displayed the new product to her retail clients. The photo frames were an instant success in the North American market with the United States exhibiting the greatest interest in the Langs' product line. Large retail chains quickly embraced TMG frames and were soon demanding orders worth $40,000.

When Heidi was initially unable to obtain loans from the bank, she financed inventory with her credit card. Eventually, this method was impossible and did not allow TMG the means to fill $40,000 orders. The banks would not touch TMG until Heidi could produce a long-term business plan. To do this, Heidi enlisted the help of a professional business consultant. A detailed business plan outlined Heidi's five-year vision for TMG. It was this plan, a ferocious work ethic, and strong sales experience that gave one bank the confidence to support Heidi's venture.

From this experience, Heidi has learned that planning provides a clear vision that enables a company to deal with day-to-day blunders and the ability to repave future paths when the terrain becomes rough. The entrepreneur says, "A solid plan can help avoid many of the pitfalls that confront every small business, and can help stabilize problems when they do occur." In fact, planning is now a part of everything Heidi Lang does.

SOURCE: Adapted from Heidi Lang, "The Road Ahead," *Profit*, 2001, http://www.profitguide.com/firstperson/F1_lang.html.

not granted trade credit initially, whereas an existing business or franchise has far less difficulty. The savings in interest costs can be substantial.

Finally, the owner faces the risk that there will be insufficient demand for the product or service. Even if a feasibility analysis is to be carried out prior to business start-up, some uncertainty regarding the extent of the market may remain.

THE SMALL BUSINESS PLAN

More.Business.com
www.morebusiness.
com

Regardless of whether an entrepreneur starts the business from scratch, buys an existing business or signs a franchise contract, a business plan is essential. The data points to the crucial need for entrepreneurs to formulate business plans, not just for raising capital, but for organization and classification of long- and short-term goals. A business plan is a vital tool for entrepreneurs—a blueprint to be referred to again and again to keep business growth on course. *

The use of business plans by Canadian entrepreneurs is increasing. A recent study of 100 successful Canadian small business owners found that 53 percent utilized full-scale plans, 91 percent of which had a time frame and 98 percent of which were written down. On the other hand, only 4 percent of Canadian entrepreneurs did not prepare a business plan.[2] Incident 4-2 illustrates the value of a detailed plan. As mentioned by Joe Mancuso, the business plan may serve both internal and external purposes. From an internal perspective, the business plan provides a blueprint for the business which can assist in maintaining a focus essential to success. The plan can assist the entrepreneur in a business start-up as well as serve as a document which can be referred to in order to assist in the management of the ongoing business. A business plan can also assist the entrepreneur by providing a vehicle to evaluate the performance of the operation over time. Business plans should contain both

* Joe Mancuso, President of the Centre for Entrepreneurial Management

---

Incident   4-2

Planting the Seed

As coffee culture takes another foothold in the Lethbridge restaurant market, the Thistleseed Pastry Shoppe and Garden Café wants to make its mark on the more genteel, less brash part of the business.

Thistleseed's decor, complete with sofa, wooden tables and chairs, and green, pigment-coloured walls with ivy stencils, recalls a Victorian English garden.

That's exactly what owner and executive chef David May had in mind. Several other coffee shops have shared the same location, downtown on the corner of 3rd Avenue and 5th Street South. But with his partner, Jim Maruca, May believes he has the formula for success this time.

The decor is no accident, as May has a detailed five-year plan which will make the Thistleseed a successful Lethbridge business. He went to Victoria and researched the decor in tea and coffee shops there.

May and his staff want to provide Lethbridge with the best in pastry and coffee. In addition, May wants to promote his expertise in wedding cake baking and decoration as the business becomes more established.

May took journeyman training at the Lethbridge Community College, and worked there and at other restaurants for several years before setting up the Thistleseed in August.

Source: Mark Nelson, "Planting the Seed," *Southern Alberta Business* 2, no. 3 (Fall 1998), p. 46.

short-term and long-term or growth components for the business. A business plan may also serve an external purpose in that lenders and investors generally require one before lending or investing capital in the venture. There are several other reasons why a business plan should be developed. A business plan provides a sense of direction for the business, a test of the idea's viability, assistance in achieving financing and a clear-cut implementation plan.

The format and emphasis of the business plan varies depending on the user. A plan prepared for a lender should emphasize the entrepreneur's security or collateral position and the cash flow statement. It should show how the loan will be serviced in addition to the other areas. A plan prepared for a potential investor generally requires more detail to compensate for greater risk, a thorough description of the manager or management team capabilities, with emphasis on the projected rate of return. A venture capitalist will be interested in knowing the above items as well as knowing how to liquidate ownership interest in a few years. (More is said about venture capital firms in Chapter 7.)

COMPONENTS OF THE PLAN

Although each user of the plan may require a different format or emphasis, the basic components in creating a business plan are as follows:

Interactive Business Planner, Government of Canada www.cbsc.org/ibp

- Prepare a table of contents.

- Prepare a synopsis of the plan in an executive summary and background statement. This should include a mission statement indicating in general what type of business it is and what it is going to do.

- Describe the management team.

- Establish business objectives.

- Plan the marketing approach.

- Describe the selection of the location.

- Determine the physical facilities.

- Plan the financing.

- Plan the personnel.

- Investigate the legal requirements.

This chapter gives a brief overview of these components. Chapters 8 through 12 discuss the operating aspects of these areas in more detail and should be consulted before preparing a business plan. Appendix 4A at the end of this chapter presents a checklist for a small business plan, and Appendix 4B shows two actual business plans following this format. Note that a business plan may also be critical when purchasing a business, obtaining a franchise, acquiring financing, and performing other essential activities of the business. The format of the business, however, may vary depending upon who the plan is intended for.

Prepare a Table of Contents

This is mainly for the benefit of outside users of the business plan. It not only provides an overview of what is included in the plan, but it provides quick access to various parts of the plan.

Prepare a Synopsis of the Plan in an Executive Summary and Background Statement

The executive summary, written at the conclusion of the preparation of the business plan, provides a short summary of the highlights of the plan for the reader. The background statement provides a history of the project or business as well as a general statement regarding the intended mission of the venture. This mission statement is a general expression of the organization's future direction. It will identify the market, environment, strengths and management preferences.

Describe the Management Team

This section should describe the background of the entrepreneur and/or the management team. For the smaller business it may simply include a résumé. The qualifications relating to experience and education of the owner/manager are important aspects.

Establish Business Objectives

Have clearly thought-out and formally written objectives for the business. The objectives identify goals to be met in order that the mission of the enterprise can be achieved. The mission of the business indicates in a general, long-term way what the business is and what it intends to do. To be effective, an objective must be specific. Specific and quantitative objectives allow meaningful evaluation of the business's performance. Objectives can be set in the following areas for the initial year and for a few years following start-up:

- *Business size.* This includes the size of the physical facilities, financial commitments, and number of employees.

- *Production levels.* The plan should include the number of products and product lines and unit production anticipated.

- *Performance levels.* Sales, market share, and profit level should all be estimated and may form part of the plan.

Plan the Marketing Approach

The next step in the business plan is to develop a marketing plan. Considerable information regarding the calculation of market potential and market share, both essential parts of the marketing plan, is provided in Chapter 3. The following additional key aspects of a marketing plan should be investigated prior to starting the business.

Have a Clear Concept of the Target Market. It is important that the prospective small business owner have a clear idea of who the target customer is and have a well-developed customer profile. This profile should include such demographic information as age, income, occupation, and social class, as well as certain personality and lifestyle characteristics.

After determining the target market, the owner can perform the steps discussed in Chapter 3 —determining market area, market area population, market potential, and market share. Sometimes this information can be obtained using secondary data alone, but often primary research will be required. Chapter 8 illustrates a more detailed target market profile.

Understand the Target Market's Needs, Wants, and Purchasing Habits. Understanding the target market's needs, wants, and purchasing habits is essential in formulating a marketing strategy. Answers to the following questions may prove valuable:

Incident 4-3

The Grocery Go-Pher

Founded by Tracy Jeffrey before beginning studies at the University of Saskatchewan, the Grocery Go-Pher is an excellent example of a business developed based on an observed need. While working part time in a super-market pharmacy, Tracy noticed the rushed and tired expressions of many family and senior customers. This led to the idea of a business that would serve people who did not have time for or had difficulty shopping. Tracy quickly implemented and touted her service without much regard to the development of a business plan. Preliminary business research involved the development and distribution of pamphlets to seniors' residences, homecare workers, doctors' offices, pharmacies, and local businesses. Response to the Grocery Go-Pher was enthusiastic, and a client base of 25 was quickly established.

Now in her fourth year at the University of Saskatchewan College of Commerce, Tracy manages both her studies and her business. The only regret Tracy has since the start-up of the Grocery Go-Pher in 1994 is that she did not develop and implement a business plan. Despite her success, Tracy now realizes that failing to do so can be fatal to a new business. Solid planning is essential for survival in the marketplace, and even thorough preparation does not guarantee success. Tracy believes preparation is necessary if you do not want to end up five years down the road wondering what the primary objective of your business is. The entrepreneur is now developing a business plan for the Grocery Go-Pher, paying special consideration to market research, finances, and advertising costs.

Source: Adapted from Aaron Lam, "The Entrepreneurial Bug Hits Business Students before Graduation," *Business Sense*, vol. 2, no. 2 (March/April 2000) p. 32-33.

- Where do, or where will, the target customers purchase the product or service?

- When do, or when will, they purchase it?

- What product or service attributes influence the purchase decision?

- In what quantities will purchases be made?

- Most important, why do customers, or why will they, purchase the product or service?

Once again, the answers to some of these questions may be obtained using secondary data, but primary research may be required. Incident 4-3 illustrates the effort that one entrepreneur made to understand her target market.

Be Aware of Any Uncontrollable Factors That Might Affect the Marketing of the Product or Service. Several factors external to the business can affect the marketing plan and should be investigated, including the following.

Business Gateway
www.
businessgateway.ca

Exisiting or Pending Legislation Relevant to the Business. New laws relating to marketing practices such as advertising, pricing, and manufacturing can have a significant impact on the business and cannot be ignored. This information may be obtained from an office of the Federal Government or the equivalent provincial agency.

State of the Economy in the Market. The prospective small business owner should investigate whether the state of the economy is in a recovery or recessionary period. This also can influence the effectiveness of the marketing plan. Statistics Canada and private reports can provide this information.

Extent and Strategies of the Competition. The entrepreneur should attempt to evaluate the competition and look for competitive strengths over the prospective business. A recent study found that 33 percent of Canadian entrepreneurs omit this important aspect from their business plans.[3]

Cultural Norms of the Market. The entrepreneur should ensure that the new business conforms to the social and cultural norms of the market. This is especially important for exporters and for companies moving into new markets. An important aspect in this area relates to social responsibility. A code of ethics should be established for the organization's operations.

New Technology That Might Affect the Business. New technology should be reviewed and monitored regularly as it can represent either opportunities for the business or detrimental competitor strategies. Trade magazines and competitor strategies are good sources of information concerning new technology.

Plan the Marketing Program. After collecting the above information, the entrepreneur can formulate a marketing program. The essential aspects of the marketing program are as follows.

The Product or Service. This includes such information as how the product or service is developed, sources of material, and level of quality, variety, and packaging.

The Distribution System. This includes determining the path the product or service will take to reach the consumer or ultimate user and may involve selection of wholesalers and retailers.

Promotion. This involves decisions regarding promotion budgets, advertising versus personal selling, and developing appropriate communications.

Pricing. The development of pricing policies, including the calculation of specific price levels, should be planned. These elements of the marketing program are discussed in more detail in Chapter 8.

Describe the Selection of the Location

The next component of a business plan is selecting the location for the business. In setting up a new business, the prospective owner needs to determine the trading area or city in which to locate. Then the owner selects the specific site within the trading area.

The Trading Area. Several criteria are commonly used to select the trading area. Choosing the general trade area is often more critical for manufacturers than for retailers or service firms, whereas the selection of a specific site within the trade area is generally more important for retailers. The following information is valuable in selecting the trading area.

Economic Base. Information on population, employment levels, income levels, retail sales, and house values within the trading area may be needed. These elements help small manufacturers determine the availability of employees and expected pay scales. For retail and service firms, they indicate the potential for future sales. One should also examine the trends relating to these key indicators. Most of this information may be obtained from secondary data such as the government sources listed in Chapter 3.

Attitude of Trading Area toward New Businesses. Many communities are eager to attract new industry and offer various kinds of incentives for new businesses. While this benefit is usually more important for manufacturers, any small business owner should contact the local city administration or chamber of commerce regarding incentives. Often these agencies are aware of specific types of businesses their communities need.

Competition. Competitive firms in a trading area should be noted. A retail or service firm with a fixed geographic market should evaluate various trading areas on the basis of saturation levels for the type of outlet it will establish. There are many methods of calculating the saturation index. A method commonly used in the retailing industry is to divide retail sales of all competitors by the selling space of the trading area:

$$\text{Saturation} \quad = \quad \frac{\text{Competing retail sales}}{\text{Competing retail space}}$$

The saturation index can be compared to other trading areas or industry norms. The higher the index, the more attractive the opportunity. The statistics needed to compute a saturation index can be obtained from city and provincial licence and tax records, Statistics Canada reference books, or personal visits.

Costs. Obviously a key consideration in selecting a trading area is the cost of land and buildings. Another is the cost of required services and expenses once the business is operating. These include such items as utilities, business taxes, and insurance.

The trading area decision can be quantified to allow evaluation among several alternatives. Figure 4-2 shows an example of such a calculation.

The Site. After selecting the trading area, the prospective owner should investigate the following items in selecting the specific site.

Accessibility. For the manufacturer, this means accessibility of transportation services for incoming supplies and materials, as well as ease of shipping the finished product. It might also include the site's accessibility to necessary services, employees of the business, and protection services such as the fire department.

For the retailer, proximity to major arteries and transit lines and availability of parking are important to ensure maximum customer traffic. Assessing traffic patterns, both pedestrian and vehicular, may be critical to success, especially for retailers of certain types of merchandise (Chapter 8 further discusses the location considerations for retail goods). Often the chamber of commerce can provide information on traffic flows.

Site Costs. The costs of sites within a community usually vary considerably. Generally the higher-traffic areas are more expensive to buy or lease. One should also investigate other possible costs such as utilities, taxes, and licences.

Figure 4-2   Evaluation of a Trading Area

1 = Poor; 5 = Excellent

Criteria	Trading Area A	Trading Area B
Economic base		
Attitude		
Competition		
Costs		
Other		
Total		

Restrictions. When evaluating a site, any restrictive ordinances such as zoning by-laws should be investigated. Such restrictions may hinder current operations as well as future expansion.

Site History. The prospective owner should find out whether the site has had several tenants or owners over the years. If this is the case, he or she should investigate the reasons for the turnover before proceeding to purchase or lease the site.

Proximity to Other Businesses. Will the surrounding businesses have a positive or negative influence on the business? Levels of competitiveness and complementarity are two significant factors. Figure 4-3 gives examples of the positive and negative effects of these factors for both noncompetitive and competitive businesses.

Physical Characteristics. Size, frontal footage, external facade, contour, and shape are all important considerations in site selection. The business should blend in with surrounding businesses, but it should also be distinctive.

The evaluation form shown in Figure 4-4, similar to that for the trading area analysis, might be used in making the site selection decision.

The Buy-or-Lease Decision. In selecting the specific site, a major consideration is whether to own or lease the premises. Because ownership is generally more expensive, most small businesses find that to reduce the already high risk at the initial stages, leasing is the more attractive option. The small business owner should investigate several factors before signing a lease contract.

Figure 4-3   Influence of Neighbouring Businesses

Positive Influence from Neighbouring Businesses	Negative Influence from Neighbouring Businesses
Complementary—for example, a pharmacy by a doctor's office.	Uncomplementary—businesses such as a mortuary, tavern, and factory.
Competitive—could be positive for shopping goods such as clothing, automobiles, and motels.	Competitive—for nonshopping goods such as convenience stores.

Figure 4-4   Evaluation of the Actual Site

1 = Poor; 5 = Excellent

Criteria	Actual Site A	Actual Site B
Accessibility		
Costs		
Restrictions		
History		
Effect of other businesses		
Physical characteristics		
Other		
Total		

Cost of the Lease. The owner-manager should investigate the cost of the lease, how the rent is calculated, when the payments are due, and what taxes and utilities apply. Most leases are calculated on a per-square-footage basis. In retailing, a percentage of gross sales is often added to the cost of the lease in the form of royalties.

Length of the Lease. Questions concerning the length of the lease include: For how long is the contract? Is there a provision for renewal at the end of that time? What notice is required for renewal, termination, or rent increase?

Restrictions. Potential restrictions on the use of the property should be investigated. Can the site be subleased to someone else? Does anyone have the right to use a part of the property? Are there certain services or products that cannot be sold or manufactured at the site?

Repairs and Leasehold Improvements. Who is responsible for any repairs and improvements required? When the lease expires, who will own such improvements?

Insurance Coverage. What insurance does the lessor have on the property? What about liability insurance coverage? What insurance coverage will be required by the lessee?

Running the Business from One's Home. The final important consideration in site selection is the possibility of operating the business out of one's home. A 1994 study found that home businesses operated in 1.5 million Canadian households, representing 14.7 percent of the total of all businesses. A regional breakdown of this study is shown in Figure 4-5. A recent estimate pegs the percentage of small businesses that operate out of the home at 53 percent.[4] And estimates are that soon two out of every three households will be running either a part-time or full-time business.[5] Some of the best home-based businesses are business services and consulting, computer-related services, marketing and public relations, alternative medicine, independent sales, and on-line sales. A primary reason for the increase in home-based

Figure 4-5   Percentage of Penetration of Home Businesses in Canada in 1994

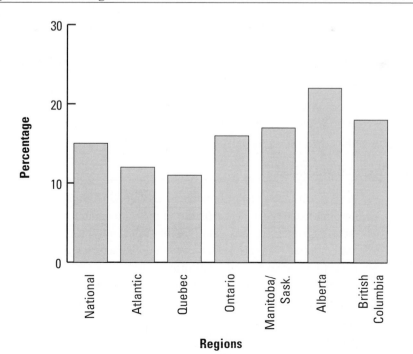

SOURCE: Market Facts – 1994 Household Equipment Survey. As reported in *The Globe and Mail,* April 10, 1995, p. B6.

businesses is the utilization of computer technology. Such equipment allows the entrepreneur access to information and communication capabilities on par with larger businesses.[6] Incident 4-4 provides an example of the advantages of home-based business.

Some situations are particularly suitable for a home-based business. First, if the business is started on a part-time basis, as many are, the costs associated with establishing a home office are minimal. Second, the lower costs associated with starting a business in one's home reduce the financial risks of a venture that may already carry a high degree of risk. Thus, a home office can serve as a temporary office until the business is more firmly established. Third, a home office is suitable for many businesses for which location is of minimal importance. Many service and some small manufacturing businesses fit in this category. Fourth, locating the business in the home offers several tax-related advantages. Chapter 13 gives more details on such advantages.

Determine the Physical Facilities

In preparing the feasibility analysis outlined in Chapter 3, the entrepreneur should already have prepared a detailed estimate of the total capital needed to acquire the building, equipment, furniture, fixtures, and possibly initial inventory. The size of investment in buildings and equipment is typically larger for a manufacturing firm, while the investment in inventory tends to be larger for the retail firm.

Prior to construction of buildings and purchasing equipment, the relevant building codes and construction standards should be investigated and required permits obtained.

In addition to these capital requirements and standards, a plan should be made of the operations flow within the business. This includes such factors as purchasing, inventory control, the production process, the interior layout, and distribution of the finished product. Chapter 11 discusses all of these items in detail.

Figure 4-6 Ways to Manage Risk

Method	Type of Risk
Self-insurance	Cover losses out of cash flow (asset values small)
Prevention	Burglar alarms, inspections, education, hiring practices
Avoidance of risk	Leasing, incorporation
Transfer of risk	Purchasing insurance (asset values large)

Insurance. Small businesses face several risks. There are four ways that an entrepreneur can deal with risk. These are illustrated in Figure 4-6. The entrepreneur should analyze the extent of such risks and determine whether they threaten the existence of the company. Generally entrepreneurs transfer risk by buying insurance when the loss would be of a serious nature. Insurance coverage for such risks should be purchased prior to the start-up of the business.

Types of Insurance. Common insurable risks for a small business include the following:

> *Loss or Damage of Property.* This type of coverage protects the business in the case of fire, theft, and similar occurrences.

> *Business Interruption.* If one of the above problems occurs, this type of insurance protects the earning power lost due to the occurrence for a short period of time.

> *Liability and Disability.* This coverage includes bodily injury to employees or customers and could include liability coverage for company officials such as members of the board of directors of the company.

> *Life Insurance.* This insurance is usually bought in the form of a group insurance plan or occasionally key employee life insurance. Partners of a business may also desire to purchase life insurance for the other partner(s).

Insurance Decisions. The entrepreneur faces three insurance-related decisions:

1. Determine what kind of insurance to purchase.
2. Determine how much coverage to take out.
3. Decide from whom to purchase the insurance.

In developing answers to these questions, the following rules of thumb commonly used in the insurance industry are helpful. The first and most important rule is: Don't risk more than you can afford to lose. In other words, if the prospective loss will put the business into bankruptcy or serious financial difficulty, insurance should be taken out. Usually the probability of occurrence of these losses is low, and the associated insurance premiums are also low. The maximum sustainable loss will, of course, vary from firm to firm and from time to time in a particular business.

A second rule of insurance management is: Don't risk a lot for a little. In implementing this second rule, the premium should be related to the potential loss and treated as savings or costs. For example, if comprehensive physical damage insurance on a $14,000 automobile costs $350 per year, the savings or return if the insurance is not purchased and the risk is assumed equals 350/14,000, or 2.5 percent. The owner is exposing a $14,000 investment to possible loss or damage for a 2.5 percent return, and that is risking a lot for a little. On the other hand, a driver who pays $150 a year for auto collision coverage with a $50 deductible, when the same coverage with a $100 deductible would cost only $125 per year, is paying a cost of $25/$50, or 50 percent for the second $50 of coverage. Here, from a cost point of view, the car owner is paying dearly for a small return. In the first case, the purchase of insurance is consistent with the rule; in the second, it is not. For this reason, it is usually advisable to purchase the largest deductible the business can afford. This can result in substantial premium savings.

The third rule is that insurance should be taken out only when absolutely necessary. Insurance always costs more than the expected value of a loss because the premium must also include the insurer's administration and selling costs, plus profit. This insurance is economically feasible only when the probability of loss is low and the severity of a potential loss is high. Therefore, in the opposite situation, the best approach may be to take preventative measures and build these losses into the cost or expense structure of the business.

The fourth rule is to buy adequate coverage. The reason is that all property insurance contracts contain a co-insurance clause. The co-insurance clause states that if the amount of insurance purchased on the property is less than some stated percentage (usually 80 percent), the insured will share all partial losses up to the face value of the policy. The purpose of co-insurance is to encourage the small business owner to buy adequate insurance coverage for the business. For example, if a small business owner has a building with a current replacement value of $110,000 and a policy containing an 80 percent co-insurance clause, $80,000 of insurance is required for collecting on partial losses. If only $60,000 of insurance were purchased and a $10,000 loss occurred, the insurance company would pay only $60,000 (coverage)/$80,000 (co-insurance), or $7,500 of the loss.

The last insurance purchasing rule involves adequately investigating both the insurance company and the agent. Choosing an insurance company with financial stability, satisfactory claims service, and competitive premiums is important, and the selection of the agent may be even more critical. The agent should have a thorough knowledge of insurance, be located where he or she can provide prompt service on claims and enquiries, and possess a genuine interest in clients' needs. The agent should be questioned regarding the claim settlement procedures, cancellation procedures, and premium rates. Many insurance companies now have special policies tailored to small businesses.

Care should be taken to ensure that coverage is current. As replacement costs rise, the level of coverage should increase. Most insurance companies now adjust policies for inflation automatically.

Plan the Financing

Four major financial aspects of the new business should be planned in advance of opening.

Establish Capital Requirements and Make Feasibility Projections. As indicated previously, these calculations are made when preparing a feasibility analysis. The results of these calculations form an integral part of the projected income statement for at least the first year of operations, and in some cases five years into the future. In conjunction with the income statement projection, enough information would have likely been obtained to prepare a projected balance sheet and cash flow statement. Although these statements are described fully in Chapter 10, Figure 7-4 in Chapter 7 (see pages 198–199) shows the format of a cash flow that would be required in a business plan. It may be advisable for the entrepreneur to enlist the services of an accountant in completing these financial statements. Proper preparation of this financial data is key to obtaining funding from investors and lenders.

Determine Sources of Funding. The projections discussed above provide an estimate of the funds required to get started and to operate the business. After calculating the required funds, the owner will need to determine a balance between his or her own funds (equity) and borrowed funds (debt). Because raising funds is such a critical area for the small business, Chapter 7 is devoted entirely to the types of funds required, sources of funding for the small business, and methods of evaluating those sources. Sufficient start-up funding is of critical importance to a new small business.

Plan the Accounting and Bookkeeping Systems. An essential part of any business is recordkeeping. Bookkeeping is the recording and classifying of the internal and external transactions of the business. This may be an area that requires professional advice. Chapter 10 reviews the types of financial records kept and the different types of bookkeeping systems used by small businesses.

Determine Financial Evaluation Measures. One area crucial to the success of the small business is the financial evaluation of operations. To perform this evaluation, the owner should determine the key indicators of the financial health of the business. These indicators include profit margins, return on investment, and inventory turnover. The owner should also set up a system of regular monitoring and reporting of these areas. This system may also require professional assistance to establish and is discussed in detail in Chapter 10.

Plan the Personnel

Chapter 12 discusses the operating details of personnel administration for a small business. Following are the major considerations in organizing for the management of personnel.

Administrative Structure. This involves setting up the responsibility and reporting procedure for all employees of the business. If there are only two owners, the administrative structure takes the form of a clear division of responsibilities. A business with several employees might require setting up an organizational chart.

Employee Recruitment and Training. The plan for hiring, training, and managing those who will work in the business should be determined.

Personnel Policies. Operating policies affecting employees should be stated explicitly and be formally prepared prior to the time the business begins operations.

Investigate the Legal Requirements

A small business can be significantly affected by the legal environment in which it operates. Considerable legislation in Canada applies to the ongoing management of the business. Typical areas covered are advertising and promotion, credit, sales contracts, pricing, distribution channels, personnel, recordkeeping, and financial relationships. Legislation pertaining to each of these aspects of managing the ongoing business is covered in later chapters.

This section discusses the legal requirements relating to the establishment of the business that should be included in the business plan. Some of the most important aspects are selecting the legal structure, investigating which licences are required, and filing for patent protection if necessary. The legal information provided here and in later chapters is intended not to replace the advice and direction of a lawyer but merely to provide a background against which the entrepreneur can work with such professionals more knowledgeably. Care should be taken in the selection of a lawyer. References from business acquaintances or a lawyer referral service could ensure that you enlist the services of a lawyer who has small business experience and expertise.

Figure 4-7   Advantages and Disadvantages of a Sole Proprietorship

Advantages	Disadvantages
1. Simple and inexpensive to start	1. Unlimited liability
2. Offers individual control over operations, profits, etc.	2. Often more difficult to obtain financing
3. Fewer forms and reports to fill out	3. The personal tax rate may be higher than the corporate rate
4. Some tax advantages	4. The life of the business terminates on owner's death

Figure 4-8   Advantages and Disadvantages of a Partnership

Advantages	Disadvantages
1. Simple and inexpensive to start	1. Unlimited liability
2. Pooling of financial and skill resources	2. Death of a partner terminates the partnership unless a provision to the contrary is specified in the partnership agreement
3. Tax advantages (i.e. income splitting)	3. Greater possibility for disagreements (buy-sell agreements should be drawn up in the event that partner(s) wants to leave the business)

Legal Structure. The owner must decide under which legal structure the business will operate. Five types of legal structures can be used.

1. Sole Proprietorship. In the sole proprietorship, the business is owned by a single individual. The proprietor has perfect freedom of operation; when business decisions are made or when actions are taken it is not necessary to get the consent of anyone else in the organization. Similarly, all profits are the property of the owner and need not be shared with anyone else. There are, however, certain disadvantages in the one-owner organization. Limited personal assets, for example, do not encourage lenders and cannot always provide the capital needed to meet the needs of the business. But perhaps the biggest disadvantage is the proprietor's personal liability for business debts; in case of business failure, the owner's home, automobile, stocks, cash, and other personal assets may be seized by creditors to satisfy the debts of the business. Registration with the provincial government is normally required and can help protect the name of the business. Figure 4-7 (above) lists the advantages and disadvantages of a sole proprietorship.

2. Partnership. In most ways, partnerships are similar to sole proprietorships except that partnerships include two or more partners. Partnerships typically provide increased resources and complementary abilities (see Incident 4-5), but they also increase the possibility of conflict (see Incident 4-6). Figure 4-8 (above) summarizes the advantages and disadvantages of partnerships. There are two kinds of partnerships a small business might use:

1. *Limited partnership.* In a limited partnership, one or more partners obtains limited liability in exchange for not taking an active part in the day-to-day management of the business or acting on behalf of the company. These partners, often called silent partners, usually provide only the financial investment as their part of the ownership interest.

Incident 4-5

A Sweet Partnership

Three Blondes and a Brownie Inc. is literally a "sweet" partnership. Nadja Piatka, Terry Lynne Meyer and Candace Brinsmead began the low-fat cake and muffin making company in 1993. The company's million-dollar success can be attributed to the expertise of each partner. Ms. Piatka is the visionary partner who began the business of making fat wise products from her home. Recipes were developed and tested on her teenage children before delivering the fat-reduced products to small stores and coffee shops. Ms. Meyer, former Miss Canada (1974), is the communicator for the business. She derives her expertise from experience in the television industry as host of her own morning show. Ms. Brinsmead is the financial expert of Three Blondes and a Brownie Inc. Ms. Meyer recruited Brinsmead for her best friend's experience as a bank manager.

   The entrepreneurial spirit of Ms. Piatka would not have been enough to build the company to where it is today. Each partner's "know-how" has contributed to the business' success. Ms. Meyer admits that if it had been just her and Nadja, the company "would have imploded in the first two years," while Meyer and Brinsmead's approach would have been too cautious. Each woman realizes that the success of Three Blondes and a Brownie Inc. is due to the individual expertise of each partner. In fact, the company's current growth in contracts with Safeway supermarkets and Co-operative grocery stores has led to the hiring of more expertise. The three blondes will rely on Kal de-Boer's expertise from Kinetic Sales and Marketing to establish new market prospects.

SOURCE: Adapted from Donna Korchinski, "Three Blondes Cook Up Sweet Success," *Globe and Mail*, August 14, 1999, p. B10.

Incident 4-6

Advanced Bioconcept

It's safe to say that Lloyd Segal is familiar with the traditional corporation. A Harvard MBA, he had spent four years as a management consultant with McKinsey & Co., working for *Fortune* 500 companies, when an interesting opportunity came his way in 1996. Clarissa Desjardins, a biotech researcher at the Montreal Neurological Institute, had co-developed a solution to a tricky, long-standing problem in new drug research: how to trace the path of a drug without using radioactive isotopes, which are difficult to handle and dispose of. With an unusually entrepreneurial flair—for an academic—she quickly sought out investors, patented the discovery and looked for ways to bring the product to the market. Then she approached Segal and Martin LeBlanc, a childhood friend who was also a McKinsey consultant, for management expertise. In exchange for equity stakes in her new company, Advanced Bioconcept, they signed on as well.

   Two years ago, Advanced Bioconcept's sales were zero; this year they will hit a healthy seven-figure number. Those revenues come from Fluo-Peptide, a non-radioactive molecule that acts like a dye, tracing the path of a drug through the body. They also have a string of promising products in their development pipeline. And they are doing it with a company that's very different from Segal's old McKinsey clients.

   "There's no question that we have a different model here," says Segal. "The old paradigm is: To be a successful company, we have to be a big company. If I can turn millions of dollars in profit with 20 people, this is a great company. The old model wanted to bring as much as possible in-house under one umbrella. My generation is saying, 'How can I minimize what I have to do so I can focus on this one small piece that really adds value, and really own that, and outsource everything else?'" Being perfectly comfortable with the notion of a virtual company is another mark of Segal's generation. "An automated Web server, two guys and 10 support people, and that's Amazon.com," he explains. "It's a virtual machine, and it's not about the number of people you have. And that is something that kind of freaks out the older generation."

SOURCE: Richard Bingham, "Rebels with a Business Plan," *Report on Business Magazine*, November 1998, pp. 77–82.

Small businesses are increasingly using this form of ownership because silent partners constitute an important source of equity funding. In addition, limited partnerships offer some tax advantages for the silent partner while retaining the positive aspects of sole proprietorship for the entrepreneur.

Business Gateway
www.
businessgateway.ca

2. *General partnership.* When the partners share in the management or control of the business, it is referred to in legal terms as a general partnership. The most obvious advantage of this form of organization over the proprietorship form is that added capital is made available by combining the assets of the partners, and money is usually easier to borrow because the partners share debts. Similarly, the personal abilities of the partners are complemented, and they may succeed together when neither could alone. However, each partner by law is equally responsible for all the debts of the partnership, regardless of the amount of capital contributed and regardless of any agreement among them to the contrary. Also, any one partner can bind the entire partnership in a business arrangement, even if it is contrary to the wishes or judgement of the majority. The general partnership has other disadvantages as well, such as the termination of the business by the death or withdrawal of any one of the partners and the inability of a partner to sell or assign his or her interest in the partnership without the consent of all the other partners. However, both of these conditions or eventualities can be circumvented by appropriate provisions in a written partnership agreement which should be prepared with the consultation of a lawyer. Although not legally required in order to form a general partnership, such an agreement is nonetheless advisable, even among relatives and close friends. At a minimum, it should specify the following:

1. Duration of the partnership.

2. Administrative responsibilities and authority of each of the partners.

3. Withdrawals and salaries of the partners.

4. Provision for the arbitration of policy disputes among the partners.

5. Provisions for the withdrawal of partners or the admission of additional partners.

6. Amount of capital invested by each partner.

7. Division of profit or loss. (Regardless of the amount of capital invested, general partners must share profit or loss equally unless there is an agreement among the partners to the contrary.)

8. Distribution of assets in the event of dissolution. (As in the case of profits or losses, this distribution must be on an equal basis unless otherwise agreed upon in writing.)

9. Settlements in the event of death or disability of a partner. This might include a buy-sell agreement funded with business life insurance in amounts equal to the interest of each partner; thus the surviving partner(s) would be assured of full title to the business, and the deceased partner's estate would be assured of receiving the full value of his or her share of the business. In the absence of such an agreement, the business might well be forced into liquidation to satisfy demands of the deceased partner's estate.

In a general partnership, unlimited liability applies to all partners.

3. Cooperative. The cooperative is used infrequently by small businesses. In most respects, its strengths and weaknesses are similar to those of a corporation (see Figure 4-9). The distinguishing feature is that in a cooperative (which needs a minimum of six members), each member has only one vote, whereas in a corporation each voting share has a vote.

4. Corporation. The corporation, or limited company, is becoming an increasingly popular form of structuring a small business. Industry Canada reports that over 50 percent of all self-employed businesses in Canada were incorporated in 1999, up from 34 percent in 1996.[7] The corporation is a legal entity that is separate and distinct from the shareholders of the business. The chief advantages of the corporation are (1) continuity in existence (2) easy transferability of ownership interest, and (3) limited liability of shareholders. The corporation is long-lived, being able to continue in existence up to the time limit granted in its charter, and may even be granted in perpetuity, whereas other forms of organization may cease abruptly with the death of the proprietor or a partner. Ownership in a corporation is easily transferred merely by the sale or exchange of stock; permission of other shareholders is not required. Care should be taken in drafting a shareholder agreement in order to facilitate the smooth transition of the ownership of the company in the event that a key owner leaves the business. Legal liability of owners or shareholders for suits for personal injury or other activities connected with operating the business is limited to the amount of funds invested in the business. The corporate form of business organization is also more attractive for raising equity capital. This is so because capital can be more readily obtained from many more sources and because of the legal limited liability of corporate shareholders. A corporation has certain disadvantages, however. Its activities are limited to those specifically granted in its charter. Similarly, its geographical area of operations is limited to the province granting its charter until permission is secured from each of the other provinces in which it desires to operate; this means that additional filing fees must be paid and additional legal requirements observed. The corporation must make numerous reports for taxation and other purposes in each province in which it does business; not only has federal and provincial regulation of corporations been increasing for some time, but the paperwork required increases greatly as the corporation grows in size.

The day-to-day operations of a corporation are handled by a manager who is appointed by and reports to a board of directors. The board of directors is elected by the shareholders. Often in very small businesses the manager, director, and major shareholder can be the same person. Many small businesses have found it valuable to enlist the services of lawyers, accountants, and other noncompeting businesspeople to serve on their boards of directors.

The vast majority of incorporated small businesses are private companies. For a business to qualify as a private company, the following conditions must exist:

- The right to transfer shares is restricted, usually requiring the approval of the board of directors.

- The number of shareholders is limited to 50. The company cannot sell new shares publicly.

Figure 4-9 (on the next page) summarizes the advantages and disadvantages of a corporation.

Figure 4-9 **Advantages and Disadvantages of a Corporation**

Advantages	Disadvantages
1. The continuity of the business exists even if the owner dies.	1. The cost to incorporate generally ranges from $800 to $1,200.
2. The owners have limited liability.	2. There is a greater reporting requirement by government.
3. The business may have a manager with professional training or expertise.	3. Flexibility may be reduced because of the binding provisions of the corporate charter.
4. It's easier to raise funds as lenders, and equity investors usually look more favourably to incorporated companies.	4. Losses cannot be deducted from other personal income of the owner.
5. The corporate tax rate on small businesses (see Appendix 13B in Chapter 13) can be lower than one's personal rate.	5. Lenders often require a personal guarantee, negating the advantage of limited liability.
6. Incorporation can assist in establishing commercial credibility.	
7. Liability insurance may be less expensive.	

Steps in Incorporation. Most entrepreneurs regard incorporation as a very complex process that requires a lawyer's assistance. While it is advisable for the small business to enlist the services of a lawyer to assist in incorporating the business, some entrepreneurs with relatively uncomplicated businesses have incorporated their businesses successfully on their own. Recently, incorporation "software" has been developed to assist entrepreneurs with self-incorporation.[8] Incorporating a business has four steps:

1. *Selection of a name for the business.* This name must be submitted to and approved by the provincial government department that handles incorporations (see Appendix 4C at the end of this chapter). The selection can be facilitated by doing a computer search to ensure that no similar names are currently being used.

2. *Development of the share structure, directors, restrictions on share transfers, and so on.* The owner must determine the number of shares to authorize, the number of shares to issue, the number of directors, the timing of meetings, and approvals required for shares to be bought or sold.

3. *A description of company operations.* This section describes what the business can and cannot do.

4. *Acquiring the necessary supplies.* This includes such items as the corporate stamp, the minute book, and the necessary journals and ledgers.

5. *Joint Ventures.* A joint venture is an agreement between one or more sole proprietors, partnerships, or corporations to participate in a business venture. Although similar to a partnership in many ways, this increasingly popular form of business allows for individual ownership of assets in the venture. Items such as capital cost allowance can be used by either party, depending on the need. Other advantages and disadvantages are similar to those in a partnership (see Figure 4-8 on page 110).

Licences and Taxes. Prior to starting a business, the prospective owner should investigate the required licences and the taxes that may be payable to the government. Licences and taxes can be levied by federal, provincial, and municipal governments, and these requirements differ among various industries. Following are the most common licences and taxes that apply to the small business. For a more detailed listing, see Appendix 4D at the end of this chapter.

Federal Government

1. *Income tax.* The income tax is a tax on both companies and individuals earning income from a business operating in Canada. The rates vary by province and by industry (see Chapter 13). Although the income tax payments are made to the federal government, part of this amount is transferred to the province in which the business earns income. Some provinces now collect their own business income tax.

2. *Goods and services tax.* The goods and services tax (GST) is a value-added tax levied on many sellers of goods and services by the federal government. The tax, which currently is 7 percent of the sale price, is collected from the purchaser by the seller and remitted to the government on a quarterly basis. Although the GST has met considerable resistance from business and consumers, it has been an effective method for increasing government revenues. Certain exemptions from the GST, relating to size of the business and type of merchandise sold, are available. The small business owner should consult Revenue Canada for the information about how the GST applies to his or her business and for information about obtaining the GST remittance number.

3. *Excise tax.* The excise tax is an extra tax imposed on certain goods sold in Canada. Payment is made by the manufacturer and is a hidden component in the cost of purchasing those goods.

Provincial Government

1. *Income tax.* A percentage of federal income tax payable is assessed by the provinces. Some provinces (Ontario, Quebec, and Alberta) collect this tax. In other provinces, the federal government collects the tax and remits the provincial portion to the province.

2. *Licences.* Many types of businesses require a provincial licence to operate. Some of these businesses may also require bonding.

3. *Sales tax.* Most provinces levy retail sales taxes on tangible property sold or imported. This tax is collected by the retailer from the purchaser at the time of the sale and remitted to the government in much the same manner as the goods and services tax. Many businesses have found the administration of the provincial sales tax more difficult since the introduction of the GST.

Municipal Government

1. *Licences.* Municipalities (cities) are authorized to license all businesses operating within their boundaries.

2. *Property taxes.* Municipalities are also authorized to levy property taxes on the real estate on which a business operates.

3. *Business taxes.* Other taxes levied on businesses by a municipality might be for water use or other services.

Intellectual Property Protection. As many entrepreneurs create new products or processes, a critical measure to ensure their success is to secure legal protection. This protection could be required for a patent, trademark, industrial design, or copyright. Copyrights are for literary, artistic, musical, and dramatic works. Industrial designs include shapes, patterns, or ornamentation of an industrially produced object. Trademarks are words, symbols, or slogans which represent origins of goods and services. A patent, the most commonly obtained for a small business, is a right granted by the government to an inventor to exclude others from making, using, or selling his or her invention in Canada for a period of 17 years.

It is important for the inventor to record the date of the invention and file for the patent as soon as possible. Registration of a patent may be made through a Consumer and Corporate Affairs office or the Commissioner of Patents, Ottawa-Hull, Canada, K1A OE1. Other helpful information about intellectual property protection may be obtained through the Strategis web site listed at the end of Chapter 3. In Canada, if the patent has been used publicly or sold within the previous two years, it may not be granted. A patent agent or lawyer can provide valuable assistance in the patenting process and may be essential if infringement on the patent occurs later. Careful screening to ensure that the invention is new, useful, and a result of inventive ingenuity are criteria used in the patent approval.

The specific steps required to register a patent are as follows:

1. Conduct a search at the patent office to ensure that the idea is not already registered.

2. File an application—the formal request for the patent, which includes a description of the idea.

A patent application may take from one to three years to receive an approval. Nearly 29,000 patent applications are received each year in Canada, and approximately 24,000 are approved. Once approved, a listing of patents is available for public perusal at most public libraries. Similar procedures for obtaining patents are followed in registering trademarks, industrial designs, and copyrights. Applications for these items are also obtained through Consumer and Corporate Affairs or the Commissioner of Patents.

Summary

1. Organizing one's own business has several advantages and disadvantages. The advantages of having a hand in determining the type of business, equipment, employees, inventory, and market are balanced against the disadvantages of uncertainty concerning demand, unforeseen problems, and the time required to establish the business.

2. A business plan provides a sense of direction for the business, determines the viability, assists in obtaining financing, and helps the owner to evaluate progress.

3. The basic steps in preparing a business plan are preparing a table of contents and synopsizing the plan in an executive summary and background statement (best done when the plan is complete), setting the overall mission of the business, establishing business objectives, planning the marketing approach, selecting the location, determining the physical facilities, planning the financing, planning the personnel, and researching the legal requirements.

Chapter Problems and Applications

1. Investigate a small business that is for sale. What are the advantages and disadvantages to you of buying this business as opposed to starting a similar one from scratch?

2. You are thinking of opening up a small business consulting company. What uncontrollable factors might affect your decision? Explain.

3. The saturation index is useful to a prospective small business owner in selecting a trading area.

   a. Using the information in the following table, which trading area would you recommend to the prospective owner?

Location	1	2	3
Number of customers for the store	100,000	50,000	25,000
Average purchase per customer	$5	$7	$9
Total square footage of the drugstore			
(including the proposed store)	20,000	15,000	10,000

   b. If you excluded the proposed store (3,000 square feet), which area would you select?

   c. Which index of saturation is more accurate—the calculation with the proposed store square footage or the calculation without it? Why?

4. Which variables are important in site location for a drugstore? Note: In answering this question, consider the variables in Figure 4-4 and rank them from 5 (most important) to 1 (least important). Justify your ranking on each variable.

5. Interview a small business owner about the details of his or her start-up plan. Find out what aspects were omitted from the plan that should have been included.

6. Choose a specific type of small business and obtain advice from an insurance agent on the types of insurance needed and the precise costs. Write a short report on your findings.

7. Contact your local patent office and find out the requirements for registering a patent.

Appendix 4A

Checklist for a Small Business Plan

Introduction

1. Have a table of contents, executive summary, and description of the management team been prepared?

Business Objectives

1. Have specific business objectives been set? At the end of one or five years, what will the size of the business be in gross sales? In production level? In number of employees? In market share? In profit?

Market Approach

1. Who is the target market in terms of occupation? Income level? Education? Lifestyle?

2. What is the target market purchasing behaviour for this product or similar products? Where are purchases made? When are purchases made? What quantities are purchased?

3. Why does the target market purchase this product or similar products? Which characteristics are preferred? What other factors influence the purchase?

4. What external constraints will affect the business? Existing or pending legislation? State of the economy? Competition? Social or cultural trends? New technology?

5. Which product characteristics will be developed? Quality level? Amount of depth? Type of packaging? Patent protection? Extent of warranty protection? Level of service?

6. How will the product get to the consumer? What channel of distribution will be used? Length of the channel? Intensity of channel distributors? Legal arrangement within the channel? Type of physical transportation?

7. How will the product be promoted? What are the promotional objectives? Which media will be used? How much will be spent on production? Who is the target of the promotion? What is the promotional theme? What is the timetable for promotion?

8. What price levels will be set for the product? Which pricing policies will be instituted? What factors will influence pricing? How important is price to the target market?

Location

1. Has the location been selected?

2. In what trading area or community will the business be established? What is its economic base? Its attitude toward new businesses? Its saturation level in terms of competing businesses? Its costs?

3. What specific site will be selected? Is it accessible to suppliers, employees, and the target market? What is the site cost? What restrictions on site use

exist? What is the history of the site? What are the neighbouring businesses? What are the physical characteristics of the site?

Physical Facilities

1. Have the physical facilities been determined?
2. What building, equipment, and start-up supplies will be needed? What are the costs? What are the depreciation rates of the fixed assets? Which building codes or standards are relevant? Which permits are required? What insurance is required?
3. How will the physical facilities be organized? Is the production process efficient and safe? Has the interior layout been carefully planned? Is the exterior facade attractive?
4. How will inventories be managed? What initial inventory is required? How will inventory levels be monitored? How will inventory be valued? What method will be used to order inventory?

Financial

1. Has a financial plan for the business been made?
2. What are the financial requirements of the business? What are the start-up costs? Ongoing operating costs? What are projected sales, expenses, income, and cash flow?
3. Which sources of funding will be used? How much equity? How much debt? Which sources will be used? Private? Commercial? Government?
4. What bookkeeping system will be instituted?
5. How will the financial information be used? Which accounts will be evaluated? How often? By whom?

Personnel

1. Has a personnel plan been developed?
2. What is the administrative structure? Is there an organizational chart? A responsibility and reporting procedure? Have job descriptions and specifications been developed?
3. Have personnel policies been developed? What are the hours of work? Pay levels? Employee benefits? Conditions and standards of employment? Grievance procedures?
4. How will the business recruit employees? Where will employees be found? How will they be screened? What guidelines will be used in selection? How will employees be trained?

Legal Requirements

1. Have legal requirements been investigated?
2. Has the legal structure for the business been determined?
3. Have the relevant licences and taxes been researched?
4. Has patent protection been obtained, if necessary?

Appendix 4B

Sample Business Plans

BUSINESS PLAN 1—RETAIL STOCKING STORE, THE SOCK HOP

Table of Contents

Executive Summary and Background

The Sock Hop is a store totally devoted to socks. The product is in the medium price range, and emphasis is on variety and quality. The Sock Hop will be located in the new Park Place Mall, Lethbridge, Alberta, which is close to the downtown core. The mall, which opened in August 1988, has a variety of products and services. It contains beauty salons, shoe repair shops, movie theatres, one anchor store (Sears), jewellery stores, men's apparel, ladies apparel, children's stores, toy stores, food fair, as well as many other specialty stores.

The majority of the customers of The Sock Hop will be between the ages of 15 and 64, both male and female. The 2001 city census indicates that there are 48,436 people between the ages of 15 and 64.[1]

The feasibility analysis shows that The Sock Hop could be a viable business within five years as it becomes well known and builds a clientele.

Description of the Management Team

The owner-manager of The Sock Hop is Sharon Stockwell. She holds a management degree from the University of Lethbridge and has eight years of experience working in the retail clothing industry full and part time. She has prepared this business plan to assist in the start-up of this venture.

Business Objectives

The Sock Hop's business plan consists of a number of objectives. The first objective relates to opportunity costs for the owner/manager. The owner would like to obtain returns that would exceed that of a salary obtained through alternate employment and the cost of capital on her equity investment in the business. Therefore,

[1] City of Lethbridge Census, 2001.

Salary at The Sock Hop ($24,000) + Additional profits > Salary if working for someone else + Cost of capital on equity

It should be noted that the cost of capital on equity investment is included because, had the person placed her life savings in a savings account, it would have been earning a stated interest amount. Thus, for the owner/manager to remain in the business, the total tangible benefits derived from the business must be greater than they would have been without the business. This objective should be met in approximately five years.

The second objective is based on performance. Market share should increase from the present adjusted 22 percent to 33 percent within five years (medium-term goal). It is hoped that as the business grows, it will have a loyal following of customers along with a good business reputation to overcome some of the weaknesses.

As a result, the sales and profits should also increase. The sales per square foot should increase from the present estimate of $278/sq. ft. As a way to increase overall profit, a minor objective is to increase the efficiency in selling the merchandise.

A third objective is a five-year long-term goal for future expansion. By the year 2006, it is hoped that the owner will be able to work out a system to franchise The Sock Hop in Western Canada. By then, the "bugs" should be worked out of the system and a franchising plan can be established. This is dependent on the Lethbridge prototype store being successful.

A fourth (short-term) objective involves the method of financing the business. The owner/manager of The Sock Hop will not be the sole contributor of equity capital to the business. However, she wishes to retain as much independence and control as possible while spreading the risk. Thus, even when equity capital is obtained, the owner/manager will retain in excess of 51 percent of the control, and there will be an option for the owner/manager to buy out other equity investors.

Market Approach

Description of the Target Market. The geographic market area for The Sock Hop is Lethbridge. However, this must be further defined into a demographic target market, since a consumer-oriented marketing strategy is to be adopted by The Sock Hop.

For The Sock Hop, the target will be anybody between the ages of 15 and 64 who lives in Lethbridge. The income level, occupation, social class, and education are relatively irrelevant for this necessary product.

The fact that this target market will be interested in quality socks at a moderate price is important. Furthermore, The Sock Hop is targeted to those who are looking for variety and fashion in socks. In addition, a good part of inventory will be devoted to high-quality socks catering to the business community.

Uncontrollable Factors. There are four uncontrollable factors that the small business owner must understand. The owner must gather information about these uncontrollables, predict or monitor trends, and adjust the internal operations to them.

Economy. At this point, the economy in Lethbridge is positive. The type of merchandise that The Sock Hop is selling, however, tends to be recession proof. Because socks are not a high-cost item, the market should remain steady. The economic environment will be continually monitored, however, with respect to its effect on this business.

Competition. There are several stores in Lethbridge that sell socks. A lot of these stores have built-up reputation and convenient location as strengths. Reputation is one of The Sock Hop's weaknesses. However, its main strength is greater variety, particularly in fashion socks.

The Sock Hop plans to monitor the competition closely through primary observation and by reviewing industry reports on a regular basis. Competitor reactions to its entrance into the market will also be noted.

Legal Restrictions. The specific legal restrictions are discussed in the legal section of this paper. Keeping abreast of new and existing laws that affect retailers and the sock industry is important. Talking to middlemen in the industry and reading association magazines and newspapers are effective ways to monitor legal effects.

Social/Cultural Trends. Since The Sock Hop has decided to adopt a consumer-oriented marketing strategy, it is imperative that new trends are monitored. Because the product is very fad-oriented at times, trends are going to be vital, especially to the portion of the target market that is young and attracted by the fashion stock. In order to keep up with these trends, industry and fashion magazines, social statistics, and government reports will be of particular help. Furthermore, observing the competition and the general surroundings will help to keep The Sock Hop management up to date on lifestyle trends, demographic changes, and purchase patterns.

Marketing Strategy

Product. The product strategy for The Sock Hop involves offering a product that can be differentiated from the competition and that will ensure a reasonable profit, anticipating the market's changes in preferences, and continuing product innovations.

The product will be differentiated by being more fashion-oriented. There will be more variety, greater selection, and better services offered at The Sock Hop than is found with competitors. The customer will be able to choose socks from both the fashion stock and the basic stock. There will be a full money-back guarantee to complete this total package offered to the customer—a package that will sway the consumer's choice toward The Sock Hop.

Distribution. It is an advantage that The Sock Hop is located close to other stores that carry socks, since it aids comparison. The Sock Hop is small and new and thus will have some disadvantages compared to department stores and chains. For this reason, it would be best for The Sock Hop to take part in a buying group. There are a lot of sock stores in Calgary and Edmonton, and many are operated as small businesses. The Sock Hop intends to investigate joining a buying group. In this way, it can obtain volume discounts, pass the savings on to customers, and thus remain competitive. Purchasing with a buying group will help keep a lower inventory, as slow-moving items can be purchased in minimum quantities.

In addition, The Sock Hop will use a more direct channel for purchasing, in accordance with the belief that the fewer the middlemen, the higher the profit margin available to the retailer. It will use a manufacturer/supplier in Canada, if one with a good reputation for quality and dependability exists. The Sock Hop will avoid foreign suppliers, if possible, since it is their policy to buy Canadian.

Pricing. Price is not the means of differentiating The Sock Hop from the competition. The Sock Hop is competing on the basis of selection, quality, service, and specialization.

Sales will be held at various times of the year to improve overall profit, to promote certain items, to counter competition, to dispose of excess inventory of inactive stock, and to improve cash flow. However, in the long term, pricing based on the full cost will be used. The economic situation, competition, market demand, and the price sensitivity of the customers also have to be taken into account when establishing a markup percentage.

Promotion. The objective here is to inform, persuade, and/or remind the target market. Five percent of sales has been devoted to advertising for the first year. This is in spite of the fact that the Dun and Bradstreet average for small businesses for advertising is 1.5 percent. Extra advertising support is needed in the first year of business because sales will not be large compared to those of other clothing stores, and the public needs to be informed about The Sock Hop and its total offering. In the next four years, advertising will be reduced to 3 percent of sales, but it will still be above the Dun and Bradstreet average.

A variety of advertising methods will be used. The normal outlets such as newspaper, radio, television, and the Yellow Pages will be used. A door-to-door flyer campaign will be considered, as Lethbridge is relatively small. For television and radio, The Sock Hop hopes to be involved in any promotional efforts in conjunction with the Park Place Mall.

At the start of the business, various contests can be held to get ideas on new designs for socks, which will help renew the product life cycle. In addition, sponsoring sock hops at the local high schools will improve public relations. This will be especially advantageous since the younger, fashion-conscious portion of the target market are high school youth. Moreover, a lot of these youngsters are innovators and thus have the power to influence a major portion of the target market.

Finally, price promotions can be used in busy months such as January, when clearances are usually held, during August and September, when it is back-to-school time, and during November.

Location

Trading Area

Economic Base. The City of Lethbridge's economy is strongly based on agriculture. The agricultural economy is supported by the food processing, packaging, distilling, and brewing industries. The city has good road and rail connections to various markets as well as to producers, and these have been important in maintaining Lethbridge's economic position. In addition, Lethbridge is in a prominent position in its region, and growth is expected in the area.

Competition. In terms of general retail and service competition in the trading area, there are 36 major retail/service clusters in Lethbridge, and they have been evaluated at a total of 3,479,000 square feet of retail and service space in addition to the square footage covered by Park Place.[2] The 3,479,000 square feet are allocated in the trading areas as follows:

2,650,000 sq. ft.	in the city of Lethbridge
829,000 sq. ft.	in the surrounding area, which comprises the trading area
3,479,000 sq. ft.	

Attitudes of the Trading Area toward Having a New Business. The new mall has increased the trading area and has shown a positive attitude toward development of the area. Lethbridge is moving ahead, and as a result most of the community is anxious for new businesses.

Specific Site

Accessibility. Park Place Mall is centrally located in the city of Lethbridge, north of the cental business district (CBD). There are major roads on all sides with good connections to the city. Careful consideration to traffic flows was given by the city before construction of the mall took place. Lethbridge is also well served by the major highway system serving Southern Alberta. Therefore, vehicular traffic is facilitated both in and around Lethbridge. The transit system facilitates customers who don't own vehicles. There is a major transit station downtown within walking distance of the mall. A proposal to move the station north of Galt Gardens has also been considered, which would bring this station on the street facing this mall. In addition, bus routes include the mall.

[2] *Lethbridge Community Profile, 1999-2000.* City of Lethbridge, Economic Development Department, February 2000.

Thus, all customers will have good access to the site, which is fairly visible from the major thoroughfares (Stafford Drive, Crowsnest Trail, First Avenue).

Site Costs. The specific site costs (information obtained from Park Place Mall administration and the city of Lethbridge) include the following:

Rent	$20–$30/sq. ft. per year
	($30 × 400 sq. ft. = $12,000 per year)
Utilities	$5–$10/sq. ft. per year
	($10 × 400 sq. ft. = $4,000 per year)
Business taxes	4.2% of fair rental value
	[4.2% × (400 × 30)] = $504
City business licence	$53 per year
BRZ fees	$3.78 per month–$45.36 per year
	(0.75% of business tax)
Insurance	$87.39 per year

The total site and operational costs add up to $16,680.75.

Total rent of The Sock Hop will be $12,000 per year. In addition, the mall offices generally set a break-even point for the store, and once this point is reached by the store, a royalty of 5 percent to 8 percent of sales in excess of the break-even point is charged in addition to the normal rent.

The typical term of this lease is between five years and 10 years. Since this aspect of the lease is negotiable, an attempt should be made to have the term reduced. In addition, advance rent of two months is required by the mall administration. In terms of recharges, the total cost of utilities, electricity, and upkeep of the common area is $4,000 ($10.00 × 400 sq. ft.).

Insurance for The Sock Hop covers the business contents such as merchandise, fixtures, furniture, and equipment. The insurance also applies to the actual business loss sustained by the owner and the expenses incurred to resume normal business operations. Thus, the insurance provides coverage when the damage caused by an insured peril results in the interruption of business. The money and securities are also covered against loss by robbery, safe burglary, and theft from a night depository in a bank or from the custodian. The insurance further covers liability for bodily injury and property damage claims arising out of the maintenance and use of premises.

Total insurance per year is equal to:

$$\$3.70 \times (\$23,618.77/\$1,000) = \$87.39$$

It should be noted that the mall administration insures the common area. (The various taxes and licences will be covered in the final section of this business plan.)

Proximity to Other Businesses. Park Place Mall has many products and services. This is advantageous in that it will generate customer traffic essential to the success of the business. Socks are defined as a shopping good, which means that consumers will usually shop around and compare before making the final purchase decision. Therefore, by locating close to competing businesses (see Figure 2 on page 132), consumers will be able to compare and choose the superior product. The Sock Hop offers good quality socks at a reasonable price, which, when compared to other stores, will draw a loyal following.

Furthermore, other stores will be selling complementary articles of clothing (shoes, pants), which will generate customer traffic for The Sock Hop by creating a need for socks. Other than the businesses in Park Place Mall, there are no other stores offering socks in the immediate vicinity of the site.

Physical Facilities

Start-Up Costs. The start-up costs for a retail store are made up of two things—capital assets and inventory. The following is a detailed breakdown of the physical items required to furnish the store. (This list was obtained from Roll-It Catalogue, National Signs, and Consumers Distributing.)

Item	No.	Each	Total Value
Furniture and Fixtures			
Multi Merchandiser (48″ × 54″)	6	$ 507.00	$ 3,042.00
End Frame Pegboard (48″ × 66″)	4	146.65	587.00
Miscellaneous hardware (pegs)	1	1,000.00	
Used Bargain Bunk	1	200.00	200.00
Counter	1	500.00	500.00
Sign	1	500.00	500.00
Filing cabinet (4 drawer, legal 24″ deep)	1	190.00	190.00
Desk (30″ × 60″, steel)	1	250.00	250.00
Swivel chair	1	50.00	50.00
Equipment (obtained from Cypress Business Equipment, AGT Business Office, Office Depot, General Fasteners)			
Software (Bedford)	1	$ 300.00	$ 300.00
Computer and printer (IBM clone)	1	2,000.00	2,000.00
Cash register	1	1,200.00	1,200.00
Telephone installation	1	40.00	40.00
Adding machine	1	75.00	75.00
Pricing gun	1	80.00	80.00
Vacuum cleaner	1	280.00	$280.00
Total			$10,294.00

Initially The Sock Hop will invest about 15 percent of projected sales in inventory. This is standard.

Inventory = Sales × 15%

$13,324.77 = $88,831.33× 15%

Layout. In the case of The Sock Hop, the layout is designed to display the merchandise effectively. While browsing is somewhat encouraged by the multimerchandisers, there isn't enough selling space to encourage a lot of creativity in layout (see Figure 1 on page 132).

Financial

Feasibility Analysis

Target Market and Trade Area. Geographically, the trade area for Lethbridge is delineated. The competitive influence of retail and service facilities in the city of Calgary limit the extension of the trade area to 70 kilometres to the north. To the east, competitive retail facilities in the city of Medicine Hat limit the trade area's extent to 95 kilometres. In the south, the trade area extends some 80 kilometres to the Canada–United States border. The trade area to the west extends 130 kilometres from Lethbridge. Here, it is primarily limited by the distance and driving times and is bounded by the Alberta–British Columbia border. The study by Larry Smith and Associates Ltd., referred to earlier, indicates that Park Place Mall expects to derive the majority of its sales volume (80 to 95 percent) from this area. The remaining 5 percent to 20 percent of market support normally reflects customer shopping derived from visitors, tourists, or people working in Lethbridge but not residing in the delineated trade area.

Market Potential

- Total 1999 Lethbridge retail apparel and accessories sales were $32,260,000 (*Lethbridge Fingertips Facts*, 1999-2000). At an inflation rate of 4 percent per year (Alberta Retail and Service Trade Statistics), the retail sales for 2002 will be:

$$\$32,260,000 \times (1.04)^3 = \$36,288,113$$

- The 2001 population of Lethbridge is 66,500 (city statistics).

- The 2001 population for the trade area excluding Lethbridge is 88,250 (city statistics).

- The amount of regional population which shop for socks in Lethbridge was estimated by clothing retailers to be 33 percent.

- It is estimated by clothing retailers and the personal experience of the owner-manager that between 3 percent and 5 percent of the expenditures on clothing are for socks. However, 3 percent may be on the high side for a low price item like socks, so a more conservative figure would be 2 percent. Based on these figures, the 2002 Lethbridge per capita socks sales figure can be calculated as follows:

$$\frac{\$36,288,113 \times 2\%}{[66,500 + (88,250 \times 33\%)]} = \$7.59$$

The market area for The Sock Hop can be safely defined as Lethbridge. Thus, in the remaining calculations, Lethbridge population figures will be used. Total market potential calculations:

- 2001 per capita socks sales in Lethbridge is $7.59 (as calculated above).

- 2001 population for Lethbridge is 66,500 (see above).

Therefore, the 2002 unadjusted total market potential figure for The Sock Hop can be calculated as follows:

$$\$7.59 \text{ per person} \times 66{,}500 = \$504{,}726.30$$

An adjustment must be made to this figure in order to take outshopping into account. Outshopping is the result of a consumer in a particular market area going to another area to make purchases. Based on interviews with store managers, the outshopping figure was said to be 20 percent. This is quite conservative, since the presence of Park Place Mall has two implications. Thus, the adjusted 2002 total market potential for Lethbridge will be:

$$\$504{,}726.30 \times 0.80 = \$403{,}781.04$$

This figure is the most accurate market potential figure. It takes into account inflation, outshopping buying habits (figure determined by primary research), and 2001 population figures.

Market Share. No statistics were available on the amount of retail space devoted to socks. Therefore, estimates were obtained through primary research (see Appendix 2). The proposed store will have an area of 400 square feet with 300 square feet devoted to selling space. Based on these figures, the unadjusted market share of The Sock Hop should be the following:

$$\frac{320 \text{ sq. ft.}}{872 \text{ sq. ft.} + 320 \text{ sq. ft.}}$$

This figure represents the unadjusted market share available to The Sock Hop. In order to adjust the figure, the strengths and weaknesses on the various aspects of the business must be considered.

The major weakness of The Sock Hop is that it is a new store. It does not have a loyal customer following, has no reputation, and has plenty of established competition. In addition, this specialty store will more than likely have higher prices than some of the discount department stores selling socks.

The major strength of The Sock Hop is its location. It is going to be located in a new major shopping mall, Park Place Mall. The customer traffic in the mall is above average. The store will be in an attractive setting with good exposure. Furthermore, there is a vast amount of parking space available for the satisfaction of the consumers. The Sock Hop provides a variety of socks in one location that is convenient and pleasant for consumers. Another area of strength is the growing trading area. The outlook is very positive for the Lethbridge economy, and this can only aid The Sock Hop.

Based on this analysis, the adjusted market share can be said to be a very conservative 22 percent. This is based on present conditions. Hopefully in the future, this percentage will increase as the business becomes more established.

Projected Income. The projected income statements for the next five business years are in Figure 3 on page 133. The figures have been derived through primary and secondary research. The revenue figure was calculated by multiplying the adjusted market potential and the adjusted market share figures together:

$$\$403{,}781.04 \times 22\% = \$88{,}831.83$$

Financing. This section pertains to the financing plan for The Sock Hop. Business start-up costs are needed in order to determine the financing needed. These costs are made up of the following:

CASE program	$ 400.00
Inventory	13,324.77
Incorporation fees	1,000.00
Physical facilities	10,294.00
Rent (last 2 months of lease + 1 month rent)	3,000.00
Total	$ 28,018.77

Most lenders require the borrower to prepare a financing proposal. This will provide answers to questions the lender will have about the owner and about the proposed business. In order for the lenders to know how a loan will be repaid, they need to look at income and cash flow projections for evidence of earnings that will support the loan. These are shown in Figures 3 and 4 (on pages 133–134).

Sources of Financing. The Business Development Bank of Canada (BDC) offers term loans to allow small business owners to acquire fixed assets such as land, building, machinery, and equipment. The loans are offered at floating rates or at fixed rates. BDC may also provide assistance through its CASE program. CASE is a counselling service offered exclusively to small- and medium-sized businesses. This program employs experienced counsellors who advise the small business owner on any aspect of business.

The interest rate for the loan is approximately 8 percent with a minimum repayment period of four years.

The term of the amount borrowed must match the actual lifetime of what is being financed. Thus the inventory portion will be financed by an operating loan with a term of two years. This will be financing from a chartered bank. It should be noted that although $13,325 is being borrowed for this purpose, a lesser amount will be needed. This is because The Sock Hop will endeavour to finance a good portion of inventory from suppliers who, due to competition in the industry, are willing to market their products through new outlets. The remaining $7,500 will be borrowed from BDC on a term of five years. The equity investment will thus be $7,500.

Accounting System. Rather than employ a bookkeeper, the manager of the business will record on a computer all transactions that occur every day. The Bedford accounting software will be used, which is priced at less than $300 (quote from computer dealer). The computer and a suitable printer priced at $2,000 will also be used.

The Bedford accounting software is a fully integrated package for the small business. It is easy to use and very user friendly. It consists of the General Ledger, Payroll, Receivables, Payables, and Inventory modules that are all posted, as applicable, through single entries. It is very versatile and easily adaptable to small business needs. It produces full audit trails and a number of other management information reports. The vendors have a good track record of maintenance and support. Computing magazines such as *PC Magazine* and *InfoWorld* have given good reviews to this software.

The services of a public accountant (CA or CGA) will be utilized for annual reviews, for tax advice, and on special occasions when necessary. The business will follow Generally Accepted Accounting Principles in maintaining the financial records.

Credit Policy. The Sock Hop does not intend to allow any credit to customers, since it is not a practice in the industry. We do not intend to start a trend in this area, as the volume per customer would not justify it. However, we will accept all major credit cards (VISA, MasterCard, American Express, etc.). With this facility to customers, there would be no need to extend direct credit, which, in any case, would entail taking some risk on the part of The Sock Hop.

Financial Evaluation. Monthly financial statements will be prepared and reviewed by the owner-manager in an effort to monitor and evaluate progress. Several financial ratios will be calculated and compared to similar businesses as well as to previous performance.

Personnel

Administrative Structure. Since The Sock Hop is not a big store, initially the number of staff employed will be limited.

Store hours for The Sock Hop will be as follows:

Monday–Wednesday, 9:30 a.m.–5:30 p.m.

Thursday and Friday, 9:30 a.m.–9:00 p.m.

Saturday, 9:30 a.m.–5:30 p.m.

Thus, the basic salary and wage expenses will be:

Store manager	$24,000.00
1 full-time clerk ($6.00 × 40 hr./week)	12,480.00
1 part-time clerk ($5.90 × 12 hr./week)	3,120.00
Total salary and wage	$39,600.00

With this staffing plan in mind, the organizational chart will be as follows:

```
                        Owner/Manager
        ┌───────────────────┴───────────────────┐
Full-time clerk                              Part-time clerk
```

Employee Recruitment and Training

Job Descriptions. A typical job description is as follows:

Duties: Greets and helps customers, keeps shelves organized and stocked, rings up sales and bags items, opens and closes store when manager is away, cleans counters and vacuums.

Responsible to: Store owner/manager.

Requirements: Must have previous sales experience, be available to work nights and weekends, be able to use a cash register, be able to learn store procedures.

Personal: Must be friendly, appropriately dressed and groomed, punctual and reliable.

Recruitment. The channels of recruitment utilized by The Sock Hop will include write-ins (applicants), walk-ins, want-advertising, and educational institutions. Job application forms will be used to collect information about recruits. These application forms will attempt to gather information pertaining to personal data, employment status, education, skills, work history, memberships, awards, hobbies, and references.

Evaluation. The first three months of employment are a period of observation for the employee as well as the owner-manager. The employee will receive professional sales training and will be taught the basics of The Sock Hop store procedures.

Beginning at the end of week three of employment, the owner-manager will initiate a coaching discussion. The employee's job performance will be evaluated, and discussions will be held to help the employee understand the job. In addition, any questions the employee has will be answered.

Training. Training will be carried out by the owner-manager and will consist of three general areas. First, the employee will be provided with information about the business and its philosophy and goals. Second, the employee will receive training about the merchandise including such things as the material they are made of, washing instructions, etc. The third area of training involves the teaching of specific selling skills—such things as approaching the customer, presenting the merchandise, closing the sale, and suggestion selling.

Policies. The following policies will be followed by The Sock Hop employees:

- An employee is assigned an identification number consisting of four digits to be used for all cash register operations.

- Work schedules will be posted at least one week in advance.

- Scheduling conflicts are to be reported to the manager as soon as possible.

- The wages for regular full-time clerks will consist of an hourly rate of $5.50 plus a 2 percent commission on sales.

- Similarly the wages for part-time clerks will be an hourly rate of $5.00 plus a 2 percent commission on sales.

- An employee who has completed six full months of continuous service by June 30th shall be entitled to one week's vacation during the summer vacation period.

- Any employee who has completed one full year of continuous service with the company by June 30 shall be entitled to two weeks or 4 percent of earnings as vacation pay (whichever is greater).

- Employees who have completed less than six months service with the company by June 30 must be paid 4 percent of their gross earnings from the date of hire until the last pay period in June.

- All full-time employees must receive vacation pay in the last pay period prior to leaving for their vacations.

- The employee will be expected to have a professional appearance. This includes proper grooming, clean and pressed clothing (no jeans), name tags, clean and proper footwear, and above all else, a smiling pleasant attitude.

- The Sock Hop emphasizes customer satisfaction. Therefore, the employee should ask all customers to retain their sales receipts. The Sock Hop will provide a full cash refund or merchandise exchanges on all returns with receipts.

- All staff will be entitled to a 20 percent discount on purchases from The Sock Hop.

- All purchases by staff members must be handled by the owner-manager. At no time is the staff member to "key in" their own purchases. These purchases are to be conducted during breaks or at the end of shifts.

- The phone is to be answered promptly, giving the store name and the employee's name. It is important that the employee be cheerful, helpful, and courteous.

- Personal calls are to be kept to an absolute minimum!

- The employee should practise the following prevention activities: (1) approach and greet all customers promptly and never leave the sales floor without coverage and (2) be aware of customers carrying merchandise from one location to another.

Legal Requirements

It has been decided that The Sock Hop will be an incorporated business. This decision was made after looking at the relative pros and cons of incorporation. The main reason for incorporating is the limited liability of shareholders. Thus, the owner is protected should the business fail. By incorporating, the owner is not risking her life savings. She is only liable for the amount invested in the business.

Regulations. Since The Sock Hop is a retail store, the regulations that apply to it are those common to any regular small business in Lethbridge. The municipal government requires that the small business owner hold a business licence ($53 per year). In addition, the city requires building and electrical inspections after renovations have been made. Municipal taxes include a business tax of about $504 per year and a Business Revitalization Zone (BRZ) fee of $45.36 per year, since the mall is within the BRZ. In addition, the small business is required to pay various taxes. The federal as well as the provincial government require the filing of yearly income tax returns. The federal GST will need to be collected on sales and remitted to the federal government.

Figure 1   Selling Space

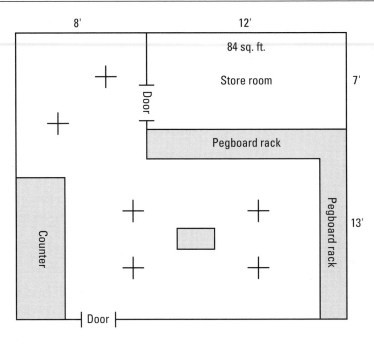

Scale: 1 cm = 2 feet
+   Multimerchandisers
▨   Bargain Bunk

Figure 2   Selling Space in the Market

Store	Number of Stores	Total Square Feet
Zellers	1	323
Safeway	3	22
Wal-Mart	1	161
Smartset	2	11
Reitmans	2	11
Winners	1	54
Sears	1	75
Shoppers Drug Mart	1	32
Tip Top	3	32
Jack Fraser	2	22
Bay	1	32
Mariposa	3	11
Error factor	00	237
Total		1,023

Figure 3   **Projected Income Statement for Five Years (in dollars)**

	2002	2003	2004	2005	2006
Sales	88,832	133,248	173,222	207,866	228,653
Cost of goods sold	44,416	66,624	86,611	103,933	114,327
Gross margin	44,416	66,624	86,611	103,933	114,327
Less expenses					
Rent	12,000	12,000	12,000	12,000	12,000
Staff wages	15,600	16,068	16,711	17,379	18,074
Owner's salary	24,000	24,000	24,000	24,000	24,000
Employee benefits	3,960	4,007	4,071	4,138	4,207
Advertising	4,442	3,997	5,197	6,236	6,860
Licences and taxes					
Business licence	53	53	53	53	53
Business tax—4.2% of rent	504	504	504	504	504
BRZ fees	45	48	48	48	48
Credit card discounts	213	360	433	520	572
Repairs and maintenance	711	1,066	1,386	1,663	1,829
Utilities and occupancy costs	4,000	4,000	4,000	4,000	4,000
Professional fees	622	933	1,213	1,455	1,601
Office and store supplies	888	1,332	1,732	2,079	2,287
Telephone—Rent	115	120	124	129	135
—Estimated toll chgs	600	624	649	675	702
Insurance	87	91	95	98	102
Interest expense	2,593	1,594	1,396	398	199
Depreciation	2,059	2,059	2,059	2,059	2,059
Other expenses	1,777	2,665	3,464	4,157	4,573
Total expenses	74,269	75,521	79,134	81,591	83,804
Net income (before income taxes)	(29,853)	(8,897)	7,477	22,343	30,523
Income taxes	0	0	1,500	4,468	6,104
Income after income taxes	(29,853)	(8,897)	5,977	17,875	24,419

Figure 4   Projected Cash Flow for Five Years (in dollars)

	2002	2003	2004	2005	2006	Totals
Cash in						
Net income	(29,853)	(8,897)	7,477	22,343	27,068	18,138
Add noncash items:						
Depreciation	2,059	2,059	2,059	2,059	2,059	10,294
Cash flows from operations	(27,794)	(6,838)	9,536	24,401	29,127	28,432
Equity contribution	35,000	15,000				50,000
Loan receipts —Operating	13,325					13,325
—BDC	7,500					7,500
Total cash inflows	28,031	8,162	9,536	24,401	29,127	99,257
Cash out						
Loan repayments—Operating	0	6,662	6,663	0	0	13,325
—BDC	0	1,500	1,500	1,500	1,500	6,000
Return of equity	0	0	0	20,000	30,000	50,000
Start up costs						
Legal	1,000					1,000
CASE counselling	400					400
Furniture and fixtures	10,294					10,294
Inventory	13,325					13,325
Two months' advance rent	2,000					2,000
Total cash outflows	27,019	8,162	8,163	21,500	31,500	96,344
Net cash flows	1,012	(0)	1,373	2,901	(2,373)	2,913

BUSINESS PLAN 2—BEAUTY SALON, QUALITY CUTS

Table of Contents

Executive Summary and Background

Quality Cuts is a new beauty salon located in the city of Lethbridge, Alberta. It will operate from the College Value Mall in south Lethbridge, will employ five full-time hairdressers, and will be managed by Sue Holland. Quality Cuts will provide haircuts, styles, perms, and colour, as well as hair products supplied by well-known manufacturers. It will also provide cosmetic and manicuring services. Quality Cuts will attempt to target the middle- to older-aged women in the Lethbridge area, which is currently the most rapidly growing part of the market. Quality Cuts will utilize a computer database to build customer knowledge and improve customer service. The feasibility analysis and business plan projections show that Quality Cuts will be a viable entry to the beauty salon market.

Description of Management Team

Quality cuts will be owned and operated by Sue Holland. She has her hairdressing certification from the Alberta School of Hair and Beauty Design and has worked as a hairdresser for 10 years in the Lethbridge area. Prior to leaving her current employment to plan the establishment of Quality Cuts, Sue was supervising four other hairdressers. Sue will be assisted in the financial and computer management aspects of the business by her husband who currently is a chartered accountant. Preliminary consultations indicate that a high percentage of Sue's current clients will continue with her in the new business.

Business Objectives

The objectives for Quality Cuts are as follows:

The first objective is to have a positive cash flow for the first year of operations. Cash flows consist of receipts and payments attributed to operating, investing, and financing activities. As can be seen from the cash flow statement, it is estimated that there will be a positive net cash inflow for each of the four sectors of the first year of operations.

A second objective deals with the prices charged to the customers of the business. The prices will be competitive with other salons. Each hairdresser will have some input into prices charged for their clients to ensure that pricing is competitive.

A third objective is to achieve a market share of at least 3 percent by the end of the first year of operation, moving up to 5 percent within five years.

Market Approach

Description of Target Market. The target market geographically consists of the city of Lethbridge and some of the surrounding trade area. Lethbridge is an agricultural service centre with a high market draw for many smaller communities within a 48-kilometre radius.

The demographic characteristics include middle- to older-aged women in the middle- to higher-income classes. Approximately 80 percent of Sue Holland's current clients fall into this range. The location of Quality Cuts is ideal for this market because the College Value Mall is adjacent to some very large seniors' apartment buildings and upscale housing projects. It is located on the south end of Lethbridge where new housing developments are taking place. The purchase characteristics for this market include concern over quality and service in a clean and friendly atmosphere.

Uncontrollable Factors. There are two uncontrollable factors which would most affect Quality Cuts. The competition is the first. There are currently 35 other beauty salons or shops in the city employing 150 hairdresser/stylists. Because this is a personal service industry customer patronage is determined to a large extent by the quality of the service provider and the level of confidence the client has in the hairdresser. Quality Cuts has determined that they will attain a competitive edge through careful hiring and training of their employees. Proximity of competitors may be a secondary factor to customer patronage, and Quality Cuts will be the only beauty salon in the College Mall which should be an advantage.

The second relevant uncontrollable is the social/cultural factor. Concern over one's looks is a major trend in North America. This suggests a continued and growing use of beauty salons. In addition, the Lethbridge market is an aging one. Both of these should be a positive influence on Quality Cuts' performance.

Product. The product that makes up a beauty salon is comprised of three distinct parts; hair service, manicures and cosmetic work, and hair products. The hair service side is by far the most important, as it includes things such as haircuts, styles, perms, and colours. This will make up 80 to 90 percent of the entire revenue of the beauty salon. The selling of hair products and providing cosmetic and manicure services, although less important, are still vital as they may serve as a draw for passing consumers. The products include things like gels, shampoos, conditioners, moisturants, hair-repair treatments, protectors, sculpting lotions, and hairsprays. These type of products are available to the consumer in pharmacies but the quality of the professional products that are only found at beauty shops makes them attractive, even if the price is slightly higher. The brands that will be stocked include Paul Mitchell, Matrix, Lanza, Zotos, and Mahdeen. Because hair grooming is a service, Quality Cuts will emphasize superior customer service with its clients. Frequent follow-up communications with consumers will be maintained through computer tracking and database programs.

Pricing. Prices will be set close to competitors' prices during the first year to ensure the transfer of existing clients with their hairdresser. Price will eventually rise to 5 to 10 percent above the competitors' as the clientele of the business stabilizes. This in turn will be in harmony with the image Quality Cuts wants to project. Markups on the products will be 50 percent of retail selling price.

Promotion. Advertising will take place at approximately the average for hair salons in Alberta. This amount will be 1.9 percent of sales, or approximately $2,836 for the first year of operations.

In addition to this amount in the first year, there will be extra "opening" advertising that will be conducted for the first month. This is to get the name of the business out to the public, and to let the hairdressers' old clients know where their hairdressers have moved. The cost of this opening advertising will be an additional $500, making the total advertising budget for the first year $3,336.

This advertising will take a couple of forms. First, the Yellow Pages is a must as it is an easy way for the public to see where certain salons reside. There are currently seven pages full of advertising just for beauty salons, with the average "large" advertisement occupying approximately 26 square centimetres.

The TV guide within the Friday edition of the *Lethbridge Herald* is also a favourite place for beauty salon advertising.

Business cards and extensive use of single-sheet advertising will also be used. These printed sheets of paper will be slid under the doors of apartments in neighbouring buildings, containing information and possible coupons to attract new customers. As mentioned previously, a sophisticated tracking system will be set up on computer to monitor customers' purchases and improve customer service efforts.

Distribution. There are four main suppliers that Quality Cuts will be dealing with, three from Calgary and one from Lethbridge. They are the following:

Emerald Beauty Supplies (Lethbridge)

Monarch Messenger Beauty Supplies (Calgary)

Consolidated Beauty Supplies (Calgary)

Obsco Beauty Supplies (Calgary)

All of these distributors can supply within two days. Quality Cuts will attempt to take advantage of quantity and cash discounts where possible.

Location

Trading Area. The City of Lethbridge has a fairly stable population into which many older people from the surrounding areas retire. The socio-economic level of the community is above average. Both of these factors will have a positive effect on Quality Cuts' performance.

Specific Site. Quality Cuts will be located in the College Mall in the southeast corner of the city. The exact location in the mall will be where North West Trust is currently located, as it is moving to a different location within the mall.

Accessibility. This location has access from within the mall and private access from outside. It also allows for a neon sign on the outside of the mall to help attract customers. Traffic flow should be quite high as Wal Mart is not too far away.

Site Costs

Item	Cost ($)	
Rent	18.50	per square foot (includes property tax)
Utilities	3,000	per year (plus $150 deposit)
Telephone	540	per year
Insurance	605	per year
Business taxes	420	per year
Licences/permits	113	per year

Proximity to Other Businesses. There are no other beauty shops within the mall, but there are many businesses which draw traffic and would be complimentary to Quality Cuts.

Physical Characteristics of the Site. The store size is 1,200 square feet. It has the front opening into the mall, but also has a side door open to the outside.

Physical Facilities

Equipment, fixtures, and supplies are an integral part of the business, and a list of these items is included below. The costs have been obtained from prospective suppliers.

Item	Cost ($)
9 hydraulic chairs	4,500
9 styling stations	2,997
10 hair dryers	2,490
10 dryer chairs	1,480
4 shampoo chairs	592
4 sinks	1,476
9 mirrors	1,350
washing machine	650
dryer	450
2 neon signs	3,000
4 lounge chairs	400
computer system	2,000
air exchanger	5,000
reception desk	300
layout additions	3,000
shelving	500
miscellaneous supplies (includes start-up product)	6,000

Layout. The layout of the shop is shown in Figure 1 (see page 145). The layout diagram shows that the shop contains three areas. The first is the reception area which houses the reception desk, the shelves of products, the coat rack, and waiting chairs. The second contains the hair salon itself, with the 9 stations, 4 sinks, 10 dryer stations, and coffee area. The third section is at the back of the location and includes a bathroom, washer/dryer area, and an 18 foot by 18 foot office/lunchroom/storage area.

The salon is set up in a way to accomplish three goals. These are to utilize the space, to be convenient for the patron, and to be pleasing to the eye. The image projected will be one of cleanliness and class, as appropriate for the target market.

Financial

Feasibility

Market Potential. The estimate of average family expenditure on hair grooming for Alberta in 2001 was $375 (Source: Statistics Canada Catalogue 62-555). It is also estimated that 45.5 percent of this amount is for women's hair grooming (Source: Statistics Canada Catalogue 63-555). Using a percentage of 50 percent should be conservative as Quality Cuts' revenue will also include sales of hair care products and cosmetic/manicuring services as well as some haircuts to male customers. The population for the target market includes approximately 20,000 households (Source: Lethbridge Community Profile 1999-2000). Market potential estimate is as follows:

$$\text{Households} \times \text{household expenditures} \times \text{percent of expenditures for target market}$$
$$= 22,000 \times 375 \times 0.50 = \$4,125,000$$

Market Share. The number of beauty salons and hairdressers/stylists in the market area were obtained through calls to all of the shops. This totalled 35 shops and 150 hairdressers/stylists. An estimate of Quality Cuts' proposed market share is shown below.

$$= \frac{6 \text{ hairdressers/stylists (Sue + 5 employees)}}{6 + 150}$$

$$= \frac{6}{156} = 3.8\%$$

This share should be decreased to 3.6 percent due to the fact that the business is new and will take some time to build sales. The start-up delay should not be significant, however, because all five hairdresser/stylists are currently working in the market area and will bring the majority of their clients to the new business.

$$\text{Projected share in revenue} = \text{market share} \times \text{market potential}$$
$$= 3.6\% \times \$4,125,000 = \$148,500$$

Projected Income. Below find the projected income statements for the first five years of operation. Revenue figures from above are used as the basis behind this information. Amounts and sources of expenses are as follows:

Cost of Goods Sold 10% (Statistics Canada Small Business and Special Surveys Division, confirmed by primary research)

Wages and Salaries 53.5% of sales (Alberta Business Profile, *Barber & Beauty Shops*, July 2001)

Depreciation   See schedule for calculation

Repairs and   0.8% of sales (Alberta Business Profile, *Barber & Beauty Shops*,
  Maintenance   July 2001)

Utilities $3,000 per year, 5% increase yearly (Primary information from College Mall management)

Phone $540 per year, 5% increase yearly (Primary information from phone company)

Rent	$10.00 per sq. foot flat rate for first 2 years, $11.00 for years 3 and 4, $12 for 5th year. $8.50 per sq. foot variable rate, 5% increase yearly (Primary information from College Mall management)
Interest Expense	See table for calculation
Legal Fees	0.7% of sales (Alberta Business Profile, *Barber & Beauty Shops,* July 2001)
Advertising	1.9% of sales (Alberta Business Profile, *Barber & Beauty Shops,* July 2001)
Insurance	See legal section for details
Licences/Permits	See legal section for details
Business Taxes	$0.35 per sq. foot (City of Lethbridge Taxation Department)
Other Expenses	1% of sales (Statistics Canada Small Business and Special Surveys Division)

The projected income for Quality Cuts is found below.

	Year 1	Year 2	Year 3	Year 4	Year 5
Sales	$148,500	$156,702	$164,537	$172,764	$181,402
Cost of Goods Sold	14,850	15,670	16,454	17,276	18,140
Gross Margin	$133,650	$141,032	$148,084	$155,488	$163,262
Expenses:					
Wages and Salaries	$ 79,448	$ 83,836	$ 88,027	$ 92,429	$ 97,050
Depreciation*	1,749	1,749	1,749	1,749	1,749
Repairs and Maintenance	1,188	1,254	1,316	1,382	1,451
Utilities	3,000	3,150	3,308	3,473	3,647
Phone	540	567	595	625	656
Rent	22,200	22,710	24,444	25,008	26,796
Interest Expense	1,894	1,056	829	578	303
Legal Fees	1,040	1,097	1,152	1,209	1,270
Advertising	2,822	2,977	3,126	3,283	3,447
Insurance	605	635	667	700	735
Licences/Permits	113	113	113	113	113
Business Taxes	420	420	420	420	420
Other Expenses	1,485	1,567	1,645	1,728	1,814
Total Expenses	$116,544	$121,131	$127,392	$132,697	$140,063
Net Income	$ 17,106	$ 19,901	$ 20,692	$ 22,791	$ 23,199

Depreciation Schedule

Assets	Capital Cost	Life (years)	YEARS			
			1–5	6–10	11–15	16-20
Equipment:						
Hydraulic chairs (9)	$4,500	20	$1,125	$1,125	$1,125	$1,125
Workstations (9)	2,297	20	749	749	749	749
Hair dryers (10)	2,490	20	623	623	623	623
Dryer chairs (10)	1,480	20	370	370	370	370
Shampoo chairs (4)	592	20	148	148	148	148
Sinks (4)	1,476	20	369	369	369	369
Washing machine	650	10	325	325		
Dryer	450	10	225	225		
Computer system	2,000	5	2,000			
Air exchanger	5,000	20	1,250	1,250	1,250	1,250
Fixtures and furniture:						
Shelves	500	20	125	125	125	125
Neon signs (2)	3,000	20	750	750	750	750
Lounge chairs (4)	400	10	200	200		
Mirrors (9)	1,350	20	338	338	338	338
Reception desk	300	10	150	150		
Total			$8,746	$6,746	$5,846	$5,846

Financing. Start-up costs are found below.

Item	Cost	Source
Initial equipment and fixtures	$30,185	See Physical Facilities section
Miscellaneous supplies and product (includes opening inventory)	6,000	See Physical Facilities section
Rent (one month)	1,850	See Location section
Utility deposit	150	See Location section
Business licences and permits	113	See Legal section
Legal fees	754	See Legal section
Advertising and promotion (first month)	500	See Promotion section
Insurance (first quarter)	151	See Legal section
Total start-up costs	$39,703	

A cash flow statement has also been calculated to determine the cash situation that might arise during the first year of operations. This is shown below.

Quarter ending	Mar 31	June 30	Sept 30	Dec 31
CASH INFLOWS:				
Sales	$29,848	$37,310	$37,310	$44,772
Bank Loan	37,000	0	0	0
Equity Investment	5,000	0	0	0
Mall Payback	25,000	0	0	0
TOTAL CASH INFLOW	$96,848	$37,310	$37,310	$44,772
CASH OUTFLOWS:				
Equipment and Supplies	$36,185	$ 0	$ 0	$ 0
Inventory	2,985	3,731	3,731	4,477
Wages and Salaries	15,969	19,961	19,961	23,953
Advertising	1,334	834	834	834
Licences/Permits	113	0	0	0
Business Taxes	0	0	0	420
Insurance Expense	151	151	151	151
Interest Expense	925	323	323	323
Legal Fees	209	261	261	313
Rent	5,550	5,550	5,550	5,550
Repairs and Maintenance	239	298	298	358
Utilities	900	750	750	750
Telephone	135	135	135	135
Loan Repayment	24,075	788	788	788
Other Expenses	$ 298	$ 373	$ 373	$ 448
TOTAL CASH OUTFLOW	$89,068	$33,156	$33,156	$38,502
NET CASH INFLOW	$ 7,780	$ 4,154	$ 4,154	$ 6,270

Financing. Sue will require approximately $40,000 to finance Quality Cuts. She intends to invest $10,000 of her own money and will borrow $30,000 from the Royal Bank. Current interest rates are 8 percent and the term of the loan is five years. The loan repayment schedule is shown below.

Year	Payment	Principal	Interest	Balance
1	$28,333	$25,933	$2,400	$4,067
2	1,340	1,014	326	3,053
3	1,260	1,015	245	2,038
4	1,180	1,016	164	1,022
5	1,104	1,022	82	0

Bookkeeping/Accounting System. The computer system that will be purchased will take care of all aspects of a beauty salon, including the financial aspects. The ACCPAC software program for small businesses will be utilized to monitor and evaluate performance. Monthly financial statements will be prepared and reviewed by Sue and her husband.

The credit policy for the shop is quite simple; cash, cheque, or charge. There will be no credit granted, except for clients in very good standing and then only with Sue's approval. Cheques will be accepted with other identification from unknown customers. Also, major credit cards like Visa, MasterCard, and bank debit cards will be accepted.

Personnel

Quality Cuts will begin operations with five hairdressers and Sue Holland as owner/manager. The organizational chart for the staff can be seen below.

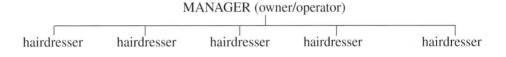

The salon hours will follow that of the mall: 9:30 a.m.–5:30 p.m. Monday to Wednesday and Saturday; 9:30 a.m.–9:00 p.m. Thursday and Friday. It will not be open on Sundays or extend its hours such as during the Christmas season.

Hairdressers work on commission, so the estimate of wages paid out over a year will make up a percentage of total sales. As stated earlier in this plan, secondary data suggests that this percentage averages 53.5 percent of total sales in Alberta, which is used to calculate the wages and salaries paid out over the first year of $79,844.

Hairdressers will work 16 to 24 hours per week. This is in accordance with industry averages as most hairdressers/stylists prefer to work part-time. A work schedule will be drawn up at least one week in advance and will accommodate client preference for certain hairdresser/stylists.

Employee Recruitment and Training. Skill training will be limited in this field of work as hairdressers have to attend a qualified beauty school and earn their certificate. However, Quality Cuts will devote extra effort to stressing to each employee the importance of customer service and projecting the right image. Explanation of company procedures and the commission payment plan will also be a part of the training.

Recruitment will also stress that the workers project the image that the beauty salon itself projects. Sue has already made contact with three hairdresser/stylists who fit the Quality Cuts image and have agreed to work for her. Interviews will be held to select the remaining employees. This should lead to the hiring of those who work well with the customers and other hairdressers.

Policies. The following policies will be in effect at Quality Cuts:

1. Employees must appear neat and clean.
2. No smoking is allowed in the customer area of the shop.
3. The approved uniform top must be worn at all times.
4. No food or drink is allowed in the customer area.
5. Employees will receive a 20 percent discount on all hair care products.
6. The customer is always right.

Evaluation. Employees' performance will be evaluated monthly on the basis of revenues generated, referrals, sales of hair care products, customer complaints, and progress toward employee objectives. As mentioned previously, employees' pay will be based partly on commissions of appointments as well as other sales.

Legal

Legal Structure. Quality Cuts will operate as a sole proprietorship. This will allow Sue to maintain flexibility and control of operations in the first few years.

Licensing. The licences necessary to operate this business are as follows:

Development application	$ 31.00
Occupancy permit	20.00
Business licence	62.00
Total licensing costs	$113.00

Insurance. Insurance is a legal necessity for this business. The breakdown of insurance is as follows:

Commercial general insurance (covering stock and building)	$190.00
Money and security insurance	75.00
Employee dishonesty bond	150.00
Malpractice insurance	190.00
Total insurance (for the first year)	$605.00

Figure 1   Shop Layout

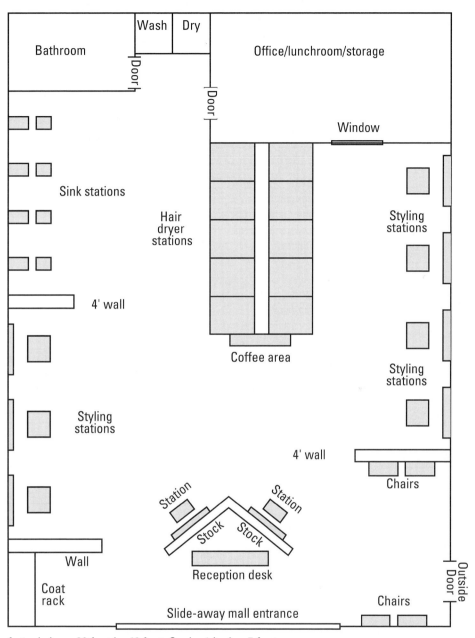

Actual size = 30 feet by 40 feet; Scale: 1 inch = 5 feet

Appendix 4C

Incorporation of Companies and Associations

Federal
Registrar of Companies
Consumer and Corporate Affairs
Place du Portage, Phase 2
Ottawa-Hull, K1A OL5

Alberta
Registrar of Companies
Alberta Consumer and Corporate Affairs
Century Place
9803 102A Avenue
Edmonton, T5J 3A3

British Columbia
Registrar of Companies
Minister of Consumer and Corporate Affairs
940 Blanshard Street
Victoria, V8W 3E6

Manitoba
Corporation and Business Names
Registration Branch
Department of Consumer and Corporate Affairs
Woodsworth Building
405 Broadway
Winnipeg, R3C 3L6

New Brunswick
Registrar of Companies
Consumer and Corporate Services Branch
Department of Justice
P.O. Box 6000
Fredericton, E3B 5H1

Newfoundland
Registry of Deeds
Companies and Securities
Department of Justice
Confederation Building
St. John's, A1C 5T7

Nova Scotia
Consumer Services Bureau
5639 Spring Garden Road, 2nd Floor
P.O. Box 998
Halifax, B3J 2X3

Northwest Territories
P.O. Box 1320
Yellowknife, X1A 2L9

Ontario
Companies Branch
Minister of Consumer and Commercial Relations
555 Yonge Street, 2nd Floor
Toronto, M7A 2H6

Prince Edward Island
Department of Provincial Secretary
P.O. Box 2000
Charlottetown, C1A 7N8

Quebec
Department of Consumer Affairs
Cooperative and Financial Institutions
800 Place d'Youville, 6th Floor
Quebec, G1R 4Y5

Saskatchewan
Corporations Branch
Saskatchewan Justice
1871 Smith Street
Regina, S4P 3V7

Yukon
Department of Consumer and Corporate Affairs
P.O. Box 2703
Whitehorse, Y1A 2C6

Appendix 4D

Jurisdiction of Licences and Taxes

Topic	Comment	Jurisdiction Municipal	Provincial	Federal
Licence and Permits				
City business permits		X		
Zoning by-laws	Applicable to certain provinces	X		
Land use regulations		X		
Business, school, water, taxes		X		
Provincial corporation income tax, estate taxes			X	
Capital tax (Ontario, Quebec, Manitoba, Saskatchewan, B.C.)	Applicable only to these provinces		X	
Quebec place of business tax	Applicable only to Quebec		X	
Sales and Excise Taxes				
Provincial excise tax	For consumer goods, must obtain a certificate from Department of Revenue, and vendor collects sales tax from consumer			X
Federal corporation income tax				X
Goods and services tax (GST)	Generally 7%, but certain goods exempted, e.g., foodstuffs			X
Export/import permit	All Canadian importers and exporters must obtain permit			X
Federal sales and excise taxes on imported goods	Levied on duty-paid value of some items			X
Custom duties on imported goods	Amount levied varies according to type of goods imported as classified by Canadian customs			X

Suggested Readings

Bingham, Richard. "Rebels with a Business Plan." *Report on Business Magazine*, November 1998, pp. 77–82.

CIBC. *Your Guide to Business Planning*. Canadian Imperial Bank of Commerce, 1995.

Dible, Donald. *What Everybody Should Know about Patents, Trademarks, and Copyrights.* New York: The Center for Entrepreneurial Management, 1986.

Drache, Arthur. "Life Insurance Can Save a Small Business." *The Financial Post,* April 2, 1990, p. 21.

Dunnett, Paul. "Entrepreneurs Can't Afford to Forgo Insurance." *The Globe and Mail,* January 13, 1999, p. B 12.

Financial Post, "How Entrepreneurs Can Develop Solid Business Plans." *The Financial Post* 85, no. 39 (September 21–23, 1991), pp. 21, 25.

Goldhirsh Group Inc. *Anatomy of a Start-Up: Why Some New Businesses Succeed and Others Fail.* Boston, 1991.

Gray, Douglas A., and Diana L. Gray. *The Complete Canadian Small Business Guide.* Toronto: McGraw-Hill Ryerson, 1994.

———. *The Canadian Home Based Business Guide.* Toronto: McGraw-Hill Ryerson, 1994.

———. *Home Inc.*, 2nd Edition. Toronto: McGraw-Hill Ryerson, 1994.

Hamdon, Clay K., "Before You Open The Door: Legal Condiserations for the Entrepreneur." *Law Now* 19, no. 3 (December 1994–January 1995), pp. 7–12.

McDonald, Gayle. "Small Business Spooked by Liability Cases." *The Globe and Mail*, October 9, 1995, p. B7.

Patents Questions and Answers. Ottawa: Consumer and Corporate Affairs, 1996.

Small Business Guide to Federal Incorporation. Corporate Directorate, Industry Canada, February 28, 1998.

"What to Consider When Insuring a Small Business." *The Globe and Mail,* October 26, 1998, p. C10.

Video Case Questions
Baron of Beer*

Winnipegger Gary DePape developed a taste for premium ales and lagers while playing hockey on the pro circuit in Germany. These days, he's playing a tough new game—building a million-dollar microbrewery in Winnipeg's highly competitive specialty beer market.

1. Briefly discuss the problems of starting from scratch, as illustrated by the Aggasiz Brewing Company.

2. How could Gary DePape have avoided these problems?

3. What would have been the advantages and disadvantages of Gary purchasing a micro-brewery instead of starting from scratch?

4. What risks would Gary have faced if he dropped the price of his product?

*Source: CBC *Venture* #729, running time 16:58.

Chapter 5

Buying a Business

Chapter Objectives

- To review the advantages and disadvantages of purchasing an ongoing business compared to the other methods of small business ownership.

- To describe the sources of businesses that are for sale.

- To explain how to evaluate a business that is for sale.

- To review the methods used in determining the price to pay for a business.

Small Business Profile

Vic De Zen
Royal Group Technologies Ltd.

Royal Group Technologies Ltd.
www.royalgroup
technologies.com

Vic De Zen was born in Traviso, Italy, in 1942. He studied as a tool-and-die maker in Switzerland during the 1960s. In November of 1968, Vic arrived in Canada with just $20 in his pocket. One hour after his flight had landed in Toronto, he began his career in the building products industry, installing doors and windows in residential housing.

In 1967 De Zen found work at Pillar Plastics Ltd. His skill as a tool-and-die maker brought the company financial success, but because of his disappointment with how the company treated him and other employees, he quit. Vic and two partners pooled their savings and founded Royal Plastics in 1970. Within one year, the company was operating in the black, but De Zen refused to take home more than $35 a week. Eight years later, Royal Plastics bought the foundering Pillar Plastics. From then on, absorbing troubled companies became another Royal Plastics strategy. In 1989 the company cut a $15-million deal with Quebec's Plastibec Ltd., turning around the failing plastic producer in two years by installing De Zen's own machinery and corporate structure. De Zen's stategy is to maintain a controlling interest in Royal subsidiaries, which are set up throughout Canada, the United States, and Mexico and are essentially autonomous.

Today, Vic acts as chairman, president, and CEO of Royal (now known as Royal Group Technologies Ltd.) which posted sales of $1.54 billion in fiscal 2000 with international operations in several countries. Under Vic's leadership, sales have advanced each year since its inception. During the last three years, annual sales have almost doubled and profit growth has been steady. Recently Royal Group Technologies Ltd. has been successful in receiving key U.S. building code approval, forming joint ventures to supply structures for education and the art industry. To meet this rapid growth, Royal Group Technologies Ltd. is currently constructing a 4 million square foot industrial complex in Woodbridge, Ontario.

Vic's entrepreneurial management style and business successes were recognized by the Governor General of Canada in 1995 when he was selected from over 1,000 candidates as "Canada's Entrepreneur of the Year." Vic's advice to would-be entrepreneurs is simple— "Listen to your customers, listen to your employees, and be prepared to work very hard!"

Used with the permission of Vic De Zen.

Incident 5-1

Don't Grow It...Buy It

It took just two years for Ric Carrick to grow his insulation-contracting company from a spare-bedroom operation to $3 million in sales. So in 1990, Carrick decided to take a break — not for some well-deserved R&R, but to study his industry and figure out a strategic path. That he'd try to grow InsulPro Industries Inc. rapidly was certain. But the tough question remained: how could that growth be best achieved?

After six months of research and discussions with experts across North America, the then-33-year-old Carrick decided on a bold strategy. He would break the industry's mom-and-pop tradition by developing a more sophisticated multi-branch operation. And rather than build new locations from scratch, he resolved to take the fast lane: growth through acquisition. By consolidating regional competitors under the InsulPro banner, Carrick reasoned, he would not only avoid creating an oversupply of contractors, but enjoy instant credibility in his new locations.

Armed with $500,000 from an initial public offering, Carrick approached target companies, primarily offering share-for-share swaps. Most of his targets resisted, suspecting it was a scheme to peek at their books. But by 1994, after pushing sales to $18 million with a dozen new start-ups in B.C. and Alberta, the climate began to change. Veteran contractors saw Carrick bringing new professionalism to the industry; InsulPro had even developed branch management software so powerful that two competitors licensed the system — at $500,000 each. Suddenly, many rivals who had spurned Carrick were inviting him back.

By the end of the year, Surrey, B.C.-based InsulPro owned six more contractors in Calgary, Edmonton, and the U.S. Today, Carrick oversees a 655-employee empire with outlets in B.C., Alberta, Ontario, Texas, and the U.S. Northwest. In all, acquisitions and start-ups have boosted InsulPro's sales from $5.7 million in 1992 to $48.7 million.

SOURCE: Adapted from Harvey Schachter "Don't Grow It ... Buy It," *Profit,* June 1999.

PURCHASING AN EXISTING BUSINESS

An alternative to organizing a business from the ground up is to purchase an existing business. Many entrepreneurs prefer this method of becoming a small business owner as the preferred method of growth. Thirty-eight of Canada's fastest growing companies have acquired other firms in recent years. Of these, 22 firms can attribute more than 20 percent of their growth to mergers and buyouts.[1] Incident 5-1 describes an entrepreneur who bought a floundering business after a careful and thorough evaluation. His experience and hard work turned the business around.

Advantages of Purchasing

Following are some reasons why buying a business may be an attractive alternative.

Reduction of Risk. Chapter 2 mentioned that high risk is associated with starting a small business. Much of this risk can be reduced by purchasing an existing business. Uncertainty about the extent of consumer demand can be eliminated to a certain degree by examining past results of an existing business. Therefore, with proper investigation, the risk associated with purchasing a small business should be less than with a business organized from scratch.

Reduction of Time and Set-Up Expenses. In an existing business, physical facilities such as building and equipment are already in place. The product or service is already being produced and distributed. Financial relationships and other important contacts have also been established. Each of these areas not only takes time to plan and organize but can be costly if unforeseen circumstances arise. Examples of such circumstances include lack of demand for the product or service, construction problems, production difficulties, and legal complications. Purchasing an existing business can minimize these potential problems.

Reduction of Competition. Purchasing an existing business can eliminate a potential competitor. This may be an especially important consideration in a fairly stable market with only a few well-established competitors. Breaking into such a market with a totally new business may be difficult, and the potential small business owner should investigate the possibility of purchasing rather than organizing. Incident 5-1 illustrates this motivation for a Canadian company.

Capitalization of Business Strength. Often a business for sale has a competitive strength that would be difficult to duplicate with a new firm. For example, the location of the business, a very important consideration in the retail and some service industries, may be excellent. Personnel, technology, or even the physical facilities of the business may be superior to those of competing firms. In such situations, buying a business that offers these advantages may be an attractive alternative. Incident 5-2 provides an example of a company that increased its competitiveness through acquisition.

Possible Assistance from the Previous Owner. The previous owner may be willing to work for the purchaser of the business, or at least provide some assistance for a short time following the purchase. This type of help can be invaluable to the new owner.

Easier Planning. Financial and market planning for a business is much easier when historical records are available. This information is not available for a start-up business. When approaching lenders or investors, projections from actual results of an existing business may generate more confidence than untested estimates.

Incident 5-2

Buying Your Competition

Transmitters, receivers, amplifiers, cable assemblies, and adapters are just a few of the products available from JDS Uniphase's comprehensive line of fibreoptics. The company did not always provide such an extensive product line. In fact, JDS Uniphase was formerly known as JDS Fitel. Fitel also specialized in fibreoptics, but certainly not to the extent the company does today.

In 1998, JDS Fitel earned a top spot on *Profit* magazine's hottest IPO's ranking. At the time, President Jozef Straus' company strategy was to provide people with the products they want. In an effort to abide by this strategy, JDS Fitel underwent a friendly merger with California-based Uniphase Corp. The merger was not a competitor buy-out, but rather two companies seeking to work together. Both JDS and Uniphase were supplying different products for the same clients, and a merger was the perfect answer to creating a one-solution company. Straus recalls, "We believed that for us to continue to bring strong value to customers, we needed to expand our product offering." Merging JDS and Uniphase, rather than entering into competition with one another, accomplished this expansion.

Merger and acquisition did not stop with JDS and Uniphase. It simply provided the company with the power to maintain healthy growth through acquisition. Since its initial merger, JDS Uniphase has acquired more than seven companies. Not all buy-outs were friendly and done in an attempt to expand the product line. The acquisition of E-Tek Dynamics was a strategic move by JDS Uniphase to wipe out the competition.

JDS Uniphase is now a $100 billion company and the industry leader in design, development, manufacture, and distribution of advanced fibreoptics products for the telecommunications and cable television industries. In the case of JDS Uniphase, "make products people want" meant acquiring companies that allowed for product line expansion.

Source: Adapted from Laura Pratt, "Up, Up and Away," *Profit*, April 2000, p. 31.

Disadvantages of Purchasing

A prospective purchaser should also be aware of the potential disadvantages of purchasing a business. Following are some of the potential disadvantages of buying a business. Many of these problems concern the condition of the assets and other aspects of the business.

Physical Facilities. The building and equipment may be old, obsolete, or below current standards. In addition, they may not be completely paid for or may have charges or liens against them. If the prospective buyer is unfamiliar with how to evaluate the condition of such facilities, he or she should enlist the services of a professional appraiser.

Personnel. The business's employees may be incompetent or unmotivated. They may also resist the new ownership and reduce their productivity or even quit once the transfer of ownership is completed. The potential buyer is well advised to visit with current employees to ascertain their attitudes toward change.

Inventory. The inventory may be obsolete or hard to sell. This factor may be especially critical in a retail store or a high-technology firm. The age of inventory can often be determined through internal records or by price-tag coding.

Accounts Receivable. The outstanding accounts may be uncollectible or at least costly and time consuming to collect. An evaluation of the length of time these accounts have been outstanding can be helpful in evaluating this potential problem.

Financial Condition. The financial health of the business may be deteriorating or less positive than it appears in the financial statements. An in-depth evaluation of the firm's financial condition should always be conducted prior to purchase.

Market. The market for the business's product or service may be deteriorating, or a strong, new competitor may be about to enter the market. In addition, such factors as the economic state, interest rates, or government policy could adversely affect the market.

Deciding on the Price. The prospective owner may have difficulty negotiating a price to pay for the business or evaluating the fairness of the listed price.

Many of the above potential problems associated with buying a business can be uncovered through a detailed investigation of the operations of the business prior to purchase. Some of the key evaluation areas are discussed later in this chapter.

SOURCES OF BUSINESSES FOR SALE

Where can the entrepreneur who has decided to purchase a business find out which businesses are for sale? The following are common sources.

Classified Ads. Classified ads are found in local newspapers or financial or business publications. Figure 5-1 gives an example. Although numerous opportunities are publicly advertised, many of the best businesses to buy have been sold prior to the time they are advertised in the print media.

Canada Business Service Centres www.cbsc.org

Government Departments. The small business or industry department in most provinces is usually aware of businesses for sale. They may also know of communities that want to attract a particular type of business to locate there.

Trade Journals. Trade journals frequently carry listings of businesses that are for sale in that industry. This may be a more effective source than more general classified ads.

Real Estate Brokers. Many entrepreneurs purchase their businesses with the assistance of a broker whose job is to get buyers and sellers together and help negotiate the sale. If the

Figure 5-1   Classified Ad for a Business Opportunity

Lucrative Business for Sale

Manufacturer of picture frames and artists' supplies. Wholesalers to photo shops, artist stores, and craft shops. Growing business with established clientele, situated near Vancouver. Excellent investment potential. $150,000 negotiable. Please reply to:

National Post
300–1450 Don Mills Road
Don Mills, Ontario M3B 3R5

---

prospective purchaser knows a certain broker fairly well, he or she might request that this individual be on the lookout for the type of business desired. Brokers are aware of most businesses that are, or soon will be, for sale, and some brokers even specialize in businesses.

Other Professionals. Other professionals such as lawyers, accountants, business appraisers, and bankers often know of businesses for sale. Some prospective purchasers have found excellent opportunities by sending these professionals letters requesting information about businesses for sale. In addition, organizations such as the Chamber of Commerce may offer "match-up" services. One example is COIN (Canadian Opportunities Investment Network).

Word of Mouth. In their association with businesspeople, entrepreneurs often learn about business opportunities through word of mouth. Executives of industry associations often hear about owners who want out of their businesses, and prospective buyers can contact these sources.

EVALUATING A BUSINESS FOR SALE

A wise purchase decision may require considerable investigation. The prospective buyer should look into several key areas of a business before making a decision to purchase.

Industry Analysis

The entrepreneur should be well informed about the industry in which the business operates. Ideally this information should come from an extensive background or experience in that industry. Some specific areas to investigate are the following:

Sales and Profit Trends of the Industry

- The degree of competition, number of competitors entering or leaving the industry, and the nature of competitors' strategies

- The state of the economy in the market area and the extent to which changes in the economy affect the industry

- Legal restrictions currently affecting the operations of the business, as well as relevant pending legislation or political pressure

- Social concerns that may adversely affect the industry in the future

One or more of these areas could be significant in determining the future success of the proposed purchase. As a result, they should be thoroughly investigated unless the buyer has considerable experience in the industry.

The Previous Owner

The entrepreneur should ask the following questions about the previous owner of the business:

- Why is the previous owner selling the business? The often advertised reason, "because of poor health," may refer to financial rather than physical health.

- Is the previous owner a well-known and respected member of the community? Has this reputation contributed significantly to the success of the business? Will this success continue once that individual is no longer associated with the business?

- Will the previous owner be available—temporarily, at least—to provide assistance and advice to the new owner? This help can be invaluable, especially to a purchaser who lacks experience in the industry or market.

- Is the previous owner willing to finance the purchase by spreading it over a number of years? This may be helpful to the purchaser and advantageous tax-wise to the seller.

- What will the previous owner do after he or she sells the business? To guard against the previous owner starting a similar business in the same market area, the prospective purchaser might insist that a noncompetitive clause be included in the sales agreement.

Financial Condition of the Business

The financial condition of a prospective business is perhaps the most important area to evaluate. Care should be taken in evaluating the financial statements and assessing their validity. It is advisable to review not only the most recent year's financial statements but also those for past years. This process can reveal any trends and extraordinary circumstances. For instance, a general negative trend in profits during the past several years might suggest a lower value for the business, or at least the need for further investigation by the prospective buyer.

If the prospective buyer lacks a basic knowledge of accounting and an understanding of financial statements, it would be wise to enlist an accountant to assist in the financial evaluation. Some specific items to investigate, either by oneself or with the help of an accountant, are the following.

Validity of the Financial Statements. Since some flexibility is allowed in preparing financial statements and a wide range of bookkeepers and accountants may be preparing them, the entrepreneur should assess the validity of the financial information obtained from the business. This can be done by obtaining audited statements and reviewing the methods used in recording such items as depreciation, inventory value, extraordinary items, repairs, owner's salary, and the treatment and terms of debt.

The prospective buyer should also investigate whether any potential hidden liabilities, such as liens or lawsuits, exist. Some industry experts recommend that if there is a possibility of such a liability but the amount is unknown, the purchaser should buy only the assets of the business. By doing this, the potential liability will accrue to the business itself rather than to the new owner.

Another task in assessing the validity of the statements is to review the income tax returns and bank deposits of the business. In addition, many prospective purchasers insist that the financial statements be audited to ensure their accuracy.

Evaluation of the Financial Statements. Once the prospective buyer is satisfied that the financial statements are complete and accurately portray the operations of the business, he or she can evaluate the performance of the business as described in these statements. Sales, expenses, profit levels, assets, liabilities, and cash flow position are important items. Application of various financial ratios can help in comparing the performance of the business to those of other firms in the industry. Chapter 10 gives a detailed discussion of ratio analysis and other financial evaluation measurements. Appendix 10B illustrates the financial evaluation of a small business.

Naturally, one would hope the business is strong financially and profitable in its operations. In some situations, however, a business may be a good purchase even if it is unprofitable at the time of evaluation. This is illustrated in the Small Business Profile that opens this chapter and also in Incidents 5-3 and 5-4. Such situations might be the following:

- The current owner is incompetent or lacks knowledge about the industry, and the purchaser has the competence and knowledge to turn the business around.

- The industry is, or will shortly be, in a growth position that might improve the firm's profitability and/or resale value.

- The major contributor to the firm's unprofitability is lack of capital leading to high interest costs, and the purchaser has the needed capital to inject into the business.

Incident 5-3

Blind Ambition
How Not to Buy a Business

David W. Clausen didn't have the slightest idea what he was doing. This, he realizes today. At the time, he simply decided to buy a business, then did it. Without experience. With little market research. And with limited financial resources. He even passed on hiring accountants and lawyers.

"I was so eager to get my hands on a business, I had faith I could make anything turn around," he says. "But I was naive. I ran into a lot of obstacles I didn't expect."

In the end, a church acquaintance who was a cartographer at Barclay Maps told him that the 40-year-old-map-publishing business was up for sale. The owner had just died, and the asking price for the company was $200,000.

Clausen walked through the facility, figured he saw about $25,000 worth of equipment, factored in $15,000 for goodwill, and offered $40,000. To his surprise, the offer was accepted.

His failure to do any research beforehand created some serious business hurdles: right away he discovered that his company was riddled with problems of outdated equipment, a dwindling customer base, and missing books. On top of that, he understood the industry barely enough to know where to begin.

Despite his inauspicious beginning, in five years Clausen has pushed annual sales from $190,000 (and falling) to projected $1 million. Barclay is now one of the country's largest suppliers of high-end digital geographic data.

Source: Adapted from "Blind Ambition, How Not to Buy a Business," *Success*, October 1997, p. 65

Incident 5-4

New and Improved

Red-L was a respected but decidedly moribund outfit when Mike Ludwig took over in December, 1991. The company's founder, retiring Phil Redl, had built a hose-and-clamp business based almost entirely on Alberta's boom-and-bust oil industry, a strategy that paid ample dividends 20 years ago, but no longer seemed viable in the 1990s.

"This was a sleepy, do-nothing company when I bought it," says Ludwig. "I came here and turned it into a monster, an aggressive and pro-active sales and marketing machine." It was no magic, he says: "All I did was inject some life into the place"—one improvement at a time.

Ludwig motivated staff by "pounding them over the head with a couple of simple messages: There is no downturn in the economy. There is no reason we can't double our sales in five years. There are no excuses." That attitude jolted employees long accustomed to sitting around waiting for orders. Before Ludwig, "our fortunes were completely tied to the oil patch," says accounting clerk Deanna Tibbetts. "Things were very unstable, especially when the oil industry peaked and crashed in the early 1980s. We went from 19 employees to 50, and then back to 19. You never knew who was going to be next to get laid off."

The bottom line: Ludwig had to kick hard to keep his head above water. He had to develop a new strategy, one that would strengthen his team and turn the company around quickly.

Ludwig's first step was to whip the organization into shape. He spent the first few days getting to know his employees by name and getting a sense of what they could offer. Then he moved people around to take better advantage of their skills.

Source: Adapted from Diane Lucklow, "Red-L Distributors," *Profit*, April 2000, p. 29.

Condition of the Assets

Several assets of a business may require thorough inspection and, for nonliquid assets, possibly an appraisal by an independent appraiser. The fee for this service is generally reasonable and may be well worth it. Assets to value in this manner are the following.

Liquid Assets (Cash and Investments). An important question to a prospective purchaser concerns how easily the liquid assets can be converted to cash. There may be special terms or conditions with respect to these assets, for example, the time period on a term deposit.

Accounts Receivable. Have accounts receivable been aged? How many may be uncollectible? (Accounts receivable ageing is discussed in more detail in Chapter 10.) Enlisting the services of a professional accountant to assist in this regard may be well worth the cost.

Inventory. Is any inventory old, obsolete, or damaged? A detailed evaluation of inventory should be done by someone with knowledge and experience in this area.

Building and Equipment. Are the buildings and equipment old or obsolete? Are they comparable to competitors' facilities? Are there any liens against them?

Real Estate. What are the land taxes and service costs? If the premises are leased, is the lease transferable? What are the terms and conditions of the lease? Has the location experienced a high turnover of businesses in the past?

Goodwill. What value does the owner place on goodwill? Goodwill is the intangible value of such things as reputation, past experience, expertise, and prominence in the industry or community. Is this value realistic and reasonable? Generally, goodwill costs should not exceed 20 percent of the cost of the assets, even for well-established businesses.

Quality of Personnel

The prospective purchaser should evaluate the efficiency of the business's personnel. How do they compare to employees in other, similar businesses? An important factor is personnel reaction to the new owner after the purchase. It may be wise for the buyer to meet with key personnel to better evaluate their reaction to the sale of the business. What is the staff turnover?

External Relationships of the Business

The investigation should include a review of those organizations or agencies currently essential to the operations of the business. Will these relationships continue, and if so, under what terms or conditions? Some organizations to contact include suppliers, financial institutions, and key customers.

Condition of the Records

Other records to review are credit files, personnel files, sales reports, contracts, and customer lists. These items can be very valuable to the operations of the business and should be included with the business when it is purchased.

Appendix 5A at the conclusion of this chapter presents a comprehensive checklist of considerations in purchasing a business.

DETERMINING THE PRICE OR VALUE OF A BUSINESS

If the preceding evaluation of the business shows positive results and the prospective purchaser decides to buy the business, he or she must make a decision concerning the price to pay for it. Is the asking price reasonable? Should a lower counteroffer be made? Several methods can be used to arrive at a price for a business.

There are four approaches to valuing a business. The first is by market value. The second relies heavily on asset value. The third uses the earnings potential of the business as a basis for determining value. The fourth uses a combination of asset value and earnings potential. Each method can help the entrepreneur make a general estimate of the purchase price. It should be kept in mind, however, that the buyer, the seller, or the business may possess unique characteristics that cannot be incorporated into a formula. Such situations will require adjustments to a formula-determined price. A more detailed coverage of the financial terms used in price determination is found in Chapter 10.

Market Value

In a free market, the right price is the one on which the purchaser and seller agree, or, in other words, where demand and supply meet. When applied to a business purchase, this price is called the market value. To use the market value method effectively, the prospective purchaser must collect data on the market values of many similar businesses. In many markets, the number of sales transactions of similar businesses is fairly small; thus, little data may be available. In such cases, other methods of valuation will be more useful.

Asset Value

There are two approaches to valuing a business using value of assets as a base: book value and replacement value.

Book Value. The book value method lists the business at the net balance sheet value of its assets minus the value of its liabilities (Chapter 10 provides the fundamentals of balance sheet assets and liabilities). This method generally understates the value of the business by a significant amount. For this reason, the book value price may form a lower limit to determining the price of the business.

Replacement Value. The replacement value method lists the replacement cost of the assets as their value. Because the assets of an existing business typically are not new, the replacement value method tends to overstate the value of the business. When coupled with the liability side of the balance sheet, the replacement cost method may result in an upper limit to the price to pay for the business.

Earnings Value

The prospective purchaser is interested not only in asset value but also in how the business will perform in the future. Therefore, earnings potential is another factor to be taken into account in setting the price of a business. Pretax earnings or income should be used, as the tax rates vary by province and by industry.

It is also important to use average earnings in calculating earnings potential rather than just the most recent year's net income figure. When using average earnings, extraordinary items that have affected income should be deleted in order to make the estimate a "true" average. This is called normalizing earnings. Many analysts will use the previous five years' average of earnings. If earnings appear to be unstable from year to year, a weighted-average calculation might be used. The determination of average earnings using the weighted-average approach is shown in Figure 5-2. This method gives a greater weight to the most recent years' earnings in arriving at average earnings.

Two specific methods of estimating the purchase value of the business use earnings as a base.

Dun and Bradstreet
www.dnb.com

Statistics Canada
www.statcan.ca

Capitalization of Earnings Method. This method is commonly used to arrive at a quick estimate of the price of a business. The capitalized value is found by dividing average earnings of the business by a specified rate of return expressed as a decimal. This specified rate of return figure can be obtained by using bank interest (a risk factor of a few percentage points should be added) or another required rate of return percentage for the investment. It can also be obtained by using average return on tangible net worth statistics from such sources as Dun and Bradstreet and Statistics Canada. Figure 5-3 illustrates the capitalization of earnings formula.

Figure 5-2   Calculating Weighted-Average Earnings for a Business

	Average Earnings	Weighted Average Earnings (Earnings × Weights Factor)				
Last year	$5,000	5,000	×	5	=	25,000
Two years ago	4,000	4,000	×	4	=	16,000
Three years ago	7,000	7,000	×	3	=	21,000
Four years ago	10,000	10,000	×	2	=	20,000
Five years ago	$14,000	14,000	×	1	=	14,000
	$40,000			15		96,000

Average Earnings
40,000/5 = 8000

Weighted Average Earnings
96,000/15 = 6,600

Figure 5-3   Capitalization of Earnings Formula

$$\frac{\text{Average earnings}}{\substack{\text{Predetermined interest rate or} \\ \text{rate of return required for investment}}} = \text{Capitalized value}$$

Figure 5-4   Capitalized Earnings Value

Line of Business	Net Profits to Tangible Net Worth as a Percentage*	Capitalized Earnings Value†
Retail		
Book and stationery stores	22.0	$45,450
Clothing, men's	12.9	77,520
Clothing, women's	12.8	78,125
Drugstores	20.7	48,310
Food stores	10.8	92,595
Gasoline service stations	23.1	43,290
Hardware	14.5	68,965
Jewellery store	8.3	120,480
Manufacturers		
Appliances, small	18.4	54,350
Bakery products	17.8	56,180
Machine shops	19.7	50,760
Meat products	11.8	84,745
Sash, door, and millwork plants	29.0	34,480
Soft drinks	34.9	28,655
Sporting goods and toys	11.0	90,910
Construction		
Building contractors	23.3	42,920
Services		
Hotels	15.5	64,515
Agriculture, forestry, and fishing		
Agriculture	12.2	81,965

*Tangible net worth is net worth less intangibles, i.e., copyrights, goodwill, trademarks, and patents. This figure can be found in Dun and Bradstreet, *Key Business Ratios*.

† Represents the investment or tangible net worth required to earn $10,000 in profits after taxes, assuming the firm is operating at median level. Calculated in the following manner:

$$\frac{\$10,000}{\substack{\text{Net profit to tangible} \\ \text{net worth as percentage}}} = \text{Capitalized earning value.}$$

Sources: Adapted from Paul Harmon, *Small Business Management—A Practical Approach* (New York: D. Van Nostrand, 1979), p. 76. Figures updated from Dun and Bradstreet, *Key Business Ratios*, 1990.

Figure 5-4 (on the previous page) illustrates a calculation of capitalized earnings value using industry averages. This method measures the firm's ability to earn profits in relation to the capital invested. For example, for a book and stationery store, it will take $45,450 paid for the business to earn $10,000 after taxes if the store were run at the median level. Figure 5-4 also illustrates Dun and Bradstreet averages for various industries.

Times Earnings Method. This method arbitrarily multiplies average earnings by a number usually between 1 and 10, based on past sales and industry experience, to arrive at the price for the business. This is often called the price-earnings ratio. Small businesses are usually sold at between four and five times earnings according to the U.S. Small Business Administration, although recently some Internet companies have sold at much higher multiples. This number can vary significantly for very small businesses. Therefore, the advice of an experienced business broker or accountant valuator should be sought.

Combination Methods

Because both the asset value and the earnings value are important components of the price of a business, some methods attempt to combine both values to estimate the price. Figure 5-5 illustrates such an example. This method utilizes historical experience in determing relevant indicators of the components of the value of a business.

As mentioned previously, determining the price of a business by using a formula may provide a good estimate of a business's worth, but the unique characteristics of each situation may alter the price actually offered and/or paid for the business.

Figure 5-5   Combination Methods for Pricing a Business

Type of Business	Price Offering Range
Apparel shop	.75 to 1.5 times net income + equipment + inventory
Beauty salon	.25 to .75 times gross sales + equipment + inventory
Fast-food store	1 to 1.25 times net income
Grocery store	.25 to .33 times gross sales including equipment
Insurance agency	1 to 1 times renewal commissions
Manufacturer	1.5 to 2.5 times net income, including equipment + inventory
Restaurant	.25 to .50 times gross sales, including equipment
Retail store	.75 to 1.5 times net income + equipment + inventory
Travel agency	.04 to .10 times gross sales, including equipment
Video store	1 to 2 times net income + equipment

Source: Gustav Belle, *The Small Business Information Handbook* (New York: John Wiley and Sons 1990), pp. 30–32.

THE PURCHASE TRANSACTION

The entrepreneur should enlist the services of such professionals as lawyers and accountants to assist in the purchase decision. Once a purchase price and other terms and conditions have been agreed upon, the buyer should enlist the services of a lawyer to draw up the purchase agreement and close the transaction. This helps ensure that clear title to the business is transferred and post-purchase difficulties are minimized. The purchase agreement should cover the following areas:

- The purchase price, including principal and interest amounts

- Payment date(s)—when and to whom payments are to be made

- A detailed list of all assets to be included in the purchase

- Conditions of the purchase—what nonfinancial requirements, if any, are part of the purchase? Many purchase contracts are signed subject to the purchaser obtaining suitable financing

- Provisions for noncompliance with conditions, including penalties for breaches of the contract

- Collateral or security pledged in the transaction (if the seller is financing the sale)

Negotiating the Deal

In purchasing a business, the first formal step is to make the offer to purchase. The offer may be made directly by the buyer or through a realtor or a lawyer. In either case, the offer to purchase should be made only after consulting a lawyer and an accountant. As part of the negotiating strategy, the potential buyer should have calculated (preferably financially) the maximum amount he or she can offer for the business using one or more of the methods previously cited. This value is generally somewhat higher than the original purchase offer. As negotiations continue, the purchase price or other aspects of the agreement may have to be altered.

Once the purchase price has been agreed upon, the transaction is usually closed and legal transfer of title to the business takes place. Typically this is carried out by both the buyer and seller's lawyer. The purchaser should exercise caution if the seller's lawyer is to close the deal. The buyer's lawyer should be permitted to review the details of the transaction in this case.

The buyer is normally required to make a deposit of 5 to 10 percent of the purchase price as a show of good faith. This amount should be minimized at least until the seller has met the conditions of the agreement.[2]

Summary

1. The potential advantages of buying a small business include the reduction of risk, time, set-up expense, and competition; capitalization of business strength; possible assistance from the previous owner; and easier planning. Potential disadvantages include problems with physical facilities, personnel, inventory, and accounts receivable; deterioration of the business's financial condition or market; and difficulty in negotiating a purchase price.

2. The common sources for locating a business for sale include classified ads, government departments, real estate brokers, word of mouth, and professionals such as lawyers, accountants, and bankers.

3. The key areas an entrepreneur should investigate in carrying out an industry analysis are sales and profit trends, degree of competition, state of the economy in the market area, legal restrictions, and social concerns that may adversely affect the industry in the future. To evaluate the internal aspects, the following should be addressed: previous owner's reputation, why the owner is selling the business, validity of the financial statements, the condition of the assets, the personnel, external relationships of the business, and the existing records.

4. There are three general approaches to valuing a business. The first method uses the asset value to determine the price. The second method uses the earnings of the business. The third method uses a combination of assets and earnings.

Chapter Problems and Applications

1. John Van Goegh wants to own his own business. His area of expertise is the sporting goods market. He has checked into opening his own store versus purchasing an existing store in the downtown area. The existing store is a seven-year-old proprietorship with sagging sales. There are four main sporting goods shops in the city (60,000 people). The existing business is in a prime location, and the market and product line are well established. The financial condition, however, includes a large amount of accounts receivable. With this information, John turns to you as a consultant. What advice would you give John regarding whether to purchase the existing business or start his own? What additional factors should he consider? Justify your answer.

2. You are investigating the purchase of a fertilizer manufacturing plant. The results of your analysis of the firm are extremely positive, except for an unidentifiable annual payment of $100,000. On further investigation, you learn that the $100,000 is being paid in fines for dumping toxic waste. The previous owner has determined that it costs less to pay the fines than it would to properly dispose of the waste by deep-well injection. In light of recent government actions, how would this situation affect your decision to purchase? Explain.

3. Sally's Bar and Grill is available for purchase. Sally's earnings for the past five years were as follows:

Last year, $50,000	Four years ago, $40,000
Two years ago, $60,000	Five years ago, $25,000
Three years ago, $30,000	

Determine the value of the business using the following methods (use current bank interest rates) using both general and weighted averaging methods.

a. Capitalized earnings formula

b. Times earnings method

4. Do an industry analysis for the existing grocery stores in your area. Complete your analysis using all the areas mentioned in the text.

5. From an advertisement in the paper, contact the seller of a business.

Find out the price and other information pertinent to the sale. Does the asking price seem reasonable? Check with industry averages to evaluate the performance of the business.

Appendix 5A

Checklist of Considerations in Purchasing a Business

The Industry

1. What are the sales and profit trends in the industry?
2. What is the degree of competition? What competitive changes have taken place?
3. What is the nature of competitor strategies?
4. What is the state of the economy in the market? How is the business's performance affected by changes in the economy?
5. What existing or pending legal restrictions affect the operations of the business?
6. What social or cultural concerns affect the industry?
7. Are there any potential competitive or trading area changes that might affect the business?

The Previous Owner

1. Why is the previous owner selling the business?
2. Has the reputation of the previous owner contributed to the success of the business?
3. Will the previous owner help you by providing assistance and advice after the sale?
4. Is the previous owner willing to finance all or part of the purchase?
5. Will the previous owner start a competitive business after the sale?

Financial Condition of the Business

1. Is the financial information provided accurate and indicative of the business's performance?
2. What is the past history of profits going back at least five years?
3. Has the business gained or lost market share in the past five years?
4. How do the various financial ratios for the business compare with industry averages?
5. Does the business have a strong identity with customers or clients? Can this identity be maintained?
6. What prospects does the business have for increasing market share and profitability in the future?
7. If the business is currently unsuccessful, what are the chances of improving it with an infusion of capital and/or managerial expertise?
8. What value does the business place on goodwill?

Condition of Assets

1. Are any special terms or conditions associated with the liquid assets?
2. Are the accounts receivable collectible?
3. Is the inventory old or obsolete?
4. Are the building and equipment up to date and paid for?
5. Are taxes and service costs paid on land?
6. Is the location good? Is it increasing or decreasing in value?
7. Is the lease good? What are the terms and conditions of the lease?

Quality of Personnel

1. Do the employees of the business compare favourably with the industry in productivity and expertise?
2. Will the employees stay on with the business after the sale?
3. Has the business been progressive in meeting competitive demands regarding wage rates and employee benefits?

Condition of External Relationships

1. Can favourable relations with suppliers be maintained?
2. Are financial sources appropriate and adequate? Can they be maintained?
3. Does the business have a strong support staff such as a lawyer, an accountant, and a consultant? Can these people be retained if needed?

Condition of Records

1. Can the purchaser obtain key records such as credit files, personnel files, customer lists, sales reports, and contracts?

Suggested Readings

Bianchi, Alessandra. "Why You Won't Sell Your Business." *Inc.*, August 1992, pp. 58–63.

Bunn, Verna A., and C. R. Steedman. *How to Buy and Sell a Small Business.* Toronto: Checkerbooks, 1987.

Gray, Douglas A., and Diana L. Gray. *The Complete Canadian Small Business Guide.* Toronto: McGraw-Hill Ryerson, 1994, pp. 79–103.

Green, Janet M. "Structuring an Acquisition Strategy." *Small Business Reports*, December 1992, p. 51.

Jacobsen, Gianna. "Mission: Acquisition." *Success*, October 1997, pp. 62–66.

Joseph, Richard, Anna Nekoranec, and Carl Steffens. *How to Buy a Business: Entrepreneurship Through Acquisition.* Dearborn Financial Publishing, 1995.

Moskal, Brian S. "The Art of the Deal" *Industry Week*, January 18, 1993, p. 23.

Shachter, Harvey. "Don't Grow it… Buy It," *Profit*, June 1998, p. 161.

Thomas, Peter. "Negotiate to Win," *Profit*, October 1991, pp. 34–36.

Tulenko, Paul. "How to Buy Yourself a Job for Life." *The Globe and Mail*, July 24, 1995, p. B7.

Video Case Questions
Merger Madness*

CBC

Conventional business wisdom says that mergers are good for business and good for shareholders. Year by year over the past decade, companies have been doing bigger deals, and more of them. But the reality is that well over half of those deals have not created value.

1. What can a prospective purchaser of a small business learn from this example?

2. What resources might assist to ensure that the price paid for a business is not too high?

*Source: CBC *Venture* #723, running time 8:24.

Chapter 6

Chapter 6

Franchising

Chapter Objectives

- To discuss the significance of franchising in the Canadian economy.

- To explain the various types of franchises available for small business.

- To list the relative strengths and weaknesses of franchising as a method of starting a small business.

- To explain how to evaluate a franchise opportunity.

- To discuss how to organize a franchising system.

Small Business Profile

Adrienne Stringer and Jim MacKenzie
Molly Maid International Inc.

**Molly Maid
International Inc.
www.mollymaid.com**

In 1978 Adrienne Stringer, a former nurse, invested $2,000 to organize a maid service business. She believed changing lifestyles and the increasing number of two-income families had created a market for the business.

By 1980 Stringer's company, Molly Maid, was grossing about $100,000 and seeing further growth possibilities. Because she lacked finances to accomplish this growth, she decided she needed to obtain equity money, either from new partners or through a franchise system. As she investigated further, she thought the franchising system would more likely provide the necessary expansion funds. She entered into an arrangement with Jim MacKenzie to franchise the business. MacKenzie, a business graduate from Queen's University, purchased 80 percent of the business and immediately began developing a complete franchise system for Molly Maid. Stringer became the first franchisee.

Since that time Molly Maid has grown dramatically, employing over 5,000 maids and reaching sales of about $175 million in 2000. Molly Maid has sold more than 500 franchises in Canada, the United States, the United Kingdom, Portugal, and Japan.

International expansion increased when the Government of Canada introduced the G.S.T. in 1991. "The GST caused a 20 percent decline in our company so our growth was taken away," says Mackenzie. Today international operations are growing at 25 percent per year compared to 12 percent for Canada.

Molly Maid's success can be attributed to the recognition by Stringer and MacKenzie of an underdeveloped market and the business acumen needed to properly organize and administer the franchising system. A consistent dedication to marketing and consumer research has made the company the dominant maid service in Canada. In recent years, Molly Maid has also aggressively pursued international expansion.

Incident 6-1

From Hobby to Enterprise

"We're putting the spark of interest in a child's mind," says Ariel Shlien.

Fifteen years ago, Ariel and his brother Ron began pursuing their teenage passion, model rocket launching. Shortly after, the backyard hobby turned into a business. When a woman saw their demonstration at a local area YMCA, she asked the two brothers to launch rockets at her son's birthday party. The boys were happy to oblige, as payment for the one-hour demonstration was $100. Ariel and Ron were soon doing three to four shows every weekend.

Since the days of birthday party demonstrations, business growth has not stopped. The Shliens continued to do birthday party demonstrations through their university careers until the launch of the Mad Scientist Group in 1993. The objective of this business was to transform science education into fun-filled shows that helped kids understand the wonders of nature. Delivering fun, interactive workshops in classrooms, theme parks, and at various special events has increased sales by an astronomical 1,233 percent. The Montreal-based firm generated $3.7 million in1999 profits. This landed the Shlien brothers on the *Profit 100* List of Canada's Fastest-Growing Companies.

By changing their boyhood hobby into a premium service, the Shlien brothers were able to capture millions of dollars in profits. Mad Scientist Group has experienced red-hot growth since its establishment in 1993. In order to contend with such growth, Ariel and Ron turned their business into a franchise operation. Today, 114 franchises operate in over 18 countries, and Ariel Shlien says, "We've turned Mad Science into the McDonald's of this business."

SOURCE: Adapted from Ian Portsmouth, "Agents of Change," *Profit*, June 2000, pp. 34-40.

HISTORY AND BACKGROUND OF FRANCHISING

Franchising is becoming an increasingly popular method of establishing and operating a small business. Many entrepreneurs find the opportunity to operate their own business with slightly less risk an attractive option (see Incident 6-1). Others enter franchising out of necessity, having lost jobs with larger organizations. Franchising now occurs in most industries and is experiencing rapid growth in the service sector.

Franchising has not only been successful for the entrepreneur. Many large organizations also recognize that this method of doing business benefits their operations (see Incident 6-2).

From the franchisor's point of view, franchising provides a source of capital and a stable and motivated work force, thus usually leading to higher performance. For the franchisee, it offers a turnkey operation with valuable assistance from the franchisor.

One dilemma the entrepreneur often faces is that as the business grows, funds are needed for expansion. As the profile at the beginning of the chapter illustrates, franchising is one answer to this financing question.

In addition, expansion of a business usually requires the addition of new employees. The new employees often lack the same incentive as the owner to make the business succeed. Some franchisors have used innovative methods to increase interest and motivation (see Incident 6-3).

Although the concept has been around for decades, franchising has experienced its most rapid growth in North America only since the 1950s. It began with the automobile manufacturers, oil companies, soft drink bottlers, and breweries and has since spread to many different industries throughout the world. Through franchising, many organizations with a proven concept or product were able to expand much more rapidly to meet demand. This

---

Incident 6-2

Managing Partner Plan Rejigs Franchise Contract

Douglas Casimiri opened a 600-square-foot fish-and-chip stand when he was just 17, using a loan co-signed by his father. Located in midtown Toronto, the tiny take-out joint thrived because he sold fresh fish and home-cut potatoes that he got from a farm north of the city.

Building on its success, Mr. Casimiri opened two more outlets in suburbs, both of which also did a booming business. By the late 1980s, Caz's was serving 150,000 customers a month. The sheer size of the portions — a half pound of fish and a pound of fries — was Caz's claim to fame. "That was my marketing tool."

With this rapid growth, however, Mr. Casimiri noticed that it was becoming more difficult to manage the operations in each outlet when he wasn't there. Motivation of employees was also a problem. In 1987, he started franchising as a means of addressing the labour problems associated with a growing business. The franchising concept brought in franchisees as partners. The outlets continued to prosper as franchisees now had a greater stake in the business.

He discovered there were investors interested in his concept, and eventually the chain grew to 10 units.

SOURCE: Adapted from John Lorinc, "Managing Partner Plan Rejigs Franchise Contract," *The Globe and Mail*, December 24, 1998, p. B1.

---

growth was so rapid that toward the end of the 1960s, several problems developed in the industry that resulted in the formation of franchisee associations and the passage of legislation to protect the rights of both franchisees and franchisors. Currently several provinces are looking at requiring greater financial disclosure by franchisors to better protect potential franchisees.[1] Alberta and Ontario have already passed such legislation.

Incident 6-3

Managing Partner Plan Rejigs Franchise Contract

Douglas Casimiri, a jaded veteran of the franchise wars, thinks he's found a way to smooth over the traditionally litigious relationship between chains and franchisees.

And he's offering up his own 25-year-old fish-and-chip chain, Caz's International Inc., as the guinea pig to test a novel partnership arrangement designed to attract new investors, reduce franchisee-franchisor conflict, and improve operations.

Beginning in January, Caz's will offer conventional franchise packages but also special deals under its "managing partner" plan.

At most chains, the acquisition of an outlet involves costs such as an up-front fee, equipment purchases, and continuing royalty payments. This typical arrangement is contractual. However, many franchisors and franchisees face difficulties when terms of the contract are not met. Under Mr. Casimiri's scheme, investors will enter into a legal partnership with Caz's, acquiring a 49-per-cent stake in a new outlet in exchange for a 55-per-cent share of its profit.

The franchise price is less expensive than the traditional franchise price, although the projected long-term returns to franchisees are comparable.

The managing partner offer provides the franchisee extra security because the chain has a direct interest in the viability of each location, while the franchisor has more say over matters such as quality control and cleanliness.

SOURCE: Adapted from John Lorinc, "Managing Partner Plan Rejigs Franchise Contract," *The Globe and Mail*, December 24, 1998, p. B1.

Within the last decade, over 40 percent of all retail sales ($432 billion) resulted from franchising in North America.[2] Estimates are that this figure may be as high as 60 percent of sales by the year 2005.[3] Franchise growth in Canada has paralleled the rapid growth in the United States, with recent estimates indicating $130 billion in sales in 2000[4] which accounts for 48 percent of total sales from more than 1,300 franchise systems and 65,000 franchised outlets.[5] This trend is shown in Figure 6-1. Studies by Price Waterhouse and Peat Marwick Thorne show that franchising is growing faster than the general economy.[6] In addition, over 100 Canadians are now franchising internationally, with the United States being the prime location.[7]

Figure 6-2 illustrates the industries in which franchising has had the most significant impact. The percentages denote industry sales as a percentage of total franchise sales. Traditional franchising includes motor vehicle, oil, and soft drink companies which sell their products through franchises.

Canadian Franchise Association
www.cfa.ca

Figure 6-1   Franchise Sales in Canada (in billions)*

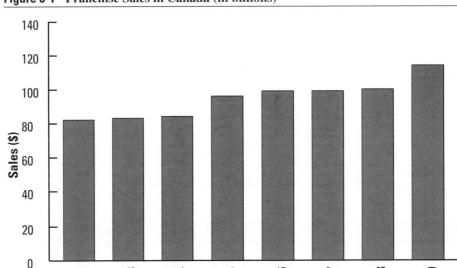

* Sales figures are estimates of the Canadian Franchise Association.

Figure 6-2   Franchising by Industry

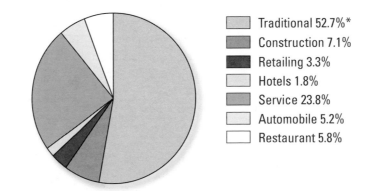

Traditional 52.7%*
Construction 7.1%
Retailing 3.3%
Hotels 1.8%
Service 23.8%
Automobile 5.2%
Restaurant 5.8%

* Includes motor vehicles, oil companies, and soft drink bottlers.

SOURCE: *Market Research Handbook* (Ottawa: Statistics Canada, 2000), p. 191.

Figure 6-3   Canada's Leading Franchising Companies

Franchise	Gross Revenue (000's)	Parent	Type of Business
Canadian Tire	$5,207,574	Billes Family	Retail hardware
Metro-Richelieu Inc.	4,657,500	Widely held	Convenience food
A&P Co.	2,937,000	A&P U.S.	Food retailer
McDonald's Restaurants	2,070,000	McDonald's Corp.	Fast food

SOURCE: Taken from the 2001 annual reports of these companies.

Franchises exist in almost all industries today. A major reason for the large recent increase in the number of franchises is expansion into the service sector, which is the fastest-growing sector in the Canadian economy. The profile at the beginning of this chapter exemplifies this trend. Figure 6-3 lists the largest franchises in Canada today.

WHAT IS FRANCHISING?

Franchising is a system for selectively distributing goods or services through outlets owned by the franchisee. A common definition for a franchise arrangement is a patent or trademark licence entitling the holder to market particular products or services under a brand or trademark according to prearranged terms or conditions. Today many applications of this definition translate into a broad range of franchising relationships. The brand identification is an important aspect of this form of distribution. It consists of standardization throughout the system. The various outlets in the system are similar as to class of trade, merchandise carried, or services rendered, and other factors that have a bearing upon joint merchandising and management through common policies. Also, all of the outlets in a franchise system are identified as members of the system. They operate under a common name and/or insignia, and the establishments often have a distinctive appearance common to all members of the system. This standardization is ensured and controlled by the terms of the franchise contract.

A franchise system is therefore a "voluntary" chain, that is, a chain of individually owned businesses. Franchising, in fact, has been the salvation of many independent wholesale and retail merchants in the face of increasing competition from corporate chains and discount operations. By joining a jobber-sponsored voluntary chain, for example, an independent retailer can get all the benefits that are available to a corporate chain store: central buying as well as assistance in merchandising, promotion, and management.

The franchising or licensing technique is more often utilized today, however, when a company comes up with an idea for a product or service and finds that it does not have adequate resources to market its own idea. By licensing prospective entrepreneurs to perform the marketing function for it, the franchising company is enabled to achieve rapid expansion at relatively low cost, a substantial part of the investment being contributed by the franchise holder. The various types of franchises are grouped into three categories.

Manufacturer-Directed Franchise. In this type of franchise, the manufacturer of a product grants a dealer the right to sell the product. This right, which tends to be geographically exclusive, often requires no initial fee. (See Figure 6-4 for further details of this type of franchising.) Manufacturer-directed franchising is common in such industries as automobile sales, gasoline distributorships, and farm implement dealerships. This type of franchising is successful only when the manufacturer has an established name, a solid reputation, and considerable consumer loyalty.

Wholesaler–Retailer-Directed Franchise. In this arrangement, one member of the distribution channel, such as the wholesaler or retailer, initiates the organization of the franchise. The primary purpose of such an organization generally is to centralize many managerial and operational functions and take advantage of volume buying for a group of sellers. As with the manufacturer-owned franchise, there is usually no initial fee, but an equity investment in the franchise may be required. Figure 6-4 illustrates some of the other operating details for this type of franchise and the industries in which it is prevalent.

Franchising Company. This type of franchise usually involves a company that sells a product or service in exchange for an initial predetermined fee and an ongoing royalty. The franchisee gains the right to sell under the franchisor's name and receives the franchisor's assistance and managerial expertise. Franchising companies are commonly found in the retail and service industries. In recent years, many companies using this method of franchising to expand their operations have experienced rapid growth. Figure 6-4 provides further details of the franchising company arrangement.

Figure 6-4   Types of Franchises

		Details of Agreement		Examples	
Title	**Method of Franchising**	**Franchisor Provides**	**Franchisee Provides**	**Industry**	**Company**
Manufacturer	Franchisee has right to sell product	Product sales support	Selling function	Automobile	Ford GMC
		Exclusive territory	Facilities	Farm machinery Oil companies	Hesston ESSO GULF
Wholesaler– retailer	Franchisee owns equity in supplier company and purchases product from the franchise	Product and other technical assistance and service	Selling function Buys equity Board of directors	Retail grocery Hardware	Associated Grocers Home Hardware
Franchising company	Franchisee buys the right to sell service and/or product	Method of operations Training Location, building, etc. Financing Proven name Advertising	Fee Royalties Compliance with conditions of contract	Fast food Auto rental	McDonald's Kentucky Fried Chicken Avis Budget Hertz

ADVANTAGES OF FRANCHISING

Compared to the other two methods of starting a small business (buying and organizing), franchising offers many specific advantages.

Proven Market for the Product or Service. Except for newly established franchises, a known market for the franchisor's product or service exists. Information about the performance of existing franchises is normally supplied or can be obtained by the franchisee. Such a track record makes it much easier to make projections for future operations.

The instant pulling power of the product also greatly helps the small business owner shorten the duration of the initial stage of the business, when the market is being developed and resulting revenues are low. A study by the University of Toronto showed that franchised businesses had higher sales per outlet than independents in almost all types of businesses.[8] Another study of franchisors found that during the last recession, franchised outlets were less affected than nonfranchised outlets.[9]

Services the Franchisor May Provide. A franchising company typically provides many valuable services to a franchisee. Figure 6-5 shows the incidence of some of these services. A description of franchisor services follows.

Selection of Location. Assistance in selecting the location can be very important, especially if location is critical to the success of the business, such as in retailing and often in the service industry. Often a franchisor has considerable site selection expertise that can be used in establishing the business.

Purchase or Construction of Site, Buildings, and Equipment. The franchisor's experience and financial resources in this area may mean considerable savings of time and money. In addition to providing expertise, the franchisor may even purchase or construct the facilities for the franchisee.

The Royal Bank
www.royalbank.com

Provision of Financing. Some franchisors will provide financing for franchisees, and their association with the franchisees often helps the franchisor obtain financing. For example, the Royal Bank, through its Franchise Assistance Program, allows favourable interest rates on franchisee loans because of a franchisee's association with a well-known franchisor.

Standardized Methods of Operating. Standardized operating procedures and manuals are often part of the services the franchisor provides in the areas of cost accounting, control systems, and customer service standards. Such methods can result in considerable savings for the small business.

Advertising. Most franchisors will provide national advertising that may benefit the franchisee. Such a level of promotion may be difficult and costly for the franchisee to develop unassisted.

Figure 6-5   Characteristics of Canadian Franchise Agreements

Contract Provision	Percent Yes	Percent No
Require franchisee to be owner/operator	79	21
Offer renewal option	88	12
Provide training	94	6
Offer financing	25	75
Franchisor owns franchise property	6	94

SOURCE: *Franchising in the Canadian Economy 1990–1992* (Toronto: Canadian Franchise Association and Price Waterhouse, 1992), pp. 36–39.

Incident 6-4

Franchising Provides Many Advantages

Franchising can provide several advantages over buying or starting a business from scratch, especially for those who lack experience in the industry. Second Cup is a franchise that has very strong brand name recognition in Canada. This recognition is one of many advantages obtained when purchasing a Second Cup franchise.

Since its founding in 1975, more than 350 franchise operations have been opened across Canada. This has resulted in a positive brand image of the company. Second Cup receives over 4,000 inquiries a year for those interested in buying a franchise. Tim Sinclair, Second Cup's vice president of business development, says this affords the company the opportunity to be choosey about those who are granted a franchise. In fact, "Of those 4,000, less than 1 percent will be allowed into our system."

But positive brand recognition is not solely responsible for the success of Second Cup's franchise operations. The strength of the franchisee network is a key factor in the company's success. According to Sinclair, "Our franchisees really drive a sense of community in their cafés, and make people want to come back again."

But what other advantages does Second Cup provide for its franchisees? Each one attends a three-week mandatory coffee college that teaches new owners franchise basics including a business section that covers hiring, staffing, and managing books. Eleven territory managers also create a support network for new franchise operators and can assist in servicing the cafés as well as with the development of a business plan. This training advantage, in addition to strong brand recognition, makes Second Cup an attractive franchise for Canadian entrepreneurs.

SOURCE: Adapted from Anne Hoekstra, "Franchising: Your Ticket to Entrepreneurship," *Business Sense*, November/December 2000, pp. 32-34.

Purchasing Advantages. Because the franchising company purchases large volumes of inventories for its franchisees, it can pass the resulting cost savings on to franchisees on purchases made from the franchisor.

Training. Most franchisors provide training to new franchisees. This may take the form of an instruction manual or thorough training at a franchisor's school. A McDonalds franchisee, for example, receives training at Hamburger University in Illinois and can even receive a bachelor's degree in Hamburgerology! Because of the extra training provided, franchising (as opposed to buying or organizing) is often more suited to someone who lacks experience in the industry. Recently, knowledge-based businesses such as consulting or research have experienced rapid growth of franchising. The capital investment to get established in these businesses is typically low and flexibility is high (see Incident 6-4).

Because of the foregoing advantages, a franchisee's chance of success in the business is higher than with the other two methods of starting a small business. The franchising industry advertises a failure rate of only 4 to 8 percent, which is much lower than the rate for non-franchised businesses.[10] Some claim however, that this low failure rate is greatly exaggerated by franchising companies. In the United States and Canada an increasing number of franchisees are complaining—sometimes in court—about the problems incurred when they sign a franchise contract.

POTENTIAL DISADVANTAGES OF FRANCHISING

Because of the apparent advantages just discussed, many individuals have signed franchise contracts. However, many suffered disillusionment and failure a short while later. Evidence shows the level of franchise litigation is growing. Often franchisees misinterpret the franchise agreement concerning such things as use of advertising funds, restrictions, and services provided by the franchisor. It is critical that the prospective franchisee be aware of the difficulties that can arise when one enters the world of franchising. There are several areas of potential conflict discussed in this section. The franchisee should have a clear understanding of how disputes will be resolved in the event that they occur. Following are some of the more common dangers.

Lack of Independence. In signing a franchise contract, the franchisee can expect to receive a certain amount of assistance from the franchisor. The franchisor will monitor the business, however, to ensure that the conditions of the contract are being met. This condition restricts the franchisee's freedom and independence.

Cost of the Franchise. Most franchises have a price that often consists of an initial fee and ongoing royalties based on operations. To enter most franchise organizations, individuals will have to accumulate a certain amount of capital either to pay the fee and/or to provide the facilities and the associated set-up costs. Appendix 6A provides details on this subject, including the financial requirements of some of the better-known franchises in Canada.

Unfulfilled Promises. Most franchising companies indicate they will provide such services as training and advertising. In some cases, however, this assistance does not materialize or is inadequate. A recent study of 470 franchisees in the U.S. found considerable disillusionment with the promises made (see Figure 6-6).

Restrictions of the Contract. The franchise agreement may contain some restrictions that inhibit the franchisee's freedom. Such restrictions include the following.

Product or Service Offered. The franchisee may not be allowed to offer for sale any products not procured by the franchisor.

Line Forcing. The franchisee may be required to offer the franchisor's complete line of products for sale, even if some are not profitable in the franchisee's market area.

Figure 6-6 Franchisee Experience with Franchising

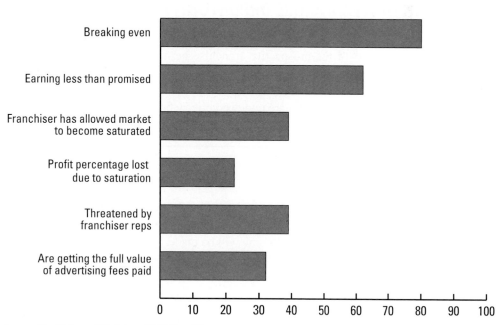

SOURCE: *The Globe and Mail*, June 12, 1995, p. B7.

Termination. The franchisee may not be able to terminate the franchise contract without incurring a penalty. The franchisee may also be prohibited from selling the business or passing it on to family members.

Saturation of the Market. In some industries, franchising companies have allowed over-saturation to occur in a particular geographic market. Saturation in established markets is a growing problem in North America. Careful examination of the franchise contract should be made to ensure that this does not occur. This puts financial pressure on those franchisees operating within that market. If a franchisor has a large initial fee and no royalties, its major concern may be the selling of franchises rather than their ongoing success. Such franchises seem particularly vulnerable to oversaturation.

Lack of Security. A franchisor may elect not to renew a franchise contract once it has expired or may terminate the contract prior to its expiry if the franchisee has violated the terms or conditions. Many franchising companies operate company-owned outlets as well as franchised outlets. The number of company-owned outlets is only about 18 percent of total franchise outlets, but recent figures show slight increases in this percentage.[11] Some argue that franchising companies take over the outlets after the franchisees have successfully established them.

Cost of Merchandise. The cost of merchandise purchased from the franchisor may exceed the price the franchisee can obtain elsewhere. However, the contract may require the franchisee to purchase solely from the franchisor.

Effectiveness of Promotion. Most franchisors provide promotion and advertising for their franchisees. In some situations, however, the promotion is not effective for the franchisee's market and may be time-consuming and costly for the franchisee to participate in. Often a franchisee does not wish to participate in these programs but is required by the contract to do so.

Exaggeration of Financial Success. Most franchising companies provide promotional literature for prospective franchisees. This information generally contains financial statements for the typical franchisee. In some cases, these estimates have been overly optimistic and the actual results for the franchisee are disappointing.

EVALUATION OF A FRANCHISE OPPORTUNITY

In view of the potential disadvantages just mentioned, it is critical that a thorough investigation of the prospective franchise be made before signing the contract. Several key areas should be examined in evaluating a franchise. Thorough investigation of the franchisor, the product or service, the franchise contract, and the market should be carried out. Sources of this information are reviewed briefly below.

Franchisor

The franchisor should provide a prospective franchisee with information in several areas (a more detailed list is found in Appendix 6C):

- A complete set of financial projections for the franchise should be provided. These should include indications of net income to be earned, when income will be made, what financial investment is required (franchise fee plus other costs), and when payments are required. The prospective franchisee should ensure that these projections are applicable to their own market area and personal situation.

- The franchisor should provide details on what financing is required and whether the franchisor provides financial assistance and at what cost.

- The proposed location should be calculated along with the number of other locations and protection against saturation of the market that will be provided.

- The extent of training, ongoing management support, and promotion that the franchisor will provide should be made available.

- The supplies purchasing arrangement, costs and level of mandatory purchasing from the franchisor should be identified.

Each of these should be analyzed carefully with professional help if necessary to ensure their accuracy.

Industry Associations

Such organizations as the Canadian Franchise Association (Toronto), the local chamber of commerce, and various other industry associations may provide valuable information about a franchisor's history, reputation, operations, size, and number of operating franchises. In addition, considerable franchise information may be obtained on the Internet. *The Franchise Handbook* may be found at http://www.franchise1.com. Information about specific franchising companies may be found by searching the Net under the company name. Appendix 6B at the conclusion of the chapter lists several agencies that can provide assistance. Some publications also offer assistance, including the *Franchise Annual*, published by the Canadian Franchise Association in St. Catharines, Ontario; the *Franchise Yearbook*, published by *Entrepreneur Magazine*; and the *Info Franchise Newsletter*, published by Info Press in St. Catharines, Ontario. In addition, regular franchise shows are held in major cities in Canada. Such events allow the prospective franchisees the opportunity to evaluate and compare several franchise opportunities in a short period of time.

Professionals

A prospective franchisee is well advised to enlist an accountant to review the financial side of the franchise to ensure that the information provided is accurate. Often financial statements do not conform to Generally Accepted Accounting Principles (GAAP) or are unrealistic.

A lawyer's expertise should also be used in reviewing the terms and conditions of the contract. Because the franchising industry is becoming so specialized, it may be worthwhile to enlist a lawyer who is knowledgeable about franchising issues. The franchisee should ensure that his or her rights are protected and that there is a clear understanding of both franchisee and franchisor responsibilities regarding the following items:

- Initial fee—how much and when paid?

- Royalties—how much and when paid?

- Additional costs for training and management assistance

- The total investment required and how the balance will be financed

- Assistance offered by franchisor

- Product pricing fees

- Termination conditions—are they specific and realistic?

- Advertising provided

- Any merchandise requirements and/or restrictions

- Liability insurance—who carries it and what is covered?

- Geographic territory—what is the geographic territory of the franchise, and is it exclusive?

In addition, lending institutions and other business organizations may be aware of attractive franchise opportunities.

Other Franchisees

One of the most valuable sources of information for the prospective franchisee is communication with other franchisees from the same organization. Because the largest incidence of fraud in franchising today is due to misrepresentation made by the franchisors, interviewing current franchisees can be helpful. Has the franchisee been happy in his or her association with the franchisor? Other specific questions to ask a franchisee are as follows:

- When was the franchise purchased?

- Why was this one selected?

- Have the franchisor's promises been fulfilled?

- What problems have developed?

- How have they been resolved?

Government Agencies

The Consumer and Corporate Affairs departments or their equivalents at the federal and provincial levels of government may also provide information about the practices of franchisors. In addition, the provinces of Alberta, Ontario, and Quebec require franchisors to register and provide disclosure of information that could be helpful to the franchisee in this investigation. The industry division of Statistics Canada also offers a fraud checklist for potential investors.

Additional Areas to Investigate

McDonald's
www.mcdonalds.com

Dairy Queen
www.dairyqueen.com

Checking with the above sources can provide much valuable information to aid in the franchise decision. However, some final and critical questions remain. How much drawing power does the franchise name and product or service have? Is the franchise fee worth the drawing power and services provided? The latter may not be a critical question for well-established franchises such as McDonald's or Dairy Queen, but it may be very important for a lesser-known franchise. Market research obtained through secondary sources or even collected by the prospective franchisee may provide enough information for evaluating the strength of the franchise's drawing power. Specific areas to investigate include industry trends, consumer acceptance of the concept, and franchisability of the concept.

One should also evaluate whether they have the financial capacity, the willingness to accept direction from the franchisor, and the ability to manage the business. Because most franchises involve a fixed-term contract, one should be sure that they are ready to make a long-term commitment.

Because the signing of a franchise contract is a major step for the entrepreneur, the investigation should be thorough. Appendix 6C at the end of this chapter provides a comprehensive checklist for the prospective franchisee to use in this evaluation.

THE ENTREPRENEUR AS FRANCHISOR

An increasingly popular method of entrepreneurship in franchising is not being a franchisee but selling franchises and becoming a franchisor. Incident 6-5 illustrates this type of franchising.

Before a prospective franchisor attempts to sell franchises, several requirements must be met. Is the type of business franchisable? What information is required? How much capital is needed? All of these questions should be addressed in the process of becoming a franchisor.

What Businesses Can Be Franchised?

Treats
www.treats.com

Franchises abound in many industries today. This phenomenon is reflected in the following statement by the U.S. Commerce Department: "Any business that can be taught to someone is being franchised."[12] The franchise business must have a sound concept. The franchise should be distinct, be practical, and fill a need. It must also be easy to teach and clearly communicate to others. It must be capable of being replicated and transferred to other geographical areas. Suzy Okun, a co-founder of the franchise Treats, which specializes in desserts, elaborates on this idea: "We sell a concept. We take what the palate already knows, and we make it electric! We take what the customer has already seen and do it differently."[13] Consumer research may be required to solidify the concept. Estimates based on sound research will be much more attractive to the prospective franchisee.

Incident 6-5

Death by Chocolate Franchise Ltd.

Death by Chocolate
www.
deathbychocolate.ca

Latin Lover, Height of Passion, and Crumble in My Arms are just a few of the extraordinary desserts being served up by Death by Chocolate Franchise Ltd. President Shakil Adam along with two partners, a Vancouver optometrist and a Toronto radiologist, launched the first Vancouver franchise in 1996 after obtaining rights from New Zealand-based, Milloy Reid and Wong Co. Ltd.

The three partners were looking to purchase a hospitality business, and the New Zealand firm just happened to be looking for a Canadian Franchisee. "When we saw Death by Chocolate, it looked unique," Adam says. "We didn't want to look at just a coffee bar, or a bagel or a muffin place." Deliciously unique is certainly what the three partners found in this scrumptious franchise. Soon after the successful establishment of Death by Chocolate in British Columbia, the partners purchased exclusive Canada-wide rights to the company. The company has eight stores in Vancouver, one in Toronto and plans to open more in Edmonton, Kelowna, and Victoria. The new Toronto location is corporate owned as Adam continues to "tweak the new concept as he goes along." Of the nine dessert outlets, seven are franchises. Typically, franchisees invest $300,000 and annual sales average about $550,000.

The focus on sweet treats and specialty coffee puts Death by Chocolate in direct competition with mom-and-pop pastry shops and chains such as Second Cup Ltd. and Starbucks Corp. However, Adams believes the unique deserts and continually revamped ice cream-based treats provide something special and fresh to his customers. The success of Death by Chocolate will ultimately depend upon the quality of franchise operators it attracts. As Roger Dent, an analyst of Second Cup Ltd., says, "With any of these things, if you get the right franchisee, it's fabulous. And if you get the wrong people, it's a disaster."

SOURCE: Adapted from Wendy Stueck, "Franchise Peddles Sweet Dreams," *The Globe and Mail*, February 11, 2000, p. M-1.

How Does One Become a Franchisor?

Once the prospective franchisor is satisfied that the business is franchisable, he or she must take several steps to develop the franchise. Some of the most important steps are the following.

1. Establish a Prototype. The franchisor should set up and operate a prototype business long enough to iron out the bugs and get a clear picture of market demand. This business can also serve as a reference point for prospective franchisees to use in their evaluations. To be useful, the prototype should be earning a consistent profit.

2. Prepare the Necessary Information. Information prospective franchisees will require includes promotional literature regarding the franchise and detailed financial data not only for the company but for a typical franchise. A prospective franchisee requires information on capital needed, potential income, cash flow projections, and future trends in the industry to make an informed decision. It is recommended that someone with accounting expertise be retained to assist in preparing this information.

3. Investigate the Legal Requirements. The franchisor should investigate the legal requirements in setting up a franchising company. Some of these requirements might be:

- Registration and disclosure with government agencies. As mentioned earlier, some provinces require detailed information before franchising can begin.

- The required business licences and incorporations.

- Other laws regulating the operations of franchises.

In addition, the franchise contract should be drawn up by someone with legal expertise to ensure that the rights of both parties are protected. The legal operations of the franchise and the responsibilities of both franchisor and franchisee are formalized in the franchise contract. The franchisor needs to decide which services and what assistance to provide, what restrictions to impose, and what to require from the franchisee in return. A more detailed listing of typical contract provisions appears in Appendix 6D.

Molly Maid International Inc.
www.mollymaid.com

4. Develop a Planned and Standardized Program of Operations. Standardization of procedures is an essential part of a successful franchise and enables the franchisor to monitor operations more easily. The following quote about Molly Maid, the business profiled at the beginning of the chapter, illustrates the effective use of professionals in the development of the franchise system:

> *MacKenzie made full use of experts in setting up his company. He used two well-known accounting firms, one to develop an internal accounting system, and the second to construct a package for franchisees. A legal expert on franchising developed the franchise agreement, and a firm specializing in trademarks and patents set up the rules for use of the logo.*[14]

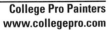

College Pro Painters
www.collegepro.com

The operations manual is generally developed using the experience of the prototype business. As mentioned above, the methods or "system" used are typically the "service" that is franchised. The franchisor must ensure that the operations manual is understandable and easy to integrate into franchisee operations. The following quote about College Pro Painters shows the time and care taken in preparing the operations manual:

After graduation in 1974, he took a year off to travel around the world, and started to put together a manual for the operation of College Pro Painters. Drawing on the knowledge he had acquired at school, he developed a chronology for starting a business and systematically attached every topic from "Business Plan" to "Close Down" in what would become his corporate bible.[15]

5. Obtain Adequate Financing. To franchise successfully, the franchisor will need capital to set up the prototype business, do the necessary market research, prepare the promotional literature and financial estimates, and develop the system of operations. A rapid expansion program may even require outside equity financing from a venture capital company or other financial institution.

FRANCHISING IN THE FUTURE

Franchising is expected to continue its rapid growth as new types of businesses incorporate franchising principles into their operations. Several trends are expected to surface in the future. The retail food industry, the largest sector of Canadian franchising, is expected to continue its growth, but in more specialized areas such as ethnic foods. This growth will provide numerous opportunities for entrepreneurs but it also means greater competition for existing small businesses in certain industries. As mentioned previously, more and more service businesses are expected to become franchises. A high percentage of Canada's fastest growing franchises are in the service industry.

McDonald's
www.mcdonalds.com

Wal-Mart
www.wal-mart.com

Some franchises are experimenting with "piggybacking," in which two or more franchises operate in one outlet. This concept has been tried with gas stations/convenience stores and restaurants/video stores. The practice of converting existing chain outlets to franchises, or "branchising" is expected to continue as chains search for new sources of interest-free capital. Additional growth areas in franchising are "mini-franchises" which are small satellite versions of larger franchisees (McDonald's in Wal-Mart) and mobile franchises that move from location to location on a seasonal basis.

Recent trends show a more sophisticated group of franchisees participating in the industry. These individuals tend to have higher educational qualifications and more business management experience. This trend is not only leading to higher success rates for franchises but also the creation of more organizations to protect franchisee rights. Other dominant franchising trends include the growth of service-based and home-based franchises.

Summary

1. Franchising has enjoyed phenomenal growth in recent years. One reason franchising is popular is the increased incentives for franchisees. Franchising continues to allow many organizations with a proven concept or product to expand much more rapidly to meet demand.

2. The three types of franchises are (a) the manufacturer-directed franchise, in which the manufacturer of a product grants a dealer the right to sell the product; (b) the wholesaler–retailer-directed franchise, in which one member of the distribution channel, such as the wholesaler or retailer, initiates the organization of the franchise; and (c) the franchise company, in which a company sells a product, service, or system in exchange for an initial predetermined fee and an ongoing royalty.

3. Franchising offers the following advantages over the other two methods of starting a small business: a proven market, services such as selection of location, purchase or construction of

the site, financing, standardized methods of operating, advertising, volume purchasing, and training. The potential disadvantages of franchising are lack of independence, cost of the franchise, unfulfilled promises, restrictions of the contract, saturation of the market, lack of security, cost of merchandise, and possible exaggeration of financial success.

4. Several key areas should be examined in evaluating a franchise. Information can be obtained from several sources including the franchising company, the Association of Canadian Franchisors, professionals such as lawyers and accountants, other franchisees, and government agencies.

5. Becoming a successful franchisor entails five steps. The first step is to develop a franchise prototype to iron out any difficulties. The second is to prepare the necessary information for the prospective franchisee. The third is to investigate the legal requirements in setting up a franchise company. The fourth is to plan and standardize the program of operation to facilitate the monitoring of operations. The last step is to ensure that adequate financing is available to keep up with possible rapid expansion.

Chapter Problems and Applications

1. Contact a franchisor and obtain information about becoming a franchisee. Using the procedures discussed in this chapter, evaluate the attractiveness of this opportunity.

2. What possible benefits does Death by Chocolate Ltd. realize in franchising its businesses instead of expanding through company-owned outlets?

3. Discuss in detail the steps you would follow in developing a maid cleaning franchise system.

4. Visit a local franchise in your city and ask the manager what he or she thinks are the advantages and disadvantages of franchising.

5. Using the same franchise as in question 4, gather information from government agencies and other sources about that franchise. From your collected information and the results of question 4, would you invest in a franchise of this company? Justify your answer.

Appendix 6A

A Sampling of Franchises Operating in Canada

Franchisor	Total Locations	Initial Fee	Total Investment	Total Royalty
Arbys	116	$42,500	$400,000	4%
Chem-Dry Carpet and Upholstery Cleaning	140	$15,950	$32,950	$285/month
Cullingan of Canada Ltd.	59	$1,000–$20,000	$75,000–$100,000	5%–10%
Dairy Queen of Canada Inc.	504	$35,000	$450,000–1,200,000	4%
Japan Camera	150	$20,000	40% of purchase price	7%
Kernals Popcorn	63	$25,000	$110,000–$125,000	9%
Kwik Copy	76	$25,000	$200,000	9%
Mail Boxes Etc.	211	$29,950	$120,000	6%
McDonalds Restaurants	1,062	$45,000	$600,000–$800,000	17%
Minute Muffler	126	$5,000–$25,000	$120,000–$150,000	4%

Franchisor	Total Locations	Initial Fee	Total Investment	Total Royalty
Molly Maid	160	$14,000	$14,000	6%
Mr. Lube	84	$50,000	$200,000	7%
Nutri-Lawn International	38	$15,000	$45,000	6%
Orange Julius Canada Ltd.	106	$20,000	$150,000–$200,000	6%
Pet Land	17	$25,000	$150,000–$250,000	4.5%
Sports Experts	280	$30,000	$300,000–$400,000	4.5%
Subway		$10,000	$150,000	10.5%
The Great Canadian Bagel	166	$30,000	$260,000–$300,000	6%
Thrifty Car Rental System	157	$8,000–$150,000	$80,000–$250,000	8%
Tim Hortons	1525	$50,000	$275,000–$360,000	3%

SOURCE: *1999 Franchise Annual*

Appendix 6B

Trade Associations and Government Departments That Assist Franchisors and Franchisees

Business Development Bank of Canada
http://strategis.ic.gc.ca

Canadian Franchise Association
5045 Orbitor Drive
Building 9, Unit 401
Mississauga, ON L4W 4Y4

Canadian Franchise Fact Sheet
http://www.francom.com/canadian_facts.htm

Franchise Handbook Online
http://www.franchise1.com

International Franchise Association (IFA)
1350 New York Avenue
#900 Washington, DC 20005

International Franchise Opportunities
11 Bond Street
St. Catharines, ON L2R 4Z4

Retail Council of Canada
Franchise Division
214 King Street West, Suite 212
Toronto, ON M5H 1K4

Ontario Ministry of Consumer and Commercial Relations
Investigation and Enforcement Branch
555 Yonge Street
Toronto, ON M7A 2H6

Appendix 6C

A Checklist for the Potential Franchisee: Questions to Answer Affirmatively before Going into Franchising

The Franchisor

1. Has the franchisor been in business long enough (five years or more) to have established a good reputation?

2. Have you checked better business bureaus, chambers of commerce, government agencies, Association of Canadian Franchisors, industry associations, or bankers to find out about the franchisor's business reputation and credit rating?

3. Did the above investigations reveal that the franchisor has a good reputation and credit rating?

4. Does the franchising firm appear to be financed adequately so that it can carry out its stated plan of financial assistance and expansion?

5. Have you found out how many franchisees are now operating?

6. Have you found out the "mortality" or failure rate among franchisees?

7. Is the failure rate low?

8. Have you checked with some franchisees and found that the franchisor has a reputation for honesty and fair dealings among current franchisees?

9. Has the franchisor shown you certified figures indicating exact net profits of one or more going operations that you have checked yourself?

10. Has the franchisor given you a specimen contract to study with the advice of your legal counsel?

11. Will the franchisor assist you with
    a. a management training program?
    b. an employee training program?
    c. a public relations program?
    d. obtaining capital?
    e. good credit terms?
    f. merchandising ideas?
    g. designing store layout and displays?
    h. inventory control methods?
    i. analyzing financial statements?

12. Does the franchisor provide continuing assistance for franchisees through supervisors who visit regularly?

13. Does the franchising firm have experienced and highly trained management?

14. Will the franchisor assist you in finding a good location for your business?

15. Has the franchising company investigated you carefully enough to assure itself that you can successfully operate one of its franchises at a profit both to it and to you?

16. Have you determined exactly what the franchisor can do for you that you cannot do for yourself?

The Product or Service

17. Has the product or service been on the market long enough to gain broad consumer acceptance?

18. Is it priced competitively?

19. Is it the type of item or service the same consumer customarily buys more than once?

20. Is it an all-year seller in contrast to a seasonal one?

21. Is it a staple item in contrast to a fad?

22. Does it sell well elsewhere?

23. Would you buy it on its own merits?

24. Will it be in greater demand five years from now?

25. If it is a product rather than a service,
    a. is it packaged attractively?
    b. does it stand up well to use?
    c. is it easy and safe to use?
    d. is it patented?
    e. does it comply with all applicable laws?
    f. is it manufactured under certain quality standards?
    g. do these standards compare favourably with similar products on the market?
    h. if the product must be purchased exclusively from the franchisor or a designated supplier, are the prices for you, as the franchisee, competitive?

The Franchise Contract

26. Does the franchisee fee seem reasonable?

27. Do continuing royalties or percent of sales payment appear reasonable?

28. Is the total cash investment required and the items for financing the balance satisfactory?

29. Does the cash investment include payment for fixtures and equipment?

30. If you will be required to participate in company-sponsored promotion and publicity by contributing to an advertising fund, will you have the right to veto any increase in contributions to the fund?

31. If the parent company's product or service is protected by patent or liability insurance, is the same protection extended to you?

32. Are you free to buy the amount of merchandise you believe you need rather than required to purchase a certain amount?

33. Can you, as the franchisee, return merchandise for credit?

34. Can you engage in other business activities?

35. If there is an annual sales quota, can you retain your franchise if it is not met?

36. Does the contract give you an exclusive territory for the length of the franchise?

37. Is your territory protected?

38. Is the franchise agreement renewable?

39. Can you terminate your agreement if you are not happy for some reason?

40. Is the franchisor prohibited from selling the franchise out from under you?

41. Can you sell the business to whomever you please?

42. If you sell your franchise, will you be compensated for the goodwill you have built into the business?

43. Does the contract obligate the franchisor to give you continuing assistance after you are operating the business?

44. Are you permitted a choice in determining whether you will sell any new product or service introduced by the franchisor after you have opened your business?

45. Is there anything with respect to the franchise or its operations that would make you ineligible for special financial assistance or other benefits accorded to small business concerns by federal, provincial, or local governments?

46. Did your lawyer approve the franchise contract after studying it paragraph by paragraph?

47. Is the contract free and clear of requirements that would call on you to take any steps that your lawyer thinks are unwise or illegal in your province, county, or city?

48. Does the contract cover all aspects of your agreement with the franchisor?

49. Does it really benefit both of you and the franchisor?

Your Market

50. Are the territorial boundaries of your market completely, accurately, and understandably defined?

51. Have you made any study to determine whether the product or service you propose to sell has a market in your territory at the prices you will have to charge?

52. Does the territory provide adequate sales potential?

53. Will the population in your territory increase over the next five years?

54. Will the average per capita income in your territory remain the same or increase over the next five years?

55. Is the existing competition in your territory for the product or service not too well entrenched?

56. Are you prepared to give up some independence of action to secure the advantages offered by the franchise?

57. Are you capable of accepting supervision, even though you will presumably be your own boss?

58. Are you prepared to accept rules and regulations with which you may not agree?

59. Can you afford the period of training involved?

60. Are you ready to spend much or all of the remainder of your business life with this franchisor, offering this product or service to the public?

Appendix 6D

Franchise Contract Clauses

The following are individual clauses commonly found in franchise agreements. The clauses are listed in the order in which they are most frequently found in a franchise agreement.

1.	Term and Renewal	13.	Franchisor—Right to Inspect
2.	Site Selection	14.	Standard of Cleanliness
3.	Franchisor Approval of Lease	15.	Standard of Operations
4.	Exclusive Territory	16.	Franchisor—Right to Audit
5.	Trademark Restriction	17.	Noncompetition
6.	Training by Franchisor	18.	Confidential Information
7.	Franchisor Help with Operating	19.	Permitted Incorporation
8.	Operating Manual	20.	Termination by Franchisor
9.	Advertising by Franchisor	21.	Termination by Franchisee
10.	Advertising by Franchisee	22.	Right of First Refusal
11.	Advertising, Control of	23.	Sale Approval by Franchisor
12.	Royalty	24.	Sale of Equipment to Franchisor

Suggested Readings

Buying A Franchise — Doing It Right. Royal Bank of Canada, 1990.

Canadian Franchise Directory (annually).
www.cgb.ca/directory/html

Canadian Franchise Handbook
www.cgb.ca/handbook/html

Franchise Annual. St. Catharines, Ontario: Canadian Franchise Association, yearly. (905) 688-2665.

Franchise Canada (bi-monthly).
www.cfa.ca

Franchise Directory. *Entrepreneur* (annually).

Franchise Financing. Toronto: Canadian Imperial Bank of Commerce.

Franchise in Canada. Industry Canada (613) 941-1240.

Franchising in the Canadian Economy, 1990–1992. Toronto: Canadian Franchise Association and Price Waterhouse, 1992.

Opportunity Canada: Franchise and Dealership Guide (905) 277-5600.

Serwer, Andrew. "Trouble in Franchise Nation." *Fortune Magazine*, March 1995, p. 115.

Southerst, John. "How to Succeed In Franchising." *The Globe and Mail*, June 14, 1996, p. B 3.

Zaid, Frank, and Jerry White. *The Canadian Franchise Guide*. Toronto: Richard De Boo Publishers, 1986.

Comprehensive Case
The Framemakers: Part 3

Robert and Teresa Norman immediately went to work organizing their new business. They had contemplated signing a franchise contract with U-Frame-It, but decided against it when they found out they would have to pay a $20,000 franchise fee and royalties of 10 percent of sales just for the name and set-up assistance. In addition, the franchisor required that the stores follow a set format and that all supplies had to be purchased from them.

Robert's college training had taught him the importance of drawing up a business plan, so they prepared the following outline for their business:

- *Target market.* Robert and Teresa thought the new store should cater to the price-conscious individual who wanted to save a few dollars by doing his or her own framing. What they had learned about the do-it-yourself market seemed particularly suitable for the new business. They judged that the target market was between the ages of 35 and 60 and could spend up to an hour in the store. This was based on their observations of the other framing store in Brandon.

- *Financial.* Based on data from the U-Frame-It franchise, Robert estimated start-up costs to be about $100,000. Since they were planning to lease space for the store, the capital requirements included only the purchase of shelves, fixtures, initial inventory, and tools. Because he and Teresa had $25,000 in equity to put into the venture, they expected to be able to borrow the remaining $75,000 from a local bank.

- *Personnel.* Robert and Teresa were hesitant to hire any employees until they were sure the business would be successful. In addition, they wanted to be totally involved in the business to better learn about all aspects of framing. The two would work full time, each doing whatever needed to be done.

- *Regulations.* They knew The Framemakers would need a business licence, which they would obtain from the city hall. They would operate the business as a proprietorship until the need to incorporate became evident.

- *Layout.* After looking at the U-Frame-It shop in Winnipeg, Robert drew up an interior layout plan he believed allowed efficiency and convenience for the store.

- *Location.* Although there weren't many available locations in Brandon, Robert and Teresa recognized the need to locate in a high-traffic area of the city. This would not only be convenient for regular customers but hopefully would attract some walk-in customers as well.

After developing this business plan, Robert and Teresa began making contacts to get the business going. Within the next month, they were busy negotiating with suppliers, landlords, his banker, and the city hall to get the business started as soon as possible.

One particularly troublesome decision was the location. Brandon had three available locations, all in high-traffic areas of the city. The first was an older downtown outlet leasing for $500 per month; the second was space along a major artery into Brandon that rented for $600 per month; the third was in a small mall on the south side of the city and cost $550 per month. Although Robert and Teresa were partial to the mall location because it was closer to their home south of Brandon, they chose the space on the major artery on the advice of a friend who operated a business in the city. He had indicated that the most expensive space was usually the best because of the level of customer traffic.

Questions

1. From the information provided, evaluate the business plan Robert and Teresa have prepared for their new business.
2. Weigh the relevant pros and cons for the Normans of operating a U-Frame-It franchise instead of starting their business from scratch.
3. What are the factors that Robert and Teresa should have considered in selecting the location for The Framemakers? Did they make the right choice?

Video Case Questions
Reading the Fine Print*

CBC ◉

It's August, 1999, and Paul Dahlin is not happy to be moving out of his Second Cup coffee shop. He paid $150,000 for the franchise three years ago, after being downsized out of his position with a large corporation. The thought of running a neighbourhood coffee shop with a sure-thing national chain seemed worth the price.

1. Briefly discuss the advantages and disadvantages of franchising which are identified in this example.
2. What could prospective franchisees do to reduce the risks of the problem identified in this example?
2. What sources of assistance are available for franchisors in Canada?

*SOURCE: CBC *Venture* #750, running time 8:52.

Chapter 7

Financing the Small Business

Chapter 7

Chapter Objectives

- To discuss financing problems experienced by small businesses.

- To identify the types of start-up capital the entrepreneur may require.

- To illustrate a method for determining the amount of capital required.

- To identify the sources of equity and debt funds available to start and operate a small business.

- To explain the considerations in obtaining equity or debt financing.

- To discuss how to prepare a proposal to obtain financing for the small business.

Small Business Profile

Ron Paley
OMT Technologies Inc.

OMT Technologies Inc.
www.omt.net

OMT Technologies Inc. (OMT) is a Canadian company established in Manitoba in 1970 to service a market niche in the professional audio and recording industry. In 1972 the Company was federally incorporated to accommodate a growing geographic market for its professional and broadcast audio products and services.

During the first decade, very few changes were made to the analogue audio product lines that OMT distributed to broadcasters. In the early 1980s, the advantages of computers and software applications became evident as the company began to digitize its own accounting, inventory, and desktop publishing functions. OMT secured the Canadian distribution rights to the products of Median Touch Systems Inc., a U.S.-based digital audio storage solution provider that integrated networks, computers, and software for radio broadcasting.

At the end of the last decade, economic downturns saw radio broadcaster's advertising revenues shrink, especially those stations located in small to mid markets. The radio industry turned to digital automation systems such as MEDIATOUCH to provide a high level of efficiency, mission critical reliability, and improved programming quality. Within four years, OMT had marketed MEDIATOUCH in Canada to a 20 percent market share.

A deregulated American broadcast market offered tremendous opportunities for expansion of the company using its Canadian expertise in the integration of the MEDIATOUCH software product. In 1995, thanks to a Western Economic Diversification loan and two Business Development Bank of Canada venture loans, the company bought exclusive worldwide rights to sell MEDIATOUCH software. "Venture loans left room for many options," says president, Ron Paley. "We didn't dilute ownership and now have the opportunity to attract very good strategic alliances with other companies through the exchange of shares."

Through a strategy of technological leadership and innovative development by its management team of Paley, his brother Ted Paley, and Scott Farr, the company has diversified MEDIATOUCH into other parallel markets that offer tremendous opportunities for continued growth and expansion. In 2001 OMT received recognition for another new product. This product, Media Ads Cast, is an online streaming content stabilization system for broadcasters.

SMALL BUSINESS FINANCING

The inability to obtain adequate funding has often been cited as a major small business frustration, if not a primary cause of some small business failures. Incident 7-1 illustrates that cash is a common problem in establishing a software business. The entrepreneur may require financing not only to start the business but also to provide capital to fund ongoing operations. Figure 7-1 shows some of the uses of financing for already established businesses.

One dilemma the entrepreneur often faces is that as the business grows, funds are needed for expansion. As the profile at the beginning of the chapter illustrates, franchising is one answer to this financing question.

Incident 7-1

IKE Inc.

Derek Patriquin and David Roach, founders of IKE (the acronym for Interactive Knowledge-based Enterprises or "I Know Everything") describe their five years as software entrepreneurs as a "trip through hell." Yet, with three products under their belt, they are among the only 10 percent of software firms that survived to market their first product. Three problems overwhelm most software start-up companies: cash, a saturated industry dominated by big-name players, and a product instead of a market focus. IKE still relies on "love money," cash raised from family and friends, to fund its business. And substantial funding is necessary. One industry analyst stresses that without a budget of at least a million dollars, most firms don't have a chance. Such a large budget is essential because Canadian firms must gain acceptance in both the U.S. and Canadian markets.

SOURCE: Joanna Pachner, "We've Been Through Hell," *The Financial Post Magazine*, October 1997, pp. 50–57.

Figure 7-1   Reasons for Financing of Ongoing Operations

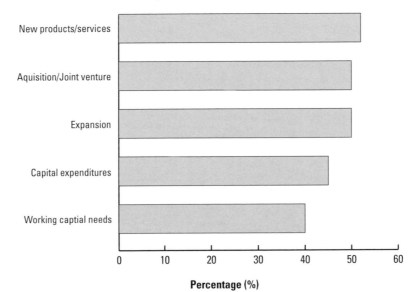

SOURCE: *First Annual Survey of Canadian Entrepreneurs*, Ernst and Young, 1994.

Although many small businesses have experienced difficulties due to their inability to obtain needed funds, statistics show that financing woes are often a symptom of other management problems.[1] Lack of managerial competence and experience can often result in the following specific financial problems:

- Underestimating financial requirements. See Figure 7-2 for an illustration of the significance of this factor in business bankruptcies.

- Lack of knowledge of sources of equity and debt capital, leading to either an inability to obtain funds or the failure to obtain them at the lowest cost

- Lack of skills in preparing and presenting a proposal for financing to a lender or investor

- Failure to plan in advance for future needs, resulting in last-minute financial crises

- Poor financial control of operations, leading to failure in payment of loan obligations

This chapter discusses each of these important areas to assist the entrepreneur in obtaining financing for establishing his or her business. Most of the information in this chapter is also applicable for the purchase of a business or for signing a franchise contract.

Figure 7-2   Financial Management Problems Contributing to Bankruptcy

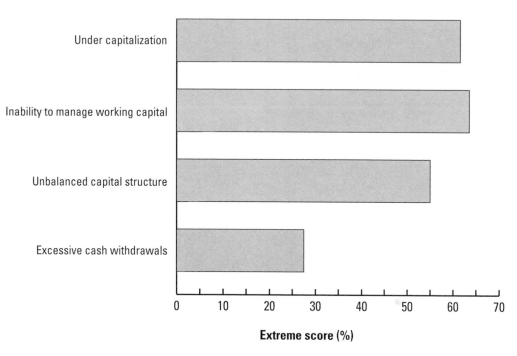

SOURCE: *Failing Concerns: Business Bankruptcy in Canada* (Ottawa: Statistics Canada, November 1997), p. 26.

DETERMINING THE AMOUNT OF FUNDS NEEDED

The first step in securing capital (funds) for the business is to determine the amount of money needed. Any lender or investor will want to see evidence of a systematic and thoroughly prepared statement of fund requirements. In this regard, it is helpful to divide required funding into two categories: start-up costs and ongoing operating requirements. The entrepreneur's own funds available for the venture can then be subtracted from the projected required amounts to obtain the capital needed from outside sources, as shown in the following formula:

$$\text{Capital requirements} = \text{Start-up costs} + \text{Operating requirements} - \text{Owner assets available for investment}$$

Start-Up Costs

Industry Canada
www.strategis.ic.gc.
ca/sc_x/engdoc/
financing.html?guides
=e_fin

Capital will be required to finance land, buildings, equipment, and other items needed to start up the business. Figure 7-3 illustrates an example of a start-up schedule for a small retail store. Note the source provided for each number in the schedule. The owner should obtain and verify quotes from sellers of these assets with owners of existing similar businesses.

Figure 7-3   Start-Up Cost Schedule

Item	Cost	Source
Land and buildings	No cost—leased	If purchased, a similar business or quotes from suppliers
Equipment	$34,000	Other similar businesses or quotes from suppliers
Initial inventory	70,000	Other similar businesses or quotes from suppliers
		Use the formula Inventory = Projected sales/Inventory turnover (300,000/4.3)
Wages (first 2 months)	6,000	Other similar businesses or current wage rates
Utilities and telephone		
First deposit	100	Quotes from provider
First 2 months	680	Quotes from provider
Rent (deposit)	500	Quotes from lessor
First 2 months	3,000	Quotes from lessor
Advertising agency or media	960	Quotes from advertising agency or media
Insurance (prepaid)	975	Quotes from insurer
Licences and permits	200	Quotes from municipal agency
Other prepaids	285	Other similar businesses
Contingency	3,300	
Total start-up requirements	**$120,000**	

Add a contingency factor for potential price increases during the planning and start-up phase.

Start-up capital will also be required to finance some of the operating costs during this period. Usually a delay in sales revenues occurs for a start-up business, but many operating expenses are incurred before the business begins operating. The entrepreneur will need to make estimates of these types of expenses and should include them in the capital requirements: The length of time until operations provide sufficient cash flow to finance expenses will vary, but usually it may be between two to six months. Some of these types of expenses are:

- Initial inventory

- First few months' payroll, including owner's salary

- First few months' utilities

- First few months' rent

- Initial advertising

- Prepaid items such as utility deposits, rent deposits, and insurance

- Licences and permits

- Other operating costs to be paid before revenues are generated

Start-up costs may be difficult to project. Note the sources of information used to prepare this statement. Also note that operations of the business in the first two months should provide some cash to offset the initial start-up requirements although this has not been included in this example.

Ongoing Operating Costs

The entrepreneur should prepare a cash flow statement to calculate financial operating requirements after the start-up period. A cash flow statement, explained in more detail in Chapter 10, is simply a record of all projected cash inflows and outflows. An example of such a statement for the same business for which the start-up schedule appears is found in Figure 7-4 (on the next two pages). In this monthly cash flow for a hypothetical business, it has been calculated that up to $65,285 may be needed to finance operations. This occurs in the first month.

If debt financing were used, the entrepreneur would most likely attempt to arrange a $66,000 line of credit (operating loan), with a lender to cover this amount when required. Such a method of financing would allow the business to withdraw and deposit funds on an ongoing basis as long as the total amount withdrawn at any point in time did not exceed $66,000.

The Owner's Net Worth

After estimating start-up and operating capital requirements, the owner should prepare a personal net worth and capability statement. Preparing this statement not only will help determine the amount of the owner's funds to invest in the business but will probably be required by a lending institution if the owner needs to borrow the necessary capital. The essentials of the personal net worth statement are the same as those for a business's balance sheet. An example of a net worth statement appears in Figure 7-5 (on page 200).

Figure 7-4   Sample Cash Flow Statement

	Pre- Start up	Feb.	March	April	May	June
Opening balance	$ 0	$(69,000)	$(65,285)	$(48,595)	$(31,905)	$(55,173)
Bank loan	$ 35,000	0	0	0	0	0
Sales:						
Cash	0	12,000	12,000	12,000	13,750	13,750
Credit	0	0	12,000	12,000	12,000	13,750
Total receipts	$ 35,000	$(57,000)	$(41,285)	$(24,595)	$ (6,155)	$(27,673)
Disbursements						
Furniture and fixtures	$ 34,000	$0	$0	$0	$0	$0
Rent		1,500	1,500	1,500	1,500	1,500
Utilities		200	200	200	200	200
Promotion (2% of sales)		480	480	480	550	550
Telephone		140	140	140	140	140
Wages and salaries		3,000	3,000	3,000	3,000	3,000
Inventory	70,000	0	0	0	41,820	0
Maintenance and repairs		240	240	240	270	270
Professional fees		330	330	330	330	330
Insurance		975	0	0	0	0
Interest and bank charges		1,420	1,420	1,420	1,208	1,208
Loan repayment						
Total disbursements	$104,000	$8,285	$ 7,310	$ 7,310	$ 49,018	$ 7,198
Cash (+/–)	$(69,000)	$(65,285)	$(48,595)	$(31,905)	$(55,173)	$(34,871)

Note: 50% of monthly sales are cash and 50% are credit. The credit sales are collected in the next month.

DETERMINING TYPES OF FINANCING

Two general sources of funds can be used to finance a small business. The first is equity or ownership financing. The second is funds obtained from borrowing, usually referred to as debt financing (including trade credit). Many small businesses use both forms of financing to get established. A recent study of small business financing found that 90 percent obtained debt financing from a lending institution, 36 percent from personal credit cards, 18 percent from family members, 7 percent from external investors, 6 percent from retail companies, 5 percent from friends, and 5 percent from government agencies.[2] This section discusses each of these types of financing.

Figure 7-4 Sample Cash Flow Statement (concluded)

July	Aug.	Sept.	Oct.	Nov.	Dec.	Jan.
$(34,871)	$(14,569)	$(36,839)	$(17,289)	$2,261	$(19,811)	$ 1,967
0	0	0	0	0	0	0
13,750	13,750	13,750		13,750	14,250	14,250
13,750	13,750	13,750	13,750	13,750	14,250	14,250
$(7,371)	$12,931	$ (9,339)	$10,211	$30,261	$8,689	$30,467
$ 0	$ 0	$ 0	$ 0	$ 0	$ 0	$ 0
1,500	1,500	1,500	1,500	1,500	1,500	1,500
200	200	200	200	200	200	200
550	550	550	550	570	570	570
140	140	140	140	140	140	140
3,000	3,000	3,000	3,000	3,000	3,000	3,000
0	41,820	0	0	43,350	0	0
270	270	270	270	270	270	290
330	330	330	330	330	330	330
0	0	0	0	0	0	0
1,208	1,960	1,960	1,960	712	712	712
0	0	0	0	0	0	35,000
$ 7,198	$ 49,770	$ 7,950	$7,950	$ 50,072	$6,722	$ 41,742
$(14,569)	$(36,839)	$(17,289)	$2,261	$(19,811)	$1,967	$(11,275)

Equity Financing

Equity financing involves giving up ownership of the business in return for capital. The three sources of equity financing are private investors, corporate investors, and government.

Private Investors. This source includes funds from friends, relatives, or private investors in exchange for shares in an incorporated company or for a percentage of ownership in a sole proprietorship. It is especially critical from an investor's point of view that there be a clear understanding of conditions, authority, and responsibilities of all the investors under such an arrangement. The investor's degree of involvement can vary greatly. Some investors expect only a reasonable return on their investment, while others expect to be full operating partners in the business in addition to receiving a return on their capital.

Figure 7-5   Suggested Format for a Personal Net Worth Statement

Personal Net Worth Statement For:_____

As of _____, 19_____

Assets		*Liabilities*	
Cash on hand and in banks	$ _____	Accounts payable	$ _____
Savings account in banks	_____	Notes payable to banks	_____
Canada savings bonds	_____		
Accounts and notes receivable	_____	Notes payable to others	_____
Life insurance—cash surrender value only	_____		
Other stocks and bonds	_____	Installment account (auto)	_____
		Monthly payments $_____	_____
Real estate	_____	Installment accounts (other)	_____
		Monthly payments $_____	_____
Automobile—present value	_____	Loans on life insurance	_____
Other personal property	_____	Mortgages on real estate	_____
Other assets	_____	Unpaid taxes	_____
		Other liabilities	_____
		Total liabilities	_____
		Net worth	_____
Total	$ _____	Total	$ _____

An increasingly popular form of private financing is the selling of ownership interest to the employees of the business. Many companies have found that in addition to providing a source of funds, this method of financing results in dramatic increases in productivity. Incident 7-2 illustrates such a situation.

Incident 7-2

Employees Invest in Royal Group Technologies Ltd.

An increasing number of entrepreneurial companies are using employee investment as a form of financing. An example of this is found with Royal Group Technologies Ltd. (formerly known as Royal Plastics), a custom plastics extruder, which has grown to be a major high-tech supplier of building products and systems in North America.

In aggregate, over 70 percent of Royal's shares are owned by management, thereby aligning the interests of management with those of shareholders at large. This culture enables managers to work together to expand their business, thereby creating wealth for investors and themselves. Each plant manager is a company shareholder, and over 500 employees throughout the organization, including lead hands and die makers, have been awarded over 8.7 million stock options. This ownership/incentive program serves to motivate employees at all levels. Vic De Zen, Royal's Founder, President and CEO maintains a controlling interest in Royal, thereby fostering rapid decision making.

SOURCE: *Royal Plastics Group Annual Report* for year ended September 30, 2000, p. 5.

Another form of private equity investment is the sale of shares in the business to anyone who is interested. This is known as going public, wherein shares in the company are sold on a public stock exchange. This form of financing is discussed in detail in Chapter 15. Generally, small businesses are not large enough to seek public equity for the business start-up. For businesses that require smaller amounts of money, private investors (sometimes referred to as "angels") may be helpful. "Angels" are thought to invest some $1 billion per year in small businesses.[3]

Corporate Investors. Many companies are interested in investing in a small business in the hope that the value of their investment will increase over time. Often they then sell their ownership interest back to the original owners when the owners are in a better position to finance the business independently.

Companies whose major activity is investing in smaller and medium-sized businesses are called *venture capital companies.* These companies use highly sophisticated evaluation techniques and accept only a small percentage of applications.[4] A venture capital company typically looks for a business within a growth industry, with sound management and the potential for a return on investment of between 20 and 40 percent.

Canadian Venture Capital Association www.cvca.ca

In 2000, the 125 members of the Association of Canadian Venture Capital Companies invested some $6.3 billion in almost 1,500 small businesses in Canada, 80 percent of which were technology companies. Total venture capital investment stood at $8.4 billion in 1999.[5] The majority of the investments fell in the $1,000,000 range.[6] Incident 7-3 provides an example of how venture capital helped a Canadian entrepreneur. An entrepreneur seeking venture capital assistance should be aware of the areas of the business to which investors will pay specific attention. Normally such factors as the abilities and expertise of the management team, the level of development of the product or service, and industry trends are key elements in this evaluation.[7] Appendix 7D presents a list of some of the more active venture capital companies in Canada.

Incident 7-3

Growth and Retention

Relying on outside investors is a common source of financing for small businesses. However, one should be wary of just how much of the company outside lenders control. Investors owned so much of one entrepreneur's Markham, Ontario-based business that he was unable to stop the board from voting him out.

Michael Grenier's first venture was Star Data Systems, a supplier of on-line financial data. Most of Star Data's financing was obtained through outside sources and left Grenier holding just a fraction of his own company. In 1994, Star Data's board of directors decided to hire a more experienced CEO. Grenier could do nothing to save his position.

Grenier has since overcome the loss of his first company and has moved on to his second business venture, Starfire Technologies Inc. Through this company, Grenier launched Star Pages, a Yellow Pages-type listings for small businesses who lack either the vision or the funds necessary to produce a full Web site. Ultimately, Starfire's goal is to provide effective, feasible on-line strategies for businesses that lack the Internet "how to."

Grenier recently raised $5.5 million in venture capital for Starfire Technologies. Despite the outside injection of funds, the entrepreneur retains a healthy 56 percent of his company. Michael Grenier is living proof that one can both "grow and retain equity." It is simply a matter of ensuring that you own the greater part of your life's work!

Source: Adapted from *Profit,* April 2000, p.12.

Government. Traditionally the government has hesitated to provide equity funding to small businesses. However, programs have been developed in recent years that permit government funding and incentives for venture capital firms or allow for direct equity investment by the government in the business. Some of these programs and agencies are described next.

Business Development Bank of Canada
www.bdc.ca

Business Development Bank of Canada (BDC). The BDC will participate with other investors as a principal in the provision of investment capital in businesses it views as promising. Generally the purpose of such financing is to provide an adequate equity base for the firm to receive funding from additional sources. In July of 1995 the Government of Canada changed the name of the old Federal Business Development Bank to Business Development Bank and lifted the loan ceiling of $3.2 billion in an effort to increase service to small businesses.

Canada Development Corporation (CDC). CDC is a Crown corporation set up by the federal government to act as a venture capital company. This agency, however, provides funds primarily for larger businesses and large-scale projects.

Provincial Programs. Provincial governments have provided tax and rebate incentives for the formation of small business investment companies, which function similarly to venture capital companies. A brief listing of current provincial government equity capital programs appears in Appendix 7A at the end of this chapter.

Advantages and Disadvantages of Equity Financing. Before proceeding to obtain equity capital, the entrepreneur should be familiar with the advantages and disadvantages of equity financing versus debt financing.

Equity financing offers the following advantages:

Pan Canadian
Community Futures
Network
www.community
futures.ca

Western Economic
Diversification Canada
www.wd-gc.ca

Atlantic Canada
Opportunities Agency
www.acoa.ca

1. There is no obligation to pay dividends or interest. This flexibility allows the firm to invest earnings back into the business in its early years, when these funds are usually needed most.

2. Often the original owner benefits from the expertise the investor brings to the business in addition to the financial assistance.

3. Equity capital expands the borrowing power of the business. Most lenders require a certain percentage of equity investment by the owners before they will provide debt financing. Thus, the more equity a business has, the greater its ability to obtain debt financing.

4. Equity financing spreads the risk of failure of the business to others.

Disadvantages of equity financing include the following:

1. Equity financing dilutes the ownership interest of the original owner and leads to decreased independence. Because of this drawback, many owner-managers are hesitant to follow this route in obtaining capital.

2. With others sharing the ownership interest, the possibility of disagreement and lack of coordination in the operations of the business increases.

3. A legal cost may be associated with issuance of the ownership interest.

Debt Financing

Few small businesses are able to get established and continue operations without some sort of debt financing. About 30 percent of the money loaned to business in Canada is held by small businesses.[8] A national survey found that 85 percent of small- and medium-sized businesses used a bank for financial support, 75 percent have lines of credit, and 50 percent have loans.[9] Because of the high possibility that debt financing will be required, it is essential that the entrepreneur be aware of the advantages and dangers of using it. It is also important that he or she understand the sources of debt capital and the characteristics and requirements of various financial lenders.

Advantages and Disadvantages of Debt Financing.
Some of the positive benefits of using debt are as follows:

1. It is possible to obtain a higher return on investment by using leverage debt. If borrowed funds earn a higher return than the associated interest cost, it is possible to increase the overall return on investment for the business through debt financing. Figure 7-6 illustrates this concept. The $10,000 investment could be any productive asset or change in the business.

2. Interest costs in a business are tax-deductible expenses (assuming a profit is being made), whereas dividends paid as a result of equity ownership are not tax deductible.

3. Debt financing may allow greater flexibility in that there is no loss of ownership control.

4. Many small businesses have found it is often easier to obtain debt capital than equity capital.

Some of the potential negative aspects of debt financing are as follows:

1. Interest must be paid on borrowed money. Interest costs can be high, and high interest expenses are a common problem in many failing businesses. During the period from 1975 to 1985, interest rates in Canada were extremely high. This caused serious hardship to many

Figure 7-6   Leveraging —Using Debt Financing and Return on Investment

Basic Information

Amount to invest = $10,000

Interest rate = 8%

Investment cost = $10,000

Estimated return per year = $2,500

Calculation of percentage return after one year

1. If no debt was used:

$$\frac{\text{Return}}{\text{Investment}} = \frac{\$2,500}{\$10,000} = 25\% \text{ return}$$

2. If debt was used (assuming only $2,000 was invested, $8,000 was borrowed to purchase the investment, and the interest on $8,000 is $640):

$$\frac{\text{Return}}{\text{Investment}} = \frac{(\$2,500 - \$640)}{\$2,000} = \frac{\$1,860}{\$2,000} = 93\% \text{ return}$$

Note: The potential investment income that could be earned on the $8,000 not invested in the project could be added to this amount.

small businesses, and the inability to pay interest costs resulted in the foreclosure and/or bankruptcy of many businesses. Although interest rates are currently at low levels, the small business owner must monitor rate changes closely.

2. Debt financing creates additional paperwork requirements for the entrepreneur, and the lender may monitor the business.

3. When using debt financing, the total risk of the venture lies squarely on the owner's shoulders. There are no other partners or shareholders to assume some of this risk.

Sources of Debt Financing. Several sources of debt financing are available to small businesses, including private lenders, corporate lenders, private lending institutions, and government agencies.

Private Lenders. One increasingly common source of debt capital for small business is the borrowing of funds from the owners of the business. These funds are called shareholders' loans, and they offer some unique advantages. A study by *Venture* found that 34 percent of small business owners made a start-up loan to their own businesses.[10] While the interest paid is a tax-deductible expense for the business, the repayment terms are often flexible. In addition, lenders often view shareholders' loans as equity as long as the funds are left in the company. Some believe this method combines the advantages of equity and debt financing.

Another source of private debt is borrowing from other individuals such as friends or relatives. As with shareholders' loans, it may be possible to structure flexible repayment terms.

Corporate Lenders. In some circumstances, other companies may lend funds to a small business. Often these are larger firms that have established some connection or working relationship with the small business. One example of such funding would be the granting of trade credit by a company to a small business that purchases merchandise from that company. Most small businesses use this source of financing wherever possible. Trade credit for inventory is normally financed for 30, 60, or 90 days, with discounts for prompt payment. Equipment is usually financed for up to five years, with a 20 to 30 percent down payment required.

Another type of lender associated with accounts receivable is a factor. Factor companies purchase accounts receivable from a business at a discount. The business obtains needed cash, and the factor collects the accounts receivable. An increasing number of businesses in Canada are enlisting factoring companies to obtain short-term financing.

The sale and leaseback is another form of financing involving other businesses. In this arrangement, the business sells an asset to another company, which in turn leases it back to the seller. The advantage of the sale and leaseback is that the seller not only has the use of the funds of the sale but also benefits from the tax deductibility of the lease payments.

Canadian Youth Business Foundation www.cybf.ca

Recently a private foundation has been established in Canada to provide start-up financing and mentorship to young entrepreneurs. This organization is the Canadian Youth Business Foundation (see Appendix 7B).

Regular Private Lending Institutions. This category includes companies whose major purpose is the lending of funds. The most common of these firms are the following: (See Figure 7-7 for an indication of bank financing to small business.)

- *Trust Companies.* Trust companies are geared primarily for mortgages on long-term capital assets such as land, buildings, and equipment.

Figure 7-7   Small Business Market Share, 1989-2000

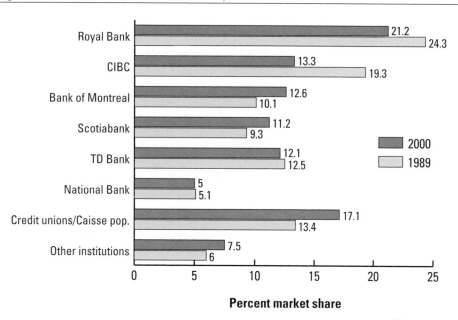

SOURCES: *Banking Survey,* CFIB, 2000, and *Our Members' Opinions Survey,* no. 24, CFIB, 1989.

**Canadian Bankers
Association**
www.cba.ca

Bank of Montreal
www.bmo.com/
business/business
.html

Royal Bank
www.royalbank.com/
sme/index.html

**Canadian Imperial
Bank of Commerce**
www.cibc.com/
english/business_
services/index.html

Scotiabank
www.scotiabank.com

TD Canada Trust
www.tdcanadatrust.
com/smallbusiness

**Business Development
Bank (BDC)**
www.bdc.ca

- *Credit Unions.* Credit unions are usually locally owned. They tend to be concerned primarily with personal loans, but in some communities they also provide significant financing to small businesses.

- *Finance Companies.* These are high-risk lenders that charge a higher rate of interest than other agencies. As with credit unions, the majority of their loans are personal loans.

- *Chartered Banks.* A major source of small business financing is Canada's chartered banks. A survey of Canadian small businesses indicated that 78 percent use bank financing.[11] At present, six major Canadian chartered banks and a multitude of foreign-controlled banks operating in Canada account for nearly 80 percent of all small business lending. Chartered bank loans to small- and medium-sized businesses in Canada in 2000 totalled $104.5 billion.[12] In many larger cities, some of these banks are even creating specialized business branches. The majority of small business loans range from $20,000 to $50,000.

An additional source of small business financing that seems to be increasing is the entrepreneur's use of their credit cards to provide temporary assistance. The Canadian Bankers Association states that 46 percent of small businesses help finance their start-up in this way.[13]

Government Lenders. Government agencies at both the federal and provincial levels lend money, provide grants, and give counselling assistance to small businesses. At the federal level, the major small business lender is the Business Development Bank (BDC) of Canada which currently has over $5 billion in loans with small business. Initially government lending agencies were established to assist those small businesses unable to obtain financing from conventional sources because of high risk. In recent years, however, they have relaxed this attitude and become more similar to other lending institutions.

The potential advantages of approaching a government agency are the following:

1. The agency may finance higher-risk or lower-equity ventures, which characterize many small businesses.

2. Government lenders may be more willing to rewrite loan terms and conditions if the business gets into trouble. They also tend to be less quick to foreclose on a failing business.

3. Government agencies may provide a lower interest rate than the chartered banks. Many provincial government lenders fall into this category. BDC rates, which are adjusted periodically, are usually similar to chartered bank rates.

4. Government lenders may provide some equity capital in the form of temporary ownership or grants, depending on the type of business and its location.

5. Government lenders may provide management counselling along with funding to assist the business.

Although the above advantages may make borrowing from government agencies attractive, there are some potential disadvantages of which the small business owner should be aware:

1. A government agency usually requires more information to review a loan application than other lending institutions do.

2. The time period required for approval of a loan tends to be a longer than with private lending institutions.

3. Most government agencies exert more monitoring and control over the businesses they lend to and often require regular reports on operations.

In addition to the government agencies established to provide both debt and equity financing, several specific federal government programs also provide financial help for the small business. Appendix 7B at the end of this chapter briefly reviews those most helpful for the small business.

Most provinces also have various programs designed to provide financial assistance to the small business community. Appendix 7C at the end of the chapter reviews some of these programs.

DETERMINING THE TERM OF FINANCING

The small business owner should carefully evaluate the characteristics of the above sources of financing to ensure their suitability to the needs of the business.

The length of term and type of financing required may assist in making the decision among lenders, as Figure 7-8 shows. This figure also illustrates the typical assets covered by the various terms of financing. The length of the term allowed by a lender is normally equivalent to the useful life of the asset, except in the case of land, which is often carried on a 20-year term.

An often costly mistake that some owner-managers make is to use funds obtained for long-term purposes to get them through short-term crises. Inevitably, this practice creates a more serious financial crisis a short while later. If capital requirements were underestimated, the owner should approach the lender again with this information and attempt to have the lender adjust the funds provided.

Figure 7-8   **Matching Financing to Assets**

Type of Loan	Sources	Use	Security	Loan Characteristics
Short-term (demand) loans	Banks, private sources, factoring houses, confirming houses	Receivables inventory (working capital items)	Assignment of receivables and inventory, personal guarantees, assignment of life insurance	Can be withdrawn on short notice; no fixed payment terms; interest, principal rates fluctuate
Medium-term (3–10 year) loans	Banks, term lenders, financial houses, leasing companies, foreign banks, private sources, and government programs	Equipment, furnishings, vehicles, leaseholds, and new business investments	Chattel mortgages, conditional sales contracts, or assignment of equipment insurance	Specific repayment terms; interest either fixed or floating with prime rate
Long-term (15–25 year) mortgages, bonds, debentures	Trust companies, foreign banks, private sources	Property, land, and buildings, new business investments	Collateral mortgages, assignment of property insurance	Fixed repayment terms; fixed interest rates

Source: Geoffrey Brooks, "Matching Your Financing to Your Assets," *Small Business Magazine*, September 1983, p. 38.

PREPARING A PROPOSAL TO OBTAIN FINANCING

Incident 7-4 describes an all too common situation for the small business. In attempting to obtain financing, a small business owner should be aware of those areas about which the lender requires information. In addition to completing the loan application, the owner should include the financial projections. A detailed and well-prepared loan proposal goes a long way toward ensuring the approval of a loan application.

Criteria Used in the Loan Decision

Most lenders make the loan decision by evaluating the following three criteria.

1. The Applicant's Management Ability. The lender will want to be sure the applicant has the skills, experience, and ability to make the business succeed. To evaluate the applicant's managerial ability, the lender will specifically want to know the following.

Incident 7-4

Reclino-Bath

Harold Taylor had a problem. He had withdrawn his total savings of $20,000 to purchase the mould required in the manufacture of a plastic bathtub accessory he had invented. To begin production, he needed additional funds but had been turned down by both chartered banks and government agencies. The lenders not only were unconvinced there was a market for the product but could see Taylor's lack of planning in estimating his financial requirements. They wanted him to prepare detailed information on what he needed and a projected statement of income based on objective research to estimate consumer demand for his product. Taylor didn't know where to turn. He lacked both the expertise to prepare the statements or do the research and the funds to hire an outside agency to do it.

SOURCE: D. W. Balderson, University of Lethbridge.

How Much the Applicant Knows about the Business. The lender will probably ask questions about the business or industry to ascertain the applicant's level of knowledge. The lender will also be interested in any previous experience the applicant has had that relates to the proposed business.

How Much Care Was Taken in Preparing the Proposal. The lender will want to see a detailed plan of what the loan is for, as well as a listing of the other sources of financing for the project. The steps of a business plan outlined in Chapter 4 should provide the basis for the financing proposal. Several statements will be required, and it is important that the applicant document the source of the information in those statements. The first statement is the lending proposal, which typically follows the format shown in Figure 7-9.

In addition to the lending proposal, the lender will probably want to see a proposed income and cash flow statement for at least the first year of operations, and probably longer. A balance sheet may also be required. These statements should be carefully prepared following the formats discussed in Chapters 3 and 10. As mentioned above, each item on the statement should be well researched and documented. The lender will want to know what provision has been made for the owner's salary and for potential contingencies. Often an entrepreneur is advised to enlist an accountant if he or she is weak in financial statement preparation. Incident 7-5 discusses advice from one entrepreneur regarding the essential aspects of the proposal.

Figure 7-9   Loan Proposal Format

Program		Financing	
Land	$20,000	Bank Loan	$60,000
Building	50,000	Own funds	20,000
Equipment	10,000	Total	$80,000

Incident 7-5

On the Road Again

As a co-founder of one-time forms-software leader Delrina Corp., Mark Skapinker knows too well the trials of the software business. But when Skapinker and friends sold Delrina for $400 million in 1995, his entrepreneurial urges hadn't been satisfied. For 18 months, Skapinker pondered electronic commerce and how virtual vendors could deliver real life customers. The result is Balisoft Technologies Inc., which develops software that allows customer-service reps and Internet shoppers to communicate on-line in real time.

Even with $500,000 of his own behind the project, the banks weren't interested in Skapinker. "Because we had no hard assets, the banks basically said, 'Sorry, we can't help you'," he says. "they take a very conservative view." But that's not such a bad thing: "It's dangerous for a high-risk [start-up] to have too much debt financing. You don't want your financing to radically affect your ability to take calculated risks."

Still, Skapinker did tap friends and family for $1.5million. "Most of the investment in that round was based on credibility from Delrina, not the business plan of Balisoft," he admits. But venture capitalists and corporate investors were sufficiently impressed to pony up $12 million last May, which funded marketing, R&D, and a staff increase from 15 to 40.

Skapinker's advice to those seeking financing? "Most investors are looking for credibility and simplicity — the more well thought out your story, the easier it is," he says. "And keep it simple. We use the 'fifth floor elevator' test: you have to explain your concept in the time it takes [an elevator] to travel that distance."

SOURCE: Adapted from *Profit*, November 1998, p 8.

2. The Proposal. Obviously the lender will assess the idea or proposal itself. Using the income statement and cash flow projections, the lender will assess the chances of repayment of the loan. The lender will evaluate not only the specific business but industrial trends, including the extent of competition and the experiences of similar businesses. The lender may also check with experts in the industry. Many chartered banks now have industry specialists on staff to assist in this type of evaluation.

Some specific types of evaluation used in the lending industry are:

- *Level of working capital*—the dollar difference between current assets and current liabilities. Working capital should be sufficient to meet current obligations as they become due and to finance delays in revenue caused by such items as accounts receivable.
- *Current ratio*—current assets compared with current liabilities. A healthy current ratio is 2:1.
- *Quick ratio*—current assets less inventories compared to liabilities. A healthy quick ratio is 1:1.
- *Debt-to-equity ratio*—percentage of owner's equity compared with debt. A minimum debt-to-equity ratio is 4:1 (25 percent equity). For smaller businesses, most lenders prefer to see 50 percent equity.

Chapter 10 discusses each of these ratios in greater detail.

The lender will also want to see projections for the basic financial statements such as the balance sheet and income statement. The fundamentals of these statements are also covered in Chapter 10.

Collateral. Because of the security position on the loan, the lender will want to know whether another lender is also providing funding for the project and, if so, what collateral it has taken as security for the loan. The lender will also want to ensure that the funds loaned will be secured by some form of saleable collateral. On capital assets, a lender generally allows only about 80 percent of the value of the assets as security. The reason is that if the lender needs to realize (repossess) on the security, obsolescence, selling, and administration costs will reduce its value.

At this point the entrepreneur may realize that he or she does not possess the required equity to secure adequate financing. In such cases an investigation of the possibility of leasing instead of buying could be made. An increasing number of businesses are leasing assets to free up capital for other purposes. A recent study carried out by Trimark Seg Fund found that over one-half (53.5 percent) of small business entrepreneurs have given personal guarantees to secure loans. Forty percent have used their homes, while 20 percent have used their savings.[14]

3. Applicant's Background and Creditworthiness. In addition to the project itself and the applicant's managerial ability, the lender will require some additional information in judging the applicant's creditworthiness.

Personal Information. In filling out a loan application, an applicant is usually required to file information typically included in a personal resume—items such as age, marital status, education, and work experience. (Be careful to check the legal implications of certain questions.)

Present Debt and Past Lending History. The lender will want a list of the current state of any loans outstanding and may require information about the applicant's past loan history as well. Most lenders are members of credit bureaus that can provide a complete credit history of the applicant. Lenders will generally use this source to verify the information provided by the applicant.

Amount of Equity the Applicant Has Invested. All lenders want to know the amount of the applicant's personal funds going into the project. Usually cash equity is required, but occasionally capital assets or even "sweat equity" may be acceptable. The amount of equity funds required will vary depending on the risk associated with the project, but as mentioned above, few lenders will provide financing if the applicant has less than 20 to 25 percent equity to invest in the business.

Will the Applicant Bank with the Lender? Many lenders will request that the applicant's business accounts be transferred or opened with the lending bank. They may also require that a compensating balance be held in the account as collateral. If the loan request is turned down, it is important that the entrepreneur find out the reasons for the refusal and make adjustments to the proposal. Alternatively, several lenders should be visited to secure the necessary funding.

Incident 7-6

Getting the Best from Your Bank

David Horowitz, president and CEO of Priva Inc., concluded that working for a bank would allow him to understand the inner operations of small business lending. After receiving his MBA from McGill University, Horowitz landed a job as a commercial account manager. This position provided the entrepreneur with the insight he needed to secure financing for his manufacturing company. Ten insider tips to establishing a healthy relationship with your banker are as follows:

1. Know what your banker is looking for. Account managers want to see comprehensive business plans as well as the management skills needed to successfully execute the plan. A detailed proposal for repayment of the bank loan will also increase your chance of loan obtainment. Be sure to include how you will use the loan, timing, source of repayment, and appropriate cash flow projections.

2. Do not "tell" your banker, "show him or her." Show your account manager your business' product and/or service.

3. Turn the tables and interview your banker. Remember you are looking for a bank that is right for you. This means being prepared to visit several banks. Some entrepreneurs have even been so bold as to ask bankers, "Why should we do business with you?"

4. When obtaining large business loans, having a partner can provide credibility to your request.

5. Be sure to exude passion when pitching your business idea to the account manager. Bankers find strong entrepreneurial passion very persuasive.

6. Ask for more money than you need, as it ensures that you will be able to deal with the growth of your small business. Having to approach your bank for a loan adjustment makes account managers concerned and reflects poorly on your ability to plan for the future.

7. Involving your banker with the business makes him or her a part of the "team." This not only establishes a positive rapport for future financing, but may also open up a huge network of valuable contacts.

8. Extend your credit when you do not need it. Sourcing funds at least 12 months before needed ensures you with adequate time to shop around for the financial institution that is right for you.

9. Introducing your accountant and lawyer to your banker lends an air of professionalism to your business.

10. If all else fails, keep looking. Most entrepreneurs do not receive financing on their first try. Be persistent, as it will no doubt pay off.

Source: Adapted from David Menzies, "Getting the Best from Your Bank," *Profit*, November 1998, p. 26-32.

Lender Relations

Once financing has been obtained, it is important that the business provide up-to-date information to the lender regarding current operations and future plans. Regular financial statements and lease contracts can help establish trust between the banker and the owner-manager. Many businesses have found that maintaining a close working relationship with lenders helps ensure adequate levels of financing in the long run. Advice about how to do this is found in Incident 7-6.

What do entrepreneurs do if they have investigated both equity and debt sources and are unable to obtain the needed capital? Probably the first thing to do is find out the reasons for refusal and possibly rework the proposal to bring it more in line with the lender's requirements.

Changes may be necessary to make the proposed business more attractive to lenders and/or investors. One option that is increasingly being used to reduce the amount of funds required for capital purchases is to consider leasing or renting the asset. Leasing the asset generally does not require a down payment. The ability to obtain the lease is usually based more on the earning power of the asset and the business than on the background of the owner. Later, when the company is in a more stable condition, the owner may succeed in obtaining funds to make a purchase if he or she desires. Specific conditions of leases are discussed in Chapter 4.

Summary

1. Lack of managerial competence and experience can often result in such financing problems as underestimating financial requirements, lack of knowledge of sources of capital, lack of skills in preparing and presenting a proposal for financing to a lender, failure to plan in advance for future needs, and poor financial control in payment of loan obligations.

2. Start-up capital includes initial inventory, deposits, and first month's payments for payroll, utilities, rent, advertising, insurance, licences, and permits. Accounts receivable and any other operating costs that need to be paid before revenues are generated should also be planned for.

3. An essential step in determining the amount of capital needed is to calculate the owner's net worth. This helps determine the amount of funds the owner(s) has to invest in the company and will probably be required by a lending institution.

4. Three general sources of equity financing are private investors, corporate investors, and government programs. Sources of debt financing include owners of the business, corporate lenders, regular lending institutions, and government agencies.

5. The advantages of equity capital over debt financing include interest obligation, expertise of the investor(s), expanded borrowing power, and spreading of risk. The disadvantages of using equity financing include dilution of ownership, increased potential of disagreements, and the cost incurred in the issuance of the ownership interest. The potential advantages of debt financing over equity capital are a possible higher return on investment, deductibility of interest, flexibility, and ease of approval. The disadvantages include interest expense, additional paperwork, and lack of diversification of risk to other investors.

6. Criteria most lenders use in making the loan decision are the applicant's managerial ability, the proposal itself, and the applicant's background and creditworthiness.

Chapter Problems and Applications

1. Indicate whether each of the following is a start-up cost (S), an ongoing operating cost (O), or both (B).

   a. $1,000 for first month's rent

   b. $25,000 for store fixtures

   c. $1,000 for third month's rent

   d. Weekly cleaning fee of $250

   e. Purchase of $50,000 of inventory

   f. Payroll expense

   g. $50,000 for TV advertising

   h. Prepaid insurance

   i. Delivery expense

   j. Operating licence

2. What other sources of financing could the owner of IKE Inc. (Incident 7-1) have used?

3. What are some potential drawbacks of the profit-sharing system as explained in Incident 7-2?

4. Imagine you are preparing a business plan for a small manufacturing firm in your province. Using Appendixes 7A and 7B, determine what programs are available for possible assistance. How could each program help your client's business?

5. a. Using Figure 7-8 as a reference, match the following list of assets to the type of financing, source, and loan characteristics needed.

   (1) Capital for building of manufacturing plant

   (2) Company car

   (3) Inventory purchase

   (4) Equipment (life expectancy two–three years)

   b. Why is it important to match financing to your assets?

6. Interview an employee at one of the government agencies that offer equity or debt financing to small businesses. Determine the purpose, the merits, and the weaknesses of that program.

7. Interview a banker to determine what he or she looks for in a loan application.

8. Using Figure 7-5, calculate your personal net worth.

9. ABC Laundry is considering the purchase of 10 new washing machines. The cost is $5,000 and current interest rates are 8 percent. Should the laundry use equity or debt financing if the expected extra income from the machines is $2,000 per year?

10. Prepare a start-up cost schedule for a new computer training/consulting operation.

Appendix 7A

Provincial Equity Capital Programs

Alberta
Small Business Equity Corporation

British Columbia
Small Business Venture Capital

Manitoba
Venture Capital Program

New Brunswick
Venture Capital Support Program

Newfoundland
Venture Capital Program

Nova Scotia
Nova Scotia Venture Corporations

Ontario
Small Business Development Corporations Program
Venture Investments Corporations

Prince Edward Island
Small Business Development Corporations
Venture Capital Program

Quebec
Societés de placement dans l'entreprise Quebecoise
Societés de developpement de l'entreprise Quebecoise

Saskatchewan
Community Bond Program
Equity financing available through SEDCO
(Saskatchewan Economic Development Corporation)
Labour-Sponsored Venture Capital Program

SOURCE: "Provincial Venture Capital Corporations: A Comparative Analysis," *Journal of Small Business and Entrepreneurship—Canada* 4, no. 5, (Fall 1986), p. 22.

Appendix 7B

Federal Government Assistance Programs for Small Business

Program	Type of Assistance	Limits	Purposes	Contact Offices
Canadian Small Business Financing Act	Provides guarantees on loans for a variety of capital purposes.	No refinancing of existing debt. Annual revenues can't exceed $2 million. Interest: prime plus 1%. Maximum 10-year repayment period.	Improve and modernize equipment and buildings; purchase land.	All approved lenders
Program for Export Market Development	Shares costs of specific export marketing efforts. Encourages and assists export.	Provides up to 50% of the costs incurred by a company in penetration of new markets. Repayable if sales are made.	Specific project bidding; market identification; participation in trade fairs abroad; bringing in foreign buyers; export consortia development; sustained export market development.	Industry Canada regional offices
Self-Employment Incentive Program	Provides temporary grants while entrepreneurs establish business.	$200 per week.	To assist with living expenses while an entrepreneur establishes a business.	Employment and Immigration Canada

Federal Government Assistance Programs for Small Business

Program	Type of Assistance	Limits	Purposes	Contact Offices
Atlantic Canada Opportunity Agency	Financial assistance for economic development and capital costs.	Varies by type of project and industry.	Improve the economic viability of businesses in Atlantic Canada and encourage entrepreneurship.	ACOA offices in Atlantic Canada
Western Economic Diversification Fund	Financial assistance through grants.	Maximum amount of assistance depends on which tier the applicant is in. Level of support depends on nature of the project, need for support, value, and government economic objectives.	Promote industrial and regional development in Western Canada.	Industry Canada regional offices
Industrial Research Assistance Program	Financial assistance through grants and technical assistance.	Varies according to which aspect of the program is applied for.	Increase the calibre and scope of industrial research and development through the use of available technology.	Industrial Research Assistance
Small Business Development Bond	Assistance through reduced interest rates on loans.	Eligible small business corporations that use all their assets in an active business. One-to-five-year loan. Specific time restrictions on past loans to qualify.	Relieve the financial burden of interest rates on the small businessperson.	All approved lenders
Technology Outreach Programs	Financial assistance.	Small businesses can access information, receive grants and loans for implementing new technology.	Promote innovation and use of new technology.	Industry Canada
Business Development Bank	Loans and equity investment.	Extend debt financing to small businesses. Can also extend venture capital to small firms wanting to expand.	Increase viability of small business.	BDC offices
Patient Capital Program	Financial assistance.	$230,000 for early-stage technology companies.	Improve chances of success of new companies.	Industry Canada
Micro Business Program	Financial assistance.	$25,000 for very small companies.	Improve chances of success of new companies.	Industry Canada
Student Business Loans Program	Training and financial assistance.	$2,500 to assist students at educational institutions to start businesses during summer months.	Help students to start businesses.	BDC

Federal Government Assistance Programs for Small Business

Program	Type of Assistance	Limits	Purposes	Contact Offices
Aboriginal Economic Economic Programs	Financial assistance.	Up to 40% equity and 75% for marketing, innovation and R&D for aboriginal businesses.	Support and encourage formation and growth of aboriginal businesses.	Aboriginal Programs, Industry Canada
Young Entrepreneur Financing Program	Financial assistance.	Up to $25,000 and 50 hours of counselling.	To help start-up entrepreneurs between the ages of 18 and 34.	Business Development Bank of Canada
Canadian Youth Business Foundation	Financial assistance and mentoring.	Up to $15,000 to candidates 18–29 unable to raise funding elsewhere.	To help youth start businesses.	Private

Appendix 7C

Provincial Government Financial Assistance Programs and Agencies for Small Business

Alberta

Alberta Opportunity Company. This is a Crown corporation that provides financial and managerial assistance. The AOC is a lender of last resort. Loans are made or guaranteed for capital assets, plant buildings, machinery and equipment, material and inventories, research and development, and general working capital.

Small Business Assistance Program. This program provides access-fixed-term loans (3 to 10 years) with fixed rates to qualifying small businesses throughout the province. Loans can be for refinancing or consolidating business debt or for improving, constructing, or acquiring capital assets. Limit $150,000.

Small Business Equity Corporation Program. Essentially this program provides a cash grant of 30 percent of the capital invested by a resident of Alberta or a refundable tax credit of 30 percent of capital invested by a corporation with a "permanent establishment in Alberta."

British Columbia

B.C. Development Corporation. The BCDC is a provincial Crown corporation set up to further economic development in British Columbia through financial, advisory, and information services. Under its low-interest loan plan, the BCDC provides funds for establishing, modernizing, or expanding manufacturing and processing industries.

Small Manufacturers Assistance Program and Assistance to Small Enterprise Program. These programs create jobs by assisting with the establishment, expansion, or modernization of small manufacturers. They also give other assistance to small enterprises in the province. These programs provide interest-free, forgivable loans to British Columbia companies that may be used for start-up, expansion, or modernization.

Manitoba

Design Assistance for Small Projects. This cost-shared program will pay up to 50 percent of design costs to improve product, graphics, and packaging to a maximum contribution of $1,000.

Venture Capital Company Program. This program aims to stimulate the flow of equity capital into Manitoba businesses by providing an investment vehicle for the private sector. The province participates jointly on a 35/65 percent basis with private investors, who must contribute $25,000 at the time the venture capital company is registered and a minimum of $65,000 within one year.

New Brunswick

Department of Commerce and Development. The Minister of Commerce and Development may provide financial assistance to aid and encourage the establishment or development of manufacturing or processing industries in the province. Assistance may take the form of a direct loan, bond guarantee, or acquisition of shares in a company.

Financial Assistance to Small Industry. This program makes interest-free, forgivable loans to new or existing industries for start-up, modernization, or expansion. Loans are calculated on the basis of approved capital costs.

Newfoundland and Labrador

The Newfoundland and Labrador Development Corporation. This Crown corporation is funded jointly by the federal and Newfoundland governments. It is mandated specifically toward small business. The NLDC offers both term loans and equity finance, but it does not guarantee loans.

Northwest Territories

Small Business Loans and Guarantees Fund. This program gives loans and guarantees to small businesses in the territory that are not eligible for the Eskimo Fund or the Indian Business Loan Fund. Funds may be used for purchase and for improvement or expansion of land, buildings, equipment, and inventory.

Nova Scotia

Industrial Estates Limited Financing Program. This program provides appropriate loan financing to new or expanding manufacturing operations. The minimum loan financing available is $250,000. Repayment is normally by way of a 20-year amortization.

Product Development Management Program. This program assists manufacturers in developing new products and upgrading the design quality of existing products. Grants under the program provide up to 75 percent of the product development costs submitted by a consultant designer. The maximum grant is $15,000 per project.

Small Business Development Corporation. This program provides loans to businesses with annual sales of less than $2 million or employing fewer than 50 people. Interest rates are fixed for the life of the loan, and repayment terms are flexible.

Ontario

New Ventures. This program offers loans to new companies to a maximum of $15,000 if approved by a participating financial institution. These loans are guaranteed by the Ontario government (Ontario Ministry of Industry, Trade and Technology) and matched by the owner's equity.

Ontario Development Corporation. This agency and its complementary development corporations within Ontario stress the importance of small business and the desirability of a private sector share in small business financing. Although commencement of repayment may be deferred, loans may be interest free or at a rate lower than the ODC's prevailing rate.

Small Business Development Corporation Program. This program acts as a private sector investment firm in which individuals and corporations are encouraged to buy equity. These firms then invest in small businesses eligible under the act. Money invested may be issued only for expansion or improvement of fixed assets, development, or start-up debt. Corporations that invest in SBDCs are granted a credit of 25 percent against Ontario corporations' income tax.

Prince Edward Island

Department of Industry and Commerce. The PEI Department of Industry and Commerce administers five general assistance programs. Those occupied with direct assistance are run jointly with DREE. Eligible recipients of these programs are manufacturers and services in the small business sector.

Quebec

Quebec Industrial Development Corporation. This Crown corporation aims at spreading economic power within the population, improving and rationalizing the business structure. Assistance may come in the form of a rebate on the company's borrowing cost, a loan at the usual market rate, a loan guarantee, or acquisition of a minority interest in a company.

Small Business Assistance Program. This program was established to assist firms that are usually profitable and well managed but face temporary working capital shortages. Financial assistance takes the form of an interest subsidy and loan guarantee.

Saskatchewan

Community Bond Program. This program provides financing for communities in the area of economic development.

Labour-Sponsored Venture Capital Program. This aims to stimulate growth of the province's small business sector. It provides provincial tax incentives to both individuals and corporations that are willing to invest in Saskatchewan small businesses.

Saskatchewan Economic Development Corporation (SEDCO). This Crown corporation is a major internal provincial government vehicle of economic development and as such deals with enterprises of all sizes and sectors. There is no upper limit on loans, and interest rates are set according to type of loan and current market conditions.

Yukon

Yukon Small Business Assistance Program. This program offers both financial and nonfinancial assistance to entrepreneurs wishing to start a new business as well as those seeking to expand an existing business. Financial assistance takes the form of loans and loan guarantees.

Appendix D

Venture Capital Firms in Canada

BG Acorn Capital Fund
Toronto
Focus: all sectors

Business Development Bank of Canada
Venture Capital Division
Several offices across Canada
Focus: small businesses

Canadian Venture Founders
Oakville, ON
Focus: environmental and high tech/information management

DGC Entertainment Ventures Corp.
Toronto
Focus: entertainment, communications, primarily Ontario-based

Fonds De Solidarite Des Travailleurs De Quebec
Montreal
Focus: all sectors, preference for small and medium-sized businesses in Quebec

Grieve Horner Brown & Asculai
Toronto
Focus: technology related to health care, information processing, communications

Helix Investments (Canada) Ltd.
Toronto
Focus: technology

Horatio Enterprise Fund L.P.
Toronto
Focus: Toronto-area telecommunications services, education

Innovatech Grand Montreal
Montreal
Focus: information technology, biotech, pharmaceuticals, telecommunications

Innovation Ontario Corp.
Toronto
Focus: all sectors; high-tech R&D ventures based in Ontario

MDS Discovery Venture Management Inc.
Vancouver
Focus: medical and biotechnology

MDS Health Ventures Inc.
Etobicoke, ON
Focus: health care and biotech

Native Venture Capital Co. Ltd.
Edmonton
Focus: Alberta ventures operated by aboriginal peoples

Novacap Investments Inc.
Montreal
Focus: medium- and high-tech manufacturing

Saskatchewan Government Growth Fund
Regina
Focus: Saskatchewan-based ventures

Soccrent
Jonquiere, PQ
Focus: aluminum, forest products

Societe En Commandite Capidem Quebec Enr.
Quebec City
Focus: manufacturing

Soquia
Quebec City
Focus: agri-food technology

Vencap Equities Alberta Ltd.
Calgary
Focus: all sectors

Ventures West Management Inc.
Vancouver
Focus: technology

Vision Capital Fund
Winnipeg
Focus: all sectors, Manitoba-based preferred

Wesport Capital Inc.
Toronto
Contact: D. T. Waite
Focus: small businesses

Working Ventures Canadian Fund
Toronto
Contact: Ron Begg
Focus: small businesses

Suggested Readings

Gray, Douglas A. *Raising Money, The Canadian Guide to Successful Business Financing*. Toronto: McGraw Hill Ryerson, 1994.

Gray, Douglas A., and Diana L. Gray. *The Complete Canadian Small Business Guide.* Toronto: McGraw-Hill Ryerson, 1994, pp. 145–63.

"Lending, A Forest of Challenges for Small Business." *The Globe and Mail,* October 26, 1998, p. C2.

Lister, Kate, and Tom Harnish. *Finding Money: The Small Business Guide to Financing.* New York: Wiley.

Small Business in Canada. Ottawa: Industry, Science and Technology Canada, 1991, pp. 57–69.

Sources of Venture Capital in Canada. Ottawa: Department of Industry, Trade and Commerce, 1997.

"The Online Definitive Guide to Small Business Financing," Royal Bank of Canada, www.royalbank.com/sme

Walton, Dawn. "Big Banks Crank Up Efforts to Win over Small Businesses." *The Globe and Mail,* September 15, 1998, p. B13.

———. "Venture Capitalists Like Mad Markets," *The Globe and Mail*, October 8, 1998, p. B14.

"Where Small Businesses Can Go to Get Financial Help." *The Globe and Mail,* October 26, 1998, p. C5.

Comprehensive Case
The Framemakers: Part 4

After selecting their location, Robert and Teresa Norman began securing merchandise for their initial inventory in earnest. They soon learned, however, that suppliers wanted to be paid before making deliveries. Therefore, Robert approached his local bank's manager to obtain the money he needed to get started. Although he had known his banker for a long time, he was surprised to find a less than positive reaction toward his proposal. Robert requested a $75,000 business loan, with he and Teresa contributing $25,000 of their own money to the estimated $100,000 cost of the venture.

The bank manager asked Robert to go home and prepare a detailed description of their needs, as well as a projected operating statement for the first year's operations. The Normans were upset by this negative reaction and decided to visit other banks to obtain the funds they needed. But they found out they would need to provide the requested information to obtain the money no matter where they went. Robert and Teresa spent two days working feverishly and came up with the statements shown in Figure 1 (on the next page).

When Robert took the proposals to the bank, the manager seemed impressed but still would not give approval for the loan. Some uncertainties about the statements still bothered the banker. Finally, after two weeks of collecting information—and pleading—the Normans' loan for $75,000 was approved. A major reason for the approval was their past dealings with the bank and their good credit standing. Now they could begin purchasing supplies to get started.

Before long, however, the Normans realized that they had underestimated many of their expenses. They learned, for example, that utilities, rent, and telephone all required initial

Figure 1

The Framemakers
Financial Requirements, Year 1

Item	Amount	Source of Information
Inventory	$ 45,000	General estimate
Equipment and fixtures	35,000	Approximation
Opening promotion (trade show)	2,000	Price of booth
First month's rent	2,000	From landlord
Three months' salary (Robert and Teresa)	12,000	Estimated $4,000/month
First three months' advertising	3,600	One ad in TV, radio, and newspaper
Miscellaneous	400	Estimate
Total	**$100,000**	

The Framemakers
Projected Income Statement, Year 1

		Per Customer (Professional Picture Framing Association Figures)	20 Customers a Day for 240 Days
Sales	$32	100%	$153,600
Expenses	24	75	115,200
Profit	8	25	38,400

deposits of $200. They also needed some additional supplies, even though they had overbought some unnecessary supplies from especially persistent salespeople. The landlord required the first and last months' rent before letting them move in. The equipment costs and inventory levels were higher than they had estimated. Finally, since the Normans had decided it would be better to incorporate their business, they faced additional legal costs for which they had not planned. The result of all these additions was that The Framemakers needed another $10,000—and the Normans hadn't even opened the doors!

Robert and Teresa didn't know what to do. They were hesitant to go back to the bank and ask for more money because of the difficulty they had had obtaining the first loan. On the other hand, they knew their chances of obtaining funding elsewhere were slim. On top of that, the time for the grand opening was rapidly approaching.

Questions

1. Evaluate the Normans' initial approach to obtaining financing for The Framemakers.
2. Assuming you are the banker, evaluate the financial requirements and projections Robert and Teresa prepared.
3. What should the Normans do now?

Video Case Questions
Cottage Cheesecake Industry*

CBC ⬤

Brad Miller bakes cakes in his garage in Sydney, Nova Scotia. At least he did until the business grew so big that Brad decided to move the bakery into a full-sized factory. But growing up is hard to do.

1. What aspects of Brad Miller's background would be positive for him to obtain financing for his business? What aspects would be negative?

2. What are the advantages and disadvantages of equity financing for this business?

3. What other sources of financing might he have accessed?

*Source: CBC *Venture* #726, running time 9:04.

Cases for Part II

Clark's Sporting Goods	Johnson Enterprises
Garden City Petroleums	Kelly's Grill
Jensen Roofing	Nevada Bob's Discount Golf and Tennis

CLARK'S SPORTING GOODS

D. Wesley Balderson
University of Lethbridge

Dave Clark plans to open a sporting goods store in London, Ontario, as soon as he graduates from university there in the spring. He did a market demand analysis for such a store for one of his course projects and is confident the opportunity exists.

Dave's major problem is determining the amount of funds he will require. His father, who is quite wealthy, will give him $30,000 as a graduation gift to invest. He has located a store that rents for $2,000 per month (in advance) and has made an itemized list of the start-up costs as follows:

Merchandise (4 months)	$100,000
Shelves, racks, displays	5,000
Remodelling	4,000
Cash register (used)	800
Check-out counter	500
Office supplies (4 months' supply)	200
Telephone: $50/month, $100 deposit, $25 installation fee	
Utilities: $200/month, $200 deposit	

Dave has made the following estimates:

- He can completely turn over his inventory every four months.
- In the first year, he plans a 60 percent markup on cost of merchandise.
- He can get by on a salary of $2,000 per month.
- He plans to hire one full-time employee at $1,500 per month and one at $1,000.
- He plans to spend $2,000 in opening promotion in the first month and $500 a month after the grand opening for advertising.
- He estimates that 50 percent of his sales will be on credit and will be paid in 30 days.
- The interest rate is 10 percent, payable every four months.
- The depreciation rate is 10 percent.

Questions

1. Estimate how much money Dave will need from outside sources to start his business.
2. Assuming Dave receives start-up financing from a bank, as calculated in question 1, will he require an operating line of credit during the first four months of operation? If so, how much?
3. Should Dave pursue debt or equity sources of funds to get started?

GARDEN CITY PETROLEUMS

D. Wesley Balderson
University of Lethbridge

Bernie Gryant was a licensed mechanic working for a large garage in Coalbanks, a city of 65,000 in southern Alberta. Although he had worked with the same employer for seven years, he felt his chances for promotion were limited. Bernie lived on a small farm outside Coalbanks, and commuting each day was getting fairly expensive. All of these things had made him start thinking about opening his own business.

One day on the way home from work, he noticed a "for sale" sign on the old service station located on the highway just outside Garden City, a small town halfway between Coalbanks and Bernie's farm. The prospect of quitting his job and purchasing the business hit him immediately. The location was currently owned by a local fertilizer company. On talking to the owner, Rod Grainger, Bernie found out the asking price was $80,000, plus the value of the fuel in the tanks at the time of purchase. The owners also indicated a willingness to finance the purchase over three years at 10 percent per year if Bernie could provide a down payment of $20,000. Bernie didn't have $20,000 to invest, but he discussed the proposal with a good friend, Tom Duncan. Tom, a lawyer, agreed to enter a co-ownership arrangement with Bernie in return for the $10,000 needed for half of the down payment. They discussed the background of the proposal and obtained the following information:

1. The town of Garden City had a population of 2,000 but only one other gas station (affiliated with a major oil company). Although the owner of this station was very prominent in the community, he had no mechanic and was open only from 8 a.m. to 5 p.m. six days a week.
2. This station was the only outlet for bulk farm fuel within a 20-mile radius— and this was a farming community. If they decided to pursue the bulk fuel market, however, they would have to buy a bulk fuel truck.

3. Only one mechanic operated in Garden City; two others in the area did mechanical work from their farm garages.
4. Although the location of the proposed purchase was on the outskirts of Garden City, it was on the major highway between Coalbanks and the province's third major recreational area, Waterville National Park.
5. The present owner was willing to finance the purchase with favourable terms.

All of these points seemed positive, and Bernie and Tom agreed to make an offer subject to viewing the financial statements. The offer was accepted. Figures 1 and 2 show the income statement and balance sheet for the service station.

Figure 1 and 2

Garden City Petroleums
Income Statement for Year Ended March 31, 2001

Gasoline sales		$255,480
Expenses:		
Cost of sales	$215,162	
Bad debts	1,008	
Depreciation	2,000	
Equipment repairs	2,206	
Insurance and taxes	3,000	
Office supplies and postage	1,540	
Telephone and utilities	2,525	
Wages and benefits	23,000	
Total expenses		250,441
Net income		**$ 5,039**

Garden City Petroleums
Balance Sheet March 31, 2001

Assets		**Liabilities**	
Cash	$ 1,191	Accounts payable	$ 3,658
Accounts receivable	8,425	Notes payable	5,000
Fuel in stock, 3/31/96	12,500	Total liabilities	$ 6,658
Other inventory	3,880		
Building and equipment		**Owner's Equity**	
Less: depreciation	38,000	Owner's equity	$68,680
Land	20,000		
Total assets	**$83,996**	**Total liabilities and owner's equity**	**$83,996**

After viewing the financial statements, Bernie and Tom were a bit disappointed. However, although the business's income was low, they believed that with the addition of Bernie's mechanical capability, money spent on advertising, and the purchase of a bulk fuel truck, they could improve this figure substantially. They went ahead with the purchase.

Now, approximately six months later, Bernie is getting discouraged. He is working from 7 a.m. until 10 p.m. every day, and he feels profits are not as high as he had planned.

Questions

1. Evaluate the purchase of Garden City Petroleums. What further analysis should have been done prior to the purchase?
2. How could Tom and Bernie have gone about assessing the market potential and market share for this business?
3. Do you think the price paid for this business was too high, too low, or about right?
4. What recommendations would you make to Tom and Bernie at this point?

JENSEN ROOFING

D. Wesley Balderson
University of Lethbridge

Robert Jensen had just completed a short entrepreneurial course at a local college as preparation for establishing his own roofing business. One of the main things that he learned in the course was the necessity of preparing a business plan for the enterprise. As a result Robert went to work and within a few days had put together the following business plan for Jensen Roofing.

Background

I, Robert Jensen, will be the sole owner of this proprietorship which will install and repair roofs in the Lethbridge, Alberta market area. I have completed an entrepreneurial course at the Lethbridge Community College and have had several years experience in the roofing business working for Charles Hill Roofing, the largest roofer in the Lethbridge area.

I am desirous of starting my own business in order to be independent and to obtain a higher financial compensation than I am currently receiving. I want everyone in Lethbridge and surrounding areas to know my company and the quality work we do.

Market Approach

The target market will be every person who owns a house, apartment building, warehouse, condo, or office building. The services we provide will cater to all people who own buildings that need roof repair or construction. We will provide all types of roofing materials and services. Eavestroughing will also be included in our business. Quality workmanship will be the building block of our business. We will ensure a one-year guarantee on all workmanship.

Because the service Jensen Roofing will provide is of high quality, I will charge a slightly higher price on our product. I will try to maintain a 20 percent markup over costs to keep our prices fair to every customer. Jensen Roofing will utilize several forms of promotion. Brochures and pamphlets will be prepared and sent through direct mail to every homeowner in Lethbridge. Newspaper ads and the Yellow Pages will also be used to promote the business.

Physical Facilities

The business will be located in my home at first. This will save a considerable amount of money until the business gets established. Equipment, supplies, and opening inventory will be purchased from local suppliers. The following schedule provides a listing of the equipment and supplies that will be needed to get started.

Physical Requirements

1 work truck (used half ton)	$ 5,000
3-tonne dump truck	5,000
1 hoist	500
4 ladders (25 foot)	1,500
Computer system	3,000
Office equipment and supplies	1,000
Total	$17,000

Financial

To estimate potential revenue for Jensen Roofing for new houses, I have multiplied the average roofing job for new houses ($8,000) by the number of new houses constructed in Lethbridge (400) in 1998 for a total of $3,200,000. For repair jobs I have taken the average dollar expenditure per household for the Lethbridge area (Urban Family Expenditure Data) of $100 and multiplied it by the number of homes (26,000) for a total of $2,600,000. Of this total of $5,800,000 I estimate that Jensen Roofing will obtain a 10 percent market share for a total revenue of $580,000. There are currently eight other roofers in the city, but because of my quality workmanship, I hope to increase the market share of Jensen Roofing to 20 percent within five years.

Projected income based on these estimates are found below:

Jensen Roofing Projected Income—Year 1	
Sales	$580,000
Cost of goods sold (45%)	261,000
Wages	100,000
Depreciation	2,000
Advertising	2,600
Insurance	1,200
Repairs and maintenance	5,000
Licences and permits	200
Professional fees	800
Interest (8% on $15,000)	1,200
Total	374,000
Net Income	$206,000

Jensen Roofing will obtain a loan from a local bank to finance $15,000 of the start-up requirement. The remaining $2,000 will be supplied by myself, the owner. The financial records of the business will be prepared and maintained by an accountant.

Legal Requirements

The necessary business licences and permits will be obtained from the City of Lethbridge. Initially the business will be operated as a proprietorship, and when the business becomes more established I will consider forming a limited company.

Personnel

The personnel required to keep Jensen Roofing operating will vary from season to season. Due to the uncertainties of the weather, part-time employees will be utilized. Ads will be placed in the local newspaper to find workers for the business. I will also utilize the government employment agency of Canada Manpower. During the summer months I may also look at hiring students. I estimate that on average I will have about five workers on the payroll. Training will take place on the job which is appropriate for this type of work.

Questions

1. Evaluate the Jensen Roofing business plan from an investor's and a lender's point of view.

JOHNSON ENTERPRISES

Rick Heyland
University of Lethbridge

Steve Johnson, a resident of Winnipeg, Manitoba, spent 10 years trying to manufacture the Triple-Tool in his spare time. He found many retailers and wholesalers that were willing to buy the product if he could manufacture it.

Steve had worked on drilling rigs and mine sites for many years; it was here that he saw the need for the Tool. The Triple-Tool is a tool with a fibreglass handle and three attachable heads: shovel, pick mattock, and axe. A heavy-duty rivet holds a steel sheath onto the formed fibreglass handle. A forged steel wedge lock forms a positive lock for holding the axe, shovel, and pick mattock in place. Steve holds the patent rights for his invention.

The Triple-Tool is more cost effective, convenient, and durable than conventional tools. Rather than having three different bulky tools, the Triple-Tool comes all together in its own carrying case. It also assembles without tools. Replacing an axe head with the Triple-Tool takes minutes rather than hours.

Steve has found a strong interest in the product by some top hardware chains in Canada and the United States. The target market for this product is campers, recreational vehicle owners, mining companies, oil companies, and farmers. But Steve has been unable to get it manufactured.

Steve has made contacts throughout Canada, the United States, West Germany, Japan, and Sweden in an attempt to have the Triple-Tool manufactured, but has been unsuccessful. Initially Steve was looking for a manufacturer that could make the whole product, but manufacturing was so specialized that no one company could make it. As a result, Steve decided to try to find a group of manufacturers. Recently he found a manufacturer that could make the axe head, but it demanded $5,000 to make the die and a minimum of 10,000 units for an initial order.

Unfortunately, Steve has spent most of his funds on trying to determine the market and finding someone to make the product. He has calculated that to get an order of 10,000 units with all three heads, carrying case, and handle, he would need close to $250,000. Steve has tried everywhere to find an appropriate investor, but all prospects are either "a two-bit operations" or "want too much of the pie."

Questions

1. a. Where can Steve get the necessary financing?
    b. How can Steve get the necessary financing?
2. How would you recommend that Steve find a manufacturer for the Triple-Tool?
3. If Steve can get the Triple-Tool made, what distribution channel should he use to get the product to the consumer?

KELLY'S GRILL

D. Wesley Balderson
University of Lethbridge

Kelly Orr worked as assistant department manager in the ladies' wear department of a large department store in Kingston, Ontario. She enjoyed her work but saw that chances of further advancement in her $35,000-a-year job were limited. For the past few years, Kelly had been thinking about starting her own business. As a teenager, she had worked summers in a fast-food franchise and had always desired to own her own restaurant. As she had two children, she resented having to work Thursday and Friday evenings and Saturdays and thought that by owning her own business she could more easily take time off to be with her family. Her husband, a schoolteacher, had supported her working in the past, but was a bit hesitant about Kelly risking her savings of $20,000 to go out on her own. They agreed, however, that Kelly should investigate a few possibilities and obtain as much information as she could about the restaurant industry in Kingston.

For the past six months, Kelly has visited with several of her friends, looked at some prospective businesses, and checked with public officials to find out what information was available. She has obtained the following information:

Population of Kingston	95,000
Per-family away-from-home food expenditures	$80/month
Number of families in Kingston	28,000
Number of restaurants in Kingston	110
Average square footage per outlet	1,500
Cost of goods sold as percentage of gross sales	50%
Bank's lending rate	10%

Operating expenses, excluding rent, interest, and franchise advertising royalties, are estimated to be 35 percent of gross sales.

From several restaurant possibilities, Kelly has narrowed the decision down to three: a site in a new shopping mall, a downtown restaurant that is for sale, and a fast-food franchise. All three involve a greater investment than Kelly was planning on. To get sufficient funds, the Orr's may have to remortgage their house.

Possibility A

The first potential site is a new shopping centre just nearing completion in a new and growing part of Kingston. The centre is anchored at each end by two national department stores. The space Kelly is considering contains 3,000 square feet and carries a rental of $10 per square foot, plus a royalty of 2 percent of gross sales. Although the rental costs would be high, Kelly is confident that the mall would generate considerable customer traffic, which would outweigh the rental costs. Also, the mall location is within a few minutes' drive from her home. However, the space is unfinished, and Kelly estimates she would need a minimum of $40,000 in equipment and $20,000 in leasehold improvements to get the restaurant started. Since not all the space was leased out, she was not able to find out how many other restaurants were planning to locate in the mall.

Possibility B

The second potential site is a 1,500-square-foot, busy downtown lunchtime café that is for sale. The present owner is asking $50,000 for the restaurant and is willing to finance the sale at $25,000 down and $10,000 per year for three years. The space had been leased at $12,000 annually and was due to be renegotiated in three years. The location of this restaurant makes it attractive to lunchtime and late-afternoon customers. The restaurant has operated successfully for six years and is located close to several large office buildings.

Possibility C

The third possibility is to sign a franchise contract with a national fast-food franchise chain that wants to expand into Kingston. The typical outlet size is 2,000 square feet. The initial franchise fee is $20,000, plus an additional $50,000 to be financed through Kelly's bank with the franchise guarantee, which would lower the interest rate by 2 percent. Kelly would also pay 6 percent of gross sales as a royalty. They would train Kelly in one of its company-owned outlets at no charge and help with the start-up of her own outlet. She would, of course, be constantly monitored by the franchise—a point that makes her a bit uneasy.

Kelly needs to make a decision soon. All three prospects might be lost if she waits too long.

Questions

1. How well has Kelly thought out and prepared for her decision to start her own restaurant?
2. Based on the information provided, which of the choices open to Kelly would you advise her to make?
3. What additional information should she obtain before making this decision?

NEVADA BOB'S DISCOUNT GOLF AND TENNIS

D. Wesley Balderson and Rick Heyland
University of Lethbridge

James Durant had opened a small golf supply shop in downtown Saskatoon, Saskatchewan, in June 2001. Named Durant's Golf Accessories, it handled clubs, balls, bags, and carts, as well as a limited line of golf-related clothing. James, an experienced golfer himself, had done what he felt was a thorough job of assessing the market for the shop. However, after five months of operation and with winter approaching, the performance of the store was not what he had expected. The store was averaging only one-half of the projected $20,000 per month in sales. James was not sure why, but he suspected part of the problem was lack of awareness of his store among the golfing public. His product line included major brand name merchandise, and he was attempting to be price competitive. This was difficult, however, because of his lower volume of purchases, which resulted in higher merchandise costs. James believed he would have to advertise more but had put all of his savings (approximately $20,000) into getting the business started. He felt fortunate that thus far he hadn't needed to borrow any money.

In November 2001, James was contacted by the Nevada Bob's Discount Golf and Tennis franchise about the possibility of becoming the franchisee for Nevada Bob's in Saskatoon. Nevada Bob's is a well-recognized and respected golf and tennis supply wholesaler in the western United States and was in the process of expanding into Canada. James would be one of the first franchisees in Canada and would have exclusive rights for Nevada Bob's in Saskatoon.

Upon further investigation, James learned that Nevada Bob's would provide information on sources for merchandise at discount prices. He was not obligated, however, to purchase from these suppliers. James would also automatically receive any catalogue sales in the Saskatoon area that the franchise advertised nationally. The franchisor indicated this had amounted to $18,000 in 2000. James received from the franchisor a cash flow statement for a typical franchisee (see Figure 1), which looked very positive. He visualized that such performance would certainly be an improvement over his existing business.

The Nevada Bob's franchise would cost James $25,000, with an additional 2 percent royalty on sales. Although no formal training program or operations manual was available, the franchisor indicated they would help James if he needed some assistance. The franchisor has given James two weeks to make his decision.

Figure 1

	Nevada Bob's Discount Golf and Tennis Statement of Projected Cash Flow as of 2001		
Opening cash balance		$ 15,000	
Cash sales		876,000	
Cost of goods sold		(663,200)	
Total			$ 227,800
Cash disbursements			
Accounting and legal		$ 5,350	
Advertising		31,500	
Automotive		1,200	
Insurance		3,600	
Licence and dues		2,400	
Office and sundry		5,100	
Rent		24,000	
Credit card discount		8,760	
Repairs and maintenance		9,000	
Telephone and utilities		8,400	
Salaries		39,000	
Sales commission		3,600	
Travel and promotion		13,500	
2% royalty of gross sales paid quarterly		$17,520	
Total			$172,930
Cash balance			$ 54,870

Questions

1. If you were James Durant, what other sources would you contact? What information, if any, might you require, before making the decision?
2. What specific questions might be raised about the cash flow statement provided by Nevada Bob's?
3. What course of action would you recommend for James Durant?

Part III

Managing the Small Business

Part II of this text dealt with issues relating to the organization and establishment of a small business. Once the business has been established, the owner-manager should follow several management fundamentals to ensure that the business stays viable and competitive. Part III discusses five of these management areas. Chapter 8 focuses on the marketing principles essential for understanding the market and getting the product or service to the consumer. Chapter 10 covers the recording and controlling of the financial aspects of the business. Both marketing and finance are areas in which many entrepreneurs lack training and competence. Chapter 11 discusses some fundamental components of the internal operations or production aspects of the business. Chapter 12 reviews the principles of personnel management applicable to the small organization. Chapter 13 outlines the most relevant tax considerations for the small business.

Chapter 8

Chapter 8

Marketing Management

Small Business Profile

Ben Varadi, Anton Rabie, and Ronnen Harary
Spin Master Toys

Spin Master Toys
www.spinmaster.com

The history of Spin Master Toys is part Wright brothers, part Roots—a tale of what happens when innovation meets savvy marketing. Childhood pals who met at summer camp a few years after their families moved to Toronto from South Africa, Anton Rabie and Ronnen Harary both attended the University of Western Ontario in London, where they met fellow biz-student, Ben Varadi. The three established a business under the name Sieger Marketing, selling a locally sponsored frosh-kit calendar as their first product. Their success from this project allowed them to build up enough money so that in 1994 when Harary's grandmother brought back a novelty gift from Israel—a sawdust-filled stocking with a face that sprouted grass for hair—they knew they had found it. The Earth Buddy was born.

In the years to follow, the company continued to identify and successfully market interesting novelty and toy products. After the Earth Buddy came Devil Sticks, a three-rod juggling game which went on to become Canada's number one non-promoted toy for 1995. Then came Spin-A-Blo, Growthings, and a dozen others. The company's success owed much to their "grass-roots" approach to marketing and promotion, combining innovative point-of-purchase displays, highly visible promotions, and intense PR campaigns. The Earth Buddy caught Canada's attention with its direct product displays—two Earth Buddies side-by-side, one bald, the other sprouting a full grassy head. For Devil Sticks, they took the product to the people—literally paying college students to travel the country demonstrating the toy at public events.

In 1997, the company was approached by a set of British inventors with the idea that would change their course and launch them into the forefront, establishing them as a legitimate player in the international toy marketplace. The concept was simple—an air-pressure powered toy airplane that relied on a theoretically sound, yet unproven, engine design. All the major companies passed on the idea, but Rabie, Harary, and Varadi saw something special—a chance to corner the market on flight, delivering a great flying toy at a great price point. It took more than a year, a sink-or-swim course in Far East manufacturing, and close to $1 million in development costs before they had a plane that would fly. The Air Hogs line was born, and it was a huge hit, eventually cracking the top three best-selling toys of the year.

The success of the Air Hogs stemmed from two main drives—innovative product development and powerhouse PR and marketing. If developing the product was tough, the Air Hogs press campaign was only slightly less difficult. By generating a legitimate success story, spinning it for the media, and packaging it all in a series of eye-catching press kits (an Air Hog along with a bag of airline peanuts and a sickness bag), the company became the darling of the media. Over the past four years, the company has continued its record of major successes with trend-setting items like Flick Trix extreme sports toys, Key Charm Cuties, dozens of Air Hogs spin-offs, and a new line-up that includes an R/C airplane, an interactive plush monster with a split-personality, and a re-launch of the 1970s classic, Shrinky Dinks.

With sales topping the $100 million mark in 2000, Spin Master has entered into direct competition with multi-billion dollar companies like Mattel and Hasbro. While they have accordingly stepped up their marketing techniques—to compete on a grand scale, multi-million dollar TV advertising campaigns are essential—much of their game plan remains very similar to their Earth Buddy and early Air Hogs days. By cultivating close relationships with the top retailers, they have developed innovative, interactive in-store displays designed to show off what are after all new, unseen and inherently complex, must-try products. The results from the merchandisers have been seen to increase sales by more than 40 percent in some instances. At the same time, PR to this day remains the backbone of the company—a throw back to their days of super-low budget, most-bang-for-the-buck strategizing—though through their reputation alone, they have had to up the creative ante with every new campaign. Their latest efforts involve an intricate series of humourous mailings, cryptic phone calls, buzz-building packages, and personal greetings from a dedicated team of PR representatives—a requisite, all-out push that could make or break performance for one of their key holiday items.

THE ROLE OF MARKETING MANAGEMENT IN THE SMALL BUSINESS

Marketing activities are often overlooked by owner-managers after the business has been established. Some possible reasons for this are: (1) owner-managers do not fully understand what marketing is; (2) owner-managers may not think it is necessary—that is, they may believe that if they have a good enough product, it will sell itself; or (3) owner-managers tend to be so busy with the day-to-day activities and problems of the business that they do not take the time to assess the market and develop a marketing plan.

Regardless of the reasons for failing to apply marketing principles in the small business, it is critical that the owner-manager understand and apply those principles. The business will likely be unable to hire a specialist in marketing. Therefore, the owner-manager will have to do a considerable amount of marketing, not only to potential customers but to suppliers, employees, bankers, and perhaps even government agencies. The Small Business Profile of Spin Master Toys Inc. illustrates how important marketing and meeting consumer needs was to the successful establishment of Spin Master Toys.

www.
businessgateway.ca

The major purpose of this chapter, then, is to introduce the fundamentals of marketing that can help sustain the growth of the business. Some of the principles also apply to establishing a business and are mentioned briefly in Chapter 3. Other marketing principles form an important part of a business plan and are discussed in Chapter 4.

An owner-manager may become involved in the following marketing activities:

- Defining the target customer (market niche), target customer characteristics, and information concerning that customer's product/service wants and needs

- Understanding those influences outside the business that will affect its operations

- Developing the product or service

- Developing the channel(s) of distribution

- Setting price levels for the product or service

- Providing information or promoting the product or service to those who are influential in its purchase

This chapter will discuss the relevant aspects of each of these components of marketing separately. It is important to note, however, that these components need to be coordinated to prepare a marketing plan and managed together as a system to be most effective.

THE TARGET CUSTOMER

In preparing the feasibility analysis in Chapter 3, we stressed the need to define the target customer. The ability of the entrepreneur to clearly identify the specific market is critical to success, as the Small Business Profile that opens this chapter shows. This is important in calculating a quantitative estimate of the size of the market. The small business owner might attempt to reach and collect information about the following target markets:

1. The consumer market

2. The organization market

3. The export market

Each of these markets has unique characteristics that must be taken into account in developing the marketing program.

The Consumer Market

The owner-manager should obtain information about several characteristics of the consumer market. Some characteristics that may be most helpful in developing the marketing program are the following:

Ideasite for business
www.
ideasiteforbusiness.
com

1. *Demographic characteristics.* These include items such as age, income, education, occupation, and location of residence.
2. *Lifestyle characteristics.* This category includes such things as activities, interests, opinions, media habits, and personalities of target market individuals.
3. *Purchase characteristics.* These include what, when, where, and how much of the product or service the market purchases. Figure 8-1 gives an example of purchase characteristics for various age groups.
4. *Purchase motivations.* This area contains one of the most important items of information: It explains the reasons behind consumer purchases. In addition to understanding the "why" of the purchase, the entrepreneur should attempt to understand the factors that might influence the purchase. Common sources of influence are members of the consumer's reference group, social class, and/or family. Current prominent motivations are service and value of the price/quality relationship.

Figure 8-1   Purchase Characteristics for Various Ages

In Their Teens

This group has an increasing amount of money to spend on clothing, cosmetics and entertainment products. They also have a major influence with family purchases.

In Their 20s

This group is not yet financially secure. It demands instant gratification, lasting values, and tangible benefits. Purchase decisions are often based on subjective factors.

In Their 30s and 40s

These people have high incomes and high debt. They are individualistic, striving for self-fulfillment, and concerned about social and environmental issues. They look for information before buying.

In Their 40s and 50s

Prosperous and facing retirement, they purchase for sentimentality, brand loyalty, and convenience.

In Their 60s and 70s

They tend to have lots of leisure time. They seek financial security, quality, and value. They rely on knowledge and experience.

In Their 80s

This group spends heavily on health care, travel, and security products.

SOURCE: *The Globe and Mail,* February 13, 1995, p. B8.

Once this type of information has been obtained, the development of the marketing program—including product characteristics, pricing strategy, distribution channels, and method of promotion—becomes much easier, and the program is usually more effective.

Much of the above information about the target customer can be obtained through secondary data or primary research, as discussed in Chapter 3. It is important for the small business owner to realize that collecting information about the target consumer is not a one-time event used only as the business is getting established. It should be used continuously to help the owner stay responsive to changes in consumer needs and wants.

Most successful companies, whether large or small, stay that way because they are close to the consumer and incorporate consumer wants and needs into their marketing programs.[1] This philosophy, called the marketing concept, has been taught in introductory marketing courses for a number of years. Incident 8-1 illustrates how two entrepreneurs applied the marketing concept in meeting a consumer need. Many small businesses are successful initially because they fill a consumer need, but as they grow they often fall out of touch with their customers. This situation usually leads to difficulties, particularly in competitive markets. A recent survey of Canadian entrepreneurs who have been nominated for Canadian Entrepreneur of the Year awards indicated that customer relations were their most important issue.[2]

Other companies define their consumer markets too broadly. As a result, their marketing programs may fail to satisfactorily meet the needs of any one group in the market. The practice of tailoring the marketing program to each specific market is known as market segmentation.

Incident 8-1

IKE Inc.

Entry barriers into the software market are substantial. Big-name firms, such as Microsoft, Electronic Arts, Broderbund, and SoftKey, dominate the industry. Unless firms can successfully license their product with one of these giants, it is almost impossible to get retail distribution. The big-name firms that license and then publish other's software are viewed as the talent scouts of the industry. Without the logo of one of these companies, retailers are reluctant to take a chance distributing an unknown product. The final flaw in the strategy of many software entrepreneurs is their lack of market orientation. They fall in love with their product and believe that if it's good enough, the world will beat a path to their door. "The failure to do market research before ploughing tens of thousands of dollars into development is perhaps the most common blunder that trips up software start-ups." Derek Patriquin and David Roach have learned a lot about marketing, distribution, and business management since 1992 when they conceived their company in a St. Catharines pub. They have been determined that their products must meet a consumer need and are not just those that they find interesting themselves. As a result they have been successful in this highly volatile market where others have failed. Rapid changes in technology can change an industry overnight and this hope keeps dreams of riches dancing in the heads of these two entrepreneurs.

SOURCE: Joanna Pachner, "We've Been Through Hell," *The Financial Post Magazine,* October 1997, pp. 50–57, p. 54.

The Organization Market

The second type of market the small business might attempt to reach is the organization market. This market includes companies, institutions, or even individuals who purchase the product to assist in the manufacture of other products. Government purchases, an ever-increasing market for small business, are also classed as an industrial market.

In consumer markets, buying influences include the emotional as well as the rational. Industrial goods, on the other hand, are purchased primarily for rational reasons. Such characteristics as price, quality, dependability of supply, ability to manufacture to specification, speed of manufacture and delivery, and services offered are commonly considered in making industrial purchases. The purchasers, often acting as a committee, are well informed about the product category and are also aware of competitive offerings. Generally the information the purchaser requires is of a technical nature, requiring a well-trained and knowledgeable sales staff on the part of the small business.

In attempting to reach the industrial market, the following areas should be investigated: (1) which companies and government agencies purchase from small businesses, (2) the influences on industrial demand, and (3) how the bidding-tendering process works.

**Canada Business
Service Centres
www.cbsc.org**

**Contracts Canada
(Government of Canada)
www.contractscanada.
gc.ca**

Companies and Government Agencies That Purchase from Small Businesses. Many large organizations purposely look to small business to fill their product and service needs. Such businesses find that the efficiency and service of the small enterprise meet their needs adequately and the price is competitive. Another form of selling to other businesses is through barter—the trade of goods or services. Bartering has grown to a $50 million business in Canada and may benefit the small business by opening new markets and reducing the need for higher levels of cash.[3]

Influences on Industrial Demand. Demand for industrial goods is derived from demand for the final product. Because of this relatively delayed response, industrial demand changes can be easier to predict than consumer demand changes. Some of the key indicators of industrial demand changes are:

- The state of the economy and its effect on the purchase of the end product

- Government legislation or regulations

- Potential competition for the purchasing company

- Specific bodies or agencies that exert influence on the purchases

The Bidding-Tendering Process. The small business owner should be aware of how the purchase decision is made and which criteria or specifications are used to make the decision in the industrial market. Because many industrial goods, particularly those purchased by the government, are purchased on a tender-bid basis, it is essential that the small business owner know how to prepare and submit bids within such a system.

The Export Market

**Export Development
Canada/Exportation et
développement Canada
www.edc.ca/**

Canada has always been known as a trading nation. The value of exports has contributed an estimated 20 percent of Canada's employment and 30 percent of GDP.[4] Export sales increased from $40 billion in 1977 to $360.6 billion in 1999.[5] The importance of exports to the Canadian economy is underscored by the fact that for every billion dollars worth of exports, 9,000 new jobs are created.[6] In the past, a large portion of exports have come from the primary and resource industries, which consisted of large companies and government agencies.

Incident 8-4

Digigraph Systems Inc.

Three years ago, during a trade mission to Latin America, architect Bernard McNamara realized that there was a market for quality, affordable housing. He also noticed that traditional construction methods appeared insufficient to meet the growing demand.

With this in mind, McNamara, President and Managing Director of Digigraph Systems Inc., set to work designing a product that would draw on Canadian industrial know-how and be made of materials readily available in Central and South America. By 1996, he developed an affordable, lightweight polyvinyl chloride (PVC) house frame that is made in Canada, shipped in segments, and easily assembled at the building site. His company focuses exclusively on export markets.

Digigraph is currently filling its first orders for 49 homes in Chile, Colombia, and Costa Rica. It has established a network of distributors in many Latin American countries and will promote its homes at industrial trade fairs over the coming year.

SOURCE: "Readiness for Exporting," *Profits* 17, no. 2 (Business Development Bank of Canada, Spring 1997), p. 3.

Recently, however, many small businesses have successfully exported manufactured goods to foreign countries (see Incident 8-4). The number of small- and medium-sized businesses that export has increased by 32 percent from 1993–1999. From 1993–1999, the value of goods and services exported by small- and medium-sized businesses grew by 35 percent.[8]

Because of both the vast potential in these foreign markets and the considerable encouragement and assistance provided by the government, the small business owner should not overlook this option. The North American Free Trade Agreement between Canada, the United States, and Mexico is rapidly opening up new markets for Canadian small businesses,[9] as is the current direction of policy formation by the World Trade Organization. Recent surveys indicate that Canadian entrepreneurs expect exports to increase significantly in the next few years.[10] Top international markets that Canadian entrepreneurs export to are the United Stated (85 percent), Asia (85 percent), Western Europe (44 percent), and South America (38 percent).[11] In order to determine the readiness for exporting, several questions should be answered. A brief review of some of these questions is shown in Figure 8-3. In addition, it is estimated that a certain amount of money will be required for such things as travelling to markets, drafting brochures, working trade shows, and meeting potential customers. Estimates range from $10–15,000 to cover these expenses.

World Trade Organization
www.wto.org/

The small business owner who plans to export needs to investigate (1) the forms of government assistance available for exporting, (2) the unique characteristics of the foreign market, and (3) the mechanisms of exporting.

Government Assistance Available for Exporting. Many government programs are designed to encourage and assist the entrepreneur who desires to export a product or service to another country. Some of the more active agencies and programs follow.

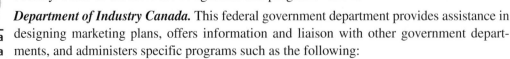

Industry Canada
www.strategis.ic.gc.ca

Department of Industry Canada. This federal government department provides assistance in designing marketing plans, offers information and liaison with other government departments, and administers specific programs such as the following:

1. *Promotional Projects Program.* This program promotes Canadian goods and services abroad through trade fairs, missions, and other foreign contacts.

2. *Program for Export Market Development (PEMD).* This program shares part of the financial risk associated with foreign trade by providing grants to

Figure 8-3   Readiness for Exporting

Some of the questions that should be asked to determine readiness for exporting:

1. Are you entrepreneurial?
2. Do you have a reliable, service-oriented character?
3. Are you a natural networker, building and maintaining relationships?
4. Do you see yourself as highly organized and research-oriented?
5. Do you have good communication skills?
6. Do you pride yourself in your strong negotiating skills?
7. Are you experienced in handling complex documentation?
8. Are you an avid follower of global politics?
9. Can you speak and write more than one language?
10. Are you sensitive to different cultures?
11. Do you adapt ideas easily, even under pressure?
12. Are you well-travelled or curious about other cultures?

SOURCE: *Profit*, September 1993, p. 21.

Export Hotline
www.exporthotline.com

the entrepreneur for travel to identify foreign markets, participate in trade fairs, and bring foreign buyers to Canada. Recently the emphasis for this program was changed to target firms with sales of less than $10 million.

3. *World Information Network for Exports (WIN Exports).* This computer-based information system is designed to assist in matching foreign needs to Canadian capabilities.

4. *Technology Inflow Program.* This program is designed to help locate, acquire, and adopt foreign technologies by promoting international collaboration.

Team Canada Inc.'s
Export Source
www.exportsource.gc.
ca

5. *New Exporters to Border States (NEBS)—to U.S. South (NEXUS)—to overseas (NEXUS).* This program provides counselling assistance as well as organizing trade missions to businesses planning to export to these areas.

6. *New Exporters Overseas (NEXPRO).* This is a training and counselling program for new exporters provided by Industry Canada. The 1998 Team Canada trade mission led to the signing of 306 agreements for a total value of $1.78 billion of which 90 percent were concluded with small and medium Canadian businesses.[12]

Export Development Corporation (EDC). As mentioned previously, the EDC is a Crown corporation of the federal government that essentially provides three services to exporters:

Export Development
Canada/Exportation et
développement Canada
www.edc-see.ca

1. *Export insurance.* This is a protection service for the exporter to ensure payment for export sales in the event of buyer default or detrimental foreign government action. The required screening to obtain the insurance assists small business in selecting creditworthy partners in foreign countries.

2. *Export guarantees.* Guarantees can be provided to financial institutions to assist exporters in obtaining financing for the export operations.

3. *Export financing services.* The EDC also has authorization to provide medium- and long-term financing for exporters to help them compete in the international marketplace.

EDC also provides a 1-800 number to help smaller firms get instant access to financial and insurance assistance of goods and services abroad.

Canadian Commercial Corporation
www.ccc.ca

Canadian Commercial Corporation (CCC). CCC is another Crown corporation that responds to requests from foreign governments and international agencies seeking Canadian goods and services by attempting to match those requests with suitable sources of supply.

Canadian International Development Agency (CIDA). CIDA is a federal government agency that administers Canada's development cooperation programs around the world, many of which employ private consultants, contractors, suppliers, and manufacturers to underdeveloped countries.

Canadian Trade Commissioner Service
www.infoexport.gc.ca

Department of Foreign Affairs and International Trade—Trade Commissioner Service. This referral service maintains an extended network of over 134 trade offices around the world. Its primary focus is to assist Canadian companies seeking export markets. A directory of the trade offices throughout the world may be obtained through the Department of Foreign Affairs or the Department of Industry Canada. In addition, entrepreneur exporters who register with WIN exports have free access to more than 600 market reports.

Forum for International Trade Training (FITT). This agency offers training for entrepreneurs in international trade.

Royal Bank Small Business Exporting Guide
www.royalbank.com/
sme/guides/export/
index.html

Canadian Export Association (CEA). The CEA is a national nonprofit association concerned with improving the environment for Canadian exporters. It provides information, contacts, education, and lobbying support for exporters.

Export Clubs. Many cities have established export clubs that meet regularly to exchange ideas and information about exporting.

Provincial Government Programs. Most provincial governments actively encourage exports and may offer specific incentive programs to assist in this regard. The Department of Industry, Trade and Commerce or its equivalent in each province can provide information about their programs. In addition to the above, trade missions facilitate the creation of a large number of agreements.

As we have seen, considerable assistance is available for a prospective exporter. Specific addresses of the above agencies are given in Appendix 8A.

Unique Characteristics of the Foreign Market. A second requirement for success in exporting is to understand the peculiarities of the foreign market. Many companies have experienced difficulties in marketing internationally because they failed to obtain enough information about the various markets. Several of the agencies mentioned above can provide information to answer the questions listed in Figure 8-4.

Figure 8-4   Key Areas for Developing a Foreign Marketing Strategy

1. What needs does the product fill in this culture?
2. What products (if any) currently meet these needs?
3. What are the differences in the way the product is used (consumed)?
4. What are the characteristics of the consumers who will buy the product?
5. Can the consumers afford to purchase the product?
6. What are the political or legal restrictions to marketing the product?
7. How stable is the political situation in this country?
8. What are the distribution and media capabilities in the culture?
9. What language differences exist?
10. What nonverbal communications should be noted?
11. What information-collecting restrictions might exist?

Figure 8-5   Major Barriers to Success Abroad

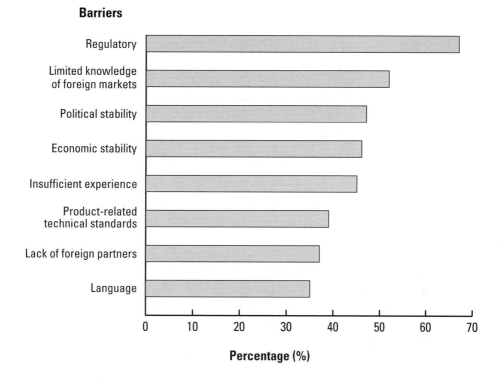

SOURCE: First Annual Survey of Canadian Entrepreneurs as reported in *The Globe and Mail,* June 24, 1995, p. B7.

Figure 8-5 illustrates the areas which constitute the greatest barriers to international markets. Additional analysis may be required in these areas. Incident 8-5 (on the next page) illustrates how these barriers affected one Canadian entrepreneur.

Because of the volatile condition existing in many countries as well as implications of foreign exchange fluctuations, the entrepreneur will need to constantly monitor conditions of the foreign market. Hedging is a way the entrepreneur can achieve foreign exchange protection.

Mechanisms of Exporting. The agencies discussed earlier can also provide information about the mechanisms of exporting. Some of the essential features of an exporting arrangement are as follows:

- *Documentation.* Contracts, invoices, permits, insurance, and bills of lading must be drafted or obtained.

- *Methods of credit offered.* Letters of credit, accounts receivable, and consignment sales are often a part of the process.

- *Physical distribution. The type of shipment, transfer of title, and inspection* points will have to be determined.

- *Channel of distribution.* Sales representatives, government agencies, export agents, and trading houses will need to be identified and contacted.

- *Security.* Export insurance and guarantees must be obtained.

Incident 8-5

Ani-Mat Inc.

Owners, Rosaire Croteau and Ange-Albert Allard, have a whole lot riding on recycled tires. Since its establishment in 1983, Ani-Mat Inc. has become a business that handles everything from manufacturing to installation of their rubber mat product line. Being in the right place at the right time, offering a low-cost, versatile product, and knowing how to make the most of a niche market has contributed greatly to the success of this Quebec-based company.

Specializing in rubber mats designed for animal comfort has been largely responsible for tripling Ani-Mat's sales in the past three years. Narrowing the company's focus, from tools that help increase farm animal productivity to the production of mats made from recycled rubber tires, permitted the exploitation of a niche market. Although Ani-Mat's niche marketing strategy has allowed them to target key clients in the dairy industry, the company's products have proved to be useful as protective arena coverings. Croteau and Allard attribute the majority of Ani-Mat's success to offering a turnkey product and service that has simplified the lives of their dairy farm clientele.

Ani-Mat's president forecasts a sales increase of 150 percent in the next year. These ambitious figures are not going to be reached relying solely on the company's niche marketing strategy. In fact, Ani-Mat's past exponential growth has been due to its rapid exploitation of international markets. A Productivity Plus Loan from BDC enabled the upgrading of Ani-Mat's manufacturing equipment. This allowed the company to deliver more products faster and meet the large demand of U.S. clientele. Developing a sound export strategy was key to meeting international demand for Ani-Mat's products and services. Today, 50 percent of Ani-Mat's products are delivered to the United States and 10 percent to Europe.

SOURCE: Adapted from "A Whole Lot Riding on Recycled Tires." *Profit$*, Fall 2000, p.3.

Because many of these items are complex, it is recommended that the entrepreneur seek assistance from the agencies mentioned earlier to ensure that he or she follows safe and proper procedures in carrying out the mechanics of exporting. Many Canadian exporters have found that one of the most effective ways to do business in another country is to strike a partnership with firms in that country.

A recent study by Neil Abramson of successful Canadian exporters to the U.S. found the following five factors being followed.[13] Successful Canadian exporters:

1. *Are Larger or Appear Larger.* According to Abramson, "Americans seem to prefer to do business with larger suppliers because the American buyers have a greater confidence that a larger suppler is more likely to remain in business." Some successful small companies in the researcher's survey had formed strategic alliances or joint ventures in order to appear larger or to have more product than their competitors.

2. *Have Built Effective Relationships.* The ability to resolve conflicts, acquire trust, and develop shared goals results in higher overall performance and more effective channels of distribution in the U.S. The less-successful smaller companies surveyed were not always noted for their conflict resolution skills. For example, the CEO of one company sur-

veyed, convinced that the Canadian way of selling software was the only way, insisted that U.S.-based sales representatives take training on Canadian sales methods. When the U.S. sales manager's complaints that sales declined after each training program went unanswered, she tried, unsuccessfully, to have the CEO removed. The CEO closed the manager's sales office and began using a few local representatives. Sales fell off dramatically.

3. *Have Sales and Service Offices in the U.S.* Abramson's research found that transferring to the U.S. any R&D, manufacturing, marketing, sales, or service was related to higher gross sales. Transferring R&D was related to the greatest increase in sales, and the companies that did so had 2.95 times the U.S. sales of companies that did not.

4. *Have Experience in the Market.* More experience in the U.S. and more commitment to American markets was related to higher performance. However, the researcher notes that companies with negative U.S. experience were more likely to have negative views about American customers and were, therefore, less likely to commit themselves extensively to U.S. markets.

5. *Sell Higher-Priced Products.* Products priced at the higher end of the scale were more likely to result in increased sales. "This may be because American customers equate higher prices with leading-edge products." While Canadian customers seem to want "tried and true" products, their U.S. counterparts are looking for a competitive edge. "American customers were perceived to be fairly price insensitive when new innovations were available."

INFLUENCES EXTERNAL TO THE ORGANIZATION

In any market, several conditions exist that may have a significant impact on the small business but are outside the control of the owner of that business. Incident 8-6 (on the next page) shows a company which has been successful by effectively dealing with export markets and such uncontrollable elements as the weather where their product is grown. Nevertheless, the owner-manager can do some things to effectively respond to these external influences:

- Identify which external conditions affect the business.

- Set up a system to continually monitor the relevant external influence(s). For the owner-manager, this might mean regularly obtaining reports, newsletters, and studies that contain up-to-date information on these conditions.

- Adjust internal operations to respond to changes in these external influences most effectively.

Some of the most common external influences that can affect the small business and thus affect the information to be collected are the economy, the competition, legal restrictions, and the social and cultural environment.

Incident 8-6

Pass the Mustard Please...

The Sakai Spice Canada Corporation processes raw mustard seed — both yellow and the spicier oriental — and exports the finished mustard flour to Japan for use in such varied products as Wasabi, the hot, green paste found in sushi, and in traditional "wet" mustards like French's table mustard. Mustard powder is also the secret ingredient in mayonnaise.

While the Sakai plant has been operating in Canada only since 1996, Canada has exported mustard seed for almost four decades, says Steve McDonnell, Sakai Spice Canada Corp.'s general manager. Under Demeter Agro Corp., he says, the raw mustard seed was exported to Japan for processing there.

In 1996, Sakai Spice first threw its hat into the international spice manufacturing ring by opening a plant in Lethbridge — the only one of three Sakai plants to exist outside of Japan.

Considering production, McDonnell says Canada is also the logical location. He says Canada produces about 85 percent of the mustard traded globally. While mustard production in countries like India may rival Canadian production, McDonnell says the mustard-producing foreign nations consume much of what they produce.

McDonnell says their mustard seed comes from all across the prairies. Sakai keeps a wide base to guard against the possibility of a bad crop in one particular area, and to ensure a consistent supply.

McDonnell says between four and five thousand tonnes of raw mustard seed is stored, cleaned, de-oiled, sifted and milled by his plant every process year, in two separate lines: one for yellow mustard and one for oriental mustard.

The finished product is trucked to Calgary, carried by train to Vancouver, and then shipped to foreign shores.

Source: Clayton Grose "Pass the Mustard Please...," *Southern Alberta Business 2*, no. 3 (Fall 1998), pp. 16–17.

The Economy. The state of the economy in the market area is a critical external condition. For most products and services, market demand is directly related to upturns and downturns in the economy. The small business often is able to react more quickly than large businesses to changes in the economy.

Competition. As mentioned in Chapter 1, a small business usually finds itself competing against larger firms over which it has no control. New technology used by competitors is another factor in assessing competition, especially in many growth industries. In some cases, the small business may gain competitive advantages because of its size. The North American Free Trade Agreement between Canada, the United States, and Mexico has not only opened up new markets for Canadian entrepreneurs but also increased competition for Canadian businesses as U.S. companies continue to enter Canadian markets. These situations are discussed in Chapter 1. By accurately identifying prospective competitors and their strengths as well as weaknesses, the entrepreneur can develop a more effective strategy. Attempts should be made to clearly identify the competitive advantage for the business.

Legal Restrictions. This potential influence includes the laws and regulations with which the business is required to comply. The owner-manager should keep up to date with any legislation that might affect business operations.

Social and Cultural Environment. This factor encompasses trends in the culture in which the business operates that may affect demand. The culture may dictate norms the population is generally hesitant to violate or suggest new growth industries that can be attractive opportunities.

Figure 8-6 Management of the External Influences

External Influence	Possible Characteristic	System to Monitor	Possible Internal Adjustment
Economy	Inflation rate Unemployment level	Collect relevant government and industry reports regularly	Lower prices Increase advertising
Competition	Identify competitor Competitor strengths and weaknesses Competitor's use of new technology	Competitor's new products Competitor's reaction to your strategies	Product or service alterations Selection of specific target market
Legal	Laws affecting your business What changes in laws are pending	Regular receipt of legislative changes from government documents and industry reports	Product or service alterations Promotional changes
Social and cultural	Lifestyle trends Demographic studies Purchase patterns	Industry and government reports recording social statistics and purchases	New products or services Distribution channel changes Promotional themes and levels
Technology	Trends	New product reports Fast growing company literature	Product alteration

Technology. New technology can be a significant factor in the success of a small business. Failure to recognize and adopt technology can spell disaster for the entrepreneur. Likewise, developing and utilizing it can be an important competitive edge.

Figure 8-6 illustrates how the owner of a small business can work with these uncontrollable conditions.

DEVELOPING THE PRODUCT OR SERVICE

As we mentioned at the beginning of this chapter, the product or service to be offered should be designed to meet target market demand. To ensure responsiveness to consumer demand, the owner-manager should think of the product or service in terms of the ways and extent to which it satisfies consumer need. A prototype of the product should be prepared and tested with a representative sample of the market. This type of information should be collected prior to finalizing the production decision.

Some major decision areas about which the small business owner should be knowledgeable when developing a product strategy are discussed next.

Develop Product or Service Policies. Product policies should cover such items as quality level, product or service depth and width, packaging, branding, level of service, and warranties.

Decide How the Product Will Be Manufactured. For many small businesses, contracting with another firm to manufacture the product is advantageous. This may be an especially viable alternative during the early stages of a business, when the risk is usually higher. Once the product has achieved market acceptance and the volume of production has increased, it may be more cost effective to acquire the manufacturing capability.

Understand the Product Life Cycle. All products and services have a life cycle, as Figure 8-7 shows. As the product moves from the introduction to the decline stage in its life cycle, the marketing strategy for the product and even for the business may also change. This means changes may be required in pricing, in distribution, in promotion, and even in the product or service. Knowing that the product or service has a life cycle helps the owner-manager plan for any necessary adjustments to the marketing strategy when the maturity stage is reached. Such modifications can help prolong the life cycle of the product or service. Strategies include the following:

- Appeal to a new target market.

- Adjust the product or service to meet changes in customer needs.

- Increase promotion to enhance frequency of purchases.

- Emphasize different uses or characteristics of the product or service.

- Offer a new product or service.

Product life cycles in many industries, notably the high-technology areas, are getting shorter. This has an impact in the long-term planning of the entrepreneur.

Figure 8-7   Product Life Cycle

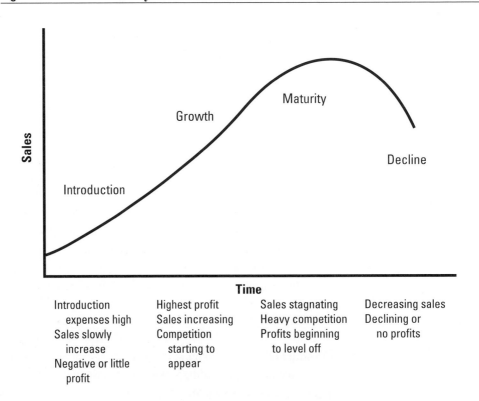

Determine Factors That May Accelerate Product or Service Adoption. Research shows that consumers generally adopt new products or services at different rates. Those who purchase first are the innovators or early adopters. These people often are the opinion leaders in a social group. The innovators and early adopters typically make up about 15 percent of the market, but they have a far greater influence because the rest of the market usually looks to this group before purchasing.[14]

After the small business owner has identified the innovators and early adopters within the target market, every attempt should be made to test market the product or service to that group first. If the early adopters accept the product or service, they may even do much of the initial promotion. Early adopters and opinion leaders also tend to be very vocal about the products and services they try and use. In addition, they tend to have higher income and educational levels, be more socially active, be more willing to take risks, and have greater exposure to printed media.

In addition to understanding the characteristics of innovators and early adopters, the small business owner should be aware of the factors that can speed up product adoption and attempt to capitalize on them. Following are some of the more important factors.

Relative Advantage. If the product or service appears to have a significant advantage over existing ones, and if this advantage can be communicated effectively, it is more likely to have a faster adoption.

Complexity. If the product or service is difficult to understand, the adoption rate is typically longer. In such a case, promotion should have an informational or educational content.

Divisibility. A product or service that can be purchased in small amounts with a minimum of social or financial risk usually has a quicker adoption rate.

Communicability of Results. If the results of using the product or service are quickly evident and easily communicated to others, its adoption will be more rapid.

In summary, the less risk associated with the purchase decision, the more rapid the adoption rate. The owner-manager therefore should do whatever is possible to reduce such risk when introducing a new product or service. Providing information and offering a guarantee or warranty as part of the purchase are commonly used methods for reducing risk.

Understand How the Consumer Classifies the Product or Service. Marketers use a standard classification system in categorizing consumer products. This system can be valuable in developing the marketing strategy for the small business. The classifications are as follows:

- *Convenience products.* Convenience products are purchased with minimal effort. They may be necessities, unplanned purchases, or emergency goods.

- *Shopping products.* Shopping products are purchased only after comparison with similar products. Comparisons may be made on the basis of price if competing products are viewed as similar or in terms of quality or style if competing products differ.

- *Specialty products.* Consumers have substantial brand or product loyalty with specialty products or services. As a result, they are willing to spend considerable effort to locate and purchase the brands and products they desire.

Figure 8-8 Strategy Implications for Product Classifications

Type of Product	Price	Distribution	Promotion
Convenience	While usually lower priced goods, the markups tend to be high.	Located close to consumers, either in relation to where they live or within the store.	Promote availability. Point-of-purchase displays for impulse goods.
	Within a certain range, price is not important to consumer.	Availability important to customer.	
Shopping	For similar products the price must be competitive, as consumers are price sensitive.	Located close to competing products to aid comparison.	Promote price advantage for similar products or quality/style advantage for dissimilar products.
	For dissimilar products that are still competitive, price is not as important to the consumer.		
Specialty	Within a certain range, price is not important to customer.	Location not important to customer.	Promote the outlet that carries the product or or brand.

Figure 8-8 illustrates strategy implications for each of these classifications. The focus of the marketing strategy is determined by how the target consumer classifies the product or service.

DEVELOPING THE DISTRIBUTION SYSTEM

Many entrepreneurs develop an excellent product but lack the knowledge about the best way to get it to the consumer. Such a situation is illustrated in Incident 8-7. An effective distribution system should provide the product or service to the right consumer, at the right place, at the right time, and in the right quantity.

The distribution channel is the path the product or service follows from the producer to the consumer. It includes the different organizations or individuals who will assist in this movement toward consumption.

The small business owner needs to address three main distribution decision areas: the type of channel to use, the length of the channel, and the number of distributors authorized to sell the product.

Channel Options

A small business can follow essentially two channel paths, although various combinations of these types of channels are possible.

Incident 8-7

Bringing Distribution Home

In 1988, a line of sparkling water beverages provided many a drinker with a burst of flavourful fruit indulgence. The product line was called Clearly Canadian Sparkling Flavoured Water and was launched by Vancouver-based Clearly Canadian Beverage Corporation. When the sparkling beverage hit the market, Clearly Canadian had arrangements with a network of master licencees, distributors, and sub-distributors to distribute and sell its products.

Aggressive manufacture and distribution outsourcing proved to be a successful strategy for President Douglas Mason. 1992 sales reached US$188 million. However, it was not long before a mob of copycat competitors penetrated the market that Clearly Canadian had so carefully pioneered. By 1995, sales for the company dropped to US$48 million. Clearly Canadian fought back by introducing innovative new beverages, including Orbitz, a texturally-enhanced drink containing gel spheres that stayed suspended in the beverage.

Although new and innovative, product introductions were not enough to regain Clearly Canadian's market share. The company realized that in order to become closer to its customers, it would have to take control of distribution. 1995 symbolized the beginning of Clearly Canadian's re-engineering efforts with the repurchase of distribution rights from master distributors to establish Company Managed Territories. Removing the master distributors from the marketing and distribution process enabled the company to reinvest revenues into local brand support. "This closer relationship with customers gives us a more immediate insight into what the market wants," says Mason.

Clearly Canadian continues to look for new strategies and opportunities to build its business, including entering into a licensing agreement with Reebok International Ltd. to create, package, market, and distribute Reebok Fitness Water in North America. The Reebok brand enables Clearly Canadian to gain access to national distribution in major grocery, convenience, and drug store chains and provides strong sports/fitness credentials to the new beverage concept of "enhanced water beverage." Mason says, "The brand equity of Reebok will provide Reebok Fitness Water significant consumer exposure and strengthen our relationships with key distributors and retail accounts."

Courtesy of Clearly Canadian Beverage Corporation.

Manufacturer to Consumer (Short-Direct Channel). This type of channel involves distributing the product or service directly to the consumer. The transportation and selling functions are carried out by the owner-manager or the sales staff. Often small businesses lack the financial capacity or expertise to hire and train their own sales forces.

Manufacturer to Wholesaler/Retailer to Consumer (Long-Indirect Channel). In this type of distribution channel, the wholesaler or retailer purchases the product and resells it to another channel member or to the consumer. The manufacturer assumes less risk with this method but generally has less control over the distribution and a lower profit margin. The small business may use this type of distribution channel by going to a retailer or wholesaler directly or visiting a trade show attended by these intermediaries. Many products receive their initial start from successful trade show experience.

Figure 8-9   Deciding Channel Length

Direct-Short Channel (Manufacturer to Consumer)	Indirect-Long Channel (Manufacturer to Wholesaler/Retailer to Consumer)
Implications for Manufacturer	
More expensive to set up	Cheaper to set up
Greater potential return	Least return
More risk	Less risk
More expertise needed	Less expertise needed
Product Characteristics	
Perishable	Standardized
Technical	Inexpensive
Large, bulky	Proven demand
Expensive	
Market Characteristics	
Geographically concentrated	Geographically dispersed
Low product awareness	High product awareness
Sales effort required	Less sales effort required

Channel Length

The decision regarding channel length will depend on the concerns of the manufacturer mentioned above. It also involves examining the product and market characteristics listed in Figure 8-9 (see above).

Channel Intensity

Another channel decision is how many distributors/dealers will be allowed to sell the product. Generally speaking, products that require greater selling effort, seller knowledge, and sales expertise are best distributed through a more exclusive type of arrangement. Standardized or convenience-type products usually call for a more intensive channel system. Because product availability is important in such a system, many dealers are allowed to carry the product.

SETTING THE PRICE FOR THE GOOD OR SERVICE

Another marketing strategy variable within the control of the owner-manager is the setting of price for the product or service. Pricing is a critical part of the marketing strategy; the small business cannot afford to make a pricing mistake in a competitive industry.

To approach price setting effectively, one must understand the factors that affect prices. These factors can be classified as either external or internal. External influences, as discussed earlier, include the state of the economy in the market area, the extent of competition, possible legal restrictions, cultural or societal attitudes toward certain price levels, and target market demand. Typical internal influences on pricing policy are internal costs, the firm's long-run objectives, and pricing policies as set by the owner-manager.

In setting price levels for the product or service, one may find that some of these factors are more influential than others. As a result, businesses use three general bases for price setting that take these influences into account: cost, demand, and competition.

Cost-Based Pricing

In cost-based pricing, the major influence is the cost of producing the product for the manufacturer, of purchasing and selling the product for the retailer, and of providing the service for the service firm (internal influence). Figure 8-10 illustrates the use of cost-based pricing in each of these types of business.

Once the costs have been determined, a percentage markup is added to reflect the profit objective of the firm. The owner-manager should realize, however, that the initial markup is seldom achieved. Markdowns and inventory shrinkage should be estimated (see Figure 8-10) and built into the markup calculation.

Figure 8-10   Cost-Based Pricing Methods

Manufacturing Firm

Direct material cost per unit	$ 18.00
Direct labour cost per unit	21.00
Variable overhead (manufacturing)	10.00
Fixed overhead (factory)	30.00
Total manufacturing cost per unit	79.00
Selling cost per unit	3.00
General overhead (allocated per unit)	5.00
Total cost per unit	87.00
Desired profit	13.00
Selling price	$100.00

Retail Firm

Cost of merchandise	$50.00
Selling and storage (estimated)	20.00
Estimated markdowns	5.00
Desired profit	25.00
Selling price	$100.00

In retailing, the difference between the price and the cost of inventory is known as *markup*. In this example, it is $50 and is usually expressed as a percentage in the following manner:

$$\text{Percentage} = \frac{100-50}{100} = 50\%$$

Service Firm

Estimated cost of providing service per customer	$ 60.00
Estimated overhead costs per customer	20.00
Desired profit per customer	20.00
Selling price	$100.00

Figure 8-11   Consumer Price Sensitivity: Demand Pricing

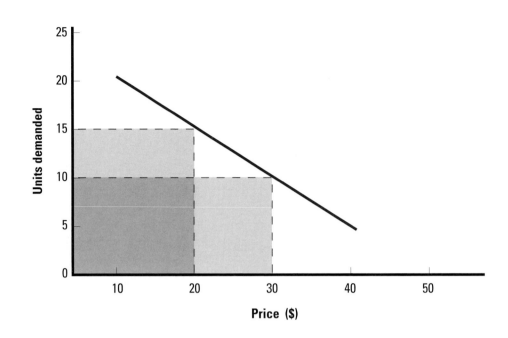

Demand-Based Pricing

Demand-based pricing uses consumer sensitivity to price as the major factor in arriving at the final price level (external influences). Usually primary research in the form of surveying will be required to assess acceptable prices for new products. Figure 8-11 (see above) illustrates the results of such a survey incorporated into a demand curve. Each point on the line shows the quantity demanded at the related price. For example, at a price of $30, demand would be 10 units; at $20, demand increases to slightly more than 15 units. In this example, the total revenue at the $30 price is $300 (30 × 10), whereas at $20 the total revenue is $320 (20 × 16). This situation can be described as price elastic. In price-elastic situations, price increases result in a negative effect on demand. For some types of products (convenience and specialty) and some industries (those with little direct competition), price may be less important to the purchaser, and thus a change in price may not significantly affect demand. If this condition exists, it means the business has much more freedom and flexibility in setting prices than it would in a more competitive and price-sensitive situation.

For products and services already on the market, existing price levels and industry experts may provide valuable information to assist in setting demand-based prices.

Competition-Based Pricing

Firms in a growing number of industries are using competitive pricing in which the major consideration in setting prices is the price levels and policies of competitors (external influences). Many firms conduct ongoing price checks on the competition to guide their own pricing. The small firm may wish to set prices at a fixed percentage above, equal to, or below competitors' prices.

The small business owner should not rely too heavily on only one of the above methods of pricing. All these methods are important in most industries, and each should be taken into account when setting the final price for a product or service.

PROMOTION

Gone are the days of the philosophy "build a better mousetrap and the world will beat a path to your door." Today most businesses must actively provide information to the purchaser.

Types of Promotion

Canadian Federation of Independent Business www.cfib.ca

A small business can use essentially four methods to provide information about its product or service: advertising, sales promotions, public relations, and personal selling.

Advertising. Advertising is a nonpersonal form of promotion. It is directed at a mass audience through various forms of media such as television, radio, newspapers, magazines, billboards, and direct mail. A small business owner should be aware of the strengths and weaknesses of each of these types of media and exactly when each is appropriate. This information is presented in Figure 8-12 (on the next page). One of the most rapidly growing vehicles for small business advertising is through the Internet. Recent surveys carried out by the Canadian Federation of Independent Business and Deloitte and Touche found that an increasing number of small business owners used the Internet regularly.[15] It is not only an effective means of advertising but also an excellent tool for securing customer feedback. More will be discussed about small business and the Internet in the next chapter.

Harcourt Canada www.harcourtcanada

Sales Promotions. Sales promotions are also nonpersonal forms of promotion but are directed at a much more restricted audience than is advertising. Examples of sales promotions are point-of-purchase displays, coupons and discounts, trade shows and exhibitions, and contests. All of these mechanisms are very effective forms of advertising for the small business, and some are relatively inexpensive. Appendix 8C provides information regarding Canadian trade shows.

Spin Master Toys www.spinmaster.com

Public Relations. Public relations, or publicity, can be a very effective form of promotion for the small business. This is particularly the case when the product or service is innovative or extraordinary in some way. The profile at the beginning of this chapter illustrates how Spin Master toys was successful in utilizing public relations to launch new products. This form of promotion may involve public-interest news stories, sponsorship by the business of community projects such as sporting teams or events, or specialty advertising such as calendars, pens, hats, and the like. Public relations is generally inexpensive and can be very helpful in promoting not only the product or service but the business itself.

Trade Show News Network www2.tsnn.com

Personal Selling. The conditions conducive to a short distribution channel or an emphasis on personal selling are discussed earlier in this chapter. Most businesses will require some personal selling as part of their marketing strategy. Owner-managers will undoubtedly be required to promote themselves, their businesses, and their products to customers, bankers, suppliers, and government agencies through personal selling. If salespeople are employed, they will need to be trained, not only with respect to product or service knowledge, but also in selling skills. Other aspects of training, supervision, and motivation of a sales force are discussed in detail in Chapter 12. A type of personal selling which is significant for small business is the use of direct marketing. Common methods of direct marketing are mail, phone, cable television, and the Internet.

Figure 8-12 **Advertising for Small Business**

Media Type	Advantages	Disadvantages	Particular Suitability	Typical Costs

Newspapers	Flexible
	Timely
	Local market
	Credible source
		May be expensive
		Short life
		Little "pass along"
		Nonselective
		  audience
			All general retailers
			  or for definable
			  market areas
			  similar to
			  circulation
				One-page ad: large
				  market
				  ($1,800–$3,000)
				small market
				  ($500–$800)
				(prices dependent on
				  length of contract)

Television	Sight, sound, and
	  motion
	Wide reach
		Cost
		Clutter
		Short exposure
		Less selective
			Definable market area
			  surrounding the
			  station's location
			  for certain products
				30 seconds of prime
				  time:
				large local market
				  ($750–$1000)
				small local market
				  ($200–$300)

Direct mail	Selected audience
	Personalization
	Flexible
		Relatively expensive
		  per contact
		High "throwout" rate
			New and expanding
			  businesses; those
			  using coupon
			  returns or catalogues
				Approximately $1 per
				  contact

Radio	Wide reach
	Segmented audience
	Inexpensive
		Audio only
		Weak attention
		Short exposure
			Business catering to
			  identifiable groups:
			  teens, commuters,
			  housewives
				30 seconds of prime
				  time:
				large local market
				  ($175–$250)
				small local market
				  ($35–$60)

Magazines, including trade publications and catalogues	Very segmented audience Credible source Good reproduction Long life Good "pass along"	Inflexible Long lead times Costly	Restaurants Entertainment Identifiable target Markets Mail order Chains	Approximately $30,000 for one-page, four- colour ad in *Chatelaine* (French and English)
Outdoor	Flexible Repeat exposure Inexpensive	Mass market Very short exposure	Amusements Tourist businesses Brand name retailers	1 month of prime location billboard, large market ($2,500–$3,000)

Telephone directories	Users in market
	  for goods or
	  services
	Continuous ads
	Costs relatively low
		Limited to active
		  shoppers
		Limited visibility
		Not dynamic
			Services
			Retailers of brand
			  name items
			Highly specialized
			  retailers
				Inexpensive—
				depends on size of
				ad

Internet	Inexpensive
	Requires computer
	  hardware and
	  expertise
		Limited market (but
		  growing)
		Can't see and try
		Lack of privacy
		Viruses
			Products that do
			  not require trial
			Information products
				"Sign on" fee
				varies by type of ad

Trade Shows	Many buyers High Exposure Time Saving	Cost	Product sold in chain stores	Varies

STEPS IN A PROMOTIONAL CAMPAIGN

How does the owner-manager prepare the promotional program for the product or service and/or the business? Following are the essential steps in carrying out a promotional program that can be used as a guide for the small business.

1. Set Promotional Objectives. Specific objectives should be set prior to the promotion. Typical examples are the desired percentage increase in sales, the amount of traffic to be generated, and the percentage of awareness increase desired.

2. Determine the Target of the Promotion. While in many cases the target will be the ultimate consumer, often it may be a middleman in the distribution channel or another group that has considerable influence over the purchase.

3. Understand the Target's Needs and Perceptions of the Product or Service. Once the target of the promotion has been determined, it is essential that information be gathered about that group with regard to their needs, media habits, and perceptions of the product category or specific product or service. This information is very similar to the consumer profile discussed earlier.

4. Develop the Relevant Theme. The next step is to develop a theme for the promotion that will reflect responsiveness to target needs and perceptions and help achieve the promotional objective. It is important that only one theme be used, since too many themes or too much information can confuse the consumer and lead to unsatisfactory results. Research has shown that the most important factor in the success of a small business is to promote credibility.[16]

5. Determine the Method or Media to Use. The decision about which promotional type to use often depends on the relative importance of creating awareness and/or closing the sale. Figure 8-13 lists the strengths of each previously mentioned type of promotion with respect to these purposes. As the figure illustrates, advertising and public relations and some sales promotions tend to be more effective in creating awareness, whereas personal selling tends to work better for achieving or closing the sale.

6. Develop a Specific Promotional Message. Once the theme and medium have been determined, it is possible to develop the specific type of message to be used. As Figure 8-13 points out, some types of information are not appropriate for certain types of media. Care should be taken to ensure that the benefits of the product are clearly communicated.

Figure 8-13   Effectiveness of Promotion Types

	Personal Selling	Sales Promotions	Public Relations	Advertising
Create awareness of product or business	Weak	Weak	Strong	Strong
Develop interest in product	Weak	Medium	Weak	Strong
Increase desire to purchase product	Medium	Medium	Weak	Medium
Achieve product purchase	Strong	Medium	Weak	Weak

7. Setting the Promotional Budget. Once the method of promotion is determined, it is possible to estimate the cost of the promotion. Several methods are used to determine amounts to spend on promotion. The most common approach is the percent of sales method. Standard percentages for various businesses can serve as a guide in using this method. (See Appendix 8B for examples.) The percent of sales method is theoretically weak but simple to apply, which explains its high rate of use by small businesses. A business owner should remain flexible in using these percentages, however, as market and product conditions may necessitate a deviation from the averages.

8. Implement the Promotional Program. An essential feature of implementing the program is proper timing. Certain times of the year, the week, and even the day may be inappropriate for promoting the product or service to the target market.

9. Evaluate the Effectiveness of the Promotion. The owner-manager should attempt to evaluate the promotional effectiveness to aid in future promotions. Evaluating effectiveness is much easier if specific objectives such as those mentioned earlier are set. Observations of results and surveys may be used in this evaluation. The mechanics of using primary research methods are discussed in Chapter 3.

As this chapter illustrates, many aspects are involved in the marketing plan of a small business. The way all of these aspects are integrated so that they comprise a clear and coordinated strategy often spells the difference between a successful and unsuccessful business. Appendix 8D at the conclusion of this chapter provides a marketing plan checklist.

DATABASE MARKETING FOR THE SMALL BUSINESS

A customer database is an organized collection of comprehensive data about individual customers or prospects, including geographic, demographic, psychographic, and behavioural data. The database can be used to locate good potential customers, tailor products and services to the special needs of targeted consumers, and maintain long-term customer relationships. Database marketing is the process of building, maintaining, and using customer databases and other databases (products, suppliers, resellers) for the purpose of contacting and transacting with customers.

A small business can use databases for both business-to-business as well as business-to-consumer marketing. In business-to-business marketing, the salesperson's customer profile may contain such information as the products and services the customer has bought, past volumes and prices, key contacts, competitive suppliers, status of current contracts, estimated customer expenditures for the next few years, and assessments of competitive strengths and weaknesses in selling and serving the account. In consumer marketing, the customer database may contain a customer's demographics, buying behaviour, and other relevant information. Several simple and inexpensive database software programs are now available to assist small businesses to be more responsive to their customers.

CUSTOMER SERVICE AND RETENTION FOR SMALL BUSINESSES

One of the most critical keys to the success of the small business is retaining its customers. An increasing number of organizations are realizing that the cost is much higher to attract a new customer than to retain an existing one. As a result, expenditures for customer retention activities have now surpassed expenditures on customer attraction in North America.[17] The entrepreneur needs to identify the reasons why customers do not return to their business, and then work to rectify areas that contribute to loss of patronage. Several studies show that by far the largest reason given for a customer terminating business with a company is because of a negative experience with, or bad attitude of, a staff person.[18] Furthermore, North American business, in general, is not given a very positive evaluation in the area of customer service. This problem is even more serious for a small business because of the small customer pool available to the business. In addition, when a current customer switches to a competitor because of poor service, the business not only loses that person's sales but also additional sales of those that this person influences. It is a well-known fact that customers tell more people about a bad experience that they have had with a business than they do when they have a good experience.

The small business should have a natural advantage over large businesses in the area of customer service and retention because of the ability to develop a more personal relationship with the customer. Many large businesses, in their attempts to increase volume of sales, simply cannot provide the level of service that a small business can. This is because service tends to be individualized and time consuming to provide. The small business needs to remember that in most situations the offering of excellent service is what will set it apart from large business and provide an important competitive advantage. (See Incident 8-2 on page 238.)

In order to provide an effective customer service and retention, the small business should do the following:

1. Identify the types of service to offer. These service activities, of course, should be tailored to the needs of the target market of the business as exemplified by the innovations of Boardwalk Equities Inc. in Incident 8-8.

Incident 8-8

The Customer Service Specialists

Calgary-based Boardwalk Equities Inc. is Canada's largest residential property manager. Since its establishment in 1993, Boardwalk has acquired over 25,000 apartment and townhouse units in Alberta, Saskatchewan, and Ontario. Annual revenues have skyrocketed to over $186 million in the past two years. To what does Boardwalk attribute its success? Excellent, unfaltering customer service is Boardwalk's secret.

Gone are the days when tenants surreptitiously slipped maintenance requests under the doors of burly landlords. Boardwalk's exemplary approach to customer service is revolutionizing the property management industry. The company refers to its tenants as "customers" and then treats them in that manner. "We're here to serve their needs, says Boardwalk president Sam Kolias. "Not just their housing needs—their carefree living needs."

Serving tenants' "carefree living needs" has resulted in the development of several unique customer services. Boardwalk has implemented a 24-hour customer call service where tenants are encouraged to call in with maintenance and cleaning requests. Virtual concierges have been installed in many of Boardwalk's apartment lobbies. These computers provide tenants with a further means to submit maintenance and cleaning requests, as well as make rent payments. If tenants are busy, the virtual concierge is capable of fielding grocery delivery requests that are filled by Boardwalk's partners.

The property management company does not intend to stop here with its customer services. In fact, Boardwalk is hoping to become both a long-distance telephone and cable service provider. When all of these services are set up, Boardwalk intends to sell them to other landlords both in Canada and the United States.

SOURCE: Adapted from "Composition of the Profit 100," *Profit*, June 2000, p.40.

2. In order to provide effective service, the business needs to budget adequate funds for this activity. Employee training, guarantees, and other service activities will require a financial investment.

3. The small business should be sure to handle customer concerns and complaints effectively. Research has shown that if a business handles a complaint quickly and satisfactorily, 70–95 percent of customers will continue to patronize the business.

4. It is important that the service level does not disappoint the consumer. While the business may need to advertise the service, many have found the the best policy is to provide better service than their customers expect. Christine Magee, founder of Sleep Country Canada, reflects this point of view. "When a customer comes in the door, we want to exceed their expectations."[19]

5. The small business should move toward utilizing a database of its customers, if possible. As technology becomes more affordable, many small businesses are finding database management of customer information to be a valuable tool in better serving their customers' needs.

6. Any program such as customer service and retention should be regularly evaluated to ensure effectiveness and that it meets the needs of customers.

Summary

1. Marketing activities include defining the target customer's needs and wants, monitoring the relevant outside influences, developing the product or service, selecting the channel of distribution, setting the price, and developing the promotional program.

2. The three types of target markets a small business may attempt to reach are consumer markets, industrial markets, and export markets. It is important that the entrepreneur identify the needs of the target market in developing the marketing strategy.

3. Some of the most common external influences affecting the small business are the economy, the competition, legal restrictions, and the social and cultural environment. In dealing with external influences, the owner-manager must identify which external conditions affect the business and then set up a system to monitor and effectively respond to changes in those influences.

4. The classifications of consumer goods include convenience, shopping, and specialty goods. The marketing strategy will differ for each type. The major decision areas in distribution include being aware of the channel options, deciding on the length of the channel, and determining the channel intensity. The three methods of setting price are cost-based, demand-based, and competition-based pricing. There are four methods of providing information about a product or service: advertising, sales promotion, public relations, and personal selling.

Chapter Problems and Applications

1. Define the target market for Nordel Home Hardware (see Incident 8-2). What are the target market demographics, lifestyle characteristics, purchase characteristics, and purchase motivations (see Figure 8-2)?

2. Illustrate how Digigraph Systems Ltd. (Incident 8-4) successfully completed the three steps in developing an export market outlined in the chapter.

3. Discuss the uncontrollable variables that might affect Digigraph Systems Ltd. in the development of its overseas markets.

4. Develop a marketing mix (i.e., product, promotion, price, distribution) for a bakery.

5. Where is Kellogg's Corn Flakes in the product life cycle? What has Kellogg done to prolong the life cycle of this product?

6. What could a new cereal company do to speed up the adoption rate for its cereals?

7. How would you classify the following products (see Figure 8-8)? How would you promote and distribute these products? Explain.
   a. Discount clothes
   b. Quality furniture
   c. Chocolate bar
   d. Bread

8. Why was Clearly Canadian's (Incident 8-7) original distribution system ineffective? Which channel are they now using? Is it appropriate? Why?

9. Which pricing system would you use for the following products? Why?
   a. Campbell's Soup
   b. Montreal Expo season tickets
   c. Patio furniture
   d. Automobiles

10. Using a scale of -1 to $+1$, how would you rate the following products for elasticity ($-1 =$ inelastic, $0 =$ neutral, and $+1 =$ elastic)? Justify your answers.
    a. Salt
    b. Porsche automobile
    c. Lawn mower

11. If the cost of merchandise is $100 and it is sold for $150, what is the markup on cost? On selling price?

12. You have been approached to develop an advertising campaign for a new local discount golf franchise. The owners realize they need to develop awareness among consumers but have a very limited amount of funds available for advertising. Using Figure 8-12 as a guide, decide which media type to use for the advertising campaign. Justify your decision to use or not use each media type.

13. Choose the promotional types (advertising, personal selling, sales promotion, and public relations) you would use for the following list of products. Explain why.
    a. Medical supplies
    b. Hula Hoop™
    c. Recreational vehicles
    d. Coca-Cola™
    e. B.C. Lions football team

14. Interview a local small business owner and find out what his or her marketing strategy is. Determine the promotional strategy. Are these strategies similar to those discussed in the chapter?

Appendix 8A

Agencies Providing Export Assistance

Canadian Commercial Corporation (CCC)
Bental Tower IV
P.O. Box 49158
Vancouver, BC V7X 1K8

Canadian Export Association (CEA)
99 Bank Street, Suite 250
Ottawa, ON K1P 6B9

Canadian Export Newsletter
Dept. of Foreign Affairs and International Trade
125 Sussex Dr.
Ottawa, ON K1A 0G2

Canadian International Development Agency
(CIDA)
200 Promenade du Portage
Hull, PQ K1A 0G4

Canadian Management Network
This is a database of 170 consultants
assisting in reporting to foreign markets.

Department of Industry
1st Floor, East Tower
235 Queen Street
Ottawa, ON KIA 0H5

Export Development Corporation (EDC)
Box 655
Ottawa, ON K1P 5T9

External Affairs and International Trade Canada
125 Sussex Drive
Ottawa, ON K1A 0G2

Forum for International Trade Training

Open Bidding Service (OBS)
This is an electronic bulletin service which
announces government contracts up for tender.

Web site for Exporters
www.worldexport.com

Appendix 8B

Advertising as Practised by Selected Small Businesses

Type of Business	Average Ad Budget (percent of sales)	Favourite Media	Other Media Used
Gift stores	2.2	Weekly newspapers	Yellow Pages, radio, direct mail, magazines
Hairdressing shops	2.0–5.0	Yellow Pages	Newspapers (for special events), word of mouth
Home furnishing stores	1.0–3.2	Newspapers	Direct mail, radio
Pet shops	2.0–5.0	Yellow Pages	Window displays, shopper newspapers, direct mail
Restaurants and food services	0.3–3.2	Newspapers, radio, Yellow Pages, transit, outdoor	Television for chain or franchise restaurants

Type of Business	Average Ad Budget (percent of sales)	Favourite Media	Other Media Used
Shoe stores	0.5–0.8	Newspapers, direct mail, radio	Yellow Pages (especially for specialty shoe vendors)
Bars and cocktail lounges	1.0–1.2	Newspapers (entertainment section), local magazines, tourist bulletins	Specialties
Bookstores	1.5–1.6	Newspapers, shoppers, Yellow Pages	Direct mail
Building maintenance services		Direct mail, door-to-door, Yellow Pages	Signs on company vehicles and equipment
Camera shops (independent)	2.0–3.5	Direct mail, handouts, Yellow Pages	Newspapers (except large urban)
Drugstores (independent)	1.0–3.0	Local newspapers, shoppers	Direct mail (list from prescription files)
Dry cleaning plants	0.9–2.0	Local newspapers, shoppers, Yellow Pages	Store front ads, pamphlets on clothes care
Equipment rental services	1.7–4.7	Yellow Pages	

SOURCES: Adapted from Dennis H. Tootelian and Ralph M. Gaedeke, *Small Business Review* (Sacramento, Calif.: Goodyear Publishing Company), pp. 154–155; Dun and Bradstreet Operating Statistics, 1990 (Toronto: Dun and Bradstreet).

Appendix 8C

Directories of Trade Shows and Exhibitions

Canadian Industry Shows and Exhibitions: Annual Directory
Toronto, Ontario: Maclean Hunter
Frequency: annual
Canadian trade and consumer shows are arranged by category of product or service. Access is by date, name, and location of the show.

Trade Shows and Professional Exhibits Directory
Detroit: Gale Research
Frequency: annual
Covers over 3,500 exhibitions, trade shows, and conventions in Canada, the United States, and the world.

Appendix 8D

Checklist for a Marketing Plan

The Target Market

1. Has the target market been clearly defined geographically?
2. Has the target consumer been clearly identified?
3. What are the target consumer's characteristics—age, income, education, occupation?
4. What are the target consumer's lifestyle characteristics—activities, interests, opinions, media habits, personalities?
5. What are the target consumer's purchase characteristics—what, when, where, how much of the product or service does he or she purchase?
6. What are the reasons the target consumer purchases the product?
7. Are there any government programs that can assist in marketing to the target consumer?

The Environment

1. What economic forces will affect the business?
2. What is the competitive situation? How many competitors? What are relative market shares? What is the nature of competitors' strategies? What are competitors' strengths and weaknesses?
3. What legal restrictions will affect the marketing of the product or service?
4. Are there any social or cultural trends that will affect the business?
5. What adjustments have been made to accommodate any of the above environmental constraints?

The Product

1. What are the objectives and policies for the product?
2. How will the product be manufactured?
3. What is the estimated length of the life cycle for the product?
4. What can be done to increase rate of adoption of the product?
5. How does the target consumer classify the product?
6. What will be the product quality, depth, and variety?
7. What warranty and service standards will be set?
8. Does the product or service possess the features or characteristics the target consumer wants?

Distribution

1. What channel options are available to reach the target consumer?
2. Can the product be marketed better through a short-direct channel or a long-indirect channel?

3. Who are potential buyers for the product?

4. What trade shows exist for the industry?

5. What level of intensity should exist in the distribution channel?

6. Will the selected distribution channel provide the product to the target consumer at the right place, at the right time, and in the right quantities?

Price

1. What price policies have been set?

2. What price is the target consumer willing to pay?

3. How important is price to the target consumer?

4. What levels of markup are required to cover selling and overhead costs?

5. What are competitors' prices, and how do they compare with our product price?

Promotion

1. What are the objectives of the promotional program?

2. Does the theme reflect the target consumer's needs and attitudes?

3. What specific media will be selected to carry the message to the target consumer?

4. Does the product require personal selling?

5. How much will be spent on promotion?

6. What is the timing of the promotional program? Has a calendar timetable been prepared for this?

7. How will the results of the promotion be evaluated?

8. Will the business offer credit to the target consumer? If so, what procedures will be followed to screen, monitor, and collect accounts?

Suggested Readings

Blake, Gary, and Robert Bly. *How to Promote Your Own Business.* Scarborough, Ont.: Canadian Small Business Institute, 1990.

Bullock, John F. "Competing in a Global Economy." *Journal of Small Business and Entrepreneurship,* July–September 1991.

Carroll, Jim. *Opportunities for Canadian Business.* Scarborough, Ont.: Prentice-Hall, 1995.

Davidson, Hillary. "Why Canadians Can't Market," *Profit,* April, 2001, p. 18-22.

Davidson, Jeffrey P. The Marketing Source Book for Small Business. New York: John Wiley and Sons, 1989.

Foot, David, and Daniel Stoffman. *Boom, Bust, and Echo 2000: Profiting from the Demographic Shift in the New Millenium.* Toronto: MacFarlane, Walter and Ross, 1998.

Gordon, Ian. *Relationship Marketing.* New York: Wiley, 1998.

Lewis, Herschell Gordon, and Robert D. Lewis. *Selling On The Net — The Complete Guide.* Lincolnwood, Illinois: N.T.C. Business Books, 1996.

Lucklow, Diane. "Sell for Real in Cyberspace." *Profit Magazine,* April–May 1997, p. 71.

Roadmap to Exporting, 2nd Edition. Ottawa: Government of Canada, 2000.

Stone, Robert. *Successful Direct Marketing Methods,* 6th edition. NTC Publishing Group, Nov.1996.

Team Canada Inc. *A Step-by-Step Guide to Exporting.* Ottawa: Government of Canada, 1999.

Comprehensive Case
The Framemakers: Part 5

Saturday was the big day! Robert and Teresa had been able to obtain the needed financing after considerable difficulty and were now ready to open their store. The few weeks leading up to the grand opening were hectic. The interior remodelling and layout organization took longer than they had expected. Some of the inventory did not arrive on time. The Normans learned they needed many items they hadn't planned for. As a result of these difficulties, the opening had to be postponed for a few weeks.

Once ready, they placed advertising in newspapers, on radio, and even on television announcing the store's opening. They soon found out that the $2,500 budgeted for opening promotion didn't go very far. The quarter-page ad in the local newspaper totalled $500 for three days. The Normans paid $700 for radio advertising the week before opening on the two Brandon radio stations. This included production costs. They also placed an advertisement on a local television station that cost $1,300, including production. Robert wished he had had more money for promotion, but realized that if he hadn't purchased the lowest advertising rate, he wouldn't have received even the coverage he did. He wondered how other framing shops got much promotion done using the 1 percent of sales figure the Professional Picture Framers Association (PPFA) had suggested.

When Saturday rolled around, Robert and Teresa were a bit disappointed to note that the store wasn't as busy as they had hoped. In addition, several people who came in looked around and left without making purchases. They hoped this was characteristic of a typical store opening. Some purchasers of frames indicated that The Framemakers had good prices on the merchandise. Others, however, complained prices on some items were way out of line. This troubled the Normans as they had been sure to follow the suppliers' suggested retail prices on most of the merchandise. A few customers also complained of poor parking and of difficulty finding the store.

At the end of the day, Robert and Teresa were exhausted and disappointed. They had rung up sales of only $542. They were concerned about the negative comments they had received and wondered if this was just an occupational hazard or if the business had some real problems.

Questions

1. Evaluate The Framemakers' opening promotion program. Suggest any changes that might have improved its effectiveness.
2. Evaluate The Framemakers' pricing procedures. Make recommendations regarding what, if anything, should be done at this point.

Video Case Questions
High Flyers*

CBC ⊛

Back in 1993, Anton Rabie was just 23 years old, but already a born entrepreneur. Anton and two buddies from business school were manufacturing Earth Buddies, little grasshead guys on the Chia Pet model.

1. What inexpensive forms of promotion have been used by Spinmaster?

2. What are the advantages and disadvantages of an Air Hog section in a toy store?

3. What are the risks associated with operating a business in this industry?

*Source: CBC *Venture* #748, running time 10:24.

Chapter 9

Small Business and Electronic Commerce

Chapter Objectives

- To explain what electronic commerce is and how a small business can utilize it.

- To describe the advantages of electronic commerce to a small business.

- To discuss the potential difficulties associated with establishing electronic commerce.

- To describe how to construct an electronic commerce web site, select a web host, and attract customers to it.

Small Business Profile

Michael Furdyk
Buybuddy Inc.

Buybuddy Inc.
www.buybuddy.com

By 2005, consumers in the U.S. will spend $632 billion on-line. Buybuddy Inc. provides the means to facilitate this on-line shopping projection. In fact, Buybuddy is the pioneer of a unique technology that has made the company the Internet's leading community-driven commerce provider. Many on-line shoppers spend the majority of their time using group-buying sites that lead to links that simply do not have the means to carry out educated price comparisons. Canadian, Michael Furdyk, American, John Brown, and Australian, Michael Hayman, recognized the need for a system that would help consumers more easily navigate the Internet to find information needed to make informed buying decisions. In 1998, the three partners quickly capitalized on their idea and launched the driving technology behind Toronto-based Buybuddy.com.

CEO Mike Ambramsky says, "What we have created is an essential on-line commerce service—one that combines commerce with community, and our user base is really starting to respond positively to the type of value we can provide for them." The user-friendly web site provides tens of thousands of customers with the ability to make side-by-side comparisons in over 100 categories of products ranging from hardware, software, video games, movies, and music.

Buybuddy's aim has been to revolutionize the on-line comparative shopping experience. This has been accomplished by offering more than just price comparison services. Product reviews by customers and web sites are also available and serve to create the community atmosphere on which Buybuddy prides itself. Consumers can instantly place on-line orders and are even given the chance to bargain if lower prices can be found.

"From a technology perspective, our heritage in creating a superior user experience based on community development is what separates us from our competition," declares VP of Product Development, Michael Hayman. Buybuddy's innovative technology has put them miles ahead of the competition. But rather than keep it to themselves, Buybuddy is capitalizing on the global market potential of its revolutionary technology through syndication. Buybuddy provides customized systems to syndicate partners who wish to use Buybuddy technology but retain their own look and feel. Customers simply see a new, enhanced site with the same familiar branding.

Buybuddy partners Furdyk, Brown, and Hayman want to provide the best in community and commerce. A previous collaboration for an on-line publishing company called MyDesktop.com sold for US$1 million in 1999. Buybuddy technology is sure to surpass this last venture, as instant access to Buybuddy's content and services is available on PDAs, cell phones, pagers, and other handheld wireless devices in both North America and Asia. VP Michael Hayman adds, "And with the next generation of our product suite due out soon, it's only going to get better from here."

SOURCE: Adapted from www.buybuddy.com

SMALL BUSINESS AND ELECTRONIC COMMERCE

internet.com
www.internet.com/
home-d.html

Electronic commerce (e-commerce) is pervasive in society today. A person cannot pick up a newspaper, magazine, turn on the television or radio without being flooded with information about some aspect of e-commerce. A recent Ipsos-Reid survey found that three out of four Canadians say that e-commerce or "the Net" has significantly impacted their lives.[1] Business managers are given the impression that they must get on the e-commerce bandwagon or risk being left behind by their competitors. Many small business owners recognize the need to incorporate e-commerce into their operations but do not know how to do so. This chapter will provide information to guide the small business owner in evaluating the merits of e-commerce and establishing it in their organization.

WHAT IS ELECTRONIC COMMERCE?

Electronic Commerce
in Canada
www.e-com.ic.gc.ca/
english/index.html

Electronic commerce, or e-commerce, refers to the use of computers and electronic communication networks to connect with other relevant organizations. E-commerce covers a wide range of activities from electronic mail (e-mail) to Internet-based sales, transactions, and web-based marketing. E-commerce is a worldwide phenomenon, which will significantly impact national economies, businesses, and consumers over the next few years. It is a new way of conducting business, which will supplant many traditional commercial relationships.

The majority of people think e-commerce means on-line shopping. However, web shopping is only a small part of the e-commerce portrait. The term also refers to on-line stock-and-bond transactions, and buying and downloading software without ever going near a store. In addition, e-commerce includes business-to-business connections that make purchasing easier for large as well as small organizations.

E-commerce can help small business improve the ways it does business with customers, other businesses, and the government. Small business involvement in e-commerce can take a number of forms, with varying levels of cost and complexity, depending on the business's needs. The basic use of e-mail by small business can provide a rapid and reliable way to communicate with suppliers, to receive and respond to customer queries, or even to initiate customer contact. For example, product information and quotations can be e-mailed, manufacturers and wholesalers can accept orders on-line, and businesses can quickly and easily put potential customers in touch with their retail outlets.

A small business can improve its operations by greater use of electronic bookkeeping and records management. The Internet offers a means for business to order its supplies on-line, resulting in faster and more efficient provision of goods and services, potentially reducing the need for the physical warehousing of inventory. Small businesses can also improve their efficiency by making use of a wide range of on-line banking services, such as electronic bill payment, funds transfer, and payroll management, all now offered by most large financial institutions.

GROWTH OF E-COMMERCE

Over the last decade e-commerce has seen dramatic growth. On a global basis Forrester Research forecasts that worldwide e-commerce will reach $6.8 trillion by 2004.[2] While North American activity represents a majority of this trade, its domination will fade in the future as Asian-Pacific and Western European countries experience increased growth.[3]

Small Business Canada
www.sbinfocanada.
about.com/cs/
ecommerce/index.html

Canadian expenditures on the Net have also increased dramatically over the past few years. Combined consumer and business transactions stood at $11 billion in 1999 and are expected to grow to $94 billion by 2003.[4] Recent research indicates that 5 million Canadian adults have bought products or services over the Net, and another 2 million indicate that they intend to do so within the next year.[5] In addition, Canadians appear to be plugged into the Internet more per capita than almost any other country[6] with recent estimates pegging Internet access at close to 70 percent of the population.[7]

The major growth areas of e-commerce, in terms of tangible goods, are computer products, consumer products, books and magazines, and music and entertainment products. Although a significant portion of Canadian consumer expenditures in these areas were made from non-Canadian companies, mostly from the U.S., an increasing number of Canadian companies have begun to enter the market. The proportion of Canadian businesses using the Internet advanced in almost all industry sectors over the past year. Internet use was most common in information and cultural industries (93 percent), private sector educational services (89 percent), and professional and technical services (84 percent).

Grocery Gateway
www.grocerygateway.
com

Canadian business received $7.2 billion in customer orders over the Internet in 2000, up 73.4 percent from $4.2 billion in 1999. However, only 6 percent of businesses reported selling goods and services on-line in 2000, so it appears that the potential for growth is great.[8] One successful Canadian e-tailing business is Grocery Gateway which combines the expertise of several organizations to sell groceries on-line.

While Internet purchases receive much attention, there are other important uses of e-commerce for small business which are also experiencing growth. For example, of the businesses that used the Internet in 2000, 43 percent did so to access databases of suppliers, 23 percent did so for education and training, and 16 percent did so to access databases of customers. Figure 9-1 illustrates the incidence of some of these other types of use of the Internet for various sizes of business.

Figure 9-1   Types of Internet Usage Among SMEs

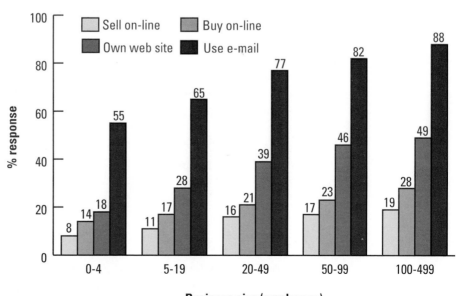

SOURCE: Canadian Federation of Independent Business, results of *Our Members' Opinions Survey* #46 (Q2, 2000).

TYPES OF E-COMMERCE

There are several types or methods that a small business can follow to utilize e-commerce in their operations. The following describes these options.

Business to Consumer (B2C)

gosolo
www.gosolocanada.
com

With this type, the focus is on the business-to-consumer transaction processes. This type of e-commerce has experienced very rapid growth recently as has just been discussed. Consumers are increasingly going on-line to procure goods and services, arrange delivery and financing, and acquire after-sale service. B2C e-business includes retail sales (e-tail) and other on-line purchases such as software, music, entertainment venue tickets, airline tickets, travel products, and financial products. Many existing brick-and-mortar retailers (including many small businesses) are now also e-retailers with a web storefront. These combined brick-and-mortar/on-line businesses are known as "brick and click." Those businesses whose whole channel is on-line are known as "pure play" e-commerce businesses. The largest business-to-consumer e-tailers are shown in Figure 9-2. There are a number of business models that B2C businesses use to generate revenue. These models will be covered in the next section.

Business to Business (B2B)

Although B2C is the most familiar type of e-commerce at present, B2B is expected to represent a much larger share in dollar terms in the future. There are a number of methods that businesses use to conduct B2B on-line. Many businesses use intranets to allow employees to

Figure 9-2   Top E-Tailers of March 2001
Ranked by Share of Purchasers

Rank	Site	Unique Audience (000)	Purchaser Share (%)
1.	Amazon.com	22,751	15.1
2.	eBay*	18,987	14.5
3.	BMG.com	4,762	4.3
4.	Barnes & Noble	5,948	3.8
5.	ColumbiaHouse.com	2,723	3.7
6.	Half.com	4,939	3.1
7.	JCPenney.com	3,339	3.0
8.	Travelocity	7,966	2.5
9.	CDNow.com	5,295	2.2
10.	Southwest.com	3,954	2.0

*Does not include Half.com subsidiary.

SOURCE: Nielson/NetRatings & Harris Interactive

view and access web sites that are only for internal organizational use and not for the outside world. The use of intranets, which use Internet technology, can add value to small business in a number of ways. These include increased productivity and decreased costs. Small businesses are also using extranets, which connect a business intranet to selected suppliers and buyers. This can improve a small business's procurement in B2B exchanges. Since both intranets and extranets use web technologies, end users need very little training to become proficient in their use.

Many small businesses utilize web sites that bring several buyers and sellers together in a digital market space. B2B exchanges can add value to small business by allowing small businesses to buy and sell goods and services to each other at dynamic (market-driven) prices. Their purchases and sales can be aggregated with other small and large businesses so that they can compete in the market on an equal footing with businesses and markets that are much larger.

B2B e-commerce sites work in various ways and are broken into two major groups: the verticals and horizontals. Verticals are B2B sites designed to meet the needs of a particular industry, such as retail. Vertical sites are the most likely to contain community features like industry news, articles, and discussion groups. Horizontal sites provide products, goods, materials, or services that are not specific to a particular industry or company. Horizontal B2Bs provide services and products that any industry could use. Horizontals might provide travel, transportation services, office equipment, or maintenance and operating supplies. Horizontals and verticals can perform as intermediaries which facilitate transactions or connect buyers and sellers together directly. There isn't one predominant model for B2B electronic commerce. B2B sites vary from those providing simple lead generation, to multi-faceted marketplaces serving a diversity of buyers and sellers, to private extranets.

Business to Government (B2G)

Merx
www.merx.bmo.com

The primary focus with this type of e-commerce is toward government agencies at the national, provincial, or local level. The method is similar to the B2B exchange type but focuses on the government procurement model. This is a very large market in Canada. Before the establishment of e-commerce, many small business were unable to obtain access to this market due to the significant barriers of entry. The Canadian Federal Government estimates that it procures $8–9 billion in goods and services per year. Most provincial and federal agencies and departments across Canada are required to advertise potential purchases over $25,000, with many others choosing to post contracts under that dollar value to ensure open competition. Experts estimate that as government agencies and departments streamline processes and amalgamate departments, governments will look increasingly to the private sector to provide goods and services. E-commerce tools have opened the way for small business to enter this market on a more equal footing with larger business. Merx is one B2G exchange on which Canadian Federal Government contracts are advertised.

Consumer to Consumer (C2C)

ebay Canada
www.ebay.ca

In this method consumers sell directly to one another via on-line exchanges and auctions. A good example of this model is ebay Canada. Ebay has been very successful at generating repeat business. Some dealers of antiques and collectibles are, in fact, making a living using ebay as their sole storefront. Many people, who started off as consumers, have turned these auction C2C models into a business.

Consumer to Business (C2B)

priceline.com
www.priceline.com

This type of e-commerce is called a reverse auction. This method lets consumers name the product or service they are interested in and the attributes they want in the product or service. The consumer might dictate such things as quantity, physical attributes, and price. Businesses are then able to match their offerings with what the consumer wants in order to complete the transaction. Examples of this type of e-commerce are priceline.com and reverseauction.com.

E-COMMERCE MODELS

Within the types of e-commerce discussed previously, there are many e-commerce business models. A business model is the way a business conducts business in order to generate revenue. A good business model is an important part of a business plan for a brick-and-mortar business. It is just as essential in the world of e-commerce. For a firm to be successful, it needs to be able to describe how it can generate revenues that exceed costs in order to be profitable over the long term. There are nine basic business models that can be used on the Internet.[9] These will be discussed below.

Brokers

Brokers are market makers in that they bring buyers and sellers together and facilitate transactions. They can be business to business (B2B) or consumer to consumer (C2C) markets. A broker charges a fee for each transaction it enables. Brokerage models can take a number of forms. An example of this model is eTrade which allows consumers to buy stocks on the Internet.

Advertising Model

altavista
www.altavista.com

The web advertising model is an extension of the traditional media-broadcasting model. The broadcaster, in this case a web site, provides content (usually for free) and services (like e-mail, chat forums) mixed with advertising messages in the form of banner ads. The banner ads may be the major or sole source of revenue for the broadcaster. The broadcaster may be a content creator or a distributor of content created elsewhere. The advertising model only works when the volume of viewer traffic is large or highly specialized. Examples are ExciteCanada.com and Alta Vista.

Infomediary Model

Deja.com
www.groups.google.
com

Data about consumers and their buying habits are extremely valuable, especially when that information is carefully analyzed and used to target marketing campaigns. Some firms are able to function as informediaries by collecting and selling information to other businesses An example is Deja.com which allows one to search the Net for keyed-in information.

Merchant Model

chapters.indigo.ca
www.chapters.indigo.ca

This is a classic model of wholesalers and retailers of goods and services; one with which most people are very familiar. An example is chapters.indigo.ca, an on-line seller of books.

Manufacturer Model

Flowerbud.com
www.flowerbud.com

This model relies on the power of the web to allow manufacturers to reach buyers directly and thereby compress or disintermediate the distribution channel. It is important to remember that the services performed by the middleman in the distribution channels are just being transferred somewhere else. It is likely that the manufacturer or the consumer now has to provide the middleman's functions. An example of this type of model is Flowerbud.com, a fresh flower distribution company.

Affilliate Model

The affiliate model provides purchase opportunities wherever people may be surfing. This model gives financial incentives to other web sites to promote products and services. An example is BeFreeze which receives a commission for sales resulting from referring people to business web sites.

Community Model

National Public Radio
www.pbs.org/npr

The viability of the community model is based on user loyalty (as opposed to high-traffic volume). Users have a high investment in both time and emotion in the site. In some cases, users are regular contributors of content and/or money. Having users who visit continually offers advertising, infomediary, or specialized portal opportunities. The community model may also run on a subscription fee for premium services. An example of a community model site is National Public Radio.

Subscription Model

Slate
www.slate.msn.com

With this model users pay for access to the site. High value-added content is essential for this model to be effective. An example is *Slate*, a magazine that regularly publishes on-line news and information.

Utility Model

fatbrain
www.fatbrain.com

The utility model is a metered usage or pay-as-you-go approach. This works very much like an electric bill in that the more electricity that is used, the higher the bill. An example of this type of model is fatbrain, which contains a comprehensive listing of computer, programming, and technology books as well as training and certification programs.

In utilizing an e-commerce model there may be overlaps with some of the models mentioned above. As a result, a firm may combine different models as part of its web business strategy. A brokerage model may be blended with a subscription model to yield an overall strategy that is profitable. It is likely that in the future new and innovative models will be introduced to the e-commerce landscape.

ADVANTAGES OF E-COMMERCE FOR THE SMALL BUSINESS

While some of the advantages of e-commerce use for a small business have already been mentioned briefly, this section will discuss some of the major reasons why small businesses should give consideration to this too.

Incident 9-1

Small Business Clicking on Electronic Commerce

John Connolly's 10-year-old company has enjoyed dramatic growth since setting up shop on the Internet in 1995.

Annual sales at Image Control, which sells and recycles toner cartridges for fax machines, printers, and copiers, have doubled to $500,000 in the three years following its web site launch.

The Toronto retailer now uses the Internet to process credit card payments, offer free advice, and provide information about its products and services. Last year, the three-person company shipped products to customers in 39 U.S. states and nine countries.

"It's all off the Internet," says Mr. Connolly, referring to Image Control's foreign customers. "I've never paid for an ad in recent years in the U.S."

According to a survey released yesterday, more than 60 percent of Canadian small businesses are using the Internet and one-quarter have conducted financial transactions in cyberspace.

Data collected by SES Canada Research Inc. also suggest that there will be a boom this year in the number of entrepreneurs participating in electronic commerce.

Source: Dawn Walton "Small Business Clicking," *The Globe and Mail*, Wednesday, May 5, 1999, p. B10. Reprinted with permission from *The Globe and Mail*.

Expand Markets

E-commerce can give a small business greater visibility and the possibility of expanding existing markets and finding new customers. This is a great attraction for many small businesses. An example of such a business is found in Incident 9-1. The Internet overcomes many of the challenges of geographic location for small businesses to achieve access to geographically dispersed domestic and foreign markets. By using the web, customers all over the world will have access to the business. Many organizations are caught off guard by this sudden international presence and have not planned for it.

For many Canadian small businesses, it may be something as simple as gaining access to the large U.S. market in an inexpensive way. A web presence can provide visibility without the expense of physically setting up in these markets. For the Canadian small business, the U.S. market has the advantage of a common language, banking, and legal systems.

A web presence makes entering and having a visibility in foreign markets a real possibility, with a reduced investment and expertise. However, having a web presence and conducting business in foreign markets still bears considerable risks that a small business must be prepared for such as legal, logistical, and currency exchange differences and problems. These were discussed in detail in Chapter 8.

Maximize Customer Relationships

Experience has shown that it is much less expensive to service existing customers than it is to find new ones. This was discussed in Chapter 8. For this reason many firms concentrate on satisfying and developing existing relationships with their customers. E-commerce technologies can help the small business maximize customer relations and improve its ability to improve customer responsiveness such as quick turnaround in answering customer queries. Through the use of a web site and e-mail, a small business can have a 24/7 presence and access for its customers. Product information and a frequently-asked-questions section on a business web site can provide first access for customers to get satisfaction to concerns or questions before, during, and after purchase of the product or service. E-mail is also an important tool for achieving customer satisfaction through the answering of queries and concerns. One frequently used area of software development is a web-based software tool called a CRM package. CRM is the acronym for Customer Relationship Management. These packages allow large and small businesses alike to keep better track of their customers and to better satisfy their needs and wants. CRM software is designed to leverage existing customer relationships, increase sales, and reduce the cost of finding new customers.

Create New Services

The materialization of e-commerce has permitted many small businesses to add new digital products and services to their product line in a cost-effective manner. Examples of this are adding information products, or adding value to existing products and services. An illustration of this is found in Incident 9-2. Many small businesses use web sites or e-mail to help customers in their information search by highlighting those attributes or comparing their product to that of their competitors. Mass customization is made much easier by the use of e-commerce.

Although mass production of standardized goods was the source of a business's economic strength for generations, this is changing. The new paradigm of management is mass customization, which allows for large production runs while at the same time customizing each product for each customer. A good example of this is Dell Computer's web site. Each customer selects or designs what he or she wants his or her individual computer to look like, and then Dell is able to assemble that computer in a low-cost way on an assembly line. This is made possible by the use of information technology using the computer and the web.

Incident 9-2

The Evolution of a Dot-Com

After 10 years, Gerry Stanton ended his teaching career and entered the world of high tech. Stanton's smooth talking and flair for spotting opportunity landed him a job with Mitel Corp. In 1984, the entrepreneur retired from his position as Mitel's Human Resource manager and started Stanton & Associates, an HR consulting company. Stanton then purchased the rights to Drake Beam Morin, and launched an HR outplacement firm.

Stanton continued to pursue his interests in human resources and was thrilled when the introduction of the World Wide Web allowed him to move a portion of his outplacement business to the Internet. In 1996, Stanton started Careerbridge.com, a company that developed and maintained electronic job placement boards. Throughout this venture, Stanton continued to provide high-tech clientele with HR consulting expertise.

Eventually, Stanton moved away from the electronic job posting business and created a new entity called E-Cruiter.com Inc. Running two separate companies proved to be challenging for the entrepreneur. "When you have two different business models, you risk not doing either well," says Stanton.

E-Cruiter is a company that offers two HR packages to its clients. A $995 package called E-Cruiter Express provides companies with the means to place high-tech job postings on relevant job boards. If companies require more extensive services, E-Cruiter Enterprise can be purchased. Enterprise is a total hiring solution for companies that lack the skills needed to manage the career portion of their web sites. Despite its innovative concept, E-Cruiter has yet to turn a profit, a problem that many e-commerce companies face.

Source: Adapted from Harvey Schachter, "E-Cruiter.com Inc.," *Profit*, May 2000, p. 38.

Reduce Costs

Small business can achieve substantial cost reductions using e-commerce technologies. These reductions can be achieved in many of the core business processes such as purchasing, production, marketing, and human resource management. The selection of suppliers, cost comparison, aggregation of purchases on-line with similar business buyers, order, and reduction of delivery time are examples of purchasing advantages. In the area of production, a small business can develop more accurate forecasting, order delivery times, and monitor work in progress, resulting in less cash tied up in inventory. Marketing savings might include less expensive advertising messages which are achieved in digital format. Costs such as recruiting, hiring, and training can also be reduced and improved for small businesses by using Internet-based tools.

PROBLEMS WITH E-COMMERCE FOR SMALL BUSINESS

Even though statistics show that the e-commerce market is rapidly growing, there are still many problems which can result from the attempt to adopt it. Figure 9-3 illustrates the results of a survey conducted by Statistics Canada that indicates many of the perceived concerns that non-user businesses have with e-commerce. Among businesses that did not buy or sell over the Internet, 56 percent believed that their goods or services did not lend themselves to Internet transactions. Thirty-six percent preferred to maintain their current business model. Smaller proportions of these enterprises felt that security was a concern (14 percent), or that the cost of development and maintenance was too high (12 percent).

Figure 9-3 Why Businesses Have Not Adopted E-Commerce

	% of Enterprises That Do Not Buy or Sell On-Line
Goods do not lend themselves to Internet transactions	56.4
Prefer to maintain current business model	35.6
Security concerns	13.9
Cost of development and maintenance is too high	11.8
Lack of skilled employees	10.3
Uncertain about benefits	9.9
Customers not ready	9.6
Concern about competitors analyzing company information	5.7
Suppliers not ready	5.6
Internet available to us is too slow	3.6

Source: http://www.statcan.ca/Daily/English/010403/d010403a.htm

Incident 9-3

Cansupply.com Inc.

Beware! Some customers are not "net-ready." Brad Mitchell, president and founder of Cansupply.com Inc., has realized that the Canadian marketplace is slow to adopt on-line purchasing habits. Mitchell heads an office supply company that deals with clients over the Internet. His business idea is simple. Customers place orders on Cansupply's web site. These orders are then passed on to distributors and manufacturers that deliver the goods within 24 hours.

Despite the quick embracing of on-line shopping by those south of the border, Canadians have been less than zealous in using the new purchasing medium. Mitchell estimates Canadian consumers to be 18 months behind the U.S. This lag in buying behaviour has resulted in the redesign of Cansupply's growth strategy. "I'm not going to be as aggressive as I was going to be a year and half ago," says Mitchell. "I won't have 40 or 50 sales reps—instead of the six I have now—because I don't think the business is there yet." Company representatives have had to spend way too much time educating customers on how to buy over the Internet, and many large companies remain reluctant to purchase on-line. This is something entrepreneurs need to be aware of before launching new on-line ventures.

SOURCE: Adapted from "Ahead of the Curve," *Profit*, March 2001, p. 50.

Other frequently mentioned concerns with the adoption of e-commerce include Internet availability, complexity of getting started, inconsistent tax laws, and legal issues. Incident 9-3 describes a company that found the hesitancy on the part of consumers to use e-commerce a problem.

Three factors that appear to be major stumbling blocks to a more successful experience with e-commerce are security concerns, protection of property, and payment systems. These will be discussed in more detail below.

Security Concerns

For many consumers security is a major reason for not using the Internet as was shown in Figure 9-3. Once a business is connected to a public network such as the Internet, it is exposed to security risks that are associated with that network. E-commerce security is the protection of assets from unauthorized access, use, alteration, or destruction. Any act or object that poses a danger to computer assets is known as a threat. Although this section will identify major threats and countermeasures being used today, new threats to network security are emerging with surprising frequency.

When a small business encounters security concerns, the display of security measures and privacy policies can alleviate some of the reservations consumers may have about conducting on-line transactions. A small business should start with a security plan or policy. Generally, the plan should state what is to be protected, who is to be allowed access, and what resources will be allocated to e-commerce safety. There are tradeoffs that a small business must make with regard to security. The greater the security that a business desires for its electronic commerce assets, the greater the cost to protect those assets will be. There is no foolproof system of security, and there will always be some degree of security risk in the digital world just as there is in the physical world. A security policy should address the following specific concerns.

Authentication is the process of determining whether someone or something is, in fact, who or what it is affirmed to be. In private and public computer networks (including the Internet), authentication is commonly done through the use of log-on passwords. Knowledge of the password is assumed to certify that the user is authentic. The weakness in this system for transactions that are significant (such as the exchange of money) is that passwords can often be stolen, inadvertently revealed, or forgotten.

Access control or authorization is the process of giving someone permission to do or have access to the e-commerce system. Different users may have different degrees of access to e-commerce assets. Managers must make important decisions regarding, for instance, the extent to which internal workers and customers have access to information.

Data Integrity determines who will be able to change or modify data. Obviously a business wouldn't want employees able to change their wage information at random, or customers to change price information.

To assess the existence of e-commerce threats, it is useful to look at the entire e-commerce process, beginning with consumer and ending with the business server. The three general e-commerce assets to protect are client computers, electronic commerce channels, and the commerce server. Key security provisions in each of these areas include secrecy, integrity, and available service. Encryption provides secrecy, and there are several types or forms available for e-commerce. Encryption includes the use of codes that only certain parties may be aware of.

Digital certificates provide both integrity controls and user authentication. The idea and process is much like an individual going into the bank to cash a cheque. A teller would want to authenticate one's identity by requiring some I.D. such as a driver's licence and/or birth certificate. The same sort of trust of proof is needed to make people secure with e-commerce transactions. Trusted third parties, known as certification authorities, provide digital certificates to users and organizations. Verisign is a leader in the certification authority industry. The two most heavily used Internet browsers, Explorer and Navigator, have built-in protocols to protect electronic commerce channels. There are several Internet protocols that provide secure Internet communication channels such as Secure Sockets Layer (SSL) and Secure HTTP.

The commerce server must also be protected. Protections for the server include access control and authentication, which are provided by user name and password log-in procedures and client certificates. Firewalls provide a hardware and software solution that separates the trusted inside computer networks and clients from the untrusted outside networks.

Copyright and Intellectual Property Threats

Copyright and intellectual property rights are security threats and risks that should be understood and managed by the small business. Copyright law secures for the originator of a creative effort the exclusive right to control who can make copies, or make works derived from the original work. There are a lot of subtleties and international variations of copyright law. If one creates something, and it fits the definition of a creative work, that person receives control of who can make copies of it and how these copies are made. Under the Berne copyright convention, which almost all major nations have signed, every creative work is copyrighted the moment it is fixed in tangible form. No notice or registration is necessary, though these are helpful in legal cases. The copyright lasts 50 years after the author dies.

An intellectual property is any product of the human intellect that is distinctive, new, and unobvious. Intellectual property is defined as any new and useful process, machine, composition of matter, life form, article of manufacture, software, copyrighted work, or tangible property. Intellectual property may or may not be patentable or copyrightable. It is created when something new and useful has been conceived or developed, or when unusual, unexpected or non-obvious results, obtained with an existing invention, can be practised for some useful purpose. Intellectual property can be created by one or more individuals, each of whom, to be an inventor, must have conceived a critical element or have contributed considerably to its theoretical development.

These two issues are of great concern in e-commerce because the material on the Internet is in a digital format. This characteristic makes copying, theft, and the distribution of one or numerous copies of the information very quick and of high quality. This was not the case with other analog products such as cassette or VHS tapes where the quality of copies was usually quite inferior to the original.

The financial loss caused by breach of use of copyright and intellectual properties usually has a smaller impact on a business or an individual than other e-commerce security breaches. However, if the business depends on the marketing of copyright material of intellectual property, it can have a significant effect. An example is organizations that "share" music files on the web. Napster was a pioneer in this area and instantly had millions of users "sharing" files over the Internet. The recording industry has recently shut down the free sharing of music files on the Napster web site through legal methods. However, many more sites and technologies have emerged that still make this "sharing" possible and presently out of reach of the recording industry.

Payment Systems

In the physical world when an item is purchased, there are a number of options for payment—cash, cheque, credit, or debit cards. The e-commerce industry is trying to duplicate the attributes of these payment systems in the digital world. There have been many companies attempting to introduce electronic payment systems that they feel will increase e-commerce purchase activity. Many of them have not been successful. Effective implementation of electronic payment systems is still developing. When customers access a web site and are ready to make a purchase, it is important that they feel it is safe, convenient, and widely accepted. The small business must provide the choices that are best suited to their target market.

Some of the options that are available to the small business include: electronic cash, electronic wallets, stored value cards, and credit/debit cards. Each of these will be discussed briefly below.

Electronic Cash. Electronic cash has not seen widespread use in North America at the present time. For electronic cash to be functional it must have certain characteristics in common with real money; a person must be able to spend e-cash only once and it must be anonymous. The business must be able to determine that e-cash is not counterfeit or being used in two different e-commerce transactions at once. There are many e-cash systems on the market including the following: checkfree, clickshare, Digicash, ecoin.net, Internetcash, Millicent, Paypal.com (very popular with ebay users), Beenz, and Flooz.

Electronic Wallets. As customers shop on-line, one of the negative aspects includes the amount of personal information that is required in order to purchase a product. Research has shown that many people abandon their purchase screen or digital shopping cart because of the need to fill out this information repeatedly as they go to various sites. An electronic wallet is encryption software that works like a physical wallet during electronic commerce transactions. To speed up transactions, a wallet can hold a user's payment information, a digital certificate to identify the user, and shipping information. The consumer benefits because the information is encrypted against piracy and because some wallets will automatically input shipping information at the merchant's site and will give the consumer the option of paying by digital cash or cheque. A merchant benefits by receiving protection against fraud. Most wallets reside on the users' computer but recent versions, called "thin" wallets, are placed on the credit card issuers' server. Netscape and Microsoft now support wallet technology on their browsers.

Electronic wallets hold a great deal of promise both on the consumer and business side of the transaction. For the consumer, the advantages include saving the time and effort required to type in information in order to purchase an item. For the business, the advantages include a better chance of the information being accurate, the authentication of the buyer, and a decreased rate at checkout of abandoned shopping carts filled with digital purchases.

The biggest problem facing the use of wallets is the standard that is used. There are a number of vendors attempting to establish themselves in the e-wallet market. This fragmentation of standards has made adoption and use of this promising technology slow. Consortiums are now working to standardize the wallet technology across the industry.

Smart Cards. Smart cards are plastic cards (like a credit card) with an embedded microchip, which contain large amounts of information. At present, a smart card can store over 100 times the information that the typical magnetic strip credit card will hold. Smart cards are much more secure than current credit cards because the information is encrypted on the embedded microchip rather than being visible.

The adoption of smart card technology and standards has been very successful in Europe, Japan, and Australia. It has been slower to catch on in North America. Mondex has been a pioneer in this area and has many years of experience in the industry. Recent developments such as the entrance of Visa and American Express into the smart card market should contribute to more rapid adoption in North America in the future.

Credit and Debit Cards. Credit and debit cards are still the most popular forms of payment on the Internet. They are universal, convenient, and simple to use. There is a large installed base of users of these cards, and they are in use on a global basis. The incidence of credit card fraud over the Internet, however, is a major problem. Recent research estimates that e-commerce fraud totalled $1.5 billion in 1999.[10]

In order for a small business to accept credit/debit cards over the Internet they must obtain what is called a merchant account. A small business will receive a numbered account into which they deposit the accumulated card sales amount. There are also several third-party Internet- and web-based businesses that are available to handle all the details of processing payment card transactions. Pay Pal has been successful for its credit card services. In such a system the business simply inserts Pay Pal Web Accept buttons on the site. Members can also use Pay Pal to request payments. Fees are charged on a per-use basis, making the service a cost effective solution for small companies that are still in the developing stage.

PLANNING AND BUILDING A WEB SITE

Canadian Internet Registration Authority www.cira.ca/en/home. html

One of the challenges that the small business owner faces in establishing e-commerce is developing the web site. A good web site should answer the following four questions about the firm.[11]

1. Who we are.

2. What we do.

3. How we do it.

4. How to contact us.

Figure 9-4 illustrates an example of an effective web site for a small Canadian specialty business. Figure 9-5 (on the next page) shows the information which is quickly accessed by clicking on the "What Is Everything Garlic" icon.

Figure 9-4   An Effective Internet Site

EVERYTHING GARLIC

Your One-Stop Shop For Garlic Lovers!

What Is "Everything Garlic"?

Sizzling New Garlic Tidbits & Facts

How To Order (2)

Garlic Cookbooks (17)

Garlic Oils (5)

Garlic Vinegars (3)

Pickled Garlic and Garlic Olives (3)

Garlic Salsas and Sauces (4)

Garlic Spreads (4)

Garlic Mixes and Seasonings (4)

Garlic Condiments (5)

Garlic Bread Mixes

Garlic Braids, Wreaths and Swags (4)

Garlic Keepers (9)

Garlic Bakers (6)

Garlic Baker & Keeper Gift Sets (2)

Garlic Tools (4)

Garlic Presses (6)

Garlic T-Shirts and Linens (3)

Great Gift Ideas (6)

On Line Response Form - SAVE 10% !

Hot Garlic Info Links

Figure 9-5 An Example of a Menu for an Internet Site

about our company

call or fax toll free: 1-800-668-6299
9:30 am - 6 pm pacific standard time
p.o. box 91104, west vancouver, b.c.
v7v 3n3 canada
tel: (604)926-3154 fax: (604)926-3154

everyone's garlic specialty store...
fresh garlic, specialty garlic food
products, supplements, utensils, books,
gifts, and more!

some things are worth making a big stink about!

you've found it! whether your interests lie in gourmet foods, improving your
health or finding a garlic press that actually works, everything garlic is the place
for you.

you're even sure to find something for the hard-to-buy-for person on your list. after
all, everyone appreciates a gift of food, and our products are always in good taste!

we have the most complete and varied supply of garlic products you'll find anywhere.
check us out for everything from garlic mist to garlic t-shirts. in this web site you
will find some of our best sellers and personal favourites.

if you're in the vancouver, b.c. area, please take the time to visit our retail store at
lonsdale quay market in north vancouver. we carry a wide array of unique products,
including many unavailable elsewhere.

please note: all prices are in canadian dollars ($1.00 canadian is equal to
approximately $.75 us).

check out the garlic information hotline:
1-800-330-5922 9 am - 5 pm e.s.t.

cornell university provides information on research findings regarding garlic's
preventative and therapeutic qualities.

how to order in canada

how to order in the u.s. and internationally

Identifying Objectives

Stars Online
www.stars.com

The small business owner who wants to use e-commerce alone or in conjunction with a brick-and-mortar business must first identify the objectives of using e-commerce. The following questions should be answered in order to determine such objectives as the first step in web site development.

Will the web site be able to:

- allow customers to order products and services over the Internet?
- advertise and promote products and services?
- provide technical support for the firm's products and services?
- create and/or support brand or image development?
- conduct market research on-line about current and potential customers?
- give links to related web sites that will help the customer?
- provide general and/or industry information?
- recruit new employees?
- serve international customers?
- serve multiple or single market segments?

It is probable that the web site may have multiple objectives. As with most aspects of small business, it is important to keep the target market or customer at the centre of the strategy. For example, as Figure 9-6 shows, faster connection was one of the things that would increase consumer use of the Internet. Currently 1/4 of Canadians have high-speed access at home.[12] It is therefore important that the site be constructed so that it downloads very quickly as the time it takes for a visitor to leave a site for the competitor site is less than ever before. Understanding who the target customer is and what their characteristics are in relation to e-commerce, such as their level of experience and what type of technology they currently use, is very important in web site development.

Figure 9-6   **What Would Increase Your Usage of the Internet?**

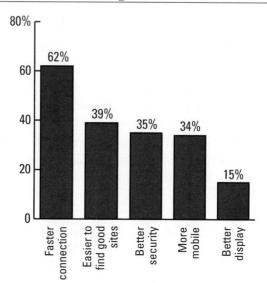

Source: Canadian Business Magazine and Bluespark Survey as reported in *Canadian Business Magazine*, April 2, 2001, p. 37.

Incident 9-4

An E-Commerce Crisis!

TD Waterhouse Group Inc. is a 15-year-old discount brokerage firm that began offering on-line transaction services in 1997. The introduction of Internet trading increased transaction volume substantially for Waterhouse, and the company's clientele base exploded. Waterhouse was servicing over 4 million customers worldwide, of which 72 percent completed transactions on-line. This unexpected boom in on-line trading left Waterhouse scrambling to deal with a daily volume of 70,000 to 80,000 transactions.

The Toronto-based brokerage firm had only partitioned enough resources to process 20,000 transactions a day. This shortfall in human resources and hardware resulted in poor service and dissatisfied customers. Transactions were not processed in time and did not accurately reflect stock price changes. Vice-chairman, John See, says, "Our clients saw immediately what happened in their account with the transaction, what price they got it at and how many shares."

See and his team at Waterhouse moved quickly to end the crisis. Managers and employees worked side by side to quickly process large transaction volumes. See sent out letters addressing the issue facing his company and how the matter would be resolved. Open, honest communication was foremost in re-establishing positive customer relations. "We tried to communicate with our clients and told them what to expect and what we were doing about it," says See.

Although this was a short-term solution to the problem, Waterhouse managers sought out a more permanent resolution. The shortage in staff trained to facilitate on-line transactions was partially due to e-commerce securities regulations that required new staff to undergo a supervisory period of 90 days. After increasing licensed employees from 600 to 1,500, Waterhouse began lobbying the securities regulators to reduce the supervisory period to 30 days. See expects this change to increase the company's ability to staff up more quickly if ever faced with a similar situation.

SOURCE: Adapted from Chad Heard "Dangers of Success," *Profit*, February–March 2001, p. 46.

Another issue in strategy development is the business's ability to handle the estimated increase in business the company will generate by being on the web. Resources should be allocated to deal with this growth. This problem is illustrated in Incident 9-4.

By defining the objective of the business's e-commerce strategy, the firm can determine which web site level would be most appropriate to incorporate. There are three levels of e-commerce that a small business may utilize.

Level 1—Read Only. This is a static site on which to post company and product information. Providing a toll-free number (linked to the company's call centre) encourages visitors to call in and request products and other information.

Level 2—Electronic Request Capability. Sites at this level provide level-1 features as well as e-mail communication. Organizations typically use this type of site to improve customer service. For example, software companies may allow customers to download software files. Airlines provide flight schedules, and manufacturers of all kinds may provide product specification and price lists. Visitors can ask questions and request information electronically.

Level 3—Transaction Capability. Sites at this level have firewalls and secure socket layers installed to protect information. Customers can place orders and make electronic payments. "E-commerce programs" can be used to build this kind of interactive site. Predictions about the future of e-commerce point strongly to integrated business systems and increasingly complex sub-sites that offer a higher degree of customization and self-service capabilities for customers. As the business web site's self-service capability and complexity increase, it becomes more operational and able to do e-commerce. Ability to reach out to customers is strengthened, and web revenues are likely to grow as well. Likewise, the costs of building and maintaining a site increase to the next level.

Strategies for Web Site Development

Once the web site objectives and levels have been determined, the next step is to start developing the site. There are three options to examine with this step.

Buy a Ready-Made Solution. This is an off-the-shelf solution. Therefore, one would attempt to choose an e-commerce package that most closely matches the features needed to achieve the objectives. The advantage of this option is that development can be very quick. Most of such services state that they employ best business practices in the various industries in which they compete. For example, an industry might have a pre-set package tailored to that industry. The disadvantage is that these solutions are typically not very flexible. This option may meet the business objectives in the early stages but may not be flexible enough to meet the changing needs and objectives as the business grows. Examples of these types of packages are Intershop or IBM WebSphere. Incident 9-5 provides an example of a small business that has successfully developed a web presence.

Incident 9-5

Storefront Software

Interested in setting up an on-line business? This process is no longer as tedious and skill demanding as it once was. Thanks to innovative software companies, merchants can now set up on-line stores in mere hours. Brad Lawryk established his football-memorabilia store in one evening using Actinic Catalog, a storefront software package designed by New Jersey-based Actinic Software LLC. Lawryk sells over 50 items on his web site including trading cards and jerseys worn in Canadian Football League games. Also available in Lawryk's store are team standings, team information, and an area for fan discussion. All make for an impressive on-line store customized to Lawryk's specifications.

Actinic Software LLC is one of many software companies designing and selling storefront packages. Catalog software is the equivalent to an empty store with shelves, cash registers, and sales clerks. All that is required of merchants is the entering of product descriptions and prices. This can be further simplified by importing the information from an excel file. "It's all about making it easy for the merchant to get his site up and then keep it running," says Actinic CEO Kevin Grumball.

Although Actinic boasts over 10,000 customers, Miva Corp. of San Diego has served over 60,000 on-line merchants. The Miva Merchant package provides on-line vendors with software capabilities similar to the Actinic Catalog. Also based in California, is Miva-rival Kurant Corp., a company that produces StoreSense. StoreSense is generally sold to Internet service providers. The ISPs then provide customers with a complete package that includes hosting a web site and supporting a storefront by using software. These deals range from $700 to $800. This price is cheap considering the hundreds of hours that are required to develop a storefront from scratch. Both the cost and time savings make this an incredibly attractive alternative. It is important to remember that these software packages only make it easy to launch an on-line store; they do not ensure the continuation of business operations. Product quality and pricing are still the key to a business' success.

SOURCE: Adapted from Grant Buckler, "Software Can Build a Store in Hours," *Report on E-Business*, March 30, 2001, p. E6.

Rent Space in a Network-Based E-commerce Solution. Depending on the business objectives, this solution has many common e-commerce features and is relatively inexpensive. This solution is fast because there is no need for additional software. The site is administered over the web. One selects a look, configures some settings, and enters product information for an instant storefront. These services would include a customer storefront that can be built in the browser, tools to design, manage, and promote the business, user-friendly shopping cart, secure credit card processing, and competitive monthly pricing with tech support for merchants. The disadvantage is that these services may not support the features or the look and feel that is wanted. They help the small business from having to deal with the complexities of installation and configuring, but they only offer a few ways to do these things. This may be acceptable if there exists a good match between what they provide and what is needed. Examples of these types of packages are Yahoo Stores or Escalate Direct.

Build the System from Scratch. This option will give the small business the exact solution it needs but will require expertise, time, and a sizeable budget to implement. The advantage is that the business can build into the system the required features and functions which may be necessary to be unique and competitive in the marketplace. When taking this route, the organization will need to design databases from scratch and then integrate tax, shipping, and payment processing software modules with the mail application. The small business needs to be comfortable developing applications on this level. If not, professional e-commerce systems developers can be hired to get the web site developed. Examples of these types of packages are Macromedia's ColdFusion, Intershop 4, and Microsoft's Site Server Commerce Edition.

When evaluating these solutions, one should consider not only the cost of the package but how much it will cost to customize it to suit the individual needs of the business. What may look like an inexpensive set-up at the outset can end up being very expensive if it becomes necessary to add new features or redo the design.

CHOOSING A WEB HOST

Once the site has been developed, the small business owner must next decide on how to get the site onto a computer that is connected to the Internet or web host. An Internet service provider (ISP) or a web host provides access to a host computer. Many large businesses, colleges, universities, and government agencies may already have a computer network that is part of the Internet. For most small businesses the cost of having their own computer host connected to the Internet can be a large financial barrier.

To be a self-web hosting organization, the business will need hardware, electronic commerce software, and a T-1 connection just to get started. The cost of setting up an in-house web hosting capability can cost in excess of $75,000 which is beyond the budget of many small businesses.

Types of Web Hosts

There are a number of other options the small business can select to obtain the web host. They are discussed briefly below.

Shared Hosting is where the web site resides on a web host's server with several other web sites. It is inexpensive, requires very little of the business's time to maintain, and it may have a very fast connection to the Internet. Shared hosting can have some disadvantages also. There might be a loss of direct control; at times updates are slow due to the large quantity of traffic to the server's other on-line businesses. There could also be some security problems resulting from numerous businesses sharing the same server.

Dedicated Hosting occurs when an ISP or web host provides a server just for the small business in question. The advantages include more web and commerce options, a high-speed connection, and more decision-making and site design control. Disadvantages include higher software costs, higher maintenance costs, and very little control over the hardware containing the site.

Colocated Hosting is closer to self-hosting. The server is owned by the on-line small business but is located at the ISP or web host's site. Even though the server is dedicated, it is necessary to have a secure, environmentally controlled location in which to house it. The web host will provide the needed space along with fast, reliable connectivity and full UPS (uninterruptible power supply) backup. The business gets the benefit of a direct connection to the Internet backbone at dramatically reduced costs. The web host of ISP provides maintenance. Advantages are the same as self-hosting. The disadvantages include maintenance costs that are higher than self-hosting, occasional difficulty getting access to the server to implement changes, and more expensive software.

Advantages of Using a Web Host

For the majority of small businesses, the advantages of using a web host far outweigh the disadvantages. Most business owners find that setting up a web server infrastructure is both complex and costly. But the web host already has the infrastructure in place. A web host can combine a dedicated server with management and monitoring service. A web host can provide a reliable, stable, continuous, and secure system. The web site content can be updated at any time. Disk space is available for the web site and can be provided with a unique domain name. The cost is usually reasonable and the contracts can be very short term (as short as one month), and payment for services is usually on a monthly basis. This helps the small business with cash flow and does not require the capital investment of self-hosting.

A domain name is registered with a central registrar for a period of one to ten years and costs about $50 to $65 per year. The easiest way to register is through the web hosting service when the web space is purchased. To register the name before finding a web host, the small business can utilize a service like Network Solutions or Register. Com. When the site is ready, the web hosting provider can arrange the transfer. The web host or ISP costs range from $30 to a few hundred dollars per month. For a business that decides to host their own web site that cost could reach over $1,000 per month.

ATTRACTING CUSTOMERS TO THE WEB SITE

Once the site has been developed and the host determined, the small business must plan how to attract customers to the web site. Traditional methods of advertising such as printed or broadcast media may be effective but expensive for the small business. Other methods that are related to the technology tend to be more effective and less expensive. Some of these methods are listed below.

Register with a Search Engine

Many people go to search engines to find what they are looking for on the web. Registration with the search engine will provide exposure of your business when people do searches. Some service companies will register the site with the top search engines for a fee. Many businesses also buy advertising space on the home pages of search engines or other companies. Recent research indicates that 9 percent of Canadian Internet users clicked on on-line ads, a much higher success rate than conventional advertising is able to achieve.[13]

Request Links on Industry Sites

This type of promotion involves contacting the industry association related to the small business and allowing the business to be listed on their web site. Although there may be a cost to do this, it is usually worth the contact that can be made.

Include URL on Stationery, Business Cards, and Literature

Although it seems like an obvious way to promote the business, many small businesses fail to include their web site address on printed materials of the business.

Request Reciprocal Links

The small business could request that their link be placed with suppliers' and customers' web sites.

Issue News Releases

The small business can find newsworthy events (such as launching new products or services) and send news releases to print and web periodicals in the industry.

Capture Visitor E-mail Addresses and Request Permission to Send Updates

On the web site, include a checkbox where a visitor can provide permission to receive e-mail updates about products or services. The e-mails to visitors are not "spam" because they have been requested.

Publish an E-mail Newsletter

Although it can be very time consuming, publishing a weekly, monthly, or quarterly newsletter is one of the best ways to keep in touch with current and potential customers. It also allows the small business to build up brand awareness, trust, and future business. The newsletter can be distributed by using an e-mail program, or by people subscribing on the web site directly. Recent research shows that 78 percent of Canadian Internet users subscribe to e-mail newsletters.[14]

Set Up a "Signature" in the E-mail Program

Most e-mail programs allow the customer to choose a "signature" to appear at the end of each message that is sent. It should be short and include such things as the company name, address, phone number, URL, e-mail address, and a one-phrase description of unique business offerings.

Promote the Site in Mailing Lists and News Groups

The Internet offers thousands of very targeted mailing lists and news groups made up of people with very specific interests. Helpful messages about the product or service where a related discussion is taking place can be an effective way to find new business. Do not use hard-line marketing and be sure to place the "signature" at the end of the e-mail message.

Begin an Affiliate Program

An affiliate program pays a commission to those sites whose links result in an actual sale. This commission acts as an incentive to provide more prominent placement of the web site.

THE FUTURE OF E-COMMERCE AND SMALL BUSINESS

E-commerce is still in the embryonic stages of development. Despite its rapid growth, the industry is still struggling with many problems and challenges that affect a small business. It appears, however, that most successful new businesses are embracing e-commerce as a vital part of their operations. Recent studies of the top start-up companies in Canada have found that the majority use e-commerce.[15]

E-commerce is an exciting and dynamic area in which products, services, and ideas have very short life cycles. It is widely recognized that any book attempting to describe and instruct on e-commerce is somewhat outdated by the time it is published. It is therefore necessary that the small business owner be aware of current news articles, trade publications, and stories on the web to keep up to date on the trends relating to e-commerce.

Summary

1. Electronic commerce involves the use of computers and electronic communication networks to perform business such as electronic mail, marketing, and making transactions.

2. Electronic commerce can take the form of business to consumer, business to business, business to government, consumer to consumer, and consumer to business.

3. Advantages of small businesses using e-commerce include expanded markets, maximization of customer relationships, creation of new services, and the reduction of costs.

4. Some of the challenges of using e-commerce include security issues, copyright and intellectual property rights, and payment systems.

5. The small business owner should use a well-planned approach to building a web site, choosing a web host, and attracting customers to the site.

Chapter Problems and Applications

1. Briefly describe what is meant by electronic commerce.

2. Which of the e-commerce types as described in the text are employed by the following?

   A. Amazon.com

   B. Priceline.com

   C. E-cruiter (Incident 9-2)

   D. Image Control (Incident 9-1)

3. Describe how a small business can benefit by implementing e-commerce.

4. Briefly describe the potential problems for a small business of establishing an e-commerce system.

5. How could you determine whether a business should proceed with each of the three models of e-commerce: Model 1—advertise only, Model 2—communication ability, and Model 3—transaction ability?

6. How could one go about selecting a web host?

7. Interview a small business owner that has a web site to determine which of the "methods of attracting customers" the business is using.

8. What are the characteristics of an effective web site?

9. Interview a small business owner that has a web site about the problems/challenges he or she experienced establishing e-commerce.

10. Interview a small business owner that has a web site to determine the steps he or she followed in establishing the site.

Appendix 9A

E-COMMERCE WEB SITES

E-Commerce Daily/Weekly News Services

C-NET E-Commerce News—News.com
CIO Web Business—CIO Communications
Cybertimes E-Commerce Report—NY Times (registration)
E-Commerce Times—Triad Commerce Group
E-Commerce Today—Phillips Publishing
E-Commerce Watch—WebReference.com
E-Commerce World—Thomson EC Resources
E-Commerce Guide—The Mining Company
E-Business Magazine—Hewlett-Packard
Electronic Commerce Guide—Internet.com
Industry Standard E-Commerce News—IDGnet
InternetNews E-Commerce News—Internet.com
InternetWorld E-Commerce News—InternetWorld Daily
I-Commerce News—InfoWorld.com
PlanetIT E-Commerce—CMP.net
Servers & E-Commerce—WebTools.com
Webmonkey—Hotwired
ZDNet E-Business—Ziff-Davis
ZDNet E-Commerce Alert—Ziff-Davis

Wire Services:

All E-Commerce News—V-Networks
CommerceNet EC Today—Commerce.net
Competence Network E-Commerce—European news service
E-Commerce NewsNow—UK news service
NewPage E-Commerce News—NewsEdge $
Web Commerce—Netscape NetCenter

Web-Related News Services

Business 2.0—Imagine Media
BusinessWeek eBiz—Businessweek.com
C-Net—News.com
Computerworld—IDG.net
Cyberscape Daily—Faulkner.com
Cyberscope—Newsweek.com
Fortune: Technology—Fortune.com
Digital Daily—Time Digital
HotWired—Wired Digital
The Industry Standard—IDG.net
Inter@ctiveWeek—ZDnet
InternetNews.Com—Internet.com
InternetWeek—CMP.net
InternetWorld Daily—Internet.com
Internet Business Journal—Netscape NetCenter
NewMedia—Newmedia.com
PC World Online—PC World Communications
Salon Technology—Salon.com
SiliconValley.com—San Jose Mercury News
TechWeb—CMPnet
Watching the Web—Wall Street Journal

Special Reports

A Guide to Succeeding in the Net Economy—Sun-Netscape Alliance
E-Commerce Special Section—NY Times (9.22.99)
The High Price of Auctions—News.com (2.24.99)
Cashing In on E-Commerce—Network Computing (12.15.1998)
Amazon.com: The Wild World of EC—BusinessWeek (12.14.1998)
Selling Point—Wall Street Journal (12.14.1998)
Mining for E-Commerce Gold—Webtools.com (10.08.98)
Spotlight on E-Business—CMPnet.com (1998)
The Internet Economy—Policy.Com (07.27.1998)
The "Click Here" Economy—BusinessWeek (06.22.1998)
Spotlight on E-Commerce—C-Net Builder.com (1998)
Buying Into E-Commerce—PCWeek (02.02.1998)

Investment and Stock Indexes/Economic Indicators

Internet Economy Indicators—Cisco and UT-Austin
Internet Stock Index (ISDEX)—FastQuote.com
@Net Index—Inter@ctiveWeek
CBOE Internet Index—News.com
CMGI—Internet venture fund
Internet Stock Report—Internet.com

RedHerring Online—Herring Communications
Silicon Investor—Technstocks.com
C-NET Investor—News.com

Conferences

Electronic Commerce—Search the Internet Calendar.Com
Internet Commerce Expo—IDC
Internet World & ISPCON Events—Penton Media
EC 2000 Conference—TMA and NACHA
Calendar of E-Vents—Wired News

Cyber Law and Public Policy

Advertising Law—Arent Fox Kintner Plotkin
Berkeley Technology Law Journal—UC-Berkeley
Computer Law Review & Technology Journal—SMU
Cyberspace Law Institute
Cyberspace Law Abstracts—Harvard Law School
Cyber Law Journal—Cybertimes
E-Commerce Law Update—Mallesons Stephen Jaques (Australia)
Harvard Journal of Law and Technology—Harvard Law School
IDEA—Journal of Technology and Law
Journal of Online Law—William & Mary
Kuester Law
Richmond Journal of Law and Technology—University of Richmond
Stanford Technology Law Review—Stanford University
Texas Intellectual Property Law Journal—UT School of Law
Virginia Journal of Law and Technology—University of VirginiaCenter for Democracy and Technology
Consumer Project on Technology
Electronic Commerce Forum
Electronic Frontier Foundation
Electronic Privacy Information Center
Global Internet Project
Internet Law & Policy Forum
Online Privacy Alliance

Suggested Readings

Chatterson, Del. "E-Commerce Challenges for Small Business." *Small Business Canada*, Barrie: May/June 2001, vol. 3, no. 3, p. 32.

Collett, Greg. "Dot Com Heaven—Internet Boom or Bust?" *Small Business Canada*, Barrie: May/June 2001, vol. 3, no. 3, p. 28.

"Strategies and Solutions for the Digital Economy." *E-Business Journal*—Plesman Communications Inc., a monthly journal on current e-commerce trends and activities.

Mallet, Ted. E-Business Update. Canadian Federation of Independent Business. Ottawa: August, 2000.

Thirgood, Keith. "Why Should a Business Have a Web Site?" *Small Business Canada*, Barrie: July/August 2001, vol. 3, no. 4, p. 29.

Yuhas, Danna. "How to Write an Effective E-Marketing Plan." *Small Business Canada*. Barrie: July/August 2001, p. 30.

Video Case Questions
E-Commerce*

CBC

Lights. Camera. Leather! It's an advertising photo shoot for Danier Leather. But that's not all that's going on here. They're also shooting with a digital video camera. And that's for the Danier web site so consumers will be able to see all of the outtakes, the actual shoot, and interviews with the models and photographers. It's all part of Danier's drive to move into the new frontier of retail-Internet shopping.

1. What are some of the problems of starting an E-commerce business?

2. How might adding e-commerce assist a small business?

*Source: CBC *Venture #723*, running time 6:20.

Chapter 10

Financial Management

Chapter Objectives

- To review the fundamentals of small business accounting.

- To discuss the various types of accounting systems a small business can use.

- To describe the considerations in purchasing a computer for the small business.

- To show how to develop and use budgets and financial planning tools.

- To illustrate how to evaluate the financial operations of the small business.

- To discuss the important aspects of credit management for the small business.

Small Business Profile

Dr. Éric Dupont
Æterna Laboratories Inc.

Æterna Laboratories Inc.
www.aeterna.com

Dr. Éric Dupont is a 33-year-old scientist and businessman at the head of a Canadian biopharmaceutical company involved in the development of new therapeutics for unmet medical needs, principally cancer. Dupont's passion for applied research led him to found Æterna Laboratories in 1991 as he was completing a PhD in physiology-endocrinology and a certificate in administration at Laval University (Québec City).

Anxious to make his mark in the biotechnology sector, Dupont built a unique company where R&D of new drugs and development of ingredients favouring well-being are performed at the same time. The development of successful products in the cosmetics, nutrition, and nutraceutical areas helps Æterna finance part of the drug development activities in an independent manner.

As a visionary, Dupont took a keen interest in a field that used to be neglected by researchers but that is now very popular, namely angiogenesis. Furthermore, Dupont targeted high-incident diseases such as cancer and psoriasis. The discovery of an angiogenesis inhibitor looks like the medical breakthrough of the next millenium.

Up to this day, Dupont's team of researchers have focused on angiogenesis inhibition. Æterna's lead compound, Æ-941, is being investigated in three major indications: oncology, dermatology, and ophthalmology. The product is entering a pivotol clinical trial sponsored by the U.S. National Cancer Institute (NCI). In a strong position because of a unique expertise in the development of new therapies, Dupont will now tap into his experience in the development of Æ-941 complementary technologies aimed at treating cancer. This strategy should enable Dupont to ensure the harmonious growth of the company he has been running since its inception.

Éric Dupont realized that the success of his company would depend on his ability to select products that were financially feasible. "I started emphasizing products that would generate profits," Dupont says. "Many companies start with too many products and don't prioritize." As a result of this planning Æterna has launched successful products in many areas such as nutrition, cosmetics, and health care. In an industry where less than 20 percent of companies make money, Æterna has been profitable since its foundation with a significant portion of sales made abroad.

THE NEED FOR FINANCIAL RECORDS

Canada Customs and Revenue Agency
www.rc.gc.ca

Incident 10-1 illustrates how financial management problems spelled disaster for a small business. This situation occurs often with small businesses. One survey found that from 24 to 45 percent of Canadian small business owners did not understand basic financial measurement ratios used in evaluating their businesses.[1] Failure to understand and manage the financial aspects of a business can be disastrous for the small business owner. The need for competence in this area is continually growing as new technology and greater competition in many markets necessitate closer monitoring of operations and quicker decision making. Keeping proper records can warn the owner-manager in advance of future financial difficulties and assist in planning the growth of the business.

Another reason for proper recordkeeping is to satisfy government requirements. While most owner-managers don't revere the Canada Customs and Revenue Agency, the fact that this agency requires accurate recordkeeping to calculate a business's tax liability may actually benefit the small business.

Recordkeeping is also necessary if a business must borrow money. Lenders will require that proper recordkeeping be followed to ensure that debt obligations are met. Incidents 10-2 and 10-3 illustrate how two Canadian entrepreneurs could have benefited from a better understanding of financial implications of debt.

The availability of accurate and current records of the operations of the business is also essential for the evaluation and control of business operations. Figure 10-1 (on page 300) illustrates the various uses of accounting information.

Small business owners may be tempted to neglect the financial aspects of the business in favour of the day-to-day operational aspects such as production, personnel management, and marketing. Often this is because they have an incomplete understanding of how to manage the recordkeeping system effectively. Understanding the managerial aspects of recordkeeping requires reviewing some basic accounting fundamentals.

Incident 10-1

Bollum's Books Grows Up Too Fast

The financial plight of Vancouver's Bollum's Books Ltd. is a case study in overzealous expansion, industry observers say, not an indictment of the mega-bookstore concept the company helped pioneer in Canada.

The book industry was absorbing the news this week that two-year-old Bollum's, with a megastore in Vancouver and Calgary, had filed for protection from its creditors in Vancouver. Founder Tom Bollum acknowledged that rapid expansion prompted the company's current cash crunch.

"I think [Bollum's situation] is an isolated case," said Scott Baldwin, marketing manager at Duthie's Books Ltd., a 40 year-old chain of smaller-sized bookstores in Vancouver. "With Bollum's, it was a matter of growing too quickly."

Even before Toronto-based Chapters Inc. launched its superstores, Bollum's sprawling Vancouver outlet was opened in July, 1995 by Mr. Bollum, a U.S.-born entrepreneur who made a fortune in eye glasses.

He offered readers a vast array of titles and a "package" concept with something for everyone, including an in-store coffee bar, where customers could plop on a comfortable chair to read their books or magazines.

But documents filed to the Office of the Official Receiver in Vancouver show that Bollum's creditors are currently owed $2-million and 12 shareholders, including Mr. Bollum, are owed $2.4-million for loans they made to the company.

SOURCE: Ann Gibbon, "Bollum's Books Grows Up Too Fast," *The Globe and Mail,* Thursday, April 10, 1997, p. B 17. Reprinted with permission from *The Globe and Mail.*

Incident 10-2

The High Cost of Expanding Downhill

Sea to Sky Condominium Rentals looked like the perfect acquisition. As owners of a Vancouver yacht-charter business, we figured renting condos to skiers at Whistler Resort would provide synergies up to the gunwales.

Our target markets were identical; experience has taught us that most sailors ski. Even the business concepts were similar: Sea to Sky managed 150 condominiums for individual owners; Cooper Yacht Charters marketed 50 privately owned sailboats just the same way. Even our company's software system was originally designed for condo rentals.

Best of all, profits for our four shareholders would soar as we reduced overheads at both firms through parallel marketing and centralized management. This was an opportunity too good to pass up—or so it looked at the time.

In retrospect, things went wrong from the outset. The purchasers were forthright but our due diligence was sloppy. We made some very bullish assumptions about our ability to market these properties. Plus, we should have spotted certain operating problems. Splitting revenues with condo owners 60–40, how can you make money renting our units for $85 a night when they cost $35 just to clean? Overall, our analysis resulted in overly optimistic revenue projections and understated operating costs. A little more time with the books would have helped.

What did we learn? If you suspect a problem, deal with it now. Don't try to defy basic business principles. Our major mistakes come right out of B-school case studies:1. The purchase was undercapitalized. This is the most common cause of business failure. We attempted a leveraged buy-out from cash flow. We couldn't do it, and you probably can't either. 2. We couldn't control what we didn't know. Without financial statements, management's cardinal tools, pin-pointing problems was impossible.

SOURCE: Barrie Jackson, "The High Cost of Expanding Downhill," *Profit,* September, 1995, p. 15.

Incident 10-3

Nuytco Research Ltd.

Dr. Phil Nuytten's passion for undersea diving has led to a life-long career in deep-diving technology and one-atmosphere systems (pressure-proof mini-submarines and armoured diving suits). Nuytten founded Can-Dive Services Ltd. in 1966 and in 1969, it and two small American diving companies co-founded Oceaneering International Inc. (OII) which would become one of the largest underwater technology companies in the world (currently measuring annual revenues in excess of a half billion U.S. dollars). Nuytten sold out his interest in OII in 1984 and reacquired Can-Dive from the American parent, now in its 36th year of commercial diving operations. He is currently the majority shareholder.

In 1984, Nuytten patented a flexible rotary joint, and Can-Dive spun off a company called International Hard Suits Inc. (IHS) to exploit that technology. Nuytten led a skilled team to produce the world famous "Newtsuit." The "Newtsuit" allows commercial and military divers to work at depths in excess of 1,000 feet with no need for lengthy decompression to avoid the potentially crippling or fatal "bends." In 1996, Hard Suits was the subject of a hostile takeover. Nuytten's "Newtsuit" (now called "Hardsuit") and the submarine rescue system "Remora" are still being successfully manufactured by Hardsuits, today.

Nuytten continued the development of one-atmosphere work systems through his wholly-owned Nuytco Research Ltd., which currently builds and sells the manipulator-equipped "DeepWorker 2000" (a 2,000-foot, Lloyd's-certified, mini-submersible) along with new underwater lighting, communications, manipulators, and life-support items. One of Nuytco's most anticipated new developments is the lightweight Exosuit TM. Nuytco is currently booked to capacity on "DeepWorker" orders—which only goes to show that success sometimes involves sales being "down."

SOURCE: Courtesy of Nuytco Research Ltd.

Figure 10-1   Uses of Accounting Information

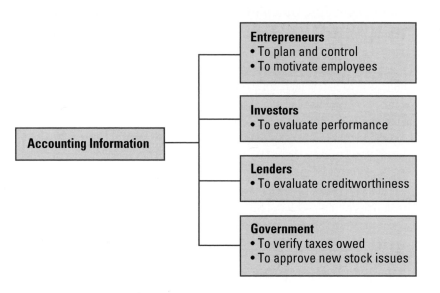

THE ACCOUNTING CYCLE

Figure 10-2 illustrates the basic process by which transactions of the business are translated into financial statements.

Recording Transactions

Transactions are recorded chronologically (as they occur) in a record called a *journal.* Many types of journals are used. In a business where few transactions occur, these entries may be made manually. In many retail businesses, the daily cash register tape total may be used to record the revenue journal entries. The cheque register can be used to record payments or disbursements. In businesses with a large number of transactions, the journal may be kept mechanically by a bookkeeping machine or by a computer.

Accounting uses double-entry recording. This means the amounts of each transaction are recorded twice. This procedure accurately reflects the fact that each transaction affects two parts (accounts) of the business. Often a decrease in one means an increase in another. For example, if a desk costing $400 is purchased and paid for in cash, the amount of cash in the business decreases by $400 and the value of the office furniture in the business increases by $400. The use of double-entry accounting also allows double-checking of the accuracy of the entries.

Figure 10-2   The Accounting Cycle

Recording of		Classification of		Summarizing of
Transactions	$\longrightarrow$	Transaction Totals	$\longrightarrow$	Data
(journal)		(ledger)		(financial statements)

Figure 10-3   Typical Journal Entries

		DR.	CR.
Jan. 1, 2002	Cash..	2,000	
	Accounts receivable.....................		2,000
	Received from Bill Smith on account.		
Jan. 5, 2002	Equipment	4,500	
	Cash		4,500
	Purchased equipment for cash.		
Jan. 20, 2002	Inventory	2,000	
	Accounts payable.........................		2,000
	Inventory is purchased on account.		
Jan. 31, 2002	Accounts Payable.....................................	500	
	Cash		500
	Liabilities of $500 are paid with cash.		
Jan. 31, 2002	Cash..	8,000	
	Sales Revenue.............................		8,000
	Sales of $8,000 are made during the month.		

Figure 10-3 illustrates how some typical recording entries might appear in a small business journal. In each of these transactions, for every increase in one account a corresponding decrease occurs in another account. At the end of the period, the totals of increases and decreases at the bottom of the page for a number of transactions should be equal.

Classifying Transaction Totals

Once the transactions have been accurately and properly recorded, the next step is to group or classify similar transactions together. These groupings or classifications are called accounts and are entered into a book called a *ledger*. The ledger keeps a running balance of the dollar amounts in each account so that the net totals may be known at the end of each period. Like journal entries, a ledger may be kept manually or by computer. Figure 10-4 shows some accounts of a typical ledger for service, retail, and manufacturing firms. The recording and classifying steps of the accounting cycle are usually referred to as *bookkeeping*. Many small businesses have found it valuable to hire an accountant to set up the bookkeeping system most appropriate for their businesses.

Figure 10-4 Typical Ledger Account Titles Utilized for Some Types of Businesses

Service Firm	For a Retail Firm Add These Accounts	For a Manufacturing Firm Add These Accounts
Sales	Sales returns and allowances	Machinery
Cash	Sales discounts	Accumulated depreciation: Machinery
Accounts receivable	Furniture and fixtures	
Accounts payable		
Land	Accumulated depreciation: Furniture and fixtures	Cost of goods sold: Raw materials Direct labour Factory overhead
Building		
Accumulated depreciation: Building	Merchandise inventory	
Office equipment		
Accumulated depreciation: Office equipment Office supplies inventory Retained earnings Salaries expense Telephone expense Advertising expense Office supplies expense	Cost of goods sold: Purchases Purchase returns Purchase discounts Transportation in	
Depreciation expense: Building		
Depreciation expense: Equipment		
Miscellaneous expense		
Salaries payable		
Utilities expense		
Licences and taxes expense		
Insurance expense		
Accounting and legal expense		

Summarizing Data

The third step in the accounting cycle (which is usually carried out by an accountant) involves taking the account totals from the ledger and putting them together to form the financial statements. These statements indicate the past success and current position of the business. It is important that the small business owner understand what financial statements mean and how to use them.

Essentially three financial statements are important to the small business owner: the balance sheet, the income statement, and the cash flow statement.

Balance Sheet (Statement of Financial Position). The balance sheet presents, in summary form, a snapshot of what the business owns and owes at any point in time. Those items the business owns are termed assets, and those owed are either liabilities (owed to sources outside the business) or equity (owed to owners). Figure 10-5 illustrates a balance sheet for a hypothetical small business. Assets and liabilities are generally listed in order of liquidity, with the most liquid being first. Usually assets and liabilities are divided into current (to be consumed in one year) and noncurrent (in more than one year).

Figure 10-5

Small Business Corporation
Balance Sheet
As of December 31, 2002

Assets

Current assets:		
Cash	$ 3,449	
Accounts receivable	5,944	
Inventories	12,869	
Prepaid expenses	$ 389	
Total current assets		$22,651
Fixed assets:		
Land, buildings, and equipment cost	26,926	
Less accumulated depreciation	$13,534	
Total fixed assets		$13,412
Other assets:		
Investments	$ 1,000	
....		$11,000
Total assets		$37,063

Liabilities and Shareholders' Equity

Current liabilities:		
Accounts payable	$16,602	
Other current liabilities......................	$ 845	
Total current liabilities		$ 7,447
Other liabilities:		
Mortgage payable.........................	3,000	
Total liabilities		10,447
Shareholders' equity:		
Common stock	15,000	
Retained earnings.........................	11,616	
Total shareholders' equity..................		26,616
Total liabilities and shareholders' equity		$37,063

Income Statement (Statement of Profit and Loss). The income statement shows the results of the operations of the business for a given time period. This statement, introduced in Chapter 3, is an integral part of the feasibility analysis and the business plan. The profit or income is determined by taking revenue from operations and subtracting expenses incurred in earning that revenue. Figure 10-6 illustrates an income statement for a hypothetical small business.

Cash Flow Statement and/or Statement of Changes in Financial Position. The importance and format of the cash flow statement was discussed in Chapter 7. This statement is similar to the income statement except that only cash inflows and outflows are shown.

In recent years, it has been common to examine not only the cash flow position of a firm but all of the asset/liability accounts over time. This practice has led to the popularity of a statement called "the statement of changes in financial position." As the name implies, this statement presents balance sheet account changes from one period to the next. It can help explain why a business has a positive net income but a decrease in cash for the same period of operation, a situation that mystifies some small business owners. The examination of the statement of changes in financial position can be complex. An example of a cash flow statement for a hypothetical small business appears in Figure 10-7.

Figure 10-6

Small Business Corporation
Income Statement
For the Year Ended December 31, 2002

Net sales	$197,000
Cost of goods sold	123,000
Gross margin on sales	74,000
Operating expenses	
Selling expenses	
Advertising expense	1,200
Sales salaries expense	18,300
Depreciation expense—store equipment	2,000
Total selling expenses	21,500
General expenses	
Depreciation expense—building	3,000
Insurance expense	675
Miscellaneous general expenses	425
General salaries expense	7,200
Total general expenses	11,300
Total operating expenses	32,800
Net operating margin	41,200
Other expenses	
Interest expense	2,750
Net income before income taxes	38,450
Income taxes	14,450
Net income	$ 24,000

Figure 10-7

Small Business Corporation
Cash Flow Forecast 2002

	Jan.	Feb.	Mar.	Apr.	May	June
Cash receipts:						
Sales in 2000	—	$ 5,000	$ 7,500	$10,000	$10,000	$ 10,000
Accounts receivable for 1999 ..	$19,000	13,000	6,000			
Other:						
Equity funding		10,000				
Total cash receipts	$19,000	$28,000	$13,500	$10,000	$10,000	$ 10,000
Cash disbursements:						
Cost of sales						
Labour	$ 5,000	$ 5,000	$ 5,000	$ 7,000	$ 7,000	$ 7,000
Materials	400	800	800	1,000	1,100	1,100
Transport	300	400	400	500	400	400
Accounts payable from 1999	12,000	10,000	10,000	6,000		
Selling expense	400	800	800	800	800	800
Administration	250	550	550	550	550	550
Fixed-asset investment						
Long-term repayment			2,500			2,500
Income tax installment			3,000			3,000
Interest on debt						
Long-term debt			680			640
Bank loan (other cash source) ..	$ 400	$ 350	$ 270	$ 370	$ 430	$ 440
Total cash disbursements	$18,750	$17,900	$ 24,000	$16,220	$10,280	$ 16,430
Monthly cash surplus (deficit) ...	$ −250	$10,100	$−10,500	$−6,220	$ −280	$−6,430
Accumulated cash surplus (deficit) for 2000	250	10,350	−150	−6,370	−6,650	−13,080

ACCOUNTING SYSTEMS FOR THE SMALL BUSINESS

Small businesses use several types of accounting systems today. Variations occur because of differences in size, type of business (retail, service, manufacturing), industry, number of transactions, and expertise of the owner. Following is a brief description of some of the more common general systems used.

One-Book System

The one-book system is most appropriate for the very small business with few transactions. It combines the recording and classifying steps of the accounting cycle into one step and presents this information on one page in a typical columnized ledger. Figure 10-8 illustrates a typical one-book system. In this example, the journal entry is recorded in columns 1 through 5 and the ledger accounts are entered in columns 6 through 10. The double-entry procedure is followed, and column totals at the end of the period are taken to prepare the financial statements.

One-Write System

A simplification of the one-book system is the one-write or "pegboard" system used by many small businesses. The format is the same as that for the one-book system. However, special carbon cheques are used so that when a disbursement cheques is made out, it automatically enters the name and amounts into columns 2, 3, and 5 of the journal. This eliminates one operation and reduces the potential for error in transposing the information from the cheque register to the journal columns. The ledger part of the entry is the same as that for the one-book system.

One-write systems are commercially available and are usually reasonably priced.

Multijournal System

For businesses that are larger or have a large number of similar transactions, the journal and ledger entries may be separated into two books. It is common for the business to use more than one journal, such as a sales journal, a disbursement journal, a payroll journal, and others. This practice can simplify the entry procedure and allow easy transfer of the journal totals to the ledger accounts.

The multijournal system, along with the one-book and one-write systems, are manual systems whose use is decreasing as more and more small businesses adopt automated systems.

Outsourcing Financial Activities

A business can outsource such financial activities as cash receipts and disbursements, payroll, accounts payable, bank reconciliations, general ledger maintenance, budgeting, and preparing interim financial statements. Some small businesses have found that this option can be quicker, easier and less costly and does not require financial expertise.

Figure 10-8   **Illustration of a One-Book Accounting System**

1	2	3	4	5	6	7	8	9	10
			Bank		Revenue		Expenses		
Date	Description	Cheque Number	In	Out	Sales/Miscellaneous		Wages/Advertising/Other		
Sept. 1/02	Wages paid for August	25		5,000			5,000		
Sept. 8/02	Sales for week 1		8,000		8,000				
Sept. 12/02	Paid utility bill	26		800					800
Sept. 15/02	Sales for week 2		6,500		6,500				
Sept. 19/02	Paid advertising bill	27		400				400	

Another outsourcing option for many small businesses that cannot afford their own computerized accounting system is to use a computer service bureau. Most of these services are offered by accounting firms. For a monthly fee, a small business can take its journal and/or ledger totals to such a bureau and within a few days receive detailed financial statements for the period (usually monthly). Much of the bookkeeping will still need to be carried out by the business, but a good portion of steps 2 and 3 of the accounting cycle can be provided by the service bureau. The big advantage is that the details contained in the reports can be valuable in operating the business.

Small Business Computer Systems

CNET
www.builder.cnet.com/

Many small businesses are finding that computer systems are no longer reserved solely for large companies. Not only has the cost of computers come down, making a computer affordable for the small business, but numerous software programs exist that are written especially for small businesses. In addition to the many benefits of owning a computer (see Figure 10-9), computer systems can manage several types of information requirements for a business. Some of the most commonly used operations are the following:

- *Word processing.* A simplified and efficient method for producing any written correspondence.
- *General ledger.* A complete bookkeeping/accounting system of all business transactions.
- *Database files.* Storing, monitoring, and retrieving of information on inventory, personnel, customers, and suppliers.
- *Payroll.* Simplified payroll systems, including cheque writing.
- *Financial planning.* Spreadsheet packages to prepare actual and projected financial statements.
- *Capital investment decisions.* Programs calculate interest costs, payback, and present values.

Figure 10-9   Some Benefits of Using a Small Business Computer

Applications	Reduce Labour Expense	Shorten Billing Cycle	Carry Less Inventory	Increase Sales	Control Costs	Manage Cash	Plan and Control Growth
Accounts payable	X				X	X	X
Accounts receivable	X	X	X	X		X	X
Business modelling				X	X	X	X
General ledger	X			X	X		X
Inventory control	X	X	X	X	X	X	X
Order entry	X	X	X	X		X	X
Payroll	X				X		X
Word processing	X			X			
The Internet		X		X			X

Source: Data General Corporation, *The Insider's Guide to Small Business Computers* (Westboro, Mass: Data General Corporation), p. 8.

In all of these functions, the computer can allow for increased speed and accuracy of maintaining records, improved service to customers, improved and more timely information to managers, and reduced operating costs. Note that the selection of software is the most important aspect of the computer decision. Software that will carry out the operations the small business requires should be selected first, followed by the hardware on which the software will run. This ensures that the hardware is powerful enough to handle the demands the software places on the computer.

Despite the benefits, purchasing a computer does not automatically solve an owner-manager's financial problems. Some entrepreneurs have learned to carefully evaluate what benefits a computer will provide for their businesses. Such an example is illustrated in Incident 10-4. It is important that the small business owner fully understand the potential pitfalls of computer ownership as well as the benefits. Some of the potential disadvantages include the following.

Cost. Although microcomputer prices are coming down, an adequate total system for most small businesses could still cost over $2,500.

Obsolescence. The rapid changes in the computer industry are resulting in very short life cycles for most computers. Often, by the time a computer is purchased and operating, new, improved versions hit the market.

Employee Resistance. Employees within an organization may resist the introduction of a computer. The owner may need to involve such employees in the decision and purchase process to help dispel any such resistance.

Incident 10-4

Here's How You Can Save Money

When it came to saving some of her precious capital upon opening her business last year, Teresa Marshall came up with some excellent inspirations.

An accountant by background with all the cost-consciousness that implies, Marshall started Action Personnel Inc. as the only home-growth business of its kind in Surrey, B.C. a booming community of 290,000 people and the second-largest municipality in the province.

"The type of business I'm in is a very cash poor business," notes Marshall, who today has a personnel consultant, account executive and receptionist working for the company. "I needed to make sure I kept my monthly costs down."

In Marshall's case, that meant buying rather than leasing office furnishings and equipment, the monthly bill being less and the company being in business for an intended long haul. It was in choosing the digs in which the furnishings would go, however, that Marshall brought her negotiating skills to bear and won a solid bargain.

"As an accountant, you can imagine that my eyes were on the bottom line all the time," says Marshall with a chuckle. "I did a lot of leg work, a lot of looking."

How much looking? In fact, three years worth, which was the overall research period before starting up, a clue to how planning paves the way for predictable and prudent spending.

"As for the computers, you need to buy what will work for you, and you don't need all the bells and whistles," Marshall says. That was also true of the second-hand photo copying machine Marshall purchased, the kicker being that she backed up the move by getting a maintenance contract on it.

Conversely, there were instances where spending more was wise. When it came to the laser printer, for example, Marshall spent the extra $1,000 to get 600 dot-per-inch quality, but I've saved an incredible amount of money with it because I do all my own layouts for advertising."

SOURCE: *The Globe and Mail*, March 17, 1995, p. C5.

Capabilities. Many types of computers are available, all with different capabilities and characteristics. Some computers cannot do what the small business owner requires them to do. Thorough investigation of the business's needs and computer capability is required to avoid this situation. Business owners should purchase computers with future growth and expansion in mind, recognizing the possible need to add to existing capacity.

Set-Up Time. Installing a computer system, educating those who will use it, and eliminating the bugs will take time. It is recommended that the system previously used by the small business be continued for a short period of time in case such a problem arises.

Failure to Compensate for Poor Bookkeeping. Some small businesses purchase a computer hoping it will clean up their bookkeeping systems. However, a computer will not help a bookkeeping system that is sloppy and inaccurate. After all, the same information entered on a manual basis must be entered into the computer. A common rule of thumb used in the computer purchase decision is that if the information generated by a manual system is accurate but takes a long time to prepare and retrieve, a computer may be of great assistance.

As the preceding discussion shows, the decision to purchase a computer is not one to be made haphazardly. It should be approached systematically and with thorough investigation. Appendix 11A presents a checklist for use in making the computer purchase decision.

MANAGEMENT OF FINANCIAL INFORMATION FOR PLANNING

The first part of this chapter deals with the fundamental aspects of collecting and maintaining the financial information within the business. This information is of minimal value, however, unless it is used to monitor, evaluate, and control current operations as well as plan for the future. Incident 10-5 illustrates the importance of financial management in helping a business to be successful.

Incident 10-5

The Fashion Industry Knows Multipliers

In Toronto, the company to watch is Snug. Since its 100 percent home-grown beginning in 1995, Snug's $100 start-up budget has flowered into dreamy seven-figure annual sales digits. What started with Greg Blagoev and Tony Elston hovering over dodgy sewing machines in an attic has become 4,300 square feet in Toronto's swanky fashion district. What was once silver vinyl record-sized bags is now a full line of clothing that has grabbed a big chunk of the Canadian market and is expanding into promising international sales territory.

"We didn't even take any draws for the first year-and-a-half. Nothing," says Elston. That meant sacrifices. "We basically paid our rent and ate mashed potatoes," says Blagoev, "just to get our product out there, just to do what we wanted to do." But Elston says, "It was what we loved to do, so it wasn't like it was a big sacrifice in the sense that we weren't giving up this time and energy that was going to someone else's dream."

Brent Micks joined in September, 1996, to help Blagoev and Elston with the finances and day-to-day management. But it wasn't until August, 1997, that Snug started to run ads in *Vice*, a music and street-scene magazine distributed free out of Montreal. Until that point, all their success had been garnered with practically no advertising budget. That's not playing by the rules of the fashion biz. But, by then, they were already past the halfway mark on the way to the golden mile, with sales well into six figures thanks to word of mouth, flyers distributed in clubs, and Noise, a store on Toronto's Queen Street West that was the first — and is still the largest — distributor of Snug duds.

SOURCE: Richard Bingham, "Rebels with a Business Plan," *Report on Business Magazine,* November 1998, pp. 77–82.

Short-Term Financial Planning

Short-term financial planning consists of preparing an estimated future financial result of operations of the business. Such pro forma (projected) financial statements serve as a blueprint for planning operations. The projected income statement is generally referred to as a budget and was described in Chapter 3 in the preparation of the feasibility analysis. Although budgets can provide many benefits to an organization, relatively few small businesses prepare or work with budgets. Using a budget, however, can be a very valuable financial tool for the following reasons.

Clarification of Objectives. A budget forces an organization to anticipate future operations and set goals and procedures to accomplish them.

Coordination. The budgeting process draws employees and/or departments together and brings them into the planning process to input into the budget information relevant to their responsibilities.

Evaluation and Control. A budget allows the owner-manager to quickly determine discrepancies that may require investigation. Such an investigation is often called variance analysis. It also allows comparison of planned (budgeted) amounts with actual results, which can improve effectiveness in the long term. Figure 10-10 shows how a budget might be established and used. After the comparison of budgeted (planned) and actual results, attempts can be made to explain the reasons for any differences. Consequently, changes might be made to correct the differences or refine the budgeting process.

Long-Term Financial Planning

Three types of long-term financial planning decisions could affect the small business—decisions regarding capital investment, capacity, and expansion.

The Capital Investment Decision. Most long-term planning includes the question of future capital purchases. This may involve the acquisition of land, buildings, equipment, or even another business. The small business owner needs to have a simple but accurate way to determine whether the decision will be financially sound. Some of the more commonly used methods of estimating future return for capital investments are discussed below.

Rate-of-Return Method. This method estimates the annual rate of return of the new investment. After this value has been determined, it can be compared to alternative investments. Figure 10-11 (on page 312) shows how a rate of return for a capital asset is determined.

Present Value Method. This method employs the time value of money in looking at future cash inflows and outflows. Future inflows and outflows of cash are discounted because cash held today is worth more than cash received or paid in the future. Present value rates are collected from present value tables, which most accounting and finance texts provide. The rate required to equalize discounted outflows (for the purchase of the assets) and discounted inflows (income from the assets) represents the discounted rate of return of the asset.

Payback Method. This method, which is similar to the rate-of-return method, estimates the number of years required for the capital investment to pay for itself. Figure 10-12 (on page 312) illustrates how the payback method is used.

The Capacity Decision. Another important financial planning decision for the small business, especially the small manufacturer, is the size and extent of operations. Financial management techniques related to capacity help answer such questions as how many units should be produced and how large the plant should be. A useful technique for answering these questions is break-even analysis.

Figure 10-10

Small Business Corporation
Income Statement
For the Year Ended December 31, 2001

	Budgeted	**Actual**	**Difference**	**Explanation**
Net sales	$197,000	$180,000	$17,000	Sales targets not reached
Cost of goods sold	123,000	120,000	3,000	Material costs increase
Gross margin on sales	74,000	60,000	14,000	
Operating expenses				
Selling expenses				
Advertising expense	1,200	1,200	0	
Sales salaries expense	18,300	18,300	0	
Total selling expense	19,500	19,500	0	
General expenses				
Depreciation expense—store				Additional equipment
equipment	2,000	4,000	2,000	purchased
Depreciation				
expense—building	3,000	3,000	0	
Insurance expense	675	1,200	525	Premium increase
General salaries expense	7,200	7,200	0	
Miscellaneous general				
expenses	425	600	175	
Total general expenses	13,000	16,000	2,700	
Total operating expenses	32,800	35,500	2,700	
Net operating margin	41,200	24,500	16,700	
Other expenses				
Interest expense	2,750	3,200	450	Rate increase
Net income before income	38,450	21,300	17,150	
taxes				
Income taxes	14,450	7,455	6,995	Marginal rate decrease
Net income	$ 24,000	$ 13,845	$10,155	

The *break-even point* is the point at which the level of output (in units or dollars) is equal to fixed and variable costs. By applying break-even analysis, the small business owner can determine the minimum level of operations required to financially break even. The use of break-even analysis could form an important part of the feasibility analysis discussed in Chapter 3. The formula for break-even analysis is shown on page 312 (following Figure 10-12).

Figure 10-11   Rate-of-Return Method

Steps	Example
1. Calculate total cost of investment.	$50,000
2. Estimated depreciable life of investment.	5 years
3. Calculate average value of investment over life. Beginning value ($50,000) plus end value (0) divided by 2 equals average value.	$\dfrac{\$50,000}{2} = \$25,000$
4. Estimate average annual profit over depreciable life (net of depreciation).	$10,000
5. Average profit divided by average investment.	$\dfrac{\$10,000}{\$25,000} = 40\%$

A reasonable rate of return on a capital investment is between two and three times the prime rate of interest. Using this criteria, the 40 percent rate of return in this example represents an attractive investment.

Figure 10-12   Payback Method

Steps	Example
1. Calculate total cost of investment.	$50,000
2. Estimate depreciable life of investment.	5 years
3. Calculate annual depreciation charge.	$10,000
4. Estimate average annual profit over depreciable life.	$10,000
5. Cost of investment divided by cash inflow (profit + depreciation)	$\dfrac{\$50,000}{\$10,000 + \$10,000} = 2.5$ years

The payback period for the capital investment would be 2.5 years. As this is considerably less than the depreciable life of the asset, it appears to be an attractive investment.

$$\text{BEP} = \frac{\text{Fixed costs}}{\text{Contribution per unit}} = \text{BEP in units}$$

or

$$\text{BEP} = \frac{\text{Fixed costs}}{\text{Contribution as \% of sales}} = \text{BEP in dollars}$$

where

Fixed costs = Costs that will not vary as production increase (e.g., costs of plant, equipment, and some overhead expenses)

Contribution per unit = Selling price − Variable costs

The resulting graph (Figure 10-13) illustrates at what price and output the break-even point occurs given fixed and variable costs.

Figure 10-13   Break-Even Analysis

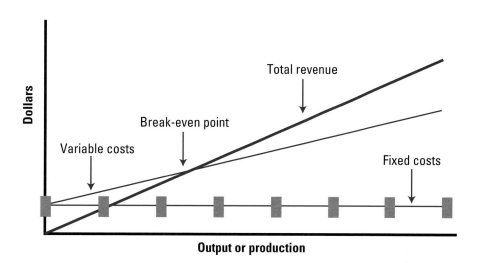

The Expansion Decision. Break-even analysis can also be used to help the owner-manager decide whether to expand the scope of operations. The same formulas can be used, but only on an incremental basis as follows.

The Effect of Fixed-Cost Adjustments

$$\text{BEP} = \frac{\text{Additional fixed costs}}{\text{Contribution per unit}} = \frac{\text{Additional unit volume needed to cover additional fixed costs}}{}$$

$$\text{BEP} = \frac{\text{Additional fixed costs}}{\text{Contribution as percent of sales}} = \frac{\text{Additional sales volume needed to cover additional fixed costs}}{}$$

The Effect of Variable-Cost Adjustments. Another use of incremental break-even analysis is to measure the effects of changes in the components of the formula, such as variable costs. The following example illustrates this calculation:

$$\text{BEP} = \frac{\text{Fixed costs}}{\text{New contribution/unit}} - \frac{\text{Fixed costs}}{\text{Old contribution/unit}}$$

= Additional unit volume needed to cover additional variable cost

$$\text{BEP} = \frac{\text{Fixed costs}}{\substack{\text{New contribution as} \\ \text{percent of sales}}} - \frac{\text{Fixed costs}}{\substack{\text{Old contribution as} \\ \text{percent of sales}}}$$

= Additional sales volume (in dollars) needed to cover additional variable costs

EVALUATION OF FINANCIAL PERFORMANCE

Quantitative evaluation of the performance of the business is an essential management task. Because they lack a financial background, many small business owners rely on their accountants to look after the complete financial end of the business. An accountant may be essential for preparing year-end financial statements, but few small businesses can afford ongoing financial management advice from this source. The small business owner is well advised to acquire a basic working knowledge of some key financial evaluation components of the business. This can enable the owner to monitor and control operations throughout the year, not just at year-end.

Several measures also can be used to evaluate the results found in the financial statements. Some of the more common techniques are described next.

Management of Current Financial Position

One critical problem many small businesses face is a shortage of cash to finance operations. Some small business owners find it hard to understand that as their businesses become successful and grow, this problem tends to create a strain on operating funds. Equally hard for many to understand is the situation in which the income statement shows a profit, but the cash position of the business has deteriorated.

The reason these situations occur is that most small businesses do not operate on a cash basis of accounting. (Some service businesses, farmers, and fishermen do use cash basis accounting methods, however.) The system used is called an accrual-based accounting system. With an accrual system, a transaction need not involve a cash transfer to be recorded. For example, a sale of merchandise is recorded as revenue for income statement purposes whether it is paid for in cash or purchased on credit. Likewise, many noncash transactions may affect the income statement, whereas some cash transactions may not.

The above discussion illustrates the need to closely monitor the cash position of the business. As we saw, this is difficult to do by examining only the income statement. The balance sheet and cash flow statements are essential components of monitoring cash position.

If the cash position of the business needs to be improved, an effective way to do so is to reduce the length of time from payment for inventory to receipt of payment for the inventory once it is sold. This cycle has three essential components:

1. Time taken to pay accounts payable

2. Time taken to sell inventory

3. Time taken to receive payment for inventory

Figure 10-14 illustrates how to use these components in reducing this cycle for a hypothetical business.

Evaluation of Financial Statements

Once the financial statements have been prepared, several relationships between various account totals can assist in evaluating the operations of the business. This evaluation of relationships is called ratio analysis. It can be used to compare the financial performance of the business with those of other similar businesses or to previous results for the same business.

Reports of financial ratios for other businesses are prepared by industry associations, Statistics Canada, and can be found on the Stats Canada or Strategis web sites. These reports are collected from many businesses across the country; thus, when using them it is important to use comparable businesses from the same industry.

Statistics Canada
www.statcan.ca

Figure 10-14

Small Business Co. Ltd.
Balance Sheet
at Dec. 31, 20—

Assets		Liabilities	
Accounts receivable $100,000		Accounts payable ....$ 40,000	
Inventory 50,000		Bank loans 100,000	
Fixed assets $140,000		Shareholders' equity $150,000	
		Total liabilities and shareholders'	
Total assets $290,000		equity $290,000	

Small Business Co. Ltd.
Income Statement
for Year Ended Dec. 31, 20—

Sales $750,000	
Cost of goods sold 500,000	
Gross profit 250,000	
Expenses 200,000	
Net profit ....$ 50,000	

1. Time taken to pay accounts

$$= \frac{\text{Accounts payable}}{\text{Cost of goods sold}} \times 365 \text{ days}$$

$$= \frac{\$40,000}{\$500,000} \times 365 \text{ days}$$

$$= 29.2 \text{ days}$$

This means that, on average, it takes 29.2 days to pay for inventory purchased.

2. Time to sell inventory

$$= \frac{\text{Inventory}}{\text{Cost of goods sold}} \times 365 \text{ days}$$

$$= \frac{\$50,000}{\$500,000} \times 365 \text{ days}$$

$$= 36.5 \text{ days}$$

This means that, on average, it takes 36.5 days to sell the inventory.

3. Time to receive payment

$$= \frac{\text{Accounts receivable}}{\text{Sales}} \times 365 \text{ days}$$

$$= \frac{\$100,000}{\$750,000} \times 365 \text{ days}$$

$$= 48.67 \text{ days}$$

This means that, on average, it takes 48.67 days to receive payment for inventory sold. The business cycle for this company is:

$$229.2 \text{ days} + 36.5 + 48.7 = 56 \text{ days}$$

Figure 10-14 **(continued)**

To increase the cash position, suppose the business was able to increase the accounts payable and decrease the turnover and receivable day totals for each component by five days. The result of these actions is shown in the paragraphs below.

1. *Time taken to pay accounts:* A five-day increase substituted in the formula would increase accounts payable from $40,000 to $46,849 with a resulting increase in cash of $6,849 (46,849 – 40,000) by using the above formula. This five-day increase might have been accomplished by obtaining extensions from suppliers or simply not paying accounts payable until absolutely required.

2. *Time to sell inventory:* A five-day decrease substituted in the formula would decrease inventory from $50,000 to $43,150 with a resulting increase in cash of $6,850 (50,000 – 43,150). Such a decrease might be as a result of increased advertising, more careful purchasing, or greater incentive to salespeople.

3. *Time taken to receive payment:* A five-day decrease substituted in the formula would decrease accounts receivable from $100,000 to $89,733 with a resulting increase in cash of $10,267 (100,000 – 89,733). Such a decrease might be accomplished by increasing the intensity of collection procedures and/or submitting charge card receipts more often.

The total effect of these measures on the cash position of the company would be $6,849 + $6,850 + $10,267 = $23,966 increase. The owner-manager, of course, would have to balance this increase in cash against the costs of accomplishing the five-day increases or decreases.

Financial ratios can also help in isolating and analyzing weaknesses within the business. Four categories of ratios are commonly used in evaluating a small business. Each is discussed next with a general statement regarding whether the ratio is acceptable. The ratios of certain industries, however, may deviate from these averages. Illustrations of these ratios for a small business appear in Appendix 10B.

Liquidity Ratios. Liquidity ratios assess the business's ability to meet financial obligations in the current period. Two liquidity ratios are commonly used: the current ratio and the acid test or quick ratio. The calculations for these ratios are as follows.

$$\text{Current ratio} = \text{Current assets: Current liabilities}$$

This figure, expressed as a ratio, should be higher than 1:1 and usually between 1:1 and 2:1.

$$\text{Acid test or quick ratio} = \text{Current assets} - \text{Inventories: Current liabilities}$$

The quick ratio is more suitable for businesses that have a high level of inventories. A ratio of 1:1 is considered healthy. If the liquidity ratios are lower than they should be, the business may have difficulty meeting obligations within the year and will have a hard time raising further debt capital. Actions which could improve the liquidity ratios are increasing current assets without a corresponding increase in current liabilities such as equity financing or increased long-term debt.

Productivity Ratios. Productivity ratios measure the efficiency of internal management operations. They include the inventory turnover ratio and the collection period ratio.

The calculation of the inventory turnover ratio is as follows:

$$\text{Inventory turnover} = \text{Cost of goods sold: Average inventory at cost}$$
or
$$\text{Inventory turnover} = \text{Sales: Average inventory at retail price}$$

Inventory turnover reveals the number of times the inventory is turned over (sold) in a year. Average turnover rates vary considerably by industry but usually should not be lower than 2 to 3 times. An inventory turnover that is too low may reflect poor inventory buying in terms of either being overstocked or buying low-demand inventory.

The collection period is calculated as follows:

$$\text{Collection period} \quad = \quad \text{Accounts receivable: Daily credit sales}$$

This ratio reflects the average number of days taken for purchasers to pay their accounts to the business. Normal collection periods are in the 20-to-40-day range. If the collection period is too long, it may mean the credit-granting policy is too loose, the administration of billing is too slow, or the collection of accounts is too lax. Solutions to poor productivity ratios include better buying, more emphasis on selling and collections.

Profitability Ratios. Profitability ratios measure the effectiveness of operations in generating a profit. There are four ratios in this category.

The first ratio is gross margin:

$$\text{Gross margin} \quad = \quad \text{Sales} \; - \; \text{Cost of goods sold}$$

This figure, usually expressed as a percentage of gross sales, can be used for comparisons. Gross margin for an individual product is calculated by subtracting cost from selling price and is commonly called markup. Average gross margins usually range from 20 to 50 percent. If gross margins are lower than they should be, the cause may be poor buying, failure to emphasize high-margin items, theft or spoilage, or price levels that are not current.

The profit-on-sales ratio measures profit as a percentage of gross sales:

$$\text{Profit on sales} \quad = \quad \text{Net profit (before tax): Sales}$$

Typically the average percentages fall within 1 to 5 percent. A lower than average profit-to-sales percentage can reflect a problem with either pricing or expenses. Pre-tax profits are normally used, since the tax rates may vary by province and industry. In addition, reporting agencies that publish industry standards may use pre-tax profits as a comparison.

The third profitability ratio is the expense ratio:

$$\text{Expense ratio} \quad = \quad \text{Expense item: Sales}$$

Many specific expenses on the income statement may be expressed as a percentage of gross sales. These figures can then be compared to those for similar businesses.

The return-on-investment ratio reflects the profitability of the owner's investment:

$$\text{Return on investment} \quad = \quad \text{Net profit (before tax): Owner's equity}$$

This ratio may be compared not only with those for other similar businesses but also with alternative investments. If compared to the bank rate of interest, it is important to remember the risk associated with the business. Thus, the return on investment should be higher than the bank rate to compensate for this.

Debt Ratio. The debt-to-equity ratio measures the solvency of the business, or the firm's ability to meet long-term debt payments:

$$\text{Total debt to equity} \quad = \quad \text{Total debt: Owner's equity}$$

Acceptable debt ratios vary, but generally speaking it should not be greater than 4 to 1. A lender normally will not provide further financing to a firm with a higher ratio. To improve the debt ratio the small business may need to increase the equity investment or reduce debt through operations.

CREDIT AND THE SMALL BUSINESS

A major concern for many small businesses in their attempt to reduce the length of the business cycle is control of credit. The owner/manager should understand the fundamentals of credit granting and management to effectively control receivables. Before deciding to extend credit, the owner/manager should be aware of the costs and potential difficulties involved in granting credit as well as the advantages of its use. The attractiveness of such a program is less today, since the majority of consumers can use bank credit or debit cards for their purchases.

Advantages of Credit Use

The advantages of offering credit include the following:

- A credit program will undoubtedly result in increased sales and will probably be necessary to remain competitive.

- Credit customers are more likely to be loyal to the store or business.

- Credit customers tend to be more concerned than cash customers with quality of service as opposed to price.

- The business can maintain information about and a record of credit customers and their purchases that can help in formulating future plans.

Disadvantages of Credit Use

A credit program can also create certain difficulties:

- There will generally be some bad debts when using a credit program. The number of bad debts depends largely on how strict the credit-granting policy is and how closely accounts are monitored.

- Slow payers cost the business in lost interest and capital that could be used for more productive investments. It is estimated that in many businesses, losses resulting from slow payers are greater than losses from bad debts.

- A credit program increases bookkeeping, mailing, and collection expenses. Purchase records need to be kept, statements mailed, and accounts monitored and collected. As a result, many small businesses decide against offering their own credit programs.

Management of a Credit Program

If the small business owner decides to use a credit program, some essential steps should be followed to ensure maximum effectiveness.

Determine Administrative Policies. This includes such items as application forms, credit limits for customers, procedures to follow on overdue accounts, determining which records to keep, and deciding when to send statements.

Set Criteria for Granting Credit. A small business owner-manager may want to assess many of the same areas a lender would evaluate in considering a small business loan, although perhaps not in the same detail. Some essentials would be past credit history, other accounts held, monthly income, references, and bank used. A small business is well advised to use the services of a credit bureau located in most cities or a commercial agency such as Dun and Bradstreet to evaluate customers' creditworthiness.

Dun and Bradstreet
www.dnb.com

Set Up a System to Monitor Accounts. Proper management of accounts receivable involves classifying accounts by the length of time they have been outstanding. This process is called ageing of accounts receivable. Common categories used are under 30 days, 30 to 60 days, 60 to 90 days, and over 90 days. Experience shows that the longer an account is outstanding, the smaller is the chance of collecting it. Therefore, special attention should be paid to overdue accounts.

Establish a Procedure for Collection. A uniform procedure should be set up regarding the use of overdue notices, phone calls, credit supervision, legal action, and/or a collection agency. Lax supervision of accounts has led to many small business failures, so this is an area of credit management that cannot be ignored. An example of such a collection policy appears in Figure 10-15.

One form of collection sometimes used by small businesses is a factoring company, which, as discussed in Chapter 7, can also be a source of small business financing. This type of company purchases accounts receivable for cash and attempts to collect them. In some cases, a factoring company handles the overall credit program for the business and even provides debt financing.

Use of Bank Credit Cards

Visa
www.visa.com

Mastercard
www.mastercard.com

Because of the high costs and risks involved in operating their own credit programs, many small businesses find the most effective way to offer credit is to use bank credit cards such as Visa and MasterCard. The use of credit cards and electronic banking by consumers has now surpassed that of cash and cheques in Canada. The credit card companies assume the risk of bad debts and cover much of the administration costs of bookkeeping and issuing of statements in return for a fee—usually of from 2 to 6 percent of sales, depending on volume. Because of the high ownership of these cards by consumers today, most retail and service firms find their use essential to enhancing sales.

Although not considered a credit program, most small businesses also offer electronic banking (debit cards) in the form of such programs as Interac card capabilities. For a monthly fee the business can be assured of on-the-spot transfers to their bank for a transaction.

Figure 10-15   An Example of a Collection Policy

	30 Days	45 Days	60 Days	75 Days	90 Days
Communication	Letter, telephone; copy of statement	Letter, telephone; copy of statement	Letter, telephone	Letter, telephone	Registered letter or lawyer's letter
Message	Overdue account, please remit	Pay in 15 days or deliveries will be stopped	Deliveries stopped; pay immediately	Pay in 15 days or account will be turned over for collection	Action is being taken
Action	None	None	Stop deliveries	None	Use collection agency or small claims court

Source: *Small Business Review,* pamphlet (Toronto: Thorne Riddell Chartered Accountants)

Many businesses allow the use of debit cards, such as Interac. Much like the bank credit card, the debit card automatically transfers the sale amount from the customer's account at the bank to the business's account. The obvious advantages of debit cards are the quick repayment and reduction of accounts receivable. The costs of offering this service are approximately $50 per terminal per month.

Summary

1. The three-step process of the accounting cycle includes (1) recording the transactions (journal), (2) classifying the transaction totals (ledger), and (3) summarizing the data (financial statements). The three financial statements important to the owner-manager of a small business are the balance sheet, the income statement, and the cash flow statement.

2. The common types of bookkeeping systems used by small businesses today are the one-book system, the one-write system, the manual multi-journal system, outsourcing certain functions, computer service bureaus, and small business computers.

3. Some of the more common operations computers can perform are word processing, general ledger, database files, payroll, financial planning, and capital investment decisions. Some potential disadvantages of computer ownership are cost, obsolescence, employee resistance, restricted capabilities, and set-up time.

4. Short-term financial planning consists of preparing an estimated future financial result, or a budget, and comparing it to actual results. The three types of long-term financial planning decisions are capital investment, capacity, and expansion decisions.

5. Ratio analysis enables the small business owner to compare the financial performance of the company to those of other firms in the industry and to the company's own past performance. Common financial ratios include liquidity ratios, productivity ratios, profitability ratios, and debt ratios.

6. The advantages of offering credit are a likely increase in sales, increased store loyalty, and improved information about purchases. The disadvantages are bad debts, slow payers, and administration costs. Essential aspects of administering a credit program are defining administrative policies, establishing credit-granting criteria, setting up a system to monitor accounts, and establishing a procedure for collection.

Chapter Problems and Applications

1. For the following transactions, indicate which accounts are changed and by how much.
   a. Feb. 14, 2002—Received $1,000 from Frank Johnson on account.
   b. Feb. 14, 2002—Purchased equipment for $1,500 (paid cash).
   c. Feb. 15, 2002—Paid owner Bill Cartwright $2,000 for January's salary.
   d. Feb. 18, 2002—Paid telephone bill of $90.87.
   e. Feb. 19, 2002—Bought ice cream on account, $395.00.

2. Discuss what can be done to ensure the purchase of the right computer for a small business.

3. Calculate the rate of return for the following investment. The total cost of the investment is $250,000, the depreciable life of the investment is 10 years, and the annual profit (net of depreciation) is $30,000. What considerations other than financial ones exist?

4. Assume the annual depreciation charge for the investment in Problem 3 is $25,000. Determine the payback period of the investment.

5. Determine the break-even point, in dollars, for an investment with fixed costs of $100,000 and an estimated contribution of 60 percent. How much revenue would it need to produce before you would invest?

6. a. From the balance sheet and income statement of Sam's Paint and Drywall, determine the following ratios.

    (1) Current

    (2) Inventory turnover

    (3) Profit to sales

    (4) Return on investment

    (5) Total debt to equity

  b. From Dun and Bradstreet's *Key Business Ratios* on industry norms, evaluate each of the above ratios.

SAM'S PAINT AND DRYWALL
For Year Ended December 31, 2001 (in thousands of dollars)

Assets		**Liabilities and Net Worth**	
Cash	$ 12	Accounts payable	$ 15
Inventory	41	Notes payable—bank	4
Accounts receivable	18	Other	20
Total current assets	71	Total current liabilities	39
Fixed assets:		Long-term liabilities	41
Vehicles	10		
Equipment	15		
Building	22		
Land	23	Total net worth (owner's equity)	61
Total fixed assets	70		
Total assets	$141	Total liabilities and net worth	$141

Income Statement
December 31, 2001
(in thousands of dollars)

Sales	$280
Less: cost of goods sold	186
Gross margin on sales	94
Less: operating expenses	81
Net profit	$ 13

7. Conduct an informal survey with three small businesses to find out which accounting system they use. Determine whether their systems are working effectively.

8. Why would a small gasoline retailer drop its credit program?

9. Dick's Draperies has gross sales of $15,000 per month, half of which are on credit (paid within 30 days). Monthly expenses are as follows: wages, $3,000; utilities and rent, $2,000; advertising, $300; and miscellaneous, $500. Inventory is purchased every three months and totals $30,000 for each order. Yearly expenses paid for in advance are insurance of $1,000 and a rent deposit of $700. Prepare a six-month cash flow statement for Dick's Draperies. What advice would you give this business based on the cash flow statement?

Appendix 10A

Checklist for Buying a Small Business Computer

1. Take an introductory computer course, or read a book on small business.
2. Invest in independent consulting advice.
3. Determine the potential benefits your organization can obtain from EDP.
4. Examine your existing systems and their deficiencies.
5. Define your information needs.
6. Estimate your current costs.
7. Prepare and send out a request for proposal.
8. Consider feasibility questions:
   a. Will it work?
   b. Will it pay?
   c. Will we use it?
   d. Will it cause adverse effects?
9. Avoid potential risks:
   a. Availability of proper personnel.
   b. Availability of suitable computer programs.
   c. Continued support of software.
   d. Expendability of the equipment.
   e. Security of the computer installation.
   f. Security of files and programs.
   g. Availability of a disaster recovery plan.
   h. Adequate formal management and personnel discipline.
   i. Careful selection of the computer system.
10. Deal carefully with suppliers:
   a. Get everything in writing.
   b. See a realistic demonstration.
   c. Check the suppliers' references.
   d. Negotiate a contract.

11. Develop and follow an implementation plan:

   a. Form a conversion and installation team.

   b. Involve top management.

   c. Plan your conversion carefully.

   d. Emphasize careful system testing.

SOURCE: Harvey S. Gellman, *A Buyer's Guide to Small Business Computers* (Toronto: The Canadian Information Processing Society, 1993), p. 12.

Appendix 10B

Use of Financial Ratios for a Small Business (Automotive Dealer)

Ratio	Method of Computation	Motor Vehicle Dealer			Explanation
		Last Year	Previous Year	Industry Average	
1. Liquidity a. Current ratio	Current assets/Current liabilities	1.09 times	1.05 times	1.1 times	Satisfactory: This dealer has the same ability as is common in this industry
b. Quick ratio	Current assets inventories/ Current liabilities	.33 times	.45 times	Not available	
2. Productivity a. Inventory turnover	Cost of goods sold/Average inventory (at cost) or Sales/ Average inventory (at retail)	7.41 times	7.41 times	6.0 times	Good: This dealer has a higher turnover rate than the average dealer. This may indicate a higher sales level or lower inventory levels.
b. Collection	Average inventory at retail/Daily credit sales	13.56 days	16.01 days	12 days	Fair: The collection period is longer than average which may indicate the need to tighten the credit policy; however, it seems that some action has already been taken.
3. Profitability a. Gross margins	Gross sales — Cost of goods sold or a percent of sales	10.71%	12.28%	16.70%	Poor: The inventory may be obsolete or company prices may be too low.
b. Profit on sales	Net profit (before tax)/Gross sales	.85%	– (.6%)	.6%	Good: Expenses are being kept in line

c. Expense ratio	Expense item/ Gross sales	11.69%	13.59%	Not available	Good: The company is making an effort to cut expenses.
d. Return on investment	Net profit (before tax)/Owner's equity	10.49%	– 1.74%	9.0%	Good: This company is more profitable than most in the industry. It is clear that action is being taken to improve profitability of this firm.
4. Debt a. Total debt to equity	Total debt/ Owner's equity	325.89%	376.09%	398.20%	Good: This dealer depends less on debt financing than is common in this industry. An intentional move has been taken in this direction.

Note: / denotes division sign.

Suggested Readings

"Accounting Software: What's New?" *Small Business Canada*, vol. 2, no. 4, Fall 2000, pp. 31–34.

Bartholomew, Douglas. "4 Common Financial Management Mistakes . . . And How to Avoid Them." *Your Company*, Fall 1991, p. 9.

Cornish, Clive G. *Basic Accounting for the Small Business*. Vancouver, B.C.: International Self-Counsel Press, 1985.

Fundamentals of Record Keeping and Finance for Small Business. New York: Center for Entrepreneurial Management, 1986.

Maynard, Roberta. "Smart Ways to Manage Cash." *Nation's Business*, August 1992.

McMahon, Richard G. P., and Scott Holmes. "Small Business Financial Management Practices in North America: A Literature Review." *Journal of Small Business Management*, April 1991.

Comprehensive Case
The Framemakers: Part 6

Robert and Teresa were able to overcome their first-day blues as they continued to work hard, gain experience, and make adjustments to their operations. It seemed that business was picking up gradually as the first year progressed. However, six months after the opening sale, the bank called and indicated that The Framemakers' account was overdrawn beyond the authorized operating line of credit. This was especially alarming to the Normans because a bank payment was due soon. They visited the bank and, on the basis of the steady record of deposits and increasing sales, were able to obtain an increase in the amount of operating credit and postpone the bank payment until the end of the year. The bank manager indicated that he wanted to see The Framemakers' financial statements for the first year when they were completed.

During the last few months of the year, it seemed to the Normans that business had picked up considerably, especially during December. As a result, they were able to meet the bank payment at the end of December. Robert and Teresa were beginning to feel confident that their business was turning the corner. Teresa gathered up the box of cash register receipts, invoices, and cheque register stubs and dropped it off at the accountant's office in January so the year-end statements could be prepared.

The Normans were shocked, however, when they received the statements about a month later (see Figure 1). Although business for the year had been slower than expected, they did not anticipate the $9,810 loss that had occurred. The Normans were concerned about the loss and were now very hesitant to take the statement to their banker. Teresa contacted the industry association and obtained some operating results for framing shops to better understand what had happened. The data are as follows:

Current ratio	1.2 to 1	Collection period	5.8 days
Gross profit	70%	Debt to equity	.8 to 1
Profit on sales	20%		

Figure 1

The Framemakers
Statement of Income or Loss
For the Year Ended January 31

Sales revenue	$62,000
Less cost of goods sold	$24,800
Gross profit	37,200
Expenses:	
Accounting and legal	748
Advertising and promotion	3,500
Auto costs	2,895
Bank charges and interest	2,500
Building maintenance and repairs	3,280
Depreciation	1,560
Equipment rentals	800
Office supplies	942
Rent	7,200
Travel	2,105
Utilities	3,480
Wages	$18,000
Total	$47,010
Net income	($9,810)

The Framemakers
Balance Sheet
Assets

Current:	
Cash	$872
Accounts receivable	3,601
Inventory	8,204
Prepaid expenses	350

Total current assets	13,027
Equipment and fixtures	7,773
Organization expenses	500
Total assets	$21,300

Liabilities

Current:

Bank indebtedness	$15,000
Accounts payable	9,010
Current part of long-term debt	$ 1,000
Total current liabilities	25,010
Long-term debt	6,000
Total liabilities	$31,010
Share capital	100
Owner's equity (deficit)	($9,810)
Total liabilities and owner's equity	$21,300

Questions

1. Evaluate the Normans' financial management practices during the first year of operation.
2. In view of the industry statistics obtained, evaluate The Framemakers' statements and make suggestions for improvement.

Video Case Questions
Appliance Recyclers*

CBC ◉

One man's junk is another man's fortune. Follow the entrepreneur who is building his business on junk.

1. Discuss the financial problems created by growth as identified in this example.
2. What strategy was followed to improve the cash flow for Canadian Appliance Centres?
3. What finally helped Anthony Giuffre to be successful?

*Source: CBC *Venture* #760, running time 11:21.

Chapter 11

Chapter 11

Operations Management

Chapter Objectives

- To review the methods of planning the production process.

- To discuss the management of the components of the physical facilities of a small business.

- To explain the types of layouts used in small businesses.

- To illustrate methods of purchasing and controlling inventories in the small business.

Small Business Profile

Randy Marsden
Madentec Ltd.

Madentec Ltd.
www.madentec.com

Randy Marsden, a soft-spoken native of rural southern Alberta, has been a trailblazer. As a third-year engineering student at the University of Alberta, he and a colleague developed a computer aid to help a severely disabled friend communicate by touching a switch with his lips when, for example, he was thirsty or tired.

With that, Marsden and his partner garnered awards, professional recognition and job offers from large technology companies across the United States. While his partner headed south of the border, Marsden stayed in Edmonton to establish Madenta in 1989 and eventually bought out his colleague's interest.

Madenta designs and produces cutting-edge computer technology for severely disabled people. But until three years ago, he couldn't get his products to those who needed it most. No one had set up a distribution channel for this kind of "adaptive technology," says Marsden, 35, president and chief executive officer. "It was a real ad hoc, mishmash way of selling and an industry-wide problem, which was affecting us."

Madenta's products help people with quadriplegia, cerebral palsy, muscular dystrophy, multiple sclerosis, or other disabilities to use computers and gain access to the Internet. But in the mid-nineties, it was nearly impossible to get his products to market. After trying some direct sales options, including telephone marketing, Marsden took the step of setting up his own retail channel.

Marsden's approach to the challenge was hands on; he hit the road in major cities across Canada and the United States to demonstrate his products to would-be vendors, mostly wheelchair retailers who were looking for higher-margin items to round out their stock. Recently, Madenta was restructured to better meet changing market demands and new technology; the company is now called Madentec Ltd.

Its future success is closely linked to an efficient distribution channel, Marsden says. "The ultimate indicator for this network is we're selling a lot more now. I don't think we've reached near its potential, but time will tell."

MANAGEMENT OF INTERNAL OPERATIONS

The management of internal operations is part of the physical facilities section of the business plan (see Chapter 4). Operations management is one area in which many small business owners have their greatest strength. They know how to produce a quality product or provide a quality service, and their primary interest often lies with this aspect of the business. Incident 11-1 illustrates the potential problems of inefficient management and production. Although they may have production expertise, many entrepreneurs lack the management skills of maintaining quality and control. Typical areas needing attention might be cash flow, production costs and product quality, inventory management, and physical facilities issues. As mentioned in earlier chapters, the entrepreneur is typically weaker in the areas of marketing and financial management than in managing the production process. As a result, many entrepreneurs find it advantageous to outsource some of these services. A recent study by Price Waterhouse–Coopers found that 73 percent of Canadian businesses outsource one or more business processes.[1] Some of the typical services are financial management, human resource management, income tax preparation, marketing, call centre and customer care, and mail-room operations.

THE PRODUCTION PROCESS

The production process involves the conversion of inputs such as money, people, machines, and inventories into outputs—the products or services provided. Figure 11-1 illustrates this application for manufacturing, wholesaling, retailing, and service businesses. The owner-manager's task is to organize the production process of the business so that the outputs (products) can be produced efficiently. Incident 11-2 illustrates how one Canadian firm is accomplishing this.

Incident 11-1

"Damn the Expenses, Just Get the Sale"

With sales of $264 million in 1999, Ontario-based Skyjack Inc. attributed its success to the strategy, "Damn the expenses, just get the sale." President and CEO, Wolf Haessler envisioned his company to be a one-stop shop for movable scissor lifts. Achieving this dream was accomplished by buying a lavish integrated manufacturing facility that employed over 250 people. This lackadaisical approach to financial operations nearly resulted in Skyjack's demise.

During the company's beginnings, Haessler's entrepreneurial style of management allowed Skyjack to successfully penetrate the movable platform market. However, this strategy was not enough to contend with the boom that followed market penetration. By 2000, Skyjack was $127 million in debt and on the brink of bankruptcy. The banks declared, "Unless you do something quick and drastic, we're going to ask for the keys." At this point, Haessler turned his position over to Jos Wintermans, a veteran corporate executive. Wintermans immediately hired experienced management, cut expenses, and installed efficient management operations systems.

The debt is now under control and Wintermans remains president and CEO of Skyjack Inc. Scrimping and saving during the first six weeks of his employment reduced company expenditures from $5 million a week to less than $2.5 million. Personally tracking the company's cash flow and installation of internal controls in all levels of Skyjack's operations has reduced the debt by $70 million. This stronghold approach to operations management will no doubt play an important role in bringing Skyjack's operations into a new profitable state.

Source: Adapted from Camilla Cornell, "Out of Control," *Profit*, April 2001, p.43.

Figure 11-1 Examples of Production Systems

Type of Business	Inputs	Process	Outputs
Apparel manufacturer	Cloth, thread, buttons	Store—Cut—Sew—Press—Ship	Dresses
Wholesaler	Large volume per order of each product	Store—Sort—Package—Ship	Smaller volume of a product in each order
Retailer	A volume of each of many products to the ultimate customer	Store—Customer display—Package	Low volume of a few products to each customer
Laundry (service firm)	Dirty clothes	Sort—Wash—Press—Store	Clean clothes

Source: Adapted from Curtis E. Tate, Jr., Leon C. Megginson, Charles R. Scott , Jr., and Lyle R. Trueblood. *Successful Small Business Management.*, 3rd ed. (Georgetown, Ont.: Irwin-Dorsey of Canada, 1982), p. 244.

The Priority Evaluation and Review Technique (PERT) and other flowchart systems have been developed to assist in organizing the production process. A simple example of such a system is shown in Figure 11-2 for a manufacturing firm. By visually plotting the tasks and required time, the owner-manager can minimize down-time and ensure the most efficient production. Continual effort should be made throughout the process to ensure quality control. This Total Quality Management (TQM) can be used by small business as a means of ensuring customer satisfaction, improvement of products and services, and full involvement of employees.

PHYSICAL FACILITIES

Planning the physical facilities is discussed briefly in Chapter 3 as part of the preparation of the feasibility analysis. Selection of the location for the business is introduced in Chapter 4 as one of the steps in organizing a business.

Incident 11-2

earls Philosophy

The sights, sounds, and smells — mouthwatering smells emanating from earls restaurants — are something to behold. Fresh food displays are everywhere. In the background are the sounds and smells of cooking: the sizzle of the sauté pan, the hypnotic orbit of the fresh chickens turning in a rotisserie oven, the whisper of a paddle against the tile bed of a forno oven. Dining at earls is an experience you won't likely forget.

earls started in 1982 as a single restaurant in Edmonton, the brainchild of Bus Fuller and his son, Stan. Today there are 50 locations and it is the dominant chain for quality casual dining in Western Canada. The recipe for success is quite simple and has not changed since the beginning: emphasize freshness, quality, and variety in a relaxed, friendly environment. Starting with a great idea, earls has grown because of the high standards that were set and maintained in every area: food quality, staff training and motivation, customer satisfaction, and ambience.

Source: Adapted from Bob Bryant, "Ads as Fresh as Food," *Marketing*, June 9, 1997, p. 13.

Figure 11-2 Priority Evaluation and Review Techniques (PERT)

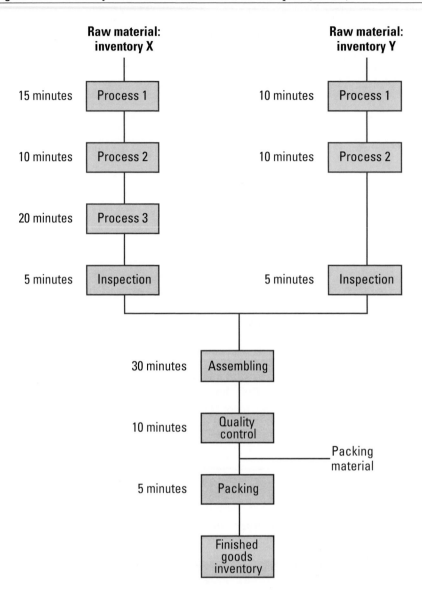

Total work time = 120 minutes   Critical path time = 95 minutes

While it is not necessary to review that information again, it is critical for the owner-manager to recognize that the physical facilities must be closely monitored and maintained to ensure they are efficient and up to date. Locations are never static—populations, businesses, and traffic patterns shift continuously. This trend has caused many excellent locations to deteriorate over the years.

Some aspects of the physical facilities that should constantly be evaluated are illustrated in Figure 11-3. The figure ranks the importance of each physical facility characteristic based on the type of small business.

Figure 11-3   Business Building and Site-Rating Table

Factors	Retailing	Service	Manufacturing	Wholesaling
Building feature:				
Age	1	4	3	4
Space	1	3	1	4
Configuration	1	4	4	3
Appearance	1	3	3	4
Frontage	1	4	4	4
Access	1	2	1	1
Interior utilization:				
Floor space	2	3	1	1
Room dimensions	1	3	1	4
Ceiling heights	2	2	2	4
Stairways, elevators	3	3	1	1
Window space	1	3	4	4
Utility services	3	1	1	3
Improvement potential:				
Building exterior	1	3	4	4
Building interior	1	3	2	2
Site	1	2	3	4
Surrounding	2	2	3	4
Streets and walks	2	3	3	3
Access	1	3	2	1
Expansion	2	1	1	1
Site and environment:				
Street and service areas	1	2	2	3
Setback and frontage	1	3	4	4
Parking	1	2	2	3
Surrounding businesses	2	3	4	4
Area environment	2	3	4	4

Key to ratings: 1 = critical; 2 = very important; 3 = not ordinarily important; 4 = minimum importance

SOURCE: John B. Kline, Donald P. Stegall, Lawrence L. Steinmetz, *Managing the Small Business* (Homewood, Ill.: Richard D. Irwin), 1982.

LAYOUT

Effective management of the interior layout of the business can greatly enhance productivity. Small businesses use several types of layouts. The layout selected varies by industry and by scope of operations. In determining layout, it is advisable to draw up a floor plan to better utilize available space.

Layouts for Manufacturing Firms

Here are some key areas to consider in planning the interior of a manufacturing plant:

- Location of utility outlets for machines
- Location of receiving and shipping areas for raw materials and finished goods
- Safety aspects
- Adequate lighting capability throughout
- Provision for ease of maintenance and cleaning of the plant

Essentially three types of layouts are used by small manufacturing firms: product layout, process layout, and fixed-position layout.

Product Layout. The product layout is suitable for the business that manufactures just one or only a few products. It closely resembles the production line of a large factory. Figure 11-4 illustrates the floor plan of a typical product layout. The product layout generally allows for economy in both cost of and time required for production, as each part of the manufacturing process is carried out in sequence.

Process Layout. The process layout is designed for factories that manufacture many different or custom-made products. In this layout, similar processes are grouped together and the product moves back and forth among those areas until completed. The process layout is often more expensive and requires more management time to ensure efficiency. Figure 11-5 illustrates a process layout for a small factory.

Fixed-Position Layout. In the fixed-position layout, the product remains in a fixed position throughout its manufacture. The production processes move to the product. As one might

Figure 11-4 Product Layout

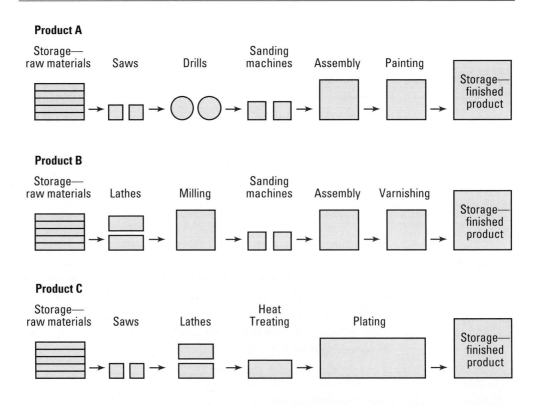

Figure 11-5   Process Layout

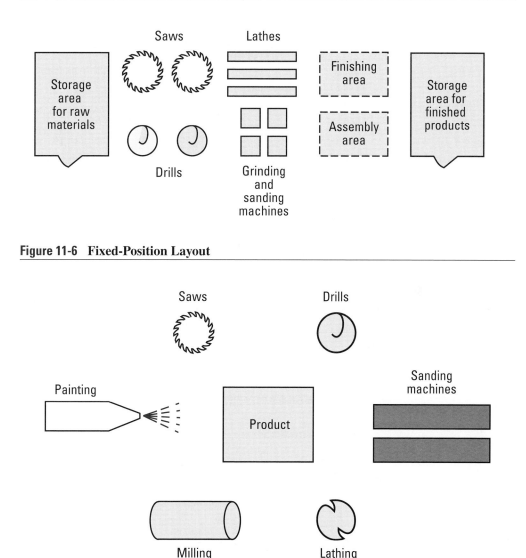

Figure 11-6   Fixed-Position Layout

expect, this type of layout is used for very large and cumbersome products and is used infrequently by the small business. Figure 11-6 illustrates the fixed-position layout.

Layouts for Retail Firms

As noted in Figure 11-3, interior layout is a very important factor in the success of a retail store. As Incident 11-3 (on the next page) illustrates, sensitivity to consumer needs and shopping patterns is critical to the development of an effective layout. In planning the layout, the retailer will need to analyze several key areas.

Allocation of Selling versus Nonselling Space. Experience in retailing shows that some areas of a retail store are more productive and draw more traffic than others. This phenomenon is illustrated in Figure 11-7. Generally, the space at the front and to the right is more productive space. Obviously, selling space should be planned for the most productive areas of the store.

Incident 11-3

Need a Strategy

The spring of 1994 is one that Eddy Calderon will never forget. In three months, two big boxes opened up within 15 minutes of his tiny hardware store in the Montreal suburb of Laval. Instantly, his customers had another quarter million square feet of store space to shop in — a Réno Dépôt and a RONA L'entrepôt (owned and operated by Calderon's fellow members in the RONA buying group).

As his customers checked out the giants down the road, Calderon wondered if this was it for the business started by his dad in 1957. "My manager and I had to sit down and re-evaluate our situation to the point of saying, 'Okay. Do we close and do something else?' We asked each other, 'Do you want to be an employee at a warehouse store?' Because that's where our future was headed. 'No way!' we said."

That sort of soul-searching jump-started Calderon into action. He immediately doubled the size of the store, Quincaillerie Métro, to 6,000 square feet. The colour scheme was modernized and Calderon re-evaluated his layout and product selection. Racks were strategically lowered to eliminate the claustrophobic feel often associated with the small corner store. The bottom line was he tried to be different.

SOURCE: Robert Gerlsbeck, "Need a Strategy," *Hardware Merchandising*, July–August 1998, pp. 31–37.

Figure 11-7   Rankings of Space Importance in a Typical Retail Store

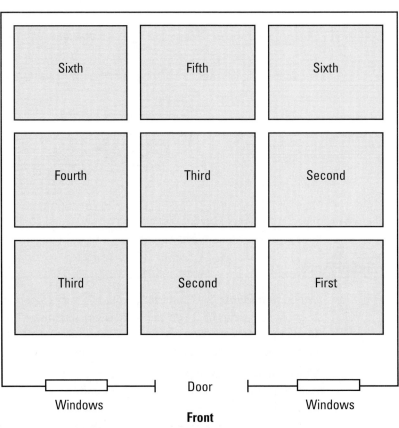

Allocation of Space among Departments and/or Products. The same principle discussed above should be applied in allocating space among departments and products, with the most profitable being placed in the high-traffic areas if possible.

Classification of Merchandise. Chapter 8 discusses the classification of consumer goods—convenience, shopping, and specialty goods. Each merchandise classification may require a slightly different placement in the retail store based on the purchase motives associated with that class of goods. For example, convenience items are often found close to heavier customer traffic flow. Shopping goods might be placed by competing brands, and specialty or demand items at more inaccessible parts of the store.

Location of Displays and Products on the Shelf. The small retailer should acquire expertise in a number of display techniques. Placement of merchandise on the shelf or counter can lead to increased sales, as certain areas are more productive than others. Merchandise placed at eye level and at the ends of aisles generally sells better. Two types of layouts are used by retail stores: the grid layout and the free-flow layout.

Grid Layout. The grid layout is organized with customer convenience and retailer efficiency in mind. Grid layouts have traditionally been used in stores like supermarkets and hardware stores. Figure 11-8 illustrates a grid layout.

Free-Flow Layout. Some types of merchandise are purchased in a more relaxed atmosphere that allows customers more time to browse. For such merchandise it is common to use the free-flow layout, illustrated in Figure 11-9 on the next page. This type of layout is suitable for clothing and many specialty types of merchandise.

Many larger retail stores use combinations of the grid and free-flow layouts. Most small retailers, however, generally use one or the other type.

Layouts for Service Firms

Because the operations of service firms are so diverse, it is difficult to provide standard information on layouts. Some service firms, such as restaurants, more closely approximate

Figure 11-8   Grid Layout

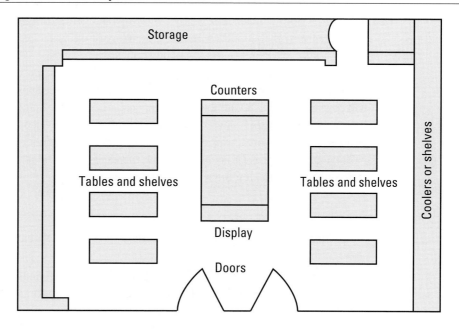

Figure 11-9   Free-Flow Layout

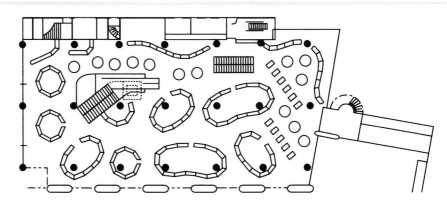

the layouts of retail stores. Many of the principles discussed earlier for retailing apply here. For those service firms that are more similar to manufacturing firms, such as repair shops, the principles of manufacturing layouts may be more appropriate.

PURCHASING AND CONTROLLING INVENTORIES

The cost of purchasing and holding inventories can be substantial. Because a small business generally has limited economic resources, it is critical that such a firm give inventory management a high priority. The following sections discuss areas about which the small business owner should be knowledgeable in purchasing and controlling inventories.

Sources of Supply

Chapter 8 discusses various aspects of the distribution channel from the seller's point of view. The same principles apply in this section, but from the buyer's position. The owner-manager should know which suppliers are available. Purchases can usually be made directly from the manufacturer, from an agent of the manufacturer, from a wholesaler, or from a retailer. While sources vary considerably among industries, most small businesses purchase their inventories from wholesalers. Many owner-managers import merchandise that uses sources of supply from other countries. In this case, many of the concepts discussed in Chapter 8 with respect to the exporting section may be applicable.

One question most small businesses face is whether to purchase from one supplier or many. In purchasing from only one supplier, the buyer is assured of consistent quality and will probably receive favourable treatment such as discounts and guaranteed supply in case of shortages. On the other hand, other suppliers may offer lower prices from time to time. The business may also spread risk by purchasing from many suppliers. The small business owner must weigh these pros and cons in making this decision. Incident 11-4 illustrates the possible consequences of making the wrong supplier decision.

Evaluating Suppliers

Small business owners generally use certain criteria to evaluate suppliers. Following are some of the more common criteria.

Dependability. The owner-manager should evaluate how dependable the prospective supplier will likely be. Dependability will undoubtedly be more important for some companies and even for some types of products than for others.

Incident 11-4

Bill's Service Station

Bill Andrews, owner of Bill's Service Station in Montreal, Quebec, was in a dilemma. He ran out of antifreeze early in the winter of 2000, and most of his regular customers were growing impatient and going elsewhere to winterize their cars. In the past, Bill had prided himself on shopping competitively for antifreeze. To obtain the lowest prices, he frequently changed suppliers and had been able to pass some of this saving on to his customers. With the onset of the antifreeze shortage, however, this practice had come back to haunt him. Suppliers were providing the scarce product only to the retailers who had been loyal to them and had previously purchased larger volumes. Bill's Service Station was one of the first outlets to be cut off. Now Bill wished he had stayed with one supplier, even if it meant paying a few dollars more.

SOURCE: D. W. Balderson, University of Lethbridge.

Cost. Obviously the cost of inventories will play a major role in supplier selection for the small firm.

Services Offered. Typical services offered by suppliers are delivery, discounts, credit, promotion, promotional support materials, return policies, guarantees, and technical assistance. Willingness and ability to provide these services at all hours may be an important factor in the selection of a supplier.

Determining Order Quantities

Estimating the quantities of inventories to order will require several essential items of information.

Order Lead Time. The time taken to process the order at both shipping and destination points, as well as to transport the item(s), should be estimated. This is called order lead time and is illustrated by the distance between points B and C in Figure 11-10 (on the next page). An increasing number of businesses have instituted a just-in-time inventory policy. In this approach, the order is placed so that the inventory arrives "just in time" to be utilized in the production process. This system is appropriate for manufacturers that have computer capabilities, are confident in the dependability of suppliers, and require large amounts of inventory.

Sales or Production Estimate. The owner-manager will need to make a realistic projection of inventories to be sold or consumed in the manufacture of the finished product for the period. Methods of obtaining this type of information are discussed in Chapter 3. Such a rate of sale throughout the period is shown by the diagonal line A–C in Figure 11-10.

Minimum Inventory Levels Required. No business wants to run out of inventory, especially if the inventory consists of important items. It is therefore common to carry a minimum basic inventory for many items. Such inventory is often called safety stock and is shown as the distance between D and E in Figure 11-10. The size of safety stock usually depends on such factors as the importance of the inventory, volatility of demand, and dependability of sources of supply.

Inventory Currently on Hand. The owner-manager should have an accurate estimate of inventories on hand. To monitor current inventory levels on a continuous basis, a perpetual inventory system can be used. Details of this type of system will be discussed later in this chapter. For many businesses, a perpetual system requires a computerized inventory system.

Figure 11-10   Order Points

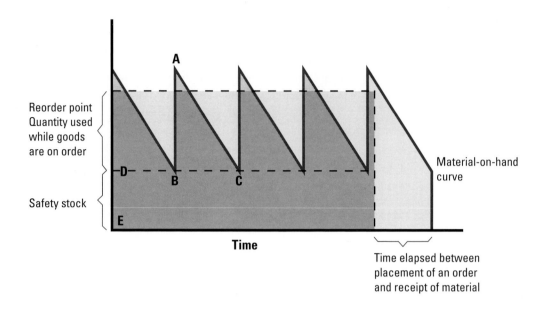

As mentioned in Chapter 10, an increasing number of small businesses can now afford such systems. Once current inventory levels have been determined, the owner-manager can incorporate those amounts into various methods to determine order quantities.

Methods for Determining Order Quantities. Some of the more common methods used to determine order quantities follow.

Minimum Turnover Method. This method uses the inventory turnover formula (discussed in Chapter 10) for the business in determining amounts of inventory required. For example, if inventory turnover for the business is 4 (four times per year) and projected sales for the period are $200,000, the required inventory is calculated as follows:

$$\frac{\text{Sales}}{\text{Inventory}} = \text{Inventory turnover}$$

$$\frac{\$200,000}{\text{Inventory}} = 4$$

$$\text{Inventory} = \frac{\$200,000}{4} = \$50,000$$

Hence, the minimum required inventory at retail value for the period is $50,000.

Maximum and Minimum Method. Some small businesses set acceptable maximum and minimum limits on inventory levels. Whether inventory is measured in dollar amounts or number of units, reaching these limits indicates when it is time to order and specifies the amount to order. This method is used frequently by small businesses for merchandise of lower unit values.

Open-to-Buy Method. This method of calculating order quantities, used extensively in retailing, uses the following formula (the components are discussed earlier):

Open-to-buy = Maximum inventory – Merchandise on order – Merchandise on hand

where

Open to buy = Inventories that can be purchased

Maximum inventory = Expected sales + Safety stock required

Economic Order Quantity (EOQ). This formula is used infrequently in small businesses but may be helpful for important items or in manufacturing businesses. It allows for the calculation of the minimization of the ordering and storage costs of inventory. Generally speaking, if ordering costs are higher (more frequent orders), storage costs are lower (less inventory required). Through this formula, the owner-manager can arrive at the least-cost combination of ordering and storage costs. The EOQ formula for dollar amounts is as follows:

$$EOQ = \sqrt{\frac{2AB}{i}}$$

where

A	=	Annual or period demand in dollars
B	=	Costs of making an order in dollars
i	=	Inventory carrying costs (storage costs) expressed as a percentage of inventory value

For obtaining the economic order quantity in units, the formula is

$$EOQ = \sqrt{\frac{2AB}{Pi}}$$

where

PI   =   Unit price

Although this formula has proved unwieldy for many small businesses in the past, the increasing accessibility of computers and the ability to enter the formula into the appropriate software has allowed more businesses to take advantage of the EOQ formula.

A-B-C Analysis. This method of inventory management recognizes that some items of merchandise are more important to the business than others. The level of importance is influenced by such factors as higher sales, high unit value levels, higher profitability, or importance in the manufacture of the finished product.

With A-B-C analysis, the most important inventory (A items) is watched more closely to ensure they are managed efficiently. The B and C items, being less important, may require less detailed monitoring and control. Figure 11-11 gives an example of A-B-C analysis.

Administration of the Buying Process. The owner-manager should be familiar with the mechanics of purchasing. Knowledge of the different kinds of discounts and purchase terms and conditions is essential, as are efficient receiving, checking, and marking of merchandise to minimize inventory costs and reduce shrinkage.

Inventory Control

As discussed earlier, efficient purchasing requires proper monitoring and control practices. Three essential aspects of inventory control are determining the unit of control, the method of valuing inventories, and the method of monitoring inventory levels.

Figure 11-11 A-B-C Analysis

	A Items	B Items	C Items
Percent of total inventory value	65%	25%	10%
Percent of total list of different stock items	20%	20%	60%
Inventory method used	Minimum turnover EOQ Maximum turnover	Minimum turnover	Eyeballing
Time allocation	Time-consuming and precision needed	Less time-consuming estimates	Rough estimates only

Unit of Control. Most firms keep track of their inventories by dollar amounts. This approach is called dollar inventory control. Dollar inventory control is suitable for firms with large amounts of inventory at a relatively low per-unit value.

Some businesses that have relatively small amounts of inventory keep track of inventories in numbers of units. This method is called unit control.

Valuation. Generally accepted accounting principles allow inventories to be valued at the lower of cost or market value. It is very important that an accurate valuation of inventory levels be calculated, because, as Figure 11-12 shows, inventory levels directly affect the net income of the business at the end of the period.

Monitoring. There are essentially two methods of monitoring inventories. The first, periodic inventory, involves physically counting and recording the merchandise to determine inventory levels. Periodic inventory calculation is required at least once each year for income tax purposes. It is costly and time-consuming to carry out, however, so most businesses use this method no more frequently than required.

The second type of inventory monitoring, perpetual inventory, involves continuous recording of inventory increases and decreases as transactions occur. Historically this system was feasible only for a small business with low levels of high-unit-value inventory. Recently, however, microcomputer database management programs have made the perpetual inventory system a reality for many small businesses. Inventory control is also enhanced by performing various evaluation analyses such as calculating turnover, comparison of budgeted amounts with actual inventories, and analysis of inventory disappearance (shrinkage). Incident 11-5 illustrates how the use of computer technology can assist the small business in inventory management.

Figure 11-12 Valuation of Inventories

Sales – Cost of goods sold – Other expenses = Net income

where

Cost of goods sold = Beginning inventory + Purchases – Ending inventory

Using the relationships in these formulas, one can see that if ending inventory is overstated, cost of goods sold will be understated by the same amount and net income overstated by that same amount. Therefore, a valuation error of $100 will translate into either an overstatement or an understatement of net income by $100.

Incident 11-5

Competing with a Computer

Home Depot
www.homedepot.com

Even with a Home Depot only 10 minutes away from his store, Ron Cicuttini doesn't worry too much about how to compete with the big box giant's on-shelf offerings. Despite his small size, he's able to sell thousands of items not usually available in the store.

How does he do it? About a year ago he eliminated his clunky microfiche catalogue and installed an electronic catalogue system that is hooked up directly to his buying group's warehouse. When a customer comes into the store asking for a particular product, staff direct them to the PC station set up at the end of the power aisle. There they can browse an incredible selection.

While on-line ordering is helping to sell product, Cicuttini is also using technology to cut costs. His drive to improve profitability has led him to install an inventory management system that keeps stock at a minimum. The result? "Our sales have increased and our inventory has decreased," he answers.

And while he may seem a bit over-enthusiastic about the advantages of retail technology, Cicuttini says there is a calculated reason for his attitude. If you want to get your staff to accept technology, you have to hype up the system in front of them, he says. "How the staff reacts to changes in technology really comes down to the owner or manager."

Cicuttini also made sure his staff could not go back to doing things the old way. "When I got [on-line ordering], I took the old system right off the floor so there was no choice about using it. We held staff meetings and they saw I was enthused. That attitude trickled down."

SOURCE: Sonya Felix, Tech Files, *Hardware Merchandising*, July–August 1998, p. 38.

Security of Inventory. Preventing loss of inventory (shrinkage) is a major challenge for most small businesses. The business should develop a detailed procedure for ordering, receiving, marking, handling, and monitoring all inventories. The system selected will vary depending on the type of business.

The Small Business-Supplier Relationship

One of the critical keys to the success of operations management is the relationship that the business maintains with its suppliers. Because of the size of the business and resulting relatively small volumes of purchases, the small business tends to be at a disadvantage compared to large businesses in receiving favourable treatment from suppliers. It is therefore important that the owner-manager implement policies and procedures that can ensure a successful relationship with the supplier. Examples of such policies and procedures are as follows:[2]

1. Define clear, identifiable, and measurable objectives for your supplier management strategy.

2. Be prepared to work with the supplier to identify and define the roles that each will perform. Consider your relationship a partnership to achieve the goals stated in number one above.

3. Attempt to employ technology to share data relating to forecasting, product movement, and financial evaluation.

4. Evaluate suppliers regularly with an objective standardized framework that is both quantitative and qualitative.

Summary

1. The production process involves the conversion of inputs such as money, people, machines, and inventories into outputs—the products or services provided.

2. The physical facilities must be continually monitored as the conditions that contribute to their effectiveness will not remain static.

3. The three types of layouts used by small manufacturing firms are the product layout, process layout, and fixed-position layout. The product layout is used when the business manufactures large numbers of just one or a few products. The process layout is designed for factories that manufacture smaller numbers of many different or custom-made products. The fixed-position layout is used for very large or cumbersome products.

4. In planning the interior layout of a retail store, the retailer needs to analyze the allocation of selling versus nonselling space, the allocation of space among departments and/or products, classification of the merchandise, and the location of displays and products on the shelf. The two types of layouts used by a retail store are the grid layout and the free-flow layout. The grid layout, typically used in a supermarket, is organized with customer convenience and retail efficiency in mind. The free-flow layout has a more relaxed atmosphere that is conducive to browsing. This type of layout is suitable for clothing and many specialty types of merchandise.

5. In estimating the quantities to order, the essential items of information required are the order lead time, the sales or production estimate, minimum inventory levels required, and the inventory currently on hand. Some methods used to determine order quantities include: the minimum turnover method, which uses inventory turnover calculations; the maximum and minimum method, which indicates the time and amounts to order; the open-to-buy method, used in retailing; the economic order quantity, which calculates the minimization of the ordering and storage costs of inventory; and A-B-C analysis, which prioritizes types of inventory.

Chapter Problems and Applications

1. What kind of layout should be used for the following manufacturing firms?

   a. Golf club manufacturer

   b. Independent bottler

   c. Bob's Machine Shop

2. What kind of layout should be used for the following retail firms?

   a. Clothing store

   b. Motorcycle shop

   c. Small grocery store

3. Answer the following questions regarding the location of food items in a grocery store.

   a. Where are the bread and milk located? Why?

   b. Where are the chocolate bars and other candy located? Why?

   c. Where on the shelf are the top name-brand items located? Why?

   d. Where are the high-margin items positioned in the store and on the shelf? Why?

4. Visit a small retail store or manufacturing plant and evaluate the layout.

5. Frank Newhart is opening a new video store, but he has not determined which VCR supplier to use. Frank has narrowed the choice to two sources. Supplier 1 is newly established and sells the units for $260 apiece. Supplier 2 is a well-established firm and sells the units for $275 each, with a 7 percent discount on orders over 50. Evaluate each supplier from the information given. With this information, develop different scenarios in which Frank would choose supplier 1 or supplier 2.

6. Rick Smith, owner of Smith's Men and Boys' Wear, must determine how much inventory to purchase and in what amounts. For the upcoming year, he has forecast $200,000 in sales. He has calculated that the average ordering cost is $50, and the average inventory holding cost is 5 percent. His average inventory turnover is 3.4.

   a. Calculate the per-order quantities in dollars.

   b. Calculate the required inventory for the year.

   c. How many times during the year should Smith order?

7. Interview three business owners to determine which inventory ordering system they use and why.

8. Interview a small business owner to learn why he or she selected a particular supplier. Find out what criteria were important to the owner in making the choice.

Suggested Readings

Berman, Barry, and Joel R. Evans. *Retail Management: A Strategic Approach.* New York: Macmillan, 1995, pp. 392–416.

Hatten, Timothy S., *Small Business Entrepreneurship and Beyond.* Saddle River, New Jersey: Prentice Hall, 1997, pp. 423–442.

Levy, Michael, and Barton A. Weitz. *Essentials of Retailing.* Chicago: Irwin, 1996, pp. 271–293.

Lewison, Dale, and D. Wesley Balderson. *Retailing,* Canadian Edition. Scarborough, Ont.: Prentice Hall, 1998, pp. 236–259.

Longnecker, Justin G., and Carlos W. Moore, J. William Petty, Leo B. Donlery. *Small Business Management—An Entrepreneurial Approach.* Toronto: Nelson, 1998, pp. 410–452.

Total Quality Control: A Winning Strategy for Small Business. Montreal: Federal Business Development Bank, 1990.

Varnicchio, David. "Affordable Computer Solutions to Help You Market," *Small Business,* vol. 4, no. 2, Fall, 2000, p. 10.

Comprehensive Case
The Framemakers: Part 7

Although The Framemakers' financial statements for the first year of operations were disappointing, sales had picked up during the last few months by enough to allow the Normans to make their bank payment. The Normans also were learning that the majority of their customers appeared to be repeat business. Thus, instead of experiencing a post-Christmas slump, sales continued to climb steadily. Now Robert and Teresa were sure the business had turned the corner.

The increased sales made it necessary to hire two employees and substantially increase the money spent on inventory. The inventory ordering area troubled Robert. It seemed that at the same time they had too much of some inventory, they frequently ran out of some of their more popular items. Both Robert and Teresa had initially placed orders when they thought an item was getting low. They tried to order a week before they expected the item to run out to allow for the seven days' delivery required for their supplies, which came mostly from Ontario or the United States.

Another inventory problem was determining the amount to order. Frequently they ordered a larger amount of inventory on some items than they thought they needed. Some suppliers, however, required a minimum-volume purchase to grant a discount, and others would not deal with them unless the order was substantial. The Normans also differed on which inventories they thought were needed. Robert felt Teresa ordered too much of some items that she especially liked to work with herself. He hesitated to bring it up, however, as they were already experiencing enough strain.

To deal with these problems, the Normans hired another employee and implemented a card system to control inventories. However, it became clear toward the end of the second year that the card system had failed to solve the inventory problems. Inventory always seemed to be behind, and frequently cards were not updated as items were sold. The Normans realized they had to do something about the problem. The Framemakers' inventory turnover figure and gross profit had been far too low in the first year, and if a better system were not adopted, Robert suspected it would be worse the following year.

Robert investigated the possibility of purchasing a computer to help solve these inventory difficulties. Despite the company's still weak cash position, he found an inexpensive used Apple II computer that the salesperson said would be adequate for their needs. The Normans were pleased they would finally be able to get better control over the business.

The implementation of the computer system turned out to be another disappointment. First, the employee who had developed the card system for inventory control and would be doing much of the ordering was sceptical about the benefits of the computer, continued to make errors, and eventually quit. The Normans also found that the computer they had purchased lacked the capacity to handle their expanded inventories. Finally, some information concerning inventory and the accounting system had been completely lost when entered on the computer and then cancelled.

Robert and Teresa not only continued to worry about inventory control but were completely disillusioned with the computer. They were considering scrapping it altogether and going back to their manual system.

Questions

1. Why did The Framemakers experience inventory management problems?
2. Aside from purchasing a computer, what could the Normans have done to alleviate these problems?
3. Evaluate the Normans' computer purchase decision and its implementation.

Video Case Questions
Mohair Sock*

CBC

South Mountain, Ontario is an hour's drive south of Ottawa. There's actually no mountain here, just four churches, a gas station, and the farm of local entrepreneur, Theresa Bergeron. She is a trader on the world specialty fibres market. She deals in the volatile market of Mohair—that's the fleece of angora goats.

1. Identify the production problems that Theresa Bergeron is required to deal with in operating South Mountain Mohair Incorporated.

2. How could she avoid these problems?

3. What suggestions might be made to improve her marketing efforts?

*Source: CBC *Venture* #723, running time 8:14.

Chapter 12

Human Resources Management

Chapter Objectives

- To explain the importance of human resources management to the small business.

- To illustrate the methods of planning for hiring and training of employees.

- To discuss skill areas the owner-manager can strengthen to improve personal leadership and people skills within the organization.

- To illustrate principles of effective human resources management for the small business.

- To review the procedures of administering a small business payroll.

- To review the legal requirements relating to personnel of the small business.

Small Business Profile

Gailen Drost
Drost Save Easy

Canadian Federation of Independent Grocers
www.cfig.ca/

It's the career he never planned on. But, 44 years later, Gailen Drost, owner of Drost Save Easy in Bath, N.B., and the new chairperson of the Canadian Federation of Independent Grocers (CFIG), says he has no regrets whatsoever.

Drost packed groceries at his father's 2,000 square foot store in Bath during high school, then went on to university in 1954 to study engineering. However, he wasn't convinced that engineering was the right career for him. "Like most young people, I wasn't sure what I wanted to do, and I made the mistake of telling my dad," Drost says.

The rest, as the saying goes, is history.

John Drost bluntly told his son that if he couldn't decide on a career, he should work for a year at the store. That year has turned into over four decades of success as an independent grocer in a tiny rural village in western New Brunswick.

CFIG has recognized the store for its cleanliness and friendly staff. In 1994, it received the CFIG Platinum Award, after placing among the top three independent stores in Atlantic Canada for 10 consecutive years. In 1987, Drost was named Grocer of the Year for stores up to 10,000 square feet in size.

Using a combination of training programs from the CFIG and franchisor Atlantic Wholesalers for his 32 staff members (18 of whom are full-time), Drost essentially teaches his employees the importance of delivering top-notch customer service, by example. "I have always enjoyed meeting my customers and giving them personalized service," Drost says, adding that he savours being literally the last grocer in the region to still carry customers' packages to their vehicle.

"I like the idea of being on the floor and serving my customers, and I still like carrying groceries out for my customers," he says.

Drost's emphasis on family values is evident with his staff's work schedules. Some of his part-timers have chosen to work fewer hours so they can spend more time with their children, and Drost is more than happy to accommodate them. With all his staff, he strives to be flexible. "We've always felt our staff is like a big family, so for anything—time off, or whatever—we do our best to give them what they want," he says.

While supporting his staff where their families are concerned, Drost also likes to see employees involved in community activities, projects, and organizations. Four of his staff, as well as Drost himself (who also served as mayor for 11 years), are members of the village's volunteer fire department, although Drost admits he's been cutting back his time after 40 years in the brigade.

Employees at Drost Save Easy have also helped out in fundraising projects like the annual Children's Miracle Network Telethon, reconstruction of the local pool and others. "We believe in supporting all worthwhile causes," Drost says. In the fall of 2000 Drost received the Canadian Federation of Independent Grocers Award in recognition of a well-run store.

HUMAN RESOURCES MANAGEMENT AND THE SMALL BUSINESS

**Canadian Federation
of Independent
Business
www.cfib.ca**

Management in an organization has often been defined as getting things done through other people. The small business owner is a personnel manager even if his or her main strength or interest lies in the production, financial, or marketing aspects of the business.

Often the small business owner is reluctant to learn personnel administration fundamentals because he or she believes these principles apply only to larger organizations. The result is often personnel problems such as frequent turnover of staff, lack of motivation and initiative, lack of harmony among employees, high absenteeism, frequent grievances, and high overall employee costs. The incidence of these problems appears to be high in small business. One study of 77 successful entrepreneurs indicated that owner-managers' number one headache was personnel.[1] The same study pointed out that the demands of running the business usually prevented owner-managers from paying as much attention to their employees as they should. Another study, conducted by the Canadian Federation of Independent Business, found that over half of small businesses had difficulty finding qualified labour at a reasonable wage.[2] On the other hand, CFIB has found that employees in small companies are significantly more likely to rate their workplace as "good" than those in large firms. This is shown in Figure 12-1. The reasons for this apparent high level of satisfaction are increased flexibility in the workplace and a closer relationship with the owner.[3] Small businesses have a natural advantage over large businesses in these areas. It is critical that the entrepreneur take advantage of the techniques described in this chapter to maintain that advantage.

As the business grows, the owner-manager's workload generally expands. Because there is a limit to what one person can do, the business may suffer if the owner fails to hire new employees and delegate responsibilities to them.

The reputation of a business in the community can be affected by employees' satisfaction with their jobs. The level of employee satisfaction can be enhanced or lowered by the owner-manager's use of personnel management principles. This is especially true in the retail and service industries. Motivated and competent personnel are one characteristic of a business that the competition may find difficult to duplicate.

Figure 12-1   Job Satisfaction Among SME Employees and Self-Employed Is High

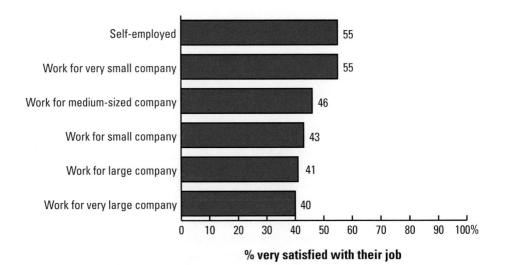

SOURCE: Canadian Federation of Independent Business, *Small Business Primer*, June 2001, p. 10.

Given all these factors, it is essential that the owner-manager have some knowledge of personnel administration principles to sustain the success of the business. This chapter covers planning for personnel, hiring, and ongoing personnel management in the small business.

PLANNING FOR HUMAN RESOURCES

There are essentially four human resource planning steps in an organization. This section discusses each of these steps briefly.

Determine Personnel Requirements. The first step in planning for personnel is to determine the number of jobs or tasks to be done, the level of expertise required, and the number of people needed to perform those tasks. This process may already have been carried out as part of the feasibility analysis discussed in Chapter 3.

Set Organizational Structure. The second step in personnel planning is to integrate tasks and employees so that the owner can visualize how the different parts of the plan will work together. This formalized plan is commonly called an organizational chart. In the very small (two- or three-person) business, the organizational chart may simply be a division of responsibilities, as in Figure 12-2. In a larger business, the organizational chart shows the lines of responsibility for each member of the organization. An organizational chart for a small retail store appears in Figure 12-3. Each business possesses unique characteristics that dictate how to set up the organizational chart. Some of the more common approaches are to organize by (1) function performed, such as sales, purchasing, or promotion; (2) type of merchandise or department, as in Figure 12-3; and (3) geographic territory.

Figure 12-2   Division of Responsibilities for a Very Small Business

Partner A	Partner B	Partner C
↓	↓	↓
Marketing	Production	Finance

Figure 12-3   Organizational Chart for a Retail Furniture Store

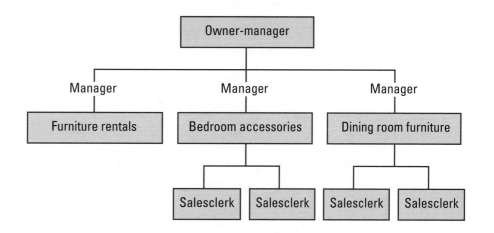

In setting up the organizational structure, some rules of thumb have been found to contribute to a successful operation:

- Each employee should report to only one supervisor. This arrangement is called unity of control or command.

- Similar functions should be grouped together if possible.

- There is a limit to an individual's span of control. Span of control is the number of people who can be directly supervised by one person. The proper span of control varies according to the combined characteristics of the manager, the subordinates, and the job.

Prepare Job Descriptions. The third step in personnel planning is the preparation of job descriptions and specifications. Before hiring employees, a detailed listing of the job or task duties (job descriptions) must be made. The job description briefly explains what is to be done, how it is to be done, and why it is done. This information goes into the job specification—a statement of the skills, abilities, physical characteristics, and education required to perform the job. As mentioned earlier, part of the job description may be included in the policy manual. Figure 12-4 illustrates a job description and specifications for an employee of a small business.

Develop Personnel Policies. The fourth step in personnel planning is to formally develop personnel policies. Including these policies in an employee policy manual can help prevent many personnel problems. For the very small business, this may simply be a list of some do's and don'ts; a larger business may provide a booklet to each new employee.

Figure 12-4   Job Descriptions and Specifications Sales Manager, Hardware Store

Job Duties Description:

Reports to the general manager

Directly responsible for floor salespeople

Suggests markdowns on slow items

Controls inventory

Authorizes merchandise returns

Occasionally meets with suppliers to learn about new products

Maintains good customer relations at all time

Takes care of written correspondence concerning sales

Does any other task relevant to the job as requested by the general manager

Personal Requirements Specifications:

High school diploma or equivalent

At least two years' experience in a similar job

Initiative; "instinct" for sales; convincing manner; aptitude for managing people

Self-disciplined; good appearance; willing to work overtime

Policy manuals are used infrequently in small businesses. The uncertainty that can result may create serious employee difficulties. The common areas to be covered in a policy manual are described below. Minimum standards for many of these areas are set by government labour departments in each province.

- Job descriptions clearly outline the duties, responsibilities, and reporting lines for employees, as mentioned previously.

- Working conditions include such things as hours of work, coffee breaks, and other expectations of management.

- Holidays and leaves outline statutory holidays, paid vacations, and procedures for taking a leave of absence.

- Remuneration and pay consist of a listing of details of the payroll such as date of payment, time periods included, and reviews of pay levels.

- Employee benefits provided by the firm, such as bonuses, profit sharing, medical-dental insurance plans, and employee discounts should be clearly stated.

- The grievance procedure consists of a description of the procedure employees are to follow if they have a concern or grievance within the organization.

THE HIRING PROCESS

Once the personnel plan has been developed, the next step is to review various sources for potential employees and make the selection.

Sources of Employees

Following are some potential sources of employees for the small business.

Recruitment from Within. For most organizations, recruiting from within the firm is the most common course if current employees have the qualifications. Hiring an outsider to perform a supervisory job instead of someone within the organization usually has a negative and disruptive effect on the business.

Other Businesses. To reduce training costs, employees from competing firms or similar industries can be hired. Such employees generally will have some background about the industry and/or business that can be easily transferred. The recruiter, however, will have to use this approach carefully to avoid a negative reaction from the competition, particularly in smaller markets.

Employee Referrals. Present employees may be asked to recommend acquaintances to fill available jobs. This method has the advantage of some prior knowledge of the individual's background. It may have a negative effect, however, if the new employee proves unsatisfactory.

Advertising. Some small businesses advertise for employees in local newspapers. The cost of this type of advertising is minimal.

**Human Resources
Development Canada
www.hrdc-drhc.gc.ca**

Employment Agencies. Employment agencies sponsored by provincial governments are one source. Human Resources Development Canada offices also have lists of employees looking for work. This can be a potentially valuable source of employees, particularly for positions that do not require highly technical expertise. Private employment agencies typically are not used by small businesses to recruit employees, but they may be helpful in recruiting highly skilled employees.

Educational Institutions. Some small businesses that require employees with technical expertise use universities or colleges as sources. These sources can be helpful in manufacturing and some service businesses and retailing.

The Screening Process

Once potential employees have been identified from one or more of the above sources, the owner-manager faces the task of selection. Several screening devices can be used to aid in the selection of employees.

**Human Resources
Development Canada
www.hrdc-drhc.gc.ca**

Application Form. Many small businesses do not use an application form. If new employees are hired infrequently, such a formal document may be unnecessary. However, the application form can be a valuable screening tool and a time saver for the owner. An application form need not be lengthy to be useful, as Figure 12-5 illustrates. The owner-manager must be careful not to violate provisions of the Human Rights Act in preparing the application form.

The Employment Interview. Although the application form may screen out several potential employees, an interview is usually required in making the final decision. The employment interview is particularly important for jobs requiring interpersonal contact, as it allows the interviewer to judge appearance, poise, and communication ability. A helpful tool in interviewing is an interview guide, which focuses the discussion and provides a constant base of information with which to compare applicants. Appendix 12A illustrates an interview guide. Again, human rights legislation precludes the use of certain questions during an employment interview, and the owner-manager should be aware of such legislation.

Checking References. The third screening device is the checking of references. Most application forms require the applicant to list both personal and business references. As might be expected, business references are more valuable because they provide information regarding the individual's past work record. Incident 12-1 illustrates the value of checking references for one small business.

Checks made by telephone or in person with business references are preferred to written responses. The writer of a letter of reference may have little or no idea of the requirements of the job. Also, past employers are sometimes reluctant to write uncomplimentary letters of reference. Specific questions should be asked about the candidate's performance, as well as about whether employers would consider rehiring the person.

Incident 12-1

Home Hardware

The owner of the Home Hardware store in Magrath, Alberta, was looking for an assistant manager for hardware. After interviewing several applicants, the owner decided to hire an individual who had several years' experience in a hardware store in a distant town. All indications were that this individual was the best choice. Before making the offer of employment, the owner decided to check with the previous employer. He was grateful he did, because he found out that the chosen applicant had an unsatisfactory work record as well as questionable honesty. As a result of this reference check, another applicant was chosen and proved to be an excellent employee.

**Home Hardware
www.homehardware
dealers.com**

SOURCE: D. W. Balderson, University of Lethbridge.

Figure 12-5   Application for Employment for a Small Business

Name _____   First Name _____

Address (Home) _____   Tel. _____

Address (Work) _____   Tel. _____

Social Insurance No. _____

Languages: Spoken _____   Written _____

Secondary Education

| Years | School | City | Diploma |

Postsecondary Education

| Years | School | City | Degree |

Work Experience

(begin with most recent)

From _____ To _____   Employer _____

Title _____   Nature of Duties _____

Salary _____

Reason for Leaving _____

_____

Work Experience

From _____ To _____   Employer _____

Title _____   Nature of Duties _____

Salary _____

Reason for Leaving _____

Other Information

| References: | Name | Address | Title |

1.

2.

3.

Signature   Date

Tests. Many large businesses use various types of intellectual, ethical, and physical tests as part of the screening process. Some specific tests being used increasingly in small businesses are proficiency and skill tests (to perform a particular trade, craft, or skill), vocational interest tests (to assess long-term interest in the job or company), aptitude tests (to determine how a person might perform on a given job), and polygraph tests (to measure level of honesty). Because some of these tests are technical, the owner-manager should seek professional assistance in administering them.

Notification of the Hiring Decision

Once the hiring decision has been made, an offer of employment should be made to the successful applicant. This notification should be in writing, with a clear indication of the terms and conditions associated with the job. Most businesses require written confirmation of acceptance of the offer by the applicant.

All unsuccessful applicants should also be notified. Failure to provide this courtesy can have a detrimental effect on the reputation of the business.

PERSONNEL MANAGEMENT

HRM Guide Canada
www.hrmguide.net/
canada/index.html

Once the employee has been hired, the owner-manager's responsibility is to see that he or she is properly trained, satisfied enough with the working conditions to continue working there, and—probably most important—motivated to work hard and show initiative. Most small businesses are not in a position to hire a professional personnel manager to ensure that these desirable conditions exist. However, the owner-manager can foster these conditions by using the concepts of personnel management discussed in this section.

The Introduction Period

The first few months on the job are crucial to the employee's overall satisfaction and length of stay with the business.

The First Week. One of the most frequently mentioned characteristics of good working conditions is the way the owner-manager makes the employees feel like part of the organization.[4] Much can be done in the first week to communicate to the employee that he or she is a valued member of the business. The new employee should be introduced to co-workers, shown the locations of employee facilities, informed of any company regulations, and encouraged to ask for additional information if needed. The employee should be talked to frequently during the introductory period, not simply left alone to read the company policy manual as larger companies sometimes do.

Many employers find it helpful to set some short-term goals toward which the employee can work within the first week or two. These goals can be discussed at the conclusion of the agreed-upon time. This communicates not only that the employer is interested in the employee but also that the business is results- and goal-oriented.

The Probationary Period

Most employers find it advantageous to use a probationary period of three to six months for new employees. The probationary period allows the employer to further assess the new employee's suitability for the job. At the conclusion of a satisfactory probation period, the employee becomes permanent and may be entitled to a pay increase and other benefits of a permanent employee.

Training

Small Business Human Resources Guide
www.royalbank.com/
sme/guides/hr/index.
html

The purpose of the training program is to increase productivity. In addition, successful training programs can reduce employee turnover, allow for less supervision, and increase employee morale. Properly trained employees acquire a sense of worth, dignity, and well-being, as well as increased skill levels. Businesses use many forms of employee training. Some of the more common are discussed next.

On-the-Job Training. This is the least structured and most frequently used method by small businesses. It is perhaps the best method of training for routine and repetitive types of work. The business may assign another worker to work closely with the new employee in a buddy system or apprenticeship.

Formal Classroom Training. Businesses use many varieties of formal classroom training, but only a few have been used by small businesses. One such system is a cooperative type of program with an educational institution. This allows the employee to attend classroom instruction and training on a part-time basis. In Canada, the government provides financial assistance for employee training programs. These programs are discussed later in this chapter. Some businesses hold periodic seminars in which they bring experts from various fields to the business.

The Owner-Manager as Personnel Manager

Leadership Style. The first step in this process is a self-evaluation to obtain an understanding of one's own leadership or management style. Sometimes the owners are so preoccupied with running the technical or market side of the business that they give little thought to the kind of leadership example they set for employees.

Among leadership styles of entrepreneurs, several styles appear to be successful. A recent study of Canadian entrepreneurs found five different types of leadership. Figure 12-6 describes each type.[5]

The effectiveness of the owner-manager's leadership style may vary depending on the characteristics of the business and its employees. However, certain styles generally are more successful in the long run. Whatever the owner-manager's style, concern for both the people within the organization and the production process is important. The resulting team management approach found in many Japanese companies is particularly adaptable to the small business.

Time Management. A second critical aspect of successful people management is efficiently managing one's own time. Time management is often difficult to apply in the small business. So many operating crises and interruptions take place in the normal course of a day that the

Figure 12-6   Leadership Styles in Canadian Small Business

Solo	Osmosis	Managerial	Systems	Figurehead
Does everything	High level of control over business, but does spend time developing managers	Sets objectives and lines of authority	Develops systems and direction	Owns business but has little to do with it
Little delegation				
Very small firms		Controls results but delegates more on procedures	Allows employees to set some objectives and determine how they are met	Complete delegation
	High level of contact with employees	Less employee contact		

owner-manager may feel much of the advice in time management literature is impossible to employ. However, some basic time management concepts can be used successfully in the small business. Some of the more important concepts are discussed below.

Recognize the Importance of Time. Much time wasting results from a failure to recognize the importance of one's time. The first step in improved time management, therefore, is to have a sincere desire to use time more efficiently.

Reexamine and Clarify Priorities. Priority planning may be long or short term. Long-term planning involves setting objectives that the owner and business are projected to meet over a period of months or years. Long-term objectives, which are a part of the business plan, as discussed in Chapter 4 as part of the establishment plan of the business, provide direction for the firm. This strategic plan serves as the guideline for all operations of the business. Short-term priority planning deals with the utilization of time on a daily or weekly basis. It involves prioritizing tasks and working on those that are most important.

Analyze Present Time-Consuming Activities. This step requires keeping a diary of the daily activities of the owner-manager. Most people find the results of this step surprising. Often they find they spend time on less important items at the expense of more important ones. One small business owner spent several hours arguing over a $25 increase in building rental instead of using that time to evaluate the suitability of the overall location.

Implement Time Management Principles. The owner-manager may be able to eliminate common time-wasting traps and become more efficient in his or her use of time by implementing the following practices:

- Avoid procrastinating on difficult but important decisions in favour of easier but less important ones.

- Use the most productive time of the day for the more important decisions or analyses. For some people this may be early in the day, and for others it may be later. Many have found it beneficial to schedule routine or enjoyable tasks during their least productive time.

- Read only relevant information. Stop reading and start searching. Use travel, waiting, or otherwise unproductive times for reading.

- Use letters less and the telephone more. If possible, handle letters only once in a given period of time.

- Operate with a minimum of meetings. Make sure meetings are results-oriented and have definite starting and ending times.

- Delegate as much work as possible, recognizing that the owner-manager is still ultimately responsible for the decision or action. A more detailed discussion of delegation in small businesses appears in Chapter 14.

Motivation and Loyalty

Employers Online
www.hrdc-drhc.gc.
ca/common/home.
shtml

Successful managers are able to generate strong loyalty from their employees. They also succeed in motivating employees to work hard and be creative. They have open communication lines that provide a comfortable work environment (see Incident 12-2). It is no accident, however, that these conditions exist in some companies and not in others. In a recent Angus Reid survey, reasons for employee dislike of their jobs were examined. The results are shown in Figure 12-7. Some owner-managers understand and are able to apply these critical principles in human relations management. Two important principles concern working conditions and employee needs.

Incident 12-2

Advanced Bioconcept

The keys to Advanced Bioconcept success are its pay practices and management style. Advanced Bioconcept pays its employees well, taking the very Gen-X approach of sharing the wealth and embracing the culture of getting rich on stock options. Base salaries range between $30,000 and $60,000, but on top of that there are healthy performance-based bonuses and share purchase plans. Flex-time allows employees to customize their workweek. Segal and his partners hire people who are adaptable and comfortable with a minimum level of supervision, then let them reach their highest level of potential and responsibility very quickly. "We're incredibly willing to let people make mistakes," says Segal. "I'd rather apologize and do what I can to correct the mistakes than start getting really hierarchical. Our only credo is, just don't make the same mistake twice."

Finally, they make sure that people have fun. And the best way to do that is to keep scientists away from administrative drudgery. "The biggest part of my job is making sure everybody here is pumped to get out of bed and come to work in the morning. How can I make this fun today? It's a non-trivial thing, because the degree of fun makes a big difference in whether they want to be here. My employees are damn good, and they could all be someplace else. So I reduce, wherever I can, the amount of hierarchy and bureaucracy and paperwork, because it's no fun. And it's not great leverage to have my best scientists spending half a day filling out expense forms."

SOURCE: Richard Bingham, "Rebels with a Business Plan," *Report on Business Magazine*, November 1998, pp.77–82.

Figure 12-7 Reasons Employees Dislike Their Jobs

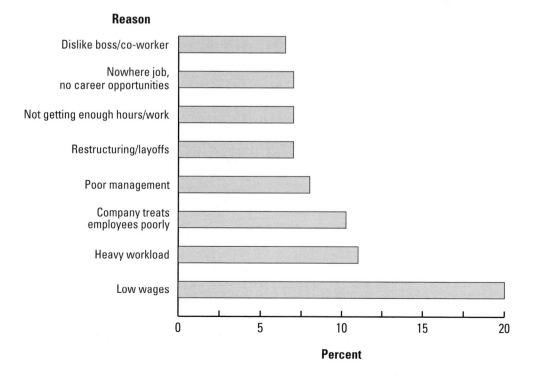

Working Conditions. Employee satisfaction with general working conditions has been shown to reduce employee turnover. Although these factors may have minimal motivational impact, they are important in developing loyalty to the organization.[6] Some working conditions that may have this effect are the physical characteristics of the workplace, the level of supervision, relationships with co-workers, and company policies.

Employee Needs. Understanding employee needs and providing the means whereby employees can fulfill unmet needs can be a powerful motivational tool for the owner-manager.[7] These needs include adequate pay, feeling they are a valued part of the organization, the possibility for advancement, extra responsibility or authority, recognition and praise by management, esteem by peers, a sense of achievement, and the challenge of the job. Incident 12-3 provides a good example of how Westjet Airlines utilizes several methods to meet employee needs.

One real challenge to the owner-manager is to encourage employees to have the same interest and enthusiasm for the business that she or he has. A recent Angus Reid survey found that 46 percent of Canadian workers are encouraged and expected to think of new and innovative ways of doing things.[8]

Incident 12-3

Westjet Staff Flying High

Westjet president, Stephen Smith, says, "We're a customer service company first and an airline second." Westjet is a no-frills, low-fare air service that provides superior customer service. It is this cheerful service and can-do attitude of Westjet staff that brings people back.

A "weeding the garden" approach is used to select and retain employees even after hiring has occurred because "not everyone hired measures up," says Smith. When dealing with employees that do not meet company standards, Westjet likes to encourage coaching to assist meeting standards. In addition to management coaching strategies, peers are very effective in assisting one another to meet and maintain Westjet standards. An employee who continues to work below peer and company standards after management efforts have been exerted is quickly removed. This is important if high employee morale is to be preserved within the company.

In order to maintain low, competitive airfares, Westjet employs only 90 people per aircraft versus Air Canada's 145 people per aircraft. Consequently, flight attendants and pilots must both join in on the grooming efforts of the plane. Less staff per plane and lower wages than offered by the competition could have a potentially negative effect on human relations. Yet keeping morale high and employees committed to superior standards of customer service has not been difficult for Westjet.

Profit-sharing plans, stock options, and celebrations keep Westjet staff happy and ready to serve customers. Westjet not only offers employees the chance to purchase profit-sharing plans and stock options, but the company also contributes toward employee purchases of stock. This approach creates a sense of ownership within Westjet staff, which positively influences the delivery of cheerful, high-quality service to the airline's customers. High levels of performance are encouraged by this method because employees reap the rewards of increased profits when their company does well. In fact, Westjet stock soared from $10 to $20 within one year, effectively a 30 percent bonus on employees' paycheques.

Celebrating the commitment and positive attitudes of Westjet staff, providing employee profit sharing, and encouraging staff to be themselves and have fun at work—these are the secrets behind the airline's success. Developing positive human relations among staff and management creates a positive people culture that results in enhanced customer service and profits for Westjet Airlines.

Source: Adapted from Dave Mabell, "Staff Praised for Westjet Success," *The Lethbridge Herald,* March 14, 2000, p. B-6.

Paying Employees

Small business owners face stiff competition from large companies and even the government in paying their employees. In September 1997, people in companies with fewer than 20 employees earned an average of $462 a week, compared with those in companies with upwards of 500 workers who earned an average of $778.[9] Many think they cannot afford to meet this competition. However, the value of a key employee cannot be overstated for many small businesses. As a result, many owner-managers have recognized that they must be competitive in paying key employees.

Employees are concerned not only about absolute but also relative wage levels. This means employees are usually aware of and concerned about their level of pay relative to those of their co-workers. Employee pay levels are very difficult to keep confidential in a small business. Often a wage increase for one employee will be seen by other employees not as a reward for that employee but as a decrease in pay for themselves. This, of course, can cause unrest within the organization.

Wage levels are generally set using external and internal factors as a guide. Externally the owner-manager may want to assess wage levels in similar or competing industries. Many provincial governments publish wage survey data that can assist in this regard. Most owner-managers can find out what the wage levels are in their communities through an informal survey. Other external considerations in arriving at wage levels might be cost-of-living increases, the demand/supply situation for employees, and government regulations. Internal considerations employers use in setting salary levels are ability to pay, employee performance levels and requirements, and, as just mentioned, relative pay relationships.

Remuneration for employees can offer employees security and also have a motivational effect. There are many methods of paying employees, each with advantages and disadvantages. The owner-manager needs to tailor the pay plan to meet the needs of employees and the goals of the organization. An example of how one Canadian entrepreneur did this effectively is found in Incident 12-4. Figure 12-8 (on the next page) lists some of the more common methods of paying employees in small businesses and describes their advantages and limitations. Many organizations use combinations of these plans. A recent survey of top employees who left large organizations to work for smaller companies revealed that the main reason was the possibility of owning equity in the firm.[10]

Incident 12-4

New and Improved

Firing up Red-L's sales team was simple. Top sellers are heaped with praise, and, if possible, rewarded with promotions. "Underachievers feel uncomfortable in our environment," says Mike Ludwig, the entrepreneur who took over the company. For those who go along, Ludwig offers rewards including a new bonus system based on profits. The better the company does, the more money there is for everyone. "When the bonuses came around last year, it was in October. Red-L invited customers and suppliers to tout its expanded head office and warehouse, wooing their good will with food, drink, and door prizes.

With a re-energized staff and aggressive marketing, sales jumped from $7 million to $11 million in three years, and the profits started to roll in. Sales for 1999 were $20 million, and Ludwig says 2001 appears even more promising. Such was his success that in October, Ludwig was named the first Turnaround Entrepreneur of the Year in Western Canada. The company has grown so fast that Ludwig realizes he has to let the managers "manage."

Source: Adapted from Diane Lucklow, "Shake Rattle and Roll," *Profit*, April 2000, p. 29.

Figure 12-8 Salary Plans for a Small Business

Type of Plan	How Calculated	Advantage	Limitation	Businesses Using the Plan
Salary	Per hour or per month	Security Simplicity	Lack of incentive	Many businesses—routine tasks
Commission	Percent of sales	Incentive	Lack of control	Automobile sales Housing industry Some retail products requiring extra selling effort
Cash bonus on individual performance	Bonus upon reaching objectives or quota	Security Incentive	Can be complicated	Retailing Manufacturing
Profit sharing on company performance	Percent of profits distributed	Incentive Cooperation in organization	Can be complicated Amounts too small to motivate	Manufacturing Retailing Knowledge based/service
Stock bonus	Predetermined percent to employees based on objectives	Long-term interest in organization Incentive	Some employees want only cash	Manufacturing Knowledge based/service

Fringe Benefits

Although one survey found that fewer than half of Canadian small businesses offer incentive plans,[11] increasingly a small business needs to provide fringe benefits to attract and retain employees. A recent survey of the 100 fastest growing small businesses in Canada indicated the opinion that only 65–75 percent of employee compensation should be salary. The rest can be made up of bonus, profit sharing, stock options, and commissions.[12] Some benefits becoming common in industry today are employee discounts, pension plans, disability and life insurance, and dental insurance. If the small business has enough employees, it may be able to qualify for group insurance plans that reduce the cost of providing this benefit. Frequently these plans are available through industry associations.

Other work-related fringe benefits the business might offer to increase employee satisfaction and motivation are discussed below.

Job Rotation. With job rotation, employees are periodically allowed to exchange jobs with other employees. Used in factory situations, this program can not only increase employee interest and motivation but also assist in training workers.

Job Sharing. Some firms have found success in allowing employees to share their jobs. The possibility of two part-time workers may satisfy the job requirements and increase the satisfaction of those who may not wish to work full time. In 1995, 171,000 Canadians were job-sharing according to Statistics Canada.[13]

Statistics Canada
www.statcan.ca

Working from Home. An increasing number of businesses are allowing employees to complete some or all of their work at home. This may not be appropriate for all types of small business but may be viewed as a valuable benefit to some employees. Statistics Canada has found that close to 10 percent of working Canadians did at least part of their jobs from home.[14]

Figure 12-9   Five Hottest Employee Benefits

1. Spending Accounts	Many firms that can't afford flexible-benefit plans are turning to spending accounts, funded by company or employee contributions. They can be used to cover a range of health or dental expenses. When employees contribute a portion of their salaries (say 2 percent) to these funds, that income isn't taxed.
2. Health Promotion	More employers offer non-medical benefits aimed at "wellness." Staff are allowed certain sums for such items as gym memberships, health-risk assessments, psychological counselling, and personal training.
3. Increased Choice	There's more choice in structuring benefit plans. Staff choices depend on how much they wish to spend, or on other variables such as their state of health or access to other benefits.
4. Flexible Work Hours	To help families juggle increasingly complex schedules, more firms let workers set their own hours. It could be 9 to 5, 7:30 to 3:30, or four 10-hour days.
5. Employee Input	More employees are being asked for their input on operational matters, but at a cost. Staff who suggest benefits changes, for instance, are held responsible for the program's success. If costs exceed plan, they must make up the balance.

SOURCE: Daphne Woolf, William M. Mercer, *Profit*, September 1998, p. 38.

Flexible Hours. Some firms have experienced increases in productivity by allowing employees a work schedule other than the 9-to-5 schedule common in many industries. An Ipsos Reid survey found that 25 percent of Canadians had flexible work schedules in 1995 up from 17 percent in 1991.[15]

Employee Suggestion Systems. Many companies have some form of employee suggestion system. Recently some companies have taken this idea a step further by offering employees money to implement their suggestions. The National Association of Suggestion Systems reports that some 3,000 formal suggestion systems operate in the United States, generating over 300,000 ideas and saving companies more than $800 million annually.

Figure 12-9 provides a description of five fast growing employee benefit programs.

Controlling and Evaluating Employee Performance

Zigon Performance Group
www.zigonperf.com

Many of the practices previously mentioned may contribute to a more motivated and loyal work force. It is essential, however, that this motivation be directed toward the achievement of the firm's objectives. In this regard, the owner-manager needs to effectively evaluate progress toward goals and objectives and inform employees of their progress. This can be done through a regular performance appraisal.

Another method that can accomplish this is the management by objectives approach (MBO), which is used in many organizations. A simplified version of MBO that is suitable for the small business is described in *Putting the One Minute Manager to Work*.[16] The five steps in this method (called the PRICE system) are as follows:

- *Pinpoint:* Define the performance area to be evaluated (i.e., sales for a retail clerk).

- *Record:* Set up a system to monitor and record performance in that area (i.e., the cash register tape).

- *Involve:* Manager and employee jointly set goals and a strategy for reaching those goals in that performance area (i.e., dollar sales per month).

- *Coach:* The manager observes performance periodically, perhaps making suggestions but allowing the employee considerable freedom to work toward the agreed-upon goals.

- *Evaluate:* At the end of the agreed-upon time period, an assessment of performance is made; positive results are rewarded, and future goals are set.

As can be seen, the value of the PRICE system is the clear line of communication between employer and employee in directing the employee toward goals and evaluating his or her progress.

HANDLING GRIEVANCES

Employee grievances, or concerns, arise in most organizations. They can have a negative effect on the morale of the organization, but they can also be positive and helpful if handled properly. Following are some principles for effective grievance management:

1. Implement a precise method whereby employees can express grievances. It is important that the organizational lines of authority be followed in this case. If at all possible, the grievance should be expressed to the immediate supervisor. This procedure should be laid out in the policy manual.

2. Employees need assurance that expressing their concerns will not jeopardize or prejudice their relationship with the employer. A wise employer will recognize that many grievances are legitimate and, if acted on, can help the organization.

3. There should be minimal red tape in processing complaints. Employees need to feel that someone is really listening to their concerns.

4. Owner-managers need to understand that some employees may be hesitant to raise a concern directly. In these situations, the suggestion box is effective.

Unionization and the Small Business

Most small businesses do not have unions operating within the organization. As the firm grows, however, and as employees become further removed from the owner, the possibility of union-related activity increases. The owner-manager should recognize that unions are formed when a majority of employees believe that a union would better serve their employment needs than the existing system. Effective human relations policies can go a long way toward discouraging union establishment in the firm. Some small businesses in certain industries may be required to hire unionized employees.

In both of these situations, there are certain requirements for both the employer and the union as set out in the Labour Relations Act in each province. Some of the more common aspects of collective bargaining that may affect the small business owner are the following:

- The contents of an agreement must deal with wages, benefits, and working conditions.

- Both parties must meet and bargain in good faith. However, an employer need not reveal company data that he or she prefers to keep confidential.

- The owner cannot discriminate against an employee for union involvement.

- Both employers and unions are bound to the terms and conditions of the collective agreement.

- Disputes concerning interpretation of the agreement must be resolved by an arbitrator.

GOVERNMENT REQUIREMENTS AND ASSISTANCE

The owner-manager should be aware of relevant government labour laws and programs that affect the management of personnel. A brief discussion of such laws and programs for all levels of government follows.

Federal Government

The federal government provides training and employment programs to 400,000 Canadians each year. Through the Canadian Jobs Strategy program, approximately $1.7 billion is spent to increase training and expand opportunities.[17] Some specific programs of Jobs Strategy include the following:

- *The job entry program* provides training for unemployed or undertrained people for up to one year.

- *Skill shortage and skill investment programs* provide financial assistance and training for up to three years for skill upgrading as a result of technological change within the company.

- *The job development program* provides training and financial assistance for the unemployed, disadvantaged persons, women, disabled persons, mature people, and visible minorities.

- *Innovation programs* provide funds to test new solutions to labour-market-related problems.

- *The Community Futures Program* helps finance local committees for development training and employment initiatives in areas experiencing economic hardship.

For more information on each of the above programs, contact the local Canada Employment Centres.

The federal government also has some legislation in the areas of employment standards, employment and pay equity, and hiring practices. Because of some overlaps in jurisdiction with the provinces, details are discussed in the next section. Appendix 12B at the end of this chapter illustrates these jurisdictions for the various programs and standards.

Provincial Governments

Each province in Canada, through its human resources or labour department, has set labour standards with which every owner-manager should be familiar. Appendix 12C lists the agencies that administer these standards in each province. Some of the more important areas that the provinces administer are discussed briefly below.

Job Discrimination. Each provincial government has passed legislation concerning human rights in the workplace. Entitled Bills or Codes of Human Rights, they are administered by provincial human rights commissions; provincial legislation has jurisdiction over businesses not federally owned or regulated. Like its federal counterparts, these provincial regulations are designed to prevent discrimination in the workplace.

Pay and Employment Equity. Recently, some provinces have enacted legislation to ensure equality of pay and employment opportunity regardless of gender, race, religious affiliation, or ethnic origin.

Working Conditions and Compensation. Numerous legal requirements govern the conditions under which retail employees work. Of importance to the small business owner are wage and hour requirements, restrictions on the use of child labour, provisions regarding equal pay, workers' compensation, unemployment benefits, and the Canada Pension Plan.

Employment Standards. Both the federal and provincial governments administer a considerable amount of legislation related to employment standards and labour relations. At both levels of government, ministries of labour have primary responsibility in this field of regulation. In addition, both levels have legislation that allows for the establishment of unions and collective bargaining agents in the form of provincial labour relations acts and the federal Canada Labour Code. The Canada Labour Code also deals with many aspects of fair labour standards, labour relations, dismissal procedures, severance allowances, and working conditions. Similarly, each province enforces statutes covering minimum wage rates, hours of work, overtime, holidays and leaves, termination notices, employment of young people, and information requirements on the statement of earnings and deductions.

Employment Safety and Health. Employment safety and health programs are designed to reduce absenteeism and labour turnover. Most provinces have passed industrial safety acts to protect the health and safety of workers. These laws govern such areas as sanitation, ventilation, and dangerous machinery. In addition to legislation, provincial governments, as well as employers, provide programs and training designed to accomplish similar purposes.

Workers' Compensation. Workers' compensation is an employee accident and disability insurance program required under provincial law. It covers the employees who are accidentally injured while working or are unable to work as a result of a disease associated with a particular occupation. While these programs vary among the provinces, they generally provide for medical expenses and basic subsistence during the period of disability. Employers help pay for the program through assessments from the Workers' Compensation Board. The assessment rates represent a substantial operating expense; thus, they must be planned for and managed with considerable care.

Wage Subsidy Programs. These programs provide financial assistance for up to six months for small businesses that hire unemployed persons.

Provincial Training Programs. These programs provide job training and skill development incentives to upgrade the labour force. Often such programs include a wage subsidy to small businesses that hire new employees. Contact your provincial labour department (see Appendix 12C) for details of these programs.

Municipal Governments

Local or municipal government regulations related to industry generally are confined to such areas as licensing, zoning, hours of operation, property taxes, and building codes. For example, one issue of current debate in some areas relates to Sunday openings of retail stores. Generally jurisdiction has been left to the municipal government by the provinces. This issue has significant implications in terms of operating costs and competitiveness.

Municipal authorities also exercise an especially strong influence over food establishments. For instance, a municipal licensing system for restaurants and other food services establishments may be in effect. Also, health inspectors may make periodic and sometimes unannounced inspections. (Any store that sells wine, beer, and/or liquor may require a licence from provincial liquor-licensing authorities.)

RECORDKEEPING FOR EMPLOYERS

Every employer should maintain an employee file that includes such information as the employee's original application form, work record, salary level, evaluation reports, and any other pertinent information. One of the most important employee recordkeeping tasks for the owner-manager is completing the payroll. There are several essential steps in managing a payroll system for employees.

Canada Customs and Revenue Agency
www.ccra-adrc.gc.ca

Employee Remittance Number. As an employer, the owner-manager collects employee income tax on behalf of the government as a deduction from the employee's wage. Before remitting this amount to the Receiver General, the employer must obtain a remittance number, available by contacting the nearest office of the Canada Customs and Revenue Agency. Along with the remittance number, the appropriate tax deduction tables and forms will be provided.

Payroll Book. The employer should obtain a payroll book or record that contains space for recording time worked as well as all of the required deductions. These books can be obtained from most business supply or stationery stores.

Monthly Remittance. As mentioned above, each payday the employer is required to make the appropriate deductions and remit them, as well as the employer's share of Canada pension (2 times the employee's share) and unemployment insurance (2.4 times the employee's share), to the Canada Customs and Revenue Agency. This remittance is made on a prescribed form similar to that in Figure 12-10 on the next page. This form contains the remittance number, the current payment amount, and a cumulative record of payments to date.

Year-End Statements. At the end of the calendar year, the employer is required to total and reconcile the year's remittances with the Canada Customs and Revenue Agency's totals. This is done on a T4-A summary form provided by the Canada Customs and Revenue Agency.

It is also the employer's responsibility to fill out for each employee a record of earnings and deductions for the year on the T4 slip. The T4 slip (see Figure 12-11 on the next page) is completed by reviewing totals from the payroll book and is required to be sent to the employee by the end of February of the following year.

Figure 12-10 Remittance Form

Revenue Canada Revenu Canada

STATEMENT OF ACCOUNT FOR CURRENT SOURCE DEDUCTIONS

PD7A (E) Rev. 96

1

Statement of account as of — Account number — Employer name

You can make your payment where you bank or to:

Balances on last statement		Current balances	
Amount paid for	Assessed amount owing	Amount paid for	Assessed amount owing

EXPLANATION OF CHANGES

Pierre Gravelle, Q.C.
Deputy Minister of National Revenue

2 Revenue Canada Revenu Canada

CURRENT SOURCE DEDUCTIONS REMITTANCE VOUCHER

PD7A (E) Rev. 96

Account number

For departmental use only

Amount of payment

Month for which deductions were withheld — Year — Month

Gross monthly payroll (dollars only) — 0 0

Number of employees in last pay period

Figure 12-11 T–4 Slip

1 Return with T4 Summary
À retourner avec le T4 Sommaire

Employer's name – Nom de l'employeur

Revenue Canada Revenu Canada

Year Année

For departmental use Réservé au Ministère 001727

T4

STATEMENT OF REMUNERATION PAID
ÉTAT DE LA RÉMUNÉRATION PAYÉE

VOID ANNULÉ

Employment income Revenus d'emploi — 14

Income tax deducted Impôt sur le revenu retenu — 22

Business Number Numéro d'entreprise — 54 — R P

Province of employment Province d'emploi — 10

Employee's CPP contributions Cotisations de l'employé au RPC — 16

EI insurable earnings Gains assurables d'AE — 24

Social insurance number Numéro d'assurance sociale — 12

Exempt – Exemption — CPP/QPP — EI — 28 — RPC/RRQ — AE

Employment Code Code d'emploi — 29

Employee's QPP contributions Cotisations de l'employé au RRQ — 17

CPP/QPP pensionable earnings Gains donnant droit à pension - RPC/RRQ — 26

Employee's name and address – Nom et adresse de l'employé

Surname – Nom de famille

First name – Prénom

Initial – Initiale

Address – Adresse

Postal code – Code postal

Employee's EI premiums Cotisations de l'employé à l'AE — 18

Union dues Cotisations syndicales — 44

RPP contributions Cotisations à un RPA — 20

Charitable donations Dons de bienfaisance — 46

Pension adjustment Facteur d'équivalence — 52

RPP or DPSP registration number N° d'agrément d'un RPA ou d'un RPDB — 50

Other information (see the back) Autres renseignements (voir au verso)

Box / Case — Amount / Montant

T4 (98)

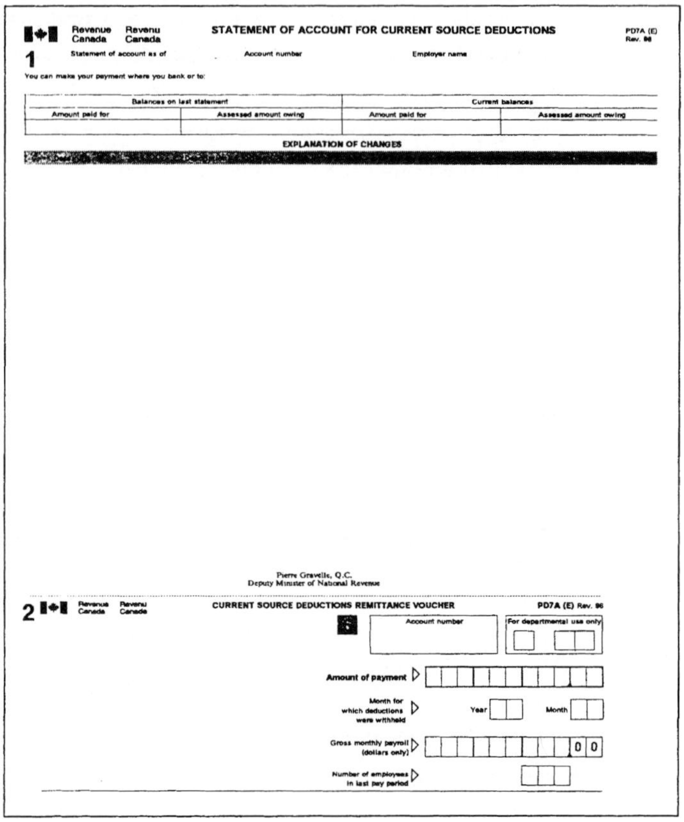

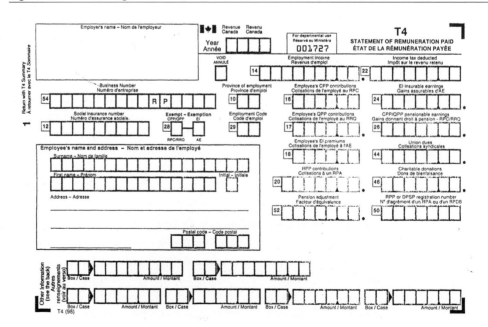

Summary

1. Sound personnel management is a key to the success of a small business, because motivated and competent personnel is one aspect of a business that may be unique and difficult to duplicate.

2. The organizational chart integrates tasks and employees so that the owner can visualize how the different aspects of the plan will work together. An effective way to prevent many personnel problems is to have a policy manual covering such areas as job description, working conditions, holidays and leaves, remuneration, and employee benefits.

3. The owner-manager should apply the following concepts of personnel management: assess his or her leadership style, work on time management by avoiding procrastination on important decisions or tasks, assess priorities, and use the most productive time of the day for the more important decisions.

4. The screening devices used in hiring employees include an application form, the employment interview, references, and various kinds of tests. An interview guide helps focus the interview and provides a constant base of information with which to compare applicants.

5. The steps in administering a payroll system are to obtain an employee remittance number, obtain a payroll book, make the appropriate deductions and remit them with the employer's share to the Canada Customs and Revenue Agency, total and reconcile the year's remittance at the end of every calendar year, and send out T-4s.

6. Legal requirements for the personnel aspects of small business are applicable from federal, provincial, and municipal governments.

Chapter Problems and Applications

1. Discuss the relative advantages and disadvantages of the various compensation plans used in small businesses.

2. What industries can you think of in which profit sharing would be less successful? Why?

3. Discuss the relative advantages and disadvantages of the different types of fringe benefits for a small manufacturing company. If possible, interview employees of such a business to find out which of these benefits are the most attractive.

4. Recently a small business increased the wages of its employees, but its productivity is still inadequate. What could be some possible reasons for this low level of productivity?

5. ABC company employee deductions for July are EI $98.72 and CPP $110.17. For what amount would the employer be liable?

6. Interview two small business owners to find out their personnel policies and how they communicate those policies to their employees.

7. Ask three employees of small businesses what they like and dislike about their jobs. What personnel policies could be used to remedy the dislikes?

8. Determine how three employees of various small businesses were recruited for their present positions. What seems to be the most popular source from which to recruit employees for small businesses? Why?

Appendix 12A

Interview Guide for a Small Business

Job:

Applicant:

Interviewed by: Date:

Check off or comment on the items you observed or found out. Do not guess at the other items: leave them blank. Not all items are relevant for every job. Your answer should be "yes" or "no," "we cannot hire," "maybe," or "not certain." You can qualify your "yes" or "no" under "Comments."

	Yes/No	Comments
Evaluate the applicant on the following:		
1. Work experience necessary to perform the job satisfactorily		
2. Skills with machines, tools, equipment		
3. Skills with job procedures		
4. Experience with special projects		
5. Formal education		
6. Trade or vocational education		
7. On-the-job training		
8. Will need training for this job		
9. Ability to get along with supervisor		
10. Ability to get along with fellow employees		
11. Ability to work as a member of a team or work group		
12. Applicant's comments about former supervisor		
13. Applicant's plans		
14. Attendance record		
15. Punctuality		
16. Safety record		
17. Health		
18. Physical strength to perform job		
19. Good work habits		
20. Supervisory experience		
21. Prefers to work alone		
22. Primarily interested in money		
23. Prefers nonfinancial rewards		
24. Likes the work		
25. Blames others		
26. Flexible: can adjust to changes		
27. Has a part-time job		
28. Off-the-job activities		

Appendix 12B

Labour Legislation Jurisdiction

		Jurisdiction		
Topic	**Comments**	**Municipal**	**Provincial**	**Federal**
Minimum age: contact Provincial Department of Labour	Varies among provinces		x	
Minimum wage: contact Minimum Wage Commission	Each province has its own industrial relations legislation		x	
Hours of work; annual vacations, holidays: contact provincial Department of Labour	Varies among provinces; general standard is two weeks; other holidays depend on the province		x	
Workers' compensation: contact provincial Workers' Compensation Board	Contributed by employer		x	
Industrial safety and health: contact provincial Department of Labour	Major jurisdiction from provinces; some federal jurisdiction		x	
Unemployment insurance: contact Canada Employment and Immigration Commission	Contributed by employer			x
Canadian pension plan: contact Revenue Canada, District Taxation Office	Except in province of Quebec, where contributions are made to Quebec Pension Plan and both employer and employee contribute			x
Employment equity contact provincial Department of Labour	Ontario has legislation; some federal guidelines		x	
Hours of operation	Contact city hall	x		

Appendix 12C

Provincial Labour Departments

Alberta
Ministry of Human Resources and
   Employment
324 Legislature Building
10800–97 Avenue
Edmonton, T5K 2B6
http://www3.gov.ab.ca/hre/
index.html

British Columbia
Ministry of Labour
Stn Prov Govt
PO Box 9594
Victoria, V8W 9K4
http://www.gov.bc.ca/sdl/

Manitoba
Manitoba Labour and Immigration
611–401 York Avenue
Winnipeg, R3C 0P8
http://www.gov.mb.ca/labour/
index.html

New Brunswick
Department of Training and
   Employment Development
470 York Street
P.O. Box 6000
Fredericton, E3B 3P7
http://www.gov.nb.ca.htm

Newfoundland
Department of Labour
Confederation Building
P.O. Box 8700
St. John's, A1B 4J6
http://www.gov.nf.ca/labour/

Northwest Territories
Labour Services
Panda Mall 3rd Floor
Box 1320
Yellowknife, X1A 2L9

Nova Scotia
Department of Environment and
   Labour
5151 Terminal Road
P.O. Box 697
Halifax, B3J 2T8
http://www.gov.ns.ca/enla/

Ontario
Ministry of Labour
400 University Avenue
Toronto, M7A 1T7
http://www.gov.on.ca/LAB/
main.htm

Prince Edward Island
Prince Edward Island Department
   of Community Affairs and
   Attorney General, Labour and
   Industrial Relations Divisions
31 Gordon Drive
P.O. Box 2000
Charlottetown, C1A 7N8
http://www.gov.pe.ca/commcul/
lair-info/index.php3

Quebec
Ministere du Travail
700, Boul. René-Lévesque
Quebec, G1R 5Z2
255, Boul. Cremazie
Montreal, H2M 2V3
http://www.travail.gouv.qc.ca/

Saskatchewan
Saskatchewan Labour
1870 Albert Street
Regina, S4P 3V7
http://www.labour.gov.sk.ca/

Yukon
Department of Justice, Labour
   Services
2134–Second Avenue
Box 2703
Whitehorse, Y1A 2C6
http://www.gov.yk.ca/services/l.
html#LabourServices

Suggested Readings

"How to Motivate? Allow Employees to Buy Into the Business." *The Globe and Mail*,
October 26, 1998.

Small Business in Canada. Industry, Science and Technology Canada, 1991, pp. 57–69.

Szonyi, Andrew J., and Dan Steinhoff. *Small Business Management Fundamentals.* Toronto:
McGraw-Hill Ryerson, 1991, pp. 268–277.

"The Definitive Guide to Managing Human Resources for Small Business Owners." *Profit,* October 1998, p. 20.

"What Do Employees Really Want Anyway?" *Hardware Merchandising,* February–March 1999, p. 36.

Comprehensive Case
The Framemakers: Part 8

Throughout the second year of The Framemakers' operation, sales and customer traffic continued to increase steadily. When the financial statements were returned from the accountant, gross sales in year two had exceeded first-year sales by a whopping $30,000—almost a 50 percent increase.

This was especially gratifying to the Normans. They had worked much harder than they had anticipated and had experienced many unforeseen problems. In addition to the inventory difficulties, one of their biggest concerns in year two was their employees. They had a difficult time attracting good ones. It seemed wage rates were too high, particularly with government agencies and larger businesses. The Normans could not afford to pay those kinds of wages. Their total wage bill was already higher than the industry average for similar-sized stores. Subsequently, those employees who were hired appeared unmotivated and unknowledgeable. They dealt poorly with customers, as the large number of customer complaints confirmed. As a result, either through employee resignations or firings, considerable employee turnover had occurred. New employees were sought through ads in the local newspaper and seemed to be in ample supply.

Firing employees had caused tense moments between Robert and Teresa on more than one occasion. Teresa tended to be the tougher of the two and would often reprimand employees and even let them go without Robert's knowledge. The most serious problem, however, was Robert's growing disillusionment with having any employees at all. He would complain to Teresa, "Why can't they take some interest in the job? They constantly watch the clock, ask for time off for this or that, and dress and behave so carelessly around the customers. Maybe we would be better off to stay small so we could do all the work ourselves!"

Questions

1. What are the causes of the Normans' personnel problems?
2. What recommendations can you make for solving them?

Video Case Questions
Patriot Computers*

CBC ◉

Stand still, you die: These days, companies have to be able to innovate and change quickly. How do you do that? Well, what if everyone in the company is trained to think and act like entrepreneurs? Colin King found a company that is doing just that.

1. What innovative personnel practices have the Durst twins implemented?
2. What is the danger of giving too much authority to employees? How might this be prevented?

*Source: CBC *Venture* #585, running time 9:29.

Chapter 13

Tax Management

Chapter Objectives

- To explain the importance of understanding the nature of the Canadian tax system.

- To discuss key tax management principles the owner-manager can follow.

- To describe specific tax-related programs that apply to small business.

Small Business Profile

Doreen Braverman
The Flag Shop

**The Flag Shop
www.flagshop.com**

In 1974 Doreen Braverman's career had been anything but entrepreneurial. She had worked as a telephone operator, receptionist, and teacher, as well as in advertising. Her decision to purchase a small premium and incentives business changed the direction of her working life.

The company she purchased—Vancouver Regalia, located in downtown Vancouver— did reasonably well, but Braverman became convinced that one of its products, flags, had more potential than the rest. She decided to focus on selling flags of all kinds to a ready market. Braverman renamed the company The Flag Shop and soon found that because of the high sales growth, she would have to make her own flags to ensure an adequate supply. She therefore added a silk screening business and moved into flag manufacturing with the establishment of Atlas Textile Print Ltd.

Growth of the companies has been steady. The Flag Shop has topped $2.5 million in sales, has over 50 employees, and has opened up six additional stores.

Braverman realized early in her entrepreneurial career that she would have to understand how to manage her business to make it remain successful. To this end, she earned an MBA degree by correspondence from the Canadian School of Management in Toronto. This training has helped her maintain tight financial control over The Flag Shop. She receives weekly sales and operations reports from her managers and prepares monthly reviews on the company's progress, which she compares to the planned budgets. Braverman recognizes the value of financial planning; she prepares annual plans three years in advance.

Doreen Braverman is also active in industry associations. While she has contributed considerably to these organizations, she has also gained valuable contacts and assistance from them. She is a strong advocate for free enterprise and believes the government should not subsidize businesses.

Braverman continues to work 50-plus-hour weeks and indicates that she "loves every minute of it." Her daughter, Susan, now manages the Vancouver shop. Doreen handles the marketing functions such as advertising and franchising.

TAXATION AND SMALL BUSINESS

Chapter 4 presents a brief outline regarding the tax requirements of a small business. It is noted that various types of business and property taxes are levied by federal, provincial, and municipal governments. The calculation of and liability for most of those taxes are relatively straightforward and are not discussed again in this chapter. Income taxes, however, can be more complicated, be more subject to interpretation, and have a greater impact on the planning and cash flow of the business. This chapter therefore focuses primarily on this area.

The income tax was instituted in Canada as a "temporary" measure in 1917. But income taxes not only are here to stay but are becoming increasingly complicated and generally more burdensome for most Canadians:

> *The average Canadian family pays more than 52 percent of its income in taxes. With changing governments, high unemployment, and crippling interest rates every consumer must find ways to save on tax bills and manage money more effectively.*[1]

Canadian Federation of Independent Business www.cfib.ca

The Canadian Federation of Independent Business reports that the total tax burden is the top concern of small- and medium-size enterprises. This is shown in Figure 13-1. Individuals who reside and corporations that operate in Canada are liable for federal and provincial income taxes. These taxes are applied on income that is received or receivable during the taxation year from all sources, less certain deductions. Federal and provincial tax agreements govern the procedures by which the federal government is empowered to collect taxes and remit portions to the provinces. Some provinces, including Quebec and Alberta, now collect their own corporate income taxes.

Because of the complexity of tax principles and the frequency of legislative changes concerning taxes and the provincial differences in application, a detailed treatment of tax management for small business is beyond the scope of this book. This chapter briefly discusses some general tax management principles and programs. While it is essential that

Figure 13-1 Total Tax Burden Remains Top SME Concern

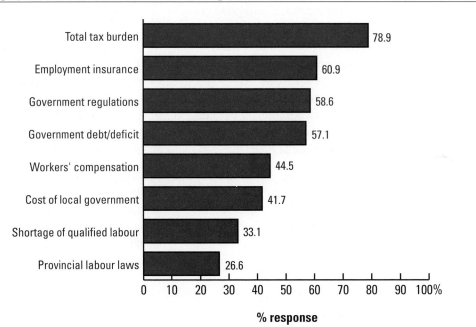

Concern	% response
Total tax burden	78.9
Employment insurance	60.9
Government regulations	58.6
Government debt/deficit	57.1
Workers' compensation	44.5
Cost of local government	41.7
Shortage of qualified labour	33.1
Provincial labour laws	26.6

% response

SOURCE: Canadian Federation of Independant Business, *OnLine Report*, Toronto, p. 16.

Incident 13-1

A Warm Welcome from the Canada Customs and Revenue Agency

Canada Customs and Revenue Agency
www.ccrc-adrc.gc.ca

It's a hard life being an entrepreneur, harder still if you're an immigrant. Take the case of Erhard Budzisch of Kitchener, Ontario, who has just won a six-year fight with the Canada Customs and Revenue Agency (CCRA), formerly Revenue Canada, that cost him his clothing import business and very nearly landed him in jail.

Budzisch and his wife, Beate, came to Canada from West Germany in 1983. Shortly after, he set up his company, Olsen Ltd.–European Fashions, hired an accountant, and opened an account at a local branch of Toronto-Dominion Bank.

For a while all went well, although Budzisch was concerned that his accounting methods might not be acceptable to the CCRA. Not to worry, said his chartered accountant, Calvin Siefert, Budzisch would be audited one day and that would be the time to resolve any difficulties.

Sure enough in 1989 the CCRA, in the person of auditor Brian Walkey, asked to look at the books. But instead of helping him out, Walkey conducted a lengthy inquiry aimed at launching a prosecution. He even asked Budzisch's TD branch to secure information, instructing an employee not to inform Budzisch. In due course, Budzisch and his wife found themselves facing 11 counts under the Income Tax Act.

SOURCE: Adapted from Brian Banks and David North, "Other Business," *Canadian Business*, November 1995, p. 27.

owner-managers have some knowledge of these principles in managing and planning their businesses, they are strongly advised to seek professional advice in preparing tax returns and investigating methods of minimizing tax liability. A basic knowledge of tax principles may assist the entrepreneur to avoid the difficulties which are illustrated in Incident 13-1.

The income of the organization which the government required the small business owner to report refers to the profits the business makes (for tax purposes). This should not be confused with the income the owner makes from the business which may or may not be taxable depending upon the legal form of the organization. This chapter deals primarily with the income tax considerations of the organization.

Some owner-managers may not be overly concerned with income taxes and thus may do little tax planning. This lack of concern may be due to one of two factors. First, the business may currently have no tax liability; in other words, it is losing money. This situation, of course, will be only temporary because the business will eventually become profitable or cease to exist. Second, the owner-manager may not understand the impact of taxes on the cash flow of the business. As Figure 13-2 illustrates, an increase in the tax rate of only 10 percent translates into a tax liability that would require an additional $100,000 in sales to offset. When the owner-manager understands the full effects of a lower or higher tax liability, he or she will want a working knowledge of tax principles and programs.

Figure 13-2 Impact of Tax Rate on a Business

Taxable income	$50,000
Increase in tax rate from 20% to 30%	20% of 50,000 = $10,000
	30% of 50,000 = $15,000
Increased tax liability	15,000 − 10,000 = $5,000
Profit as a percentage of sales	5%
Sales required to offset tax	5,000/5% = $100,000

Note: The extra $100,000 in sales would also incur an additional $1,500 tax liability.

GENERAL TAX MANAGEMENT PRINCIPLES

The owner-manager should be aware of nine fundamental areas of tax management.

Continual Tax Planning

Canada Customs and Revenue Agency www.ccra-adrc.gc.ca

One of the most disturbing aspects of tax statement preparation for the owner-manager is learning that he or she has incurred an unnecessary tax liability. This situation usually arises because the accountant received and prepared the return too late to take advantage of favourable programs and deductions.

It is critical, therefore, that the owner-manager be aware of the tax consequences of business operations throughout the year, not just at or after the year-end. Up-to-date income statements (as discussed in Chapter 10) can assist in forecasting income trends, allowing some advance tax planning. Many simple software programs are now available that could assist the entrepreneur in the information and tax management function. Incident 13-1 (on the previous page) illustrates the difficulties a lack of tax planning can create and Incident 13-2 stresses the importance of recordkeeping to manage taxes effectively.

The Canada Customs and Revenue Agency (CCRA), formerly Revenue Canada, requires that income tax be paid in installments throughout the year. Individuals operating proprietorships and partnerships are required to remit quarterly installments for the amount of taxes they incur. Corporations must submit monthly installments based on their estimated tax liability. Again, prior planning will be required to allow compliance with this regulation.

Tax Deferral

One unwritten rule of tax management concerns tax deferral. This means that one should attempt to put off paying taxes as long as legally possible. There are at least two good reasons

---

Incident 13-2

Prepare Records before Taxman Calls

Canada Customs and Revenue Agency www.ccra-adrc.gc.ca

Evelyn Jacks, author and tax specialist, indicates that small business owners face a higher-than-average chance of a visit from the Canada Customs and Revenue Agency. While employees of larger companies have their taxes deducted by the company, the CCRA has to trust small businesses to correctly assess the amount of tax they owe and remit it. So small business owners should expect audits and file their returns accordingly, says Ms. Jacks. However, if they fail to keep their receipts and do not keep good records they could face difficulties at the hands of the taxman.

This preparation also means retaining documents that verify sources of income such as invoices, bank records, and vouchers for cash receipts. Verification of expenses such as an auto expense log and documentation of paying family members are also records which should be kept. This is not the type of thing that can be pulled together only at the end of the year as many small businesses are prone to do.

Home-based businesses may also be viewed suspiciously by the Canada Customs and Revenue Agency as hobbies to defray tax. To prove legitimacy a business journal should be kept. All of these things can help the small business owners be better prepared should they receive a visit from the tax man.

SOURCE: Adapted from "Prepare Records Before Taxman Calls," *The Globe and Mail,* April 8, 1999, p. B9.

to defer taxes. First, one has the use of the tax money for the period of the deferral. This money can be put to productive use in the business or other investments. Second, tax laws may change, resulting in a decreased liability in the future.

Several specific programs facilitate deferral of tax liability. Some of these programs are discussed later.

Income Splitting

The tax system for individuals in Canada is a progressive system whereby a higher taxable income results in a higher percentage tax liability (see Appendix 13A for current federal and provincial tax rates for individuals in Canada and Appendix 13B for federal and provincial tax rates for corporations). Because of the progressive nature of taxes, splitting incomes between spouses and other family members or among partners will result in a reduced overall tax liability, as Figure 13-3 shows. If done within a family, the spouse and/or children will likely be taxed at lower rates, which would further reduce this tax liability.

Care should be taken when splitting income within the family to ensure that wages paid to the spouse or children are a reasonable amount considering their contribution to the business and that payroll withholding taxes, if applicable, are deducted.

Marginal Tax Rates

Canada Customs and Revenue Agency
www.ccra-adrc.gc.ca

The marginal tax rate is the tax rate applied by the Canada Customs and Revenue Agency to the next dollar of income earned. Knowledge of an individual's marginal rate can be helpful in planning income and expenses. For example, if an owner-manager has a marginal tax rate of 30 percent, he or she knows that each dollar of income earned will incur a tax liability of 30 cents, whereas each dollar of expense incurred will save 30 cents in tax liability. Thus, awareness of the current marginal rate allows the owner-manager to calculate the after-tax effects of extra income and expenses.

Another benefit of knowing the marginal rate is the possibility of moving that rate to a lower bracket by incurring some additional expenses prior to year-end—provided, of course, that the expenses are necessary. Like income splitting, this principle has the most value for the proprietorship and partnership.

Figure 13-3   Income Splitting—Federal Perspective

Business income = $40,000

A. If one person declared the income:

   Income = $40,000

   Tax rate = $4,921 + 22% of $9,246

   Tax liability = $6,955.12

B. If two people split the income:

   Income = $40,000

   Partner A = $20,000

   Partner B = $20,000

   Tax rate for each = 16% of $20,000

   Tax liability A = $3,200

   Tax liability B = $3,200

   Tax liability for A & B = $6,400

Tax savings by splitting income = $6,955.12 − $6,400 = $555.12

Deductibles

The small business owner should be familiar with those expenses that are deductible in the calculation of taxable income. The onus is on the taxpayer to keep proper records, since the burden of proof for these expenses lies with him or her. This means the owner-manager must keep receipts of business expenses. An often neglected aspect of this practice is the failure to obtain or keep receipts of expenses for which the owner-manager paid personally on behalf of the business. These expenses may seem too small to justify keeping track of them. However, if the tax rate is 25 percent, a mere $4 expense unrecorded can result in an increased tax liability of $1. According to Generally Accepted Accounting Principles, an expense is defined as a payment or a liability created to earn income. To determine whether certain expenses are deductible the owner-manager should consult an accountant, Revenue Canada, or such publications as the *Master Tax Guide* published by Commerce Clearing House. Some of the more common small business expenses that may require explanation follow.

Canada Customs and Revenue Agency
www.ccra-adrc.gc.ca

Accounting and Legal Expenses. Only those expenses incurred to earn income are deductible. Expenses incurred to incorporate the business or prepare a personal tax return are not deductible.

Advertising. Advertising expenses are deductible only if used in Canadian media and targeted to Canadian consumers.

Business Entertaining. Business entertaining expenses incurred in one's home are not deductible. Neither is the purchase of club memberships or yachts. Other types of legitimate business entertaining, however, are deductible.

Automobile Expenses. For a personal auto, the portion of expenses used for business purposes is deductible, but records must be kept to verify those amounts. Usually the business portion is the number of kilometres expended on business travel. In addition, automobile lease costs are also deductible business expenses.

Interest Expense. Interest expense is deductible for business loans but not for personal loans. Some experts counsel that to maximize this deductible, personal savings should be used to finance personal expenses if possible, rather than business expenses.

For a corporation, another interest-related matter is a loan to the business by a shareholder. This is a fairly common form of financing a business, because it offers some significant advantages. The interest is a deductible expense to the business, but the repayment terms may remain flexible depending on the ability of the business to pay and the wishes of the owner-lender. In a sense, the shareholder's loan combines the advantages of both debt and equity financing.

Repairs and Improvements. Repairs are deductible expenses, but improvements should be depreciated at the specified CCA rates. CCA (capital cost allowance) rates are percentages that can be subtracted from a capital asset cost and allocated as a business expense. It is often unclear what portion of the expenditure is a repair and what portion is an improvement. An accountant should be consulted in making this allocation.

Office Expenses. Office expenses are deductible and can be an important area for the owner-manager whose office is in the home. In such a case, a portion of household expenses such as utilities, mortgage interest, insurance, repairs, and taxes can be listed as business expenses. The portion to deduct depends on the size of the office relative to the size of the house. Care should be taken in including depreciation as an office expense, since it could be deemed to be recaptured and added to taxable income. A small business owner should consult with an accountant to verify the level of home expenses which qualify as a deduction.

An increasingly popular way of taking advantage of these expenses is contracting out. Many employees have left employment with an organization and have contracted out their services to that company. While this may allow them to take advantage of some of the above deductions, care must be taken to be sure that it is not an employment arrangement. Discussion with a tax accountant should be held if such a plan is being contemplated.

Government Tax-Related Programs

Numerous government programs and policies in Canada affect the tax management practices for the small business. It is important that the entrepreneur be aware of these programs in order to take advantage of their benefits. Some entrepreneurs have even built their businesses around government tax programs, although this can be a risky approach as is illustrated in Incident 13-3. Following is a summary of some of the more important items for the owner-manager.

Special Tax Rate Deductions
Small Business Deduction (SBD). The small business deduction is 16 percent (from 28 to 12 percent) of active business income for an incorporated, Canadian-controlled, private business. This special rate applies to the first $200,000 of income each year. For income above $200,000 but not exceeding $300,000, the federal tax rate is 22 percent (28 percent minus 6 percent). Figure 13-4 illustrates the significance of this program for a small business. In addition provincial tax rates for small businesses range from 4 to 9 percent. These lower rates allow small businesses to retain more of their earnings in the business for reinvestment.

Incident 13-3

A Tough Lesson to Learn

The owners of Three Buoys Houseboat Charters Ltd. learned an important lesson: Never build a business based on a tax loophole. Before Gord and Brenda Bushell and six others owned Three Buoys Houseboat, Phil Carroll and David Steele ran the company. In 1982, the entrepreneurs took advantage of a government regulation that allowed a 100 percent tax write-off on marine investments. Carroll and Steele entered the lucrative houseboat market shortly after discovering the neat regulation.

Three Buoys Houseboat Charters Ltd. was established in British Columbia's Shuswap Lake region and quickly began generating annual sales of $30 million. By 1987, the company had built and chartered over 875 houseboats throughout North America. Carroll and Steele were sailing high and did not foresee the government's change on marina investment. A 1988 legislation amendment closed the tax loophole on which Carroll and Steele had based their company. Shortly thereafter, Three Buoys fell into receivership.

Despite the company's financial setback, Gord and Brenda Bushell, employees of Three Buoys, did not lose hope. Three Buoys had developed a positive reputation in its six years of operation. "The name was well known, the boat owners liked us—and we didn't want to lose our jobs," says Gord.

The Bushell's embarked upon a three-year crusade that resulted in boat owners taking over the Sicamous, B.C. marina. During this time, Gord and Brenda petitioned investors for money. In 1993, the Bushells and six investors reclaimed Three Buoys Houseboat Charters Ltd. After undergoing significant restructuring, Three Buoys has now become a company that builds only three or four houseboats a year. Seventy-five percent of the company's revenues are now generated by only 30 boats chartered in the Shuswap Lake.

Source: Adapted from Kara Kuryllowicz, "Where Are They Now?" *Profit,* April 2000, p. 37.

Figure 13-4   Effect of the Small Business Deduction

Business income = $50,000

No small business deduction:

Tax rate = 38%

Tax liability = $19,000

Small business deduction:

SBD = 38% − 16% = 22%

Tax liability = $11,000

Difference in tax liability = $8,000

Manufacturing and Processing Deduction. This program provides for an additional reduction of 7 percent in tax liability for any business involved in the manufacturing or processing industries. This deduction is available for income that is not eligible for the SBD mentioned above (only for income over the $200,000 limit cited above).

Investment Tax Credits. Only the Atlantic Provinces and the Gaspé are eligible for investment tax credits on purchases of qualified property. All taxpayers are eligible for tax credits on qualified scientific research expenditures (SRTCs). Canadian-controlled private corporations may apply for a 35 percent SRTC, while all other taxpayers may apply for a 20 percent SRTC. In the Atlantic Provinces and the Gaspé, the rates for SRTC are 35 and 30 percent, respectively.

Deferral Programs. Some programs that allow tax deferrals have been very popular with owner-managers of small businesses:

1. *Deferred profit sharing.* DPS allows for a deferral of part of the business profits that have been registered for payment in the future to employees. The payment amount is taxable to employees only when received, but is a deductible expense in the year in which it is set aside or registered.

2. *Registered retirement savings plan.* RRSPs allow the owner-manager to put money into a registered plan that will be taxed only when received at a future date, presumably when the taxpayer is in a lower tax bracket. Budget changes have increased the contribution limits of RRSPs.

3. *Bonus deferral.* This program permits the business to deduct as an expense an accrued bonus or wage but allows a certain time period (180 days) to pay the amount. This amount is not taxable until received. The bonus deferral thus may effectively allow the business an expense in one year, but defer tax liability in the hands of the recipient to the following year.

Accelerated Capital Cost Allowance. This program allows an increased depreciation rate (capital cost allowance) to be applied as noncash expenses to certain classes of assets in calculating taxable income. Capital cost allowance rates can be obtained from an accountant or the tax department or by consulting the *Master Tax Guide*.

Small Business Financing Programs. For the incorporated business, these programs allow the business to borrow money from a chartered bank at a reduced interest rate. This is made possible because of special tax treatment these banks receive from the CCRA. Only businesses unable to obtain ordinary debt financing are eligible for this program.

The Incorporation Question

One decision regarding the establishment or growth of the business that owner-managers face is incorporation. Chapter 4 discusses the relative merits and weaknesses of the proprietorship,

Figure 13-5   Income Tax for Different Legal Forms of a Business

	Bob Johnson Ltd. Corporation	Bob Johnson Proprietorship	Bob and Sue Johnson Partnership
Revenue	100,000	100,000	100,000
Expenses	80,000	80,000	80,000
Net Income	20,000	20,000	20,000
Tax Consequences	Taxed at the corporate rate. (Bob's salary is a business expense.)	Income brought into and taxed at personal rate. (Bob's salary not a business expense.)	One-half of income partner's income and rates. (Salary to Bob and Sue not business expenses.)

the partnership, and the incorporated company. Some significant differences in tax treatment also exist among these different forms of business.

As mentioned above, with the small business deduction the tax rate for an incorporated business is about 25 percent. If the business is a partnership or a proprietorship, the business income is brought into the owner-manager's personal tax return. This return includes various other personal deductions and exemptions. The individual's personal rate (see Appendix 13A) may be higher or lower than the rate for an incorporated business (see Appendix 13B). If the minimization of tax liability were the major concern, the owner-manager would pursue incorporating when the tax rate for the business was lower than the personal rate. The incorporation question is influenced not only by the tax liability for the different legal forms of business; many government programs are available only to incorporated businesses. Examples of the tax consequences of the different legal forms of business are shown in Figure 13-5.

The Remuneration Question

Another difficult decision owner-managers must make is how to be paid by the business. In the proprietorship and the partnership, payment to the owner is treated as a drawing from the business and is not a deductible expense (or taxable income). In the corporation, an owner can be paid with a salary or with dividends. These methods of payment receive significantly different tax treatment as Figure 13-6 illustrates. The owner-manager should consult with an accountant prior to making a decision in this area as federal budgets have changed the difference in tax treatment of salary and dividends. Currently surtaxes imposed by the federal and some provincial governments result in a slightly higher income tax paid when remuneration is taken in dividends if the owner's taxable income exceeds $55,000. Beginning in the year 2000, dividends paid to children will be taxed although a family trust can still be used. This change reduces the effectiveness of income splitting with family in an incorporated business.

Transferring the Business: Capital Gains

Many small business owners wanting to transfer their businesses to others have encountered considerable difficulty. Some tax considerations significantly affect how the business is transferred. Tax changes involving capital gains exemptions have made it much easier to transfer the business to family members or others. This topic is discussed in more detail in Chapter 15.

Figure 13-6 Dividend versus Salary Income

	Salary	*Dividend*
Corporate income	$ 1,000	$1,000
Salary	21,000	—
Taxable income of corporation	—	1,000
Corporate tax @ 23%	—	230
Available for dividend payment	—	770
Income to shareholder	1,000	770
Dividend gross-up @ 25% of dividend received	—	193
Net income	1,000	963
Personal tax @ 29% on salary or dividend	290	279
Less: dividend tax credit @ 13⅓ of grossed-up dividend	—	2,128
Net federal tax	290	151
Plus: Provincial tax (50% of net federal tax)	145	75
Total personal tax	435	226
Corporate tax	—	230
Personal tax	435	226
Total tax	$ 435	$ 456

Figure 13-7 Goods and Services Tax Return

Goods and Services Tax (GST) and Provincial Sales Taxes (PST)

Although the GST and PST are value-added taxes which are not levied on the income or profits of the small business, they are taxes on sales revenues achieved by the small business and require a significant amount of effort on the part of the small business. The federal GST is currently set at 7 percent of the sale price whereas the PST rates vary by province. The amount of both taxes is added to the retail price of the product. Accurate recordkeeping is required to collect, record, and remit GST amounts to the government. Figure 13-7 illustrates the type of information required for submission to the Canada Customs and Revenue Agency by the small business. If the small business has sales of less than $30,000 per annum, no GST collection and remittance is required. The small business owner should consult the CCRA or the provincial revenue department for information about how the GST and PST applies to his or her business.

Summary

1. Basic tax knowledge allows the small business owner to save money that would otherwise be paid in taxes. Continual tax planning ensures that the owner-manager is aware of the tax consequences of business decisions throughout the year rather than just at the year-end.

2. The nine fundamental areas of tax management of which the owner-manager should be aware are (a) continual tax planning, (b) tax deferral, (c) income splitting, (d) marginal tax rates, (e) deductibles, (f) knowledge of government tax-related programs, (g) the incorporation question, (h) the remuneration question, and (i) capital gains.

3. Some of the more important government tax-related programs are the small business deduction, manufacturing and processing deductions, investment tax credits, deferral programs, accelerated capital cost allowances, and small business financing programs.

Chapter Problems and Applications

1. Explain why the year-end date is significant in tax planning.

2. The year-end for Wave Waterbeds is soon approaching. The proprietor, Tom Newcombe, estimates that the company currently has taxable income of $5,500. He would like to purchase a new cash register worth $2,000. Determine the tax liability if Newcombe purchases the cash register before or after year-end (use Appendix 13A); cash registers are depreciated at 20 percent. When would you advise Newcombe to purchase the cash register? Why?

3. The owner-manager of L.A. Construction has just incurred the following expenses. Which expenses are tax deductible?

    a. Incorporation expenses

    b. Advertising expense in the United States and in Canada

    c. Truck repairs of $2,000

    d. Costs of maintaining a residential phone used for business purposes

4. What is the tax liability for the following proprietorship's taxable incomes?

    a. $5,496

    b. $10,942

   c. $34,999

   d. $63,000

5. Which variables affect the decision to incorporate?

6. Determine the tax liability for the following companies.

   a.   A Canadian-controlled incorporated company with $25,000 taxable income

   b.   A Canadian-controlled incorporated company with $25,000 taxable income that qualifies for a small business deduction

   c.   Same as part *b*, but the business qualifies for the 5 percent manufacturing credit

   d.   A proprietorship with taxable income of $25,000

7. Ask a consultant or an accountant when a business should incorporate. What are the important considerations?

8. Discuss with an accountant the advantages and disadvantages of the different owner compensation methods in a corporation.

9. Calculate the marginal tax rate for yourself or for someone you know.

Appendix 13A

Federal and Provincial Income Tax Rates for Individuals

Federal Tax Rates

Taxable Income	Tax on Lower Limit	Tax Rate*
Up to $30,754	$ 0	16%
$30,755 –$61,509	$ 4,921	22%
$61,509–$100,000	$ 11,687	26%
$100,000 and over	$ 21,694	29%

*Income of sole proprietorships is taxed at personal rates. The taxable income brackets are indexed to the annual inflation rate in excess of 3 percent. A surtax of 5 percent must be added after taking any applicable credits into account. The 1992 federal budget decreased the basic surtax to 3 percent effective January 1, 1993.

Provincial Tax Rates

Each of the provinces in Canada levy income taxes at a percentage of the Federal tax rate. These rates range from 7.3 percent to 18.02 percent and vary by income level except for Alberta, which has a flat rate as a percentage of the Federal rate. For specific rates, see the latest Master Tax Guide or consult an accountant.

Appendix 13B

Tax Reference Tables

Federal Income Tax Rates for Active Business Income

	Effective January 1, 2001*				Effective January 1, 2000*		
	General Non-manufacturing Income	General Manufacturing Income	Small Business Income up to $200,000 (a)	Small Business Income from $200,000 to $300,000 (b)	General Non-manufacturing Income	General Manufacturing Income	Small Business Income up to $200,000 (a)
General corporate rate	38.00%	38.00%	38.00%	38.00%	38.00%	38.00%	38.00%
Less federal abatement	(10.00)	(10.00)	(10.00)	(10.00)	(10.00)	(10.00)	(10.00)
	28.00	28.00	28.00	28.00	28.00	28.00	28.00
Add surtax @ 4% (c)	1.12	1.12	1.12	1.12	1.12	1.12	1.12
	29.12	29.12	29.12	29.12	29.12	29.12	29.12
Less rate reductions (d)	(1.00)	(7.00)	(16.00)	(7.00)	—	(7.00)	(16.00)
	28.12	22.12	13.12	22.12	29.12	22.12	13.12

*See the following Notes for the actual dates on which these rates and other rate changes are effective.

Provincial Income Tax Rates for Active Business Income

	Effective January 1, 2001*				Effective January 1, 2000*		
	General Non-manufacturing Income	General Manufacturing Income	Small Business Income up to $200,000 (a)	Small Business Income from $200,000 to $300,000 (b)	General Non-manufacturing Income	General Manufacturing Income	Small Business Income up to $200,000 (a)
British Columbia (e)	16.5%	16.5%	4.5%	16.5%	16.5%	16.5%	5.5/4.75%
Alberta (f)	15.5/13.5	14.5/13.5	6.0/5.0	15.5/5.0	15.5	14.5	6.0
Saskatchewan (g)	17.0	10.0	8.0	17.0	17.0	10.0	8.0
Manitoba (h)	17.0	17.0	6.0	17.0	17.0	17.0	7.0
Ontario (i)	14.0	12.0	6.5	14.0	15.5/14.5	13.5/12.5	8.0/7.0
Québec (j)	9.0	9.0	9.0	9.0	8.9	8.9	8.9
New Brunswick (k)	16.0	16.0	4.0	17.0	17.0	17.0	4.5
Nova Scotia	16.0	16.0	5.0	16.0	16.0	16.0	5.0
Prince Edward Island	16.0	7.5	7.5	16.0	16.0	7.5	7.5
Newfoundland	14.0	5.0	5.0	14.0	14.0	5.0	5.0
Yukon Territory (l)	15.0	2.5	2.5/6.0	15.0	15.0	2.5	2.5/6.0
Northwest Territories/Nunavut	14.0	14.0	5.0	14.0	14.0	14.0	5.0

*See the following Notes for the actual dates on which these rates and other rate changes are effective.

Combined Federal and Provincial Income Tax Rates for Active Business Income

	Effective January 1, 2001*				Effective January 1, 2000*		
	General Non-manufacturing Income	General Manufacturing Income	Small Business Income up to $200,000 (a)	Small Business Income from $200,000 to $300,000 (b)	General Non-manufacturing Income	General Manufacturing Income	Small Business Income up to $200,000 (a)
British Columbia (e)	44.6%	38.6%	17.6%	38.6%	45.6%	38.6%	18.6/17.9%
Alberta (f)	43.6/41.6	36.6/35.6	19.1/18.1	37.6/27.1	44.6	36.6	19.1
Saskatchewan (g)	45.1	32.1	21.1	39.1	46.1	32.1	21.1
Manitoba (h)	45.1	39.1	19.1	39.1	46.1	39.1	20.1
Ontario (i)	42.1	34.1	19.6	36.1	44.6/43.6	35.6/34.6	21.1/20.1
Québec (j)	37.2	31.2	22.2	31.2	38.0	31.0	22.0
New Brunswick (k)	45.1	39.1	17.6	39.1	46.1	39.1	17.6
Nova Scotia	44.1	38.1	18.1	38.1	45.1	38.1	18.1
Prince Edward Island	44.1	29.6	20.6	38.1	45.1	29.6	20.6
Newfoundland	42.1	27.1	18.1	36.1	43.1	27.1	18.1
Yukon Territory (l)	43.1	24.6	15.6/19.1	37.1	44.1	24.6	15.6/19.1
Northwest Territories/Nunavut	42.1	36.1	18.1	36.1	43.1	36.1	18.1

*See the following Notes for the actual dates on which these rates and other rate changes are effective.

Suggested Readings

Beam, R. E., and S. N. Laiken. *Introduction to Federal Income Taxation in Canada,* 13th ed. Don Mills, Ont.: CCH Canadian Limited, 1992.

Canadian Master Tax Guide. Don Mills, Ont.: Commerce Clearing House, yearly.

"Canadian Tax Letter 1997—KPMG Canada." http://www.ca.cch.com/

Carter, Robert. "Insure Your Retirement." *Profit,* May 1999, p. 622

Cohen, Bruce. "A Taxing Proposal." *Profit,* April 1999, p. 84.

Corporate Tax Return Handbook. Toronto: Canadian Institute of Chartered Accountants, 1992.

Fisher, S. Brian, and Paul B. Hickey, eds. *The Canadian Personal Tax Planning Guide.* Toronto: Thomson Professional Publishing, 1992.

Krishna, Vern, C.G.A. *Income Tax Law.* Tax Research Centre, University of Ottawa, 1997. Irwin Law, Concord, Ontario.

Mintz and Partners, Chartered Accounts. *1997 Canadian Federal Budget Analysis.* 1446 Don Mills Road, Ste. 100, North York, Ontario M3B 3N6.

Video Case Questions
Fields of Seeds*

CBC ⬤

Alberta's Spitz Sunflower Seeds has one barrier between it and a national distribution deal with a major retail chain. Owner Tom Droog has to find a distributor in Quebec and crack a market and culture that finds public spitting deplorable. Venture follows the adventures of the acerbic Alberta entrepreneur as he tries to conquer the Quebec market.

1. How do husband and wife complement each other in managing Spitz Sunflower Seeds?

2. How might they organize the business to minimize tax liability?

3. What might be the best strategy for Spitz to move into the Quebec market?

*Source: CBC *Venture* #734, running time 9:24.

Cases for Part III

Alliance Cosmetics
BioStar Inc.
Derocher's Market
Home Mart Hardware Store
Martha's Designs
My Own Meals

Super Organizer
Suzie's Fashions
Taylor Construction Company
Tot-Switch
Vitality Health Food Store
Winston's Jewellers

ALLIANCE COSMETICS

Gordon McDougall
Wilfrid Laurier University

Alliance Cosmetics, a small cosmetics manufacturer in Manitoba, has a well-positioned set of mid-price-range facial cosmetic products. The quality of this product line, which retails in the $4 to $7 price range, is slightly above that of the major competitors such as Max Factor and Bonne Belle. The firm had sought and gained distribution through major pharmacy stores in Ontario and Manitoba, and chains such as Shoppers Drug Mart had responded well to its product line.

The line's success was due to more than just the slightly higher quality–price relationship. The firm had initially contracted representation from an aggressive set of manufacturer's agents. This was necessary to get quick high-volume distribution which appeared to be possible only through the drug mart chains. The majority of the agents had long-term relationships with the chain buyers and were able to open the doors for the firm's products. This rapid and fairly intensive distribution was a key factor.

Drug mart chains are interested in high turnover and good margins. Therefore, above-average retail markups—in the neighbourhood of 120 percent versus the more typical 100 percent on cost to retailer—were offered. In addition, the firm spent $200,000 on advertising in the introductory three-month launch of the initial product line three years ago and has spent about $600,000 per year on advertising.

With the success of the current mid-price-range product line, three drug chains had recently expressed an interest in the firm's producing top-of-the-line facial cosmetics. The firm had the following major facts to consider in pursuing this opportunity:

1. The plant had ample capacity. It could produce an extra 1,000,000 product units without overstraining the capacity of the equipment.

2. The fixed costs the company now faces per year are estimated at $650,000. This would likely increase by $175,000 with an additional product line.

3. The current average retail price of the company's product is $5.50. The company has an average selling price to retailers of $2.50 per unit.

4. The direct manufacturing costs per unit for the current line are $0.80. The direct overhead costs of the new line would be $1.00 per unit. Agent's commissions are 4 percent of the company's selling price.

5. Total advertising for all lines would be in the neighbourhood of $1 million in the year the product is launched.

6. The average retail price of the line would have to be a minimum of $7.75 for it to be perceived as a high-quality good.

7. Some product samples had been produced and these were very well accepted by cosmeticians and models who had tried them.

This firm faces some interesting pricing problems. Price is often equated with quality in products like cosmetics. Here the consumer is purchasing, in a very real sense, "the total product concept." Cosmetics represent much more than the physical attributes of the product to the consumer. They represent glamour, beauty, and hope! Many buyers see price as a significant determinant of the quality of a product. To signify a premium-range product, a premium price has to be set. Unfortunately, as this premium price strategy is constrained by the firm's advertising budget, it cannot match the dollar volume of the large competitors in the industry. The higher the price, the greater the need for heavy and extensive advertising and promotional push. The company must have an advertising budget that will allow it to convince the public to pay the high price. The basic question is whether the planned $1 million in advertising expenditures is enough to support both product lines.

Questions

1. What pricing approach would you recommend for the new product line?
2. What price would you set for the new line? Why?

BIOSTAR INC.

D. Wesley Balderson
University of Lethbridge

In 1992 Stephen Acres was a successful veterinary scientist at the University of Saskatchewan in Saskatoon. At 49 he was at the top of his career, running an internationally recognized research institute in infectious diseases. Because of his position many were surprised when he left the university to start his own business—Biostar Inc. Dr. Acres had no reservations about leaving academia. "You always worry a little that you may not be successful, but it's the same with any undertaking. If you're not prepared to take those risks, you probably shouldn't be doing anything."

Biostar develops and holds the commercial rights to animal health products which have a place in the world marketplace. Biostar is building on two broad technology platforms: vaccines to prevent infectious disease and enhance protection in animals, and biological mechanisms to deliver vaccines and drugs to specific cell types or organs.

Dr. Acres sees his company as a player in a global biotechnology race. "Because this is a relatively young industry, everyone is trying to get improved products to the market before their competitors do," says Acres. By 1996 Biostar had developed, received regulatory approval, and marketed three genetically engineered animal health products which provided revenues of $1.5 million.

Biostar's 21 employees carry out their research and product development close to the university which still provides financial and research support to the venture. Additional financial support has come from the provincial government and a private share placement which was made in 1993. Several venture capital firms invested in Biostar at that time and this money is provided on a gradual basis as the company grows.

Stephen Acres is faced with several major decisions that will affect the future success of the company. The first challenge is one of marketing. It currently has eight new products in development, including a contraceptive vaccine for livestock and house pets. (Because of the staggering cost of regulatory approval for human health products, Biostar plans to stick mainly to animal health.) Although the domestic market appears lucrative (preventable disease costs the Canadian livestock industry alone more than $750-million a year), Acres is also considering the development of the international market. Therefore, Dr. Acres is contemplating the development of a Canadian and an international marketing strategy which the company can follow to be successful in the future.

The second decision flows from the first. If the company continues to grow, it will require a major expansion of physical facilities, its organization, and its financial resources. In the past Biostar has attempted to remain organizationally compact by forging alliances with other companies to provide certain services. As Dr. Acres puts it, "Very few companies today are fully integrated and can do everything that's required to get a product from the concept stage to the market." However, some growth would take place and Acres is uneasy about how best to manage such an organization.

Acres is also contemplating which would be the best method to finance this expected growth. He is considering selling shares on the public stock exchange to finance its growth. Although Acres will profit from such a sale, he realizes that considerable ownership of the company may move outside of his control.

Questions

1. What considerations should be made for the development of a marketing strategy for Biostar?
2. Discuss the implications of a public stock offering as a way of obtaining financing.

DEROCHER'S MARKET

D. Wesley Balderson
University of Lethbridge

Derocher's Market opened a new store in Quebec City in January 1999. Although the firm had been in business for three generations, the neighbourhood in which the original store stood had become shabby, and many of its loyal clientele had moved to the suburbs. The present owner, Claude Derocher, decided to follow the population move. The new store was located in a small shopping centre adjacent or close to more than 70 four-story apartment buildings that housed over 400 families. Many more apartment buildings were under construction, as well as three- and four-bedroom, single-family homes in several nearby housing developments. The nearest competition was located approximately two miles northeast of the present shopping centre.

In preparation for the grand opening, Claude Derocher purchased many varieties of canned juices, fruits, and vegetables. In addition, he carried a number of varieties and lines of cheeses, frozen foods, other dairy products, fruits, vegetables, and meats. To display and sell all the stock, it was necessary to use valuable aisle space as islands for various bulk cheeses, canned fruits, and dry groceries such as potato chips, pretzels, and the like. The store size was 55 by 90 feet. The store layout, shown in Figure 1, is as follows:

Figure 1   Present Store Layout—Derocher's Market

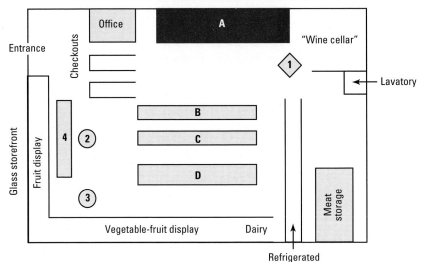

- A: display area for crackers, breads, and cookies
- B: refrigerated area for frozen foods, frozen desserts, and packaged cheeses
- C: display area for olives, pickles, other condiments, canned fruit, and fruit juices
- D: display area for canned vegetables, canned fish, breakfast cereals, and dried fruits.
- 1: island display for bulk cheeses
- 2, 3: island display for soft drinks
- 4: area for shopping carts

The store employed eight full-time people. These consisted of six clerks and two assistant managers—one manager for meat and dairy and the other for grocery, produce, and frozen foods.

During the first four weeks of operation, it was found that:

1. There were far too many employees for the type of work needed.
2. There was far too much congestion of shoppers at certain in-store locations.
3. There was a build-up of customers at the checkout stations.
4. Many customers inquired as to where to find various food items.
5. Several of Derocher's employees indicated that some changes needed to be made to the interior layout of the store.

After receiving this input, Derocher was not sure what to do. The present layout seemed unsatisfactory, but he did not want to spend a lot of money making changes.

Questions

1. Based on Figure 1 and the observations of the first four weeks, what are the weaknesses of the present store layout?
2. Develop a layout that might solve these problems.
3. How should Claude Derocher go about implementing such changes?

HOME MART HARDWARE STORE

D. Wesley Balderson
University of Lethbridge

Home Mart is a small hardware store located in Weyburn, Saskatchewan, an agricultural community with a population of about 9,000. Merchandise stocked includes automotive and farm supplies, furniture and appliances, sporting goods, plumbing and electrical supplies, and giftware.

The owner is David West, a prominent businessman in the community who also owns another business that occupies a large portion of his time. Because of this, West has delegated considerable authority to the manager of the store, John Burns. In July 1997, West and Burns decided to hire a new employee to be trained as an assistant manager. They first discussed the possibility of promoting one of the store's existing employees, but Burns thought none of them would be suitable as assistant managers because they were either too old or did not want the extra responsibility. Doug Burns, John's uncle, was already 63 years old and, though working full time, had indicated he wanted to work fewer hours and begin to ease into retirement. Sue Mikita, 52, had been with the company for 12 years but had concentrated on the giftware side of the department. Burns did not think she had an adequate knowledge of the farm supply side of the business, which produced the most revenue in the store. Ruth Huddy, 61, had worked for the company for only six years, mostly part time, and although she was very competent and knowledgeable, Burns felt she was also too old to fill the position. The only other employees were part-time students who worked Saturdays and summers.

West and Burns decided to advertise for an assistant manager in the local paper. This resulted in a few enquiries but no applicants who met the two criteria Burns and West considered most important: familiarity with the people in the community and a knowledge of agriculture. West and Burns met again in August to discuss the lack of prospects. West suggested that he might contact Noel Branlen, an acquaintance who lived in Weyburn, about coming to work for the company. Branlen currently worked in a town some 25 miles away, and perhaps he could be attracted back to his home town. Branlen was young—only 25—and knew the people in the community. West approached him and found out he was interested in working for him but required a salary higher than West and Burns had planned for this position. If they agreed to pay the salary he requested, Branlen would be paid a higher wage than the other hardware department employees except Burns himself. Although West and Burns were worried about this, they decided to hire Branlen and requested that his salary be kept confidential. Branlen would be in a training position for approximately six months and would then assume the position of assistant manager of the store.

Things went smoothly at first, but after a few months it was evident to West that some problems were surfacing. West noticed antagonism between Branlen and the other three regular employees, and so did the store's customers. In discussing Branlen's progress with Burns, West learned that Branlen was frequently late for work, his appearance was unsatisfactory, he was very slow in gaining essential product knowledge, and Burns had had several complaints from customers about him. In addition, Branlen himself had contacted West directly and expressed his disillusionment with the job and with his supervisor, John Burns. He indicated that Burns was not providing adequate training for the products or the authority to order inventory, set prices, and so on. Also, when Burns had his day off, several sales were lost because none of the employees knew the information customers required. Branlen also mentioned that as assistant manager he shouldn't have to sweep the floors as he had been required to do on several occasions. He further requested that he be granted time off two afternoons a week to take a management course at a local college to help him prepare for the managerial aspects of his job.

West discussed the problem again with Burns, who said that as soon as Branlen proved himself he would be given the requested authority—and he was very opposed to letting Branlen take time off for a management course, so this request was turned down.

Toward the end of November, Branlen contacted West to see if he could take some of his holidays just before Christmas. When West mentioned this request to John Burns, Burns was very opposed to it because this was the busiest time of the year for the store; furthermore, in the past employees had worked for a year before they took their holidays. However, West allowed Branlen to take the holiday.

The store got through the Christmas rush and inventory taking without serious incident, but things got progressively worse thereafter. Nine months after his hiring, Branlen handed in his resignation, saying he was going back to university. West was relieved that this problem employee was leaving and hoped that the same problems would not recur next time.

Questions

1. Comment on the possible reasons why Noel Branlen's employment did not turn out successfully.
2. How could Home Mart successfully compete against the threat of competition from Wal-Mart or Home Depot?

MARTHA'S DESIGNS

D. Wesley Balderson
University of Lethbridge

Martha Millwork needed to make some important decisions regarding her clothing manufacturing business. Started as a hobby in the 1970s, the business had grown to the point where she had opportunities to expand the scale of operations so that it could become a full-time commercial enterprise. She was unsure of which markets to pursue, which marketing channels to utilize, and the extent of product line that would be the most effective.

Martha lived in Grenfel, Saskatchewan and had started sewing clothing for herself and her children in the 1970s. Her skill and talents were first shown publicly during the summer agribition celebration at Regina in 1982 at a fashion show she organized. As a result of this initial show she had received orders from interested buyers, and the hobby soon became a part-time busines which she operated out of her home in Grenfel. Company sales had grown steadily since that time and reached close to $30,000 in the latest fiscal year. Although this only brought a profit of $5,000, Martha had fine-tuned the business so that an increase in sales would also mean a larger profit percentage.

Martha's Designs specializes in high-quality, fashionable women's and men's coats made from canvas, denim, and Hudson's Bay and Pendleton wool blankets. The coats were designed to be comfortable, sophisticated, and original. They also featured fur and leather trims. Several coat designs were available and Martha modified existing designs and created new ones on an ongoing basis. The coats were well made, with high-quality materials, and were priced from $300 to $600. The clothes were fashionable and modern. This blend of fashion, function, and tradition made a unique finished product which she had successfully sold to buyers from across North America and Europe.

As the owner-manager, Martha designed the coats and cut the fabric. She usually ordered materials only after receiving an order for a particular coat. The cut pieces, trim, and notions were sent to one of two part-time local seamstresses who did the sewing in their own homes. Martha carefully inspected each garment upon completion. The purchasing of materials was an important aspect of the production process, since the cost of materials was such a large part of the cost-of-goods. Fabric was purchased at the lowest possible price, but Martha was aware that better prices would be available as she increased the size of her orders. The unique trims used on the coats were purchased primarily from local suppliers.

Recently, Martha was approached by the town of Wolseley (estimated population 1,000), which is about 10 miles from Grenfel to be a part of a sewing plant which the village was planning to establish. The village intended to purchase sewing machines and other equipment and contract out the sewing services of the workers to interested firms such as Martha's Designs. Martha realized that to make such a change in operations worthwhile, Martha's Designs would have to increase its production volume dramatically. This proposal was attractive because of its low financial risk, the opportunity for increased production efficiencies, and the flexibility to produce a greater volume of coats.

Martha's marketing efforts to date consisted primarily of fashion shows, displays at events, some newspaper advertising and a brochure. Each year she organizes several fashion shows in Alberta, Montana, North Dakota, and Saskatchewan. In the past, some of these were in conjunction with other events such as the Agricultural exhibitions, rodeos, and athletic events. Each show is the result of coordinating the individual efforts of models, commentators, hairdressers, make-up artists, sound specialists, musicians, and publicity staff. Displays have been set up at various trade shows and even such events as the Calgary Winter Olympics. A small amount of advertising has been done in newspapers such as the *Regina Leader Post* and other local papers. Martha uses advertising to promote general awareness and to promote good community relations.

With a potential increase in production capacity, Martha had to plan the company's future marketing strategy. She was confident that demand for her company's unique clothing existed, and that volume could be increased enough to result in significant material purchase savings which would lower production costs. A major decision was which marketing channel to use. Until now, sales had been made directly to purchasers of the clothing. Martha thought she might achieve an increase in volume by selling through retail stores or clothing wholesalers, but she was unsure which type of retail store would most effectively reach her target customer. An alternative would be to continue selling directly to customers, and expand on these efforts by distributing a mail-order catalogue.

Another important decision was where to focus the firm's marketing efforts. Her sales to date had been mainly through buyers from Alberta, Saskatchewan, and North Dakota but there was also the possibility of increasing sales to other parts of Canada, the United States, and Europe. Martha was also thinking about increasing the sales of men's and children's coats. Although this strategy would add to her product line and create additional design work, it could also make the line more marketable by broadening its appeal.

A final decision to be made was how to support the sales efforts. Should she use more advertising, or should she concentrate on setting up sales booths at trade shows? There were many trade shows, and deciding which to attend would be difficult.

As Martha considered the alternatives available to her, she was beginning to realize that her company was at an important crossroads—in order to continue its growth it would have to enter new markets and expand production capacity. Martha's Designs was a cottage industry on the verge of becoming a small manufacturer.

Questions

1. Discuss the implications of Martha Millwork's potential expansion.
2. Evaluate the distribution channel options and promotional implications associated with them if Martha's business expanded.

MY OWN MEALS

William Rudelius
University of Minnesota

"The kids generally like the fast-food meals, I tend to not like them because I try to stay away from the high fat," says Angela Hamon, mother of three young girls. "I have to have something that is nutritious and fast," remarks Mary Champlain, mother of two. Comments like these and her own experiences led Mary Anne Jackson to conclude that there was an opportunity to provide parents with better children's food options. As Mary explains, "being a busy working mother, I knew that there was a need for this type of product in the marketplace."

The Idea

Mary's insight about the marketplace was supported by several socioeconomic trends. For example:

- More than 65 percent of working mothers now have school-age children, the highest percentage ever.
- About 90 percent of children under the age of seven eat at McDonald's at least four times per month.
- More than 80 percent of homes in Canada now have microwave ovens.
- Women already represent almost half of the total workforce. By the year 2000, two out of three new entrants into the labour force were women.

With this evidence, some food industry experience and business education, and a lot of entrepreneurial spirit, Mary Anne Jackson set out to satisfy the need for nutritious, convenient children's meals. Her idea: develop a line of healthy, microwaveable meals for children 2 to 10 years old.

The Company

Ms. Jackson started by founding a company, My Own Meals, Inc., with a line of five healthy microwaveable meals. The meals were offered in shelf-stable "retort" packages, which are like flexible cans. This created a whole new category of prepared foods and raised more than a few eyebrows among the major food companies. Mary observed that "the need for children's meals was not being addressed in the past, and I think this was because most major food companies are run by men." Eventually, however, the big companies challenged My Own Meals with their own entries into the new category. The competition reinforced Mary's efforts. "Having competitors come into the marketplace justified the existence of the category," she explains.

The product line was developed using a lot of marketing research — hundreds of busy mothers provided input about product quality, usage rates, and price. The results indicated that customers would serve their children high-quality meals between 3 to 4 times each month and that they would be willing to pay approximately $2.30 for each meal.

The Issue: Setting Retail Prices

"We were trying to decide if we were priced appropriately and competitively for the marketplace, and we decided that we would look at the price elasticity for our product line," observes Mary Anne Jackson. "We found that the closer we came to $3.00 a unit, the lower the volume was, and overall we were losing revenues and profits," said Jackson.

To arrive at final retail prices for her company's products Mary Anne Jackson considered factors related to demand, cost, profit, and competition. For example, because lower-quality brands had entered the market, My Own Meals needed a retail price that reflected the superior quality of its products. "We're premium priced because we're a higher-quality product than any of our competitors. If we weren't, our quality image would be lowered to the image that they have," explains Jackson. At some stores, however, prices approached $3.00 and consumer demand decreased.

To estimate the prices consumers would see on their shelves, Jackson needed to estimate the cost of producing the meals and add My Own Meal's markup. Then she determined the markup of each of the distribution channels – retail grocery stores, mass merchants, daycare centres, and military commissaries – would add to reach the retail price. The grocery stores were very concerned about the profitability and used a concept called direct product profitability (DPP) to determine prices and shelf space. "They want to know how much money they make on each square foot of shelf dedicated to each product line. I had to do a DPP analysis to show them why they were making more on our products for our space than the competition," remarks Mary Anne Jackson. Finally, Mary considered competitor's prices which were:

- Looney Toons $2.49
- Kids Cuisine $1.89
- Kid's Kitchen $1.19

Mary knew that it was important to consider all of these factors in her pricing decisions. The price would influence the interest of consumers and retailers, the reactions of competitors, and ultimately the success of My Own Meals.

Questions

1. In what ways are the demand factors of (a) consumer tasted, (b) price and availability of substitute products, and (c) consumer income important in influencing consumer demand for My Own Meals' products?
2. How can (a) demand-oriented, (b) cost-oriented, (c) profit-oriented, and (d) competition-oriented approaches be used to help My Own Meals arrive at an approximate price level?
3. Why might the retail price of My Own Meal's products be different in grocery stores, mass merchants, daycare centres, and cafeterias?

SUPER ORGANIZER

Cameron Roberts
University of Lethbridge

Ross Blacker is in his mid-40s and has lived in Windsor, Ontario, all his life. A foreman for a large cabinet manufacturer, he has worked for the same company for 18 years. Recently he became intrigued by the possibility of making a simple drawer insert he had invented into a profit-generating venture. The idea was spawned from his ongoing struggle to find the proper utensils in his kitchen drawer. He had tried using different loose-fitting plastic inserts to keep the utensils sorted, but before long the drawer usually returned to being a complete mess. What started out as a simple request for a pickle fork inevitably turned into a pile of scrap metal on the floor.

Blacker knew that if the utensils could be properly sorted and secured in their own appropriate, attractive wooden stalls, the irritation that accompanies a junk drawer would be eliminated. Over the next few months, whenever he had spare time, he was in his basement shop creating different prototypes. These eventually went to his relatives, all of whom were very happy with the inserts and declared them a dream come true.

The drawer sorter, later to be named the Super Organizer, could be made to match any wood cabinets customers had in their kitchens. The Super Organizer consisted of a two-level system that held the utensils at a 17-degree angle so that handles could be easily gripped and the utensils removed. The furthest tier contained a series of slots that held the knives so that only the handles were exposed, making it impossible to cut one's hand (which often happened while rummaging through a junk drawer). The front and back tiers had special partitions that held spoons and forks securely in their proper spaces, eliminating any chance of mayhem (see Figure 1).

What made the Super Organizer unique was the metal adjusters underneath the tiers. They allowed the insert to increase or decrease in length or width, enabling it to fit any standard drawer available on the market (most drawers vary in size by only a few inches). As the system expanded in width, additional slots and lips became available from within the present system. At the front and back of the insert was storage space to hold ill-fitting or special items such as can openers, potato peelers, and skewers. The Super Organizer was unique, tastefully attractive, and very neat. It would probably appeal to the homemaker who was conscientious, disciplined, and highly organized.

Blacker went to a patent lawyer to find out about protection laws for his product. The lawyer told him the design of his product could be protected but another, different design approach to the same problem could be marketed by someone else, which the patent on Blacker's insert could not prevent.

Nevertheless, Blacker decided to go ahead with the project. His brother-in-law, Bill, who was very personable and had a sales background, decided to join ranks with Blacker on this new business venture.

The company where Blacker worked was largely industrial and usually did work brought in from various contractors. Blacker discussed his idea with the people at the company, and they all encouraged him to go ahead with it. The company had the production facilities and capacity to produce the insert, but they were not set up for its marketing application.

Together Blacker and Bill came up with $60,000, mostly from personal savings. After considerable work they decided they had enough money, an innovative product, and access to production facilities. The only problem was how to market the Super Organizer.

Figure 1   Super Organizer

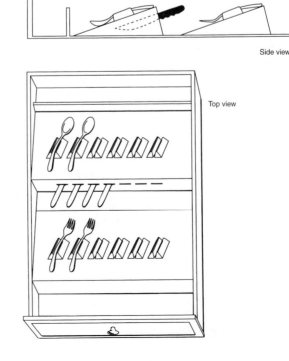

Side view

Top view

Develop a marketing strategy for the Super Organizer.

SUSIE'S FASHIONS

D. Wesley Balderson
University of Lethbridge

As part of his course requirements in completing his MBA at Simon Fraser University in British Columbia, Darren Richards had received a student consulting assignment with a small clothing manufacturer in Vancouver. The firm had been in operation a little over a year and had received funding from the government agency funding small businesses. However, it was experiencing cash flow problems. There was a concern that the business, Susie's Fashions, would have to either close or obtain additional funds. Richards spent considerable time wading through the financial data and finally came up with the approximate statements shown in Figure 1.

Susie Mikado had emigrated to Canada from Hong Kong about five years earlier. Being a hard worker and having worked in a clothing factory in Hong Kong, she got a job immediately at a dress-manufacturing factory. After three-and-a-half years, she accumulated some funds and decided to start her own small business making selected clothing primarily for the large Asian population in the Vancouver area. Mikado had an obvious talent for selecting fabrics and designing garments and, through her family and friends, developed a reputation as a skilled seamstress.

Mikado located her business in the Chinatown district of Vancouver in a leased space of about 1,800 square feet. To make renovations, buy equipment, and pay other initial expenses, she had borrowed $5,000 and put $2,000 of her own funds into the venture. She had hired two full-time employees, paying them $6 per hour to assist in sewing the clothing items. The production process was simple: Each employee and Mikado would make a garment from beginning to end.

Darren Richards visited Susie's Fashions to assess the situation and determine what could be done to solve the cash flow problem. He was impressed with the product line, which exhibited quality craftsmanship. Susie's produced primarily two garments. The first was a Chinese-style dress retailing at $55, and the second was a kimono-like robe retailing at $45. Sales were based almost entirely on word of mouth, as Mikado spent no money advertising. In examining the production process, Darren noticed numerous interruptions occurred as family and friends of the workers frequently came by to visit. He estimated, however, that on average the dresses took four hours to make and the robes took three hours. The average dress took about three yards of material, and the robes averaged four yards. The fabric for both items cost Mikado about $6 per yard.

Richards was concerned about the management of the firm. Although Mikado had hired two full-time employees, she often hired family or friends to help for a few days at a time when they, as she put it, "needed some money." He was most concerned, however, with the financial procedures Susie was following. Because there was no recordkeeping system, he had difficulty determining paid and unpaid bills from the assortment of receipts, scraps of paper, invoices, and notes Mikado kept. Deposits and withdrawals from the bank account had been made but not recorded. Mikado's salary was not recorded, but Richards learned that she withdrew $200 per week. Credit sales were frequent and informal, with Mikado allowing customers to take garments without leaving a down payment.

Figure 1   Susie's Fashions

Susie's Fashions
Balance Sheet
As at January 31, 2001

Assets		Liabilities and Owner's Equity	
Current assets:		Current liabilities:	
Cash	$ 95	Accounts payable	$ 8,450
Accounts receivable	3,815	Current portion of debt	1,000
Inventory	4,765	Total current liabilities	9,450
Prepaid expenses	275	Long-term liabilities	
Total current assets	8,950	Debt	4,000
Fixed assets:		Total liabilities	13,450
Equipment	3,500	Owner's equity	(1,000)
Total assets	$12,450	Total liabilities and owner's equity	$12,450

Income Statement
For Year Ended January 31, 2001

Sales:		
352 dresses	$17,600	
298 robes	11,920	
Other miscellaneous	5,200	
Total sales		$ 34,720
Cost of goods sold:		
Dresses	6,336	
Robes	7,152	
Other miscellaneous	2,500	
Total cost of goods sold		15,988
Expenses:		
Wages (including Susie's)	20,400	
Rent	4,800	
Utilities and phone	3,200	
Interest	1,000	
Repairs and maintenance	3,000	
Total expenses		32,400
Total cost of goods sold and expenses		48,388
Net profit (loss)		**$(13,668)**

Questions

1. Briefly evaluate Susie Mikado's approach to starting her own business.
2. Examine the pricing system for Mikado's clothes.
3. Assuming miscellaneous clothing and robe sales stay the same, how many dresses would Susie's have to sell to break even?
4. Evaluate the financial statements prepared by Darren Richards in both form and content.
5. What kind of financial recordkeeping system would you advise for Susie's?

TAYLOR CONSTRUCTION COMPANY

D. Wesley Balderson
University of Lethbridge

In September 2001, George Taylor realized a lifelong dream by starting his own construction company. He had worked for several construction firms in the province of Quebec over the years, and prior to the time he started his own firm, he had been a foreman on several large projects. He was a hard worker and had developed a reputation as a capable and sought-after foreman by many companies. Since starting Taylor Construction Company, George succeeded in obtaining several profitable contracts, which kept him very busy.

One day he was visiting with a friend, Rob Dumont, over lunch. The following conversation revealed that things were not so great at Taylor Construction.

Rob: How is your business doing, George? You've sure been busy lately.

George: Yes, we've got lots of work, but you can't imagine the problems I've had with employees. I never dreamt it would be such a hassle.

Rob: What kinds of problems are you talking about?

George: Take your pick! When we started up and got our first contract I needed six labourers, so I ran an ad in the paper. I got 19 applicants, and I was surprised that most hadn't finished high school. Even the ones I hired were lazy and undependable. I spent half my time replacing those who quit or whom I fired. Since then things haven't really improved much.

Rob: Maybe you should spend more time training them.

George: More time? As it stands now, I have to be with them almost constantly on a job and tell them what to do every step of the way. If I leave one of them in charge when I have to be away, the others resent it. It seems like they're always bickering with each other.

Rob: I wonder if you should train a foreman to supervise the workers.

George: I tried that. The work that he supervised was poorly done, and on top of that he padded his hours. I even noticed a few tools missing. When I confronted him with it, he up and quit.

Rob: Can't you spend a little more money and find some better-qualified and motivated employees?

George: My labour costs are too high already! Even though I don't hire union workers, I have to pay pretty close to those rates, and they are high. Once in awhile a hard worker will come along, but before long peer pressure from the others seems to drag him down to their level.

Rob: It sounds pretty hopeless.

George: The worst part is that just last month I gave all my employees a bonus. I distributed it based on how long they had worked for me and thought I had explained it to them. However, after I gave it out, several of them were upset, and I even had two quit on the spot. Can you believe that? I'm seriously considering shutting down the business and going back to work for my old firm.

Questions

1. Why do you think George has gotten into this situation?
2. What recommendations would you make to George?

TOT-SWITCH

Robert Wyckham
Simon Fraser University

Jim Halstrum, the inventor of the Tot-Switch, was confronted with an interesting and perplexing dilemma. He was faced with the choice of leaving his product in the hands of Innovation Promotions Limited or using legal means to obtain control over Tot-Switch and finding another method of producing and marketing it.

The Tot-Switch was created by Mr. Halstrum to solve a problem he had observed in his own home. While recuperating from an illness, he noticed how often his two children, aged two and three years, asked their mother to turn lights on. He also noticed that the lights were left on as the children moved from one area to another in the house to play. He thought that if he could devise some method whereby the youngsters could turn the lights on and off he would save his wife innumerable steps and perhaps cut his hydro bill.

After tinkering with pulleys and switches, Mr. Halstrum was able to develop the prototype of the Tot-Switch. A string-and-pulley system allowed the children to operate the light switches. He put a number of these crude attachments on light switches throughout his house and immediately discovered a bonus. The children were able to light their own way to the bathroom at night.

Mr. Halstrum received encouragement from friends who were impressed by the system. Some asked him to put together sets for their homes. During the next few months he made numerous changes in design and materials until the light switch system was durable, easy to install, and easy to use.

After 10 months of experimentation, Mr. Halstrum took two major steps. First, he made arrangements to patent his invention. He took out patents on five different designs in Canada. He also applied for patents in the United States and Japan. The total cost of his patents in the three countries was $4,050. Second, he consulted with Dr. Roger Vergin, a professor of business administration at Simon Fraser University. Professor Vergin agreed to install the switch system in two daycare centres with which he was associated in Bellingham, Washington.

Six months of heavy use by the children in the two daycare centres indicated that the switch systems worked very well. They did not break down, and the youngsters found them easy to use. At this point Professor Vergin recommended to Mr. Halstrum that he try to sell the concept to a manufacturer.

Initial Marketing Efforts

Jim Halstrum's next step was to mail 50 prototypes of his switch to manufacturers and distributors across Canada. Over the next month or so he received a varied response:

1. McDonald's restaurant chain expressed interest in the switch as a promotional item. They would be willing to purchase 2.5 million units if Halstrum could sell the units for eight cents apiece.
2. A number of electric utility companies were favourably disposed toward the product. They were orienting their promotion toward conservation, and the switches fit this theme. However, because of federal regulations, none of the utilities was able to help develop and market the product.
3. A sizable number of small manufacturers and distributors felt the product had merit. They wrote asking for additional information.

At this point, a friend told Mr. Halstrum about a company called Innovation Promotions Limited. Innovation Promotions had been formed recently by a lawyer, John Pobst, and an engineer, Fred Jamison, for the purpose of new product development. In their separate professional practices, Pobst and Jamison had observed the problems that inventors have in exploiting their new products. They decided that they could assist inventors and build a healthy business in new product development. At the time that Mr. Halstrum contacted Innovation Promotions, the company had one product under contract for development.

The Contract

After a number of meetings with Pobst and Jamison, Mr. Halstrum agreed to a contract which would give Innovation Promotions Limited control over the product for five years. The contract, which was signed in October, contained the following conditions:

1. Innovation Promotions would research the market, develop the product for mass production, and handle sales of the product.
2. Mr. Halstrum was to receive a royalty of 25 cents on each unit sold.
3. Innovation Promotions must sell a minimum of 30,000 units in the first year and 450,000 units over the next four years.
4. If at any time Innovation Promotions failed to fulfil their agreement, Mr. Halstrum would regain control over the product.

During the late fall, Innovation Promotions contracted with a plastics manufacturer in Vancouver to produce the product. The switch was modified and engineered to allow mass production. A two-cavity model was produced at a cost of $5,600. This resulted in a production costs of $0.27 per unit. An eight-cavity model, which would have cost $18,000, would have reduced production costs to $0.10 per unit.

A creative director from an advertising agency was hired to develop a name for the product and to design the package. The name chosen was the Tot-Switch. It was selected because it described the product in use and was catchy. The package design was executed by a local packaging firm. Mr. Jamison decided to use an innovative skin-tight plastic-coated package, which, although expensive ($0.35 per unit), was thought to be a selling feature to the trade.

It was decided that the Tot-Switch should retail at $4.99. Up to this point no market or consumer research had been done. Pobst and Jamison were of the opinion that the six-month test at the daycare centres was an adequate evaluation of the worth of the product.

An initial production run of 2,500 units was completed by the end of January. The costs of production and markups for the first production run are shown in Table 1.

Table 1   Selling Price and Costs

	Per Unit
Retail selling price	$4.99
Retail margin	2.50
Wholesale selling price	$2.49
Production cost	.27
Packaging cost	.35
Royalty to Halstrum	.25
Taxes	.16
Royalty to Innovation Promotions, Shipping, and Advertising	1.46
	$2.49

As a first thrust into the marketplace, Innovation Promotions decided to use a mail-order marketing approach. An advertisement was prepared and placed in the Ontario, British Columbia, and Alberta regional editions of TV Guide for the first and third weeks in February. The advertisement encouraged multiple purchases by offering a quantity discount. Prices, including mailing and handling costs, were as follows: one, $5.49; two, $4.75 per unit; three, $4.58 per unit; five or more, $3.75 per unit.

Mr. Halstrum's Reaction

Mr. Halstrum was very disappointed with the performance of Innovation Promotions Limited. He felt that the $4.99 price was much too high. His original idea was to sell the product for about $1.99. Although he could understand the benefits of using mass advertising to make people aware of the Tot-Switch, he felt that the mailorder idea was a waste of time. Only about 500 units had been sold on the basis of the TV Guide ads. In discussing the situation with a friend, he made the following comments:

> They are never going to sell the required 30,000 units by September. Sales at the Thunderbird Electrical stores are not going well. I understand a California manufacturer has shown interest, but he wants national advertising support. Pobst and Jamison are negotiating with a local wholesaler on a deal for 300,000 units, but I can't see anything resulting from the discussions. They have also talked with the Paraplegic Society of British Columbia. Apparently the society wants to promote the product through their magazine and is asking for a 50-cent fee for each unit sold. As far as I'm concerned they just haven't been able to put the thing together. They probably should have gone the traditional route through the department stores. McDonald's is still interested, and if I could get the production costs down and McDonald's price up I might be able to move a fantastic number of units in one quick sale.

Mr. Halstrum wondered what he should do. He felt only two options existed at this time, to hope for the best and leave the product with Innovation Promotions, or to use legal means to regain control of Tot-Switch and design a new marketing strategy for the product.

Questions

1. What options are open to an inventor in bringing a new product to the market?
2. What steps can be taken to determine the size of the market for a new product?
3. Evaluate the current marketing mix for the Tot-Switch.
4. Assume Mr. Halstrum regains control of the Tot-Switch. What would you recommend as a future strategy?

VITALITY HEALTH FOOD STORE

Fredrick G. Crane
QMA Consulting Group Limited

Vitality Health Food Store will open for business in the fall of 2002. It will be an independently owned retail store run by John Carter, a university graduate with a degree in business. It will be located in a strip mall in a growing, upscale suburban neighbourhood. Carter decided to open the business because of his interest in health food and because of the impressive sales growth that has occurred in the sector over the past decade (9 percent annually). Vitality has no other specialty health food stores to compete with in its trade area. However, many supermarkets in the area do offer some health food sections in their stores in response to consumer demand for health food.

Carter has projected sales of $500,000 for his first year of business, which is about average for a store of this type and size. His basic marketing strategy is to penetrate the market by positioning the store as the one-stop shop for the consumer's health food needs. Customer service, convenience, and variety will be integral elements of the marketing strategy. Carter and all employees will be knowledgeable, friendly, and are committed to the concept of "relationship marketing."

Carter conducted some research on the health food shopper. He had determined that this primary (potential) customer will have the profile outlined in Figure 1. He selected his location given the numbers of potential customers living within close proximity to the store who fit the profile. But Carter realizes that customers must be made aware of the store, be persuaded to visit and to make purchases. Moreover, those customers must be reminded to return and encouraged to become regular shoppers. He strongly believes that the promotional element of the marketing mix will play a major role in the success of the business. Accordingly, he has allocated about $25,000 for promotion activities, excluding the costs of retail sales personnel. However, he still has to determine how to spend this money.

Figure 1

Demographics	Female, aged 25–49, college educated, working in professional occupations, earning over $30,000 per year
Lifestyle	Health and fitness oriented, environmentally conscious, and concerned about preservatives and additives in food
Benefits sought	Wants high-quality, safe, and healthy food, product variety, and knowledgeable and helpful retail staff
Media habits	Most likely to read consumer magazines, the Sunday edition of the newspaper, listen to FM radio, and watch late-night television

Questions

1. Outline an appropriate promotional mix for Vitality Health Food Store.
2. What specific sales promotion activities would you recommend for the store? Why?
3. What specific public relations activities would you recommend for the store? Why?

WINSTON'S JEWELLERS

Patricia Elemans
University of Lethbridge

Winston's is a jewellery store located in Kamloops, British Columbia. Kamloops is a city of approximately 70,000 people. Ten to 40 percent of its retail trade comes from the 25 surrounding agricultural communities. The total trading area of Kamloops is approximately 200,000 people. During the past three years, the area has experienced severe droughts and thus poor farming conditions. This situation, coupled with generally poor economic conditions, has had an adverse effect on sales at Winston's.

Winston's opened its doors in 1992. A five-year lease was signed at this time and was renewed for five more years in 1997. The store was opened with an image that Fred Winston believed was consistent with his own lifestyle: upper-class.

Centre Mall, where the store is located, was the highest-traffic mall in Kamloops in 1997. Its retail mix catered to the middle- and upper-income consumer. Winston's was designed to appeal to this market as well. All aspects of the store's marketing targeted the "discriminating" consumer. Winston's carried a superior-quality, distinctive product, ran professionally produced television advertisements, employed a knowledgeable, experienced sales staff, used prestige pricing, and limited the number of sales promotions. Also, Fred Winston was the only certified gemologist in the city, meaning he was the only person in Kamloops qualified to complete jewellery appraisals. The other jewellery stores sent their merchandise to Creston, approximately 200 kilometres away, to be appraised, which took approximately two weeks. Winston's could have items appraised and returned to customers within 24 hours.

For the first four years of operations, Winston's enjoyed considerable success. Sales in the store climbed steadily. Over time, however, the market in Kamloops changed. Competition for the jewellery market increased. The number of stores selling jewellery rose from 13 to 17 in four years. Of these, two stores catered to the upper-income market. One store was a prestigious chain store that had been in Kamloops for five years. The other was a well-established, independent store owned and operated by a local businessperson who was well known and respected in the community. This store has been open for approximately 15 years.

The composition of Centre Mall's patrons also began to change. The upper- and middle-income consumers were now shopping at the newer mall in Kamloops. Centre Mall was now patronized predominantly by middle- and lower-middle-income consumers. Due to the changing clientele of the mall and the increased competition, Winston's began changing certain aspects of its marketing program to appeal to this new market. Initially, the store brought in low-priced, lower-quality jewellery items. In 2000, in an effort to overcome slumping sales due to bad economic conditions, Mr. Winston decided to introduce giftware to the store's product line. The gift items were of average quality and could be purchased at most other jewellery stores and in some department stores. Also at this time, Mr. Winston introduced a "buy now and pay later" plan for customers. On approved credit, customers had one of two options. With no down payment they could take the merchandise they wanted and pay nothing for four months, at which time the balance was due. The second option was to take the merchandise and begin making 12 equal, interest-free monthly payments. The plan met with good response in 2000 and was continued into 2001. Most of the people who took advantage of the plan were in the lower- and middle-income ranges. The average value of items purchased on the plan was $700.

In early 2001, one of Winston's direct competitors closed its doors following the owner's retirement. The store had been open for more than 25 years and had captured approximately 25 percent of the upper-income jewellery market. The closing of this store, coupled with two large diamond sales of $12,000 and $10,000 in December 2001, led Mr. Winston to believe that there was a large market that was not being catered to. This was the upper-income market, who he felt were "floating around" and had not yet decided where to bring their business. Mr. Winston decided he wanted to attract these people to his store. Since he was not quite sure how to go about doing this, he hired a consultant to help him develop a marketing plan to attract this "floating" market.

Questions

1. What marketing-related problems does Winston's face?
2. What would you, as the consultant, suggest to Mr. Winston to get his business back on the right track?

Part IV

Looking to the Future

Part IV focuses on management of the small business for the long term. If a business is being managed effectively and increasing sales and profitability have resulted, the owner-manager will face the question of expansion. If growth of the business is desired, some changes will be required within the organization. Chapter 14 discusses the preparations needed in such a situation.

Chapter 15 (appropriately) discusses the methods of transferring ownership of the business to someone else. Many key considerations in this regard have legal and tax implications with far-reaching consequences for the owner-manager. An option other than transferring of ownership to another person is involving family members in the business. The majority of small businesses are, in fact, family owned and operated. Thus, Chapter 15 also examines the special characteristics of such businesses.

Chapter 14

Managing Growth

Chapter Objectives

- To describe the potential problems that success and growth can bring to the small business.

- To review the characteristics of the stages in the business life cycle.

- To discuss how to sustain the business despite the difficulties created by growth.

- To illustrate the importance of planning for growth.

Small Business Profile

Frank Commisso
Commisso's Food Markets

Commisso's Food Markets Ltd.
www.commisso.com

Thirty-nine years ago in 1962 Frank Commisso's father Mike, then in his early 50s, opened a neighbourhood food store called Commisso's Grocery. From the outset the store was a family-owned and operated business. Frank looked after the day-to-day operations and doubled as butcher; one of his sisters took care of the cash; and his two brothers, Tony and Rocco, both still in school, helped out on a part-time basis.

Commisso's did quite a brisk business within its mere 1,300 square feet, and with just one aisle, a checkout counter, and a fruit stand on the sidewalk outside. In its first five years, sales increased 105 percent annually, and this success led to the opening in 1967 of a second store, 4,000 square feet in size and located in Welland. Three years later, the original Beamsville store was closed and replaced with a bigger store down the street, just a stone's throw away.

Over the years, Frank, along with Tony and Rocco, continued to expand the business, and today, they are at the helm of Commisso's Food Markets Ltd., a fast growing chain of 16 independently owned and operated supermarkets located across the Niagara Peninsula, Hamilton, Burlington, Orangeville, Brantford, Cambridge, and Mississauga. The chain consists of three stores in St. Catharines, two in Welland, two in Hamilton, one each in Niagara Falls, Fort Erie, Port Colborne, Beamsville, Burlington, Orangeville, Brantford, Cambridge, and Mississauga. The stores range in size from 24,000 square feet to 42,000 square feet.

"Commisso's is one of the most entrepreneurial independents we have in the country," says John Scott, president of the Canadian Federation of Independent Grocers. "They're a very impressive company—extremely entrepreneurial and aggressive."

Technology is one area where Commisso's is progressive. It started utilizing front-end scanning back in 1978, long before many independents made the move. And it was one of the first grocery stores to develop its own web site. "We're very proud of our Internet site; I think it's one of the nicest of any retailer in Canada," says Frank, adding that hits are doubling every month. Launched five years ago, the site lets web surfers check out the week's specials and job openings, enter contests, call up recipes, read the corporate history, and much more.

Commisso's also spent two years developing an exciting new merchandising software program that it has just implemented chain-wide. Called "Cnet," the user-friendly program contains all of the company's SKU (stock keeping units) performance history (margins, units sold, etc.) which category managers can efficiently access to plan ad features, do projections, and all their "what iffing" scenarios.

Commisso's and its employees are also dedicated to supporting their communities and focus their efforts on health care, education, and children-related groups. In 2000, the company raised more than $500,000 for local charities and organizations through various fundraising efforts, and this year plans to contribute more.

"What I really love to do is help build great communities," says Frank. "I get real satisfaction from watching the various communities develop, whether it has to do with little league sports or community services like hospitals and playgrounds." It's also important to staff, he believes. "They don't want to be known as people who feed off the community; they want to stimulate the community to grow and be healthy and strong. And that benefits everyone."

SMALL BUSINESS AND GROWTH

As Incident 14-1 illustrates, short-term success and subsequent growth do not always lead to a trouble-free business operation. Often success and growth may compound the complexities and difficulties of managing the business.

To avoid the pitfalls of growth and changes in the market, the owner-manager should try to ensure long-term viability early in the life of the business. First, the owner-manager needs to understand the life cycle of the business to effectively plan for the future. Second, he or she should be aware of some of the more common growth problems a business is likely to face. Finally, the owner-manager should take certain specific steps in planning for growth of the business.

THE BUSINESS CYCLE

The business cycle of the small enterprise is similar to the product life cycle discussed in Chapter 8. For many small businesses that have only one or two products, the business cycle and the product life cycle may be one and the same.

Figure 14-1 illustrates the shape and characteristics of a life cycle for a small business. The vertical axis represents the growth index, usually measured by gross sales, market share, or profitability. The horizontal axis measures the time taken to pass through the stages of the cycle. The length of time a business stays in one stage depends on several variables. Many small businesses take several years to move through the life cycle, while others pass through all four stages within a couple of years. This shorter life cycle is common in high-technology industries. The characteristics of the stages of the business cycle are discussed next.

Incident 14-1

Growing Beyond the Basics

Since the early 1990s, Linda Hamilton and George Traini have watched the sales of their Cotton Basics store decline dramatically. The Toronto-based clothing store is experiencing the decline stage of the business life cycle. Quick, assertive action will be required if Hamilton and Traini want to remain competitive in the clothing retail industry. According to the two owners, keeping the business alive means expansion will be inevitable.

Because Cotton Basics is an independent retail store, suppliers are often unwilling to handle the small fabric volumes it demands. This meant that Traini, store product designer, had to open and run a five-person factory that would meet the manufacturing needs of his store. Now faced with declining sales, Hamilton and Traini must evaluate the possibility of growth. Keeping the factory open in Canada means that Cotton Basics will have to expand, and expansion into a high-traffic area will be the key to their future success. In fact, Hamilton and Traini have already begun implementing the necessary expansion plan. Their objective of expansion is to increase product exposure enough to maintain a level of demand that will keep the five-person factory open. After evaluating alternatives, Hamilton and Traini have decided that opening a new store on the busy Toronto street of Danforth Avenue would be the best solution to meet their expansion goals. Only time will tell if this expansion will prove strong enough to keep Cotton Basics competitive with expanding national and international retail chains.

SOURCE: Adapted from Elizabeth Church, "A Struggle to Grow Beyond the Basics," *The Globe and Mail*, May 26, 1999, p. B-7.

Introduction. Stage 1 is the start-up stage of the small business. It is characterized by expenditures made for both product development and introductory promotion and by low profits, particularly at the beginning. Stage 1 also usually includes a narrow market, a very limited product line, and involvement in most aspects of the business by the owner-manager. The owner's role tends to be more technical and entrepreneurial in this stage.

Growth. Stage 2 of the business cycle, growth, is usually characterized by the establishment of a market share, or acceptance, and expansion of the product line or markets. It may also take the form of internal or external expansion, such as a merger or franchising. During this period, sales grow at an increasing rate. At the end of the growth stage, however, competitive pressures begin to take their toll, necessitating changes in business strategy. Promoting the business to customers, investors, and employees is important at this stage of the business life cycle. Most small businesses find that this stage requires increased capital to finance the expansion. The business may have orders to purchase but only receives payment when the product or service is delivered. Therefore, financing to cover inventories, equipment, and employees is required before sales occur. Most high-growth firms indicate that this is the stage where the most severe cash flow problems occur in the life of the business.

Maturity. Stage 3 is characterized by a levelling of sales due to increased competition and/or a decrease in demand. During this stage, the owner-manager must make some important strategic decisions to avoid moving into stage 4, decline. Of necessity the strategy of the business will become more competitive. Such a strategy may involve adding new products, expanding to new markets, or adjusting or improving existing products in some way. The goal of such actions is to lengthen the life cycle, as illustrated by the increase in sales during the decline stage of the adjusted life cycle in Figure 14-1. The owner's responsibility becomes much more managerial during this stage.

Decline. As Figure 14-1 shows, stage 4 involves a decrease in both sales and profits. Unless action is taken to reverse this trend, the business will fail.

Figure 14-2 shows an example of the growth of a business and subsequent operational and strategy changes that should take place. The actual dollar level of sales relating to the stages

Figure 14-1 The Life Cycle of a Business Concept

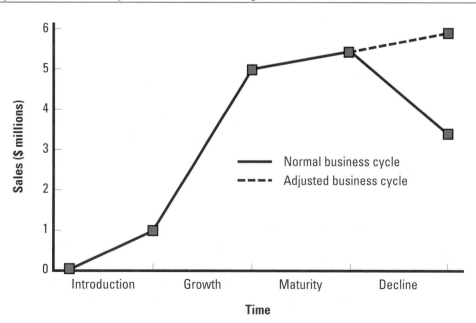

Figure 14-2 Stages of Growth

Approximate Sales Level	Market	Product	Owner-Manager
0–$1,500,000	One market	One or limited line	Involved in day-to-day aspects of the business such as buying, selling, and financial management
$1,500,000–$4,000,000	Expanding into new markets	Adding new products in same category	Some organizational change allowing supervisor to oversee greater part of day-to-day operations
			Greater need for financial evaluation
			Greater need to obtain capital to finance growth
			Some delegation required
			Development of managers
$4,000,000 +	Established markets: continued expansion to new markets	Adding new products in different categories	Managers run day-to-day operations and report to owner Communication and information important Training for management development
			Establishment of proper controls

SOURCE: Ronald W. Torrence. *In the Owner's Chair: Proven Techniques for Taking Your Business from Zero to $10 Million,* © 1986, p. 259. Reprinted by permission of Prentice Hall, Inc., Englewood Cliffs, New Jersey. Updated 2001.

of the life cycle will vary depending on the growth of the market, the type of industry, and the owner's objectives. However, Figure 14-2 points out the need to deal quickly with the changes that growth in sales can create.

PROBLEMS CREATED BY GROWTH

To be able to anticipate growth difficulties and make plans to minimize them, the owner-manager should be aware of some of the problems that can be expected to accompany growth. Figure 14-3 illustrates the importance of some of these factors as found in a survey of 1,500 Canadian Companies. Some of these are discussed below.

Owner-Manager Fatigue and Stress. Stress levels rise when the scope of the business and the magnitude of its problems increase.

Lack of Communication. As the scope of operations grows, the former closeness between owner and business dissipates. Many owner-managers have resented this loss of closeness and even curbed their growth objectives as a result (see Incident 14-2).

Lack of Coordination. Various aspects of the business may become specialized and less integrated with the overall operation as a business grows. This often results in increased conflicts among departments and/or individuals within the organization. Employees who in the early stages of the company life cycle performed many duties are often reluctant to give up some of those responsibilities to specialists. Such resentment often leads to conflicts within the organization.

Figure 14-3   Factors Contributing to Successful Growth in a Small Business

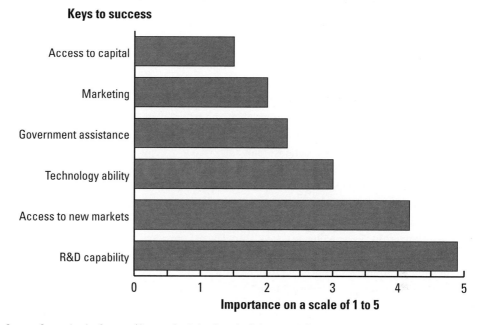

Keys to success

SOURCE: *Strategies for Success* (Ottawa: Statistics Canada, February 1994).

Incident 14-2

The Fridge

Ever wonder how to keep your beer cool on a hot summer's day? Keith Barnwell and his partners, Ross Cruikshank and Joe Luschak, wondered and designed a beer sleeve capable of just that. The three entrepreneurs called the gel-insulated plastic sleeve, "The Drink Refrigerator." The Drink Refrigerator was launched from Brampton, Ontario-based Candea in 1988. The three men projected huge sales for their simple idea and were not disappointed. Placing the beer holders in Canadian Tire and Ontario Brewers Retail Outlets resulted in first year sales of $1 million.

Despite the instant popularity of The Drink Refrigerator, Keith Barnwell learned a hard lesson. Success does not necessarily guarantee security. By 1993, Candea had annual sales of $8 million. One-hundred-and-twenty employees were employed by the company both in Canada and abroad. The future could not have been brighter for the three entrepreneurs. But it was at this point that Barnwell and his partners began disagreeing over the direction of their million-dollar company. Hoping to resolve the conflict, Barnwell invoked a shotgun clause in the partnership agreement that would have allowed him to become sole owner of the company. However, when Cruikshank and Luschak realized Barnwell's intentions, the tables quickly turned. "I found that when I loaded the shotgun, it was pointed back at me," says Barnwell. "It's a chance you take." Soon after the fiasco, Barnwell's partners purchased his 32 percent share in Candea. Cruikshank and Luschak operated Candea until selling out to Baltimore-based diversified manufacturer, Life-Like Products Inc., in 1998.

Barnwell does not regret his time at Candea and is appreciative of the chance he had to learn about business. "I learned everything about business at Candea," he says, "product development, manufacturing and automation, retailing and trade shows, how to negotiate." However, the most important lesson the entrepreneur learned from his Candea experience was "choose your partners wisely. Don't choose someone just because he's a friend. Make sure they supply skills you don't have." Barnwell now operates his own small business that specializes in product and business development consulting.

SOURCE: Adapted from Kara Kuryllowicz, "Older, Wiser," *Profit*, April 2000, p. 37.

Incident 14-3

Rostar Precision Inc.

Growth is a goal that many small businesses strive for, but it calls for careful and informed business decisions.

When Rostar Precision Inc., a manufacturer of mechanical components for the aerospace industry, decided to try and spur more dynamic growth, it meant restructuring the company. Although Rostar had grown at a respectable rate through much of its 21-year existence, it wanted to be considered for high-profile aerospace, satellite, and International Space Station projects run by companies such as Spar, Boeing, and Allied Signal. "We didn't want to be thought of as a small company that couldn't meet the requirements of these large contracts," says the director of marketing Roman Kuczynski.

Exporting is crucial to the growth of some companies almost from the very beginning, but getting the support needed to pay for and manage an expensive export and marketing program can be extremely difficult. The problem is a common one for many start-up software companies, that not only have to sell their specialized products globally in order to survive but also have to foot the bill for high research and development costs.

"Cash flow is always a challenge," says Tony Harris, president and CEO of Comdale Technologies (Canada) Inc., a manufacturer of advanced software for the industrial automation marketplace. "We never had trouble paying employees, but we had to delay some payments to suppliers." He added that the period when a software company is trying to "shrink wrap" its product to sell in higher volume is financially one of the toughest.

SOURCE: "Controlling Growth," *Profits Magazine* 17, no. 3 (Business Development Bank of Canada), p. 4.

Shortage of Cash. Growth and expansion often require financing that the business has not yet generated. Merchandise may have been sold but cash not yet received, even though cash is still needed to acquire new inventories. Incident 14-3 illustrates this difficulty for one Canadian company.

Low Profitability. Low profitability is common in rapidly growing businesses. Several of the fastest-growing companies in Canada lost money in 2000, and others earned small profits.[1] Considerable expenses have been incurred in research and development of markets during the growth period.

Breakdowns in Production Efficiency. Declining production efficiency, as evidenced by unmet schedules, increases in quality assurance problems, and consumer complaints, is common in rapidly growing companies.

Lack of Information. Lack of information with which to evaluate the business's performance often accompanies rapid growth. As the owner-manager becomes increasingly removed from day-to-day operations and the scope of the business outgrows manual information retrieval, a more automated system is often required to generate the required data. Incident 14-4 illustrates how one small business recognized the value of communications technology for growth.

Decreasing Employee Morale. Lower employee morale results in higher employee turnover and absenteeism. New people are added to the firm to accommodate growth, but they often receive insufficient training. Existing employees work harder in growth companies and may not receive adequate recognition for their efforts. This situation can lead to employee discontent.[2]

Any one of the above problems can spell disaster for an otherwise potentially successful small business. To prevent such problems, the wise owner-manager can prepare himself or herself and the business to handle growth in several ways.

Incident 14-4

Cygnal Technologies Corp.

Communication technologies is one of the fastest growing sectors in Canada. In order to be successful, one must stay abreast of competitors' technological releases. Oshawa, Ontario-based Cygnal Technologies is a company that has capitalized upon technology introduction and, as a result, now dominates the Canadian communications industry.

Nowadays, clients demand networks that can transmit voice, data, and video information at lightning speed. Cygnal provides a variety of specialized services that meet this need including the assemblage and installation of automated meter reading and wireless networks for high profile clientele such as Wal-Mart, Bell Express Vu, and Hydro Quebec. The communications giant focuses on building complex networks that meet the needs of today's high-tech sector. To do this, Cygnal has become a company that can handle any communications task. Most firms focus on one aspect of network installation and then outsource the remaining work. Cygnal is a company that completes network installation and maintenance from start to finish, and it is this capability that has made them Canada's top communications guru.

President and CEO, Doug Young, attributes Cygnal's success to its commitment to versatility. Rather than sticking to one niche, Cygnal has expanded to offer almost every service required for network establishment. Most communications companies are tech distributors that lack expertise needed for network installation and maintenance. Through acquisition, Cygnal now possesses all of the necessary capabilities. Young identifies companies with strong core competencies that lack management expertise and/or financials to deal with growth and then brings them under Cygnal's direction. The proposed acquisitions must be profitable and have established strong customer loyalty. Founders of the newly acquired companies are rewarded for their efforts by money and the opportunity to remain employed by Cygnal. In the past five years, this strategy has paid off in the form of a 41,847 percent growth in revenue. Young says this growth is because Cygnal does not simply purchase companies, but integrates and aligns them with its goals.

SOURCE: Adapted from Ian Portsmouth, "The Master Builders," *Profit,* June 2001, p. 42-44.

Owner Lifestyle. An often overlooked contributor to business failure due to growth relates to personal lifestyle decisions of the owner as the business begins to be successful. A larger house, car, or exotic vacations based on the expectation of continued growth often leaves the owner unable to meet personal obligations.

EVALUATING THE GROWTH QUESTION

The owner-manager should answer four important questions before proceeding to expand the business.

Is the Business One That Can Grow? A preliminary step in dealing with the question of growth is to evaluate whether the product or business is one that can grow. Restricted markets or products that have volume production restrictions are difficult to expand. Many service businesses that rely on the special expertise of their owners also fit into this category. Rapidly changing industries such as those found in high technology suggest concerns of rapid obsolescence. This is particularly critical if the capital investment of growth is large.

Is the Business Owner Prepared to Make the Effort? Expanding a business will require additional time and effort on the part of the owner-manager. The decision the owner-manager must make is whether he or she is ready to increase effort and prepare for the stress or be content with a smaller but less demanding business. Many successful small businesses have chosen not to grow for precisely this reason.

Does the Owner-Manager Have the Capabilities to Grow? The owner-manager should assess whether the needed capital, labour, and expertise can be obtained to deal effectively with growth. Some of these specific areas will be discussed in the following section.

How Should the Owner-Manager Pursue Growth? If growth is desired, several approaches may be taken in pursuing it. The most common strategies (some already mentioned) are as follows:

- Pursue new markets for the product or service. This may involve different geographic (domestic or foreign) or demographic markets.

- Increase sales of existing products or services by increasing the frequency of use. This can be done through increased promotion.

- Add new products or services or modify existing ones to increase sales.

- Find new uses for the product or service and promote these uses to the market.

- Acquire other small companies or merge with another organization.

PLANNING FOR GROWTH

Once the decision to expand has been made and the method of expansion has been determined, a plan for growth should be developed. A growth or strategic plan is a blueprint of future actions. Planning is an essential but often overlooked part of management. One survey found that only 5 percent of all companies do formal short-term and long-term planning, and almost 50 percent do little or no formal planning.[3]

Some small business owners fail to plan for the future because they do not understand what a plan is. A plan is more than short-term sales forecasts and budgets. It includes setting long-term objectives and outlining procedures for reaching those objectives.

In addition, most small business owners feel snowed under by the daily operations and often think planning is a nuisance. However, small business owner-managers who are able to periodically step back from the organization and objectively assess its overall direction are generally better able to cope with the environmental changes that will affect the business.

Finally, in many industries conditions change so rapidly that plans have to be altered frequently. The need for constant adjustment discourages many small business owners.

The Expansion Plan

Chapter 4 discusses the essential elements of the start-up business plan. Many similarities exist between the start-up plan and the expansion plan. The business plan as introduced in Chapter 4 includes projecting for growth and expansion as well. The steps in the expansion plan are as follows.

Set Objectives. The first step in the planning process is to set the objectives the business is to accomplish. As mentioned previously, it is important to set objectives specifically so that the outcomes can be measured. Objectives may include dollar sales, market share percentage, or dollar profits.

Determine Alternatives. The second step includes identifying possible strategies to achieve the set objectives. It also involves forecasting the possible outcomes of different alternatives.

Select the Best Alternatives. Alternatives should be selected with a view toward long-term success. The components of this success are the company's capability and the potential growth of the area.[4]

Understanding the Requirements of Growth

Rapid growth will necessitate some fundamental changes within the organization. Some of the requirements of growth are discussed next.

Greater Management Depth. The owner-manager must realize that an expansion of management depth must accompany the expansion of the business. This will require more skills or harder work on behalf of the owner-manager. Because he or she may already be stretched to the limit, such expansion usually consists of training subordinates to handle some of the managerial responsibilities. This involves training and delegation, two personnel practices owner-managers are often hesitant to incorporate into their management styles. As Figure 14-4 illustrates, the owner must spend more time thinking and less time doing. This also means he or she must move from task delegation to functional delegation, allowing key people to manage various functional areas of the business. Greater management depth can also be achieved through the use of functional specialists outside the company such as accountants, lawyers, directors, or mentors.

Intelligent Expansion. A common problem among small business owners is that in their effort to succeed, they start too many diverse projects. They often do so without evaluating whether they have the productive or marketing expertise and resources to accomplish the expansion. They may also ignore the potential effects of unplanned expansion on their existing products. The decision to expand should incorporate continuity, experience, and intelligence. Incident 14-5 (on the following page) illustrates the need for this for one of Canada's most successful entrepreneurs.

Additional Capital. Any expansion in the business will require additional money to finance added productive capacity, inventory, or personnel. Unless the business has a solid debt-equity ratio and a steady cash flow, it may have difficulty obtaining this needed financing. Chapter 7 discusses sources of financing. Incident 14-6 (on the next page) shows how one Canadian firm grew rapidly because of its ability to obtain the needed capital.

Figure 14-4 Recommended Managerial Activities

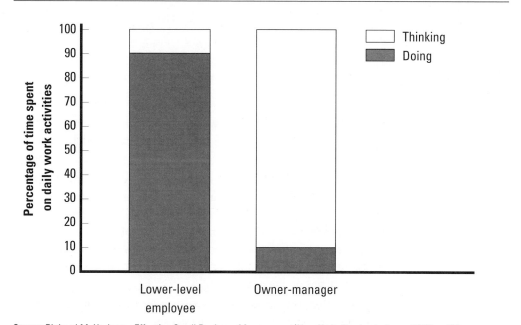

SOURCE: Richard M. Hodgets, *Effective Small Business Management* (New York: Academic Press, 1982), p. 193.

Incident 14-5

Watch Your Growth

Roots Canada Ltd.
www.roots.com

In some instances, a company's distribution channels can't handle the volume. "A classic example relates to Roots, a Canadian clothing and apparel company which at one point in time had an immensely successful advertising campaign," says Brander. "Unfortunately, their distribution infrastructure wasn't able to cope with the level of demand."

Don Green, co-founder of the highly successful Roots chain concurs. "Between 1987 and 1989, before sports-licensed merchandising appeared, there was a major fad for logo sweatshirts. Our product filled a void in the market and we caught the wave beautifully," he says. "But we had a problem in meeting demand."

Green explains that suppliers secured additional production capacity soon after, and things got smoother. Roots has since continued its expansion and now boasts 100 outlets and 1,000 employees across Canada, as well as stores in the U.S. and Asia. "We now try to plan well ahead of time," he adds. "We also own two factories in the Toronto area, which is really key in terms of ensuring supply."

SOURCE: "Watch Your Growth," *Profits Magazine 17, no.1* (Business Development Bank of Canada), p. 6.

Incident 14-6

VAW Systems

Winnipeg's VAW Systems manufactures noise control systems for commercial buildings and industrial plants. The privately-owned company is a world leader in sound and noise control technology and exports 90 per cent of its production. VAW Systems is one such Canadian growth-oriented company. "From 1980 to 1992, we were a small regional player," says Robert Jackson, the company's President. "In 1992, we decided to expand our market to include the U.S. and we grew a lot since then."

VAW Systems' sales have grown from $2.7 million in 1992 to $6 million in 1996. Customers include Motorola, Advanced Micro Devices (the world's second largest computer chip manufacturer), and the Diamond Back, a new dome stadium in Phoenix, Arizona. "The main challenge to our growth is finding and training enough technical employees," says Jackson.

SOURCE: "Growing Companies Create The Most Value," *Profits Magazine* 17, no. 1 (Business Development Bank of Canada), p. 4.

One way to achieve high growth even with limited capital may be to franchise the business or the idea. Although becoming a franchisor requires a certain amount of capital (see Chapter 6), franchising may allow a firm to expand rapidly without large amounts of funds.

Financial Information. Often increased sales obscure the fact that the profitability of the business is declining or even negative. As the business grows, it is increasingly difficult—but more important—for the owner-manager to obtain accurate information about the profitability and productivity of the business. The use of computers by many small businesses has greatly helped in this area. As the business grows there is a greater need to utilize information technology. Owner-managers should regularly project future financial requirements so that cash shortages do not occur.

Organizational Change. As the owner-manager realizes he or she can no longer be involved in every aspect of the business, the organizational structure will require alteration. This is

Incident 14-7

Balancing Life and Work

It is possible for one to balance a million dollar business and a rewarding personal life. Forty-two-year-old Grace White, owner and president of CanJam Trading Ltd., is living proof. White began the international trading business from her home in 1989 with little more than a phone and a strong dose of chutzpah. CanJam exports a range of low-cost food products including salted fish, mutton, and kidney beans to her native Jamaica and Korea. Now the exporting company boasts sales over $6.5 million and soon expects to generate sales up to $100 million.

Despite her booming business, this extraordinary entrepreneur still manages to take the time necessary to foster a healthy family life. However, this was not always the case. The death of White's husband in 1992 left her reeling with grief. In an attempt to cope with the tragic loss, the entrepreneur threw herself into her work. "For a long time I was working seven days a week, and sometimes 15 or 16 hours a day." Strenuous time demands and a taxing workload soon took their toll. Luckily, a chance encounter shed light upon White's exhausting situation.

In 1998, the CanJam president met an older woman who not only impressed her, but eventually became both a friend and mentor. The woman's peacefulness and serendipity inspired White to re-evaluate her hectic lifestyle. Soon after the friendship began, White realized the importance of her family taking priority over her business. "I realized that the order in my life should be God first, then my children, then my company, and my community," says White.

Since 1992, Grace has hired 30 employees and has filled key management positions necessary for her to spend quality time with her two children. "No more seven-day work weeks," says White. She now realizes the negative consequences that can result when one does not establish a balance between work and family.

SOURCE: Adapted from Hilary Davidson, "A Perfect Balancing Act," *Profit*, April 2000, p. 30.

necessary to establish a clear understanding of reporting and responsibility centres in the business. The aim is to reduce the owner's span of control and allow more of his or her time for the planning and long-term strategy development of the business. It can also allow the owner more time to foster coordination within the firm. Incident 14-7 illustrates how one entrepreneur found that delegation was required for her firm to grow while maintaining a balance between work and family.

At the same time, the owner-manager must resist the temptation to "overdo" the bureaucracy of the organization. An entrepreneurial culture (which likely contributed to the business's success in the first place) must be retained if growth is to continue.

Implementing Managerial Controls. As a business grows, it becomes more difficult to control. Through the use of informational and organizational methods, a system of goals, performance levels, and evaluations must be put into place. As discussed in Chapter 11, the integration of computers into the small business's operations has greatly enhanced the owner-manager's ability to control all aspects of the business. Such measures as ratio analysis, inventory turnover, margins, and cost controls are examples.

Monitoring the External Environment. The final growth requirement is that the owner-manager focus greater attention on the external environment of the business. These external forces serve as a guide to the long-term strategic planning in which the owner-manager now must engage. Important external forces, discussed in Chapter 8, are technological change, competition, consumer demand, social and cultural norms, legislation, and the state of the economy.

In the new millenium managers of companies need to:

- Invent new applications for products and services
- Find new sales and distribution channels
- Rethink internal processes
- Enhance technological content
- Provide employees with upgradeable, saleable skill sets
- Disseminate internal information use effectively[5]

Summary

1. Problems to anticipate as a result of growth are the owner-manager's increased fatigue and stress, lack of communication, lack of coordination, shortage of cash, low profitability, a breakdown in production efficiency, lack of information, and possible decreasing employee morale.

2. The four stages of the business cycle include the introduction, growth, maturity, and decline stages.

3. To acquire the knowledge to deal with growth problems, the owner-manager should address three areas. First, the owner-manager must review the business life cycle. Second, the owner-manager should be aware of the common growth problems that arise. Third, the owner-manager must know the steps he or she can take to plan effectively for growth.

4. Growth planning is often overlooked because of the failure to understand the planning process, lack of time, and the constant changes occurring in the industry. The three steps in developing an expansion plan for a small business are (1) setting objectives, (2) identifying all the possible strategies or alternatives for achieving the objectives, and (3) choosing the best and most viable alternative.

Chapter Problems and Applications

1. Describe the business cycle for Cotton Basics (Incident 14-1).

2. Which of the problems created by growth as described in the chapter could apply to Cotton Basics? Explain.

3. The owner-managers of a small, successful hair-cutting company want to expand their business. Their growth objective is to have 35 percent of the local hair-cutting market in two years' time.

   a. What steps could they take to determine the feasibility of their expansion?

   b. Outline a brief expansion plan.

4. What recommendations for expansion would you make for the following companies? Justify your answers. How does your recommendation differ from what actually happened? Why does it differ?

   a. The Fridge (Incident 14-2)

   b. Rostar Precision Inc. (Incident 14-3)

   c. Cygnal Technologies (Incident 14-4)

   d. Cotton Basics (Incident 14-1)

5. What requirements for growth would be necessary for further expansion of Cotton Basics?

6. Interview the owner-manager of a successful small business, and evaluate the potential for further growth. Would you recommend expansion for this firm? Why or why not?

7. Visit three small businesses that you suspect have varying sales levels. Determine the market, product, and degree of owner-manager involvement in each business. Are your results significantly similar to those in Figure 14-2? Explain.

Suggested Readings

Carson, David, Stanely Cromie, Pauric McGowan, and Jimmy Hill. *Marketing and Entrepreneurship in SME's: An Innovative Approach.* London: Prentice Hall, 1995, pp. 160–167.

"The Definitive Guide to Understanding Business Cycles for Growing Companies." *Profit,* June 1999, p.1–27.

Longsworth, Elizabeth. "Anatomy of a Start-up: Why Some New Businesses Succeed and Others Fail." *Inc.,* 1991, Goldhirsh Group Inc., Boston.

Mangelsdorf, Martha. "The Startling Truth About Growth Companies." *Inc.,* Special State of Small Business Issue, 1996.

Schacter, Harvey. "Don't Grow It… Buy It." *Profit,* June 1998, p. 161.

Smith, Robert H., and Paul N. Silverthorne. "Shifting into Overdrive—Strategic Business Planning for the Growth Company." *The Edge,* March, 1994.

Zimmerer, Thomas W., and Norman M. Scarborough. *Entrepreneurship and New Venture Formation.* New Jersey: Prentice Hall, 1996, pp. 485–490.

Comprehensive Case
The Framemakers: Part 9

After four years of operations, The Framemakers had developed into a thriving business. Despite their problems and difficulties, Robert and Teresa Norman were proud of its performance. Sales had reached $175,000, almost three times what they had been in the first year (see Figure 1). Sales were appearing to stabilize, however, and the Normans suspected The Framemakers had saturated the market in Brandon. They disliked the idea of this ceiling on sales and profits and were looking to expand operations. They were investigating three possibilities for expansion. Each would require additional financing. Even though interest rates were in the 10 percent range, Robert and Teresa believed their banker would lend them the money on the basis of The Framemakers' past success and a possible rate of return of at least 20 percent.

The first expansion possibility involved the purchase of the other frame shop in Brandon, The Art Studio, which was rumoured to be for sale. Robert had contacted the owner and obtained some financial information (Figure 2). The owner would not give complete financial statements without a down payment, which the Normans were hesitant to provide. Although this business was smaller than The Framemakers, it had a prime downtown location that Robert and Teresa thought would generate walk-in traffic. The asking price was $75,000. With the addition of the second store, The Framemakers would have a monopoly on the framing business in Brandon. The present owner indicated that he wanted to move to Toronto, where he saw greater opportunities for a successful business.

Figure 1

The Framemakers Ltd.
Income Statement
For the Year Ended January 31, 20—

Revenue:

Sales	$175,000	
Cost of goods sold	70,250	
Gross profit	104,750	

Expenses:

Accounting and legal	$ 1,200
Advertising	3,500
Auto	3,900
Bank charges and interest	8,100
Repairs	2,200
Depreciation	3,800
Office supplies and miscellaneous	1,200
Rent	23,150
Travel	2,700
Utilities	3,750
Wages and benefits (includes $27,000 for the Normans)	47,500
Total expenses	101,000
Net profit	**$ 3,750**

Figure 2

The Art Studio
Financial Statements

Assets

Equipment	$14,000
Inventory	18,000
Total	$32,000

Liabilities

Gross sales were about $110,000 per year.

Robert estimated profits (excluding owner's wages) to be about 10 percent of sales. He felt that about $10,000 of the equipment and inventory was of minimal value.

The second option particularly intrigued the Normans: to get into the business of manufacturing oak picture frames. Through his contacts in the industry, they had learned of a frame-manufacturing business in the United States that was for sale. The company, Frame-Line Manufacturing Company, had been operating only three years, but partnership problems and the owner's personal financial difficulties had forced him to sell. The plant had several key contracts with large retailers in the United States and Canada that they hoped to be able to maintain. The oak frame, which averaged US$25 retail per unit, had few other manufacturers and competed with the lower-priced, plastic imitation wood frames that were currently popular and that The

Framemakers stocked. Robert and Teresa thought it would be feasible to move the plant to his home town south of Brandon and still maintain the Canadian and U.S. markets for the frames. What the Normans particularly liked about this opportunity was the growth potential in sales, which appeared to be far greater than in the retailing business. (Financial information on the manufacturing plant appears in Figure 3.) The asking price for the manufacturing business was $30,000 (U.S.). They thought that if they chose this option, they might have to sell The Framemakers so that they could devote full attention to establishing the manufacturing operation.

Figure 3

Frame-Line Manufacturing Co.
Financial Information
(all figures in U.S. dollars)

Assets

Equipment (estimated life, five years)	$30,000	
Inventory	2,000	
Gross sales (200 frames per month)	60,000	per year but growing at 15% per year
Exchange rates	$1.00	U.S. to $1.30 Canadian
Freight and duty to ship equipment to Canada	$12,000	

The third option was to organize a franchising operation using The Framemakers as the prototype. With the industry growing, Robert believed that there was potential for another franchisor in the industry. He estimated they would need $50,000 to develop the literature, contracts, and promotion, and thought he could sell franchises for $10,000 each.

Questions

1. What analysis should Robert and Teresa make before they seriously investigate the three expansion opportunities?
2. Evaluate the suitability of the asking price or establishment costs for each opportunity.
3. What nonfinancial aspects of each option should the Normans consider?

Video Case Questions
Sugar High*

CBC

Winnipeggers Chris Emery and Larry Finson have a lot to smile about. Their company, Krave's Candy, has been tagged Manitoba's fastest-growing company—growing 938 percent and hitting annual sales of close to $1 million in just three years, due to their clodhoppers candy. But the founders of Krave's don't want to stop there. Chris and Larry want Krave's to become Canada's premier candy company, taking on Hershey and Nestlé.

1. What are some of the growth problems of Krave's Candy Company?
2. What could Chris Emery and Larry Finson do to solve these problems?
3. What are the advantages and disadvantages of diversifying to other products besides Clodhoppers?

*Source: CBC *Venture* #732, running time 10:00.

Chapter 15

Managing the Transfer of the Business

Chapter Objectives

- To discuss the importance of planning for the long-term future and possible transfer of ownership of the small business.

- To review the unique characteristics and problems of owning a family business and passing it on to family members.

- To explain the critical considerations in selling the business to someone outside the family.

- To discuss information pertaining to the closing down of the business.

Small Business Profile

Jean Paré
Company's Coming Cookbooks

Cooking has always been an important part of Jean Paré's life. In 1963, when her four children had all reached school age, Jean volunteered to cater the 50th anniversary of the Vermillion School of Agriculture, now Lakeland College. Working from her home, Jean prepared a dinner for more than 1,000 people which launched a flourishing catering operation that has continued for over 18 years.

With requests for her recipes mounting, Jean teamed up with her son Grant Lovig to form Company's Coming Publishing Limited. April 14, 1981, marked the debut of *150 Delicious Squares,* the first Company's Coming cookbook in what would soon become Canada's most popular cookbook series. Jean released one new title each year for the first six years. Today, an average of six new cookbooks, in various formats, are launched every year under the Company's Coming brand. In 1999, the company will have published more than 50 titles and sold over 15 million cookbooks worldwide for sales of over $10 million annually.

Printed in both English and French, Company's coming cookbooks are available in more than 6,000 retail accounts across Canada. The cookbooks are also distributed in the United States and various overseas markets. A Spanish-language edition of Jean Paré's familiar and trusted recipes can even be found in Mexico.

Jean credits much of the company's success to the sales savvy of her son, Grant, now president, who was fresh from marketing school when he developed the retail plan for the cookbooks. Grant feels the family connection is one of their great strengths. Although Jean is the primary creative force behind Company's Coming, she confides that some of her best material comes from yet another son, Brian, who lives in Kelowna, B.C. Her daughter, Gail Lovig, has been a part of the company since its inception and currently oversees all marketing and distribution efforts.

Jean and her son, Grant, are also founding shareholders of Comac Food Group Inc., a multi-concept franchise management organization headquartered in Calgary that operates four speicalty food retail brands including Company's Coming Bakery Cafes, Domino's Pizza, and Grabbajabba coffee houses.

Some advice from Jean Paré for fledgling entrepreneurs, "Keep things simple. Understand your customer's needs and never lose sight of how to satisfy them. Put profits back into the company and get going and do it!"

LONG-RANGE PLANNING

As mentioned in Chapter 14, relatively few owner-managers engage in formal long-range planning. One reason is the unpredictability of the future due to changes in the economy, technology, consumer demand, and legislation. However, one outcome that is predictable for small business is the fact that the owner-manager will not be able to manage the business forever. Someday the business will be transferred to others or closed down. Because of the time, effort, money, and commitment owner-managers have put into their ventures, they generally want the business to continue to grow and prosper and hope to realize a financial gain for their efforts in starting and building the organization.

To ensure this continuity for the business, the owner-manager needs to plan early for the time when he or she will no longer be in charge. Many small business owners are uncomfortable about this prospect. As a result they often procrastinate, avoiding the issue until shortly before the transfer of ownership is a necessity. Given today's legislation and tax laws, however, such a lack of planning can be extremely costly and damaging to both the owner-manager and the new owners of the business.

Succession problems appear to be at a high level today as many business owners who started their businesses following World War II are now retiring. According to a recent study in the United States, 42 percent of family-owned businesses expect a succession within the next five years. Only one-third admit to having a succession plan.[1] The experience with Canadian small businesses confirms this trend with an estimated 78 percent of family businesses expecting a leadership change in the next 15 years but with most not having a succession plan.

The entrepreneur should be familiar with the possible outcomes for the business, the relative merits of those outcomes, and some key implications of each.

ALTERNATIVE OUTCOMES FOR THE BUSINESS

The owner-manager can anticipate three possible outcomes for the business: transfer of ownership to heirs, selling the business to outsiders, and closing down the business on declaring bankruptcy.

Transferring Ownership to Heirs

Keeping the business in the family is a common method of transferring the business. Many Canadian family businesses have been successful. See Incident 15-1 (on page 428). Figure 15-1 shows some interesting characteristics about Canadian family businesses.[2] Many small business owners desire to pass the business they have inherited or built up to their children. In most cases, this transfer occurs with considerable tension.[3] Because a family-owned business has many unique characteristics, it is important to review the problems and potential solutions in managing this type of organization.

University of Guelph
www.uoguelph.ca/
cfww/index.html

Estimates of the extent of ownership within a single family indicate that approximately 70 to 90 percent of all businesses in Canada are family owned and operated[4] and employ close to 60 percent of the Canadian work force. The Canadian Association of Family Enterprise (CAFÉ) exists to provide assistance to family businesses relating to many areas discussed in this chapter. Although a majority of these firms are small businesses, a significant number of family-owned large companies exists. Almost 35 percent of the Fortune 500 companies are owned or controlled by a single family.[5] Family ownership of a business in Canada is similar to that in the United States. One survey of the 500 fastest-growing private corporations in America undertaken by *Inc.* and *USA Today* found that the spouse and children are involved 33 percent and 28 percent, respectively, in the business operations of the other spouse.[6]

Figure 15-1 The Status of the Family Business

How dependent is the firm on its leader?

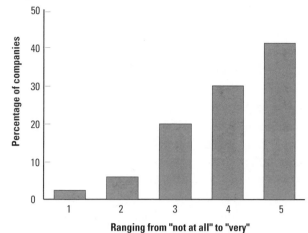

Ranging from "not at all" to "very"

How important is it that ownership remains in the family?

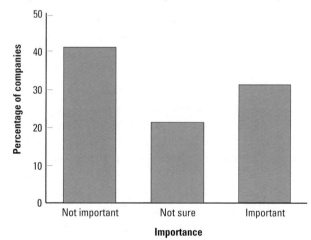

Importance

When does the firm's leader plan to retire?

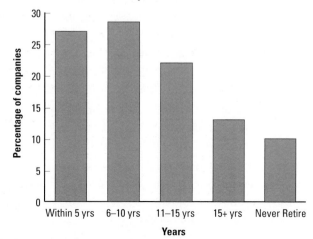

Years

SOURCE: Deloitte and Touche; University of Waterloo

Incident 15-1

The Royal Family of Kitchenware

Browne & Co. Ltd. is quickly becoming one of the world's hottest kitchenware design, manufacturing, and distribution companies. Browne's Cuisipro product line is exported throughout North America, Europe, Japan, and Australia. In fact, U.S. demand for Cuisipro kitchenware has been so great that Browne & Co. has established a separate company south of the border. Though large, the Wilmington, Delaware-based Browne U.S.A. does not compare production-wise to the Canadian warehouse in Markam, Ontario. Over 40,000 square feet are devoted to the "re-invention" of kitchen products. Any company can manufacture and sell mixing bowls, colanders, and ladles, but Browne takes these gadgets and makes them better.

Despite its success in kitchenware, Browne & Co. was not originally an exporting company. The Browne family started the business 50 years ago. Importing textiles and inexpensive kitchen supplies was Browne's focus. The 70s resulted in a decline in textile importation, as globalization allowed large companies to send sales reps overseas. Ten years later, the Brownes identified a new trend in consumer purchasing. People wanted kitchenware that was high quality and name brand. This demand resulted in an explosion of kitchenware exports. "It now accounts for more than 40 percent of our total revenues," says 57-year-old Peter Browne.

The Browne's key to success was being the first to identify, exploit, and maintain an unrecognized market. Product designer Helen Kerr's strategy has been to take the usual kitchen gadgets and rethink both design and usage. Holding focus groups with customers, storeowners, and cooking schools has allowed the Browne's to reinvent kitchenware. Demand for these product lines has sky rocketed in the past decade. Browne & Co. distributes to major companies around the world. Crate & Barrel along with several other U.S. supply chains purchase over $500,000 annually. This makes the Browne family worth a cool $45 million per year.

SOURCE: Adapted from Gerald Levitch, "Empire of the Spoon," *R.O.B.*, April 2001, p. 45.

**Canadian Association
of Family Enterprise
www.cafenational.org**

Despite the predominance of family businesses in Canadian society, relatively few survive into the second and third generations. It is estimated that only 26 percent continue into the second generation and only 6 percent into the third.[7] This succession problem also appears to be occurring more frequently today as many entrepreneurs who launched an economic boom 30 years ago are now nearing retirement.[8] What are the reasons for this apparent lack of continuity? Observation shows that if some unique considerations in operating the family business are not recognized and planned for, they can cause considerable difficulties for the enterprise. While it is an extreme example, it shows that family involvement in a business may have a detrimental effect not only on the business but also on family relationships.

Potential Problems in a Family Business. Several problems may surface in the family-owned business. Recognition of these potential difficulties is essential for the owner-manager and even for the other family members so that they can take steps to prevent them.

Over-reliance on the Founder. Most family businesses remain highly dependent for their success on their leader, who is typically the founder of the business. Most have no contingency plan covering the disability or death of this person.

Higher Emotional Level. Because of existing family relationships, some of the business decisions and evaluations may be more emotionally charged than they would be in a non-family setting. For example, the evaluation of performance or supervision affecting a family member employee may be biased positively or negatively because of the relationship. Family members often bring their personal feelings and stress to the business, which often precludes them from making objective decisions.

Blurring of Roles. In many family-owned businesses, the personal and business roles of individual family members may become blurred. For example, the chief executive officer of the business may in practice not really be in control because of his or her subordinate role in the family. This often occurs when children have "taken over" the business but their parents still exert informal control over both the children and the business.

Incompetence. The problem of incompetence may arise in the family business in two areas. The first situation involves the relative who assumes the position of chief executive simply because of birthright. The experience, education, intelligence, and work ethic required to manage the business successfully may be lacking. The second situation involves hiring incompetent family members. Helping out an incompetent family member not only may lead to disappointment and damage to the business but can have a disruptive effect on the nonfamily employees.

Nonfamily Employee Attitudes. One common characteristic of family-owned businesses is high turnover of nonfamily employees. Many young employees see no chance for promotion to management in the company because they are not part of the family. As a result, they may gain experience in the business and then leave for other organizations that offer the opportunity for promotion.

Objectives of Family Owners. In most family businesses, more than one member of the family owns shares or has an ownership interest in the business. Because these owners may be from different generations, have different levels of involvement in the business, and have various backgrounds and needs, differences of opinion regarding the operations of the business are common.

For example, owners who are actively involved in building up the business often want to reinvest more of the earnings in the business. The nonactive owners or shareholders, on the other hand, may want their share of the profits to be distributed as dividends or payments to themselves.

Objectives regarding the growth of the business may also differ. Sometimes younger members of the family want to expand the business or make capital expenditures that older family owners are more conservative or cautious about making. Both situations can lead to conflicts that have a detrimental effect on the long-term progress of the business.

Planning for Succession

Entrepreneurs.About
www.entrepreneurs.
about.com/
smallbusiness/
entrepreneurs/cs/
personnelplanning

The owner-manager has both a difficult task and an excellent opportunity in preparing children to become involved in the business. Some difficulties include providing the proper training, adequate motivation, and supportive atmosphere so that the child is able and wants to come into the business. Research shows that fewer than 50 percent of children who come from family businesses expect to return after receiving their college or university education, and only 20 percent plan to return to the business within five years of their graduation from college.[9] Other studies indicate that 70 percent of family businesses are either liquidated or sold after the founder retires.[10] It is apparently difficult for the parent to instill in the child the personal interest in the business the parent has. One school of thought is that parents may take too passive a role in attempting to interest their children in the business. They assume the children will find a profession more interesting and rewarding for them.[11] A common scenario is that of the parent-owner who is unwilling to give up control or allow the child a say in the business. On the other hand, it is also common for the inexperienced child to want to make changes the parent believes will be detrimental to the business. Incident 15-2 (on the next page) illustrates such a situation.

Incident 15-2

Charles Northstrup

Life in a family business has its ups and downs, but Brett Northstrup knew more about the downs. He had worked for his parents in the family furniture store all his life. "I grew up with the idea that I was going to work in the business; my parents told me the business was for me," said Brett. So there was never any leeway or choice as to what he was going to do as an adult. He was going to work there, so he did. But when it came time for his dad, Charles Northstrup, to retire, he wouldn't. He wanted Brett to take over the business, yet he didn't want him to do it because it was taking something away from him. Charles Northstrup now said, "I don't know if I ever will want to retire. I'd just take it a little easier someday, because I know I'd miss all the friends I've made, all the customers—they're just like friends. Besides, I'm not sure Brett can handle the business yet; he just doesn't run the business my way."

After 15 years with the business, Bret had finally had enough. He left and started over, leaving his parents to run the business their way.

Source: Rick Heyland, University of Lethbridge.

Running a family business also offers a great opportunity to provide on-the-job training and background for the child that is not otherwise possible. The parent-owner can also assess the child's progress and level of preparation over a longer period of time than would be possible if hiring an outsider to manage the business. In addition, the owner-manager's business philosophy and style may be taught to the child who is apprenticing for management and ownership of the business. Incident 15-3 illustrates this situation.

Principles of Success for Family Businesses. The preceding section has demonstrated the many difficulties that can arise in a family business. As was illustrated, these difficulties can be detrimental to the success of the business and damaging to family relationships. If the owner-manager is concerned about succession, planning for it should commence immediately rather than waiting until health or other circumstances force or prevent action. If one is involved in a family business or is contemplating bringing family members into the business, the following practices may help prevent some of the aforementioned difficulties from arising.

Draft a Succession Plan. This should clearly describe roles, responsibilities and financial arrangements including tax consequences of succession.

Recognize the Importance of Objectivity. Evaluations and supervision involving family members should be done on an objective basis. Even if tempted to do otherwise, the owner-manager must attempt to separate family discussions and emotions from business activities. Care should be taken to ensure that consistent policies are followed for both family and nonfamily employees. Many owner-managers have found it essential to separate their children physically and functionally from themselves and one another to prevent such difficulties from arising.

Create Clear Role Structures. The solution to the problem of the blurring of roles may be difficult to implement, as much of the control may be exerted informally. A clear definition of the roles, objectives, and responsibilities of all associated family members may help solve the difficulty. Separation of business and family goals and systems has also been recommended to alleviate this problem.[12]

Ensure Competence. Because an incompetent owner-manager can spell disaster for the business, providing the heir with technical and practical training, along with increasing decision-making authority, is vital. This may involve encouraging the family member to acquire some necessary skills outside the business at a college, a university, or another business

Incident 15-3

Sibling Success!

Transferring the family business to one's children can result in many problems. The Maran siblings of MaranGraphics Inc. recognized this, and with the help of their father and company founder, Richard Maran, ensured a smooth succession.

Richard Maran, now 62, started the Mississauga instructional book publishing company in 1975 out of the family's basement in Oakville, Ontario. After a futile attempt to make technological manuals user-friendly at his job with Canada Ltd., Richard quit and founded MaranGraphics Inc. The company's future management was still in diapers when Richard began designing customized software training manuals for insurance companies and banks. Eventually, the company switched from designing custom instruction manuals to mass-marketed computer books. This switch occurred after experiencing success with the design of a WordPerfect 5.1 manual for DOS. This particular manual went on to sell 80,000 copies across Canada despite its original creation for CIBC in 1990. Around this time, the Maran children became involved in MaranGraphics.

The transfer of the family business from Richard to his children was a gradual process. When the publishing company became more successful, the children took a keen interest in becoming involved. Rob, 29, who studied economics at York University and always exhibited interest in the family business, is now president. Pressure for the female siblings to join MaranGraphics came from Rob. Ruth Maran, 29, now writes the books for MaranGraphics Inc. and has sold six million copies with titles such as *Internet* and *World Wide Web Simplified*. Judy, 27, is the project manager, and Jill, 25, is in charge of accounting and human resources at MaranGraphics.

Successful succession of this family business was the result of many factors. The Marans do not allow personal grievances to hinder business obligations and opportunities. Being good friends and holding regular family events is the trick to making things work, but the key to this success is separating work from family life. "When work is done, work is done. We make a point of it," Rob says. Ensuring that each sibling has his or her own area to manage at MaranGraphics has also resulted in a successful transfer. Giving the company to his children really became important in 1996 when Richard's wife, Maxine, was diagnosed with breast cancer. Richard had no reservations about his children's ability to run the business because they were already doing it very effectively. Richard is still consulted on big, long-term decisions by his family. MaranGraphics Inc. now has 30 employees and annual worldwide sales of $30 million.

SOURCE: Adapted from Jeff Gray, "Marans Write the Book on Sibling Success," *The Globe and Mail*, November 10, 1999, p. M-1.

before returning to become fully involved. Many potential inheritors of businesses appear to follow this route to the ownership of the family business.[13] If a competent family member is not available, the remaining family owners may be able to persuade the owner-manager to let a more capable individual run the day-to-day affairs of the company.

If training does not improve the performance of incompetent relatives but for family reasons it is not possible to let the employee go, some owner-managers place such an employee in a position where he or she can do the least harm to the company.

Provide Incentives for Nonfamily Employees. To maintain the loyalty of nonfamily employees and ensure that they stay with the company, the owner-manager will need to devise various rewards and incentives. These incentives can be financial or may involve including employees in decision-making and educational programs. It may still be impossible to retain an energetic young employee who desires to eventually rise to the top of the organization unless the owner-manager is prepared to give up some of the ownership or authority of the business.

Clarify Objectives of Family Owners. To prevent disharmony resulting from differing objectives of family members, it is important to formally clarify the long- and short-term objectives of the company. These might include objectives for such areas as expansion and distribution of profits. Some firms distribute a set percentage of profits in dividends or reinvest a specified amount back into the business annually.

Planning for Succession. Care should be taken to nurture and prepare the child to take over the business with the same enthusiasm the owner has. This can best be done by including the heir in the business at an early age. It will also mean giving up a certain amount of control of the business, often before the owner-manager feels ready to do so. Incident 15-4 illustrates how this was done in one Canadian company. As mentioned earlier, it may be beneficial for the child to gain training and experience outside the business. Successful transfers between parents and children usually involve considerable compromise on the part of both parties. Figure 15-2 provides questions that should be asked before transferring the business to an heir.

Figure 15-2 Mom and Pop Quiz: How Succession-Ready Is Your Company?

Consider this a final exam that your family business should take before it advances from one generation to the next. Developed by Scott E. Freidman, an attorney, author, and consultant specializing in family-business issues, the Family Business Scorecard is a comprehensive, 100-question survey designed to identify problem areas, especially those that can directly impact a planned succession. "Three types of people should take this quiz," Friedman explains. "Adult family members who work in the business, adult family members who don't work in the business but are stakeholders, and key non-family employees and advisers, such as the firm's lawyer, accountant, and financial planner. How much of a consensus there is among the participants can be as revealing as the answers themselves."

We've adapted 10 "yes" or "no" questions from the quiz to help give readers a quick take on how they're doing.

1. Our family has customized its decision-making process to require various levels of consent (by different family members or outside advisers) for issues of varying significance.
2. Our key non-family employees are satisfied with the manner in which family members are brought into and employed by our business.
3. All family members, regardless of sex or birth order, will be considered as possible successors for the business.
4. Our succession criteria include formal education, job experience outside our business, and job experience inside our business with increasing responsibility.
5. A written agreement establishes rules for buying, selling, and transferring ownership interest in our business.
6. If our business leader suffered a catastrophe, our family would be prepared to react.
7. Spouses of family members have a meaningful form in which to air their views on subjects affecting the business.
8. Adult family members have begun working on their estate plan.
9. Senior family members approaching retirement age look forward to pursuing interests outside our business.
10. Our family has considered the merits of adopting an alternative dispute-resolution mechanism in the event of family conflict.

If you answered "no" to five or more of these questions, or if the people in your company who took the test gave different answers to the same questions more than four times, your business would benefit from a more complete analysis by an adviser. Freidman's law firm, Buffalo-based Lippes, Silverstein, Mathias and Wexier LLP (716-853-5100; sfriedman@lippes.com), charges $2,500 for a complete survey and follow-up analysis.

Source: "Mom and Pop Quiz: How Succession-Ready is Your Company?" *Success,* December 1998, p. 80.

Incident 15-4

Passing the Torch

Ralph Cator began thinking about succession planning in 1981, when he was just 45 and his four children were in their late teens and early 20s. By 1994, his oldest son, Mark, now 39, was ready to take the reins of Mississauga, Ontario-based Cardinal Meat Specialists Ltd.

On the other hand, Charles Flavelle, then 65, gave little thought to retirement or succession planning until four years ago. He had a vague notion that when the time felt right, he would put Purdy's Chocolates—his 45-store chain of retail candy shops based in Vancouver, B.C.—up for sale.

He didn't feel he was old or facing death, so it wasn't an issue, says his oldest daughter Karen Flavelle.

He had no intention of passing Purdy's to any of his three children, having encouraged them all to pursue their own passions. His son became a professional mountaineer; one daughter teaches indigenous people to map their forests. Karen, 41, the only child to pursue a business career, spent 15 years working her way up to middle management in the restaurant packaged-goods industry—before she waltzed into her father's office in 1993 with a well-thought-out plan to take over Purdy's. Charles did something unusual for a business owner of his generation. He agreed.

SOURCE: Jayne Pearl, "Passing the Torch," *The Costco Connection,* November–December 1998, p. 19.

Keeping Communication Lines Open. Perhaps the most effective aspect of operating a family business successfully is open communication. Given many potential areas of conflict, differences of opinion must be communicated to the relevant parties before they develop into a serious problem. Formalized objectives, plans, roles, and procedures can accomplish this. Incident 15-5 illustrates some of the communication problems which exist in some family businesses.

Tax and Legal Implications of Transferring the Business to Family Members. An increasingly complex consideration in transferring a business to heirs is the legal and tax implications. One specific tax consequence of transfers of business ownership within a fam-

Incident 15-5

Daughters Learn from Mentoring Moms

Daughters and mothers in business say the payoffs are many, including an up-close opportunity to learn from the mother's experience and example, often watching as the student breaks new ground or overcomes hurdles. There is a unique parental pride in watching a family business succeed.

Heather Black enthusiastically describes how her mother, Mary, was the first woman in North America to start a business in colour separation. Heather now helps run that business, Toronto-based Colour Technologies.

But the Blacks learned that a working relationship isn't for every family member. Another daughter, Brenda, worked in production with her mother but found the challenge of being the boss's daughter too much. "The third time she offered her resignation I accepted it," Mary says.

Heather says the key to a successful team is respect, adding that it is vital to recognize the nature of mother-daughter relations. "A mother will talk to a daughter differently than an employee. There's a lot of emotion and you are going to be treated differently."

Heather says one characteristic of a mother-daughter relationship may be a deeper sense of loyalty. "I've seen businesses where sons have gone into competition with their fathers. If I were to leave, I'd go off and start something from scratch."

SOURCE: Catherine Mulroney, *The Globe and Mail,* May 10, 1996, p. B7.

ily concerns capital gains. In Canada one-half of the capital gain (defined as the increase in value of the asset since acquisition of the business or 1972, whichever is shorter) upon the sale is added to the income of the person disposing of the asset (business). This rule applies a "deemed disposition" rule (to family) in that the business is "deemed" to have been sold at market price whether or not the market price was actually paid.

In the past, the federal government allowed a tax-free rollover or capital gains deferral to spouse and children up to a maximum capital gain of $200,000. This applied to Canadian-controlled private corporations. If the heir sold the shares (or business) to someone outside the family, the capital gain would be realized and a resulting tax liability incurred. In the budget of May 23, 1985, the federal government introduced a $500,000 lifetime capital gains exemption, to be phased in gradually. This provision allows for the transfer of ownership of the business with little capital gains consequence, whether or not the business is an incorporated company.

Obviously these changes have affected the tax consequences of transferring the business to heirs. While most of these changes have been positive from the point of view of the small business, they are complex and may differ by province. Therefore, counsel should be sought from a legal and/or tax expert before making a decision in this area.

Methods of Transferring the Business to Family Members. In deciding which method to use in transferring all or part of the business to the heirs, the owner-manager first needs to clarify his or her own objectives in making the transfer. Some common transfer-related objectives are the following:

- The owner-manager wants to keep a reasonable amount of control over the business until the heirs are of an age and competence level to assume their responsibilities.

- Although the owner-manager wants to maintain control of the business, he or she also wants the heir(s) to maintain their interest and commitment to the business.

- The owner-manager desires to distribute the business assets (ownership) so that the heirs (if more than one) will recognize this distribution as fair.

- The owner-manager wants sufficient access to income or assets from the transfer of the business to maintain an adequate standard of living.

- The owner-manager wants to achieve an orderly transfer of the business to minimize the tax consequences for both parties.

Some of the most common methods of transferring ownership to the heir(s) are discussed next.

Through a Will. When the transfer is made through a will, ownership of the business does not pass to the heir until the owner dies. This method may satisfy the owner's objective of maintaining control of the business, but it fails to address any of the other objectives mentioned. For example, serious tax consequences may arise if the business is unincorporated. In such a situation, the previous owner's income is calculated at the date of death. If the business has an irregular business cycle and a death occurs at the wrong time of the year, a large income (and higher tax liability) may result. The heirs would then have to deal with this tax liability.

Purchase and Sale of the Business. This method may not satisfy the owner's objectives unless it takes place gradually over a number of years. Such an agreement can remain flexible within the family to accomplish the objectives of both the owner and the heirs. A "deemed disposition" is viewed to have taken place at market value whether or not that amount was actually paid. Purchasing the business gradually may provide an incentive for the heir and also allow the parent to maintain the desired control for the required period of time.

Gifting Program. In the absence of gift taxes, part or all of the business may be gifted to the heir(s). The most common method of doing this is gradually, over several years. This option is likely feasible only if the owner is not dependent on proceeds of the sale for his or her income.

Life Estate. A life estate is used primarily when the significant assets are real property. This method transfers the ownership or title of land or buildings to the heir, with the condition that the previous owner has a position of control until he or she dies. The extent of control can diminish as the heir becomes more involved in the business. Immediately upon the parent's death, the title automatically passes to the heir. This method accomplishes many of the aforementioned objectives.

Selling the Business to Outsiders

If the owner-manager is not able or does not wish to keep the business in the family, he or she may decide to sell all or part of the business to someone outside the family. Incident 15-6 describes a recent example of such a decision for a family business. This action, of course, could be taken at any time, not just when the owner-manager is ready to retire. Regardless of

---

Incident 15-6

Business Book Store Turns New Page

Jane Cooney many not be part of the family tree. But Mary Britnell-Fisher figures Ms. Cooney shares an entrepreneurial kinship that entitles her to carry on the Britnell name.

Ms. Britnell-Fisher belongs to the family that for four generations has maintained a downtown Toronto landmark — Albert Britnell Book Shop, which dates back to 1893. Ms. Cooney is president of a business book store operation that is independent and focused on personal service.

Last week, Ms. Britnell-Smith announced, to the shock of both staff and family members, that the shop's legendary special orders division would be sold for an undisclosed price to Ms. Cooney's outfit, Books for Business.

Ms. Britnell-Fisher, widow of the store founder's grandson, is getting out of the book business after agonizing over her decision for more than a year.

"They (Books for Business), have the same philosophy as we do," she explains.

"You try to see where the fit is and see how you're going to look after your customers. Only a small independent is going to make the fit because they understand."

The special orders division of each company will be amalgamated under the name Britnell Book Wholesalers.

With the acquisition, Books for Business will expand its current offering of about 11,000 titles in size and in range of topics. While keeping its foothold in the business community, the company is positioning itself to take a larger bite out of the overall North American book trade.

"It allows us to expand our business, but still to do what we know how to do," Ms. Cooney says.

The Books for Business expansion is also a strategic move to cater to a growing number of "virtual" customers.

"The whole face of book retailing has changed dramatically," Ms. Cooney says. "There's a huge trend toward shopping from home and using electronic ordering devices of various kinds."

Len Kubas, a Toronto-based retail analyst, says special book orders placed by phone, fax, and E-mail have been increasing despite warnings by critics that the electronic era would cause the demise of the printed word.

Source: "Business Book Store Turns New page," *The Globe and Mail,* February 1, 1999, p. B 5. Reprinted with permission from *The Globe and Mail.*

when the business is sold, however, the owner-manager should realize that the last few years' performance will affect the purchase price. Therefore, careful planning should be done to ensure that the business's performance is as positive as possible prior to the sale.

Many of the aspects of selling a business are discussed in Chapter 5 regarding the informational requirements of the prospective purchaser. The seller of the business must now prepare this information and make it available to a prospective buyer. Particularly important is information on the financial condition of the business as represented by the financial statements. A listing of any hidden assets or capabilities that do not show up on the balance sheet should be made. The asset valuation and earnings methods discussed in Chapter 5 can assist in setting an asking price for the business. Most buyers will thoroughly review these statements, particularly the earnings record, to determine how accurately they portray the business.

Another critical area in selling the business includes the terms of the sale. Timing of payments may have considerable tax consequences. Some of these consequences have been reduced, however, by the alternative minimum tax provisions. Often the purchaser wants the previous owner to remain in the business in an advisory capacity. This arrangement (with appropriate compensation) can be included in the purchase agreement.

One possible outcome of selling the business may apply to a partner or other owner. As mentioned in Chapter 4, a buy/sell clause should be a part of the partnership agreement. This clause should be carefully worded to account for future differences in the value of the firm.

Sometimes small businesses are purchased by larger companies in the form of a merger. The acquiring company is usually looking to expand or capitalize on some unique advantage or capability the small business has. For example, purchasing a small business may allow a company to capitalize on such strengths as a unique product, market access, or expertise it could not otherwise obtain. In many such situations, the owner-manager of the smaller business is retained in the organization. Incident 15-7 is an example of such an arrangement.

Incident 15-7

Microsoft Buys Out Ontario Gamers

Microsoft Corporation
www.microsoft.com

Two Waterloo couples who developed a computer game business in late 1997 have sold the company to Microsoft Corp. and are moving to Washington state to work for the software giant.

When Microsoft officials made that pitch to the founder of ShadowFactor Software Inc. in April, they didn't spend a lot of time agonizing over whether they should hang on to their brainchild, which lets people playing computer games talk to each other by voice over the Internet.

Paul Newson, his wife, Isabella Carniato, and Rod and Joanne Toll established the business two years after trying out a voice over Internet communications system called Battlefield Communicator. They knew they were on to something when an announcement seeking "beta testers" to try out an early version of the product drew 1,000 e-mail responses in 48 hours.

When the four quit their jobs to work at the company full time, "it was a leap of faith," Newson said. "We knew there was potential there, but it wasn't going to be there forever."

Microsoft wanted both the technology and the people behind it, thinking "if they could do it once, they could do it again," he said.

Microsoft plans to incorporate the product into DirectX 8.0, a multimedia technology that will be part of the next Windows operating system, due for release in the summer of 2000.

SOURCE: Adapted from the *Toronto Star*, June 11, 1999, p. E4.

Often, however, this relationship is short-lived because the former owner is uncomfortable with his or her lack of independence in the new arrangement.

The owner-manager may want to sell only a part of the business. This is accomplished much more easily if the business is incorporated to allow a share transfer to take place. In such a case, the owner-manager may be able to retain control over the business while obtaining capital needed as payment for the shares.

Going Public. Sometimes a small business that has been successful but has a need or desire for a significant amount of capital sells shares to the public. This is called an initial public offering (IPO) and the corporate status changes from a private to a public company. The advantages and disadvantages of this form of equity investment are discussed in Chapter 7. Sometimes owners regret the move to go public rather than selling shares privately. Figure 15-3 illustrates a comparison of public versus private placement. Going public may also allow control of the business to remain with the owner-manager if over 50 percent of the shares are not sold. The business should address the following issues if it is planning an IPO.[14]

- Improve the company's overall capital structure and financial performance
- Review staff needs including the need for a strong management team
- Strengthen the organization through purchase or sale of particular business units
- Structure the board to include strong outside directors
- Plan for effective distribution of earnings

One or more of the following characteristics may indicate that the small business is in a favourable position to go public:[15]

- The company is in a popular specialized market.
- The company is in an above-average growth position.
- The business has a strong market niche and proven sales appeal in an emerging rather than a mature industry.
- The business can and does generate a return on equity of at least 20 to 25 percent.
- The company has at least $10 million in annual revenues.
- The company has strong management.
- The company has reached the point where it needs a substantial amount of capital for growth and expansion.

Figure 15-3 Implications of Selling Shares

	Going Public	**Private Placement**
Shareholders	Many new shareholders	Few investors
Importance of earnings	High	Low
Importance of stock performance	Short term	Long term
Investor communication required	Extensive	Limited
Board of directors	Independent members	Strategic members

Source: *The Globe and Mail,* June 12, 1996, p. B7.

If the owner-manager finds it necessary or desires that the firm's shares be offered to the public, the services of an investment dealer may be helpful. An investment dealer (or underwriter) will assist the owner by acting as the marketer for the stock. The investment dealer can use an over-the-counter market, one that includes securities that are not sold on the stock exchange. If this method is followed, a reputable investment dealer with substantial connections throughout the investment community should be selected.

Alternatively, shares can be sold on the stock exchange. To obtain a listing, however, the business must meet several requirements, and many small firms lack the performance record needed to attract investors.

Closing Down or Going Bankrupt

The third possible outcome for the business—generally a result of unsatisfactory performance—involves closing down, being placed into receivership, or going bankrupt. These are, of course, the least desirable outcomes for the small business. As discussed in Chapter 2, however, each year many small businesses end up in this situation because of lack of profitability. Closing down is much easier for an unincorporated business than for a limited company. In theory, the incorporated company is required to file dissolution forms and notify government agencies. Although this is the case if the company does not have a large debt load, the incorporated company has more protection in a debt situation because of its limited liability.

Business Bankruptcy. In 2000, a total of 10,040 business bankruptcies were declared in Canada.[16] The majority of those failures were small businesses. If the business debts are significantly greater than assets and the earning power of the business is inadequate to service future obligations, the owner-manager may face two options.

First, a major creditor may appoint a receiver and the business is placed in receivership. When a company is in receivership, the receiver enlists the services of another agency in an attempt to manage it out of financial difficulty. As this may be difficult to do, receivership is often a forerunner to bankruptcy.

The second option is to consult an accountant. If the accountant's recommendation is to see a licensed trustee for bankruptcy, an assignment usually takes place. When this happens, the debtor (the small business) assigns its assets to the trustee, who in turn meets with the creditors. The assets are converted to cash and distributed to the creditors to repay as much of the debt as possible. These assets are distributed using a priority system. Secured creditors—those who have signed security for some of the debt (including the trustee)—have first priority to proceeds of the deposition. Preferred creditors such as employees, landlords, or government departments have second priority, followed by ordinary unsecured creditors.

Frequently ordinary creditors may receive little or none of the money owed them. This is a significant point, since most small businesses themselves are ordinary creditors in their business dealings. Thus, they often lose out when a business with which they are dealing goes bankrupt.

If a proprietorship or a partnership of individuals goes bankrupt, the owner-manager is allowed to retain certain necessary assets. It is also possible for an owner of an incorporated business to declare personal bankruptcy in order to be protected from the liabilities of a failing business. It is still possible for a bankrupt individual to start another business at a later date. In fact, some businesses enter into voluntary bankruptcy, which allows them to dissolve quickly and get reestablished. Once bankrupt, however, a person's credit rating is weaker than before, and obtaining debt financing may be difficult. There are also significant "human" costs for a company that goes bankrupt. A lawyer should be consulted if this type of bankruptcy is being contemplated.

Although bankruptcy is becoming more common, it can be a difficult and damaging experience that could have been avoided in 70 to 90 percent of the cases had financial difficulties been spotted and acted on early.[17] Owner-managers who have developed and are using financial management concepts as discussed in Chapter 10 should be in a better position to avoid bankruptcy.

Summary

1. Planning for the eventual transfer of the business is an important component of small business management. Some of the more common methods of transferring ownership of a business to family members are through a will, a sale of the business to the heirs, a gifting program, and a life estate.

2. The unique problems of a family business are higher emotional levels, blurring of roles, incompetence, nonfamily employee turnover, differing objectives among family owners, and planning for succession.

3. Sometimes a small business that has been successful but needs a significant amount of capital may sell shares to the public to meet financial needs while retaining control of the company.

4. A business that cannot be transferred can be closed down, be placed in receivership, or file for bankruptcy.

Chapter Problems and Applications

1. How could Charles Northstrup have satisfied both his son's career demands and his own desires and still effectively run their furniture store (Incident 15-2)?

2. Jim Duncan is the owner-manager of a local restaurant chain. In its earlier years, the three local family restaurants were very successful. Then a recession came, and the businesses did not do as well. Jim is 60 years old and is thinking about retirement or semi-retirement. He has a son who has managed one of the restaurants, but he is not sure Jim, Jr., is ready for the problems existing in the whole operation. If you were Jim, Sr., how would you transfer ownership? Explain your decision.

3. Your father has just made you president of the family sand and gravel company. You want to computerize the payroll and the accounts payable and receivable, but your father doesn't see the need for the extra expense when expenses are already too high. What two problems exist here? How would you resolve this conflict as the newly appointed president?

4. Your parents have just made you the manager of your family's grocery store. Since the transition, problems have seldom been brought to your attention, and you have received little feedback on your instructions. What problems might be evident? How would you solve these problems?

5. Hamilton Rogers is the owner-manager of a successful machine shop. In the last year, he has promoted his sons to floor managers. Recently several employees have also left the company. What factors could be responsible for the employees leaving their jobs? How could Hamilton have prevented this problem?

6. Interview the manager of a family-owned and operated business. What unique problems are evident?

7. Interview someone who is a future heir of a family business and is now going to school or gaining business experience. What problems are evident from his or her perspective? Does this person want to go back to the business? Why or why not?

8. Pomaona Fastener Company has suffered several years of operating losses. Because of the unfavourable outlook for the firm, it filed for bankruptcy and was dissolved. On liquidation $570,000 was received, to be split among the following creditors:

Accounts payable	$100,000
Secured loans from bank	400,000
Accrued wages	10,000
Rent due on building	20,000
Government loan	300,000
Trustee's fee	10,000

What would be the priority of payment, and how much would each class of creditor receive?

9. Interview the owner-manager of a small business that recently went public, and find out what he or she learned through the experience.

Suggested Readings

"Are Canadian Family Businesses an Endangered Species?" Deloitte and Touche, Toronto, 1999. http://www.deloitte.ca/pub/tax/Familybus/highlights

Book, Howard. "Father-son Team—All We Do Is Fight." *The Globe and Mail,* April 24, 1995, p. B6.

Church, Elizabeth. "Leadership Crisis Forseen for Family Business." *The Globe and Mail,* January 18, 1999, p. B13.

Gallagher, David. "The Seven Deadly Sins of the Family Business." *Hardware Merchandising,* February–March, 1999, pp. 38–40.

Leach, Peter, Bruce Ball, Garry Duncan. *Guide to the Family Business, Canadian Edition.* BDO Dunwoody, Toronto: September 2000.

McFarland, Janet, and Gordon Pitts. "Family Firms Fumble Passing the Torch." *The Globe and Mail,* October 9, 1995, p. B7.

McLarney, Michael. "Succession. Can the Next Generation Afford to Keep the Doors Open?" *Centre Magazine,* July/August 1997, p.14.

Stern, Deborah. "Giving Your Kids the Business." *Canadian Grocer,* February 1999, pp. 39–45.

Stevens, Mark. "When to Take Your Company Public." *Entrepreneurial Manager's Newsletter* 7, no. 4 (1986), p. 4.

"Succession Planning: A Way Out for Founders." *The Globe and Mail,* October 26, 1998, p. C6.

Wuorio, Jeff. "The Succession Crisis." *Success,* December 1998, pp. 76–81.

Video Case Questions
Wild West*

CBC ⬤

A family from Southern Ontario hits the road all summer to find out whether there is an appetite for a wild west show in the '90s.

1. What does this case illustrate about the problems of operating a family business?

2. Discuss the difference in the goals of the family members in this business?

*Source: CBC *Venture* #658, running time 11:45.

Cases for Part IV

Bailey's Office Supply	James Macreary's Estate
Baker Hardware Ltd.	Rick's Place
Brian Luborsky – Premier Salons	Weiss Manufacturing Company

BAILEY'S OFFICE SUPPLY

D. Wesley Balderson
University of Lethbridge

In 1956, John Bailey left a major department store chain where he worked as the hardware department manager to open his own office supply store. John had worked for the chain for over 15 years and had become very knowledgeable about the business. He felt, however, that he could develop a successful business by offering more personalized customer service than the larger stores could. By 1966 the firm, Bailey's Office Supply, had become a large and well-known establishment in Toronto with three outlets. The firm had no particular specialties but did carry a very extensive line of all basic office supplies, typewriters, and adding machines and a limited line of office furniture. Its strength was, as John Bailey had intended, its superior customer service. John was careful to properly train his employees to know not only their products but also their customers' needs.

In 1976, John Bailey's son, Marty, was finishing college in business administration and had decided to join his father in the business. Marty had worked from time to time for his father and thought that he might enjoy the business. John had told Marty, however, to get an education first and that if he decided to work at Bailey's, he would have a job. Although John had made this offer to Marty, he was concerned because he had a younger son and an older daughter and wondered how they would react to Marty being brought into the company.

Marty joined Bailey's as assistant sales manager with the understanding that he would be given the job of sales manager upon the retirement of Kenneth Harker, which was due to take place in another three years. At the same time Marty's brother and sister along with Marty were placed on the board of directors for Bailey's. Although the board met only sporadically, it did have the authority to ratify major management decisions.

During the late 1970s both Baileys observed the phenomenal growth and development of the high-technology firms that occupied the "Golden Triangle" area in and around Toronto, Ottawa, and Montreal. This boom not only spawned the creation of many successful firms, but it signaled the introduction of many strong competitors for Bailey's. Some of these were warehouse stores, which offered a large assortment of office merchandise at very low prices. John Bailey still maintained that if Bailey's continued to offer its personal "down home" service this new competition would not seriously affect Bailey's.

Having known several persons who were a part of the technology boom, it was tempting for the Baileys to invest in newly created firms, knowing that the investments of several of their friends had been very successful. John Bailey however, was fairly conservative, and having built the business to a success was now looking forward to enjoying the fruits of his hard work by playing more golf and travelling with his wife for a month or two every year. He still retained controlling interest in the business and was opposed to making any outside investments. Marty, on the other hand, was anxious to take advantage of some of these opportunities and felt strongly that by adding lines of computer hardware and software to their merchandise line, Bailey's could increase sales. He felt, in fact, that Bailey's would have a difficult time competing with the office supply warehouses if they didn't move into this area. As this would require a rather major reinvestment of earnings back into the firm, John and his other son and daughter were reluctant to move in this direction. These disagreements were a source of frustration for Marty and he contemplated leaving the family business and starting his own high-tech office supply store.

By 1998 the effects of the competition and a cutback in building construction had reduced the total income of business and the profit of Bailey's by some 20 percent. It was a sobering turn of events for a firm that had experienced a long, steady expansion. In thinking about this, John Bailey felt that it might be wise to turn the management of the business over to Marty along with some of his ownership interest. Under John's proposal he would retain majority ownership of the company, and still come in to work part time but Marty would be responsible for the day-to-day operations. When John approached Marty with the proposal, he was shocked to hear that Marty had decided to leave the firm. John felt that he had given Marty a tremendous opportunity to learn about and then take over the business which he had built into a success. He could not understand why Marty could turn down such an offer.

Questions

1. Why would Marty want to leave the firm instead of accepting his father's offer?
2. What could be done now to salvage the situation and keep Marty with the company?
3. Assuming that Marty remained with the firm, what suggestions could be made to turn the business around?

BAKER HARDWARE LTD.

D. Wesley Balderson
University of Lethbridge

Baker Hardware Ltd. is a hardware store in the town of Souris, which is located in an agricultural area of southern Manitoba. Souris is 48 km south of Brandon (population 55,000), which is the major trading centre for many smaller towns within a 100 km radius.

Mr. Baker, the owner of Baker Hardware, is contemplating expanding his merchandise offering to include lumber and building supplies. Currently Baker's, in addition to a standard selection of hardware merchandise, carries paint and building tools; therefore, Mr. Baker thinks this new line would be fairly compatible.

Baker Hardware was a part of the Home Hardware network of dealers, a nationwide group of hardware stores and home centres located primarily in smaller towns and cities. For the past few years, Home Hardware had been encouraging its dealers to expand into building supplies. Concerned that there was another lumber yard in Souris (which happened to be next door to Baker Hardware), Mr. Baker had shown little interest in such a move in the past.

Recently, however, he became aware that this lumberyard, Banner Building Supplies, was for sale or would be closed down. Mr. Baker gathered information from both the owners of Banner as well as from Home Hardware and was in the process of making a decision. As Mr. Baker saw it, he had three choices: (1) purchase Banner Building Supplies, (2) expand into building supplies through Home Hardware on his own premises, or (3) maintain current operations (not expanding into building materials).

The Market

As previously mentioned, Souris was a small town of about 2,000 located in an agricultural area of southern Manitoba. The estimated population of surrounding area farms was 500. The town was located 48 km southwest of Brandon, the major trading centre for the area. Over the years, the retail communities in most of the small towns close to Brandon had deteriorated due to the strong competition of retailers there and the increased mobility of consumers. The building supply industry was no exception. Such chains as Canadian Tire and Beaver Lumber, which had outlets in Brandon, had attracted numerous customers from these rural communities.

The population of Souris consisted mainly of farmers, commuters who worked in Brandon, and professionals such as teachers who worked in the town. The town had experienced some growth in recent years because of its relaxed atmosphere and excellent recreational facilities. Projections indicated the population could reach 2,500 by the year 2005.

Baker Hardware

Baker Hardware had operated successfully in Souris for many years. Mr. Baker had purchased the store from his father, and with changes and modernizations, increased sales from $450,000 in 1978 to 800,000 in 2000. Although sales showed a significant increase, profits did not. The strong competition from hardware chains in Brandon in recent years had eroded Mr. Baker's profit margin. Baker Hardware's competitive strength had always been that it catered to the agricultural community. Unfortunately, farm incomes had experienced considerable volatility in recent years, and this trend directly affected Baker Hardware's profit performance.

Baker Hardware currently had 12,000 square feet of selling space and a large (8,000-square-foot) warehouse. Mr. Baker believed that if he went into building supplies he could, with some renovations, free up about half of the warehouse space to house the new merchandise.

Baker Hardware's current financial situation, while not serious, was such that if a capital investment were made, Mr. Baker would have to borrow to finance it. At the current interest rate of 14 percent, this was a concern for Mr. Baker.

Home Hardware

Home Hardware Ltd. is a well-established franchise system of dealer-owners located across Canada. Originating in southern Ontario, it has expanded to become a dominant small-town retailer of hardware merchandise. Recently Home Hardware moved into the building supply industry in an attempt to capitalize on the growth of the home centre concept. Home has been encouraging its dealers to branch into this area, and many have done so.

Mr. Baker obtained from Home Hardware a list of the recommended product assortment for a home building supply dealer. A summary of this list, along with space requirements and markups, appears in Figure 1 on the next page. Home Hardware also suggested that Mr. Baker would need a forklift (estimated cost $15,000, used), a delivery truck (estimated cost $10,000, used), and a shed of at least 5,000 square feet (estimated cost $5,000).

Banner Building Supplies

Banner Building Supplies was a family-owned business that had operated in Souris for over 40 years. It was owned by two brothers, both close to retirement age, who also owned a window and door manufacturing plant. As the manufacturing plant was much larger in size and scope of operations, the Banners had devoted most of their time and energy to this business. The retail building supplies outlet had, over the years, taken second priority in their business interests, although it provided a stable and needed outlet for the town.

Interest in selling the retail outlet resulted from two major factors. First, both brothers wanted to cut back on their work responsibilities, as both were approaching retirement age and had no family members interested in taking over the business. However, one brother had a son-in-law who was interested in the manufacturing part of the business. Second, the profitability of the retail outlet had suffered in recent years due to strong competition from larger hardware chains and home centres in Brandon. Some of these competitors could sell certain types of lumber and other supplies at lower prices than Banner's costs. The estimated profit and loss statement Mr. Baker obtained from Banners for 2000 is shown in Figure 2. Currently Banner Building Supplies has approximately $75,000 in inventory (see Figure 3) and owns a large lot containing some sheds and a showroom next door to Baker Hardware. The estimated value of real estate and buildings is approximately $25,000. The company has no debt.

Figure 1   Recommended Home Building Supply Full Product Assortment

Product	Cost	Suggested Markup on Cost	Estimated Turnover	Space Requirement
Insulation	$4,000	25%	4.0	600
Doors and mouldings (complete assortment)	6,000	30	2.5	900
Plywood (complete assortment, 2 pallets each)	10,000	15	5.5	2,100
Drywall (complete assortment, 2 pallets each)	6,000	15	4.5	600
Cement	2,000	30	5.0	180
Roofing materials	5,000	25	3.5	600
Nails	1,000	30	5.0	120
Siding, soffit, facia	6,000	30	2.0	900
Dimensional lumber, 2 3 4, 2 3 6, etc. (complete assortment, 2 pallets each)	20,000	15	6.0	3,000
	$60,000			9,000

In looking at the merchandise requirements recommended by Home Hardware, Mr. Baker noted that Banner's inventory levels were different. Mr. Baker discussed this with the previous manager of Banner's and learned that some building supplies did not sell well in Souris. He informed Mr. Baker that the standard types of lumber (plywoods, 2 3 4's, etc.) were the steady sellers, although warpage caused considerable waste in dimensional lumber. He also mentioned that it was very difficult to compete with the city building centres for the large contractors' business. The major market for Banner's had been the small contractor (renovators) and the do-it-yourself customer.

Armed with the above information, Mr. Baker was determined to make a decision.

Figure 2

Banner Building Supplies
Estimated Income Statement for 2000

Sales	$ 230,000	
Cost of goods sold (85%)	195,500	
Gross profit		$ 34,500
Expenses:		
Wages	22,500	
Taxes and licences	2,000	
Insurance	11,000	
Professional fees and admin.	500	
Utilities	2,000	
Fuel (trucks, etc.)	1,200	
Bad debts	1,000	
Depreciation	1,800	
Repairs and maintenance	1,000	
Misc. supplies	$ 500	$ 33,500
Net income before taxes		$ 1,000

Figure 3

Banner Building Supplies
Inventory Estimate

Insulation	$ 6,000
Doors and mouldings	24,000
Plywood	12,000
Drywall	7,000
Cement	1,000
Roofing materials	2,000
Nails, etc.	1,200
Siding	2,000
Dimensional lumber	35,000
Paints	2,500
Tools and hardware	2,500
Carpet and linoleum	$ 1,800
	$75,000

Questions

1. What other information should Mr. Baker obtain before he makes this decision?
2. Using the information provided, evaluate the alternatives Mr. Baker has identified. Be sure to evaluate the attractiveness of the proposed merchandise lines.
3. What other alternatives has Mr. Baker not explored?

BRIAN LUBORSKY—PREMIER SALONS INTERNATIONAL INC.

Wesley Balderson
University of Lethbridge

Brian Luborsky started out his business career as a chartered accountant with Coopers and Lybrand. It didn't take long for him to realize, however, that he wanted to be part of something that was more growth-oriented and which allowed him to be more entrepreneurial. He still remembers the day he decided to quit. His boss wanted him to write a memo, but Luborsky, who was building and buying houses on the side, was working to save $50,000 on a property to buy. "The deal was worth more than my annual salary," he laughs, "I wasn't doing myself any favours and I wasn't being fair to the company so I resigned."

Meanwhile he became interested in a new hair salon franchise called Magicuts. Magicuts had been established in 1981 as a discount haircut chain, which attempted to bring the McDonald's efficiency principles to hair salons. Luborsky joined Magicuts as a franchisee, purchasing four franchises in 1984. What lured him was the math. "There is such a high ratio of sales to assets in haircutting it was hard to go wrong," he says. "Say it costs $50,000 to set up shop. I can do $250,000 in sales in a year out of that store. Now, say I make 10 percent on that: I'm getting a 50 percent return on investment, and that's hard to beat."

In 1993 Luborsky considered expansion to the United States. He felt that his company was in a position to grow and he became aware of a chain of hair salons, which he felt could fit in with the system which he had developed for Magicuts. After difficult negotiations for financing, he was successful in acquiring a large financially troubled Minneapolis-based chain of hair salons —MEI Salons. MEI had 1,600 outlets, three times as many as Magicuts, but was in need of financial and management stability which Luborsky could provide.

Luborsky's goal for growth is now centred in three areas. First he wants to continue to emphasize superior service in order to compete with the independent mom-and-pop salons which dominate the industry. Because of the size of the company, it can take advantage of economies of scale, and this allows investment in employees. As a result, Premier has invested heavily in extensive employee training. Premier's 76 trainers teach the latest styles and trends, as well as soft skills such as dealing with clients. His second push involves "partnerships" with well-known retailers, most of which are department stores. Magicuts is now installed in more than 100 Zellers stores. "The price fits well with our customers," says Zeller's Vice-President Garnet Kinch. Luborsky's third growth strategy is to seek out compatible chains and purchase them, similar to what occurred with MEI. Recently, Premier purchased 22 Boscov's salons in Pennsylvania.

Questions

1. What are some of the problems that Brian Luborsky will likely face with the expansion to the United States? What solutions can be suggested?
2. What questions should he have evaluated prior to the U.S. expansion?

JAMES MACREARY'S ESTATE

D. Wesley Balderson
University of Lethbridge

James Macreary had built up a large farm retail store in Elmira, an agricultural community near Guelph, Ontario. He had followed the example of his parents and grandparents in working hard and persevering through good and bad times. His farm operations included 3,000 acres of prime agricultural land and a large livestock operation. He also owned a retail store in Elmira that employed 15 people full time and earned a steady but modest income. Over the years he had reinvested most of this income in the business, taking only a small salary for himself. He had an outgoing personality and was a well-respected businessperson in the community.

Macreary stayed very involved in managing all aspects of the retail and farming business well into his eighties. His major concern was to ensure that the business keep operating successfully.

Macreary had three daughters but he didn't have a son. Two were married to farmers and lived close by, while the third lived in the United States. They seemed interested in helping Macreary, but because of lack of encouragement on his part, they never became very involved with his business interests. The husbands had all developed their own careers, and grandchildren were beginning to pursue careers that were taking them away from Elmira. In November 1998, at age 87, Macreary passed away.

A few days after their father's funeral, the three daughters met in the lawyer's office to settle the estate. None of them had any idea how the estate was to be divided. They learned that one-half of Macreary's estate was going to Mrs. Macreary, who was 85, and one-half was to be divided equally among the three daughters. This perplexed the daughters, as they did not know how to proceed in operating the business. Who would manage it? They were very hesitant to sell the assets, as they knew how much the business had meant to their father. He had mentioned many times that he did not want it sold.

In addition to this problem, the lawyer informed them that Macreary's proprietorship year end was on the day he died. Being a farmer, Macreary had used a cash basis for accounting income and usually incurred many expenses in December to reduce income for tax purposes. Having passed away in November, he had not yet had a chance to incur these expenses, and as a result he left an income of over $200,000. This meant that almost half would be a tax liability. There was not nearly enough cash in the estate to pay these taxes, and the daughters were concerned that they might have to borrow or sell some assets to pay them.

To make matters worse, the daughters were upset about the way the estate was divided. The two daughters living nearby felt they should have received more than they did. The third daughter thought she was entitled to one-third of the estate. All three were upset that their mother, age 85, had one-half of the estate. What might she do with it?

The family was in turmoil. They faced the prospects of trying to run a business they knew little about, a high tax bill, and resentment within the family.

Questions

1. What could James Macreary have done to avoid this situation?
2. What advice would you give to the family at this point?

RICK'S PLACE

E. Jerome McCarthy and Stanley J. Shapiro
Michigan State University and Simon Fraser University

Mr. Rick Snow is the president and only stockholder of Rick's Place Limited, a small, successful firm in the restaurant and recreation business in the small town of Wolfville, Nova Scotia, the site of Acadia University (population of 3,235 plus 4,050 students). Mr. Snow attended the university in the 1950s and paid most of his college expenses by selling refreshments at all of the school's athletic events. As he expanded his business, he hired local high school students to help him. The business became so profitable that Mr. Snow decided to stay in Wolfville after graduation. He rented a small building near the campus and opened a restaurant.

Over the years, his restaurant business was fairly successful. Mr. Snow earned a $36,000 profit on sales of $1,462,500 in 2000. The restaurant now consists of an attractive 40-table dining room, a large drive-in facility, and free delivery of orders to any point on the campus. The only thing that hasn't changed much is Mr. Snow's customers. He estimates that his restaurant business is still over 90 percent students and that nearly three-fourths of his sales are made between 6 p.m. and 1 a.m. There are several other restaurants with comparable facilities near the campus, but none of these is as popular with the university students as is "Papa Rick's."

As a result of the restaurant's success with the student market, Mr. Snow has aimed his whole promotion effort in that direction, by advertising only through the campus newspaper and over the campus and local rock music radio stations. In an attempt to increase his daytime business, from time to time Mr. Snow has used such devices as coupon meal books priced at 85 percent off face value. And he features daily "lunch special" plates. Nevertheless, he admits that he has been unable to compete with the university cafeterias for daytime business.

In 1998, when Mr. Snow was seeking a new investment opportunity, he contacted a national manufacturer of bowling equipment and supplies about the feasibility of opening a bowling lanes operation. Wolfville didn't have a bowling alley at the time, and Mr. Snow felt that both the local and university communities would provide a good market. He already owned a large tract of land which would be suitable for construction of the bowling lanes. The land was next to the restaurant, and he felt that this would result in each business stimulating the other.

The decision was made to go ahead with the venture, and to date the results have been nothing short of outstanding. Several local and university groups have formed bowling leagues. The university's men's and women's physical education departments schedule several bowling classes each term. And the casual bowling in the late afternoons and evenings is such that at least 12 of the 16 lanes are almost always in use. Some local radio advertising is done for the bowling lanes, but Mr. Snow doesn't feel that much is necessary. The success of the bowling lanes has encouraged the developer of a small shopping centre in the residential part of town to make plans to include a similar facility in his new development. Mr. Snow believes that competition won't hurt his business, because he has more to offer in his recreation centre.

Pleased with the profitability of his latest investment, Mr. Snow decided to expand his recreational centre even further. He noted that both students and local citizens patronized his bowling lanes and concluded that the addition of an attractive, modern billiard parlour would also have a common appeal. There was one other poolroom in Wolfville. It was considered to be a "hangout" and was avoided by townspeople and students. He felt that by offering a billiard parlour operation, he would be able to supply yet another recreational demand of his market. He obtained a loan from a local bank and began to build a third building at the back of his land. The billiard parlour was outfitted with 12 tables, a snack bar, wall-to-wall carpeting, and a soft music background system.

Today, eight months later, Mr. Snow is extremely disappointed with the billiard parlour operation. After the first two or three weeks, business steadily dropped off until now only one or two tables are in use even during the evening hours when business at the bowling lanes is at its peak. Promotion for the billiard parlour has been combined with promotions for other facilities, which are still doing very well.

In an effort to discover what went wrong, Mr. Snow interviewed several of his restaurant and bowling customers. Some of the typical responses were:

A Coed: I had enough trouble learning how to bowl, but at least it's sociable. Pool looks hard and everyone is so serious.

A Fraternity Man: My idea of a good date is dinner at Rick's, then the movies or an evening of bowling. You just can't make a good impression by taking a girl to play pool.

A Wolfville Citizen: I've never allowed my children to enter the local pool hall. What's more, as a kid I wasn't allowed either, and so I've never learned the game. It's too late to teach an old dog new tricks!

Mr. Snow is thinking about selling the billiard equipment and installing some pinball machines because he has heard they can be very profitable.

Questions

1. Why has Rick Snow been successful in the past?
2. Why has Rick's latest venture been unsuccessful?
3. How could Rick ensure that the business succeeds in the future?

This case was adapted from E. Jerome McCarthy and Stanley J. Shapiro, *Basic Marketing*, 3rd Canadian Edition, 1983 (Homewood, Ill.: Irwin-Dorsey of Canada). Used with permission.

WEISS MANUFACTURING COMPANY

E. Jerome McCarthy and Stanley J. Shapiro
Michigan State University and Simon Fraser University

Bill Carson is currently employed as a sales representative for a plastic goods manufacturer located in Montreal. He calls mostly on large industrial accounts such as refrigerator manufacturers who might need large quantities of custom-made products. He is on a straight salary of $20,000 from Weiss Manufacturing Company, an established thermoplastic moulder and manufacturer. Carl Weiss, the present owner, is nearing retirement age and has not developed anyone to run the business. He has agreed to sell the business to Robert Watson, a lawyer-entrepreneur, who has invited Bill Carson to invest and become the sales manager. Mr. Watson has agreed to give Carson his current salary plus expenses, plus a bonus of 1 percent of profits. However, Bill must invest to become part of the new company. He will obtain a 10 percent interest in the business for his $20,000 investment.

Weiss is well established in the industry, with a net worth of $150,000, sales of $1.5 million, and profits of $25,000 per year. As a percent of sales, cost of materials was 45 percent; direct labour, 13 percent; indirect factory labour, 15 percent; factory overhead, 13 percent; and sales overhead and general expenses, 13 percent. The company has not been making a large profit for several years but has been continually adding new machines or replacing those made obsolete by technological developments. The machinery is well maintained and modern, but most of it is similar to that owned by its many competitors. Most of the machines in the industry are standard. Special products are then made by using specially made dies with these machines.

Financially, the company seems to be in fairly good condition, at least as far as book value is concerned. The $20,000 investment would buy approximately $30,000 in assets.

Mr. Watson feels that with new management, the company has a real opportunity for profit. He expects to make some economies in the production process and hold custom moulding sales to the present $1 million level. The other major expectation is that he will be able to develop the proprietary line of products from a sales volume of about $500,000 to $2 million a year by adding several new "novelty items" normally sold in department stores. Bill Carson is expected to be a real asset here because of his sales experience.

Questions

1. What points should Bill Carson consider before making this decision? Discuss both the personal aspects and the potential successes of the firm.
2. Evaluate the financial implications of going ahead with the decision.

Directory of Supplementary Cases

VIDEO DELIGHT

Dr. Mallika Das
Mount Saint Vincent University

Carla McDonald, Jennifer Smith, Peter Swain, and Mark Swift were marketing students at a university in Halifax, Nova Scotia. As part of a marketing course, they were asked to conduct a research study for Video Delight, a Halifax video rental store. They were to examine consumer attitudes towards the store and its pricing policy. They were reviewing the details of the research study and other relevant information that they had collected and were to make recommendations on pricing and overall marketing strategy to the owner, Peter Thompson, by December 5th, 1988—in three weeks.

Mr. Thompson was concerned about the downturn in video rentals in his Halifax store. He attributed this primarily to the recent opening of Jumbo Video, a large chain, near his store. He was also interested in customer reaction to the new pricing policy that he had introduced in July, 1998.

The Company

Peter Thompson, a commerce graduate of Dalhousie University, had begun his video rental business with one small store located in a busy area of Halifax. Soon his store had expanded, and he now offered over 10,000 titles. According to Thompson, he had enough titles to compete with anyone. After five years in the business, Thompson had opened another branch in Bedford, 15 km from his Halifax outlet. Financially, the two outlets performed well. In fact, business had been so good that Thompson enlarged his Halifax outlet in early 1998. It was at this time that a new video outlet opened in the area. Mr. Thompson thought that the new competition was beginning to affect his volume of business.

The Industry

During the early to mid-eighties, when VCRs became very popular, many video outlets had sprung up in Halifax. In addition to the video rental outlets, many corner grocery stores and even some supermarkets had entered the field. Although these stores did not offer the same variety as video rental outlets, they offered consumers greater convenience.

By the latter part of the 1980's the proliferation of video rental outlets led to severe competition in the industry. Consumers had a lot of outlets from which to choose; consequently, attracting their attention was becoming more and more difficult. Many small operators had closed, and several corner grocery stores had gone out of the video rental business. For example, the number of video outlets on Video Delight's street had decreased from ten to five—one was the same size as Video Delight and the other three were smaller. Competition was still fierce, but as the industry matured fewer competitors were entering the market and the market stabilized.

At the same time another trend developed in the industry. National chain stores were formed. Several of them, like Jumbo and SuperVideo, were late entrants into the Atlantic region. However, by 1998 these stores had opened outlets in the Halifax-Dartmouth area, and they were beginning to expand. It was as part of this expansion that Jumbo had opened a store less than one block from Video Delight.

The larger chain stores had several advantages over smaller stores like Video Delight. They had more capital to work with, more buying power and usually could withstand intense competition for longer periods of time. With their modern, well-designed storefronts and interiors, large showrooms and greater advertising budgets, these stores posed a major problem to smaller video outlets such as Video Delight.

In Mr. Thompson's opinion, the smaller stores had some advantages too—their cost of operation was usually lower and many specialized in certain types of movies. For example, one of the stores near Video Delight specialized in art films and foreign language films. Video Delight carried a good selection of children's movies and Hollywood movie classics. The other two video outlets in the area were smaller and had no special "themes." Mr. Thompson thought that stores such as Video Delight had friendlier staff and offered more personalized service to their customers.

The Customer

According to Thompson, video rental customers could be classified into three groups. The first group consisted of ardent movie fans or those who rented at least one video a week. Some of these customers rented as many as 15 videos a month. The next group—the average viewers—rented anywhere from one to three movies a month. Those who rented less than one movie a month formed the last group. Mr. Thompson had a list of all his customers with details of their viewing patterns. For example, he could pick out the top 500 customers (in terms of the number of the videos rented).

Industry reports indicated that customers tended to rent videos from stores that were located in their neighbourhood or were, in some other way, conveniently located. For example, some chose stores that were on their way to work while others chose stores located next to a supermarket where they did their weekly grocery shopping. In the case of Video Delight, Thompson knew that nearly 80% of Video Delight's Halifax clients lived within three kilometres of his store. The Bedford store, which was located in the suburbs, drew customers from up to 12 km from the store.

Parking was another factor that affected business. However, Thompson thought that in the case of his Halifax outlet, closeness to downtown and busy retail centres made his customers less sensitive to parking problems. They recognized that if they wanted to shop at any of the stores in the neighbourhood, parking would be an issue and they might have to walk a little.

Many of Thompson's customers were young adults and families with young children. Quite often, parents and children came together and chose videos at the same time. The importance of children to the industry was reflected in the recent marketing strategies of some of the chain stores. Some of these stores offered free popcorn to children and showed in-store children's movies so that their parents could browse in peace.

The Marketing Strategy

In the past, Video Delight had relied upon its extensive selection, a layout that made it easier for customers to find videos, a comfortable and homey setting, and good customer service to bring repeat clients. The store was located in an old building and had several small rooms. Each room contained a specific category of video movies and thus offered a more "private" setting to customers. While it did not carry as many multiple copies as the larger stores, it had a good variety of movies, including a better selection of old Hollywood classics than most other stores.

In July 1998, as part of his strategy to meet the new competition, Thompson changed his pricing policy. Previously he had been charging $1.99 per movie per day—the same as most of the stores in the neighbourhood. In July, Video Delight began charging $3.49 per movie for two days. Thompson thought that many customers found the single day rental inconvenient, and his method would give them the option of keeping the video for an extra day. If, however, the video was returned within 24 hours, the customer got a credit of $1 which could be applied against future rentals. The computerized system that Thompson had in place made it easy for him to keep track of the credits earned, and saved the customer the trouble of collecting coupons or making note of his/her return patterns.

The store's promotion strategy consisted mainly of pamphlets mailed to neighbouring households, a few ads in the *Mayflower* (the weekly TV guide distributed with the Halifax Herald, a local newspaper), and an occasional ad in the newspaper. As the store had been in the neighbourhood for a long time, Thompson thought that he need not advertise heavily anymore.

The Research Study

While he had some important information about his customers' needs, Thompson thought that he had to find out more about his customers, especially with the increased competition. Consequently, he contacted a local university to see if students in a marketing course would conduct a study for him. In particular, he was interested in learning about customer reactions to his main video outlet as well as their reactions to his new pricing policy.

The research study was conducted by the students as part of their course requirement. The students were asked to develop a questionnaire, collect and analyze data, and submit a report to Mr. Thompson. Carla, Jennifer, Peter, and Mark developed a four-page questionnaire and interviewed 200 people living near the Halifax Video Delight store. One hundred and forty of these people were drawn randomly from the telephone directory using a systematic sampling method. (The first three digits of the phone numbers were used to identify the area of interest.) These were primarily non-customers of Video Delight, although some (21) had rented videos from the store. The other 60 respondents were drawn, again using a systematic sampling approach, from the alphabetical list of the top 500 customers of Video Delight that Thompson had provided. The results of the study are found in Tables 1 to 6 (on the next two pages) and the questionnaire itself in Appendix 1. The interviews were conducted over the telephone during a two week period in October, 1998.

Conclusion

Carla, Jennifer, Peter, and Mark were aware that they had to start writing their report for Mr. Thompson. Although they would have liked to have certain key financial and industry information before they made their recommendations, they knew that they had to manage with the information they had. They now also realized that there were weaknesses in their questionnaire; however, due to time constraints, they had no choice but to rely on the information they had already gathered.

Questions

1. How would you rate the research study? Did it achieve the objectives set forth by Mr. Thompson?
2. Evaluate the questionnaire and the research design.
3. Based on the data collected by this group, should Thompson re-evaluate his pricing strategy?
4. What recommendations (regarding other aspects of his marketing strategy) would you make to Thompson given the results of the study?
5. What other types of analyses would you like to perform using the data?

This case was prepared by Dr. Mallika Das of Mount Saint Vincent University for the Atlantic Entrepreneurial Institute as a basis for classroom discussion. Some elements of this case have been disguised.

Table 1 Awareness of Video Outlets[1]

Store	Group 1 General Population	Group 2 Video Delight Customers
Jumbo Video	106	72
Video Delight	72	86
Store 3	40	21
Store 4	57	28
Store 5	39	18
Others	42	24

[1]Totals add up to more than 119 (140 less 21 Video Delight customers found in the general sample) and 81 (60 drawn from the customers list provided by Thompson plus 21 found in the general population) respectively as respondents mentioned more than one store.

SOURCE: Responses from Question 5 of survey (Appendix A).

Table 2 Most Favoured Store

Store	Group 1 General Population	Group 2 Video Delight Customers
Jumbo Video	60	18
Video Delight	28	54
Others	31	9

SOURCE: Responses from Question 9 of survey (Appendix 1).

Table 3 Attributes Looked for in a Video Rental Outlet

		Store Ratings	
Attribute	Overall Importance Rating[1]	Jumbo[2]	Video Delight[3]
Price	4.1	3.4	2.8
Selection	4.2	4.0	3.7
Location	3.8	3.7	3.7
Reservation System	1.7	3.2	2.9
Friendliness of Staff	2.5	2.8	3.6
Fast Service	3.5	2.7	3.8
Parking	2.7	2.9	2.8
Multiple Copies	3.2	3.9	3.2

[1]Results of Question 6, all 200 respondents.
[2]Results of Question 13 for customers of Jumbo Video alone.
[3]Results of Question 13 for customers of Video Delight alone.

SOURCE: Responses from Questions 6 and 13 of survey (Appendix 1).

Table 4 **Main Reason for Choosing Video Outlet**

	Jumbo Video Customers	Video Delight Customers
Price	40	18
Selection	56	45
Staff	17	24
Fast Service	9	16
Others	18	5

Respondents sometimes mentioned more than one reason.

SOURCE: Responses from Question 10 of survey (Appendix 1).

Table 5 **Pricing Preferences**

	General Sample[1]	Video Delight Customers[2]
Least Preferred Method		
Video Delight's Policy (A)	91	27
Pay when you take (B)	7	3
Pay when you return (C)	21	51
Most Preferred Method		
Video Delight's policy (A)	10	18
Pay when you take (B)	92	53
Pay when you return (C)	17	10

[1] Includes only non-Video Delight customers (n = 119).

[2] Video Delight sample includes respondents drawn from the general population who were customers of Video Delight (n = 81).

SOURCE: Responses from Question 7 of survey (Appendix 1).

Table 6 **Age of Respondents**

Age	Video Delight Customers	Rest of Sample
18 to 25	21	53
26 to 35	26	34
36 to 45	18	19
46 to 55	10	10
56 to 65	6	3

SOURCE: Responses from Question 15 of survey (Appendix 1).

Appendix 1

Video Delight Survey

Interviewer:	Date:
Time Start:	Phone #:
Time End:	Interview #:

Hello, my name is . . . and I am conducting a survey for a university marketing research course. I would like to ask you a few questions about video rental outlets or video stores. These questions will only take a few minutes.

Part I: Qualifiers

1. Are you over 18 years of age?   Yes   No
   (If "no" ask to speak to someone 18 years of age or over; if no one 18+ is in, terminate interview.)
2. Do you rent video movies?   Yes   No
   (If "no" terminate interview politely.)
3. If yes, how frequently do you rent video movies? (Read list.)
   a. 5 times or more per week
   b. 3 to 4 times a week
   c. 1 to 2 times a week
   d. Once every two weeks
   e. Once every month
   f. Less than once in a month
4. On average, how many movies do you usually rent per visit? 1, 2, 3, 4+
   (If less than once in a month and only one movie per visit, terminate interview politely.)

Part II: Image and Related Issues

5. When you think of video rental stores, what stores, if any, come to mind? (Take down all names provided.)

a.	d.
b.	e.
c.	f.

6. On a scale of 1 to 5, "1" being not at all important, "5" being very important and "3" being neutral, I would like to find out how important the following are to you when you choose a video rental store:
   (Read list; if respondent needs assistance, please read the scale again.)

Price of rental	Fast service
Selection	Parking facility
Store location	Multiple copies
Reservation system	Other
Friendliness of staff	(Please specify)

7. Now, I am going to describe three different ways of pricing video movies. When I am finished, please tell me which one you prefer the most and which one you prefer the least.
   (If person is not sure of "least preferred," do not insist.)
   a. Each video costs $3.49 to rent; the rental is for 2 days; you get a credit of $1.00 toward future rentals if you return the video after one day.
   b. Each video costs $1.99 to rent per day; you pay when you take the video.
   c. Each video costs $1.99 to rent per day; you pay when you return the video.
   Most preferred   Least preferred
8. How many video stores do you rent videos from on a regular basis?
   1, 2, 3, 4+
9. Could you tell me the name of the store that you rent the most videos from, please?
   (If more than one, please take down all names; if Video Delight is mentioned, insert it in all the questions below; if not, use the name of one of the other companies mentioned above.)
10. The rest of the survey deals with the video store that you rent from most on a regular basis.
    Could you please tell me your reason for renting from _____?
    (Note down the top three answers; probe if necessary.)
    a.
    b.
    c.
11. How much does renting a video cost at _____ per movie; for ____ days?
12. How far is _____ from your house? (km)
13. Using a 5-point scale with "1" being very bad, "5" being very good and "3" being neutral, how would you rate _____ on the following items?
(Read list; if respondent needs assistance with the scale, please read it over again.)

Price of rental	Fast service
Selection	Parking facility
Store location	Multiple copies
Reservation system	Other
Friendliness of staff	(Please specify)

Part III: Demographic Information

For the purpose of analyzing the data we would like to get certain demographic details about you.
14. How many members are there in your household? Of these, how many are under the age of 18?
15. Which of the following age groups do you belong to?
    18–25 26–35 36–45 46–55 56–64 65+
16. Could you please tell me which one of the following groups your total household income would fall under?   under $15,000   under $30,000 under $45,000   under $60,000   over $60,000

Thank you very much for your time.

DIEGO'S

Morris Borts
Marketec Business Consultants Ltd.

Dr. Albert Collins, a Montreal physician, faced a difficult decision as to whether or not to invest in a new fast food franchise concept specializing in Mexican food. Dr. Collins had made several good business investments, and while he thought this was a great opportunity he recognized that there was a chance it wouldn't succeed. He decided to discuss the concept with his friend, Jack Timlin, a marketing consultant who had advised him on a number of earlier ventures. Dr. Collins arranged a meeting and presented the following information to Mr. Timlin.

The Concept

About six months ago, Dr. Collins had read an article in a major US magazine about a relatively new but already successful fast food franchiser based in Phoenix, Arizona. In operation for less than five years this franchiser had opened 55 locations (some franchised, some corporately owned) in Arizona and several other southwest states and had sold (to one firm) the franchise rights for 80 locations in Florida and sold many other, soon to be built, franchises in the mid-western states.

Although Mexican food is very popular in the southern United States, this firm, in all of its advertising and store signs, always uses the phrase, "We serve marinated charbroiled chicken and Mexican food," to indicate that it offers a choice of items so that people who don't like Mexican food can also patronize the chain.

On the door of each location is a sticker stating that this restaurant is approved by the American Heart Association as a healthy place to eat away from home. Dr. Collins believed that this endorsement was obtained because of the manner in which the chicken is prepared. First it is marinated in a secret recipe of natural fruit juices and herbs and then it is charbroiled so that the fat drips out of the meat. Chicken prepared this way is lower in cholesterol than fried chicken and is juicier than barbeque (BBQ) chicken. To further enhance its healthy image, the chain does not serve french fries but does offer baked potatoes and an assortment of salads.

A quote from the article provided a very strong endorsement from at least one customer: "I do not have a great deal of experience in eating Mexican food, but the dishes were different than what I expected. The chicken was tender and juicy and had a subtle flavour—for my taste it was better than BBQ chicken. The other dishes were very tasty and definitely not spicy. If this is what Mexican food is like, I am a convert."

Dr. Collins investigated further and found out that the recipes could not be protected by patent or copyright. In fact, he learned that the Arizona chain found out how a California chain of chicken restaurants marinated their chicken and then used the recipe themselves. Dr. Collins then purchased some of the American marinated chicken, had it analyzed by a laboratory and then had a food technologist develop and test the formula and the correct procedures to cook the chicken.

He gathered a group of investors (primarily friends and acquaintances) who liked the concept and were willing to put up most of the money required to open up one or two locations to show that the concept would be successful in Canada. The plan was to sell franchises across the county.

For each location, franchisees would be charged an initial fee plus an ongoing 5 percent royalty on gross sales of the franchises. In return for these fees the franchisee would have the right to use the trade name, which the investors decided would be Diego's. The franchisee's staff would be trained to prepare the food as per set procedures and the franchisee would purchase the chicken marinade from the franchiser. The franchisee would be assisted in site selection, construction of the restaurant, the purchasing of the required equipment, and would receive ongoing mangerial assistance. In addition, the franchisee would benefit from a co-op advertising programme to be funded by a charge of 4 percent of gross sales levied on each location—franchised or corporately owned.

Preliminary Research

Dr. Collins met with the investment group several times and although nothing was formalized, a considerable amount of preliminary research had been conducted. A location was found for the first Diego's restaurant in a relatively new suburban residential area where most of the homes have been built in the last 10 years. New homes were still being built in the area and there was enough vacant land to more than double the population of the area. Most of the homes sold for $150,000 to $225,000 (compared to the current Montreal average price of $89,500 per home). Census data suggested that the typical home owner in this area was raising a young family and had a managerial job or was a professional with a practice that had not yet developed fully.

Studies have shown that most people will travel about 2.5 to 3.5 km (5 minutes) to go to a fast food restaurant. Since Diego's would be very distinctive, the first few locations probably would draw customers from a slightly larger trading area. Information was obtained from recent census data for the census tracts that would likely constitute the trading area (Figure 1).

Figure 1   Trading Area Demographic Data

Total population	114,858
Private household	38,500
Total families	31,535
With 1 child at home	6,355
With 2 children at home	8,980
With 3 children at home	3,950
No children at home	12,250
Ages of children	
0 to 4 years	8,860
5 to 9 years	9,035
10 to 14 years	8,425
15 to 19 years	8,975

SOURCE: Statistics Canada, 1986 Montreal CMA census tracts.

Investor Group Meeting

After the information was collected, the investors held a meeting where a lively debate took place about the proposed image of Diego's, the target market, and other matters.

The investment group couldn't agree what image Diego's should have and what type of customers they should concentrate on satisfying. Some of the members wanted to concentrate their efforts on attracting and satisfying families with young children (e.g., offering free magic shows on selected evenings and on weekends, offering children free balloons, and perhaps offering a special children's menu of items that will appeal to children).

One investor argued that this market segment appeared to be important. A recent newspaper article reported the results of an American study that, in 85 percent of the cases when parents go out to eat with their young children, the children make the final decision on which restaurant the family will go to.

Some of the group argued that children are known as very finicky eaters and maybe they won't like Diego's food. They suggested that Diego's should go after the teenage market, or possibly Diego's should concentrate on the adult fast food market.

One member of the investment group had conducted an analysis of the competition in the trading area. He noted that at least two competitors in the trading area, McDonald's and Chi Chi's, had special strategies for attracting children. Two other successful restaurants, St. Hubert B.B.Q. and Swiss Chalet (both specialize in BBQ chicken) have outlets in the area. Another group member provided some data prepared by statistics Canada that dealt with food purchased from restaurants (Figure 2).

Figure 2   Weekly Food Purchases from Restaurants, per Family (Canada), 1990

	Food Purchases	Income before Taxes
Average	$27.28	$45,708
1st quintile	12.63	11,808
2nd quintile	22.39	25,333
3rd quintile	32.11	39,453
4th quintile	45.39	55,813
5th quintile	63.51	96,133

Note: The average weekly food purchases from restaurants in the Montreal Metropolitan Area was $33.83

SOURCE: Statistics Canada, *Family Food Expenditures in Canada 17 Metropolitan Areas,* Cat. 62-554.

One of the members of the investor group was a practising accountant. He estimated that if the average bill at a restaurant of this type was $4.50 (excluding tax) and the actual cost of the food and the packaging was 30 percent of the selling price, the restaurant would need to serve 225,000 meals a year to break even.

Information on traffic flows was also collected. One Thursday, Dr. Collins went to the proposed site and between 12:00 noon and 1:00 p.m. counted 2,000 cars moving in the four directions at the intersection. Between 5:00 p.m. and 6.30 p.m. the street heading north in front of the site became a "parking lot" as people headed home. He felt that this was a positive sign in that people could stop on the same side of the street as they were already travelling (and not have to cut across traffic), pick up food for supper, and then continue home.

Related to the decision as to which target market(s) to appeal to, some members wondered if people would be confused if the restaurant was simultaneously promoted as a chicken restaurant and as a Mexican food restaurant. That is, would potential customers perceive the chicken as a Mexican dish or would they consider the chicken to be a suitable alternative to BBQ chicken or fried chicken?

Various members of the investment group then raised the following questions and issues:

- Will consumers recognize the fact that Diego's is really two different restaurants in one and even if a person does not like Mexican food (or is afraid to try it) he or she can order a very tasty chicken? Or will some stay away because they view Diego's as a Mexican restaurant? Is Diego's perhaps too strong a Mexican name for what we would like to achieve?

- Both images should be positive. Diego's proposed first location is not far from Chi Chi's which exposed the consumer to and expanded the market for Mexican food. According to comparisons made by some of the group, Diego's Mexican dishes taste better and will cost less than the same items at Chi Chi's.
- On the other hand, for many years chicken has been more popular in Quebec than other parts of the country. It may be due to cultural differences or may be the result of the success of the St. Hubert B.B.Q. chain which started in Quebec (Figure 3).
- In addition, over the last three or four years the consumption of chicken across Canada has increased significantly as people switched away from red meats, which are higher in cholesterol than chicken. This ties in very nicely with the emphasis that the American chain firmly places on the health aspect of its chicken meals.

Figure 3 **Estimated per Capita Regional Differences in Food Consumption**

National Average = 100 percent	Chicken	Italian	Chinese	Greek
National	100%	100%	100%	100%
Quebec	125	120	145	130
Ontario	90	75	85	80
Prairies	90	165	35	25
B.C.	90	120	100	85
Atlantic provinces	175	80	55	45

Some of the investors debated whether legally they could use an approach similar to the one Americans use and were not convinced that the "healthy" image would be a unique selling proposition that would cause people to pick their restaurant over the competition. They argued that the Canadian laws concerning food advertising were different and more restrictive than the US laws. In Canada the advertising of the cholesterol content of food (with the exception of vegetable oils such as Mazola) is prohibited. In addition, it appears that even if it wanted to, the Canadian Heart Association would be unable, given the present legal environment, to endorse the restaurant. As well, they argued that many Quebecers are not especially health conscious when it comes to food.

One person had obtained a copy of a research study conducted in Montreal about bakery products. This study concluded that French speaking respondents were less concerned with food additives than the English speaking segment of the population. It was also found that older people were less concerned with this issue than the younger generation. Quebecers consumed large amounts of especially greasy french fries and poutine (French fries, sauce, and melted cheese). In other parts of Canada the preference was for crispier, less oily french fries.

Some research conducted in the Montreal area by one of the group indicated that more than half of the respondents want french fries with their BBQ chicken. Consumers like and expect the combination that is what the chicken restaurants offer with their meals.

In spite of this information other investors would like to follow the lead of the American firm and not serve french fries but instead offer a choice of baked potatoes or Mexican rice.

One person pointed out that Quebecers love fine food and are receptive to ethnic foods. However, for some reason Mexican food has not caught on in Quebec. Taco Bell, a large U.S. Mexican fast food chain which has opened in Ontario does not, at this time, have any Quebec locations. In Montreal proper, several small Mexican restaurants have opened. None of them appears to be especially successful.

In addition, one of the investment team visited about a dozen supermarkets (some in the area of the proposed location, others in various parts of Montreal and other suburbs). Each store has a small section of packaged Mexican foods. The managers of these stores described the sales of Mexican foods as "slow but steady."

Because there was a lot of money at stake, the investors paid for some basic research. They conducted focus groups in a restaurant setting similar to what is being considered and the respondents had the chance to taste the food. (Figure 4 provides a summary of the comments.) The results of the research were interesting in that in two cases the findings go against what the investors thought the consumer might want or accept.

Figure 4   Focus Group Comments

Positive Comments

- The food is delicious.

- Great food.

- I never tasted Mexican food before; it is really good and not at all spicy.

- I am happy that you don't serve french fries. My seven-year-old son just ate nutritious food, not the junk food that he prefers.

- I enjoyed the food. The chicken was moist but not greasy.

- I liked it. I would come back again.

- I hope it opens soon. I am bored and fed up with the traditional fast foods.

Negative Comments

- The chicken looks yellow. What's wrong with it? Is it cheaper quality chicken?

- I don't think French Canadians are ready to eat BBQ chicken on paper plates using plastic cutlery.

- I don't want to see the chicken being cooked. I don't want to know that it was once a living thing.

- The chickens were brought to the grill in a pail. Do they use the same pail to wash the floors?

- For me BBQ chicken and french fries go together. Something is missing and the meal is not enjoyable without french fries.

First, it was planned to prepare the food out in the front of the restaurant where it could be seen by people inside and outside. This was intended to show that Diego's had nothing to hide and that the food was prepared under hygienic conditions. In addition, it was hoped that seeing the golden brown chicken on the grill and the aroma of cooking chicken would encourage people to order. According to the focus groups some people viewed this as a strong negative.

Secondly, while travelling through New England, Dr. Collins came across a very successful chain of seafood restaurants which, in order to keep prices low, serves on paper plates and provides plastic cutlery. This makes sense because Harvey's and other fast food chains also use disposables. Again, based on the results of the focus groups, their seems to be resistance in Montreal to eating chicken in this way.

Another research finding was of special interest and requires more study. When respondents were offered a choice between traditional BBQ sauce and salsa, a Mexican sauce, the vast majority opted for the BBQ sauce. Was it because it was something unknown? Was it the fear of something spicy? Or, perhaps, it was just habit.

The Decision

Dr. Collins concluded the presentation to Mr. Timlin with the following comments: "As you can see there is a lot of information to consider. In fact, I am confused as to what I should do. I know that the concept is successful in Arizona but I have also obtained a great deal of information, some of which is not positive, about duplicating this concept in Canada and particularly in Quebec.

"I don't know if I should invest in this project or not. If it succeeds, it will be the chance of a lifetime to make a lot of money. Should I go into it, or not? What, if anything, can be done to improve the concept so that the risk of failure will be reduced?"

Question

What would you recommend that Dr. Collins do? Why?

CLOVIS JEWELLERS

D. Wesley Balderson
University of Lethbridge

Clovis Jewellers is a small jewellery store located in Brandon, Manitoba.[1] You have been called on by the owner to prepare an analysis of the business. The owners have supplied you with a detailed description of their operation and strategy. Critically evaluate each area described in the case.

Structure

Legal Structure. Clovis Jewellers is an incorporated company under the name of Clovis Jewellers (1978) Limited. It is a privately held corporation. The only shareholders are Mr. and Mrs. Neudorf, each of whom owns 50 percent of the outstanding shares. As a corporation, Clovis Jewellers is authorized to issue an unlimited number of Class A, B, and C common shares. The only outstanding shares are 100 Class A shares. In the case of Clovis Jewellers, the shareholders are the owners, directors, and managers.

Financial Structure. The capital structure of Clovis Jewellers is financed by a combination of debt and shareholder's equity. The debt constitutes roughly 75 percent of the capital and the shareholder's equity the other 25 percent. The shareholder's equity is made up of both class A share capital and retained earnings, of which the latter is by far the larger.

The debt financing is held with the Bank of Montreal and is in the form of a long-term loan. This loan is approximately $190,000. The first $150,000 is guaranteed through a provincial government small business assistance plan and therefore carries an interest rate of 9 percent; the remaining $40,000 carries a rate of prime plus 1 percent. This long-term debt is covered by personal guarantees by Fred Meyer, a business associate of Mr. Neudorf, and from a mortgage on the Neudorfs' house.

---

1 Although this case describes an actual business, the names of the business and owners, as well as the location, have been changed.

The bank of Montreal has also authorized an operating line of credit to Clovis Jewellers with a ceiling of $20,000. This line of credit is used to assist Mr. Neudorf in managing the cash flow in the slower summer months.

Organizational Structure. There are four levels of employees in Clovis Jewellers' organizational structure (see Appendix 1 on page 472). The first level is the manager and is filled by Mr. Neudorf. The duties of this position include accounting and financial management, management of day-to-day store operations and gemologist/diamond expert. Mr. Neudorf works together with both the assistant manager and the sales staff.

The second level in the organization is the assistant manager and is filled by Mrs. Neudorf. She works as the assistant manager approximately 50 percent of the time and as a salesperson the remaining 50 percent. The duties of the assistant manager include purchasing of merchandise and control of inventory. The inventory control function is done on a very informal basis, usually by a simple visual check.

The third level in the organization includes the sales staff and the repair service administrator. The job of overseeing the repair service is held by one of the full-time salespersons and requires approximately 20 percent of her time. The number of salespersons varies with the time of year, ranging from six to seven at Christmastime to two or three during the summer months.

The fourth level in the organization is the goldsmith and repairperson. This position is filled by Mr. Neudorf and requires a great deal of his time. Mr. Neudorf works together with the repair service administrator when acting as goldsmith.

There are two positions outside of the four-level organization. One is an accountant, and the other is a lawyer. Mr. Neudorf hires these two professionals on a part-time basis as demand calls for them. Both the accountant and the lawyer interact only with Mr. Neudorf.

Personnel

Clovis Jewellers experiences very little employee turnover (one staff member every two or three years) and therefore does not engage in recruiting procedures on a regular basis. When a new staff member is needed, a small advertisement is placed in the classified section of Brandon's daily newspaper. Although an advertisement is always placed, most hiring results through word of mouth and other contacts with neighbouring businesspeople.

When selecting a new employee, Mr. and Mrs. Neudorf look for individuals with an outgoing, friendly personality. Usually the person is middle-aged and has sales experience. Application forms are screened based on these qualifications, and the applicant who best meets the qualifications is asked to come in for a personal interview. Unless there is more than one "ideal" applicant, the new employee is hired after only one interview.

The training supplied to new employees comes in two forms: product training and operations training. The product training requires the employee to learn a great deal about jewellery—a very complex area. The individual must gain knowledge about watches, diamonds, gemstones, and qualities of gold. This product training occurs as the person works in the showroom selling jewellery and takes approximately one month.

The operations training is less involved than the product training and is completed in the first week or two of employment. This training involves learning the daily routine carried out at Clovis Jewellers, as well as cash register and receipt-writing operations.

The method of employee remuneration is a straight hourly wage; no commissions are paid. Employees' hours are recorded in a payroll register, and employees are paid every two weeks based on the number of hours worked. Mr. Neudorf tried to introduce a commission pay plan in the past, but employee resistance forced him to shelve the plan.

Employee morale appears relatively high compared to other retail stores. Mr. Neudorf believes this is because he and his wife treat the sales staff with respect and as friends. The employees know the importance of selling to the company's well-being, and Mr. Neudorf continually reinforces this by verbally acknowledging an individual for his or her sales efforts. A further indication of high morale is the fact that Clovis Jewellers experiences an extremely low rate of absenteeism and lateness.

Marketing

Product. A majority of Clovis Jewellers' yearly sales consists of ring and precious stone jewellery; for this reason, its product mix heavily favours these two items. Ring sales are responsible for the single highest sales total; therefore, great emphasis is placed on the ring inventory when the product mix is evaluated. Clovis Jewellers is known for carrying good-quality merchandise; this is reflected in the purchasing habits and quality control employed at Clovis. However, Clovis has shifted to a lower-quality selection of rings and jewellery to compete with the competition. This shift appears to be temporary, as the better-quality lines remain.

Mr. Neudorf believes seasonal fluctuations in sales do not seriously affect the product mix. Relative sales of most items remain constant throughout the year.

Distribution. Clovis Jewellers is in the middle of a transition from using a traditional manufacturer-retailer distribution channel to a more direct channel. Jewellery and ring manufacturers are actually middlemen in the supply of diamonds and precious gems (the manufacturers buy the gemstones from large diamond and gemstone suppliers). This method of purchasing was more convenient for Mr. Neudorf but inevitably meant higher-priced merchandise. Mr. Neudorf has now made arrangements to buy diamonds directly from the source of supply and therefore has greatly reduced merchandise costs. This shift also gives Mr. Neudorf much greater control over diamond and gemstone quality.

Pricing. Mr. Neudorf uses several different methods in calculating the retail prices of the merchandise. Brand-name items such as watches are priced according to the manufacturer's suggested retail price, because Mr. Neudorf thinks customers will base their purchase decisions solely on price when shopping for brand names.

Merchandise whose quality the customer cannot differentiate easily, such as gold chains, are priced very competitively. Comparisons are often made with other jewellery stores to ensure that these items are priced competitively. Jewellery items such as earrings and pendants are priced according to a standard markup of keystone (50 percent), plus an additional 10 percent to make up for markdowns, which are often needed to sell the jewellery.

Mr. Neudorf finds rings the hardest items to price, as they carry no brand names or identifying trademarks. Each ring is priced individually, based on special features (or lack of them). A general markup formula is still used, but individual factors dictate the final selling price of the ring. For example, everyday solitaire engagement rings are priced below the standard markup, whereas individual modern engagement rings are priced above that markup.

Promotion. Clovis Jewellers uses a wide range of media in its advertising program, including a daily newspaper, a local television station, AM and FM radio stations, and flyers. Advertising is used to convey both a specific promotional method and corporate image advertising. Mr. Neudorf prepares much of his own advertising, especially radio and newspaper ads. He also gives the ads a personal touch by recording many of the radio ads himself and including his picture in several newspaper advertisements. Mr. Neudorf claims that Clovis Jewellers targets its selling toward middle-aged women, but this target is not evident in the advertising; rather, the advertising appears to be general, with no real objectives or target market in mind. The advertising budget is prepared by taking a percentage of projected sales. This target percentage is between 4 and 5 percent.

Mr. Neudorf uses many different forms of sales promotion throughout the year. These include diamond remount plans, jewellery repair sales, graduation promotions, Mother's Day promotions, and other general markdown sales. The number of sales promotions has increased over the past few years due to an increase in competition. The trend in promotions has switched from using them to enhance slow selling periods toward bettering higher selling periods. That is, they are now timed in conjunction with a month of already higher-than-average sales.

Personal selling is heavily used at Clovis Jewellers. Mr. Neudorf believes jewellery requires a substantial selling push and therefore uses in-store personal selling as a major marketing tool. Emphasis is on making every sale count, large or small. Monthly sales totals are updated every day and then compared to the projected sales for the month. This information is then passed on to the salespeople to keep them aware of the importance of selling.

Public relations can also be an effective marketing tool, especially in a close-knit community such as Brandon. Mr. Neudorf is involved with many community clubs and events, which give him a fair amount of low-cost public relations. Clovis Jewellers sponsors sporting events for persons with disabilities and is a member of both the Rotary Club of Brandon and the Brandon Chamber of Commerce (of which Mr. Neudorf has been president and is currently a director). Mr. Neudorf gives talks to local women's groups and at high school career days. He has also had much interaction with the Brandon City Council and has served on committees such as the Brandon Parking Commission.

Location and Layout

Location. Clovis Jewellers' trading area consists of the city of Brandon, surrounding towns and farmlands, and small communities that extend to the Ontario and Saskatchewan borders. The population of the area is slightly greater than 200,000, of which 55,000 live in the city of Brandon. The primary trading area (approximately 70 percent of the business) includes the entire city of Brandon and the surrounding towns of Virden, Souris, Minnedosa, and Neepawa.

The economy of Clovis Jewellers' trading area relies heavily on its two industries, farming and oil. Clovis Jewellers' sales experience large fluctuations due to the characteristics of each of these industries. The downturn in the oil industry has had a significant impact on the firm's profitability; sales have dropped significantly in the past three years.

Clovis Jewellers leases its site from a management firm located in Winnipeg. The basic rent is approximately $2,400 per month. On top of this expense, Clovis pays a yearly management, property tax, and insurance fee for the building. The building is a single-story structure located on Brandon's main downtown artery. The physical characteristics of the site follow the image Clovis is trying to portray; the storefront is pleasant and modern looking.

The buildings surrounding Clovis Jewellers host mostly banks and other independent retail stores. Several retail stores on the same city block appeal to Clovis's target market, including the Roset by Reid jewellery store located across the street. There is one vacant space on the street, located right next to Clovis Jewellers. The vacancy was caused by a fire over a year ago, and the building remains boarded up.

Clovis Jewellers is located on Ross Street, which is the centre downtown street. Ross Street has angle parking on both sides and is busy every weekday from 9:00 a.m. until around 6:00 p.m. This heavy vehicle traffic is due to the large number of banks in the area that deal with a high volume of customers every day. Ross Street also experiences a high volume of pedestrian traffic during the day, as it is situated in the heart of Brandon's retail and office sector.

Layout. Clovis Jewellers' present location is 1,000 square feet. Eight hundred square feet are used as selling space and the remaining 200 for office and storage space. The showroom is divided among rings, gold chains, watches, gift items, diamond jewellery, and regular jewellery. Although space is allocated to each section according to proportion of total sales, the allocation is based on rough estimates of both percentage of sales and space used.

The layout of the store is designed to make efficient use of high-traffic areas. The engagement rings, which are classified as specialty goods, are located at the back of the store, a spot that would normally see low-traffic volume. The shopping goods such as watches and gold chains are located in high-traffic areas around the cash register and front entrance.

Merchandise is displayed in either a locked showcase or behind a showcase out of the customer's reach. This method of displaying is necessary due to the high value and small size of individual pieces of merchandise. Each display case is lighted by two spotlights dropped from the ceiling. Florescent lights light the general-purpose areas of the store; other lamps are suspended from the ceiling as part of the decor. The lighting appears adequate, as the store gives a "bright" first impression.

Purchasing and Inventory Control

Purchasing. Mrs. Neudorf is responsible for purchasing the majority of the required merchandise. The salespeople often assist her, especially when the purchasing is done in Clovis Jewellers' showroom. Purchasing is done through a combination of jewellery and gift show attendance and meetings with individual supplier representatives.

The trade shows Mr. and Mrs. Neudorf attend are held throughout Canada and the United States and include cities such as Hawaii, Vancouver, Brandon, Calgary, Winnipeg, and Toronto. Roughly 20 percent of total purchases are made at these trade shows. Mr. and Mrs. Neudorf attend them for the purpose of obtaining new products and ideas as well as the actual purchasing.

Eighty percent of purchasing is done in-store and with the help of the salespeople. Mrs. Neudorf prefers in-store purchasing because it gives her the undivided attention of the company representative and allows her to compare items with Clovis's existing merchandise. Each company representative visits Clovis Jewellers two or three times a year, usually in the spring and early fall.

Mr. Neudorf has arranged special payment terms with approximately 75 percent of his suppliers. The credit terms are usually 30/60 days, 30/60/90 days, 30/60/90/120 days, or even up to six months; most companies will give these terms free of any interest charges. Mr. Neudorf finds these terms necessary for cash flow management, as the majority of purchases are made during slow sales periods.

Mr. Neudorf maintains a tight level of quality control, inspecting each piece of jewellery before it is put on sale. Each item is checked for diamond or gemstone quality, quality of stone settings, and adequate stamping of gold quality. Items that do not meet the strict quality standards are returned to the supplier for exchange.

A purchasing budget is prepared by multiplying the target gross margin percentage by the budgeted sales figure. This total purchase figure is then spread out throughout the year according to monthly sales, with the majority of purchases made in the pre-Christmas season.

Inventory Control. No formal inventory control method is used at Clovis Jewellers. Mr. and Mrs. Neudorf rely on experience when it comes to controlling inventory levels. Visual inspections determine whether inventory levels are sufficient or need replenishing. No automatic reorder procedure is used; Mr. and Mrs. Neudorf believe automatic reordering would hurt rather than enhance sales because customers expect to find unique pieces of jewellery at Clovis.

Mr. Neudorf has insurance to cover fire, loss of merchandise stored in the safe, loss of customer goods stored in the safe, and business interruption (up to six months). Insurance to protect against theft of merchandise not stored in the safe is either not available or too expensive. All of the rings and diamond jewellery are placed in the safe after business hours; therefore, most of Clovis's inventory is insured in the event of a break-in. The business interruption insurance is related to inventory; a major loss or damage of inventory would not force Clovis Jewellers out of business, as the firm would continue to have a daily cash flow.

Accounting and Financial

Recording and Classifying. The daily and weekly recording and classifying done by the staff at Clovis Jewellers basically follows a one-write system, with the addition of certain journals and a daily cash summary. The one-write system, kept by Mr. Neudorf, is used to maintain all of the sundry (nonmerchandise) accounts as well as the company payroll. The nonmerchandise accounts are paid as they arise and therefore require almost daily attention; the payroll is calculated every two weeks.

A daily cash summary is prepared by Mr. Neudorf every weekday morning (Friday's and Saturday's are prepared on Monday). This cash summary includes a summary of the day's sales, both cash sales and charge sales; a summary of how the cash flow is distributed, including cash expenses and bank deposits; and a record of returned merchandise and cheques. The main purpose of this cash summary is to ensure that the cash transactions balance on a day-to-day basis.

Mr. Neudorf also keeps an accounts payable ledger, which he updates weekly. Proper managing of the accounts payable is important to Clovis Jewellers because it relies on trade credit to purchase all of its inventories. A journal of monthly purchases is kept to maintain control over the inventory and the merchandise purchases. Mrs. Neudorf is responsible for keeping this journal up to date; usually she adds all of the invoices to the journal at the end of the month, when a total can be calculated.

One final area in which recording is done on a day-to-day basis is the jewellery repair journal and record of ring sales. Clovis Jewellers has an extensive jewellery and watch repair department. The repair department is run by the sales staff and involves entering every repair job into a journal for easy reference. Because of the quick turnover of repair jobs (usually one to two days), they must be entered into the journal the same day they are received to prevent any bottlenecks in the system. Individual ring sales are also recorded in a book for quick reference as needed.

Budgeting. Five years ago, the budgeting process was almost nonexistent at Clovis Jewellers. Except for some very rough, off-the-top-of-the-head figures, no budgets were prepared. This has changed in the last few years, and although the budgetary process still needs improvement, it has taken a definite shape and form.

The process starts with a sales budget. This budget is prepared by looking at last year's sales and then updating them based on any special considerations for the upcoming year. The budget is prepared monthly and used to make regular comparisons to actual sales figures.

Once the sales budget is complete, a merchandise purchases budget is prepared based on the specific level of monthly sales. The purchases budget includes all shares of merchandise purchases, including the cost of repairs.

An expense budget is prepared by Mr. Neudorf. Again, previous years' expense totals are used. These expense totals are evaluated as being too high, too low, or correct over the past year and are then changed accordingly for the upcoming budgeted year. The budgeting of all the expense totals is very important, as it allows for better control of these expenses as they are incurred.

The final budget prepared is the cash flow project budget. This is done by combining the projected sales, merchandise payments, and expense budgets. This cash flow projection is very important for Clovis Jewellers, because the seasonal cash inflows it experiences often creates cash shortages; the cash flow analysis allows Mr. Neudorf to plan for these shortages.

Financial Statements. Clovis Jewellers has a complete set of financial statements prepared once a year by a certified general accounting firm (see Appendix 2 on pages 473–475). The statements are prepared after January 31 of each year, which Mr. Neudorf has chosen as the year-end date due to the low volume of business and low inventory count that occur at this time. All financial statements are prepared showing the previous year's figures for purposes of easy comparison.

The balance sheet is prepared in the traditional format, with assets on the left side of the statement and liabilities and equity on the right. Current assets constitute roughly 75 percent of the total assets; inventory is the largest and most important part of the current assets. Clovis Jewellers has a long-term loan payable, which makes up the largest part of the total liabilities. This loan contract is held with the Bank of Montreal and carries personal guarantees from both Mr. Neudorf and his business associate, Fred Meyer.

An income statement is prepared based on sales and expense figures supplied by Mr. Neudorf. This statement does not include a detailed list of the operating expenses. For this purpose, a detailed statement of Operating Expenses is prepared. This statement lists each expense totalled for the year and in alphabetical order.

A statement of changes in financial position is also prepared at year end. This statement explains how funds were generated and used throughout the year. The purpose of this statement is to indicate any changes in the working capital of the business and explain how those changes occurred.

Planning

Long-Term Planning. Management at Clovis Jewellers appears to be typical of most small businesses in that a serious lack of any long-term planning exists. The only long-term planning that has occurred is the signing of a five-year lease. Although this means of planning is extremely informal by even a liberal definition, it indicates that some consideration has been given to the long-range plans of Clovis Jewellers.

Short-Term Planning. Mr. Neudorf engages in a number of forms of short-term planning. Among them are budgeting for the upcoming year, planning promotions, and cash flow planning. Budgets are prepared early in the fiscal year and extend to the end of the year. The budgets include a sales budget, a purchases budget, and an expense budget. The budgetary process is still in the early stages of development, but an increased awareness on the part of Mr. Neudorf ensures that it will be an effective form of short-term planning in the future.

Promotions are planned on an informal basis; no concrete goals or objectives are stated. Most of the promotions are planned based on the success of the previous year's promotions. If a promotion proved successful one year, it is automatically considered for the next year. This method produces mixed results, as some promotions are successful one year and quite unsuccessful the next.

One area of short-range planning that requires attention is the planning of future cash flows. Mr. Neudorf prepares a complete cash flow analysis for the upcoming year based on projected sales, merchandise purchases, and expenses. This cash flow analysis does not always prove accurate due to extraordinary items that arise in the course of the year, but at least it gives Mr. Neudorf a plan for goals for which to aim.

Appendix 1

Clovis Jewellers: Organizational Structure

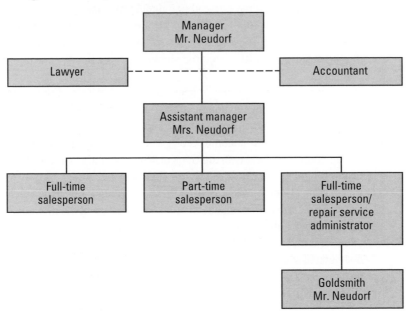

Appendix 2

Clovis Jewellers: Financial Statements

CLOVIS JEWELLERS (1978) LTD.
Balance Sheet
(Unaudited)
January 31, 2002

	2002	2001
Assets		
Current		
Cash	$ 24,886.15	$ 32,834.17
Accounts receivable (trade)	4,885.34	5,725.74
(shareholders)	18,186.40	18,462.84
Inventory	190,612.90	197,318.70
Prepaid expense	8,437.01	9,150.01
	247,007.80	263,490.46
Assets		
Investments	1,045.00	—
Fixed	10,853.69	13,566.69
Other		
Goodwill less amortization	56,672.20	59,228.20
Incorporation costs	—	373.54
Due from Neudorf holdings	15,448.95	15,448.95
	$329,027.64	$352,107.84

CLOVIS JEWELLERS (1978) LTD.
Balance Sheet (continued)
(Unaudited)
January 31, 2002

Liabilities		
Current:		
Accounts payable and accruals	$ 70,987.17	$ 92,214.96
Employee remittance payable	1,447.75	1,539.07
Corporation taxes payable	925.40	834.85
Current portion of long-term	11,316.00	8,000.00
	84,676.32	102,588.88
Long-Term	199,961.77	214,156.14
	214,683.09	316,745.02
Shareholders' Equity		
Share Capital	$ 100.00	$ 100.00
Retained Earnings	44,289.55	35,262.82
	44,389.55	35,362.82
	$329,027.64	$352,107.84

CLOVIS JEWELLERS (1978) LTD.
Statement of Income
(Unaudited)
Year Ended January 31, 2002

	2002	2001
Sales	$420,559.99	$472,035.50
Cost of Sales	218,332.01	261,016.36
Gross Margin	202,227.98	211,019.14
Selling Expenses	192,626.33	210,073.57
Operating Income	9,601.65	945.57
Other Income:		
Interest earned	350.48	213.63
Gain from sale of assets	—	1,133.00
Income before Taxes	9,952.13	2,292.22
Income taxes	925.40	834.85
Net Income	$ 9,026.73	$ 1,457.37

CLOVIS JEWELLERS (1978) LTD.
Statement of Operating Expenses
(Unaudited)
Year Ended January 31, 2002

	2002	2001
Operating Expense:		
Accounting	$ 761.20	$ 1,039.30
Advertising	11,024.93	33,265.13
Amortization	4,556.00	4,556.00
Auto expenses	1,794.77	3,146.33
Bank charges and interest	4,318.90	4,549.10
Canada pension plan	1,201.94	1,296.32
Donations	350.00	350.00
Depreciation	2,713.00	3,391.00
Equipment rental	4,200.00	2,700.00
Interest	28,016.38	30,747.77
Insurance	3,047.00	3,079.41
Legal expenses	448.54	80.09
Memberships and dues	510.00	587.74
Postage and stationery	1,382.82	2,388.12
Rent	28,965.29	28,175.00
Repairs and maintenance	432.41	464.59
Salaries	82,180.91	74,505.54
Security	711.39	681.25
Supplies	2,224.87	2,308.94
Taxes	2,603.75	3,144.88
Telephone	983.67	1,104.04
Travel and promotion	3,764.89	1,621.14
Unemployment insurance	2,492.46	2,539.19
Utilities	3,818.71	4,092.59
Workers' compensation	122.50	245.00
Total expenses	$192,626.33	$210,073.57

THOMSON GREENHOUSE

D. Wesley Balderson
University of Lethbridge

Background

Thomson Greenhouse is located just outside Sudbury, Ontario, and is owned by Earl and Lisa Thomson. It is a seasonal operation, offering many different types of bedding plants, vegetables, annuals, perennials, and specialty plants and arrangements. The business also has a two-acre tree nursery and garden offering and wide range of trees from pines to fruit trees.

Earl and Lisa Thomson have been operating the business for 17 years after taking over the business from Lisa's parents. The original business was located on land on the outskirts of Sudbury which was annexed by the city. It was at that time that Earl and Lisa decided to move from the city to a small acreage, so that they could continue the business and set up a new location. The structures were taken down and reassembled on the new acreage just northeast of Sudbury.

Much of the knowledge of the greenhouse business has been passed down from Lisa's parents and as Earl and Lisa have three sons working in the business it continues to be a solely family-run operation. Many of the aspects of the business have remained the same since it was established. Tomson Greenhouse has been serving the city of Sudbury and surrounding area for many years and has been fairly successful in establishing a name for quality products and good customer service.

Thomson Greenhouse is a form of second income to the Thomsons due to its seasonal nature and because Earl is the chief accountant for a local manufacturing company. It also has allowed the Thomson's three sons to work in the business to help finance their schooling. The oldest son Derek is currently about to graduate with a bachelor's degree in business from the local university while the other brothers (Ryan and Russel) are in grades 10 and 12 respectively. Lisa's parents, Morris and Anna Slemko, also work in the business during the busy times.

Due to the success of the business and the fact that their sons are getting to the age where they are about to leave home the Thomson's are faced with some long-term decisions about the business.

Organization

Thomson Greenhouse is a general partnership with the two partners being Earl and Lisa Thomson. Earl feels that although they have unlimited liability under this arrangement, the tax and flexibility advantages of a partnership outweigh this risk. Both partners own an equal share of the business, although Lisa spends more time working in the business because Earl has a full-time job in Sudbury.

Earl and Lisa have equal authority with regard to the employees. Both are knowledgeable regarding horticulture and care for trees and plants. Earl is more responsible for the accounting, advertising, deliveries, and seeding. Lisa handles orders, daily operations in the greenhouse, transplanting, sales, and customer service. Both Earl and Lisa know their strengths and weaknesses, and tend to do the things they each do well. Some overlapping occurs, but this is advantageous in some ways because some operations are too big to handle by themselves.

Over the years there have been few conflicts in the management of the operation or with employees as it has all been within the family. All three of the Thomson sons have worked in the business throughout the summer as well as evenings and weekends for a number of years. During the busy season Lisa's parents, from whom Earl and Lisa purchased the business, help out. Because of the fact that the business is family owned and operated no formal personnel policies or training programs have been developed. Management of the company has been carried out on an informal basis. The employees are paid on a straight salary basis with considerable flexibility available for the sons as things come up that they need to do.

One of the major concerns that Earl and Lisa have is the future of the business when the children finish their high school and university studies. The business is not currently large enough to be a full-time occupation unless a considerable capital investment is made to expand the operation. Another difficulty is that the second oldest son, Ryan, has expressed interest in becoming involved in the business but the Thomson's are concerned about how to make this transition should it take place. They are wondering what effects such a move would have on their other two sons.

Location and Physical Facilities

Thomson Greenhouse is located just northeast of the city limits of Sudbury. The market area not only includes the city of Sudbury (population 90,000) but also many of the small communities around the city which is estimated to have another 60,000 people. This location serves Thomson well because of its proximity to the city; as well, its rural location allows for plenty of space for production and expansion, if required. Distribution is carried out primarily by truck, and the highways and roads in the area are very well maintained.

Thomson Greenhouse is located on 20 acres of which 5 are used for the greenhouse and the Thomson's residence and the other 15 are rented out to a local farmer. The greenhouse building covers approximately 800 square metres. Although most of the area is taken up with plants and could be referred to as selling space, a small area at the front is devoted to customer service and a cash counter. A small greenhouse at the back is used for personal items and the holding of special orders. The building's age is a concern, and it has begun deteriorating. The frame is made of wood and the aging process has damaged many of the wooden glass frames. Much of the material for this greenhouse came from the original greenhouse that was moved from the previous site.

Recently Thomson Greenhouse purchased a new computer system. The Thomsons are in the process of converting their manual recordkeeping and inventory control over to the computer. Other equipment owned by the business are a small front-end loader/garden tractor, a truck used to deliver plants to commercial customers, roto tiller, dirt mixer, and dirt purifier, and other miscellaneous garden tools and greenhouses devices.

Purchasing for Thomson Greenhouse is carried out by both Earl and Lisa. They purchase their supply of inventory from various seed processors located primarily in Southern Ontario and the United States. Quality, dependability, and price are all used to evaluate suppliers. Lead times for ordering are about 30 days for most items. No formal inventory-ordering method is used as the business is small enough that Earl and Lisa are able to adjust their inventory levels from visual inspection and from previous experience.

Marketing

The target market for Thomson Greenhouse consists of consumers who come to the greenhouse as well as some large retail accounts to supermarkets such as Superstore and A&P. The consumer market tends to be older, those who have the resources and time to spend on their yards and gardens. The supermarket or commercial accounts purchase vegetables and some flowers while those customers who come out to Thomson Greenhouse make greater purchases of bedding plants and trees. In terms of quality and price, the commercial accounts tend to be interested in low price. As a result, the margins that Thomson achieves with the commercial accounts are much lower than with the customer accounts. Those who come out to the greenhouse desire a high quality and customer service even if it means paying a slightly higher price. Earl Thomson realizes this and sets prices to meet these preferences and also to ensure that the business is able to achieve a profit. The profit margin has to be high enough to include the discounts which inevitably occur at the end of the season due to the perishability of the product.

The busy time of year for bedding plants is during May and June as most people are preparing their yards and gardens. During the summer and fall, produce sales increase and during the winter months very little business is done.

There are several other greenhouses in the Sudbury area and many customers do price shopping. Thomson Greenhouse has always prided itself on superior customer service and despite the competitive nature of the industry seems to retain a fairly loyal following. The commercial contracts also add to the stability of operations for Thomson. Earl has an informal idea of Thomson Greenhouse market share through the monitoring of sales of their various products.

One of the trends which the Thomsons have noticed is the increasing market share which has been obtained in the gardening-nursery product category by department stores such as Wal Mart and Canadian Tire. Thomson Greenhouse currently has contracts with only two supermarkets and although these have provided steady volumes, purchases from these sources have not grown over the past few years. The Thomsons are considering attempting to obtain contracts with some of these department stores as a means of increasing sales. They realize that margins would be thin, however, and that price would be a major purchasing factor for the consumer. Many of the other greenhouses in the area are actively competing for the business of these stores and the Thomsons realize that they would have to be very competitive to be successful in obtaining a contract. If they were able to secure new purchasers, expansion of their current operation would seem to be necessary.

Thomson Greenhouse uses several forms of promotion. It places some ads in the local newspaper and utilizes the Yellow Pages. It also purchases a booth at the Home and Garden Trade show which is held in Sudbury each spring. Occasionally, direct mail promotion is used to highlight special sales or end-of-season discounts. Thomson uses business cards and has been actively involved in sponsoring minor hockey teams and karate schools as part of its public relations promotion. Earl and Lisa realize, however, that word of mouth is their most effective form of promotion so they ensure that they and their sales staff are knowledgeable about the product and courteous to the customer.

Financial Situation

Thomson Greenhouse has been profitable since its establishment, earning about $10,000 per year on about $40,000 in sales. (See Exhibit 1 for the latest income statement.) Although sales haven't increased over the past five years, Earl and Lisa have not been concerned about this because there has been an increase in competition and they are currently operating at capacity with their present facilities. They have been using a one-book system for accounting but are currently switching over to an accounting software program in conjunction with their computer purchase.

One of the concerns that Earl and Lisa have is the state of their current greenhouse, which is getting old. They are considering constructing a new one in addition to the current greenhouse. This would increase the capacity of the business and would allow for increased sales but would also increase the workload for the Thomsons, something which they are not sure they want. Alternatively, they could replace the existing greenhouse and maintain current operations but at a more efficient level.

A new greenhouse of a similar size to the current one would cost approximately $12,000 and would last about 10 years. If the Thomsons decided to go ahead with this they would finance $8,000 at the local bank at 8 percent interest. They estimate that the annual sales for a greenhouse of this size would be $30,000.

Exhibit 1

Thomson Greenhouse Income Statement For the Year Ended December 31, 2001		
Revenue		$37,000
Expenses		
Cost of Goods Sold		
Seed and materials	$ 3,560	
Containers	3,150	
Fertilizer	290	

Exhibit 1 (continued)

Water	305	
Soil	90	
Direct labour	3,000	
Contribution Margin	1,395	
Occupancy and Selling Costs	26,605	
Building repairs	130	
Truck costs	2,300	
Office expenses	1,105	
Property taxes	1,560	
Heat and power	3,450	
Advertising	2,150	
Selling labour	3,150	
Depreciation	$3,800	$17,555
Profit before Income Taxes		$ 9,050

Thomsom Greenhouse
Balance Sheet
As at December 31, 2001

Current Assets		
Cash	$1,000	
Accounts receivable	1,500	
Inventory	3,000	
Fixed Assets		
Land	26,000	
Buildings	58,000	
Equipment	$21,000	
Total Assets		$110,500
Liabilities and Owner's Equity		
Liabilities		
Accounts Payable	1,500	
Owner's Equity	$109,000	
Total Liabilities and Owner's Equity		$110,500

Questions

1. Discuss the implications of the Thomsons attempting to obtain additional commercial contracts (the department stores) for their products.
2. Evaluate the decision to construct another greenhouse from a financial as well as organizational point of view. (Use rate of return, payback, and break-even analysis in your evaluation.)
3. Comment on the financial health of the Thomson Greenhouse through a review of the financial statements.
4. Discuss the implications for succession of the business if the decision were to:
   a. pass the business to one of the sons.
   b. sell the business to someone outside the family.

Endnotes

Chapter 1

1. Naisbitt, John, *Global Paradox* (New York: William Morrow and Company, 1994).

2. As reported in *Success,* February 1999, p. 12.

3. *Growing Small Business* (Ottawa: Industry Canada/Statistics Canada, February 1994).

4. As reported in *Business Research Newsletter,* vol. #8, July 1999, p. 1, G.D. Sourcing, ed., White, John.

5. As reported in *Business Research Newsletter,* vol. #2, Oct. 1999, p. 2, G.D. Sourcing, ed., White, John.

6. *Canadian Economic Observer,* November 1997, CAICS 11-010-XPB, January–December, V-10, Statistics Canada.

7. "The Entrepreneurial Numbers Game," *Inc.*, May 1986, pp. 31–36.

8. "Small Businesses Fuel Growth," *Success,* July/August 2000, p.16.

9. "Small Business, Big Growth," *Costco Connection,* July/August 2000, p. 9.

10. *Market Research Handbook,* (Ottawa: Statistics Canada, 2000), p. 147.

11. *Small Business Quarterly,* Labour Force Information Catalogue #71-001, Statistics Canada, March 2001.

12. *Canadian Labour Force Characteristics,* (Ottawa: CANSIM, Statistics Canada, January 4, 2001).

13. *Small Business in Canada—A Statistical Overview* (Ottawa: Industry Canada, January 1996).

14. *Canadian Economic Observer,* November 1997, Statistics Canada Catalogue #11-010-XPB.

15. *Self-Employment in Canada—Trends and Prospects,* CIBC Economics Division, December 2000, p.1.

16. *Growing Small Business,* p. 1.

17. David Smith, *Why Small Business Is So Important* (Budget Brochure, Ministry of State for Small Business and Tourism, Government of Canada, 1984).

18. "Entrepreneurship Education," *Technological Entrepreneurship and Engineering in Canada,* Canadian Academy of Engineering Report, Chapter 9, Ottawa, 1997, pp. 149–160.

19. Harvey Schachter, *"I Was A Teenage Capitalist,"* Canadian Business, December 24, 1998–January 8, 1999, pp. 58–60.

20. Thomas Peters and Robert H. Waterman, Jr., *In Search of Excellence* (New York: Harper and Row, 1982).

21. Ibid.

22. *The Globe and Mail,* June 12, 1995, p. B7.

23. Code of Federal Regulations 13:121, *Standard Industrial Classification Codes and Size Standards* (Washington, D.C.: U.S. Government Printing Office, January 1, 1994), pp. 354–367; and *Growing Small Business.*

24. R. Peterson, *Small Business—Building a Balanced Economy* (Erin, Ont.: Press Porcepie Ltd., 1977), p. 64.

25. Canadian Federation of Independent Business, *Small Business Primer,* June 2001, p. 2.

26. Ibid.

27. *Growing Small Business,* p. 5.

28. *Small Business Quarterly,* Industry Canada, vol. 2, no. 3, March 2001, p. 1.

29. *Growing Small Business,* p. 5.

30. *Small Business Quarterly,* Industry Canada, vol. 5, no. 1, March 2001, p. 5.

31. Ibid.

32. *Self-Employment in Canada—Trends and Prospects,* CIBC Economics Division, December 2000, p. 7.

33. "The Young and the Restless," *Profit,* June 1993, p. 48.

34. *Self-Employment in Canada—Trends and Prospects,* CIBC Economics Division, December 2000, p. 12.

35. *Business Research Newsletter,* G. D. Sourcing, vol. 3, no. 2, November 2000, p. 10.

36. *Canadian Economic Observer,* November 1997, Statistics Canada, Catalogue # 11-010-XPB, p. 16.

37. *Women in Management* 9, no. 2 (University of Western Ontario, December–January 1999), p. 2.

38. *Self-Employment in Canada—Trends and Prospects,* CIBC Economics Division, December 2000, p. 7.

39. *Canadian Economic Observer,* November 1997, Statistics Canada, Catalogue # 11-010-XPB, p. 14.

40. *Business Research Newsletter,* G. D. Sourcing, vol. 3, no. 3, March 2000, p. 12.

41. *Small Business Quarterly,* Industry Canada, vol. 2, no. 3, March 2001, p. 1.

42. Peters and Waterman, *In Search of Excellence.*

43. Ibid.

44. *Statistics on Foreign Ownership, Small versus Large* (Ottawa: Statistics Canada, Inter-Corporate Ownership, 1984), p. 252.

45. "Would You Want Your Son to Marry a Marketing Lady?" *Journal of Marketing,* January 1977, pp. 15–18.

46. Ivan I. Stefanovic, "Sidestepping Socialism in Yugoslavia," *Venture,* September 1984, p. 60.

47. *Global Entrepreneurship Monitor,* London Business School, Summer 2000.

48. Randall Litchfield, "Turn Change into Advantage," *Small Business,* June 1989, p. 19.

49. North America Free Trade Agreement, Chapter 10.

50. North America Free Trade Agreement, Chapter 3.

51. North America Free Trade Agreement, Articles 1202 and 1204.

52. "Sunshine in the South," *Forbes,* September 16, 1991, p. 205.

53. Jason Myers, "In Praise of Open Markets," *Canadian Business,* November 13, 1998, p. 132.

54. Joe Dangor, "Thriving on Change," *Small Business Magazine,* June 1989, p. 32.

55. Cathy Hilborn, "Recession Startups Not So Risky Business," *Profit,* July–August 1991, p. 8.

56. *Growing Small Business,* p. 1.

57. John Bulloch,"Policy Guidelines to Help Make Your Venture Work," *The*

Financial Post Special Report, November 24, 1984, p. 53.

58. *Growing Small Business.*

59. *Profits,* Business Development Bank of Canada, Winter 1999, p. 2.

Chapter 2

1. "Inc. and U.S.A. Today Survey of 500 Fastest Growing Private Companies," *Inc.*, June 1986, p. 48.

2. *The Globe and Mail,* July 17, 1995, p. B5.

3. *Canadian Economic Observer,* November 1997, Statistics Canada, Catalogue #11-010-XPB, p. 21.

4. "Inc. and U.S.A. Today Survey of 500 Fastest Growing Private Companies."

5. Pat Thompson, "Characteristics of the Small Business Entrepreneur in Canada," *Journal of Small Business and Entrepreneurship* 4, no. 3 (Winter 1986–87), p. 5.

6. *The Globe and Mail,* April 17, 1995, p. B4.

7. Karl Vesper, "Freedom and Power: What Every Entrepreneur Craves," *Success,* May 1988, p. 48.

8. Thompson, "Characteristics of the Small Business Entrepreneur in Canada."

9. "Size Comparisons of Bankrupt Firms versus Non-Bankrupt Firms," *The Canadian Small Business Guide,* February 22, 1985, p. 5013.

10. *The Canadian Business Failure Record, 1994* (New York: Dun and Bradstreet, 1994), pp. 1– 19.

11. David P. Boyd and David E. Gumpert, "Coping with Entrepreneurial Stress," *Harvard Business Review,* March–April 1983, pp. 44–64.

12. "Inc. and U.S.A. Today Survey of 500 Fastest Growing Private Companies."

13. *Self-Employment in Canada—Trends and Prospects,* CIBC Economic Analysis, December 2000, p. 17.

14. Ibid.

15. Business Development Bank of Canada Survey, *Profits,* Winter 1998, p. 3.

16. *Profit,* June 1993, p. 49.

17. *The Globe and Mail,* June 17, 1995, p. B5.

18. *Self-Employment in Canada—Trends and Prospects,* CIBC Economic Analysis, December 2000, p. 16.

19. Charles A. Garfield, *Peak Performers* (New York: William Morrow, 1985).

20. Thompson, "Characteristics of the Small Business Entrepreneur in Canada."

21. "A Nation of Entrepreneurs," *Report on Business Magazine,* October 1988.

22. *Self-Employment in Canada—Trends and Prospects,* CIBC Economic Analysis, December 2000, p. 16.

23. *Canadian Economic Observer,* November 1997, Statistics Canada, Catalogue #11-010-XPB, p. 19.

24. Carter Henderson, *Winners: The Successful Strategies Entrepreneurs Use to Build New Businesses* (New York: Holt, Rinehart and Winston, 1985), p. 178.

25. *The Canadian Business Failure Record, 1994.*

26. Ibid.

27. Statistics Canada, *Market Research Handbook,* p. 94.

28. Ibid.

29. *Small Business and Special Surveys* (Ottawa: Statistics Canada, August 17, 1989).

30. *Business Research Newsletter,* G. D. Sourcing, vol. 2, no. 14, December 1999, p. 9.

31. Jeffrey A. Timmons, Leonard E. Smollen, and Alexander L. M. Dingee, *New Venture Creation: A Guide to Entrepreneurship* (Homewood, Ill.: Richard D. Irwin, 1985), p. 28.

Chapter 3

1. National Federation of Independent Business, "Bright Ideas," *USA Today,* May 11, 1987.

2. Shirley Roberts, "Harness The Future: The Nine Keys to Emerging Behavior," *Profit,* December–January 1999, p. 40.

3. Raymond Kao, "Market Research and Small New-Venture Start-Up

Strategy," *Journal of Small Business and Entrepreneurship,* Spring 1986, p. 36.

4. *The Financial Post,* October 29, 1994, p. S24.

5. *The Globe and Mail,* June 5, 1995, p. B5.

6. *The Globe and Mail,* October 29, 1994, p. B2.

7. "Incubator Update," *Inc.,* January 1993, p. 49.

8. *Profit,* October 1994, p. 62.

9. "Business Incubators Come of Age," *Entrepreneurial Manager's Newsletter,* May 1986, p. 5.

Chapter 4

1. *Business Research Newsletter,* G. D. Sourcing, vol. 3, no. 12, November, 2000, p. 9.

2. Donald Rumball, *The Entrepreneurial Edge* (Toronto: Key Porter Books, 1989), pp. 225–33.

3. Jerry White, "Canada's Free Trade Winners," *Small Business Magazine,* July–August 1990, p. 38.

4. Statistics Canada, *Perspectives on Labour and Income,* as reported in *The Globe and Mail,* September 10, 1998, p. B12.

5. *Profit,* December–January 1998, p. 46.

6. *The Globe and Mail,* April 10, 1995, p. B6.

7. *Small Business Quarterly,* Industry Canada, Spring 2000, p. 2.

8. *The Globe and Mail,* June 19, 1995, p. B7.

Chapter 5

1. Harvey Schachter, "Don't Grow It… Buy It," *Profit,* June 1998, p. 161.

2. Peter Thomas, "Negotiate to Win," *Profit,* October 1991, p. 34.

Chapter 6

1. *The Globe and Mail,* October 1995, p. B7.

2. *Franchise Annual* (St. Catharines, Ont.: Info Press, 1988).

3. Faye Rice, "How to Succeed at Cloning a Small Business," *Fortune,* October 28, 1985, p. 60.

4. "Kubas Consultants' Major Market Report 2000," *Canadian Grocers Executive Report*, 2001.

5. *Canadian Franchise Fact Sheet* 1998, Francom Canada, January 6, 1999, p. 1.

6. *Franchising in the Canadian Economy, 1990–92,* Canadian Franchise Association and Price Waterhouse, 1992.

7. *Canadian Capabilities: Key Facts about Canadian Franchise Expertise,* Industry Canada, March 4, 1998, p. 1.

8. Gordon Brockhouse, "The Franchise Advantage," *Small Business Magazine,* July–August 1990, p. 48.

9. *Franchising in the Canadian Economy 1990–1992* (Toronto: Canadian Franchise Association and Price Waterhouse), p. 3.

10. Rice, "How to Succeed at Cloning a Small Business."

11. U.S. Department of Commerce, *Franchising in the Economy, 1977–79* (Washington, D.C.: U.S. Government Printing Office, 1981), Table 3, p. 34.

12. Rice, "How to Succeed at Cloning a Small Business."

13. Kenneth Barnes and Everett Banning, *Money Makers: The Secrets of Canada's Most Successful Entrepreneurs* (Toronto: McClelland and Stewart, 1985), p. 84.

14. Ibid., p. 72.

15. Ibid., p. 144.

Chapter 7

1. *The Canadian Business Failure Record, 1999* (Toronto: Dun and Bradstreet Business Education Division, 1998).

2. Canadian Bankers Association as reported by *GD Sourcing*, Feb 1, 1999, p. 7.

3. "Where Angels Dare," *Profit,* December 1992, p. 343.

4. "Venture Capital: More Money, Still Choosy," *The Magazine That's All about Small Business,* May 1984, p. 49.

5. *Small Business Quarterly,* Industry Canada, vol. 3, no. 1, June 2001, p. 1.

6. "Risk Capital—Down but Not Out," *Profit Magazine,* December 1992, p. 60.

7. Stanley Rich and David E. Gumpert, "Business Plans That Win $$$: Lessons from the MIT Enterprise Forum," *Venture,* June 1985, p. 72.

8. *Canadian Year Book 1999,* Statistics Canada, p. 443.

9. Ibid.

10. "Venture Survey—Financing," *Venture,* October 1986, p. 24.

11. "Small Business Magazine's First Annual Survey of Canadian Entrepreneurs," *Small Business,* June 1987, pp. 49–50.

12. *Small Business Quarterly Report,* March 2001, Industry Canada, p. 5.

13. Canadian Bankers Association as reported in *GD Sourcing,* Feb 1, 1999, p. 7.

14. *Business Research Newsletter,* G. D. Sourcing, vol. 4, no. 1, June 2001, p.8.

Chapter 8

1. Thomas J. Peters and Robert H. Waterman, Jr., *In Search of Excellence* (New York: Harper and Row, 1982), p. 156.

2. *The Globe and Mail,* May 15, 1995, p. B7.

3. *Ontario Business Journal,* January 1995, p. 15.

4. John Meyer, "Canada's Exports Reach Record High—Total Sales Top $90 Billion Mark," *Export Opportunity,* March 31, 1984, p. 1.

5. *Small Business Quarterly,* Industry Canada, Spring 2000, p. 6.

6. *Growing Small Business* (Ottawa: Industry Canada/Statistics Canada, February 1994), p. 38.

7. *Small Business Quarterly,* Industry Canada, vol. 3, no. 2, September 2001, p. 2.

8. Ibid.

9. Canadian Federation of Independent Business, *Federal/Provincial Action Report, 1986.*

10. *The Globe and Mail,* May 29, 1995, p. B6.

11. *Business Research Newsletter,* G. D. Sourcing, vol. 2, no. 8, June 1999, p. 1.

12. *Profits* 18, no. 2 (Business Development Bank of Canada), p. 5.

13. *Ivey Business Quarterly*, London, Summer 1997, pp. 1, 2.

14. Everet M. Rogers with F. Floyd Shoemaker, *Communication of Innovation* (New York: Free Press, 1971), p. 270.

15. *Lethbridge Herald,* March 3, 1996, p. 27.

16. *Business Research Newsletter,* G. D. Sourcing, vol. 2, no. 6, May 1999, p. 5.

17. *Marketing—Fourth Canadian Edition,* Irwin-Times Mirror Higher Education Group, (Toronto: McGraw-Hill Ryerson), 1997.

18. *Canadian Retailer,* May/June 2000, p. 17.

19. *Power Retail: Winning Strategies from Chapters and Other Leading Retailers in Canada,* Lawrence N. Stevenson, Joseph C. Shlesinger, and Michael R. Pierce, (Toronto: McGraw-Hill Ryerson, 1999), p. 67.

Chapter 9

1. "Profitguide," *Profit,* June 20, 2001, p. 1.

2. http://www.forrester.com/Product/CoverageArea/0.4674.107.FF.html

3. Ibid.

4. *Profit,* May 2000, p. 42.

5. "Profitguide," June 20, 2001, p. 2.

6. *Small Business Canada,* May/June 2001, p. 35.

7. "Profitguide," June 20, 2001, p. 35.

8. *Canadian Business,* April 2, 2001, p. 38.

9. Rappa, Michael. *Managing the Digital Enterprise.* http://ecommerce.ncsu.edu/topics/models/

10. *Canadian Retailer,* March/April 2000, p. 21.

11. *Small Business Canada,* March/April 2001, p. 21.

12. "Profitguide," *Profit,* June 20, 2001, p. 1.

13. Ibid, p. 2.

14. Ibid, p. 2.

15. *Ivey Entrepreneur.* (London: Richard Ivey School of Business, University of Western Ontario, May/June 2001), p. 1.

Chapter 10

1. "Small Business Magazine's First Annual Survey of Canada's Entrepreneurs," *Small Business,* June 1987, pp. 49–53.

Chapter 11

1. *Profit,* December/January, 1999, p. 48.

2. "7 Steps to a Successful Relationship," Naomi Levinson, *Canadian Retailer,* May/June 2000, p. 15.

Chapter 12

1. Psychological Motivations Inc., "Dobbs Ferry, New York," *Venture,* May 1986, p. 26.

2. *Small Business in Canada,* 1990 (Ottawa: Industry, Science and Technology Canada), p. 19.

3. Linda Duxbury and Christopher Higgins, as reported in *The Globe and Mail,* Sept. 21, 1999, p. B1.

4. Robert Levering, Milton Moscowitz, and Michael Katz, *The 100 Best Companies to Work for in America,* 1984 (Scarborough, N.Y.: New American Library, 1985).

5. For a complete discussion, see Donald Rumball, *The Entrepreneurial Edge* (Toronto: Key Porter Books, 1989), pp. 159–179.

6. Frederick Herzberg, *Motivation to Work* (New York: John Wiley and Sons, 1959).

7. Abraham H. Maslow, *Motivation and Personality* (New York: Harper and Row, 1970).

8. Angus Reid Group Survey for Royal Bank, September 1997, as reported in *Profit,* October 1998, p. 16.

9. *Canada Year Book 1999,* Statistics Canada, p. 223.

10. *The Globe and Mail,* February 20, 1995, p. B6.

11. "Small Business Magazine's First Annual Survey of Canada's Entrepreneurs," *Small Business,* June 1987, pp. 49–53.

12. *Work Arrangements in the 1991's,* Statistics Canada, May 1998, as reported in *Profit,* October 1998, p. 14.

13. Ibid.

14. Ibid.

15. Angus Reid Group Survey for Royal Bank, September 1997, as reported in *Profit,* October 1998, p. 21.

16. Kenneth Blanchard and Robert Lorber, *Putting the One Minute Manager to Work* (New York: Berkley Books, 1984).

17. *Small Business in Canada,* 1990, p. 61.

Chapter 13

1. Brian Costello, *Your Money and How to Keep It* (Don Mills, Ont.: Stoddart Publishers, 1985), p. 14.

Chapter 14

1. "Canada's Fastest Growing Companies, 2000," *Profit,* June/August, 2001, pp. 32–72.

2. Paul Weinberg, "Growing Pains," *The Magazine That's All about Small Business,* May 1984, p. 26.

3. Donald L. Sexton and Philip M. Van Auken, "Prevalence of Strategic Planning in Small Business," *Journal of Small Business Management,* July 1982, p. 20.

4. Richard M. Hodgetts, *Effective Small Business Management.* Reproduced by permission of Academic Press Inc., 1982, p. 197.

5. *Profits* (Business Development Bank of Canada, Winter 1999), p. 4.

Chapter 15

1. Jeff Wuorio, *Success,* December 1998, p. 76.

2. Elizabeth Church, "Leadership Crises Foreseen for Family Firms," *The Globe and Mail,* January 18, 1999, p. B13.

3. P. C. Rosenblatt, L. deMik, R. M. Anderson, and P. A. Johnson, *The Family in Business* (San Francisco: Jossey-Bass, 1985), p. 5.

4. Jennifer Low, "Dad, When Are You Going to Let Go?" *Profit,* October 1991, p. 30.

5. S. I. Lansberg, "Managing Human Resources in Family Firms: The Problem of Institutional Overlap," *Organizational Dynamics,* Summer 1983, pp. 39–46.

6. Curtis Hartman, "Main Street Inc.," *Inc.,* June 1986, pp. 49–54.

7. B. Benson, "The Enigma of the Family-Owned Business," *Perspective* 10, no. 1 (1984), p. 26.

8. *The Globe and Mail,* October 9, 1995, p. B7.

9. S. Birley, "Succession in the Family Firm: The Inheritor's View," *Journal of Small Business Management* 24, no. 3 (July 1986), p. 36.

10. Low, "Dad, When Are You Going to Let Go?" p. 28.

11. Marshall Paisner, "Myths about Succession," *Inc.,* October 1986, p. 146.

12. Rosenblatt, deMik, Anderson, and Johnson, *The Family in Business,* p. 274.

13. Birley, "Succession in the Family Firm."

14. "Your Going Public Checklist," *Profit,* November 1998, p. 47.

15. Mark Stevens, "When to Take Your Company Public," *Entrepreneurial Manager's Newsletter* 7, no. 4 (1986), p. 4.

16. *Small Business Quarterly,* Industry Canada, vol. 3, no. 1, June 2001, p. 5.

17. William V. Curran, C.A., "Bankruptcy—What It Means," in *Running Your Own Business* (Ontario: Gage and The Financial Post, 1982), pp. 104–107.

Index

URL Index